MAYA

DIVINE KINGS OF THE RAIN FOREST

MAYA

DIVINE KINGS OF THE RAIN FOREST

Edited by Nikolai Grube
assisted by Eva Eggebrecht and Matthias Seidel

h.f.ullmann

CONTENTS

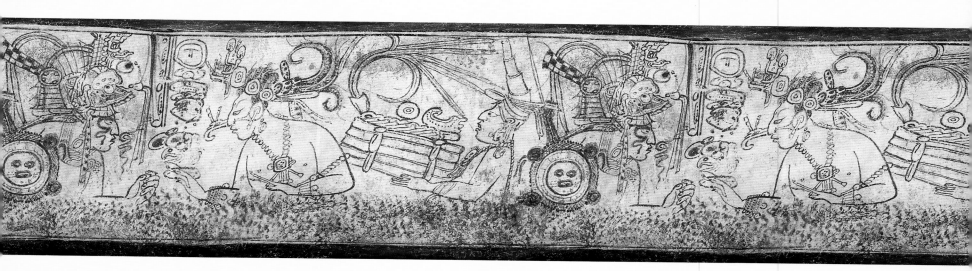

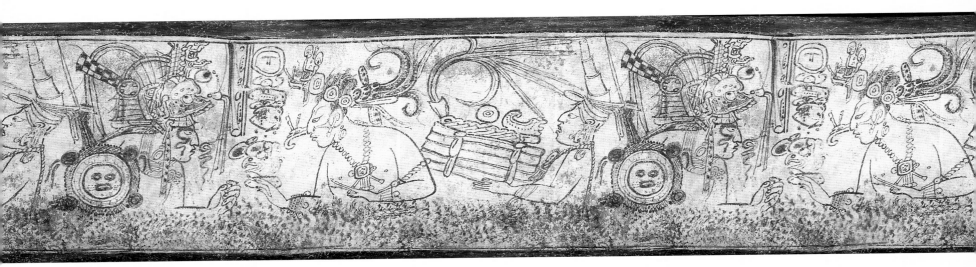

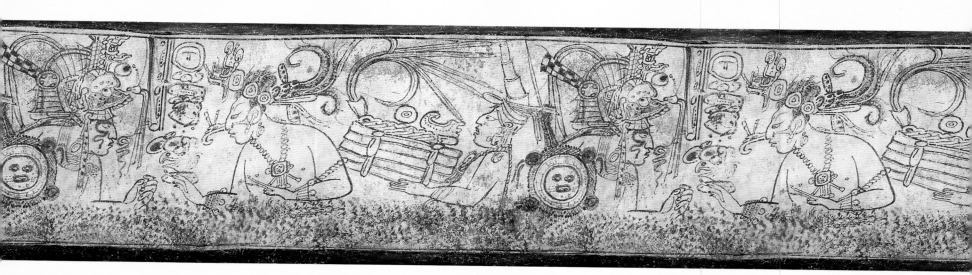

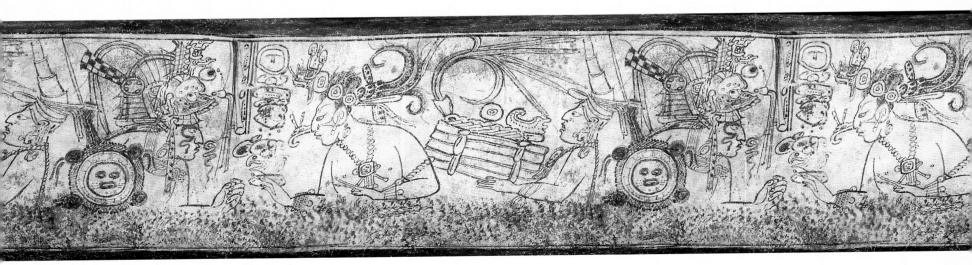

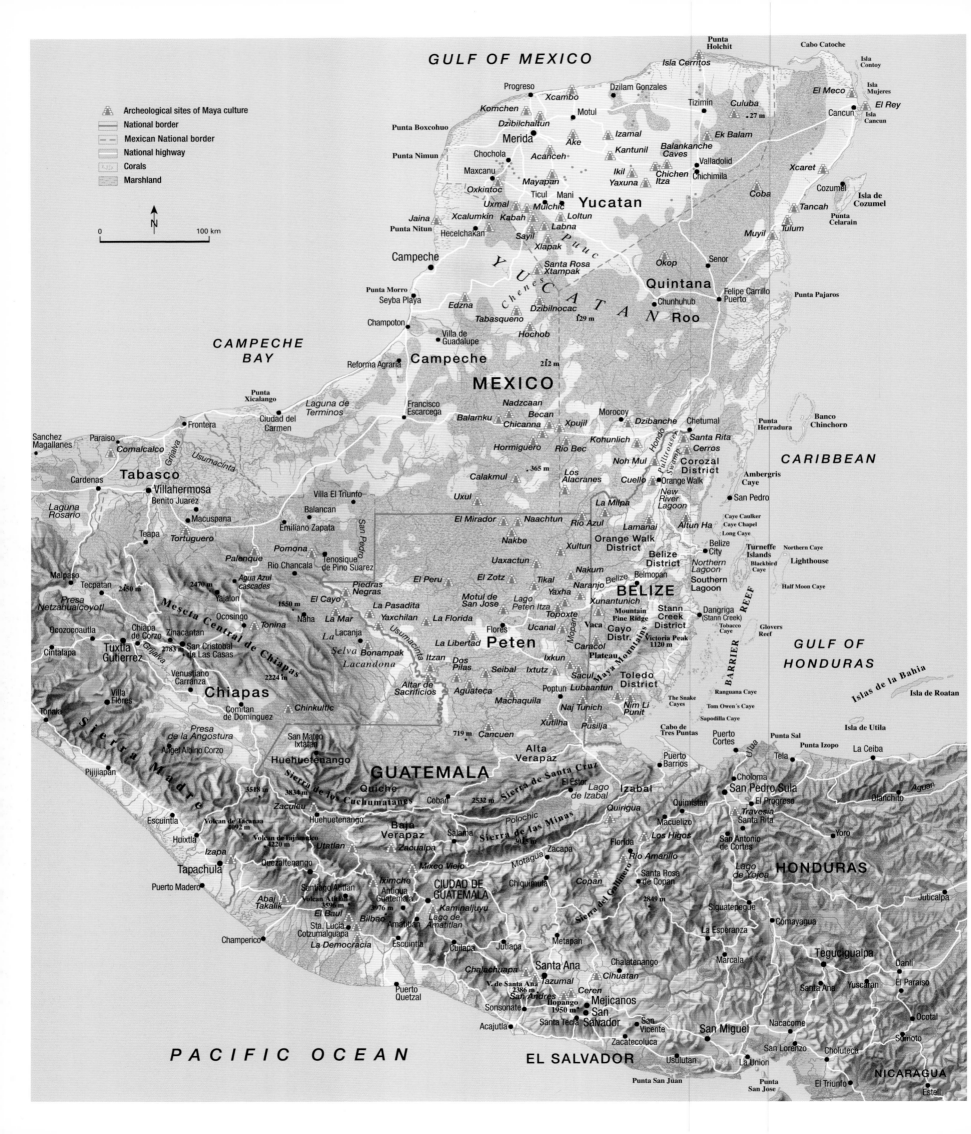

PROLOGUE

Nikolai Grube

"Who will be the prophet, who the priest, who deciphers the language of the hieroglyphs?" – this question is asked at the end of the Chilam-Balam book of Chumayel (1782), written by a Maya at the time of Spanish colonial rule; a Maya who was obviously not able to read the mysterious signs of his forefathers. No one knew anything of the large towns and cities; no one knew the names of the old kings; the inhabitants were not allowed to worship the ancient Gods any more, whose clay images lay shattered on the ground. Seldom was the old cliché of a lost culture more appropriate than to that of the Maya. When the explorer John Lloyd Stephens arrived in the steaming jungle in 1840 and found the mighty monuments of the city of Copan, he also adopted the metaphor of loss: "It lay before us like a shattered bark in the midst of the ocean, her masts gone, her name effaced, her crew perished, and none to tell whence she came, to whom she had belonged, how long on her voyage, or what caused her destruction.... All was mystery, dark impenetrable mystery...."

It was neither priest nor prophet who finally solved the mystery of the hieroglyphs, but scientists, travelers and adventurers. On foot, armed with machetes, they marched through the jungle, constantly finding new cities in the green ocean of the tropical vegetation (ill. II). Sitting at desks, surrounded by piles of books and computer printouts, they finally worked out the astronomy of this culture. Under the scorching sun, they knelt on the exposed floor of a house and, millimeter by millimeter, drew around the traces of a flattened jaw bone that belonged to a Maya who was buried 3000 years ago. Like the stones of a mosaic that slowly reveal a picture as the pieces are put together. But at last we know something about the crew; we know the name of the boat, and even of the captain who steered it. And now, one hundred years after the rhetorical question was written in the Chilam-Balam book of Chumayel, scientists are slowly unraveling the mystery of the hieroglyphs.

A new image of the Maya

There are scarcely any other areas of archeology where interpretations and ideas have changed so completely as in the field of Maya studies. It is entirely appropriate to speak of a paradigm shift. Although up to just a few decades ago it was still believed that the Maya had been peace-loving maize farmers who obeyed their priests' exhortations to observe the stars and honor time, it has now been proven that they were ruled over by kings and princes who were just as power-hungry and vain as potentates elsewhere in the world. Although many books tell us that the Maya operated a system of clearing land by fire and grew only maize, we now know that they had in fact developed intensive agricultural methods since the Preclassic period, digging raised beds and canals in marshy areas, and planning intensive horticultural and irrigation systems. The extensive Preclassic cities in northern Guatemala were unknown until just a few years ago. New excavations there have caused us to date the beginning of urban civilization back by about half a millennium. It has only been two or three years since we have learnt in what language the Maya scribes recorded their messages. New discoveries are being made all the time. Wherever archeologists start to dig, we know there will be surprises. Who would have guessed before 1997 that the rubble around the Acropolis of Ek Balam concealed amazingly an

II *Alfred Percival Maudslay in Chichen Itza. Glass plate photograph by H.N. Sweet, 1889*
The British scientist Alfred Percival Maudslay (1850–1931) was a pioneer of Maya research. At the age of 30, he heard of the ruins of Copan and Quirigua and decided to visit them. What was to have been a short stay became a lifelong passion. Maudslay went on several long trips, visiting and researching the cities of Palenque, Copan, Quirigua, Chichen Itza, Tikal, and Yaxchilan.

Previous double page:
Nobles with sacred bundles and incense pouches. Palenque, Chiapas, Mexico, bench in Temple 19, west side, limestone. Late Classic, 736 A.D.

I *Geomorphological map of the Maya region*
The region of Mesoamerica that is marked by the culture of the Maya covers an area of approximately 500,000 km², spread over five modern states.

almost undamaged stucco façade in the Chenes architectural style, the like of which is not seen anywhere else in the area? (ill. III) New finds are made every year that force us to rethink our ideas about the Maya and discard our old, familiar impressions of them.

However, it is this dynamism, with developments occurring on such a huge scale, that gives our preoccupation with the Maya its great attraction. Where else in the world are complete sites of an ancient culture hidden deep in the jungle; where else are complete regions just blank areas on the archeological map? Where else do we know so little about the economic foundations of an ancient civilization? And where else in the world have all the great cities of a culture sunk without trace, abandoned by their inhabitants for no apparent reason?

The field of Maya research is still in its infancy. It is such a new subject that only a few universities have any courses or faculties dedicated to scientific research into the Maya. One consequence of this lack of academic support is that we have no answers to many of our questions that are of tremendous scientific and cultural-historical interest. All we do know is that the race is now on between research and the destruction of the material heritage of the Maya. Maya works of art are fetching horrendous sums of money on the art market. All these

III *Stucco façade of the Acropolis. Ek Balam, Yucatan, Mexico; stone, covered with stucco and painted*
Between 1998 and 2000, archeologists of the Mexican Institute of Anthropology and History (INAH) dug in the archeological zone of Ek Balam, and found on the Acropolis a stucco frieze in a unique state of preservation and with a wealth of detail that has not been seen elsewhere in the world of the Maya. What is surprising – apart from the quality of the sculpture – is the transformation of the door into the wide-open jaws of a snake. This is something that is only seen in the Chenes architectural style, which flourished far away in Campeche.

objects have come from grave robberies, with art thieves rushing into the pyramids to loot objects with no regard for their archeological context. Archeologists lost this race long ago; most Maya sites have been emptied, and some even completely destroyed, in order to fill the display cabinets of collectors in Boston and Geneva. It would take a considerable amount of effort to research the remaining sites, to protect them and keep them for future generations. And it is not just a lack of resources that turns projects such as these into bureaucratic nightmares – but also the political division of the old land of the Maya into five modern states: Mexico, Guatemala, Belize, Honduras, and El Salvador. Although these five states have now banded together to form a "Ruta Maya," an open-border, tourist-oriented integration of the Maya world aimed at travelers, scientific research into Maya culture has not been able to benefit from this project to the same extent.

Despite these hindrances, we now have a picture of the rise and development of Maya culture that makes former representations look like rough sketches. Whereas the thrust of older works focused on the exoticism of the Maya, on their differentness and uniqueness, modern publications – such as we hope this book will reveal – show the Maya to have been people whose problems, intentions, and motives were not so different from those of other people all over the world (ill. IV). But for all the exoticism and romance that is associated with the word "Maya," they have now taken their place among the other great ancient civilizations – Egypt, Mesopotamia, India, and China.

We want to try and understand the Maya and reveal the internal logic of the history of this people. Thus the Maya also enter the stage of world history: even today, research continues to make new revelations that make our picture of this ancient culture clearer, and teach us that their monuments are much more than silent witnesses to a long-gone culture.

IV *Portrait head in stucco. Palenque archeological zone, Chiapas, Mexico; Late Classic, 600–900 B.C.; modeled stucco; H. 24.4 cm, W. 18.9 cm; Mexico City, Museo Nacional de Antropología*
The representation of heads in Maya art is usually idealized; they contain no individual features. It appears to have been only the artists in Palenque who attempted to immortalize the actual features of the people they modeled. This stucco head of an unknown Maya, presumably a prince or king of Palenque, is a masterpiece that leaves a lively impression of an important person.

V *The main plaza at Copan. Color lithograph by Frederick Catherwood, c. 1840*
"I would not dream of attempting to give an impression ... of the exciting effects of the monuments, standing there deep in the heart of a tropical forest, silent and festive, of the strange and wonderful designs, beautifully chiseled ..." wrote John Lloyd Stephens, who in 1840, together with artist Frederick Catherwood, rediscovered the forgotten ruins of Copan and opened them up to research.

Archeologists call the period in which the Maya culture slowly developed the Preclassic, and subdivided it into the Early Preclassic (2000–900 B.C.), the Middle Preclassic (900–300 B.C.) and the Late Preclassic (300 B.C.–250 A.D.). Whereas the first village communities developed during the Early Preclassic, the Middle Preclassic is noteworthy for the first examples of monumental architecture. A social order also developed in the settlements at this time, which is evident from the highly ornate tombs as well as from early stone monuments representing local dignitaries. Excavations over the last ten years have fundamentally changed our impressions of this particular period. Huge cities dating back to the Middle Preclassic have been discovered in northern Guatemala, close to the Mexican border. This makes them contemporaries of the Olmec culture on the Mexican Gulf coast; a culture that was in the past recognized as the mother culture of Mesoamerica.

Social differentiation became increasingly complex during the Late Preclassic period, and it appears that a number of states formed political structures with a clearly perceivable hierarchy of decision-makers, and with power concentrated in a central location. Monumental structures are characteristic of the Late Preclassic, especially temples and palaces decorated with over-sized stucco masks of deities. The first stone vaults also date back to the Late Preclassic. Recent excavations in Calakmul have revealed something of an architectural sensation: a Preclassic building with a genuine, that is to say self-supporting, vault, complete with keystone. However, Classic Maya used the cantilevered vault, a form of building that was unique to them throughout pre-Hispanic America and which became the foundation of all of their

VI *Stela 50. Izapa, Chiapas, Mexico, main plaza; Late Preclassic, 300 B.C.–100 A.D.; sandstone; Mexico City, Museo Nacional de Antropología*
The heyday of the city of Izapa, located in a cacao plantation close to the Pacific coast, was the Late Preclassic period. Hundreds of stone stelae and altars bear witness to ritual activities performed by the inhabitants: Stela 50 shows a seated god of death, from whose ribs spring forth lines and spirals, possibly the figure of a god or animal, possibly the depiction of an animal companion spirit.

VII *Hybrid creature, seated on a throne. Palenque, Chiapas, Mexico, Group B, Structure 3, Burial 1; Late Classic, 600–900 A.D.; modeled clay, painted; figure: H. 17 cm, W. 8.3 cm; throne: H. 6.6 cm, W. 13.6 cm; Palenque, Museo del Sitio "Alberto Ruz Lhuillier"*
Time and again, scientists researching Maya culture are stretched to the limits of their ability to explain something, such as this unusual clay figure found in a tomb some distance from the center of Palenque. It has been beautifully preserved; even some of the original painting is still visible. However, we do not know who or what the figure on the throne represents. It could be a cross between a wild turkey and a human, or simply a human wearing a mask.

Times and places

The ancestors of the Maya arrived on the American continent via the Bering Straits some time during the last Ice Age. As hunters and gatherers, they settled in the three main regions into which the Maya region is divided as a result of geological and climatic conditions: the Pacific coastal strip, the Highlands, and the Lowlands. Little is known of the early days of Maya culture (the Archaic period) but we do know that people settled in villages some time during the second millennium before the turn of the era. This happened as they turned to agriculture and began planting maize. The Maya have also left us some ceramics that date back to this period. This process did not happen simultaneously all over the region; it would appear that people settled on the Pacific coast before they did in the Highlands.

monumental architecture and urban constructions. The first stone monuments with hieroglyphic inscriptions appeared in the Late Preclassic period. The oldest texts present the script at such a level of uniformity and complexity that there must have been earlier stages; it is possible that they did not survive because of the materials used – or perhaps we simply have not yet found them.

Several major events took place towards the end of the Late Preclassic period, including natural disasters and displacements of the population. The volcano Ilopango erupted in El Salvador, burying parts of the Highlands in ash and lava, and there appear to have been climatic changes and destructive conflicts in the Lowlands. Many, but not all, Preclassic towns were abandoned. Kaminaljuyu, the biggest Maya town in the Highlands of Guatemala, was conquered by the ancestors of today's K'iche'.

The Classic period

The practice of calling the year 250 A.D. the dividing point between the Preclassic and Classic periods is a convention, an arbitrary assertion that serves to provide a rough chronological framework. In fact, though, the transition from Preclassic to Classic was gradual, and did not occur in every Maya region at the same time. Another problem with the current method of dividing up these epochs is that it was done at a time when Maya civilization was associated solely with the Classic period and its achievements. The Preclassic period was assigned the part of an incomplete precursor, and the Postclassic was seen as a time of decadence after the collapse of the cities in the Lowlands, because their material legacy was less spectacular than that of the Classic. Today, most scholars see things far more broadly, and consider the Classic period to have been only one of many forms taken by Maya culture during its long history.

VIII *Stucco hieroglyph, Palenque, Chiapas, Mexico, Olvidado Temple, door jambs at the entrance; 647 A.D.; modeled stucco, painted; H. 17 cm, W. 21 cm; Palenque, Museo del Sitio Alberto Ruz Lhuillier*
The first building by the great king K'inich Janaab Pakal of Palenque (615–683) was the so-called Olvidado ("the Forgotten") Temple, thus named because it was so far from the city center, deep in the jungle. The stucco hieroglyphs that once adorned the building, one of which is depicted here, tell us that Pakal had it built in 647 A.D. The hieroglyphs shown here have not yet been deciphered.

The Classic period is again divided into two periods, and even into three by some researchers: the Early Classic (250–550 A.D.) and the Late Classic (550–900 A.D.); the term Terminal Classic used by some scholars refers to the last 100 years of the Late Classic period, when Maya culture in the Lowlands was already showing signs of imminent collapse. During the Classic period, the Lowlands were divided by numerous competing city states; at the head of each of these small states was a king whose right to rule came from his descent from ancient gods, and he was therefore seen as an intermediary between the human world and the world of the gods. Vast, lavish palaces, conspicuous material luxury, and works of art representing the self-confident potentate bear witness to a highly developed court society. Hieroglyphic writing was also part of the culture of the nobility; thousands of texts on monumental stone pillars (called stelae by scholars), on altars, relief panels, ceramic vessels and jewelry tell of royal families and great feats, of wars and alliances, and also, at a much simpler level, name the artist who created a particular work (ill. VIII). Deciphering Maya hieroglyphic writing is undoubtedly one of the major achievements of modern scholarship; it enables us to reconstruct not only the political circumstances of the Classic period, but also the intellectual culture, astronomy and mythology of the Maya.

The Postclassic period

The Postclassic period was for a long time seen as a time of decadence, because the evidence of Postclassic culture found by archeologists was less spectacular and costly than that of the preceding Classic period. However, we now know that this difference was in fact due to a change in the self-confidence of its representatives. Whereas the Classic period was a time of despotic divine kings, the relatively small palaces and less opulent public architecture signal a reduced significance in the traditional ruling elite. As a counter-movement, a type of middle class appears to have formed that became involved in various forms of export trade and profited economically from it. Trade generally increased during the Postclassic; this is confirmed by the presence of exotic goods such as gold from southern Central America, turquoise from the south-western USA, and copper from the west coast of Mexico.

The Postclassic period is also divided into various eras. The Early Postclassic (900–1200 A.D.) is seen as the time of strong, close contact with the central Mexican metropolis of Chichen Itza which dominated the north of the Yucatan peninsula. The Middle Postclassic period (1200–1450 A.D.) is chiefly marked by the ascent of the city of Mayapan which extended its influence throughout Yucatan. This was also the time in which the K'iche' Maya ruled over and left their mark on the Highlands of Guatemala and a large number of foreign peoples. The Late Postclassic is the time immediately before the Spanish invasion. On the Yucatan peninsula, the region of the Mayapan broke down into a number of small rival states, some of which made pacts with the Spaniards at the beginning of the 16th century only so they would have allies to support them against their neighboring enemies. In the Highlands of Guatemala, the Late Postclassic is synonymous with the rise of the Kaqchikel and their capital Itzimte, whereas the importance of the K'iche' decreased. During the Late Postclassic period, another powerful state also arose in the central Lowlands, where Classic Maya culture had flowered earlier. From their island capital of Noj Peten, the Itzaj Maya resisted the Spanish conquerors until 1697.

The colonial era and the present

Most representations of Maya culture end with the Spanish invasion, as if that were also the end of Maya history. But the Maya survived, despite the terrors of military conquest, enslavement, and the introduction of new diseases, and preserved many aspects of their culture. They made an impact upon history, even under colonial rule. This is particularly evident in their countless uprisings against the colonial regime. Nor was there any improvement in the living conditions of the Maya and the continent's other Indian nations when the Latin American countries gained their independence from Spain after 1821. The original inhabitants of America had long become fringe groups at the bottom of the social hierarchy, even in areas where they still represented the majority of the population. Not even the biggest and most successful uprising by the Maya, the so-called Caste War (1847–1901), in which the Maya of Yucatan managed to conquer almost the entire peninsula, changed anything.

The Maya always suffered from oppression by force and disdain for their culture up to the present day, but today they are no longer willing to accept being patronized. Strong Maya movements have formed in Mexico and Guatemala, whose objective is to fight for political and cultural rights. The future will show whether any further chapters will need to be added to the history of the Maya, chapters which will perhaps deal with equality and cultural independence.

IX *Vault in the North Building of the Acropolis, Itzimte, Campeche, Mexico; photo by Teobert Maler, 1887*
The German-Austrian architect and explorer Teobert Maler wrote of the ruins at Itzimte, which he visited in March and April, 1887: "Itzimte is one of the biggest cities in Maya civilization and has gigantic buildings, such as one only encounters in Kabah, Nohpat, Uxmal and other capital cities. However, the proximity of a Spanish settlement - whether a village or a hacienda - makes the preservation of a ruined site completely impossible. What with the present population of the country's incurable urge to destroy things and their insuperable aversion to using the wooden tools which modern civilization has offered them to break stones from the local rocks, as the old Maya managed to do with their much more rudimentry tools, not one building, not even the most beautiful or finest of them, remains unspared."

The Early Classic period is defined largely by its contacts with the Central Mexican metropolis of Teotihuacan, the largest city of the Mesoamerican cultural region. As we now know, these connections directly influenced the politics and dynastic history of the Maya. The antagonism between the two superpowers of the Classic Maya period, Tikal and Calakmul, also arose during this time, and this finally led to the formation of two major systems of alliance. They determined politics and warfare at the beginning of the Late Classic period, but subsequently broke down, leading in turn to a process of disintegration and collapse that was hastened by ecological catastrophes and overpopulation. Throughout the 9th and 10th centuries A.D., city after city was abandoned by its inhabitants, finally leaving just a few families in the run-down ruins of former palaces.

Time for discoveries

"I saw a stela in the jungle when I was out hunting," said Andres, one of the young Maya who was helping to unearth the ruins of Caracol. No one really believed him; all too often, supposed stelae had turned out merely to be stones that nature had marked with grooves and shapes which, with some imagination, could be interpreted as representations of kings. Was it worth believing him and beating a trail through creepers, swamps and lianas, only to face disappointment again at the end of the journey? However, Andres' powers of persuasion won the day, and the expedition set off the very next morning. Kilometer by exhausting kilometer, the party walked through an area that had probably not seen humans for 1000 years – apart from Andres when he was out hunting. The metal swoosh of the machetes as they cut through the thicket was endless; mosquitoes fought to be first to suck the blood of the intrepid explorers, attracted by the smell of their sweat. Finally, the guide called out, "Here it is!" – but no stela was to be seen, not even a building. But wait – over there was a shaft that the looters had ignored. It led deep down into a shallow pyramid. Remains of ceramics and bones showed that the thieves had stumbled across a burial.

Andres pointed triumphantly to a stone beside the shaft – and yes, there was writing on it! (ill. XI). It was not a stela, but one of the capping stones that had once been used to top the burial. A sculpted capstone – that was something that had never been seen before in the southern Lowlands! A Maya artist had once used sure, fine lines to depict a mortal figure, possibly the departed, in ornate ceremony, even noting the name and date of death on the stone (ill. X). Little would he have imagined that other human eyes would one day see this stone, intended for the departed, and certainly not those of one of his Maya descendants. The time of discoveries is only just beginning in the land of the Maya, and large numbers of relics from this once flowering, highly developed culture are still waiting to be found.

X *Decorated capstone, Caracol, Belize, Conchita group; Late Early Classic or Early Late Classic, 500–650 A.D.; limestone, grooved; H. 88 cm, W. 22 cm; Caracol, Archeological Zone*
The richly dressed figure is wearing the mask of the god Itzamnaaj as a headdress. A jade bead necklace, large ear rings and cuffs on the hands and feet confirm the high position held by the person. Over the head are two incomplete hieroglyphs, which probably give the name of the artist or the deceased. At the bottom is an incomplete date – possibly that of the day on which the vault was sealed.

XI *Andres beside the open tomb and capstone*
Finally, after a long march, they arrived – at a group of nondescript buildings, hardly discernible from the hilly landscape, and completely covered by jungle overgrowth. As before, the place had already been found by looters, although they had not taken a decorated capstone from the tomb. This was probably due to the weight of the stone – and it was a huge stroke of luck for archeologists: no comparable capstones have been found anywhere else in the southern Maya Lowlands.

HABITATS AND EARLY HORIZONS

VOLCANOES AND JUNGLE –
A RICHLY VARIED HABITAT

Nikolai Grube

The region in which the Maya live today has hardly changed from the one in which their ancestors settled three or even four thousand years ago. Today, the "Maya world" embraces the southern Mexican federal states of Chiapas, Tabasco, Campeche, Yucatan, and Quintana Roo, the small state of Belize (formerly British Honduras) that finally gained independence from Great Britain in 1981, all of Guatemala, El Salvador, and western Honduras.

Geographically, the region inhabited by the Maya on the bridge of land between North and South America belongs to northern Central America. While the region is bordered by the Pacific Ocean to the south, the Yucatan peninsula stretches all the way from the Gulf of Mexico to the Caribbean (ill. 1). The entire region is south of the Tropic of Cancer, and therefore tropical.

Because of the vast differences in altitude throughout the Maya region, the fluctuating rainfall which varies from region to region, and the different soil types, scientists have divided the Maya habitat into three main zones: the Pacific coastal plain; the volcanic Highlands, and the sometimes hilly but generally flat Lowlands. Because the development of Maya culture centered around the Lowlands, where the large city-states flourished in Classic times, this cultural region is of particular importance.

A tropical climate

The climate of all tropical America north of the Equator is determined by the rainy and dry seasons. As in all the tropics, the rainy season coincides with the time of the summer solstice. The rains start at the end of May, and peak in June. Early in August the rainy period is interrupted by a short dry spell, known as the *canicula*, then becomes more intense again in September when the sun is at its highest for the second time (ill. 2). Whereas the rainy period in the Highlands ends in October, in the Lowlands it often continues until well into December. The period from the *canicula* to the end of the year is also the tropical hurricane season, with hurricanes forming extremely low-pressure weather systems over the Caribbean. When they reach land they can cause catastrophic destruction. In October 1998, Hurricane Mitch buried vast tracts of Honduras and east Guatemala under water and mud.

Along with the seasonal variations, the amount of rainfall also varies from region to region. The smallest amounts fall in the north-west of the peninsula (annual mean rainfall 475 mm/18.7 in.), the figures increasing toward the south-east. In the Toledo district of southern Belize, the annual rainfall lies between 3000 and 4000 mm (118 and 158 in.), and in the area of Palenque, Chiapas, it even exceeds 4000 mm (158 in.). The actual amounts of rainfall can vary tremendously. Some years are particularly dry; vast amounts of rain can fall in others, and both can have disastrous effects on harvests.

2 Geophysical map of the Maya region
The region, located in the modern states of Mexico, Guatemala, Belize, Honduras, and El Salvador, is marked by its great diversity of landscape forms. Landscape, climate and vegetation divide the Maya region, which is roughly the same size as the state of Oregon, into three large zones: the coastal strip along the Pacific, the volcanic Highlands, and the undulating Lowlands to the north.

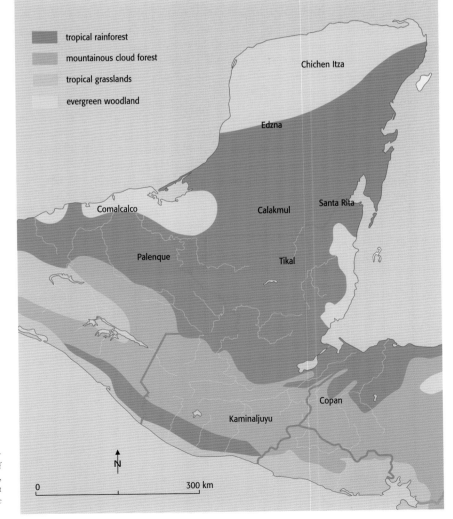

tropical rainforest
mountainous cloud forest
tropical grasslands
evergreen woodland

Chichen Itza
Edzna
Comalcalco
Calakmul
Santa Rita
Palenque
Tikal
Copan
Kaminaljuyu

N

0   300 km

1 *View of the Highlands of Guatemala*
"The country is so beautiful that it hurts," wrote Oliver La Farge in the 1920s, describing the Highlands of Guatemala and their inhabitants. Small Indian villages, smoking volcanoes, pine forests and carefully laid out maize fields still characterize the appearance of the Highlands today.

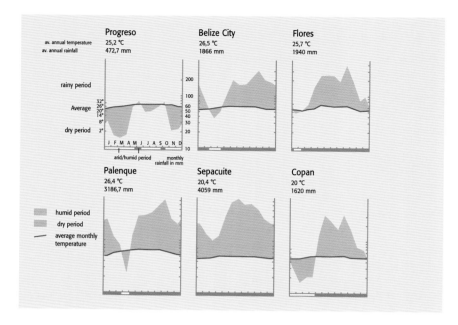

Progreso	Belize City	Flores
av. annual temperature 25,2 °C	26,5 °C	25,7 °C
av. annual rainfall 472,7 mm	1866 mm	1940 mm

rainy period

Average 32° 26° 20° 14° 8°

dry period 2°

J F M A M J J A S O N D

arid/humid period   monthly rainfall in mm

Palenque	Sepacuite	Copan
26,4 °C	20,4 °C	20 °C
3186,7 mm	4059 mm	1620 mm

humid period

dry period

average monthly temperature

3 *Climate diagrams from various Lowland locations*
The climate in the Lowlands is determined by a number of factors. On the whole, the number of rainy months increases toward the south of the region. In towns such as Flores and Palenque there are only one or two dry months a year, but in Sepacuite, the farthest south, it rains every month.

with temperatures of 35°C (95°F) and more are not unusual during the dry season. Nights are cool (14–20°C/57–68°F), and in December and January the temperature can even fall to freezing point. Daytime temperatures in the *tierra fría*, the Highlands above 2000 m (6560 ft.), are pleasant (20–27°C/69–81°F); nights are cold (below 15°C/59°F). Night frosts are not unusual between November and February.

The Pacific coastal plain

In the extreme south of the Maya region, between the Pacific Ocean and the steeply rising volcanic Highlands, is a fertile coastal strip between 40 and 100 km (25 and 62 miles) wide (ill. 4). The good quality of the soils and the high rainfall make this a good area for growing cotton and cacao. Today, banana and sugar cane plantations stretch across the wide plains; cotton and cacao are still produced, but are now less important economically than they were in pre-Hispanic times when this coastal strip was so attractive to the Maya – and to neighboring peoples, who tried repeatedly to appropriate parts of it for themselves (ill. 5). The rivers that flow down from the Highlands, and the marshland thrown up by them, are what make this coastal strip so fertile. The highly nutritious soils are dark with volcanic ash, and even the Pacific beach in this area is black. Between 3000 and 4000 mm (118 and 158 in.) of rain fall every year; from June to September, the rain in the clouds coming from the Pacific falls on the plain before the wind forces it up against the steep Highlands.

The volcanic Highlands

From Mexico to Costa Rica, the ranges of hills and mountains of the American Cordilleras form a land bridge between North and South America. The mountains in this chain reach a height of up to 4420 m (14,500 ft.) at the point where they cross into the Maya region – and yet the mighty peaks of the Sierra Madre (as the mountain chain is called in Mexico and Guatemala),

The time when the rainy season starts can also vary, and uncertainty about this and the amount of rain that will fall pose great risks to Maya farmers.

There is little temperature variation throughout the year (ill. 3). March, April, and May are the warmest months, with dry weather, clear skies and bright sunshine. When the sun is at its highest in the summer, in June and July, rain cools the air and clouds cover the sun. In the tropical Lowlands, daytime temperatures range between 29 and 32°C (84 and 90°F), and between 20 and 24°C (68 and 75°F) at night. Temperature differences between day and night are in fact greater than the seasonal fluctuations, which is why people say that night-time is the winter of the tropics.

In the milder transitional zone between the Lowlands and the Highlands, the *tierra templada* between 1000 and 2000 m (3280 and 6560 ft.) above sea level, daytime temperatures are usually mild (24–27°C/75–81°F), but hot afternoons

4 *Geological structure and vegetation on a hypothetical north-south line in the Maya region*
The principal features of the Maya environment are the volcanic Highlands and the geologically young Lowlands, which rest on karst, a porous limestone rock that rapidly absorbs rainwater. These contain underground watercourses, though access to them is possible only in areas where the limestone layer has collapsed.

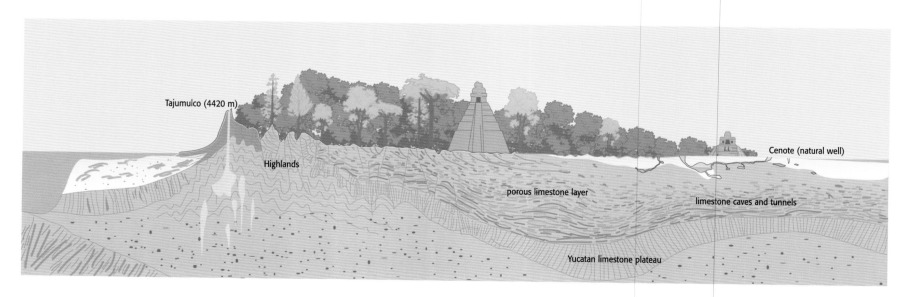

Tajumulco (4420 m)

Highlands

Cenote (natural well)

porous limestone layer

limestone caves and tunnels

Yucatan limestone plateau

with the volcano Tajumulco at 4420 m (14,500 ft.) and the Tacana at 4093 m (16,082 ft.), fall short of the snowline.

Large areas of the rugged Highlands are tectonically active; nine of Guatemala's 12 large volcanoes still pose a threat to the surrounding towns with the occasional eruption which produces ash falls and clouds of gas (ill. 6). There are also frequent volcanic eruptions in the adjoining Mexican state of Chiapas and in El Salvador, which have already driven thousands of people from their homes (ill. 7). Archeologists suspect that the eruption of the Ilopango volcano in El Salvador in about 150 A.D. caused such a massive natural catastrophe that most of the towns in the Highlands were abandoned. There is a direct link between the cultural blossoming of the Lowlands that followed and movements in the population after these volcanic eruptions. The massive earthquake that devastated Guatemala in 1976 caused demographic and political changes in the country, the effects of which are still felt today. Despite the continuing latent threat of earthquakes and eruptions, the majority of the Maya population in Mexico and Guatemala have made their homes in the Highland regions. There is a historical reason for this. When the Spaniards arrived in the 16th century, several large, newly formed Maya states were flourishing in the Highlands, and the Spaniards preferred the (to Europeans) much pleasanter climate in the Highlands to the hot, humid zones at lower levels. In order to keep the conquered Maya under better control, they relocated large numbers of them from the conquered regions of the Lowlands to the Highlands.

5 *The sculptures of Santa Lucia Cozumalhuapa in a sugar cane plantation on the Pacific coastal plain. Santa Lucia Cozumalhuapa, Escuintla, Guatemala; Classic; 600–900 A.D.; basalt*
Sugar cane, cotton, and bananas are the main export crops grown today on large plantations on the Pacific coastal plain, thanks to the excellence of the soil in this region. In pre-Hispanic times, different groups were constantly trying to win control over the coastal region so they could run the cacao plantations and foreign trade. These groups included members of the Cotzumalhuapa culture, who probably migrated from Central Mexico; their ruins contain stone stelae and altars in a style very different from that of the Maya.

6 *View of Lake Atitlan with the Santiago and Toliman volcanoes*
Embedded between the Santiago (3525 m) and the Toliman (3150 m) volcanoes is Lake Atitlan – 1300 m above sea level and the crater of an extinct volcano – and, according to Humboldt, "the most beautiful lake in the world." Coffee bushes now grow on the slopes of the volcano, and the inhabitants along the shores of the lake live primarily from maize-growing and fishing. The Tz'utujil Maya live on the south and west banks of the lake; the villages of the Kaqchikel are in the north and east and include Panajachel, now the region's center for tourism.

The volcanic soils of the Highlands were formed by massive eruptions of pumice and ash in the Tertiary and Pleistocene periods. This formed a deposit that is several hundred meters in depth and covered by a thin layer of fertile soil. Over the millennia, rain and erosion have turned the region into a rugged landscape with deeply eroded crags between the mountain ridges, together with numerous wide valleys with fertile soils (ill. 7).

At the point where the Highlands and Lowlands meet is a zone of limestone that dates back to the Tertiary and Cretaceous period. This zone contains the most amazingly eroded shapes in the more humid region on the edge of the Lowlands. The huge rainfall – an annual average of more than 4000 mm (158 in.) – and the length of the rainy season have resulted in a tropical mountain forest in this zone, the most eye-catching features of which are dripping tree ferns, mosses and lichens. This is the home of the Quetzal bird (*Pharomachrus mocino*), which is greatly prized by the Maya for its long, green and gold tail feathers growing up to 40 cm (16 in.) long, and is now featured on the national flag of Guatemala (ill. 23).

The Lowlands

As it reaches northward, the mountain jungle of the Verapaz region gradually changes into the geologically somewhat younger Lowlands, the core region of the Classic Maya culture (ill. 4). The southern Lowlands comprise the Selva Lacandona region of Chiapas, the Mexican state of Tabasco and the southern part of the federal states of Campeche and Quintana Roo, the departments of Peten and Izabal in the north and east of Guatemala, north-west Honduras and all of Belize; the northern Lowlands consists of the Yucatan peninsula, that is, the northern part of the federal states of Campeche and Quintana Roo, and the federal state of Yucatan. The Lowlands, which cover a total area of 250,000 km^2 (96,525 sq. miles), consist of an almost completely flat sedimentary limestone plateau. The landscape is interrupted by just a few ranges of hills, with the exception of the largely unexplored granite and quartz massif of the Maya Mountains in the south, where the Victoria Peak in Belize reaches a height of 1023 m (3355 ft.).

The fact that vast expanses of the Lowlands were originally covered by dense jungle is misleading as far as the soils are concerned, their quality being uniformly poor. The soil crust is extremely thin, and becomes thinner the further one travels north in the Yucatan peninsula, where it is only 50 cm (20 in.) thick in some places. Added to this, the soils of the Lowlands contain little in the way of nutrients. Although leaves fall continuously and the ground is covered in organic material, the crust does not grow thicker because the organic material

7 *Aerial view of the Santa Ana volcano, El Salvador*
At 2381 m, the Santa Ana volcano is the highest volcano in the country, but it has not erupted since 1880. Massive explosions have resulted in four concentric craters. At the center of the youngest crater is a lake, from which clouds of sulfur rise up. The Izalco volcano, which is seen behind it, is lower and still active. It appeared in 1770, and is still pushing out ash, lava and hot gases. The last major eruption occurred in 1966.

decomposes, and the nutrients are immediately used up. However, in the northern part of the Lowlands there are valleys into which more fertile soil is washed by the rain which once fed large numbers of people.

One of the major problems in the Lowlands is the porosity of the limestone, which allows any water to soak through the surface instantly. There are numerous deep rivers in the south of the Lowlands that transport water away from the Highlands (ill. 9) and have introduced an expanse of alluvial land (Pasion, Chixoy, Usumacinta, San Pedro Martir, Candelaria, Belize River, Hondo), but these become less frequent further north. The same applies to lakes and lagoons. There are countless large lakes in the southern Lowlands which are fed from underground watercourses; the largest is Lake Peten-Itza. By contrast, there is almost no surface water at all in the northern part of the Yucatan peninsula. The lack of water is a serious problem for the inhabitants of the Lowlands. In the Peten region of northern Guatemala there are wide, marshy depressions, *bajos*, that fill with water during the rainy season but are invariably dry at other times of the year. Although the water of the muddy *bajos* is not suitable for drinking, it was used intensively for agricultural purposes in pre-Hispanic times.

9 *The Usumacinta River in the Lowlands of Tabasco*
The Usumacinta River, dyed red by the loam, winds sluggishly through the Lowlands of Tabasco before merging with the river system of the Grijalva and finally running into the Gulf of Mexico. The Usumacinta is the longest river in Central America, and contains the most water. Long stretches of it form the international border between Mexico and Guatemala. One of the main trade routes of the Maya led from the Gulf of Mexico via the Usumacinta to the heart of the Yucatan peninsula.

8 *The cenote of Chichen Itza*
Where the Yucatan peninsula's limestone layer has collapsed, there are natural wells providing access to the groundwater. These funnel-shaped hollows are called *tz'ono'ot* by the Maya, and this gave rise to the Spanish word *cenote*. The cenote of Chichen Itza was an important place of pilgrimage until the Spaniards arrived. Early in the 20th century, archeologists dived down to the bottom of the cenote and salvaged a number of precious sacrificial offerings.

There are waterholes, known as *aguadas*, over wide areas of the southern Lowlands. These are to be found wherever the limestone landscape forms natural valleys that prevent rainwater from seeping away. The Maya also developed impressive natural *aguadas* by excavating large reservoirs and lining them with burnt lime to make them watertight. Many old *aguadas* are still the only source of water for the inhabitants of the southern Lowlands today. A little further to the north, natural sinkholes are the main source of drinking and bathing water (ill. 8). They are called *cenote* in local Spanish, which comes from the Mayan word *tz'ono'ot*. These are fairly circular, steep-sided waterholes between 10 and 80 m (33 and 262 ft.) in diameter. They formed when the limestone strata forming the roofs of underground caves collapsed. They have attracted humans ever since the country was first inhabited, as they are always filled with water from subterranean watercourses.

The flora

In pre-Hispanic times, large areas of the Maya regional, although densely populated, were covered by thick forests. The name of the country Guatemala bears testimony to this: it derives from the Nahuatl word *quauhtimala-tlan*, which means "lots of trees" and corresponds directly to the Mayan word *k'i'-*

chee'. The name of the K'iche' population, now the biggest group of Maya in Guatemala, also comes from this word.

The flora in the Highlands is characterized by the composition of the soil and the topography. Pine trees and grasses dominate higher up in the mountains and cliffs, whereas oak trees also thrive lower down in the valleys and gaps where there is generally more moisture (ill. 10). Nowadays coffee is grown on the fertile slopes of the volcanoes and lower down on the wind-protected expanses of the Highlands, and is the main product of the Mexican state of Chiapas and of Guatemala. The coffee bush, which came originally from Ethiopia, did not arrive in the region until the 19th century and was unknown to the pre-Hispanic Maya. In the Highlands, the Maya lived – as they continue to do today – from *milpa* (the Aztec word for "maize field" farming; see Harrison, p. 71 ff.), based on the principle of "slash-and-burn agriculture." The rugged landscape with its steep slopes obliged Highland farmers to lay out their fields in terraces. The advantages of terracing the slopes were well known in pre-Hispanic times; not only did they create a greater cultivable surface for a growing population, they also protected the mountain slopes against erosion. Today, the once dense forests of the Highlands have largely disappeared and as a consequence the fauna has been seriously decimated.

Because of the large amount of rainfalls, the fact that there are only a few dry months and the slight variations in seasonal temperatures, there is a fascinating

10 *Forest in the Highlands of Chiapas*
The exceptionally high rainfall in the area where the Highlands gradually blend with the Lowlands has resulted in a cloud forest vegetation, consisting of oak trees up to 50 m in height, laurel trees, and a variety of conifers. The floor is densely covered with ferns; lichen and tillandsia, called "beard of trees" by the Maya, thrive in the trees.

11 *Tropical jungle in the Peten, Guatemala*
The whole of the central and southern Lowlands – apart from the coasts – is noted for its dense tropical jungle. The vegetation consists of several layers, and allows practically no daylight through to the floor. This photo, which was taken at the archeological site Arroyo de Piedra in the Petexbatun region, shows the impressive roots of the jungle giants. The tree on the right is a ceiba tree (*Ceiba pentandra*), the holy tree of the Maya which, to them, represents the center of the universe.

and highly diverse tropical rainforest both on the Pacific coast and in the southern Lowlands, the main region of the Classic Maya culture (ill. 11). It is notable for an overwhelming wealth of species, although several of them are only present in small numbers. A hectare can contain up to 150 different tree species, the heights of which divide the vegetation into three to five layers (ill. 12). The roof of the jungle is formed by giant trees up to 60 m (197 ft.) high. Lower down, the crowns of the 30 m (98 ft.) high trees form a closed roof, and the younger, still growing trees form the lowest layer of the jungle.

The tallest trees include the ceiba or silk-cotton tree (*Ceiba pentandra*), which is sacred to the Maya and can grow to a height of 70 m (230 ft.). To the Maya, its slender trunk and spreading crown represent the earth's axis and the heavens. Although the ceiba tree will also grow in the Highlands, the mahogany tree (*Swietenia macrophylla*), which can reach a height of 40 m (131 ft.), the Spanish cedar (*Cedrela mexicana*) and the custard apple (*Manilkara zapota*) grow only in the Lowlands. The latter provides the raw material for chewing gum. The bark is slit during the rainy season from the crown to the stump by chicleros (gum tappers), who climb the trees with the aid of spurs and a rope. Slitting the bark gives off a quick-setting latex (ills. 13–15). These trees are all valued for their hard wood, although the number of mahogany trees has declined dramatically over the last few decades as a result of over-exploitation.

Only about one percent of sunlight actually penetrates the dense foliage of the jungle to reach the ground. As a result, there is hardly any undergrowth; not even grasses grow on the jungle floor which is always covered by a thick layer of decomposing leaves (ill. 11). Only the extremely slow-growing ferns thrive on the gloomy "ground floor" of the jungle. However, it is not easy to move around between the giant trees because of all the thick, protruding tree roots, essential for the trees to gain any kind of hold on the hard, dry ground; the lianas hanging from them form a further obstacle, some of them armed with sharp thorns. To the Maya, the jungle was not the life-threatening green hell that it was to many European travelers, but a natural resource to be used in many ways. From the timber of the logwood tree (*Haematoxilum campechianum*) they obtained a colorant used to dye materials; the nuts of the breadnut or ramon tree (*Brosimum alicastrum*) were ground and in times of need added to a maize mixture to make tamales and tortillas. The nut of the corozo palm (*Scheelea lundelli*) is still used as the source of a precious and delicious oil, and the roofs of Maya houses are covered with the leaves of the guano palm (*Sabal mexicana*) – just as they were a thousand years ago (see Hammond, p. 37).

Parasites grow in the tops of the trees and tap into the juices produced by their hosts, as well as epiphytes, the so-called "squatter plants," which want to be closer to the sunlight and therefore settle on trees but without depriving their hosts of nutrients. Some parasites, such as the "strangling fig" (*Ficus lapathifolium*) even go so far as to kill their hosts. They settle on branches of the host and grow air roots that put out suckers as soon as they touch the ground. The air roots then grow around the host tree (now no longer required as a source of nutrition), strangling it until it finally dies. Some plants exhibit quite fantastic behavior in their attempts to overcome the lack of nutrients in the soil. Special roots, such as those of Aaron's rod, absorb moisture – and the nutrients it contains – from the air; bromeliads, on the other hand, collect organic material in the rosettes on their leaves. The highly colored flowers of bromeliads and orchids are concealed from the human eye by the densely packed foliage of the tree crowns.

12 *The impenetrable forest roof*
The tops of the jungle giants – which grow up to 60 m in height – form a closed roof that totally conceals the lower layers from view, to say nothing of the remains of temples and collapsed walls, which is why many Maya settlements remain undiscovered to this day. From the air, all one can see is an apparently endless green ocean with no identifiable contours.

13 *Chiclero at work. Campamento La Toronja, Peten, Guatemala; photo taken in 1998*
During the rainy season, the chicleros (gum tappers) pass through the jungle in search of the custard apple (*chicozapote* in Spanish). When they have found one, they climb them with the aid of spurs and a rope, which they pass around the tree and their hips. Using a narrow bush knife, they slit the bark from crown to stump. The work is extremely dangerous; if the tapper inadvertently cuts through the rope, death is usually inevitable.

14 *The sapodilla tree provides "chicle" resin*
In the rainy season, the trees produce particularly generous amounts of the white chicle resin, which is used for making chewing gum. The bark of the tree is slit with the bush knife (or machete), and the resin immediately spurts from the red wood. A chiclero can work about three trees a day; the amount of chicle juice tapped from a tree varies between one and three kilograms. A tapped tree is left to rest for several years.

15 *Collecting resin*
The chicle is collected in a leather bag tied around the tree, and then boiled in large troughs (*pailas*) over wood fires. The thick fluid is then poured into blocks (*marquetas*) and sold on to dealers when solid. In the 1950s, "jungle chewing gum" was replaced by synthetic gum, and there was a strong risk that the profession of chiclero would die out. However, in recent years there has been an increased demand for natural products – including natural chewing gum.

The thorny jungle of the north

The further north one goes, the less rainfall there is. The forest gradually changes into a low, thorny jungle that lacks tall trees such as mahogany and custard apple. The dry period lasts longer here, which means that most of the trees shed their leaves. Finally, along the coast of the Yucatan peninsula, the forest becomes an impenetrable thorny scrub (ill. 16). Sisal agave was the main crop until the invention of synthetic fabrics.

Neither the thorny jungle of the north nor the evergreen rain forest of the south is actually a primary forest in the true sense. During the heyday of Classic Maya culture, the forest had undoubtedly been extensively cleared and reduced to a few "islands" of trees; this much we know from paleo-ecological research and pollen investigations. Once deprived of its trees, tropical ground soon loses its fertility and becomes unsuitable for productive use; a layer of hard laterite – the red, weathered soil that is so typical of the tropics – forms on the surface. Tropical rainfall and strong sunshine destroy the ground astonishingly quickly, which has catastrophic results on the entire ecological system and removes the population's basic source of food. An ecological catastrophe such as this was undoubtedly a contributory factor to the collapse of Classic Maya culture in the 9th and 10th centuries. Once the Maya had left their cities and towns, the jungle soon reclaimed the Lowlands.

16 *Thornbush in the north at Chichen Itza; photograph taken in 1989*
Low quantities of rain and extremely thin soils account for the thornbush forest that covers the northern part of the Yucatan peninsula. Trees and bushes shed their leaves in the dry season, between November and April, and the landscape takes on a bare and dusty appearance.

THE TWO CREATORS, ALOM AND Q'AJOLOM, CREATE THE ANIMALS

Myths concerning creation play a major role in all Mesoamerican cultures, and the subject is taken up in the Popol Wuj. After creating the Earth and the skies, the two gods decided to create the animals.

Now the gods planned the wild animals, all the guardians of the forest, all the creatures of the mountains: deer, birds, pumas, jaguars, snakes, rattlesnakes, vipers, the guardians of the undergrowth.

And Alom and Q'ajolom spoke:

"What is the point of this silence? Why does nothing move beneath the trees and bushes?"

"Indeed – they should have their guardians," replied the others. And no sooner had this been thought and spoken than suddenly deer and birds appeared.

And then every deer and bird was given a home:

"You, deer, go off to the banks of the river, and you will sleep in the glen. Be here in the glades, in the thicket, in the forests, and reproduce. You will stand on all fours," the deer were told. And then they gave all the birds, the big ones and the small ones, their nests.

"Oh, you birds, make your homes in the trees and bushes. Reproduce there, and distribute yourselves over the trees and branches of the bushes," they said to the birds. And when this act of creation was complete, they all had a place to sleep and a place to live. Thus it came about that all the animals have their home on the earth, and the homes were given to them by Alom and Q'ajolom. Now the deer and birds had been created.

And then the deer and the birds were told by the modeler and the maker:

"Speak and make calls. Do not howl or scream. Speak to one another within your own species," the deer were told and the birds, pumas, jaguars and snakes and rattlesnakes.

"Now tell us our names and praise us. We are your mother and your father. Now say this:

'Juraqan,

Ch'ipi qa qulaja, raxa qa qulaja,

The heart, the earth, the heart of the sky,

Maker, Modeler,

Alom, Q'ajolom.'

Speak, call out to us, praise us," they were told. But it transpired that they did not speak like humans, they only pretended to. They hissed, they screamed, they cackled. No one could understand their language; every one cried differently ..."

And they had to try again, and try again to praise the creators. But they were unable to understand each other, and could not make themselves understood, because they had not been made that way. That is why their flesh was sacrificed, and from that time they were eaten, they were killed, the animals on the face of the earth.

17 *Gathering of gods and animals. Rollout of a cylindrical container; provenance unknown; Late Classic, 600–900 A.D.; burnt clay, painted; H. 21.2 cm, dia. 14.3 cm; private collection (Kerr 3413)*
The cosmos of the Maya is inhabited by a large number of gods in both human and animal form. Many of them are shown here on a flight of outdoor stairs, probably the entrance to a temple. Left of center, seated on the ground, are two gods in simian form. As gods of the writers, they are having a lively discussion about a codex that is lying between them.

The Fauna

The diversity of the flora is matched by the diversity of the animal world. The fauna of the Highlands is virtually the same as in the Lowlands, but because the Highlands are more densely populated and deforested, most animal species are now only found in the Lowlands. Although the Maya did not domesticate many animals other than turkeys and dogs, to them the animal world was a resource of which they made full use.

The Maya used blowguns to hunt birds such as the toucan and the ara parrot for their brightly colored feathers, shooting them with tiny clay pellets. Larger birds such as wild pheasant and wild turkey were shot with arrows to make a tasty addition to the menu. Two types of monkey swing through the tree tops: the small and entertaining red-faced spider monkey (*Ateles geoffroyi*), and the large black howler monkey (*Alouatta pigra*), so named because of its spine-chilling call (ill. 22). Both play an important role in Maya religion as the gods of writers and artists.

The biggest animal in the Maya world was the tapir (*Tapirus bairdii*). Although a distant relative of our horse, this plump, shy giant is not suitable for domestication (ill. 18). There are no large mammals in the fauna of the Maya regions that could have been used as draft animals in pre-Hispanic times, which is probably why the Maya used the wheel as a toy rather than for transport purposes. There are two types of deer: a big one with large antlers (*Odocoileus virginianus*) and a smaller one, the brocket (*Mazama americana*) with fork-

18 *Tapir in the tropical rain forest, Belize*
The shy Baird's tapir is the biggest land mammal of Central America. It weighs more than 200 kg, and its heavy tread can be heard a long distance away. When the Maya first saw the horses used by the Spaniards, they thought they too were tapir, and therefore called them *tziimin*.

19 *Iguana*
The iguana lives close to human settlements, and is often to be seen sunning itself on the hot stones of ruined sites. Its meat and eggs are considered delicacies.

20 *Coral snake*
Although it grows to no longer than 85 cm, the coral snake is highly dangerous with a fast-acting neurotoxic venom.

shaped antlers. Both are prized and hunted for their tasty meat, their hides and antlers. The Maya also hunted a great variety of smaller animals with traps and spears, including the peccary. This member of the wild boar family goes around in groups and has a gland on its rump that gives off an extremely unpleasant smell, thanks to which it can be detected from a long way off. There was also the agouti (*Dasyprocta punctata*), a kind of rodent resembling a hare, and its relative the guanta (*Agouti paca*), a nocturnal rodent quite like a rabbit that lives in burrows, as well as the armadillo and the raccoon. The white meat of the boa constrictor, which grows up to 3 m (3.3 ft.) in length, is also suitable for human consumption. Other snakes, such as the coral snake (*Micrurus diastema*; ill. 20) can inject a seriously harmful, even fatal poison into humans. Snakes play an important role in Maya art as a symbol of transformation and of the link to the gods. The Maya prize other reptiles much more than snakes, especially different varieties of the land-bound iguana (ill. 19) and the land tortoise. Both are hunted for their meat and their eggs. Lakes, rivers and coastal regions are home to two different species of crocodile and an alligator that grows to up to four meters (13 ft.) in length; all are extremely dangerous to humans. People fished the lakes and coasts, and sharks, stingray and the plump manatee of the Caribbean coast provided plentiful amounts of meat. The spine of the stingray was used as a tool for ritual bloodletting. Shark's teeth were used as jewelry; sewing needles were fashioned from fish bones. Mussel shells were highly prized as commercial goods as they could be made into jewelry.

Holes were punched in the large shells of the Great Green Conch (*Strombus gigas*), which is found in shallow coastal areas, and they were then used as a kind of trumpet.

Of all the animals, the big cats were the most prized – and feared – in particular the jaguar (ill. 24) for its valuable shiny coat, and also the puma, which was almost the same size, the tree-dwelling ocelot, and smaller cats such as the slender long-tailed margay (*Leopardus wiedii*) and the dark Jaguarundi (*Herpailuros yaguarondi*; ill. 21). They all hunt only at night and keep away from human settlements, so it is unusual ever to encounter one of these extremely shy creatures. The denseness of the vegetation provides them with ample shelter; usually only the trained eye of a hunter will detect their presence from a few broken twigs or the disturbed mud around a water hole.

More eye-catching are the splendid butterflies, including the sparkling blue *Morpho* butterflies which flit among the trees and grow to up to 20 cm (8 in.). Cicadas and other insects create an ear-shattering noise at sunrise and sunset. The Maya made good use of the vast world of small animals and insects, such as the native stingless bee, and produces vast quantities of a very sweet honey, and wax. Honey is still important economically for Maya peasants.

The fundamental existence of this lavish animal world is now under threat as man forces his way further and further into the natural living space, cuts down trees, builds roads and develops coasts. We will undoubtedly be making the same mistakes that led to the downfall of the Classic Maya civilization a thousand years ago if we fail to protect the treasures of this tropical world.

21 *Jaguarundi*
The sleek jaguarundi is the smallest wild cat of the Central American jungle. Unlike other wild cats, it rarely lives or hunts in the branches of trees.

22 *Black howler monkey in a tree*
One of the two varieties of monkey that live in northern Central America is the howler monkey (*Alouatta pigra*) In Classic Maya mythology, the monkey was the patron of scribes and artists.

23 *Female quetzal with her prey*
The quetzal was extremely popular with the Maya because of its long green tail feathers. This shy bird lives in the mountain forests of the Verapaz region in Guatemala. Deforestation means it is now an endangered species.

24 *The jaguar – lord of the forest*
The biggest of the five predatory big cats in the Maya region is the jaguar (*Felis onca*), which grows to up to 2 meters in length. Despite international bans, its shiny pelt is still traded and processed today with the result that numbers of the animal have declined dramatically.

CACAO – THE BEVERAGE OF THE GODS

Nikolai Grube

Europeans first encountered cacao in the year 1502, when Columbus on his fourth journey to the Gulf of Honduras, came across a large Maya trading canoe that measured over 40 m (131 ft.) in length, if the story recounted by his son Ferdinand is to be believed. Not only was the canoe laden with metates (or grinding stones), copper items, fabrics and vessels, it also contained roots and grains, and a type of wine made from maize. Almonds were also on board, and they appeared to be particularly important to the Maya. Ferdinand noted that if one fell on the ground, everyone immediately bent over and carefully picked it up, as though it were someone's eye that had fallen out. These strange "almonds" were in fact the seeds of a tree that thrives in great heat, humidity and the shade of the jungle giants; a tree that in 1753 the botanist Carl von Linné named *Theobroma Cacao*. The Greek first part of the name means "food of the gods." In Europe, the tree, its fruit and seeds, and the drink that was made from the pulverized, de-oiled seeds were all known by the name cacao.

The Maya had been cultivating the cacao tree at least since the Middle Preclassic period (600–300 B.C.) on the Pacific coast, to the north of Belize and in the Lowlands of Tabasco, areas where the rainfall, soil and climate offered ideal conditions for this delicate tree.

The fruit of the cacao tree grows straight from its trunk (ill. 26). Its sweet and aromatic flesh contains 30 to 40 almond-shaped cacao beans

25 *Cacao pod, cut open*
The cacao bean is embedded in the white flesh of the pod. Although only the bean is used in the manufacture of chocolate today, the people of ancient Mesoamerica – including the Maya – also ate the delightfully sweet pulp.

26 *Cacao tree at Tapachula, Chiapas, Mexico*
Unlike European fruit trees, the blossom of the cacao tree grows in bunches directly on the trunk or on the larger branches. They are pollinated only by mosquitoes, which is why the cacao tree thrives in the shade of larger trees. The cucumber-shaped pods are between 10 and 20 cm long, and need about six months to develop and ripen. Each pod contains up to 60 cacao beans, which have to be fermented, dried and roasted before they can be ground to make cacao powder. The Maya consume the aromatic pulp around the beans as well as the beans themselves.

Theobroma Cacao L.

This is   the completion   of the script   on the drinking cup   for the (cacao) which comes from the tree of abundance   cacao

ka
wa
ka

(ill. 25). The Maya prepared delicious dishes and drinks from the pulp as well as the beans.

Almost everything we know about the way the Maya used and processed cacao has been learnt from the hieroglyphs on Maya ceramics (ill. 28). Vessels are especially valuable if there is a dedication just below the rim describing its purpose as a "cacao cup" (ill. 29). The hieroglyph for the beverage is at the end, formed by the three syllabic signs *ka-ka-wa*. The hieroglyphs preceding it describe, among other things, the various flavors. People drank bitter and sweet cacao, fruity cacao, cacao mixed with maize, and even chili-flavored cacao. It was made with water, a custom that is still practiced in many parts of Mexico and Central America today, and sometimes thickened with a little ground maize or a maize dough. The foam was greatly appreciated, and the drink was whisked or – as is shown on some painted ceramics – poured repeatedly from one container into another.

The cacao drink was so precious that banquets at which it was served were even immortalized on stone monuments. The large, beautifully painted cylindrical containers of foamy cacao were probably passed from mouth to mouth at state receptions, wedding celebrations and rituals (ill. 30). Dried cacao beans were also a precious commodity, and traders took them as far as central Mexico where, although the drink was also highly appreciated, the climate was not suitable for growing it. In the Postclassic period (909–1500 A.D.), the beans even became a kind of currency used as payment for goods and services.

28 *Dedication text on a ceramic vessel. Provenance unknown; Late Classic, 600–900 A.D.; baked clay, painted; H. 21.3 cm, dia. 18.5 cm; private collection (Kerr 1837)*
Most of the painted cylindrical ceramic vessels of the Classic period were precious cups used for drinking cacao. Most had a dedication text just below the rim that referred both to the act of painting and its use. The second part of these inscriptions named the contents – cacao – as well as the various methods of preparation and flavors. In this case, it was cacao "which comes from the tree of abundance".

29 *Early Classic vessel with cacao beans. Found north of Uaxactun, Peten, Guatemala; end of the Early Classic (Tzakol 3), c. 500–590 A.D.; baked black clay with incised hieroglyphs; H. 13.2 cm, dia. 16.5 cm; Uaxactun, Museo Juan Antonio Valdés*
The cacao vessels of the Early Classic were not as high as the tall, slim vessels of the Classic period. The incised hieroglyphs provide information about the object's owner, and the hieroglyph *ka-ka-wa* indicates the contents. The dried cacao beans in the photograph are, of course, modern.

30 *Stuccoed and painted cacao pot. Rio Azul, Peten, Guatemala, Structure C1 B, Burial 19; Early Classic, c. 500 A.D.; baked clay, stuccoed and painted; H. 23.0 cm, dia. 15.2 cm; Guatemala City, Museo Nacional de Arqueología y Etnología*
Burial 19 was discovered in 1984: a nobleman's tomb with an abundance of beautiful and exciting objects, one of which was this unusual ceramic pot. It is sealed with a screwtop lid; both the lid and the vessel were inscribed with six hieroglyphs, painted on stucco. The hieroglyphs on the lid translate as "This is the drinking vessel for *witik* cacao, for *kox* cacao"; *witik* and *kox* obviously refer to two particular flavors. Chemical analysis of residue inside this pot confirmed that it had indeed contained cacao.

27 *Cacao tree (branch with blossom and fruit); c. 1820; pen and ink lithograph, colored*
It was not until 1828 that a Dutch chemist, Coenraad Johannes van Houten, invented pulverized cacao, which replaced the old method of preparing cacao from fermented, crushed beans. Van Houten developed a hydraulic press, which was used to make a fine, long-lasting cacao powder with a very low fat content. Once it was easier to make and kept better, cacao became cheaper and available to a wider mass market. It remains as popular as ever with children and adults.

THE ORIGINS OF MAYA CIVILIZATION – THE BEGINNINGS OF VILLAGE LIFE

Norman Hammond

The first evidence of human presence in the Maya region came soon after the end of the last Ice Age, when people had already been in the New World for several millennia. Although this evidence is sparse and scattered, it suggests that both Highland and Lowland zones had been penetrated by around 10,000 years ago.

The best-documented Highland site is Los Tapiales in Guatemala, a hunters' campsite on the continental divide where obsidian and basalt tools, including a spear point, burins, and scrapers have been dated to 9600–8800 B.C. The Los Tapiales spear point fragment had a shallow channel for mounting it on a shaft, also found in the Clovis culture in North America (10,200–9500 B.C.). In the Lowlands, a chert point resembling the Clovis type was picked up at Ladyville, near Belize City (ill. 32).

These sites are tentatively put in the Paleo-Indian period of Mesoamerican prehistory before about 8000 B.C., although the lack of good context or dating leaves some cause for doubt. People were very probably hunters and gatherers. Stone tools, along with bones of extinct animals, some with marks of butchering, have been found at Loltun Cave in northern Yucatan, the Peten and Huehuetenango in the Highlands of Guatemala, but have yielded no radiocarbon dates. They could be Paleo-Indian, or from the succeeding Archaic period (8000–2000 B.C.), when the Mesoamerican climate became warmer.

The path to settlement

During the Archaic period, people moved from foraging, using different camp sites each year, to collecting resources from a semi-permanent base camp, with occasional use of other locations for specialized purposes such as hunting, gathering shellfish, or obtaining tools. The best evidence for this so far comes from the valleys of Oaxaca and Tehuacan in the Mexican Highlands. In the Maya Highlands, the Santa Marta rock shelter in Chiapas has five episodes of Archaic occupation between 7600 and perhaps 4000 B.C., while La Piedra del Coyote near Los Tapiales dates to 8700–4200 B.C. and a number of Archaic sites are known in the surrounding Highlands of El Quiche.

Indications that the Maya Lowlands were occupied in the preceramic period are provided by projectile points from coastal Belize; the broad-stemmed Lowe type is tentatively dated around 2500–1900 B.C., and the narrower Allspice and

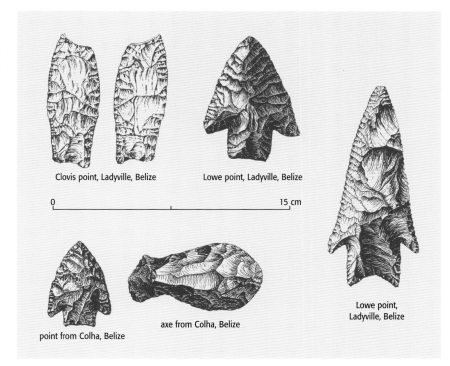

Clovis point, Ladyville, Belize

Lowe point, Ladyville, Belize

0   15 cm

point from Colha, Belize

axe from Colha, Belize

Lowe point, Ladyville, Belize

32 *Chert tools from northern Belize. Preceramic period, 9000–1200 B.C.; Belmopan, Belize Department of Archeology*
Top left: Clovis-type projectile point; Ladyville, 9000–1400 B.C., L. 9 cm; top center and right: Lowe projectile points with handle tenons, Sand Hill region, 2500–1900 B.C., L. 8.5 cm and 13.5; bottom left: Lowe point, Pulltrouser Swamp, 2500–2000 B.C., L. 4.5 cm; bottom center: axe, hammered on one side, Pulltrouser Swamp, 1300 B.C., L. 11 cm. These tools are currently the only evidence of preceramic settlements of hunters and crop farmers in the Maya Lowlands.

Sawmill types slightly later (ill. 32). Another tool type, the "uniface," probably used as a hoe or adze, has been encountered at some of the same sites, and has also been found *in situ* at Colha, later a major Preclassic and Classic chert-working center in northern Belize (ill. 32). Both a uniface and a Lowe point were found at Pulltrouser Swamp, north of Colha.

Radiocarbon dates from there, and from a soil profile at Colha which seems to document both pre-agricultural and early farming activity, suggest that the preceramic occupation dated between 2500 and 1400 B.C. Pollen from a core at Cobweb Swamp at Colha indicates that maize was being grown by 2800 B.C., with cotton and chili peppers present by around 1700 B.C. and manioc being grown as a root crop before 1000 B.C.; at Cob Swamp further north the pollen evidence suggests forest clearance around 2500 B.C.. (ill. 33).

Disturbance of the environment by human settlers, indicated by changes in the flora and fauna from those typical of tropical forest, seems to begin about

31 *Seated figure. Uaxactun, Peten, Guatemala, Structure A18, Trench 31; Late Preclassic, 400 B.C.–250 A.D.; verdite; H. 25.3 cm; Guatemala, Museo Nacional de Arquelogía y Etnología*
This carefully polished figure was offered, together with a variety of eccentric flint and obsidian pieces, when the building was dedicated. The cheeks are adorned with the hieroglyph *k'in*, "sun," which in the Late Classic was, among other things, an attribute of the sun god.

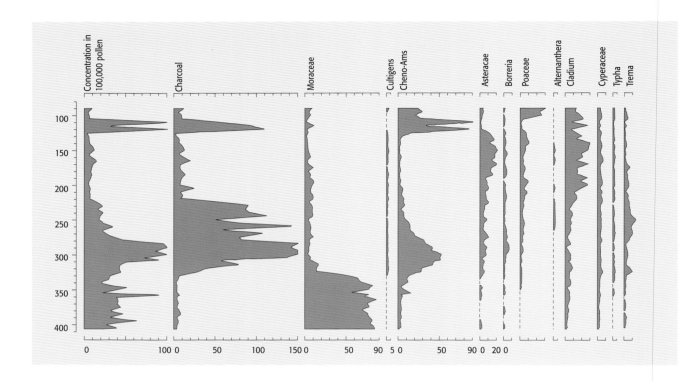

Concentration in 100,000 pollen Charcoal Moraceae Cultigens Cheno-Ams Asteraceae Borreria Poaceae Alternanthera Cladium Cyperaceae Typha Trema

33 *Pollen diagram of the Cob Swamp in northern Belize*
The pollen diagram contains indications of early crop farming c.2500–2000 B.C. It shows a sudden rise in charcoal quantities with a simultaneous reduction in forest areas and an increase in the pollen of herb-like plants and – for the first time – cultivated plants. Similar stages of early crop farming "taking over" the landscape are also seen in Europe.

2500 B.C., but agriculture may well have remained a minor constituent of an economy based also on gathering in the forest. Many undated coastal plain locations sampled by the American archeologist Richard S. MacNeish may well prove to have been occupied during the Archaic: artifacts such as milling stones suggest an increasing reliance on collected and processed plant foods.

Phases of settlement in the Preclassic

No settlement sites are yet known in the Lowlands of Belize and Peten from the time of the initial forest clearings around 2500 B.C., or for more than a thousand years after that time. The oldest so far is Cuello, occupied from 1200 B.C., and the first Preclassic Maya settlement to be extensively examined; hitherto, Preclassic deposits had usually been found buried beneath substantial constructions of the Classic period. Although a Classic ceremonial precinct was the most prominent feature of the site, which covers an area of 1.6 square kilometers (0.78 square miles), research focused on Platform 34, a large, flat-topped mound which had only minor occupation after 400 A.D. but deep stratified deposits of Preclassic date with excellent preservation of both architecture and organic remains (ill. 34).

Fourteen major phases of architectural development span some 1600 years (1200 B.C.–400 A.D.). The earliest occupants of the Swasey phase (1200–900 B.C.) built only in perishable timber and thatch, with earth floors, but later houses had plaster-daub walls and stood on thin floors of plaster and limestone rubble; by 900 B.C., they were set around a plaster-surfaced courtyard some 15 meters (49 ft.) across. These timber-framed, palm-thatched houses closely resembled modern Maya houses in Yucatan (ill. 35).

The houses stood on platforms of rubble and earth barely 30 cm (12 in.) high and rounded at the sides, and had floors of ground limestone. Later, in the Bladen phase (900–650 B.C.), the platforms were enlarged, using their predecessors as construction cores. The sides of the earlier platforms were ripped away, leaving just a raw stump: the scattering of jade beads in the resulting scar indicates that the demolition was a ritual event, not just a practical process.

Reconstruction of the appearance of these buildings can be difficult, but at least one of the Cuello buildings of this period (Structure 323) was over 11 meters (36 ft.) long and half that in width, standing a meter (3 ft.) high above the courtyard floor. One earlier building (Structure 326) escaped almost intact because it had been buried and built over (ill. 36), and is the best surviving example of an Early Middle Preclassic structure.

34 *House foundations. Cuello, Belize; current excavations, photo from 1980*
To the left and in the middle of this 30 x 10 m excavation site are the remains of houses dating back to the Middle Preclassic era (1100–700 B.C.); in the background are remains of Late Preclassic buildings (200 B.C.), and on the west side is a pyramid that was built toward the end of the Preclassic era (200–300 A.D.). The older buildings had been overbuilt by Platform 34; its white stucco remains and infill material can be seen along the top of the dig.

36 *Apse house. Cuello, Belize, Structure 326, platform; Middle Preclassic, 900–800 B.C.; 8 × 4 m*
The post holes for the wooden timber frame are clearly visible. The fragments of the loam-plastered walls confirm that this house was built in a method similar to that of Maya buildings from historical times (ill. 34). The deep trough to the right of the picture is a new grave. The floors of later buildings are seen in the background.

35 *Modern Yukatek house*
The picture shows a modern Maya house (approx. 8.5 × 3.5 m), timber framed with loam and stucco walls and a roof made of guano and palm fronds. The apse-shaped floor plan and building method are similar to the Preclassic houses excavated in Cuello (see ills. 36 and 37).

Between 650 and 400 B.C., the first rectangular buildings were larger than any previous structures on the west and north sides of the courtyard. Whether they had a ritual function is not known – their subsequent demolition removed any evidence of activities within the buildings – but the successive temples later built directly above the western structure suggest that religious architecture could have emerged from the domestic tradition by 400 B.C.

Burials provide evidence about early Maya society

The courtyard itself became more formally organized. After 800 B.C., the deep "firepits" (some of them hearths, others used for a variety of domestic purposes) that had studded its surface in earlier periods were banished to the edges, and the paved area was defined by a wall linking two of the houses (ill. 37). Around 600 B.C., the first burial took place in the center of the courtyard, where an elderly man was buried (ill. 38). He could have been the head of the clan living there, and after his death became a venerated ancestor.

Burials are among our best sources of evidence for early Maya society. The 27 individuals of the Swasey and Bladen phases found at Cuello (five from the Swasey date before 900 B.C.) include seven definite/probable male adults, ten female adults, two teenagers, and eight children.

The earliest burials may have been dug through the earth floor of a building at ground level; later graves were cut into plaster house platforms during construction, use and abandonment (ill. 39). There is no clear relationship between burial posture and age or sex: most were laid flat on their back, but

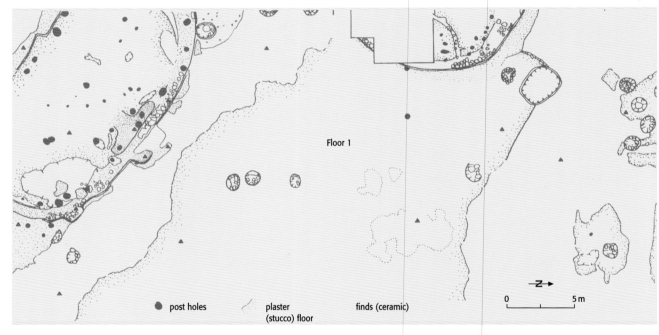

37 Settlement phase 1 in Cuello, Belize, 900–800 A.D.
Maps of excavations in Cuello, Belize indicate two phases of settlement in the Middle Preclassic era. In the older period, fireplaces were built in the courtyard, and at that time were used solely for domestic purposes. Walls were erected between the houses to close off the plastered part of the courtyard to the outside.

Floor 1

● post holes   ∕ plaster (stucco) floor   finds (ceramic)   0 ___ 5 m

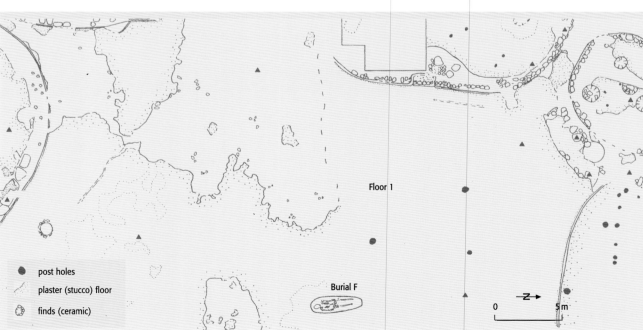

38 Settlement phase 2 in Cuello, Belize, 650–550 A.D.
In the second phase, the courtyard was enlarged around the fireplaces and surrounded by additional buildings. The fireplace was now positioned in Structure 319, top right in the drawing. A trough was excavated in the plaster floor of the courtyard for the burial of a deceased relative (Burial F49). In general, this courtyard group was now more secluded and private.

Floor 1

Burial F

● post holes
∕ plaster (stucco) floor
finds (ceramic)

0 ___ 5 m

crouched burials, some probably bound into bundles, occur early on, and by 600 B.C. the first of many seated burials occurs. Their grave goods included pottery vessels and a bird whistle, jade and shell jewelry, and tools of bone and chert. Most common was a bowl inverted over the head.

The distribution of grave goods between 1200 and 650 B.C. would suggest some social differentiation not based purely on age or sex: some of the children had hundreds of shell beads, some made from the valued red inner layer of the *Spondylus* oyster, suggesting that wealth and perhaps social status were already being ascribed by birth rather than achieved during adult life. A few objects in child burials were even more valuable and exotic, in particular blue jade pendants, which were certainly brought to Cuello from hundreds of miles away, either from the Olmec area or from a still-unlocated source of blue jade somewhere in the Highlands.

In the Late Middle Preclassic between 650 and 400 B.C. (Lopez Mamom phase), 30 burials include 20 adults and 10 juveniles. Sixteen of the adults were male, and only three female, a sex imbalance which persists into later periods. All but two of the burials were situated in houses or ancillary structures; one, as noted above, was located in the center of the patio floor. Most Lopez burials also had pottery vessels and shell ornaments, and those with grave goods had more of them. Exotic and elaborate goods were found in the best-stocked graves: the man

39 *Burial of an adult. Cuello, Belize; Middle Preclassic, c. 600 B.C.*
The burial is 80 cm wide and longer than the female skeleton, whose head faces west. One ceramic bowl has been placed over the face, another (50 cm in diameter) over the pelvis. Beneath her legs is an older burial belonging to a child. The ceramic bowl over the child's head can be seen underneath the woman's thigh bones. These burials were found in the floor near the north wall of the house.

in Burial 160 had jade beads, carved bone tubes, and a pectoral mask made from a human skull bone (ill. 40). These clearly marked his high status. Another burial lacked its skull, having a slab of chert in its place: this is the first of a succession of mutilated burials in the buildings on the west side of the courtyard, arguably those of sacrificial victims and reinforcing the suggestion of a ritual location. Thus, by the end of the Middle Preclassic in the 4th century B.C., burials suggest both increasing social differentiation and human sacrifice.

The skeletons of these early Maya also reflect some of the diseases which affected them, although the many afflictions which mark only the soft tissues of the body are archeologically undetectable, as are those for which good preservation of the bone surface is necessary. Probably the most striking evidence is that for treponemal infection, likely to have been syphilis or yaws (ill. 41). The pre-Hispanic origin of syphilis has been established elsewhere in the Americas, and the characteristic "sabering" and internal thickening of the shinbones have been observed in many Cuello burials, including one of the two earliest burials at the site, dating to around 1000 B.C. Marks of vitamin C deficiency are found both in calcified hemorrhages on bone surfaces and in the degeneration of tooth sockets. Arrested enamel growth in the teeth is the result of the withdrawal of maternal milk protein at weaning around 3–4 years of age, when it was not replaced from other sources. Public health was, however, better before 400 B.C. than later on. This is corroborated in Preclassic human remains from the Altar de Sacrificios. People also grew taller in this earlier phase, while in the Late Preclassic there was pressure on food resources as the population began to grow.

Early developments in ceramics

Stylistic change in the pottery from burials and from occupation and rubbish deposits forms the basis for relative dating at Cuello (with radiocarbon dates providing an absolute chronology). There were three successive ceramic complexes, named Swasey, Bladen, and Lopez Mamom, defining vessel forms and decoration between 1200 and 400 B.C. Swasey pottery is the earliest known in the Maya Lowlands, but is already technically accomplished in its manufacture and decoration and not at all experimental; there may have been an earlier period of development which has not yet been discovered. It is also distinctively Lowland Maya in its range of shapes, surface colors and ornamental

40 *Pendant made from a human bone. Cuello, Belize, Burial 160; Middle Preclassic, 500–400 B.C.; human skull; dia. 7.5 cm; Belmopan, Belize Department of Archeology*

The pendant shows a monster pulling a face. It was found around the neck of the adult male buried in Burial 160. Other offerings included cylindrical beads made of bone with the motif that represents royalty. A companion was buried in the same grave, beneath the man.

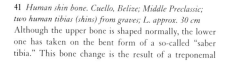

41 *Human shin bone. Cuello, Belize; Middle Preclassic; two human tibias (shins) from graves; L. approx. 30 cm* Although the upper bone is shaped normally, the lower one has taken on the bent form of a so-called "saber tibia." This bone change is the result of a treponemal

infection, as from syphilis or yaws. Although many of the inhabitants of Cuello suffered from infections such as this, they still lived to an old age. According to the work of Frank and Julie Saul, the finds made in Cuello are the earliest evidence of treponemata in the Maya region.

repertoire, without any close relationship to the pottery of the Pacific coast, the Gulf Coast Olmec heartland, or the Maya Highland zone. Even if the idea of pottery-making came from outside, the application was purely local.

Swasey vessels are fairly simple in design (ill. 43.1), mainly bowls, dishes and jars with either a red or orange surface slip or no slip at all. The latter may be decorated by pattern-burnishing with a pointed stick or bone, sometimes in elaborate checkerboard patterns; other ornamentation was created by incision, punctuation or relief-modelling of the clay before firing. Among the more striking forms are a jar with a thick, square rim, linked to the shoulder of the vessel by a handle made from two parallel cylinders of clay, and a narrow-necked bottle. Generally, these vessels were for storing liquids, and perhaps grain, and for serving food in individual portions. Drinking cups may have been made from gourds or calabashes, which are naturally hemispherical and were probably in use long before the adoption of pottery.

Bladen pottery (ill. 43.3), which succeeded Swasey by 900 B.C., is both very similar and clearly derived from its predecessor, and also distinctive in details of shapes and in the enlarged decorative repertoire. Red slips are now usually laid over a cream base, left exposed to form striped or checkered patterns; cream, brown and orange-brown slips appear, sometimes with distinctive and elaborate incised external designs. In the 7th century B.C., yet another technique was brought in, that of organic resist: the design was painted on the vessel surface using an organic substance such as honey, and this was then charred to a grey-black by holding the vessel over a fire. Organic resist can be combined with other patterning to create a three-color effect. This and other Bladen pottery types were still used in the following Lopez Mamom phase of 650–400 B.C., especially as grave goods, suggesting that ritual was more conservative than domestic usage.

Although Swasey pottery is best known at Cuello, Bladen wares have been found at nearby Colha, where the Bolay complex dates to 900–500 B.C., and at half a dozen other sites in northern Belize including Nohmul and Santa Rita Corozal. More distant and general links have been made with the Xe pottery of Altar de Sacrificios and Seibal in the Pasion valley in southern Peten, and closer at hand with the earliest occupation at Tikal in north-east Peten. Such regional ceramic traditions and links are characteristic of all succeeding periods in the Maya Lowlands.

Lopez pottery at Cuello falls within the Mamom ceramic sphere, which spans the Lowlands from Seibal in the south to Komchen in the north-east of Yucatan, and shows an impressive uniformity of pottery vessel shapes, slips, and decoration. For the first time, the same ideas about what pottery should look like were accepted by peoples across the Lowlands, including those in the north where Mamom pottery was the first to be made at many sites. That an efficient network of communications existed is confirmed by the widespread distribution, for the first time, of obsidian from sources in the volcanic Highlands of Guatemala, but differences in paste, temper, and finish show that pottery was not traded, but with few exceptions made locally.

Mamom pottery technology included the introduction of soft, very waxy slips with a crazed surface, created by the application of multiple coats of fine clay, the last of which shrank during firing to give the crackled effect. As before, monochrome red is the dominant color (ill. 44), although elaborate red-on-cream designs account for a fifth of all Lopez shards at Cuello and orange ware is also common for storage jars. The profiles of bowls and dishes are much more varied, and appendages such as flanges and spouts are quite common. Maya potters were becoming much more adventurous in their manipulation of clay even as their products became standardized over a wide area. Clay was used also to model human and animal figurines, some in the form of ocarinas playing three to five notes (ills. 31, 42). It has been suggested that some of the human figures may portray specific individuals, perhaps rulers of the Cuello community.

Stone tools and mussel shells

Apart from pot shards, the largest class of artifacts from Cuello are the fragments and manufacturing debris of stone tools, most notably those of flint-like chert and chalcedony. Chalcedony and some coarse grey and white cherts occur locally, but the better-quality brown and banded cherts came from a "chert-bearing zone" east of the New River and reaching south to the vicinity of Altun Ha. Within the zone,

42 *Fragment of a small clay figure. Cuello, Belize; Late Preclassic, 400 B.C.; clay; H. 8.8 cm*
This figure is flat-chested, so it is probably male. The eyes are represented by flat, oval hollows, each of which has a circular indentation in the middle. Nose, mouth, diadem, and ear jewelry have been added to the simply shaped head and torso.

PHASES	CERAMICS	GRAVE GOODS AND SMALL ITEMS

SWASEY
1200–900 B.C.

BLADEN
900–650 B.C.

LOPEZ-MAMOM
650–400 B.C.

COCOS-CHICANEL
400 B.C.–250 A.D.

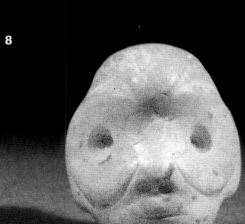

the site of Colha was notable in Late Preclassic and Classic times for its dozens of workshops producing standardized chert tool forms. Colha was occupied from at least 900 B.C. by villagers with houses, pottery, and a way of life similar to Cuello, and it seems likely that the production of chert tools had begun there at a similarly early date, perhaps with the export of finished goods to Cuello and other communities in northern Belize.

Cuello tools include a domestic tool kit of light tools, heavy-duty tools (mainly biface axes to be mounted in wooden hafts), and those of possible ritual use. The domestic kit was used for cutting, piercing, scraping, stripping, and light chopping; the heavy tools for tree-felling and breaking ground. Old and broken tools were frequently reworked and reused in other forms, until they became too small and battered to be of further use. Sharp flakes were also used, then discarded. Obsidian blades (mainly from the Pixcaya River source in Highland Guatemala), are also found in rubbish, although the earliest known piece, from a Bladen phase context, was carefully worked along all four edges and also incised; as an exotic material it may have been used for ornament rather than for its sharp edge, or it may have been retained as a curiosity after it became blunt.

Other tools of daily life were made from the harder varieties of limestone outcropping near Cuello. For *metates*, millstones, and *manos*, cylinders for grinding maize kernels to a paste, the most common material used was

limestone, although even in the Swasey phase some milling tools made from pink sandstone were imported from the Maya Mountains over 160 kilometers (100 miles) to the south. Grooved barkbeaters, mounted in a withy handle and used for making cloth or paper from the inner bark of the fig tree, first appear in the Bladen phase; although there is no evidence of writing in Maya culture until the Late Preclassic, the techniques for making screenfold books of plaster-surfaced bark paper had existed for centuries, as they also had for making many other practical objects such as clothing and headdresses.

Marine shells were procured from the Caribbean coast some 50 kilometers (30 miles) downriver from Cuello; 11 different species were imported in Swasey times, more later on. Shell scraps show that raw materials were being worked at Cuello into a range of objects, the commonest being round or irregular beads, assembled into long strands as necklaces or body ornaments. Most beads were of white shell such as conch (*Strombus*), but from the Bladen phase onwards some were made from the valued red inner layer of *Spondylus* thorny oysters; the presence of numerous shell beads in some child burials suggests high status from birth onwards, as does the presence in one burial of an entire *Spondylus* valve, scraped to reveal the red layer and perforated for use as a pendant (ill. 43.4). Bone, obtained locally from the skeletons of food animals including deer and dog, was used for beads and pendants, including one perforated disc made from

43 *The development of grave goods, ceramics, and small finds in the Late Classic at Cuello, Belize*
The oldest ceramics in the Maya Lowlands are from the so-called Swasey phase (1200-900 B.C.). Objects made at this time from other materials such as bones and mussel shells have only rarely survived. In the Bladen phase (900-600 B.C.), the increased incidence of shell objects indicates a rise in trading business. In the next phase, known as the Lopez-Mamom (650–400 B.C.), jade objects, which have also been found in children's graves, clearly indicate that prosperity and social standing were being bequeathed. In the Cocos-Chicanel phase (400 B.C.–250 A.D.), the variety of ceramic shapes increased considerably and burial objects already reveal symbolic values only slightly differing from those of the Early Classic.

44 *Jug with spout. Cuello, Belize; Late Preclassic, 400–300 B.C.; clay; dia. 12.5 cm*
Jugs such as this are often called "chocolate jugs," although there is no evidence that they were actually used for the preparation or consumption of cacao. The jug shown here was found in a mass burial containing 32 sacrificial victims, most of whom were young men, executed as part of the dedication ceremony performed for the construction of Platform 34. The platform was constructed in the Late Preclassic to cover the Middle Preclassic group of 900–400 B.C. (ill. 34).

a human skull. Splinters cut from long bones were smoothed into awls, and two deer foot bones were carved into hooks at one end, perhaps for netting. Other such bones were simply sharpened to a point and were probably used for shucking maize from the cob.

The village and its environment

The local environment yielded most of the necessities of life at Cuello. Following the careful flotation of more than 10 tons of soil from all periods, and the recovery of plant, mollusc, and animal remains, we have been able to reconstruct the nature of the countryside around the Middle Preclassic community. At the beginning of the Swasey phase, c. 1200 B.C., there was little disturbance of the natural forest, since nearly a third of the wood charcoal came from forest trees. This may reflect a comparatively long fallow cycle in maize cultivation, or fairly small and scattered fields: shrubs were characteristic of milpas abandoned for 1 to 5 years. Environmentally sensitive mollusc species corroborate the impression of a mainly forested landscape. Maize itself was the most conspicuous cultivated plant, present in over 90 % of samples analyzed for most of the Swasey and Bladen phases (ill. 46).

Beans, a second staple crop for the Maya, were smaller in Swasey and Bladen times than later on, and both beans and chili peppers could have initially been gathered in the wild. Squashes were also domesticated from wild species, and at least two kinds of root crops, manioc (cassava; ill. 45) and *malanga*, a form of arum, were cultivated from Bladen times onwards, if not earlier. Sweet potato could have been part of the diet, but has not yet been specifically identified. Fruit was collected from forest trees, including avocado, guava, cashew (ill. 48), hogplum, soursop, mamey (sapote; ill. 47), and nance. Wild fruits and those from

45 *Roots of the manioc plant (Manihot esculenta)*
The roots of the manioc plant are full of carbohydrates, but when raw also contain a poisonous hydrocyanic juice. To make manioc edible, the roots have to be peeled and grated and the poisonous juices squeezed out. The manioc mass is then washed and roasted to make manioc flour. The non-poisonous, fibrous roots of the sweet manioc are peeled, cooked for several hours until soft, and then eaten like potatoes.

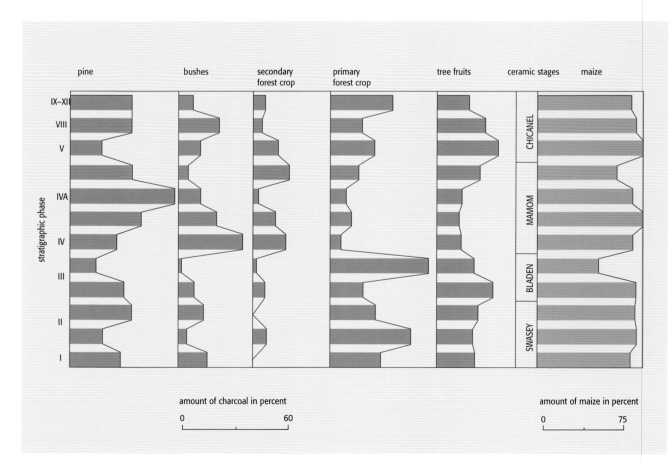

46 *The environmental history of Cuello. Charles H. Miksicek reconstructed 1300 years of environmental history in Cuello, Belize from macroscopic plant remains (seeds, fruit, charcoal)*
Phase I lasted from 1200–1000 B.C., Phases IX–XII from 100 B.C.–100 A.D. Because plenty of maize was already present in 90% of samples during Phase I, but only small amounts of charcoal from jungle trees (30%) and a high percentage of shrubs (20%), it is likely that the land had already been cleared for crop farming at this time (see ill. 33). A decline in maize was noted toward the end of Phase III, combined with forest encroachment. The soil was again cleared later for even more extensive use.

47 *Fruit of the mammey sapote tree (Achras sapota)*
Sapote is the name for several Central American tree species and their fruit. The fruits are oval or pear-shaped and between 8 and 20 cm long. The red-brown peel is thick and woody. The soft flesh is salmon pink to red. These sweet fruits weigh from 0.5 to more than 2 kg.

48 *Fruit of the cashew tree (Anadardium occidentale)*
The nut of the cashew tree, also known as semilla de Maranon, is kidney-shaped and grows at the lower end of the pear-shaped cashew fruit, which is either red, white, or yellow in color. The nuts are usually roasted before being eaten, and are also used to make oil. Delicately sweet in flavor, they contain large quantities of vitamin C and minerals.

orchards (created by either preserving trees from felling, or growing from discarded seeds in domestic rubbish dumps) cannot be told apart. Cacao beans (see Grube, p. 32 ff.), used in later times both to make a highly prestigious beverage (flavored with chili peppers) and as a currency, were not found in Middle Preclassic times.

Changes in vegetation, indicated by the seeds and charcoal recovered, and by pollen cores from Maya lake deposits, are also indicators of climate change. The rain forest became established after the end of the last Ice Age in a warm, moist period from about 8800 to 3000 years ago. A general cooling of the climate is marked at Cuello by an increase in pine charcoal between 900 and 400 B.C. The Middle Preclassic was cool and moist. Both charcoal from Cuello and pollen cores suggest a return to warmer conditions in the Late Preclassic. There seem to have been shifts in the depth of the water table at Cuello, which can be correlated with broader changes in relative sea- and river-levels between 1500 and 500 B.C., but how far these affected the Preclassic community is uncertain. Although there was a dramatic reduction in cultivation and a resurgence of forest at Cuello at the end of the Bladen phase in the 7th century B.C., this temporary shrinking of the population is more likely to have been caused by local economic or social factors, and from 600 B.C. onwards the community regained its former dynamism.

Signs of Maya culture's increasing complexity

Other Early Middle Preclassic sites of the period 900–650 B.C. have been excavated, including Colha and K'axob in the same area as Cuello; while the results have not yet been fully published, it is clear that they possess a similar material culture and reflect a similar society. Further west, the earliest period at Seibal yielded an offering of jades that matched Olmec offerings in both content and structure, and were dated to 900 B.C. Olmec-style jades from Yucatan, and Maya pottery from the Olmec site of La Venta, indicate clear contact between the two regions, as do sculptures in eastern Chiapas at Xoc (now destroyed by looters) and from near Palenque.

Komchen, in northern Yucatan, was occupied from about 600 B.C. onwards, and although the early community prior to 450 B.C. seems to have consisted of perishable buildings at ground level, there was rapid development after 450 B.C., including the construction of five substantial stone platforms around a central plaza (ill. 49). At Yaxuna, near Chichen Itza, a pyramid 11 metres (36 ft.) high was built between 600 and 400 B.C., employing masonry cut by specialist quarrymen. Similarly, the swift growth in size and density of Preclassic Seibal in 600–400 B.C., including several small ancillary ceremonial precincts outside the center, and the presence of small-scale public architecture at neighboring Altar

de Sacrificios, document the increasing complexity of Maya culture. At Tikal, Middle Preclassic buildings in the Mundo Perdido group south-west of the Great Plaza have been documented under Late Preclassic and Early Classic architecture. The large pyramid Structure 5C-54 originated around 600 B.C. as a low stepped platform (ill. 51), facing a long substructure on the east side of the plaza which subsequently supported a series of Early Classic royal funerary temples. The two structures together may have formed an early instance of the solar observation complex best known from Group E at Uaxactun, and certainly demonstrate an early formal relationship between public spaces and ceremonial structures.

By far the most compelling evidence for this, however, has come from the recent excavations of Richard Hansen at Nakbe in the northern Peten. The earliest architecture at the site dates to 900–600 B.C., and consists mainly of elongated low-walled platforms supporting timber-framed buildings with pole-and-daub walls and packed clay floors, similar to those at Cuello; some platforms stood up to two meters (6 ft.) high, larger than any of the Cuello

buildings and erected directly on cleared bedrock. After 600 B.C., large platforms at Nakbe were constructed of purpose-quarried limestone blocks, as at Yaxuna, and pyramids up to 18 meters (60 ft.) in height were built. The earliest known Lowland Maya ball court was constructed at Nakbe at the same time as a similarly low court at Abaj Takalik on the Pacific slope and markedly earlier than the ball courts at Cerros and Colha. A stone altar or marker with a double-headed image and a Kan cross, also employed as a day sign in the Maya calendar, indicates that carved monuments were being dedicated before 400 B.C.

The known area of buildings and associated Mamom sphere pottery covers over 50 hectares (124 acres) and includes a *sakbe* or causeway linking two areas of the comunity; the pottery is similar to that from Cuello and other Lowland sites, and trade links are indicated by the presence of obsidian, of which 65% came from the Pixcaya River source and 32% from El Chayal, both near Guatemala City. The obsidian was brought in as raw cobbles and worked at Nakbe, and marine shells were also imported from the Caribbean coast as the raw material for jewelry, suggesting specialist craftsmen and elite customers for

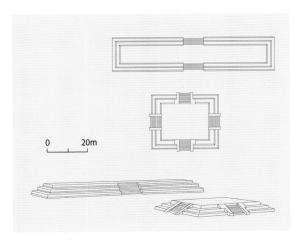

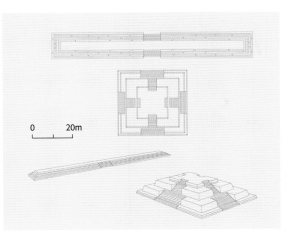

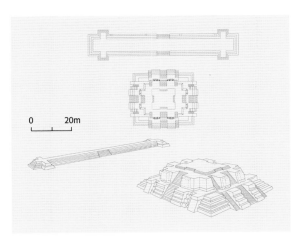

their products. The scale of late Middle Preclassic remains at Nakbe is greater than at any other Maya Lowland site explored so far, and indicates that, in the northern Peten-south Campeche region at least, a stratified society with rulers capable of exercising real economic and political power had come into existence by 400 B.C., a power dramatically illustrated by developments at El Mirador and other centers in the region in the succeeding Late Preclassic period.

51 *Preclassic beginnings of monumental architecture in the Peten. Tikal, Peten, Guatemala, Structures 5C-54 and 5D-84; Preclassic, 800 B.C.–1 A.D.*
The massive Structure 5C-54, a pyramid of the Mundo-Perdido group south-west of the Great Plaza, and the elongated Structure 5D-84 to the east, formed the earliest core of the public building complex in Tikal, and may well also have been used as an astronomical observatory or monument. The diagram on the left shows J.P. Laporte's reconstruction of the situation in the Eb phase (800–600 B.C.); in the center is the Tzec phase (600–350 B.C.) and on the right the Chuen phase (350 B.C.–1 A.D.). Each time the building was extended, the work was done without changing its basic groundplan and layout.

OBSIDIAN – THE METAL OF THE MAYA

Nikolai Grube

When the Spaniards penetrated the Maya region, they were fascinated by a civilization which seemed more refined and, in many respects, further developed than their own, even though the Maya seemed backward in certain respects. Accustomed to dealing with hard steel from Toledo, the Spaniards were amazed by the fact that the Maya and other Mesoamericans had created such outstanding artistic and cultural achievements without metal tools. Although metal hardly figured in the lives of the Maya and gold was not used for jewelry until the Postclassic, it would be wrong to classify the Maya as a "stone age" people. Maya technology was to a large extent characterized by the use of obsidian, a volcanic glass. Obsidian forms when silicon-rich lava is cooled and hardens quickly. Veins of obsidian run through a number of areas of the volcanic Highlands. They are subject to erosion at those points

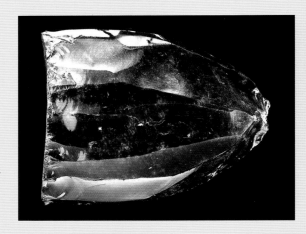

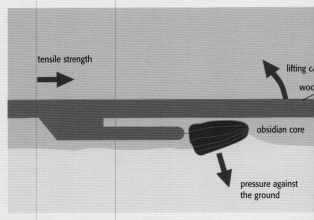

where they reach the surface, which is why there are several large sites where lumps and fragments of obsidian can be picked up off the ground.

Although obsidian consists mainly of silicon, investigations have shown that it also contains

53 *Diagram of the manufacture of obsidian blades*
Blades were produced with the aid of a wooden hook. The obsidian was pressed firmly into the ground to keep it in position. The hook was placed against the edge of the obsidian, then quickly drawn upwards, which caused a long, sharp blade to be split off.

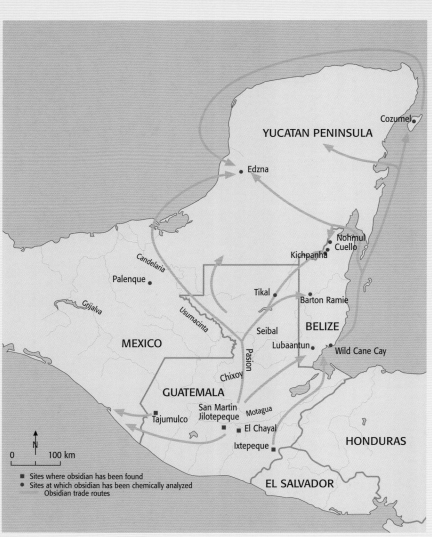

52 *Obsidian core. El Meco, Quintana Roo, Mexico; Late Postclassic, 1450–1550 A.D.; obsidian, processed; H. 10.9 cm, dia. 8.5 cm; Quintana Roo, Museo Arqueológico de Cancun*
With a carefully aimed blow, a core was taken from a lump of obsidian. This core was the basic shape from which sharp blades were made with a wooden hook.

54 *Map of the major obsidian trade routes*
By chemically analyzing artefacts, it is possible to establish the original sources of the obsidian and retrace the trade routes. It came from three main sites in the Highlands, and was transported along rivers and the Caribbean coast to the Lowlands.

varying amounts of other trace elements such as cesium, uranium, hafnium, and cobalt. The individual sites are noted for specific combinations of trace elements, which makes it possible to allocate archeological finds of obsidian to a particular site in the Highlands.

The Maya of the Lowlands had two main sources of obsidian in the Highlands of Guatemala: El Chayal, 25 km (16 miles) north of Guatemala City, and, west of there, San Martin Jilotepeque. Obsidian was already being mined there at the beginning of the Middle Preclassic, and it was most likely taken overland to the Pasion and Chixoy rivers. From there, the raw obsidian was transported to the north, probably first on canoes and then overland. The oldest evidence that obsidian was used in the Lowlands is from Cuello, and dates back to the early Swasey phase. However, the small number of obsidian finds indicates that transportation was laborious and very expensive. The trade in obsidian flourished at the beginning of the Early Classic, and merchants used two main methods of transportation to bring this highly desirable material to the consumers in the Lowlands (ill. 54). Obsidian from El Chayal and San Martin Jilotepeque was transported overland, and that from Ixtepeque, located on the border with El Salvador, was taken over the Motagua river valley to the Caribbean coast, and then along the coast in canoes to the north.

In the Classic period, there are signs for increasing competition between the merchants and the operators of the sources where obsidian was mined, which is why obsidian from El Chayal managed to supplant that from San Martin Jilotepeque. It seems there were firm commercial contracts that bound the buyers to certain providers. This is the only way to explain why the towns that bought obsidian from Ixtepeque did not buy any from El Chayal, and vice versa. However, roughly equal quantities of obsidian from both regions were found on islands just off the coast of Belize, and archeologists suspect that these islands were bases and "warehouses" belonging to neutral middlemen.

Because the metropolis of Teotihuacan in Central Mexico controlled the obsidian trade network, it influenced the entire Maya region (see Martin, p. 99 ff.). The actual city lay 55 km (34 miles) to the south of the obsidian site of Pachuca, where large, dark green, shiny lumps of obsidian could be picked up off the ground. The city's economic success was due largely to its trade monopoly in obsidian from Pachuca. As its influence over the Maya region increased, so deposits from El Chayal came under the control of Teotihuacan. The city of Kaminaljuyu, which is close to El Chayal, was taken over by Teotihuacan during the so-called Esperanza period (400-600 A.D.) and turned into a trading post.

remove the blades from the core, it was also timesaving, which made it a genuine alternative to the more expensive and labor-intensive business of processing metal.

However, the great importance the Maya attached to obsidian had less to do with their everyday work and more with its exotic origins. Obsidian became a luxury article when it had to be obtained through long-distance trade. The analysis of excavated dwellings has confirmed that obsidian tools were used only by a small, privileged stratum of Maya society. The less well-off had to make do with the more fragile silex (flint), which was also found in the Lowlands.

The precious obsidian was also used for jewelry and ritual items (ill. 56). Particularly spectacular and eccentric objects include wafer-thin, fragile creations in the form of blades, and also figures of animals and people, which were made solely for sacrificial purposes. Many such objects, sacrificial gifts made to the gods, have been found under stelae, altars and house floors (ill. 57). If a member of the ruling elite was being buried, thousands of tiny obsidian fragments were scattered around the entrance to the tomb. Although the meaning behind this ritual is not yet clear, it does show the great symbolic meaning placed on obsidian in Maya culture.

55 *Spear points and tools made of obsidian*
Obsidian was used primarily in the manufacture of weapons and tools. Thanks to clever processing with wooden tools, the Maya were able to make blades, spear points and knives in a short time. Once a tool had become blunt, it was thrown away and replaced by a new one.

56 *Anthropomorphous figure made of obsidian*
The Maya did not just use obsidian for everyday tools; they also used it for fragile *objets d'art* with no discernible purpose. These "eccentric obsidians," as they are called by specialists, are generally in the form of stylized human or animal bodies. We can only speculate as to their purpose – perhaps they were precious sacrificial gifts, placed in sacrificial caches at services of commitment in holy places.

57 *Flint ax*
More often than the precious obsidian, the Maya used silex (flint), which was also found in the Lowlands, for tools, weapons, axes and hatchets. The ax shown here was for ceremonial purposes only; unlike a "proper" ax, the head and handle are made from a single piece of stone. It may have been used to adorn the image of the god Chaak, who was thought to create thunder with an ax in his hand.

While Teotihuacan exercised its control over the obsidian trade network, not only did more obsidian from El Chayal penetrate into the Lowlands, but so did the green obsidian from distant Pachuca.

This volcanic glass was very important to the Maya because they could use the lumps to make a wide range of tools. Specialized workshops were set up in the Lowlands, where the raw obsidian was processed into almost round "cores" (ill. 52). Simply by applying skillful pressure with a wooden hook, they could remove razor-sharp blades from the core (ill. 53). With just a few carefully aimed blows, a wide range of other implements such as spear points, daggers and large knives could also be produced (ill. 55). Once a tool was worn out or broken, it was thrown away and another one made with little effort. Obsidian technology was inexpensive and, although it clearly required a certain skill – a combination of power and good timing – to

THE FIRST CITIES – THE BEGINNINGS OF URBANIZATION AND STATE FORMATION IN THE MAYA LOWLANDS

Richard D. Hansen

For a long time, there was no evidence of Preclassic occupation of the Maya region, and it was therefore assumed that the roots of Maya culture must lie outside the Lowlands. Researchers' interest turned to the climatically favorable Highlands of Central America and the Gulf Coast, the former home of the Olmec. Until just a few decades ago, scholars believed the Olmec to have been the "mother culture" of all Mesoamerican civilization, including the Maya.

The first excavations in Guatemalan Uaxactun in the 1920s revealed an archeological sensation: early traces of the Maya, which were at first classified as unusual and "primitive." However, research carried out in the 1960s and 1970s in Tikal by the University of Pennsylvania, and Norman Hammond's excavations in Cuello (see Hammond, pp. 38), confirmed that the Maya Lowlands had already been occupied and architecturally developed in the first millennium B.C. Later excavations at sites close by, such as Colha and Cahal Pech, confirmed that the Maya had indeed settled along riverbanks, trade routes, and fertile plains. Subsequent research in the Lowlands confirmed the presence of Preclassic constructions in Tikal, Altar de Sacrificios and La Lagunita, Rio Azul, the Yaxha-Sacnab region, Komchen, Dzibilchaltun, Yaxuna, Nohoch Ek, Colha, Cuello, Cahal Pech, and Blackman Eddy (ill. 59).

The Maya Lowlands provide a fascinating case study of a special kind of development of human society. The formation of a complex society in a tropical rainforest with relatively few rivers was fundamentally different from the more common socio-political and economic complexity of riverine societies in temperate arid or semi-arid regions, such as Egypt, Mesopotamia, the Indus valley, China and highland Mesoamerica.

The Mirador Basin

The Mirador Basin is a circumscribed, geographically-defined basin in remote northern Guatemala and southern Campeche (Mexico) with a large Maya occupation pre-dating most ancient cities in the Maya Lowlands of Mesoamerica. These settlements date to the Middle Preclassic (1000-350 B.C.) and Late Preclassic (350 B.C.–150 A.D.) periods with a more modest settlement during the Late Classic period (600–800 A.D.).

Early Preclassic development in the Mirador Basin is evident from the abundance of massive architectural assemblages ranging from 40 meters (131 ft.) to 72 meters (236 ft.) high. These buildings were connected by an intricate system of causeways, known as *sakbe*, which ran through individual sites as well as between them, and which joined the sites of El Mirador to Nakbe and Tintal, and possibly joined Wakna, Uxul, and Calakmul to the Mirador/Nakbe area. Similar causeways also linked Tintal to several unnamed sites to the south and east of the region.

59 *The main Preclassic sites in the Maya region*
Nothing was known of the existence of Preclassic settlements in the Maya region until just a few decades ago. However, intensive archeological excavations in numerous Highland and Lowland sites revealed evidence of Preclassic settlement in both. Northern Guatemala and Belize both contain particularly large numbers of Preclassic sites, where seasonal marshes provided the means for intensive agriculture. It is also possible, though, that the map gives an incorrect picture of the distribution of Preclassic sites, since remains from Preclassic settlements could still remain concealed beneath subsequent structures built over them.

58 *Excavation of the stucco mask of Structure 34. El Mirador, Peten, Guatemala*
Structure 34 dates to the Late Preclassic. It is a small platform to the south-east of the vast El Tigre pyramid, and is one of the most extensively researched structures at El Mirador. The stairway to the platform is stucco-covered, and flanked by two greater than life-sized masks that are so characteristic of this era. The mask is of a god with a long nose and huge eyes. The head is framed by two large ear spools with jaguar claws springing from them. The whole mask was formerly painted, and the colors and size must have had quite a dramatic impact on the visitor.

First settlements at the beginning of the Middle Preclassic

The developmental sequence for Preclassic architecture has been particularly evident in the Mirador Basin at the site of Nakbe (ill. 60). Stratigraphic studies and analyses of the few ceramics found from this period, together with information obtained from carbon dating the oldest layers, suggest that the earliest occupation began between 1000 and 800 B.C. As in Cuello, the architecture of this time consisted of wattle-and-daub residences, packed clay floors, external stone retaining walls, and post holes carved in bedrock (ills. 61, 62). Evidence of such settlements has been located in primary deposits below the platform constructions in the East Group at Nakbe.

The construction of formal stone platforms appeared slightly later, about 800 to 600 B.C. These platforms consisted of vertical walls, two to three meters (seven to ten feet) in height, and composed of roughly hewn flat stones (ill. 65). The walls were covered with a primitive lime and clay mortar or a chalky plaster, while floors consisted primarily of packed clay, limestone marl, *saskab*, or thin lime plaster. Platforms with floors such as these have been located in both the East and West Groups at Nakbe, and represent the first major architectural complexes of any size in the site.

Specialist production of figurines occurred within localized areas. Neutron activation of the Nakbe figurines by Ron Bishop at the Smithsonian Institution, Washington and subsequent comparison with the chemical composition of Uaxactun Middle Preclassic figurines revealed that, despite the close similarity in form, shape, and decoration, the vast majority of each group of figurines was manufactured at its particular site. It should be noted, however, that three figurines which had been made at Nakbe appeared in the Uaxactun collections, suggesting that an exchange had taken place during this early time.

The ceramics that were studied by Donald Forsyth from Brigham Young University between 1978 and 1989 show a remarkable variety in form and surface treatment. They include a variety of monochromes, dichromes, bichromes, incising, chamfering, resist decoration, paint, and painted stucco on vessels (ills. 63, 64). They are entirely consistent with Middle Preclassic ceramics from all over the Maya Lowlands during this early period of time, suggesting that there was extensive communication among the sites.

The early Middle Preclassic period at Nakbe, Uaxactun, Tikal, Colha, Cahal Pech, and the Pasion region is notable for the presence of a variety of shell artifacts. One of the most common types consists of large numbers of drilled conch (*Strombus*) shells (*costatus* and *pugilis*) from the Caribbean. These shell fragments (ill. 66) have a single drilled (often biconical) perforation and were cut in square or rectangular pieces but otherwise unworked. The spines and natural projections of the shells were left intact. Their unique presence in early Middle Preclassic ritual and elite deposits suggests that they may have served as indicators of political or economic status. It is significant that these diagnostic *Strombus* shells do not appear in any of the extensive Late Preclassic period contexts in the Mirador Basin or elsewhere, suggesting that the shell's function may have been speciaized and may be useful as a period marker.

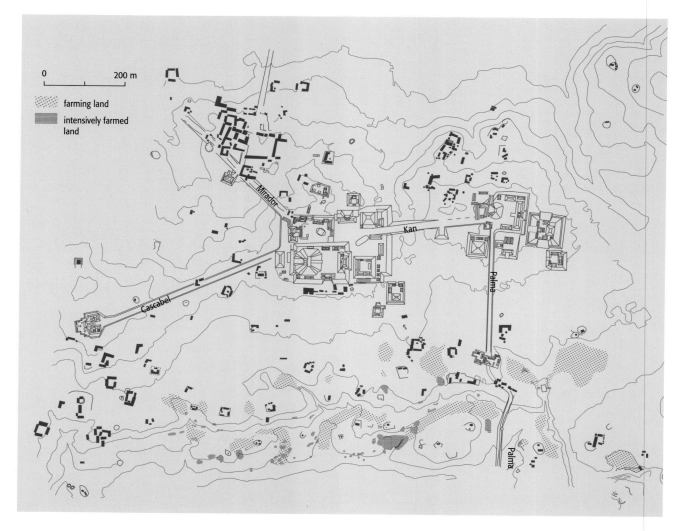

60 *Map of the center of Nakbe, Guatemala*
The large Preclassic city of Nakbe is situated in a densely forested region in northern Guatemala which is difficult to reach. Although it was first discovered from aerial photographs in 1930, it was not visited until 1962, when the Scottish archeologist Ian Graham traveled there and took cartographic measurements. The center of the city is indicated by two massive platforms. The eastern platform is 32 meters high; the western one, at 45 meters, is one of the largest acropolis buildings of the Maya. The various architectural groups are linked by causeways. A further causeway connects Nakbe with El Mitador, 13 km to the north. These causeways pass through seasonal marshes which facilitated intensive agriculture with several annual corn harvests.

61 *Excavations at the foot of Structure 51 in Nakbe, Guatemala*
Excavations to the west of the base of Structure 51 in Nakbe (right) yielded extensive finds. The shaft (below right) shows the postholes drilled into the bare rock for a building made of perishable materials under a plaster corridor; this was dated to between 800 and 600 B.C. A large, flat altar (right edge of the picture) dates from the same period as the corridor. At the top is an intact platform wall dating back to the Middle Preclassic, and to the far left in the middle is Stela 1.

62 *Middle Preclassic architecture. Nakbe, Guatemala; Middle Preclassic, c. 600 B.C.*
This vertical wall from the Middle Preclassic stands on a large plastered floor. Under the two corridor levels are the remains of an earlier Middle Preclassic building and a mound of waste from c. 800 B.C.

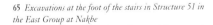

63 *Early ceramic. Nakbe, Guatemala; Preclassic, 1000–800 B.C.; baked clay*
Simple pressed decorations adorn this, the earliest engobe-free ceramic found in Nakbe. The item in question is a jug of the type "Resaca Impressed" from c. 1000–800 B.C.

64 *Early ceramic. Nakbe, Guatemala; Preclassic, 1000–800 B.C.; baked clay*
This fragment of a jug is from the period 1000–800 B.C.

65 *Excavations at the foot of the stairs in Structure 51 in the East Group at Nakbe*
The solid blocks of the stairs at the top of the excavation are clearly recognizable. The stairs and the platform were constructed at the same time. Large quantities of stone and rubble were spread over the remains of earlier settlements for the construction of the platform. A posthole in the ground close to the kneeling worker indicates the existence of an earlier building, made of wood and palm straw.

66 *Strombus shells, Middle Preclassic finds*
To the Maya, the shells of the Strombus snail (*Strombus gigas*) were particularly valuable and exotic because they had to be transported a long distance from the Caribbean coast. In Nakbe they have been found only on Middle Preclassic sites. The shells were cut into pieces and drilled so they could be threaded onto cords and worn as prestigious items of jewelry.

67 *Jade-encrusted teeth. Middle Preclassic*
Throughout the history of the Maya, decorating teeth with precious stones was considered a sign of beauty, and was also regarded as a sign of a high social standing. Remains of teeth found in Nakbe indicate that the practice of encrustation with thin slivers of jade was first practiced in the Middle Preclassic.

68 *Fragment with woven motif.*
Nakbe, Guatemala; Middle Preclassic;
baked clay
To the Maya, the mat (*pop* in Mayan) is a symbol of royal power. The motif could be a symbol of the development of rulership before the emergence of the divine kingdoms in the Classic.

69 *Ceramic fragment with a representation of the headdress of the god Hu'unal. Middle Preclassic; baked clay*
In Classic art, the god Hu'unal is always shown with a three-cornered headdress. Because it resembles a jester's cap, the god is often also referred to as the "jester god"; the name in no way reflects on the god's role as the god of royal dynasties. The ceramic fragment shown here could be part of the headdress; if so, it is the earliest representation of this motif.

The chemical analyses of Middle Preclassic obsidian blades and flakes from sealed, secure contexts at Nakbe show that about two-thirds of Middle Preclassic obsidian was imported from the source of San Martin Jilotepeque in the Guatemalan Highlands, with one-third from El Chayal (Guatemala), and a tiny proportion from Ixtepeque (border between Guatemala and El Salvador).

Physical attributes of Maya elite status, such as skull deformation, achieved by binding a plank to the forehead for the first few days after birth, and inlaid exotic stones in human teeth (ill. 67) were also apparent during the Middle Preclassic period. Figurines of the god Hu'unal, who later became god of the kings (ill. 69), and woven mat motifs (ill. 68) from early Middle Preclassic deposits, suggest that the iconography of rulership, evident in Olmec societies of the Gulf Coast region of Mexico, was also present in Maya societies prior to 600 B.C.

Beginnings of monumental architecture in the Late Middle Preclassic

By the late Middle Preclassic period, between 600 to 400 B.C., pyramidal structures of up to 18 meters (59 ft.) in height had been constructed at Nakbe. These buildings were placed on formal platforms, constructed with long linear rows of stones and paved by carefully-placed blocks. Stone fill buried the previous village deposits from the early Middle Preclassic period, and distribution of primary deposits at the site suggests that the settlement core at Nakbe was approximately 50 hectares (124 acres) in size.

The orientation of the site is in stark contrast to contemporaneous Gulf Coast and Highland centers. Olmec site orientation is primarily on a north-south axis, while the early Maya centers at Nakbe, Tintal, El Mirador, and possibly Naachtun are on an east-west axis. The east-west axis of site orientation appears to be consistent with subsequent Maya centers, and suggests that monumental architecture developed in the Lowlands independently and without outside influence.

The massive platforms – up to 40,000 square meters (43,760 square yards) in size – provided the setting for the introduction of a formal, consistent, architectural complex that was named after Group E at the site of Uaxactun where it was discovered. The construction of this form in the Middle Preclassic at Nakbe and elsewhere established a major architectural component of ritual significance that was to persist for centuries at hundreds of Maya sites. This pattern consists of at least two principal buildings constructed on a platform, with the structure on the east side consisting of an elongated, north-south platform (often with a single central building), while the western construction is a pyramid, commonly with a stairway on each side of the structure.

The Late Middle Preclassic period also witnessed the first ball court construction at Nakbe. This correlates chronologically with a Middle Preclassic ball game court found at Abaj Takalik and architecturally with subsequent Preclassic ball game courts in the Lowlands. Excavations by the Guatemalan archeologist Juan Luis Velasquez at Nakbe in the 1990s revealed the detailed sequence of three phases of ball game court modifications, before it was abandoned in the Late Preclassic period (ills. 70–72). It is worth noting, however, that Late Classic inhabitants apparently utilized this court again, since a small addition of primitive stone, one course high, was added to the ruins of the court during the Late Classic period.

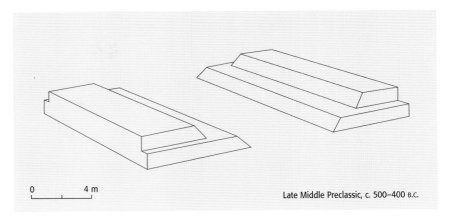

Late Middle Preclassic, c. 500–400 B.C.

70 *The ball game court of Nakbe in the Late Middle Preclassic, c. 500–400 B.C.*
The ball game court of Nakbe is situated in the south of the East Group. Excavations by the Guatemalan archeologist Juan Luis Velasquez in the 1990s revealed that it had been built in three phases, the oldest of which dates back to the Late Middle Preclassic. This makes the ball game court at Nakbe one of the oldest in Mesoamerica to be dated with accuracy. Even in its earliest phase it had the characteristic shape of two parallel low buildings with the actual court in between them.

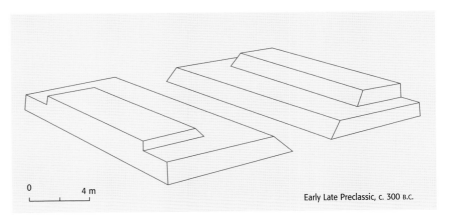

Early Late Preclassic, c. 300 B.C.

71 *The ball game court in the Early Late Preclassic*
The bases for the platforms adjoining the court were extended in the Early Preclassic, which resulted in a narrower court. The shape of the earlier ballgame court was retained.

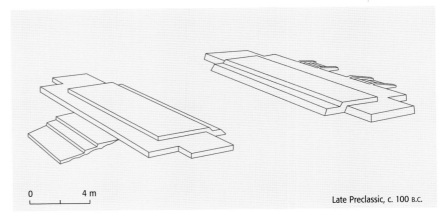

Late Preclassic, c. 100 B.C.

72 *The ball game court in the Late Preclassic*
Around 100 B.C., when Nakbe was no longer flourishing, the ball game court was remodeled a second time. Then, a part of the older platform was dismantled, and lower platforms constructed with stairs at both sides. This third phase again reflects the plan for the first ball game court.

Earliest stone sculptures

Carved stone monuments in the form of stelae and stone altars were also introduced during the Late Middle Preclassic period at the sites of Tintal, Nakbe, Isla, Pedernal, and possibly El Mirador. These monuments are similar in many ways to other examples known in the Gulf and Pacific Coast areas of Mesoamerica from 500 to c. 350 B.C. Some of the specific characteristics of these sculptures at Tintal and Nakbe consist of enormous monuments of exotic (imported) stone in celtiform shape with figures standing with legs in tandem forms (Tintal Stela 1, Nakbe Stela 1; ill. 75), carved edges of monuments with abstract symbols (Nakbe Monuments 2, 3; ill. 74), large slab altars in the center-line axis of buildings (Nakbe Altar 4), unmodified boulders with deity portraits incised on stone (Isla Stela 1), and carved circular altars with downward-looking

73 *Monument 8. Nakbe, Guatemala; Late Middle Preclassic, c. 500–400 B.C.*
This sculpted round altar is an unusual monument, the like of which is only seen in the Olmec-inspired sculptures in the Highlands of Guatemala. Around a part of the outer edge is a so-called celestial band with alligator-like creatures on the left and right; obviously people in the Middle Preclassic believed that heaven was inhabited.

74 *Monument 2. Nakbe, Guatemala; Late Middle Preclassic, c. 500–400 B.C.; limestone; H. 48 cm, W. 43 cm*
Monument 2 from Nakbe is a fragment of a flat stela that was sculpted on the front and on one of the narrow sides. Typical of sculptures from the Preclassic period are abstract symbols, curved lines, spirals, and a *horror vacui*, which led sculptors to fill the entire available surface. A strongly abstracted World Tree in the shape of a cross is visible in the top half of the monument; similar items appeared very much later on the famous reliefs of Palenque.

75 *Stela 1. Nakbe, Guatemala, Main Plaza of the East Group outside Structure 52; Late Middle Preclassic/Early Late Preclassic, c. 500–200 B.C.; limestone; H. 340 cm*
Although the Late Preclassic stelae are usually monuments about one meter high, Stela 1 from Nakbe proves that monuments from earlier times were unusually large. Stela 1 was found on the Main Plaza of the East Group. On its front are two standing figures, obviously communicating with each other, dressed in full regalia. On the front of the headdress on the right-hand figure is a mask with Olmec features – wide, flat nose, widely opened mouth with the teeth of a beast of prey – that suggest contact with neighboring Olmec settlements.

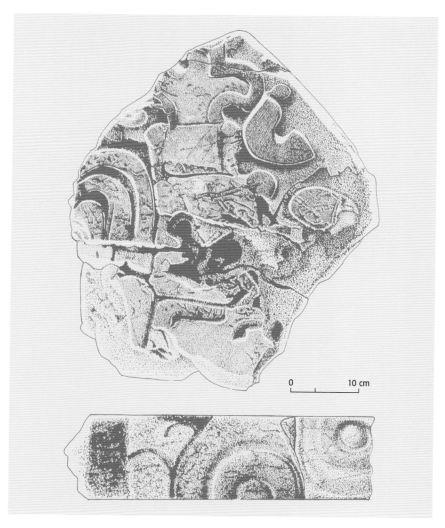

dual-headed reptiles with an early sky/water band joining them (Nakbe Monument 8; ill. 20).

The ritual veneration of early sculpture in the Mirador Basin by the later Maya inhabitants of the Late Classic period (600–800 A.D.) occurred with Tintal Stela 1, Nakbe Stela 1, Nakbe Monuments 2 and 3, Isla Stela 1, Isla Altar 2, Isla Stela 3, and six known monuments at Pedernal (Stela 1, Altar 5, Monuments 2–5). This ritual behavior included the burning of copal in spiked incense burners and the burials of important individuals near the monuments. It also included the smashing of hundreds of Late Classic ceramic vessels, which were probably most noted for containing liquids.

The practice in the Late Classic period of transporting Middle and Late Preclassic monuments from their original contexts and relocating them in Late Classic structures may explain the general absence of Preclassic sculpture in their original location in the major sites. One monument, Tintal Stela 1, was carved from a red sandstone slab that weighed at least 6.42 metric tons (6.32 tons). According to chemical analyses conducted by Paul Wallace and Thomas Schreiner of the University of California, Berkeley, the monument originated from the area of Altar de Sacrificios in the lower Pasion and upper Usumacinta Rivers and was transported 110 km (68 miles) into the Mirador Basin. This was probably accomplished during the late Middle Preclassic period (500–350 B.C.) since the Late Classic occupation at Tintal does not seem to have had the centralized organization to transport the monument the considerable distance that it came.

A complex society

Maya society gained in complexity and hierarchical structure in the Late Middle Preclassic period. This development is evident in the architecture and elsewhere. The size and shape of limestone blocks used for building changed considerably, because they now used only carefully cut stones of up to 90 cm (3 ft.) (ills. 76, 77). More lime was produced and more stucco utilized for plastering and decorating their buildings. It is likely that the general increase in social and economic complexity was due to the introduction of various intensive agricultural techniques, particularly the importation of swamp mud into upland

76 *Wall of Structure 35. Nakbe, Guatemala, Structure 35; Late Middle Preclassic; limestone*
Masonry changed in Nakbe in the Late Middle Preclassic. Instead of coarse masonry made with cut stones, the Maya began around 500 B.C. to cut the stone into large regular squares almost one meter in size. The outsides of the walls were covered with stucco. This was also the time when the façade was divided vertically into an upper sloping and lower recessed zone, a profile that is known as "apron molding."

77 *Middle Preclassic masonry. Nakbe, Guatemala; Middle Preclassic*
Although the stones used for the building are uniform in size, the design of the façade is different. Here, the lime stucco covering not only improved the appearance of the wall, but also offered protection against water seeping into the masonry.

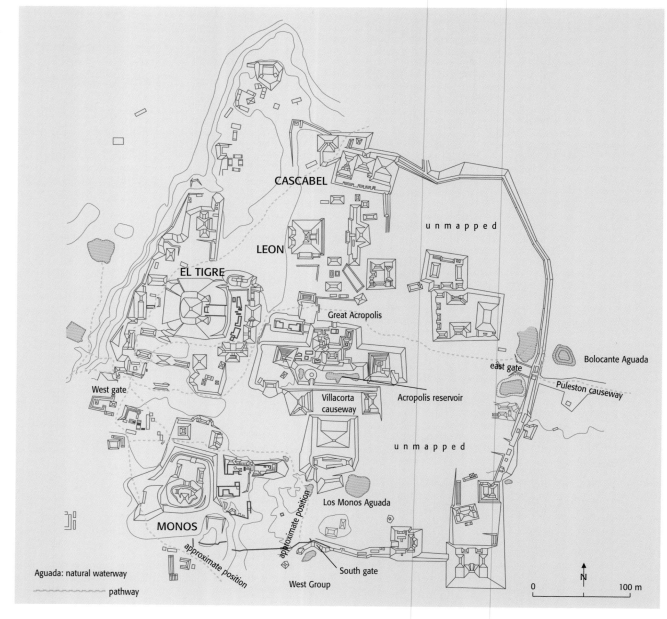

78 *Map of the West Group at El Mirador, Peten, Guatemala*
The vast Maya city of El Mirador is situated in the remote north of Guatemala, only 7 km from what is now the Mexican border. The center of the city covers an area the size of the center of Tikal. The massive pyramids and platforms make everything else built there pale into insignificance. The base of El Tigre, the biggest of all the platforms, is six times bigger than Temple IV, Tikal's tallest building. Various causeways link the center of the city with the outlying buildings as well as with other cities such as Nakbe and Tintal. The West Group is walled to the east and south; like the majority of the structures here, it dates to the Late Preclassic.

79 *Drawing reconstructing the view of the El Tigre platform from the Great Acropolis at El Mirador*
Large pyramid platforms that supported three buildings are characteristic of the architecture of the Preclassic. The El Tigre platform is the biggest of its kind in the entire Maya region. Excavations revealed a series of subsequent constructions, all of which date back to the Late Preclassic. Platform 34, which adjoins to the south and is on the left edge of the plaza, also supported three buildings. This drawing not only gives an impression of the size of the city, but also of its colorfulness; almost all of the buildings were covered with stucco and painted red.

terraces forming gardens and production areas within the civic centers of sites. It is evident from numerous excavation and sampling strategies that the surrounding swamps were the reason why the Maya settled here. Numerous multi-disciplinary investigations, including pollen, soils, geological and geographic studies, botany and paleo-botany have suggested that the areas which now form the poor-quality seasonal swamps known as *bajos* were rich wetland marshes in Middle and Late Preclassic times. Fossil remnants of these ancient wetland systems still tell of the evolutionary metamorphosis of the landscape. These marshes provided not only water, flora, and fauna, but in particular the rich renewable soils that were imported into the site centers to form a variety of civic and residential gardens (see Harrison, pp. 76).

These natural resources provided a means of effective exploitation and high yields; the abundance of food was in turn the basis for cultural innovations which allowed socially legitimate access to wealth and status. On this basis, an organized system was developed for exploiting additional natural resources, the adoption of systematic agricultural strategies, and an increasing focus on labor intensification and specialist production methods. The result of such radical transformations served to consolidate the economic and political power of an emerging elite, and led to more complex social, political, and economic structures.

Urbanization and state formation in the Late Preclassic

The economic and political growth that occurred during the Middle Preclassic period set the stage for one of the most remarkable cultural epics in Maya history: the Late Preclassic period. Major changes occurred throughout the Mirador Basin and the entire Maya region during this period (c. 350 B.C.– 250 A.D.). Perhaps the most obvious was the emphasis on monumental architecture of an unprecedented size and scale. In this era, which could be called the "Era of Monumentality," massive pyramids were built at El Mirador (ill. 78), Nakbe, Tintal, Wakna, and possibly La Manteca and Naachtun that ranged in height from between 40 and 72 meters (131 and 236 ft.). Platform constructions were built or modified involving millions of cubic meters of construction fill, indicating a significant and unparalleled control of labor and economic resources by the administrative elite (ill. 79). In addition, labor-consuming quarry and construction practices maximized the size and quantity of stone blocks, and better cutting methods meant they could be fitted more precisely into the walls (ill. 76). This created an even greater demand for labor and building materials, and significantly increased building costs.

It is curious that favorably positioned sites in river valleys, lakes or close to the coast, which later became dominant powers during the Classic period, did not have an antecedent Late Preclassic population. This suggests that population pressure, warfare, or competition for decreasing resources as argued by previous models, was not a factor in the rise of social and political complexity in the Late Preclassic; had land and natural resources genuinely been limited in this time, these regions would also have been inhabited. Although there were Preclassic settlements in favorable locations by large lakes, rivers, and lagoons, such as Yaxha (Guatemala) and Lamanai (Belize; ill. 80), it is surprising that there was not a more sustained Middle Preclassic occupation despite the fact that areas with such a wealth of resources would surely have attracted numerous pioneers. Instead, the heavy occupation at Lamanai appears to have occurred during the Late Preclassic period, around the time of the construction of the 33-meter (108 ft.) high main pyramid, Structure N10-43, in the central portion of the site. Other major constructions (Structures N 9-56, P9-2, P9-25, P 8-12) from the Late Preclassic period are concentrated in the northern section of the site, not surprisingly near what is believed to be the ancient harbor. A similar phenomenon occurred at Cerros, located directly on the coast of Chetumal Bay, which suggests that the Middle Preclassic centers of the interior regions did not establish settlements directly associated with the prime resource locations even though the importation of shell was an important component of merchant activity. Rather, settlements at Cerros and numerous other coastal sites seem to have originated almost exclusively in the Late Preclassic period and continued to thrive for several centuries before being abandoned.

In addition to the monumental size of buildings that seems to have swept throughout the Lowlands and particularly in the central core area of the northern Peten, radical changes in structural forms included the introduction of large pyramidal platforms with three summit structures, known as the "triadic architectural form." These three buildings, with a central dominant structure flanked by two smaller buildings facing each other, formed the most prevalent architectural format in the Late Preclassic. Clues to the meaning and purpose of the triad arrangement were first provided by ethnologists Barbara and Dennis Tedlock after consultations with Maya shamans about various constellations.

Tedlock noted that the three stars in the constellation of Orion known as Alnitak, Saiph, and Rigel were, according to the K'iche' Maya, the three hearthstones of the Maya kitchen, within which burned the fire of creation. The K'ich'e see the actual fire in Nebula M42 between the three stars in this constellation. This triadic form was obviously considered to be particularly sacred, since it persisted well into the Classic period. The historic Lacandon Maya still have "community houses" arranged in a triadic form today.

80 *Map of the city of Lamanai, Belize*
The archeological site of Lamanai is situated on the shores of the New River, which runs into the Caribbean and forms a wide lagoon at this point. The city was occupied consistently from the Preclassic until early historic times. The Spaniards built a small church here in the 18th century for use by their missionaries – which is why the city is also known as "Indian Church." The New River was an important trading route, which is why Lamanai had its own harbor where the dealers' canoes could be pulled onto land. Most of the settlers' remains are in the north of the site, with the exception of the 33-meter high Late Preclassic pyramid with the technical name of N10-43.

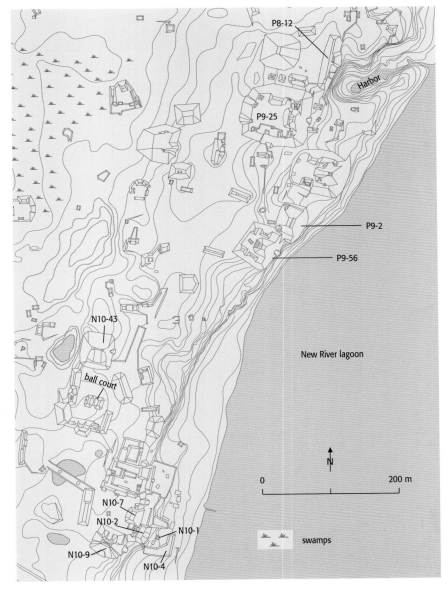

Stucco – the artistic medium of the Late Preclassic

While the monumental size and introduction of triadic architecture made for major transformations of the architectural landscape, there was to be a further innovation in the first Maya cities: monumental architectural sculpture on the primary stairways of buildings. While shallow relief art seems to have appeared in the later Middle Preclassic period, it was during the Late Preclassic that monumental architectural sculpture became the dominant medium for expressing authority and power. These sculptures consisted of deity portraits of monumental proportions, sometimes up to four meters (13 ft.) high, often flanked by profile images of the same deity with a profusion of symbolic attributes (ill. 81). Stucco on masks and reliefs was first painted cream, and then accented with red and black lines which provided a stark contrast to the red structures on which they were found. The first stucco masks of this kind were excavated at Uaxactun in the 1920s, but large numbers of similar architectural decorations have since been found at Cerros and Lamanai (Belize), Tikal, Uaxactun, El Mirador and Nakbe (Guatemala), Calakmul, Edzna, Chiapa de Corzo, and at El Tigre (Mexico).

81 *Stucco mask on the main pyramid. Acanceh, Yucatan, Mexico; main pyramid; Late Preclassic, c. 300 B.C.–250 A.D.; lime stucco, painted; H. 285 cm*
Acanceh is an important foundation of the Late Preclassic in the north-west of the Yucatan peninsula. The remains of the ancient site have now been completely built over by the modern city of the same name. Right in the center is the Preclassic main pyramid, whose four walls are decorated by four oversized stucco masks that were only excavated by Mexican archeologists at the end of the 1990s. These masks are surrounded by numerous symbolic attributes such as ornate ear jewelry, large headdresses, and spirals sprouting from their mouths.

82 *Drawing reconstructing Group H at Uaxactun*

Building complex H of Uaxactun was excavated in 1985 by a group of Guatemalan archeologists under the guidance of Juan Antonio Valdés. It consists of a Late Preclassic platform on which there were six buildings. Four buildings had corbel arches. The external façades were painted red, and decorated with murals depicting figures. Structure Sub-3 is a 5.25 m high pyramid plinth that supported a building made of perishable material. The stairs that led up to the top platform were flanked on both sides by large stucco masks painted red, black, and white. Sub-10, the small entrance building, was decorated with mat symbols and representations of deified ancestors – signs that the entire complex was used to legitimize the divine origins of a particular lineage (possibly the rulers of Uaxactun).

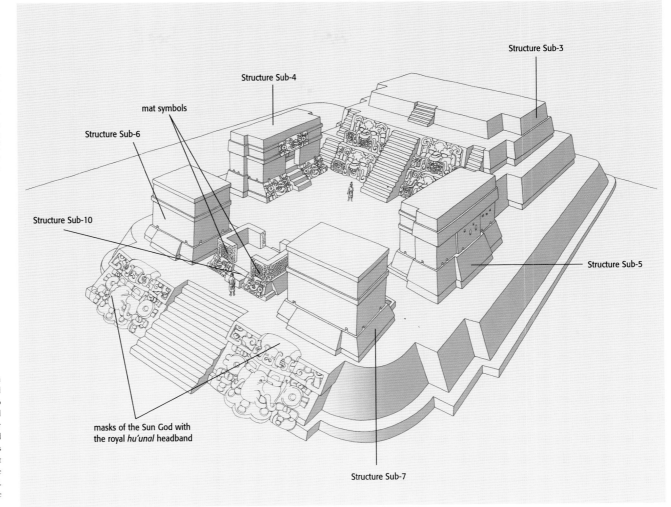

Structure Sub-4

Structure Sub-3

mat symbols

Structure Sub-6

Structure Sub-10

Structure Sub-5

masks of the Sun God with the royal *hu'unal* headband

Structure Sub-7

83 *Interpretations of one of the four stucco masks of Structure 5C-2nd of Cerros, Belize*

Cerros, which lies on the bay of Chetumal in northern Belize, grew from a small Preclassic settlement, and became an important center in the Late Preclassic due to its favorable position on major trading routes. Around 50 B.C., a part of the former village was buried under new buildings, including Structure 5C-2nd, a terraced pyramid platform with four large stucco masks decorating the south side. Two of the masks represent the gods of Venus as the morning and evening star, the others the sun in the upperworld and underworld. The mask shown here is that of the sun god in the upper world.

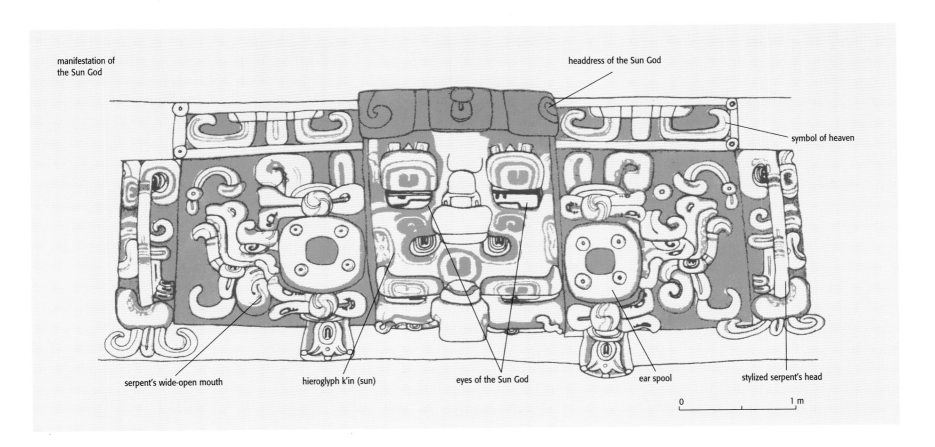

manifestation of the Sun God

headdress of the Sun God

symbol of heaven

serpent's wide-open mouth

hieroglyph k'in (sun)

eyes of the Sun God

ear spool

stylized serpent's head

0   1 m

Population increase and social differentiation

During the Late Preclassic period, sites in the Mirador Basin and other Lowland centers reached their maximum size in density and quantity of both residential and public architectural constructions, obviously because of a drastic increase in population (ill. 84). Settlement densities were such that dwellings were even placed in the seasonal swamps surrounding the major centers. The economic and political prowess of the period also included the modification or construction of large causeways to provide direct transport and footpaths between principal towns and sites. The causeways ranged between 18 and 24 m (59 ft. and 79 ft.) in width, and from one to four meters (three to 13 feet) in height. These causeways, some of which are nearly 20 km (12 miles) long, represent some of the most monumental works in Mesoamerica and merit special consideration as a consolidating factor in incipient state formation in the Mirador Basin (see Eberl, pp. 232 ff.).

During the Late Preclassic period, the extensive use of agricultural terraces and the incorporation of imported swamp mud in civic gardens was maximized. Fields consisted of terraces laid out above and beside each other, their slopes made cultivable by protective walls, imported mud within natural clay terraces, and garden terraces adjacent to the architectural complexes. Agricultural intensification is suggested by the repeated application of layers of imported swamp mud, and the fortuitous discovery of an actual terrace system with preserved small hillocks and basins. The basins are identifiable by a thin layer of lime. The field surface was covered with artificially formed, slight, circular mounds and basins, each about 80 cm to 1 meter (2.5 to 3 ft.) in diameter that were intended to collect and guide rainwater. Investigations by Steven Bozarth of the University of Kansas of fossil plant remains showed that corn, gourds, palms, and unspecified fruit trees were grown.

The accrued agricultural wealth provided the revenue for increased spending on labor, exotic and hard-to-find imports, probably a professional army, and an ambitious architectural construction program. Not least, this wealth also provided the basis for considerable social status, as suggested by the first appearance of elite royal tombs and burials, such as those at Wakna and Tikal.

The best indicator of the level of social and political complexity of a society is its monumental architecture, not least because of the quantity of resources and labor that must be marshaled into the construction effort and which goes above and beyond those of basic subsistence requirements. Attendant components include socio-political and economic developments required for planning, constructing and maintaining massive architectural complexes such as these. For example, the El Tigre Complex at El Mirador (ills. 78, 79) required 428,680 cubic meters (468,976 cubic yards) of construction fill, representing as much as five million working days only to move the fill. Detailed research into the quarrying procedures and techniques used by the Preclassic Maya have demonstrated the human days/hours of labor expended in obtaining and finishing quarried stone. Investigations still in progress into the large-scale lime production systems in the Maya area have demonstrated the quantities and types of wood and limestone, production ratios, and the techniques and strategies of lime production in the Maya Lowlands. This research has confirmed that early specialized production systems existed in the Lowlands that were either non-existent or extremely reduced in other complex groups in Mesoamerica, and serves to indicate a production and technological sofistry of early state-level development.

The Late Preclassic period is also characterized by the remarkable homogeneity of its pottery. These ceramics, known as *chicanel*, were widely produced throughout the Lowlands with engobe, waxy-textured slips in red, black, or cream the preferred surface treatment. The consistency of the ceramic slips and forms, which extended even to domestic utilitarian vessels over the whole of the Maya Lowlands, suggests a uniformity of conservative ceramic

84 *Residential area. Nakbe, Guatemala, Structure 84; Late Preclassic*
Not only large platforms but also residential buildings were found in Late Preclassic cities such as Nakbe, El Mirador, Lamanai, Cerros, and Calakmul; the platforms had probably been used to support temple buildings. These were also placed on low plinths with stairs leading up to them, and were made of perishable materials such as wood and straw; however, there were also stone buildings which already had corbel arches.

The enigmatic abandonment of Preclassic cities

The earliest cities of the Lowlands were apparently subjected to some sort of military stress in the midst of prosperity, intellectual accomplishment, and major artistic and architectural developments. Excavations by archeologists E. Wyllys Andrews IV (Tulane University, New Orleans) and David Webster (University of Pennsylvania) between 1969 and 1971 at Becan identified a Late Preclassic construction for a large moat that encircled the site (see Hohmann-Vogrin, p. 208). A similar canal/moat construction surrounded the center of Cerros. A moat-encircled "fortress" was also located at Edzna, and there was also a defensive installation at El Mirador.

While several large sites in the Lowlands prepared defensive systems, we have not yet adequately determined the perceived threat or threats that necessitated the construction of such massive fortifications. Even in Highland centers, such as Chiapa de Corzo, there is evidence of burning and destruction in the transition period from the Late Preclassic/Protoclassic period (350 B.C.–250 A.D.) and the Early Classic (250–550 A.D.). The fact that the Preclassic sites in Chiapas were relocated to more defensible sites correlates well with Lowland Maya strategies. Excavations on the summit of Tigre pyramid at El Mirador revealed numerous chert and obsidian projectile points and prism-shaped blades. The obsidian was obtained from various Mexican sources, indicating a battle in the Early Classic period (possibly 3rd or 4th century A.D.) when there was contact with Central Mexico.

One of the most remarkable discoveries at the first Maya centers is the near-total abandonment of the sites at the close of the Late Preclassic period. Residential and ritual structures were abandoned, leaving whole *chicanel* vessels (ill. 87) and stone objects directly on the plaster floors. The demise of major centers in the Mirador Basin at the end of the Late Preclassic period (c. 150–250 A.D.) occurred at numerous sites in the Lowlands, including Tikal, Uaxactun, Seibal, Cerros, Colha, Becan, the central Yucatan area, Dzibilchaltun, Komchen,

85 *Stela 2. El Mirador, Guatemala; Late Preclassic*
We still do not know whether the Maya script was created in the Highlands of Guatemala or in the Lowlands of Peten. However, the finely carved hieroglyphs on Stela 2 at El Mirador prove that writing was being used in the Mirador Basin in the Late Preclassic. Even though the text has not yet been fully deciphered, some symbols do indicate that it tells of events in the life of a prince.

86 *Stela 1. El Chiquero, Peten, Guatemala; Late Preclassic, c. 0–250 A.D.; limestone; H. 50 cm*
Small stelae were chiseled at the end of the Late Preclassic, depicting figures and areas with hieroglyphic texts. Only the lower part of Stela 1 of El Chiquero still exists; the whole monument would not have been more than one meter high. The fragment shows a pair of legs in a dynamic pose, and a rectangular area that probably contained hieroglyphs.

ideas and relatively little individual expression. Sculptures in the Mirador Basin during the Late Preclassic period were much smaller than in previous or subsequent periods (ill. 86). This interesting paradox appears contrary to what happened when important rulers commissioned large and impressive stelae and altars on the occasion of important dynastic and historic moments. Monuments of reduced size (approximately one meter/ three feet high) began to display finely-incised hieroglyphic texts on small raised panels on sculptures (ill. 85). Writing also began to appear on small portable objects, suggesting that an increasing number of people may have mastered this script, if only passively. The cumulative effort expended in the Late Preclassic monumental architecture at El Mirador, Nakbe, Tintal, Wakna, and adjacent major sites such as Calakmul, combined with the intricate web of causeways that allowed social integration, and perhaps even political and economic unification, provide a strong argument for an incipient state formation in the Mirador Basin. While it is tempting to speculate at this point that a particular area may have been responsible for the rise to statehood in the Lowlands, there is no doubt that state-level construction activities, such as the Late Preclassic canals at Edzna, were being carried out simultaneously in several areas.

the northern Yucatan coast of Cerros, Isla Cancun, Edzna, Santa Rosa Xtampak, and countless other places. Even though we do not yet know the reasons for this decline, they were undoubtedly manifold, and of a military nature. However, ecological and cultural factors would also have played a role.

The Protoclassic period in the Mirador Basin – life in the ruins of former splendor

During the brief span of time between 150 and c. 250 A.D., known as the Protoclassic period, which many researchers refer to as the end of the Preclassic, there appears to have been a dramatic decline in population in much of the Lowland Maya region, manifested by an interruption in building and other activities. Distinctive ceramic traits begin to appear during this time. For example, the waxy slips on ceramics (particularly the monochrome red, black, and cream pieces) from the Late Preclassic period became far more dull and prone to flaking. Trickle-painted and incised vessels imitated the "Usulutan" style of the eastern Highlands, which made distinctive use of orange slips painted with red and black stripes. For the first time, orange-colored clay was used as well as geometric polychrome designs. A variety of new forms were introduced, including vessels having rims, a slight "hook" on the upper surface of the rim or bowl, and four round and therefore "mammiform" (breast-shaped) feet.

Obsidian imports dropped off dramatically from the brisk trade in the Late Preclassic period, and large-scale architectural programs ceased. The major sites of the Mirador Basin seem to have been completely abandoned by the beginning of the Early Classic period (250–550 A.D.) apart from a small number of people who remained in El Mirador and a number of complexes in Nakbe and Zacatal. All extensive building work had stopped, and goods were no longer imported into the Mirador Basin. Settlements were now far more widely scattered, and tropical forest seems to have grown back over the large sites.

By the Late Classic period (550–800 A.D.), small settlements were dispersed among the ruins of the great ancient centers throughout the Mirador Basin. Residential complexes were built haphazardly, though close to the old centers, often made of stone and other materials taken from Preclassic ruins. Late Classic constructions were frequently placed directly on elevated Preclassic platforms and causeways, apparently with little regard for the original function of the constructions. There appears to have been little interaction between the different settlements during this period, since construction patterns, pottery types, tomb architecture, and burial offerings seem to vary widely within an area, or even within a site. The relatively small buildings of this time were apparently carefully decorated with painted lime plaster, murals, stucco decorations, cantilever or corbel vaults, and elaborate tombs. Murals were painted on the walls of several small constructions at Nakbe and El Mirador. Elaborate stucco sculptures of human and mythological beings are to be seen on the façades and attic stories of small and medium-sized structures. Exotic trading commodities of shell, obsidian, jade, and granite were imported to the Mirador Basin. Although evidence indicates that areas with a high population density in the Late Classic were not occupied in the Preclassic, one exception was the large site of Naachtun in the north-east of the Mirador Basin, which probably was of importance in the Preclassic and where numerous Late Classic stelae and large buildings were constructed.

Some of the most artistically important ceramics of the Late Classic were manufactured in the Mirador Basin at sites located among ancient Preclassic settlements. The style of these pottery vessels, painted in fine black line on a cream background and consisting of a wide range of forms, are known as "Codex-style," because of their supposed resemblance to and source in now nonexistent ancient codices. The scenes depicted on the vessels portray many vivid details of Maya mythology, architecture, weapons, ceramics, animals, deities, daily life activities, and hieroglyphic texts. Codex-style pottery has been found at Nakbe, El Mirador, Zacatal, La Muerta, la Muralla, and reportedly at Porvenir, each with variant chemical compositions (ill. 88). An important elite tomb in Structure 2 at Calakmul was recovered with a codex-style vessel that had the same artistic hand and the same chemical composition as the pottery from the Codex Group at Nakbe. Codex-style pottery has been actively sought by looters and collectors, resulting in the devastation of scores of Maya sites in the Mirador Basin. Many of the finest Codex-style vessels are now found in private collections throughout the world.

87 Ceramics from a looted burial. Wakna, Peten, Guatemala; Late Preclassic; fired clay
Archeologists found a looted burial in the Wakna site, south of Nakbe, in an arched tomb. The thieves were not interested in these unpainted ceramics. The monochrome black and red engobes, tapering sides, and a protruding edge on the bottom are characteristic of bowls in the Late Preclassic Chicanel style.

88 Cylindrical vessel in the Codex style. Nakbe, Peten, Guatemala; Late Classic, c. 600–900 A.D.; fired clay, painted; H. 19.5 cm, dia. 12.8 cm
Once the entire Mirador Basin had largely been abandoned in the Early Classic period, it was again occupied in the Late Classic and became an important center for the manufacture of ceramics with black painting on a cream base which resembled that of the Maya Codices. The scene on this fragment shows a god of writing with an open book in his hands.

JADE – THE GREEN GOLD OF THE MAYA

Elisabeth Wagner

Jade *objets d'art* count among the most wonderful works of art the Maya have left us. The majority of items found date back to the Classic period, but more and more artefacts dating back to the Preclassic are being discovered. The earliest of these include simple, unadorned beads found in burials in Cuello (Belize) dating back to between 1200 and 900 B.C. At this time, stone cutting was already highly developed among the Olmec, who were already working jade before the Maya.

In Mesoamerica, jade is found solely as jadeite; nephrite, the other variety known as jade, does not exist there. However, in this area of Mesoamerica "jade" is a collective term for a number of other green or blue stones, such as diopside, chrysopras, albite, serpentine and combinations of jadeite and diopside. Investigations have shown that some items are not, as previously suspected, made of jadeite, but from some of these other stones that resemble it.

For a long time, nothing was known of the sources of jade in Mesoamerica. It was not until the 1970s that it was rediscovered in the valley of the Rio Motagua in Guatemala, since when it has been used by the local jewelry industry. Mineralogical investigations have shown that all jadeite processed in the Maya region and in the rest of Mesoamerica came from this valley. The raw material is found as loose rocks and stones, ranging in size from gravel to large rocks weighing several hundred kilograms and deposited with the river sediments of the Rio Motagua. Sites of jadeite and other green stones dating back to the Classic period, when these varieties were processed, have been found in Guatemala on both sides of the Rio Motagua close to the jade beds. Surface finds in these places revealed semi-finished items and scraps with traces of

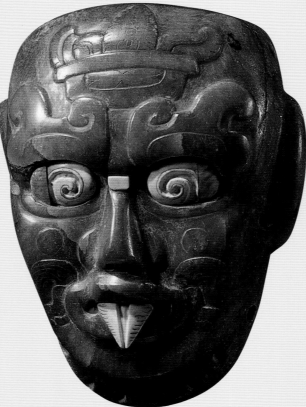

cutting, drilling and other forms of mechanical processing.

However, the raw material was not only processed close to the site where it was found, but obviously was also transported long distances as a trading commodity. This is confirmed by the 100-kg (220-lb) block found in Kaminaljuyu, for example, from which smaller pieces had already been removed for further processing. Jade from the Rio Motagua has even been found in Honduras and Costa Rica. In the province of Guanacaste in Costa Rica, there have been finds of jade carved by Maya artists, which were reworked there. To the inhabitants of the Guanacaste region – who were not Maya – inscriptions and pictorial motifs were meaningless, so they cut the original items into several pieces, which resulted in the destruction of numerous Maya works of art. Stylistically, the Maya jade from Costa Rica is of the Early Classic period.

Jade was processed using the most simple methods. Either the stone was sawn with ropes, a flat piece of hardwood, or even slate, the tool moving back and forth over the stone with the aid of an abrasive such as sand, crushed obsidian or even jade dust. Once the stone was sawn halfway through, it was turned over and the process repeated from the other side. When the join between the two sawn pieces was small enough, all that was needed was a firm blow from a hammer for the stone to be split in two.

A sharp piece of obsidian was used to score the rock. The incisions were then made deeper or extended with a sharp stick and abrasive. To make a curved line, the craftsman made a row of overlapping flat boreholes, and then rubbed the uneven areas away.

There are two known types of drill. One was a pointed wooden stick treated with sand

89 Burial mask. Calakmul, Campeche, Mexico, Structure VII, Burial 1; Late Classic, 600–900 A.D.; jade mosaic with inserts of shell and obsidian; H. 15 cm, W. 13 cm, D. 5 cm; Campeche, Museo Historico, Fuerte de San Miguel
Jade mosaic death masks were found in several royal tombs in Calakmul; the one shown here was found in a burial in Structure VII, and is the most expressive and realistic. It obviously reproduces the facial features of the deceased.

90 Burial mask. Rio Azul, El Peten, Guatemala; Early Classic, 300–600 A.D.; greenstone; H. 19.8 cm, W. 15.7 cm; Barcelona, Museo Barbier-Mueller de Arte Precolombino
This mask was probably found in a tomb in Rio Azul, since an inscription on the back records the death of an early local ruler. It shows the face of the Rain God Chaak, and was probably a death mask.

or pulverized obsidian. This type was used primarily for small holes, such as those made through a bead. The second drill type was the hollow drill, which was probably made from a bird's bone or a reed. A cylindrical borehole and cylindrical core were made with an abrasive; the core could then be used to make a cylindrical bead. Beads were often drilled through on both sides, meeting in the middle. Round beads were often made from jade gravel that had been rounded by water, and required only a little grinding and polishing. The discs used for ear spools were best made from the two halves of a small round jade stone. The half-moon pieces that were left over were then used for beads or small figurines (ill. 91). Even the smallest "scrap" pieces could be used, for example in a mosaic. These were fitted together precisely on a support, such as a shell or wood, or inserted in pre-cut grooves (ill. 94). The shape of the original object was taken into account when designing and working on the item, or else a piece of material was chosen that already

resembled the desired shape. The high polish on numerous objects was achieved by using the finest abrasive materials, such as pulverized hematite or jade and water.

Jade objects were placed in burials, used in rituals and, of course, as jewelry. As well as being used for beads, which were often strung together to make highly ornate pendants and necklaces, they were also used for ear spools (ills. 96, 97), arm, calf and foot bands, belts, pectorals (chest jewelry), and to adorn garments and headdresses. Small reliefs made of jade were a popular choice for chest jewelry, as can be seen in numerous depictions of Maya dignitaries. Drill marks on such objects indicate that they were often part of a more complicated pendant.

The inscriptions on jade objects give its name and the name of its owner. Thus several ear spools bear the incised hieroglyph *u tup*, "his/her ear spool," and then the owner's name and title. Other inscriptions on jade objects contain historical or genealogical details.

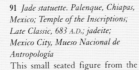

91 *Jade statuette. Palenque, Chiapas, Mexico; Temple of the Inscriptions; Late Classic, 683 A.D.; jadeite; Mexico City, Museo Nacional de Antropología*
This small seated figure from the grave of the ruler Janaab Pakal is of a deity who appears in Maya art as the personification of a tree, and in particular the World Tree or Axis Mundi.

92 *Pectoral. Copan, Honduras; Structure 10L-26; Early Classic, c. 400 A.D.; jadeite; L. 22 cm, W. 7.3 cm, D. 2.7 cm; Copan, Museo Regional de Arqueología*
Among the contents of a cache, established in 755 A.D. by K'ak'Yipyaj Chan K'awiil, the 15th ruler of Copan, was this pectoral of a standing male figure. The face, with its jaguar ears, had stylized roots instead of a lower jaw, and corresponds to the version used for heads of the hieroglyph *te*, "tree" or "wood."

93 *Jade mosaic container from the tomb of the ruler Yik'in Chan K'awiil. Tikal, Peten, Guatemala; Structure 5D-73, Burial 196; Late Classic, after 734 A.D.; jade mosaic on wood; H. 24.2 cm, dia. 10 cm; Guatemala City, Museo Nacional de Arqueología y Etnología (Kerr 4887)*
The container is a mosaic of jade platelets, placed closely together. The head on the lid shows the ruler as the god of maize, and refers also to the head of the so-called "Xook monster," a stylized shark's head which forms the god's characteristic belt decoration.

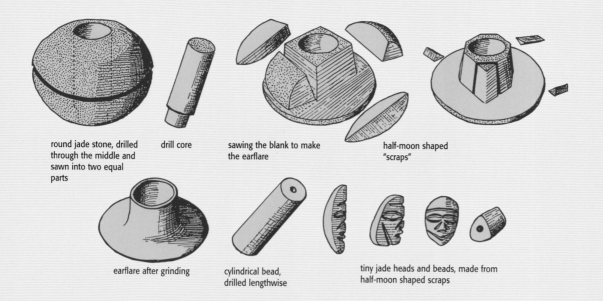

round jade stone, drilled through the middle and sawn into two equal parts

drill core

sawing the blank to make the earflare

half-moon shaped "scraps"

earflare after grinding

cylindrical bead, drilled lengthwise

tiny jade heads and beads, made from half-moon shaped scraps

placed there (ill. 98). A pectoral was discovered in a sacrificial cache at the foot of the hieroglyphic stairway outside Structure 26 in Copan, and was ascribed stylistically to the Early Classic period, whereas the actual sacrificial cache was constructed in the Late Classic when the stairway was dedicated. It is quite feasible that the pectoral belonged to an earlier ruler – or even to Yax K'uk' Mo', the founder of the dynasty, and was passed down through the generations. However, it is also possible that a burial was opened as part of a funeral ritual and the pectoral was taken from there; there is substantial written and archeological evidence, especially in Copan, that such events did occur.

It is also highly likely that jade would have been included in the dowry when a noblewoman was married to another dynasty. This probably explained why a jade head was found as part of a belt decoration near Copan, with an inscription naming a number of people from Palenque. Two inscriptions in Copan state that the mother of Yax Pasaj, the 16th ruler of Copan, came from Palenque. The jade head (exact details of where and how it was

The fact that jade was green, the same color as plants and a symbol of sprouting maize, was to the Maya – and to all other Mesoamericans – of central importance. Jade objects were placed in sacrificial caches at ceremonies of dedication and also at the ritual demolition of buildings. The most impressive examples are the rich jade finds from the cenote in Chichen Itza, where jade from all over the Maya region was dropped into the water, confirming the national importance of this sacred object. Small jade figures are often found in sacrificial caches. Such figurative representations range from plain stones, with simple sawcuts or bores to indicate limbs and faces, to perfectly modeled relief representations and small sculptures.

Jades were also handed down through generations, and worshipped and ritually buried as ancestral possessions. Occasionally, the Maya even inscribed, and possibly wore or preserved as sacred

heirlooms, objects from the Olmec era. A notable example of this is an Olmec pectoral with a Maya inscription (ill. 100). Not necessarily every object found in a burial or sacrificial cache was made either at the place where it was found or just before it was

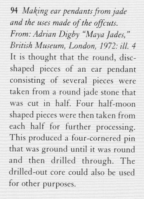

94 *Making ear pendants from jade and the uses made of the offcuts. From: Adrian Digby "Maya Jades," British Museum, London, 1972: ill. 4*
It is thought that the round, disc-shaped pieces of an ear pendant consisting of several pieces were taken from a round jade stone that was cut in half. Four half-moon shaped pieces were then taken from each half for further processing. This produced a four-cornered pin that was ground until it was round and then drilled through. The drilled-out core could also be used for other purposes.

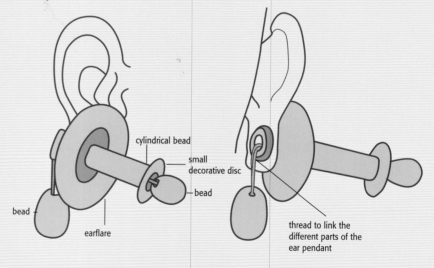

cylindrical bead

small decorative disc

bead

bead

earflare

thread to link the different parts of the ear pendant

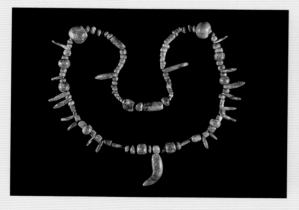

95 *Necklace. Copan, Honduras; Las Sepulturas, Structure 9N-8, Burial VIII-27; Middle Preclassic, 900–400 B.C.; jadeite; L. 80 cm; Copan Ruinas, Museo de Arqueología*
This chain was found, together with more than 300 other jade objects, in a richly furnished burial in an outer region of Copan.

96 *A pair of ear spools. Provenance unknown; Late Classic 600–900 A.D.; jadeite; dia. 8.3 cm; Denver, The Denver Art Museum (Kerr 2816)*
Ear jewelry such as this symbolizes a flower: the earflare is the calyx, and the long cylindrical bead is the pistil.

97 *A pair of earflares. Provenance unknown; Early Classic, 200–600 A.D.; jadeite; dia. 5.7 cm, D. 2 cm; Princeton, Art Museum, Princeton University*
These ear ornaments are made from simple round discs of light green jade and fashioned as stylized flowers. The flowers consist of four pierced petals arranged in facing pairs.

found are sadly unknown) could have been part of this woman's dowry.

Small jade figures representing the head of the god Hu'unal were included in the ruler's insignia, as we know from numerous representations in Maya art. Worn in the middle of the forehead – or even on three sides of the head – they symbolize the flower of the ceiba tree at the center of the universe and formed the flower diadem, which since Olmec times was the most important sign of royal dignity in all Mesoamerica. This headband put the ruler on a level with the cosmic tree at the center of the universe. When he donned the flower diadem, he was repeating a key event in creation – the rising up of the World Tree. One of the most impressive objects to symbolize this and represent the deceased ruler in his tomb as the central axis of the world is a jade head, weighing more than 4 kg (9 lb), that was found in Burial B4/7 in Altun Ha (Belize).

Flower diadems were also placed in sacrificial caches to mark the center of the sacred area thereby created. A sacrificial cache found in Cerros (Belize) contained small flower heads in jade, arranged in the same order as they would be on a diadem; the fabric had long since perished. Symbolism such as this recurs in the decoration of other jade objects found in sacrificial caches. They often depict a standing, human-like figure, a personified representation of the cosmic tree. Pieces of jade arranged in fives, especially if they contained no holes, would also have been used for fortune-telling purposes. Magicians and shamans used them to mark out the sacred area in which they carried out the ritual.

The deposition of jade objects also symbolized the placing of the three mythical hearth stones on the Day of Creation. By creating a depository of dedication, one was repeating the act of creation.

98 *Looking into the Tomb of Jasaw Chan K'awiil of Tikal. Tikal, Peten, Guatemala; Temple I, Burial 116; Late Classic, 732–734 A.D.; photograph taken in 1962*
The photo shows archeologist Aubrey Trik inspecting the remains in Burial 116, which was discovered in 1962. Virtually the entire room is taken up by a platform that bore the lavishly adorned earthly remains of Jasaw Chan K'awiil. The deceased, who had been placed on his back, was wearing costly jade jewelry. As well as ear spools, arm- and footbands, he was wearing a wide neck collar of elongated jade beads, and around his stomach another "collar" consisting of 114 large round jade beads. The gifts include a jade mosaic vessel, the lid of which bears an inscription naming Jasaw Chan K'awiil.

No other material is as durable or as resistant as jade. This explains why it was used so widely in funerary rituals, for the usually lavish gifts given to dead rulers, especially for masks of jade mosaic (ill. 89) that were placed on the deceased's face, and even used to replace skulls removed at tomb opening rituals. If the deceased ruler was buried with a large amount of jade jewelry (ills. 99, 95), it meant he was on a par with the god of maize who awaited his resurrection and renewal in the waters of the underworld, inside the mythical mountain, at the center of the universe – just like maize sown in the soil.

99 *Necklace. Palenque, Mexico; Late Classic, 600–900 A.D.; jadeite; Mexico City, Museo Nacional de Antropología*
Jade necklaces were worn as ornaments by both men and women, as is shown in numerous works of Maya art. These items often consisted of several rows of beads.

100 *Olmec pectoral with Late Classic Maya inscription. Provenance unknown; Middle Preclassic, 1000–600 B.C.; green quartzite; H. 9 cm, W. 26.7 cm; Washington DC, Dumbarton Oaks Research Library and Collections (Kerr 2838)*
In the middle of the front of this pectoral is the face of an Olmec deity which combines human features with those of a jaguar.

101 *Head of a feathered serpent. Chichen Itza, Yucatan, Mexico; large cenote; Terminal Classic period, 900–1000 A.D.; jadeite; L. 14.1 cm, W. 5.7 cm; Merida, Museo Regional de Yucatan "Palacio Cantón"*
This pectoral dates back to the Terminal Classic period. Like many other items of jewelry, it was an offering dropped into the cenote of Chichen Itza.

MAYA AGRICULTURE

Peter D. Harrison

When the Maya first appeared as an independent culture about 2000 B.C., they were already cultivating a number of important useful plants. This cultivation process took place either in the Mexican Highlands or in South America, from where their products were transported throughout the Maya region (ill. 103). Maize, beans, and squashes were the first field crops which the inhabitants of Mesoamerica planted to a schedule (ill. 107). Maize was already being harvested in what is now Mexico as long ago as 5000 B.C.; later, plants such as chili, various types of squash and some useful non-edible plants such as cotton were added. It is not known when the Maya began cultivating the cacao plant, which was so important to them because it was an addictive stimulant and eventually became a source of trade.

There is no longer any archeological evidence of fields where the Maya practiced *milpa* (shifting cultivation), because it is not possible to establish their precise locations. However, the fact that they did exist is confirmed by the field crops. Remnants of consumed foods have been found in human remains from the Archaic period (Tehuacan Cave, Mexico), and from the heyday of Maya culture.

Maya culture developed from an earlier society of hunters and gatherers, whose main form of nourishment consisted of animal protein – supplemented, of course, by plant foods such as roots, berries, and tubers. The development of agriculture as a stable foundation for the production of foodstuffs changed the balance between animal and plant foods in favor of specific cultivable plants, although hunting wild animals continued to be an important source of animal protein.

Milpa agriculture

The oldest known form of cultivation, "slash-and-burn," known in Mesoamerica as *milpa* field cultivation, was practiced alongside the growing of the first useful plants. The word *milpa* is borrowed from the Aztec. It means "field," and refers to a piece of land that has been slashed and burnt prior to sowing. This method is the oldest in the world, and the simplest process for targeted food production.

The *milpa* system of agriculture is deceptive in its apparent simplicity. It involves the clearing of land of its virgin growth, including the felling of large trees to allow access of sunlight to the soil (ill. 104). Then the felled bush and tree growth is torched and burned. This process is followed by planting, some sporadic weeding, and eventually harvest. However, much more is involved in terms of the knowledge of time and space. Even the most uneducated farmer needs to know how to "read" the seasons and how to measure space. The

103 *Agricultural expansion in Mesoamerica*
The earliest confirmation that there were several kinds of cultivated field crops came from deposits found in caves in Tehuacan in the central Highlands of Mexico, where there is evidence that maize was the earliest cultivated crop and was grown c. 3500 B.C. From this core area, field cultivation later expanded to the La Perra cave in Tamaulipas, Mexico, into the valley of Mexico, and to the Santa Marta cave in Chiapas. The latter was critical for expansion into the Maya Lowlands.

burning that preceded planting must take place the correct number of days before the first rains of the monsoon season, because the ashes that result from the burning are essential as fertilizer for the soil. If burnt too early, winds would blow the ashes away and deprive the fields of nutrients. If burnt too late, there would be a "wet" burn providing a great deal of smoke, but little ash, again disturbing the balance in the delicate system. From these needs of seasonal knowledge emerged the calendar, a product of the communal civilizations of Mesoamerica in all likelihood, long before the Maya emerged as an independent language group and identifiable culture.

A knowledge of spatial conditions was just as important as an understanding of the calendar. These conditions were already evident when a field was being planned, and ritual aspects were also taken into account. The field should not be too big or too small; either would be disadvantageous. Furthermore, it could only be cultivated for three years; after that time, the yield declined dramatically because the salts and minerals fed to the soil in the ash would be depleted. The soil was left fallow for five years to recover. A new *milpa* had to be cultivated for this time. Because there was a three-year cultivation period followed by five years of fallow, a smooth, flowing rotation was impossible and new land had to be cleared and cultivated constantly. Even a small population needed a large area for this kind of cultivation, and such an extensive use of the land would soon reach its natural boundaries – especially in times of population growth. This meant that more intensive forms of agriculture had to be developed which would allow more food to be grown in a smaller area.

With the *milpa* method, fertile soil was divided among several farmers. After three years of farming they then cleared new *milpas* as needed until the soil had recovered and farmers were able to return to the first fields.

102 *View of a terraced landscape near Solola in the Highlands of Guatemala*
The high population density forced the Maya in the Highlands of Guatemala – like their ancestors before them – to utilize every single available area for agricultural purposes. Maize, beans, squashes, and chilis were grown on even the steepest slopes. Walls were constructed on terraces for protection, permitting regular watering of the crops as well as protecting the slopes against erosion.

104 *Burning a milpa*
The time at which a *milpa* is burned is critical, and demands extensive knowledge of the rain cycle. If it is carried out too soon, the wind blows the ash away. Too late, and twigs, branches and so on will not burn completely because of the rain. In either case, the result is a poor harvest.

105 *The milpa after burning off*
After burning off, the soil is covered by a phosphate-rich layer of ash. Any large tree trunks that do not burn are simply left and the crop sown around them. This photograph was taken in May 1974 in southern Quintana Roo, close to the Dzibanche site, slightly further north than ill. 104.

106 *Sowing*
Milpas are sown primarily with maize, but yields can be increased if it is combined with other field crops. Not only does mixed cultivation provide a variety of foods from only a single clearing, but some plants provide nutrients for the soil, which helps the field to remain fertile.

107 *Milpa before the harvest*
Depending on the particular maize variety, the heads can be harvested between three and six months after sowing. As the plants grow, reaching over two meters (six feet) in height, beans entwine themselves around the stems, providing the plant with additional stability against storms.

This called for an understanding of the area, and a clear delineation of property rights. Other ideas of land allocation were religious in origin, such as the rectangular shape of the field and its orientation toward the cardinal directions. Although there are no practical explanations for this, its mandatory quality was quite clear. The Maya, who still practice slash-and-burn today, continue to observe these rules, now thousands of years old (ill. 114). Before the first crop is sown, the field has to be blessed in all four directions with incantations and the burning of incense. These customs are still practiced in parts of Yucatan and the Highlands of Guatemala, where many pre-Hispanic religious ideas have been retained under the mantle of Christianity.

A large part of Yucatan – 30 percent – consists of damp, marshy areas, *bajos*, where slash-and-burn is impossible. In the Peten in the central Lowlands of Guatemala, this figure rises to 50 percent. This means that large areas of the country are flooded during the rainy season. During the Late Classic (550–900 A.D.) these marshy areas were completely covered by water, and therefore unsuitable for habitation or agriculture. Only the hilly, constantly dry Highlands were available for *milpa*. It is no coincidence that the modern Maya are skilled in planting field crops on slopes. Despite – or perhaps because of – the lack of marshes, the large populations and complex political entanglements of the city states in the Lowlands never developed in the Highlands. The *milpa* system was a keystone to Maya subsistence. The culture inherited its knowledge from earlier societies, and depended upon it as one stable source of food supply which contributed to Maya culture flourishing for 2000 years.

MAIZE THRIVES AMONG THE ROCKS

In 1588, the General Commissioner of the Franciscans, Fray Alonso Ponce, traveled through the Yucatan Peninsula in order to evaluate the missionary works being carried out by his brothers, as well as by the official church. Traveling with him was his 33-year-old fellow monk, Antonio de Ciudad Real, who had a perfect knowledge of the Mayan language. He cherished a deep interest in and total compassion for the world of the Maya, who had found themselves under Spanish rule 40 years earlier. His tasks on returning home from his inspection on behalf of the church included reporting on the religious orders and their work; the following observations on the cultivation of maize in early colonial times are taken from this report.

From: Fray Alonso Ponce in Yucatan, 1588, translated and annotated by Ernest Noyes, Department of Middle American Research, Tulane University, New Orleans, 1932, page 311.

There have not been found, nor are there in that country, any mines of gold, silver or of any other metal nor do they grow wheat or barley in any part of it. Flour is brought from Veracruz by sea, with which they ordinarily make and sell bread in the towns of the Spaniards; but the bread common to the whole country is tortillas of maize, which is the wheat of the Indians, and of which they raise such a quantity in that province, that there is an exportation of it and it is carried in ships to Havana and Florida [...]

It seems impossible that this maize, of which we speak, is able to yield in that province because the Indians sow it among rocks, where it seems there is no moisture whatever, and nevertheless the land is so good and fertile, that without any other tillage, plowing or spading, but with only the timely burning of the bush the land is left so well cultivated by the fire and so well prepared for sowing that, sown thus, it produces very tall and stout stalks and on each of them [grows] one, two, and even three ears: and the more and the better burned the milpa is, the more and the better corn it produces, because the fire and the ashes from it serve as dung that burns the insects and roots of the weeds, and when the milpa has been recently burned and the maize sowed thus and the rains approach [of which the Indians keep careful count], it sprouts quickly and grows with the showers and when the weeds start to grow, they find the maize already up, so that they cannot grow well before they are crushed and smothered, and the maize prospers and grows very fast till it reaches full size.

Besides the maize many beans, chile-peppers, pumpkins, sweet potatoes and jicamas grow plentifully in that country and other vegetables and herbs for sustenance and pleasure of the Spaniards and Indians.

108 *Representation of cultivated plants on page 25b of the Madrid Codex. Provenance unknown; Late Postclassic, 1350–1500 A.D.; fig bark paper, coated with chalk, painted, page: H. 23.2 cm, W. 12.2 cm; Madrid, Museo de América*
This extract from the Madrid Codex depicts two types of plants with tendrils springing forth from the hieroglyph for "earth." The plants with the light stems are beans (scarlet runners) growing up a stick. The bean pods are clearly visible; the leaves are not shown. The other plant could well be a flowering squash, or a cotton plant with the seed pods that contain the cotton fibers.

109 *Amapolla tree*
Like the breadnut or ramon tree, the Maya cultivated the amapolla tree (*Pseudobombax elipticum*) in their cities. In May, just before the rainy season starts and the *milpa* is burned, its leaves turn bright red and the tree is covered in blossom. The Maya gather the juice from the tree and ferment it to make a highly intoxicating drink for ritual ceremonies. This photograph was taken in 1965, beside Temple I in Tikal.

110 *Fruit and leaves of the breadnut tree*
The fruit of the breadnut tree is extremely important to the Maya. Although it is edible, it does not contain a lot of flesh. The nut, which is high in protein, has always been valued by the Maya. It was often ground and used instead of maize to make tortillas. Today, the *chicleros* look out for breadnut trees as they ride through the forests of the Peten because they feed the leaves to their mules.

Silvaculture

Silvaculture is the practice of preserving certain varieties of wild plants in their natural habitats without cultivation or domestication. There is evidence of silvaculture among the Maya through the presence of clusters of certain species within the confines of the ruins of ancient sites. The most frequently cultivated plant was the breadnut or ramon tree (*Brosimum alicastrum*), which produced an edible nut enclosed in a thin, also edible fruit capsule (ill. 110). Modern Maya value the tree for several reasons. Its leaves are fed to pack animals such as donkeys and horses. Both animals were unknown before the arrival of the Spaniards, but in ancient times these leaves may have been fed to other semi-domesticated animals such as red deer and peccaries. These animals were kept in captivity prior to slaughter as a means of prolonging the food supply. Painted ceramic vessels contain numerous scenes of red deer with leg chains. Today, the fruit of the ramon tree is an important source of protein. Ground and made into a paste ramon is used, either as a substitute for maize (or corn) or combined with it to make tortillas. The ancient Maya may actually have preferred the fruit of the ramon tree, even in times when there was a plentiful supply of maize.

Another type of tree that is also found astonishingly often on Maya sites is the amapolla tree (*Pseudobombax elipticum*; ill. 109), which for that reason is useful as a marker for the location of ancient sites. In spring the tree bears bright red fruit, with no leaves visible. Not only was red a sacred color to the Maya, the color of the East and of the rising sun, which they worshiped as a god, but it came to represent the color of life – possibly because of the association with blood. However, this was not the main reason why the Maya cultivated the amapolla.

The tree's sap could be easily collected – and fermented to make a highly intoxicating drink. Scenes depicting revelry in excess on a number of painted vessels suggest that this activity had a strong ritual value, and that drunkenness was a spiritual activity indulged in on specific sacred occasions. The "sacred" amapolla tree provided only one of several sources of a substance that could produce the necessary ingredients for ritual imbibing.

The ancient Maya also possessed a wealth of pharmaceutical knowledge, which was far more extensive than has previously been believed. They grew many herbs and medicinal plants, but the kitchen garden was the main place for the cultivation of highly useful plants.

The kitchen garden

Like the *milpa*, it is difficult to localize and excavate the remains of a kitchen garden. The starting point for a kitchen garden is to gather a number of particular plants that will be used for seasoning, cooking, and medicinal purposes. Families sowed and tended these plants close to the home (ill. 111). Due to the irregular layout of these gardens and the area needed for them, this kind of cultivation is associated with more rural settings. Kitchen gardens are still common today, and are always located close to the home to which they belong. Small buildings adjoining the kitchen garden are used for storing provisions, and also as workshops for the manufacture and storage of farming implements. In settlements that had a large population, the most frequent pattern consisted of domestic dwellings positioned in concentric circles around the monumental ceremonial center, usually characterized by large temples and palaces. Moving outward from the center of the settlement, the distances between the buildings became greater and the buildings themselves smaller, and kitchen gardens were planted even close to the city center. The "sacred garden," which was used for ceremonial purposes, was of a higher quality and far more elegant. It was planted close to sacred buildings, specifically for the elite stratum of society, and consisted of groups of buildings that were designed, among other things, for observing the movements of the sun and seasonal phenomena, such as solstices and equinoxes. Evidence of such a "sacred garden" is reported from the E Group in Uaxactun, and possibly another one next to the large Mundo-Perdido group at Tikal. The large radial pyramid – after which the complex is named – was part of an early sun observatory. To the north of the group, on an enclosed plot of land, is a surprising variety of useful and fragrant herbs, as well as fruit trees. The meaning of these "sacred gardens" has yet to be determined by future research, but there is little doubt that they were a royal version of the traditional kitchen garden.

111 Kitchen garden
Kitchen gardens are an indispensable part of the dwellings of the simple folk. They were and are used primarily for growing herbs and medicinal plants, and also for growing basic foods. There have always been open areas around the old houses, the soil of which contains traces that prove they were used as gardens. Today, as was undoubtedly the case in former times, the yield from the kitchen gardens is so great that they are not only consumed by the grower family, but can also be sold at the local market.

112 Market scene in Chichicastenango
Agricultural products that are surplus to the family's own requirements are, as was the case in pre-Hispanic times, offered for sale. Markets are held regularly in Guatemala, especially in the Highlands, where flowers, spices, fruit, and vegetables, and also domestic animals change hands. The Sunday market in Chichicastenango, Guatemala, is one of the biggest in the Highlands.

Intensive agriculture

The *milpa* system, as the simplest and oldest form of food production, lay in the hands of individual families. The male head of the family was in charge of this duty, with the goal of producing more than his family would need in the 12 months to the next harvest. However, the farmer did not work in complete independence, but rather enjoyed the protection of the city-state ruler in whose territorial regime he lived. The ruler protected him in times of war, advised him on when to plant the crops, and could intercede with the gods for the success of the farmer's efforts. In return for these favors, the farmer had to make tribute to the royal court of the ruler in the form of food; in other words, he had to cater to the needs of a social class that was not involved in food production. Outside the growing season, his tribute could well have included working on the construction of public buildings.

The limitations of the *milpa* system have already been mentioned. They are linked to the extensive utilization of large areas of land that had to be rotated to ensure continuous production. Furthermore, agriculture depends on the seasons, and although the work is physically demanding, it is only necessary for a short period of time; in the remaining months of the year the farmer is free to pursue other activities. By the same token, although less land is required for many different forms of intensive agricultural techniques, labor is more continuous. With the *milpa* system, everything is left to nature. Its demands are followed, but not influenced.

Intensive agriculture is any method that affects natural conditions in order to increase the yield. One of the simplest methods of increasing yield is to fertilize the soil artificially. With slash-and-burn, only the nutrients that are released by burning vegetation are used to improve the soil and transferred naturally – by the rain – into the soil. Adding nutrients in the form of "night soil" (waste fertilizer) was an intensive method. Night soil was spread over the artificial agricultural fields; urine was saved for tanning hides.

113 *The chinampas of Ixtapalapa*
On the outskirts of Mexico City are a number of age-old raised fields or "floating gardens," known as *chinampas*. They were created 400–500 years ago in the bed of the former Lake Texoco, but today obtain their water from the river that is all that is left of the lake. As long as the water supply was assured, they provided up to three harvests a year. Continuous utilization and care since the time of the Aztecs increased the importance of raised fields in food production. Fruit grown on these fields is still sold on the vegetable markets in Mexico City today.

Hydraulic installations

The next, more complex step toward intensifing agricultural technique is to control the water supply to the soil. The planned collection and guiding of water is one of many facets that not only facilitates the water supply to the populace, but also to increasingly large fields. Large groups of buildings, such as the central Acropolis at Tikal, were carefully designed to direct the flow of rainfall, with the aid of sloping floors, underground drains and openings in walls, to catchment basins or to fields and gardens. This method helped to protect against natural loss through evaporation and seepage.

Channels were dug into the banks of rivers so that water could be diverted to higher areas. The Maya established artificial fields with soils from a variety of sources including from the river bed itself, although soil manipulation such as these were only possible near shallow, slow-running or standing waters. As already mentioned, over 50 percent of the Lowlands in Peten was marshy. However, the size of deposits obtained from drillings at several key points in the lower strata confirm that there were once deep lakes in these areas, long before the time of the Maya. During Maya times, they had already filled up so much that they could be used for intensive agricultural purposes.

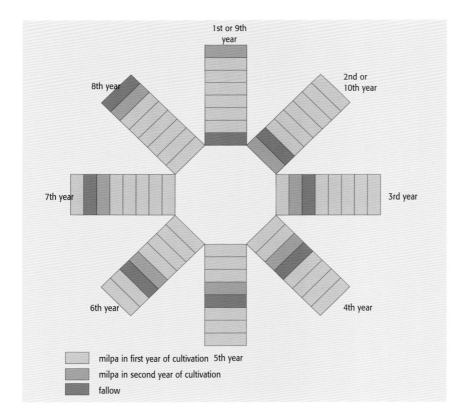

milpa in first year of cultivation
milpa in second year of cultivation
fallow

114 *Diagram of the milpa cycle*
A large amount of land is required for *milpa* cultivation. The farmer usually has several parcels of land, but only two are actually used. A new field is established in the first year; *milpa* can be practiced again in the second year, but in the third year the parcel is left so that the soil can recover. When the field has lain fallow for six years, it can again be used as before. The actual planting and regeneration times vary according to region, vegetation and soil.

On the outskirts of Mexico City, in the district of Ixtapalapa (ill. 113), the prototype of a raised field still exists, one that has been cultivated continuously for hundreds of years. The former lake bed has now dried out, but the river that travels through the district provides plenty of water to supply the fields that were established by the Aztecs in the 16th century. Although the fields have been modified since then, they have been used continuously. Due to the constant deposition of new, fertile soils, the fields are now much higher above the old water level, and modern use of pumps is now required to bring the water up to the surface of the fields. This could have been done even in ancient times, albeit by hand; yet another example of the amount of labor required for intensive agriculture.

There is evidence of excavated canals in several swamps. The swamps to the north of the site of Yaxha in the Peten and east of Tikal, as well as in the vicinity of Rio Azul in north-eastern Peten have all yielded the same forms of manipulation of the swamp bottom by canalization. Even though these methods of water manipulation are not irrigation in its true sense, they do represent a form of intensive agriculture that far exceeds the capabilities of a single family. The aim was to increase food production to levels that were not possible with the traditional *milpa* system.

There was one major prerequisite for the development and application of intensive agricultural methods: a higher degree of social organization was required to achieve such feats of engineering, and this in turn implied a central supervisory body characteristic of the water supply systems of high civilizations in the Old World. The introduction of intensive agricultural methods had consequences for the density of the population. With strict organization and control of labor, food production could be three and even four times higher than with the *milpa* system, and thus cater to the needs of far more people. This meant that hundreds of thousands of people could live in cities the size of Tikal. Large areas of raised fields would act like a "bread basket," in which hundreds of laborers worked all year round to produce food which was not for their own, or their families' consumption, but intended for parts of the population that were not involved in agriculture, such as members of the royal court.

Sociologically, this contradicts the traditional concept of the Mesoamerican "chieftainship," which was based fundamentally on familial associations. An example has been recorded in the south of Quintana Roo: aerial photographs reveal an area of 246 square kilometers (153 square miles) of fields and canals in the Bajo Morocoy, a large marshy area. The large ancient city of Tzibanche is situated on a hill adjoining this *bajo* (wetland), which means that the food

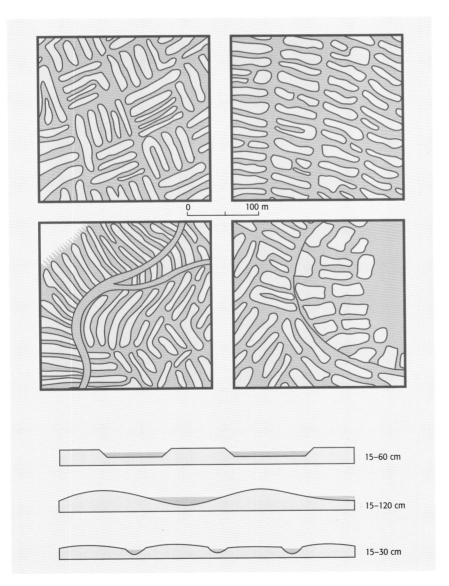

115 *Diagram of the arrangement of raised fields*
Raised fields and their canals can be laid out and managed in many different ways. Regular fields of the same size are less usual than fields that are shaped by river courses and mountains. In northern Belize, raised fields were also created by piling up mud in expanses of water. The width of the canals and the height of the beds rising out of the water vary a great deal.

116 *Raised fields in Pulltrouser Swamp, Belize*
This photograph shows the north end of the eastern arm of Pulltrouser Swamp in northern Belize. The raised fields which the Maya created in the moist basin are clearly visible. The fields and canals, which are comparable with Aztec *chinampas* (ill. 113) were used intensively for agricultural purposes by local settlers. The yield from artificially raised fields in this marshy area were about three times greater than farmers required for their own consumption. The excess was transported to large cities in the west.

produced in these fields was intended to feed people in the city close by. There were just too many of them to be fed solely by the *milpa* system.

Investigations in the wetland known as Pulltrouser Swamp in northern Belize have shown that there were several different forms of field (ill. 116), adapted to differing shoreline conditions and elevations of soil above the water level. Variations in construction include the cutting of side canals into the shore to admit water to the sides of a strip of land isolated for the purpose. Such "canalized" fields are often extended artificially into the waters of the swamp by the addition of soils imported from elsewhere or from the swamp bottom itself. A second field type is constructed as an island entirely artificially while the canals which surround the construct are deepened. Such canals require annual attention, removing the newly accumulated soils brought in by drainage from the uplands and even by water movement. This process is known as "mucking" and is performed by hand as men walk through the shallow waters scraping up the high-nutrient muck from the bottom to be replaced on the surface of the fields. A third type of field at Pulltrouser Swamp, was a combination of the previous two. A segment of the shoreline was cut free by channeling, and then the newly created island was expanded with artificially added soils.

It is probable that each wetland was used differently, depending on the prevailing conditions such as water supply sources, natural drainage of the wetland by sinkholes, seasonal variations of the water level, and the general slope of the surrounding landscape.

However, it is also relevant that the *milpa* system alone would not have sufficed to feed populations deduced from the numbers of contemporarily occupied living structures at the bigger cities. The variety of field shapes in

117 *A patchwork of fields in the Highlands of Guatemala* The entire Highland region of Guatemala is used for agricultural purposes, and the huge demand for land has greatly reduced what were once extensive areas of forest. Here, the view of a wheatfield stretches over a patchwork carpet of large and small agricultural parcels, as far as the active volcano Santa Maria close to Guatemala's second largest city, Quetzaltenango.

Pulltrouser Swamp is impressive: as well as oval L- and Y-shaped parcels, there are many square fields (ill. 115). Some fields show adaptation that is later than original construction to accomodate other functions. In one field, dams were added to service as fish holding tanks. The canals around the fields could, of course, also have been used for fish-farming (ill. 116).

There are still many unanswered questions about intensive agriculture. Were raised fields and hydraulic installations in use all over the Lowlands, or were certain cities favored because of their immediate ecological environment? What is the connection between tillage and the density of the population? And finally, the all-important question: how did the system of raised fields influence the decline of the Maya in the central Lowlands? Over a short period of observation, enormous fluctuations in the rainfall and water levels were noted in the ancient reservoirs and in the huge adjoining Bajo de Santa Fe, a huge wetland. Long periods of drought would have been catastrophic for raised field crops, which depended on constant irrigation for their yields. A relatively sudden loss of a major food source would have led to intense competition for food, increased warefare and disease, and probably to a decline in the population. This explanation for the depopulation of the central Lowlands in the 10th century is certainly just as plausible as the theory that human interference with the environment was responsible for the dramatic decline in the Maya population.

Terracing

Artificial systems of canals and terraces for irrigation purposes were widespread. Earthen terraces fronted by stone retaining walls, occur throughout the central Lowlands wherever the natural lie of the land made them possible. This process was intended as an aid to the controlled, even distribution of rainwater over a series of downslope terraces, which would catch the water and help to prevent erosion. As with the artificial raised fields, there were countless variations, ranging from simple downslope terraces that curve around hills, terracing of natural channels flanked by higher ground, to terraces at the bottom of very steep slopes which captured and held water runoff (ills. 118–120). Although terraces have been found in most explored parts of the Lowlands, they are present in particularly large numbers around the site of Caracol and in the Mountain Cow region, both in southern Belize, in southern Quintana Roo, spread across the faces of hills between the sites of Xpuhil and Francisco Bravo, and in the western Peten close to the settlements in the region of Lake Petexbatun.

118 *Cornfields near Antigua, Guatemala*
The *milpa* is no longer practiced in the mountainous, densely populated Highlands of Guatemala. The construction of terraces has meant that even steep slopes can be used. Today, land parcels are used for many years in succession with no period for regeneration. Intensive cultivation such as this is only possible with the aid of expensive artificial fertilizers.

The importance of the *milpa* system for Maya culture

The main method of supplying food was the *milpa* system, which was introduced 5000 years ago. This, the easiest and most extensive agricultural process, has never been given up, and is in fact still practiced today. The success of this method was not reduced by ecological changes, but merely by its inherently limited yield. More intensive agricultural methods, especially the utilization of artificial raised fields, were restricted to highly specific stable environmental conditions. Even small changes in the ecological conditions would have had disastrous results for such systems, expecially those located in wetland basins.

Although the *milpa* system is still practiced today, none of the intensive agricultural methods has survived, neither the raised fields nor the terraces. Perhaps these systems, which were developed later, were given up because they were more labor intensive. Free labor by demand is no longer an option, or a feature of the social system of today. A family-operated *milpa* system represents freedom of choice on the part of the participants, provided, of course, that enough land is available. Subtle changes in the environment and labor costs are two explanations why the most productive system of food production failed in the ancient Maya economy.

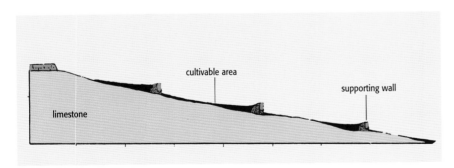

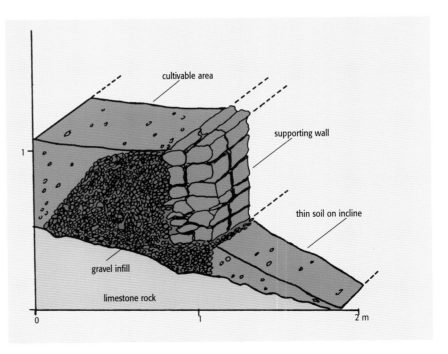

119 *Diagram of the construction of agricultural terraces*
Terraces gave the people long, level areas that were ideal for planting crops. The fertile area was made deeper by the accumulation of soil. The walls prevented erosion during the rainy season, and made it easier to control the canals and ensure an even distribution of the water. The farmers lived on the hills and tended the fields in their immediate vicinity.

120 *Cross section through the supporting wall of a field terrace*
Supporting walls on agricultural terraces, such as those found around the city of Caracol in Belize, can be up to one meter (three feet) high. They usually consist of plain, uncut stones that are gathered on the slopes and placed on top of each other without cement. One side of the wall is supported by a mass of gravel for extra support.

TORTILLAS AND TAMALES – THE FOOD OF THE MAIZE PEOPLE AND THEIR GODS

Marta Grube

The same sounds are heard in every Maya house in the early morning, at noon and again in the evening: a rhythmic slapping sound, which means that the maize dough is being shaped into tortillas, the food of the maize people – as the Maya call themselves. The round maize breads, known as tortillas all over Mexico and Central America, are eaten at any and every time of day. In fact, the average Maya obtains 60% of his or her daily calories from these flat maize cakes, so the tortilla has now become synonymous with food (ill. 122).

Tortillas are highly labor-intensive to prepare. First of all, the maize kernels have to be removed from the cob and soaked overnight in water to which a little limestone or cooking ash has been added. This results in an alkaline solution that helps

121 *Men from Tixcacal Guardia preparing sacrificial bread*
The sacrificial loaves of bread are known as *noj waaj*, and only the men are allowed to make them. Although the women make the tortillas for their daily requirements on a small table with one hand, the men use both hands to shape the bread for the gods.

122 *Loaves of Maize bread marked with a cross of toasted pumpkin seeds*
As a sign that they are sacred, the thick maize loaves are marked with a cross made of toasted and ground seeds from the *sikil* pumpkin.

to break down chemically bound amino acids in the maize, and increases its nutritional value. Early in the morning, long before the first light of dawn glimmers on the horizon, the solution is poured away, and the now soft kernels ground to a fine dough on a *metate*, stone grinding table, with a *mano*, hand pestle. The tortillas are then shaped by hand, which is when the characteristic slapping sound is to be heard. The flat loaves, about the size of a small plate, are placed on a kind of griddle on three stones over a wood fire and baked until golden. They are best eaten immediately. The tortillas are effectively the cutlery of the Maya: they tear them into small pieces, which they dip into spicy soups, bean dishes, and – after a successful hunt – meat dishes served from calabash bowls.

Although we know for certain that maize was the main food of the Maya in pre-Hispanic times, we are less certain about how it was prepared. It is assumed that, in the Classic period, maize was eaten as a loaf (*tamales* in Spanish, and *noj waaj* in Mayan) rather than as tortillas. The loaves were filled with chilis and beans, and also with meat on special occasions. Stuffed with turkey meat and wrapped in banana leaves, tamales

124 *Clay plate with a picture of a woman grinding maize. Provenance unknown; Late Classic, 600–900 A.D.; fired clay, painted; dia. 31 cm; Jerusalem, Israel Museum (Kerr1272)*
Although scenes of everyday life are rarely painted on Maya ceramics, one exception is this depiction of a woman grinding maize on a ceramic plate that could once have been used for storing tamales. The woman is kneeling in front of the grinding stone and working the maize mixture with a hand pestle. Somebody is sitting opposite her, smoking – possibly her hungry husband?

123 *Preparing sacrificial loaves of maize. Tixacal Guardia, Quintana Roo, Mexico*
The Maya of the Yucatan peninsula celebrate major religious festivals with large sacrificial loaves that are baked in an earth oven for many hours. The preparation of sacrificial food is an event in itself. Among the Cruzoob Maya of Quintana Roo, it is performed by the men because only they are seen as ritually pure. Above are some of the holders of religious offices at Tixcacal Guardia, a holy place to the Cruzoob Maya. They are standing in front of the temple of the "Speaking Cross," about to place the sacrificial loaves, wrapped in banana leaves, in the earth oven.

are today a primary food of the gods and are essential at any sacrificial ceremony held by the Maya of Yucatan. For a *ch'a chaak*, "rain bringing," ceremony at the beginning of or during the rainy season – between June and September – the men of the village all gather in a field; women are not permitted to participate in this festival. Although women are responsible for looking after the family, the Maya believe they are ritually impure, which is why the sacrificial maize loaves are only made by men (ills. 121, 123).

The *hmèen*, "maker," as the Maya priest is known, and his helper determine the type and quantity of sacrificial loaves and supervise the production procedure. Some of the loaves are made from layers of round dough cakes, others shaped into loaves from a lump of maize dough.

125 Garnishing the sacrificial loaves
Fingers are pressed into the sacrificial loaves to make holy symbols. The indentations are filled with pumpkin seeds, after which the loaves are wrapped in large leaves and secured with lianas.

126 Decorating the altar
The wooden altar table is erected on the *milpa*, the area having been cleaned in advance with incense made from the resin of the *pom* tree. The altar is a replica of the universe: the square shape symbolizes its four corners.

127 Sacrificing Balche'
To start the main part of the *ch'a chaak*, the officiating *hmèen*, "priest," kneels in front of the altar to pray at length to the Rain God Chaak and his helpers, and to invite him to the celebratory meal. The Maya believe that Chaak has a number of manifestations, each one of which is responsible for a different kind of rain.

When making these breads, the men sprinkle ground pumpkin seeds, *sikil*, in the shape of a cross and other holy symbols between the individual layers (ills. 122. 125). There is also a version that is sweetened with honey; the Maya of Yucatan call it *oxdias*, which is derived from the Spanish word *hostia*, "host." This derivation is only one of many examples of how ancient Maya ideas are combined with Christian symbolism in Maya agricultural ceremonies. Another link with the Catholic Holy Communion is the manufacture and use of Balche', a slightly alcoholic fermented drink that is made from the bark of the tree of the same name (*Lonchocarpus longystilus*). Balche' is now only brewed for religious occasions, and, by analogy with communion wine, it is known by the Spanish word *vino*. The officiating priest sprinkles the shaped loaves with Balche' to bless them. They are then wrapped in large individual banana leaves, secured with lianas or bark twine, and stacked in a shady spot.

Meanwhile, the men dig an earth oven close to the altar. In the bottom they stack firewood, then place a number of large limestones on top; the glowing stones fall to the bottom as the wood burns. Once they have removed the still glowing wood, they place the packages with the sacrificial bread among the hot stones and cover them with leaves. Finally, they cover the leaves with earth and leave the food in the earth oven for three hours. During this time, the priest and his helper decorate the altar table with flowers, candles made with wax from the wild, stingless bee (this is the only variety that is accepted as being ritually pure), pictures of Christian saints (although they are dressed in Maya clothing), with crucifixes and, finally, with a canopy made from the leaves of a tree that is believed to have a special sacred power (ill. 126). The altar is then blessed with Balche', and the priest prays long prayers invoking the Rain God Chaak and his helpers, the Christian God, and the Catholic saints (ill. 127).

At the end of the cooking time, the earth oven is opened and the steaming, hot loaves unwrapped. They are then held over *pom*, the Maya incense, and placed on the altar. Some of the loaves are broken and combined with a meat stock to make a thick soup. The soup is taken to the altar in buckets, and half a calabash with soup and pieces of meat is placed on each sacrificial loaf (ill. 128). Balche' is also poured into calabash bowls that have been arranged carefully on the altar. The order of sacrificial foods is full of meaning. Close attention is given to the number of loaves and bowls of soup and drink; they are always in the numbers 4, 9, and 13 (ill. 129), which were holy even to the pre-Hispanic Maya.

Once the sacrificial goods have been arranged on the altar, everyone kneels to ask the Christian and Maya deities to accept these "holy bites," the gifts on the altar, to look favorably upon these freely given sacrifices, and to heed the request for rain (ill. 130). The edible gifts are symbolically given to the gods as the men approach the altar table. Each one lifts up a loaf or calabash bowl and raises it to the gods in all four directions. The altar is again blessed with incense; the invisible holy essence of the sacrificial gifts rises up to the gods in the acrid smoke. This is the end of the ceremony, and the loaves of bread, soups, and calabashes with the Balche' are given first to the men, then to the women (who watch the event from a distance), and finally to the children. Any village residents and strangers who happen to be passing are invited to the meal. The end of a sacrificial ceremony is a time of joy for all concerned: it is a social banquet, and the act of sacrifice means that it will soon rain.

Maize is used to make a number of other dishes apart from tamales and tortillas. The dough can be added, with water and spices, to the drink called Atole (*ul* in Mayan), or it can be roasted and ground to make a kind of coffee, called Pinole (*k'aj* in Mayan).

Even though tortillas and tamales are at the top of every Maya menu, the way they are made has changed, especially in the more urban regions. It is no longer the rhythmic clapping that announces that food will shortly be available, but the humming and whirring of the electric maize processing plant, which in many places has replaced the stones, and the loud buzzing of the tortilla machines set up on market places and city squares and which now shape and bake the tortillas. But the Maya are convinced that the maize loaves, the food of the gods, cannot be made by machines. They still have to be shaped, lovingly and painstakingly, by hand and baked for hours in earth ovens.

128 *Calabash bowls with soup and pieces of meat*
Some of the baked *noj waaj*, sacrificial loaves, are broken into pieces and crumbled into a broth of chicken and turkey meat. The resulting soup, known as *k'ol*, is served in calabash bowls and presented on the altar with the other sacrificial foods.

129 *Sacrificial food on the altar*
The quantities of the large and small calabash bowls, gifts of candles and sacrificial loaves, have all been specified according to the symbolism of numbers, which was extremely important even in pre-Hispanic times. The cross on the altar is not the sign of Christ's Passion, but the point at which the invisible rain gods gather.

130 *Praying and offering the gifts*
The high point of the ceremony is the offering of the sacrificial foods. The *hmèen* and all the other participants kneel to pray, then raise the gifts to show and offer them to the gods. Once the gods have accepted the essence of the gifts, what is left is served as a lavish banquet to the congregation.

THE BIRTH
OF STATES

FROM CHIEFDOMS TO STATEHOOD IN THE HIGHLANDS OF GUATEMALA

Federico Fahsen

The emergence of agricultural groups into permanent settlements in southern Mesoamerica can be dated to the beginning of the Early Preclassic period around the year 2000 B.C. However, excavations at different archeological sites in the Highlands and coastal areas of Mexico and in the Pacific coastal areas of Guatemala and El Salvador point to human activity and occupation, albeit temporary, as early as 10,000 years before the present era. This occupation was in the form of hunter and gatherer groups. Their material remains are often difficult to detect because they never stayed long in one particular place, and also because the prevailing weather conditions in many of the areas that were suitable for human occupation were poor. These included extreme, rot-inducing humidity, frequently combined with torrential rainfall and storms that tore down everything in their path. In addition, the area has to be described as unstable from a geological point of view. Earthquakes and volcanic eruptions occur frequently in this part of the world, and any traces left by former settlers are therefore very difficult to find.

The first villages on coasts and river banks

By the end of the Archaic Period (6000–2000 B.C.), the areas in the vicinity of sea coasts and rivers next to the Pacific, the Gulf of Mexico and the Caribbean Sea gradually began to develop small villages where resources from the sea and rivers could be combined with limited agriculture and the hunting of animals in nearby forests and jungles.

In the beginning these village communities were organized as egalitarian societies perhaps with no more than extended family links. However, by the beginning of the Early Preclassic, social stratification began to take shape with the different lineages competing to install their respective petty chiefs, whose authority may already have been hereditary.

This social differentiation and increasing complexity, which occurred as tribes became settled, can be accounted for by two basic but interrelated factors. One is the dependence on the environment and the need for sustainable food resources in a society whose technology was limited and which did not know metal tools. Neither crop growing nor the domestication of animals was practiced to a plan, which meant that people were dependent on whatever nature by chance offered them. The other factor was the need to explain natural

132 *Preclassic sites in Guatemala*
This map of Preclassic sites in Guatemala encompasses some of the most important archeological finds investigated so far from the period between the Middle Preclassic (600–300 B.C.) and the Late Preclassic (300 B.C.–250 A.D.). The information is based on findings by a number of authors, and show that although the entire area was inhabited, certain regional groups, possibly the "cells" of states, gradually merged with each other. By the final stages of the Late Classic, some of these subregions had become fully developed states with administrative systems, their own religion and kingdoms.

phenomena in a coherent ideological system of beliefs that all members of society could accept and so give a sense to their basic daily activities.

A chief, and later an elite class were necessary to organize the provision of food by coordinating the village's activities during the planting and harvesting seasons. The chief was also responsible for distributing any excess food and for organizing alternative measures if the crop failed.

The development of an ideological system for understanding the world evolved from the need to discover the meaning of natural disasters, so prevalent in this region, and also to predict favorable conditions for farming and life in general, in which individuals, initially, and caste groups later, acted as intermediaries between the supernatural and humankind. The prestige of this priestly elite was part of a system that eventually placed a chief, sanctioned by, as it were, divine powers, at the top of a hierarchical pyramid.

Archeological material from known settlements in the first half of the Early Preclassic is difficult to obtain. This is due to the type of construction materials used (mostly pole and thatch, which rotted quickly in the humid conditions) and because of the absence of communal religious rites, which would have called for permanent religious structures made in stone. Nevertheless, mounds of some size have been found in Chiapas and a few other sites on the Pacific coast which researchers believe were man-made and intended for cultic purposes.

The little that archeologists know about the first half of the Early Preclassic period on the Pacific coast and in the Highlands has come from examining

Previous double page:
Teotihuacan, Mexico
Looking south from the Moon Pyramid, over the 1 km Road of the Dead. In the foreground is the Plaza of the Pyramid of the Moon, top left the 65-meter high Pyramid of the Sun.

131 *Seated figure from Villa Nueva. Guatemala Valley; Middle Preclassic, 700–500 B.C.; hard, fine-grained stone; H. 26.5 cm; Guatemala City, Museo Nacional de Arqueología y Etnografía*
This stone figure belongs to a late- or post-Olmec group of anthropological and zoomorphical plinth sculptures from the central Highlands of Guatemala. These figures, presumably of deified rulers, are seated on a throne or bench.

since the Pacific plain was an important trading route for people from the Isthmus of Tehuantepec and for the Olmec, who settled on the Atlantic side of the Central American straits and sought contact with the Highland Maya. These economic and cultural links were the foundation for three hundred years of prosperity at a time when the archeological site of Abaj Takalik and other sites in the east were just beginning to merge in small local chiefdoms.

A map of settlements in the Middle (800–500 B.C.) and Late (500–200 B.C.) Preclassic shows that by then the whole of Guatemala as well as a great part of Chiapas, Belize and El Salvador had communities and settlements. Many of these may have become part of sub-regional organizations or spheres of influence of a principal site (ill. 132).

Trade routes on the Pacific coast

One of these fast-developing regions centered at La Blanca and Izapa in the western Pacific Lowlands, an area with a long history of settlement. A successor state to La Blanca, situated further to the east, was Ujuxte, whose occupation has been established as dating from c. 600 B.C. A second area of human settlement is found in the central part of the Guatemalan Pacific coastal plain around El Baul, Balberta, and Monte Alto. These sites were occupied between c. 800 and 100 B.C. and later. They were located on an important long-distance trade route used by the Olmec as well as local merchants. Olmec influence is evident in numerous sculptural and ceramic remains (ills. 135, 136). The Pacific coastal plain and the slopes rising to the Highlands constitute one of the most fertile areas of Guatemala. There is no doubt that they accounted for the early interest of groups from the Gulf of Mexico in this cacao-growing area. This trade route continued to be important until the arrival of the Spaniards, and remains today an important link between Mexico, Guatemala, and the countries lying to the south.

133 *Female figure. Kaminaljuyu, Guatemala; Middle Preclassic, 900–400 B.C.; polished cream colored clay; H. 24 cm, W. 18 cm; Guatemala City, Museo Nacional de Arqueología y Etnología*
This engobe-covered clay sculpture once had movable arms. It has a prominent navel, small breasts and a cheerful smile, and is naked apart from large ear spools. It could have been a doll, and had its own wardrobe of clothing. Large-bellied figures were common in the Middle Preclassic; as well as those made of clay, stone sculptures with grotesquely swollen bellies, commonly known as "potbelly sculptures," have been found all over the Highlands.

ceramic finds. The earliest ceramics from this period are called Chantuto and were manufactured roughly between 2000–1700 B.C. Archeologists distinguish two other but slightly later early ceramic complexes, termed Barra and Locona, which lasted until 1500 B.C. These phases were followed by a more elaborate and diversified tradition of ceramic manufacture called Ocos that lasted until about 1200 B.C.

The first chiefdoms of the Middle Preclassic

The transition from the Early Preclassic to the Middle Preclassic, which took place around 1000 B.C., saw the establishment of the first known regional chiefdom of importance in the Guatemalan Pacific plains. The site of La Blanca, which was associated with the Cuadros and Jocotal styles of coastal ceramic traditions, dominates a region between the Pacific coast and the Highlands. This region had always been an area for contact between the Maya and other groups,

134 *Colossal Olmec head. La Venta, Tabasco, Mexico; Middle Preclassic, 1000–500 B.C.; basalt; H. 218 cm; Villahermosa, Tabasco, Parque Museo La Venta*
Over-sized human heads are a trademark of Olmec art. They have been found on every site of Olmec culture, the oldest city culture of Mesoamerica, and in La Venta on the Mexican Gulf coast in the state of Tabasco. It is assumed they are portraits of princes and dignitaries. We know for certain that the Olmec of the Early and Middle Preclassic had a marked influence on the Maya, and that many of their cultural achievements were adopted by the Maya.

135 *Colossal figure. Monument 4, Monte Alto, Escuintla, Guatemala; Preclassic, 600–100 B.C.; basalt; H. 157 cm, W. 180 cm, D. 170 cm; currently in the city park at La Democracia, Escuintla*
This sculpture was probably made only a few years before neighboring Monument 2, and reveals features of the region's "potbelly style." The arms and legs are close to the body, which is typical of the preferred style of the Pacific coast. The head is not separated from the body, and there are thick furrows from either side of the nose to the cheeks. The closed eyes have swollen lids, and similar styles are seen on other stone sculptures. Apart from the arms and legs, the ears are the only human attributes that distinguish this sculpture from a natural block of stone.

136 *Colossal head. Monument 2, Monte Alto, Escuintla, Guatemala; Preclassic, 600–100 B.C.; basalt; H. 147 cm, W. 200 cm, D. 180 cm; currently in the city park at La Democracia, Escuintla*
This basalt sculpture belongs to a tradition that was widespread along the Pacific coast and concurrent with the "potbelly sculptures" of the Highlands. The style encompasses the period between 500 and 200 B.C., which puts it in the so-called post-Olmec period. The inspiration of the Olmec colossal heads (ill. 134) is obvious. The human head with ears, creases around the eyes and closed eyes, a sharply formed nose and thick lips typical of the Olmec style, looks like a trophy. Because the eyes are closed, it can be assumed that the individual was either deceased or a prisoner.

La Lagunita and El Porton – minor states of the Middle Preclassic

Two other areas in the Highlands of Guatemala were also coalescing into regional political spheres during this Middle Preclassic period. The first one centered around the central El Quiche basin on both sides of the Rio Chixoy valley. Results from excavations around Santa Cruz del Quiche and extensive surveys in the western parts of the administrative districts of Baja Verapaz and El Quiche, where a large number of highly informative finds were made, reveal craft specialization and the emergence of regional artistic styles. These are signs of increasing social complexity. The development of a complex society and the emergence of kingdoms are also indicated by tombs, rich in offerings. The ceramic complexes found in La Lagunita show that these developments were contemporary with similar transformations on the Pacific coast, in Kaminaljuyu and other cities in the Lowlands.

A second region, the valley of Salama to the north of Kaminaljuyu, in the department of Baja Verapaz, exhibited an early and vigorous development. Archeologists have discovered about 15 Middle Preclassic sites with temple platforms, tombs and elite residential buildings. Around 500 B.C., the site of El Porton had probably become a regional capital in the valley of Salama with a spectacular example of early writing on Monument 1 (ill. 139). This stela bears the image of a ruler or chief, possibly with a second figure and a hieroglyphic text. The style of the carving resembles that of Stela 1 from Nakbe further north, suggesting a common artistic and ideological tradition. Both of these monuments are placed at around 400 B.C. by the archeologists who excavated them. El Porton and the entire Salama valley acted as the southern terminus of a trade route which went to the Alta Verapaz region and beyond to the Lowland Maya via Sakajut and Chisec and downriver to Chama and Salinas de los Nueve Cerros on the Chixoy river.

Kaminaljuyu – the most important Preclassic site of Highland Guatemala

Another important regional sphere was the central valley of Kaminaljuyu and surrounding sites. This region is today covered by the outskirts of modern Guatemala City. In terms of importance this site developed into the most significant Preclassic center in Guatemala with large ceremonial structures, sculptures, burials, tombs, and sophisticated management of water resources as well as intensive agricultural practices (ill. 137). Kaminaljuyu's political sphere of influence centered around the site of modern Guatemala City but extended westward into the present-day departments of Chimaltenango and Sacatepequez as far as the Pacific coast. Of great economic importance were the obsidian deposits in El Chayal, which were so important to the city states in the Highlands that they remained freely accessible despite extensive political conflict (see Grube, pp. 48).

that several monuments in Kaminaljuyu have written messages which show that they can only have been the work of scribes who spoke a language affiliated to the Ch'olan branch of Mayan languages (ill. 146). Today, these languages are spoken further north in the Lowlands; no speakers of the Ch'olan languages are present in the Highlands any more. The inscriptions from Kaminaljuyu indicate that an early variant of these languages was spoken and written there. For example, the text of Stela 10 (ill. 142) records words such as *winal*, "month," *ch'ok*, "young man," and the combination of the signs *chi* and *chan* for *chi[k]chan*, "rain serpent." The monument also has two day signs which can be read as 7 Muluk and 8 Ok. All of the Kaminaljuyu monuments with hieroglyphic inscriptions are Late Preclassic.

Other inscribed monuments such as Stela 1 at El Baul, Monuments 11 and 12, Stela 2, and Altar 13 at Abaj Takalik, and Monument 1 at Chalchuapa point to the spread of writing on monuments which portray rulers with shamanic or priestly connotations. A monument with no text but with a clear image of a ruler is the earlier Stela 11 at Kaminaljuyu (ill. 145) which shows a masked individual, probably in a ritual role, carrying a weapon made of chert in his left hand. Although the monument has no glyphic message, the image of the ruler and his dress is adorned with hieroglyphs such as the sign *ak'bal*, "night," a sign for the pronoun *u*, as well as a design with crossed bands, which soon after become part of the continuous texts in Kaminaljuyu and other sites. The sign for *ajaw*, "king"

137 *View of Kaminaljuyu*
A few unrevealing ruins are all that is left of what was once a vast city in the Highlands of Guatemala. They are in the outer western suburbs of Guatemala City, gradually disappearing in the expanding metropolis with its millions of inhabitants and increasing building activity. The first excavations in Kaminaljuyu – the name

means "Hill of the Dead" – were carried out by the Carnegie Institution of Washington in 1935. A number of rescue excavations were carried out in 1960 by the University of Pennsylvania, and since 1993 a Guatemalan project has been dedicated to systematic research into the city and its environs.

138 *Chronology of Kaminaljuyu*
This chronology was undertaken by archeologists Marion Hatch and Edwin Shook, and has now been accepted by most researchers active in this field. The Early Preclassic Arevalo phase (before 1100–1000 B.C.) is followed by the Middle Preclassic period, which is divided into three phases (Las Charcas, Majadas, and

Providencia). The Late Preclassic encompasses the well-researched Verbena and Arenal phases, and ends with the brief, and presumably turbulent, Santa Clara phase. The gradual decline of the site began with the Amatle and Pamplona phases; the other phases belong to the Postclassic.

To the north, relations with the Salama valley up to the Terminal Preclassic (0–200 A.D.) were on a coequal basis when Kaminaljuyu incorporated the area as one of its sub-regions. To the east, Kaminaljuyu controlled the obsidian deposits of El Chayal, a major source of wealth which had been exporting the material as far as the lower basin of Chiapas, the Peten region and the Pacific coastal areas since the Early Preclassic (c. 1000 B.C.). The fact that the trade routes between the site and both the Caribbean and Pacific Ocean passed through the valley was of great importance to the people of Kaminaljuyu. This allowed for trade between the rich cacao plantations on the coast and the jade deposits in the Motagua River valley. Most scholars accept now that Kaminaljuyu reached the peak of its development in the period between 400 B.C. (Verbena phase) and 100–200 A.D. (Santa Clara phase; ill. 138).

Given that over the past fifty years there have been many archeological missions to many sites in the Highlands and the Pacific Lowlands of Guatemala, it is surprising that only in recent years enough information has been gathered systematically to permit conclusions about such factors as ethnicity, statehood, trade relations, and interaction between sites.

The language and writing system of Kaminaljuyu

In 1996, the Kaminaljuyu Miraflores Archeological Project asked me to review the existing inventory of sculptures at the site, with emphasis on those that had hieroglyphic texts. These can be interpreted as one of the earliest Mesoamerican writing systems. Although there are a few known contemporary texts farther north in the Peten Lowlands, the great majority of Maya writing dates to later periods in time. A fascinating result of my epigraphic studies was

Period		Year	Phase
Postclassic	Late	1500 1400 1300	Chinautla
		1200	
	Early	1100 1000	Ayampuc
		900 800	Pamplona
Classic	Late	700 600	Amatle
	Early	500 400 300	Esperanza
		200	Aurora
	End	100	Santa Clara
Preclassic	Late	0 100 200	Arenal
		300 400	Verbena
	Middle	500 600	Providencia
		700 800 900	Majadas
		1000	Las Charcas
	Early	1100	Arevalo

139 *Monument 1. El Porton, Baja Verapaz, Guatemala; Late Preclassic, c. 400 B.C.; gray-green slate; H. 230 cm, W. 150 cm, D. 40 cm; currently in the local park of San Jeronimo, Baja Verapaz, Guatemala*
This monument bears one of the earliest texts in the Maya region. Several hieroglyphs, beginning with a hand pointing to the right followed by a dividing line, are clearly recognizable. This is followed by a hieroglyph that probably means the word *chum-il*, "enthronement." The head of a vulture follows the next illegible piece of text, and the script ends with a symbol for *ajaw*.

140 *Stela 7 and Altar 3. Izapa, Chiapas, Mexico; c. 300–50 B.C.; granite; stela: H. 178 cm, W. 127 cm, D. 35 cm; altar: dia. 146 cm, H. 40 cm*
Although the center part of Stela 7 has been destroyed, the remaining fragment depicts two people standing on the heads of a two-headed serpent. Above them arises the symbolic representation of the firmament in the shape of a heavenly serpent. As was customary in the Lowlands throughout the Classic period, an altar was placed at the foot of the stela.

141 *Stela 5. Abaj Takalik, Retalhuleu, Guatemala; Early Classic, 126 A.D., volcanic rock; H. 212 cm, W. 144 cm, D. 62 cm; Zona Arqueologica Abaj Takalik, Guatemala*
Stela 5 at Abaj Takalik was not discovered until 1976. It is one of the oldest dated monuments in Maya culture. On the raised surface at the center of the monument, flanked by two richly dressed figures, are two dates in the Long Count. Both dates are read from top to bottom in columns; the date on the left says 8.4.5.17.11 (June 6, 126 A.D. in the Julian calendar), and the right hand column appears to say 8.3.2.10.5 (May 12, 103). Unfortunately, the hieroglyphs relating to the date have been so severely eroded that we can no longer read what took place on these days.

or "lord," on the back of the skirt is a clear indication of rulership. Many of these signs later become integrated in the hieroglyphic inscriptions of the Peten Lowlands in the Early Classic and Classic periods of Maya history.

This proves beyond doubt that the language spoken and written in the Kaminaljuyu valley and nearby sites was similar to, if not the same as, that of the Lowlands to the north. Clear examples of this are Altar 1 at Kaminaljuyu and Stela 5 at Abaj Takalik, with double columns of glyphs between two individuals. The same format is found on contemporary or slightly later monuments from the Lowlands, such as on Altar 1 at Polol and the much later "Motmot" marker stone from Copan.

The Ch'olan culture of Kaminaljuyu

Part of the original home of the Ch'olan language community was Kaminaljuyu. The sudden emigration of Ch'olan-speaking groups from the Kaminaljuyu valley to the east around the end of the Santa Clara phase (c. 100–200 A.D.) may account for the resurgence of Copan and other Ch'olan-speaking Maya cities. The expansion of people belonging to the K'iche' linguistic group also forced the Ch'olan-speakers from the north and eastern Guatemalan highlands, including the peoples of Alta and Baja Verapaz, out of the region. This would have paved the way for new ethnic groups, the Poqom, Poqomchi' Q'eqchi', and Mam, to expand towards these areas. These groups replaced the earlier Ch'olan-speakers, and later split and divided themselves into more and more sub-groups.

Not only was the language of the Kaminaljuyu elite the same as that in the Lowlands, it seems that the social structure too was identical. During the late Verbena phase (c. 250–200 B.C.), the entire Arenal phase (200 B.C.–100 A.D.), and the first half of the Santa Clara phase (c. 100–150 A.D.), sculptures show rulers dressed in the clothing and paraphernalia of divine potentates. Apart from masks of gods, probably for public dance ceremonies as featured on Stela 11 (ill. 145), there are, however, no likenesses of the gods themselves. Further proof that hierarchical structures were formed in the transition from an early society to one organized like a state, is offered by the enormous size of tombs and burial offerings. For example, a burial in Kaminaljuyu (Burial 1) had 345 offerings while the later Burial 2 contained 200. The amount of artifacts is much greater

142 *Stela 10. Kaminaljuyu, Guatemala; Late Preclassic, c. 200 B.C.; fine-grain black basalt; H. 107 cm, L. 122 cm, W. 100 cm; Guatemala City, Museo Nacional de Arqueología y Etnología*
Stela 10 was presumably an altar with wickerwork motifs on the sides. The representation is of a ruler in the role of an "old" god with a chert ax in his left hand, which puts him on a par with the Rain God. A bird mask, which could be a reference to the highest bird god, is suspended behind him; kneeling beneath it is a prisoner. Two texts are engraved on the surface. There is a clearly recognizable enthronement hieroglyph, and the godly name of the individual is given in the narrative part in the form of a vulture hieroglyph, possibly a logo for "prince" and the sign for *witz*, "mountain."

143 *Stand for an incense burner. Kaminaljuyu, Guatemala, Structure D-III-6; Late Preclassic/Protoclassic, 400 B.C.–250 A.D.; sandstone; H. 79 cm, W. 82.6 cm; Guatemala City, Museo Nacional de Arqueología y Etnología*
This sculpture, in the shape of the head of an unknown god, had three vertical cones, now broken off, on which were placed bowls of incense resin. It is one of three stands for incense containers found in a large earth rampart in the south-east part of the Main Acropolis of Kaminaljuyu.

144 *Stela 9. Kaminaljuyu, Guatemala, Pyramid C-III-6; Las Charcas era, c. 1000–700 B.C.; basalt; H. 154 cm, W. 22 cm; Guatemala City, Museo Nacional de Arqueología y Etnología*
This stela, a narrow basalt column with a flat sculpture of a naked male figure, is one of the earliest sculpted monuments of Kaminaljuyu. The person is holding an unusually dynamic pose, presumably singing and dancing in ecstasy; he is looking upwards, and there are spirals winding from his open mouth. Throughout Mesoamerican art, spirals are the symbol for language and song.

145 *Stela 11. Kaminaljuyu, Guatemala; Late Preclassic, c. 200 B.C.; granite; H. 183 cm, W. 70 cm, D. 30 cm; Guatemala City, Museo Nacional de Arqueología y Etnología*
This remarkable stela has clearly cut reliefs of a person standing between two incense containers and looking to the left. The ruler is shown in the shape of a bird. He is wearing the mask of a snake bird, which covers almost all of his face. His elaborate headdress has a plant-like motif, and his robe is decorated with several *ak'bal*, "darkness," symbols. His loincloth bears a large *ajaw*, "king," hieroglyph. He carries a chert ax over his left arm, and a type of blade or rod in his right hand.

than in some of the later tombs found in the Lowlands during the Classic period. The importance and prosperity of the people buried there testifies to political power and not that of chiefdoms of a more egalitarian nature. There was an organized system of vertical as well as horizontal distribution of goods in the form of tributes, which in later phases of civic development were distributed at great public feasts and other occasions.

Evidence of internal administrative sub-centers within Kaminaljuyu politics points to its highly centralized nature. There were institutions to control and manage water resources used for irrigation (such as the canal from Lake Miraflores to the southern section of the valley), and sub-centers to control the trade to and from the coastal plains. Other resources such as obsidian from El Chayal and jade from the Motagua River valley were also monopolized and controlled by Kaminaljuyu. During the Terminal Preclassic period, Kaminaljuyu dominated the whole of the central Highlands. The city even colonized or established certain satellite cities, which for a short period of time controlled areas in the Pacific piedmont and the Baja Verapaz area to the north.

These sites, mostly located on the earlier Olmec trade routes (Abaj Takalik, Chocola, El Baul, Chalchuapa, etc.) reveal monuments with hieroglyphic texts which, although not yet deciphered, follow the format and syntax of the Ch'olan texts of Kaminaljuyu. So there was a flourishing culture in the Highlands of Guatemala in the Late Preclassic that differed little, especially in terms of language, from that of the Lowlands. Shortly after this peak, however, there was obviously a cultural breakdown in the Highlands.

The collapse of the Kaminaljuyu state

At some time – we do not yet know exactly when – there were long-term changes in the relationships between the K'iche', the inhabitants of the Pacific coast and those of the Kaminaljuyu valley. This is evident from the features on ceramic artifacts. The ceramic traditions of the central valley had strong ties with those of western El Salvador and with them formed the so-called Miraflores sphere. Strong bonds also existed between the central Highlands and the Salama Valley sites.

A shift in the population is evident from the fact that the so-called Solano ceramic tradition of the north-west began a slow but continued movement towards Kaminaljuyu, spreading out to include the area around Lake Atitlan and on to the Pacific coast. This created a difficult situation for Kaminaljuyu: among other problems it meant the loss of the San Martin Jilotepeque obsidian deposits. Very significant too was the interruption of the lucrative trade in obsidian with Chiapas. It can be shown that obsidian from El Chayal practically disappeared from the western areas.

The demise of the Ch'olan state of Kaminaljuyu is also related to the K'ichean intrusion into the Kaminaljuyu valley

and the establishment of the site of Solano, strategically located on the pass between Escuintla on the Pacific coast and the valley of Guatemala (ill. 147). In this way, traffic and trade between the two economic zones, which had lasted for a thousand years, was closed to Kaminaljuyu or at least severely hampered. In about 200 A.D., Kaminaljuyu was finally occupied by the K'iche' and its inhabitants who, probably under severe pressure for some years already, abandoned the site taking with them a tradition which had lasted for several hundred years.

The Aurora phase of Kaminaljuyu

The Aurora phase that followed (c. 200–400 A.D.) brought an actual decline in population in Kaminaljuyu, along with a change of ceramic style so drastic and final that even the utilitarian ware disappeared. At the same time, all monuments with hieroglyphic inscriptions were destroyed or broken up. A change in elite ceramics can happen when these groups accept a foreign influence or are defeated and move away. When a change of this kind occurs, archeologists believe that the lower echelons of the local population also migrate, taking with them their everyday traditions. The local traditions are then replaced by new ones introduced by the incoming population.

This massive annihilation of written history probably took place because the invading K'iche' group was illiterate. Most of the Maya groups of the Guatemalan highlands never used hieroglyphic writing, even though the Popol Wuj mentions the existence of a K'iche' script in the Highlands. Although the K'iche' gained an important role in Mesoamerica as producers and traders, they were unable to create the foundations for a truly functional, strong state until the Postclassic. Perhaps the lack of a script was one of the reasons for this.

During the two hundred years that the K'iche' Aurora phase lasted in Kaminaljuyu, massive changes occurred in the entire Maya region in both the Lowlands, the Highlands and the Pacific coastal areas. In the Lowlands, the sites of Mirador and Nakbe, which had dominated the north central Lowland area, gave way as ruling cities to the rise of Tikal and Uaxactun and many other complex states (see Sachse, p. 356 ff.).

During the Aurora era, Kaminaljuyu became a provincial center with no significant regional status. The trade agreements that had earlier been so important were no longer utilized. Access to the formerly fertile areas of Escuintla on the Pacific coast was blocked to the immigrating K'iche' from Kaminaljuyu because new groups – presumably the Xinka and Nahuatl-speaking Pipil – had penetrated to the coastal region. The result was a decline of the city-state of Kaminaljuyu, possibly hastened by the loss of the jade mines in the Motagua valley to Guayatan, an independent chiefdom that was bound to Copan.

The influence of Teotihuacan in the Highlands of Guatemala

At the same time as the K'iche' were settling in Kaminaljuyu and trying to consolidate their hold in the Highlands, foreign influences from Teotihuacan dominated in Escuintla on the Pacific coast and in Amatitlan to the south of the valley, possibly as the result of actual military conquest, or in conjunction with a monopoly on long-distance trade. Relations to this city were marked by a strong ideological substructure which was intended to justify the foreigners confiscating goods and resources. It is evident in their art, in which now Teotihuacan symbols and style elements appear (ill. 148; see Martin, p. 109).

Teotihuacan's capture of Kaminaljuyu hastened another new order, because the satellite cities of Solano and Frutal, directly to the south of Kaminaljuyu, now formed a triangle with it that exercised control over trade between the cacao-growing areas and the K'iche' Highlands.

As far as contacts between Teotihuacan, Kaminaljuyu and the Highlands are concerned, there are several theories but no satisfactory explanations

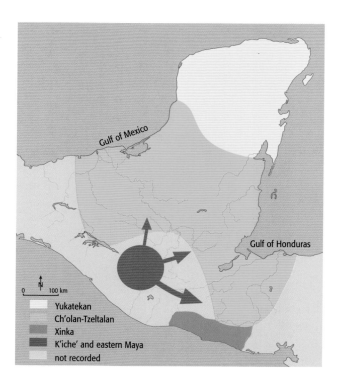

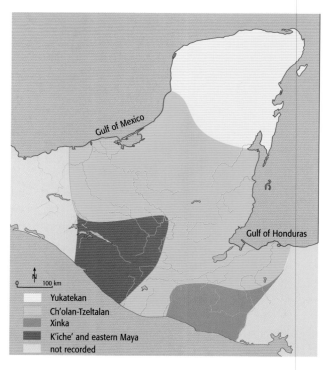

146 *The expansion of speakers of K'iche' and east Mayan languages, c. 200 A.D.*
During the Classic period, groups of Ch'olan-Tzeltalan speakers settled in a wide strip of land between the Gulf coast in Tabasco, Mexico, and western Honduras. These Ch'olan groups lived in the western Lowlands of Chiapas and further south to Copan. From texts and inscriptions from El Porton, Kaminaljuyu, El Baul, Chalchuapa, Chocola and Abaj Takalik, it can be assumed that Ch'olan races – or at least their elite – occupied a territory which to the south was far larger than their present language boundary.

147 *The wedge of K'iche' language groups, c. 300 A.D.*
The first archeological evidence of the existence of a group of proto-K'iche' speakers dates back to 600 B.C., from the heart of the Quiche administrative district around the valleys of Sajcabaja and La Lagunita. The ceramic complexes, and thus the people, shifted from this region to eastern Guatemala, to Solola (San Andres Semetabaj) and Chimaltenango (Sumpango). Finally, in the Santa Clara phase (100–200 A.D.), they conquered the valley of Kaminaljuyu and expanded further north and west. In this way they formed a wedge, through which the Ch'olan speakers were pushed further north.

148 *Lid of an incense burner. Tiquisate, Escuintla, Guatemala; Esperanza phase, 400–600 A.D.; clay, painted; H. 48 cm, W. 52 cm; private collection*
The influence of the central Mexican metropolis of Teotihuacan was evident in the Highlands of Guatemala and the Pacific foothills at the same time as in the Lowlands. Kaminaljuyu's architecture bears numerous Teotihuacan features, and the ceramics also show clear evidence of contact. In Tiquisate, which is situated between Kaminaljuyu and the Pacific coast, numerous lids of incense containers, made of clay and decorated with human figures, have been found that are otherwise only known from Teotihuacan itself. They represent lavishly clad gods from the Pantheon of Teotihuacan. The costly appliqués were shaped in molds and attached after baking. Because they are so fragile, these containers must have been made locally.

for the situation. Mounds A and B, and the Teotihuacan influenced Talud-Tablero architecture of the Palangana acropolis of Kaminaljuyu, indicate a strong presence of foreigners who could have obtained leading positions through marriage, or gained control over the city by military means.

The Esperanza and Amatle phases in Kaminaljuyu

The Kaminaljuyu Esperanza phase (c. 400–550 A.D.) is known for its Talud-Tablero architecture, a special ceramic style with magnificent cylindrical decorated tripod vases painted in stucco, and also by its construction of ballcourts and a new style of sculpture. Instead of showing images of leaders, the sculptors produced ballcourt markers in the form of tennoned serpents' heads. Clearly, there seemed to be less emphasis on the depiction of rulers and more on the assertion of belonging to a particular lineage, since each lineage appeared to have had its own ballcourt.

Because of the apparent stability brought by the influence of Teotihuacan and the revival of trading relationships with the Pacific coastal areas, population growth reached new heights. By the middle of the Amatle phase, the number of inhabitants could have reached around 15,000 before the city was finally abandoned around 800 A.D. and small scattered communities began to establish themselves throughout the central valley.

This resurgence was accompanied by the carving of new monuments in a different style and the removal of old ones to new sacred places in the Palangana acropolis. In addition, new ballcourts were built. It is possible that the withdrawal of foreign influence around the 7th century and the collapse of Teotihuacan some years later resulted in the resurgence of independent Highland Maya chiefdoms in which the K'iche', centered around Chi Izmachi and later Q'umarkaaj or Utatlan, played a pre-eminent role (see Sachse, p. 356 ff.). The rise of the K'iche' and their expansion over the Highlands marks the beginning of the Postclassic period, again a time of disturbance and close contact with foreigners from Central Mexico, whether willingly entered into or not.

The K'iche' never achieved a highly centralized state and remained a segmented political entity in which lineages vied for power, territories and tributes. This is in stark contrast to the Preclassic Kaminaljuyu system of organization, which had a strong centralized administration capable of managing water resources, organizing trade routes, developing a writing system, building monumental architecture, and extending their sphere of influence over wide areas of the Pacific costal plain and foothills, western El Salvador and the central Highlands of Guatemala. Kaminaljuyu was the first Preclassic state in the Maya area, and the way it was organized and administered may have provided a model for the Lowland Maya kingdoms of the Classic period.

THE INSIGNIA OF POWER

Nikolai Grube

The divine rulership of the Maya – indeed, their entire political system – was based on conspicuous displays of their wealth and power. Insuring it by physical means cost many human lives, huge resources and manpower. However, if a king was able to demonstrate with conviction that he possessed power, that he was a legitimate successor to the founder of the dynasty, and that the gods were on his side, then all that was required was the threat of action without the risks of actual violence. Therefore, an important function of royal art was to make the extent of royal power quite clear to the outside world. On accession, kings were given insignia to symbolize their special status. These items were of great material and symbolic value, often inherited and passed down through generations, and so were laden with spiritual energy that gave the wearer special powers.

During accession ceremonies, which probably lasted several days, the young king was given a scepter representing the god K'awiil (ill. 152). As the god of transformation and visions, K'awiil was also the god of royal dynasties, because it was the kings above all others who were able to conjure visions.

Many stelae show kings with the scepter of K'awiil in their right hand. One of the god's legs ends in the body of a serpent, serving simultaneously as the scepter's handle. Unfortunately, none of these K'awiil scepters have survived, and it is assumed they were made of wood. Archeologists have found a number of wooden scepters in the sacrificial well at Chichen Itza, which were preserved by the mud at its bottom. Although they do not depict the god K'awiil, they are an example of such designs.

For accession, kings wore the headdress of the god Hu'unal (ill. 150), which was originally probably a flower-bedecked headband made of bark or bark paper – *hu'un* in Mayan. In the Preclassic period, the flowers were replaced by jade figures which were the personification of flowers (ill. 149). The whole headband including the god figures was

151 *Oval Palace Tablet. House E of the Palace; Late Classic, c. 650–660 A.D.; limestone; H. 117 cm, W. 95 cm; in situ*
The so-called Oval Palace Tablet was set in the wall above the ruler's throne in Palenque. On the right is 12-year-old K'inich Janaab Pakal on a throne in the shape of a two-headed jaguar; in 615 A.D., he received the royal headdress from his mother, Sak K'uk', who probably performed many of her son's duties while he was still a child.

149 *Mask. Tikal, Peten, Guatemala. Burial 85 in the North Acropolis; Late Preclassic, end of 1st century A.D.; verdite, shell; H. 12.3 cm; Tikal, Museo Sylvanus Morley*
The mask could have come from the burial of Yax Eeb Xook, the founder of the Tikal royal dynasty. It has the royal headband, the three-pronged element in the center is the stylized representation of a flower, and was later replaced by the portrait of the god Hu'unal.

150 *Jade head of the god Hu'unal. Provenance unknown; Late Classic, 600–900 A.D.; jadeite; H. 13.5 cm; Salt Lake City, Utah Museum of Fine Arts*
Hu'unal was the god of royalty. He can be recognized from his headband, which has three peaks that resemble a jester's cap. Only one of the three peaks can be seen here – they are actually stylized representations of flowers – with which the kings adorned their heads.

known as the *hu'unal*, and Hu'unal himself was the god of royalty. In pictures of the god, he is shown with three points on his forehead, like the points on a jester's cap, and it is assumed they represent sprouting vegetation or petals.

Although the kings' clothing differed from that of the commoners and the nobility in lavishness and the number of attributes, it was the headdress that distinguished him from all others. There were several different kinds of headdress, but all contained the long, green-gold tail feathers of the quetzal bird (*Pharomachrus mocinno*; ill. 23). They formed the basis for masks of gods and animals and other objects of the greatest symbolic value that were intended to express that the wearer was under the protection of the gods. The exact meaning of the headdress and the identity of the gods represented by the masks are known in only a few cases. In some, the heads may conceal the patrons of the city or royal dynasty; animal masks were probably the animal doubles controlling the destiny of the king or his family (see Eberl, p. 312 f.).

Much attention is paid to the insignia of royalty in the inscriptions of Palenque. At their accession the city's rulers received various precious objects from their predecessors or parents. As well as the headband, the rulers were also given a shield and flint spearhead, symbols of war that would accompany the king into battle. Palenque also had a special royal headdress, which was a helmet made of jade discs and decorated with the picture of the god Hu'unal (ill. 151). Every king of Palenque seems to have worn this helmet as an icon of royal power, including King K'an Joy Chitam, the youngest son of ruler K'inich Janaab Pakal. Sadly, the headdress did not protect him against misfortune – K'an Joy Chitam was captured by his arch enemy, a rival king from Tonina in 711. Although we are not sure of his ultimate fate, it is likely that, rather than being killed immediately, he was held hostage in Tonina and humiliated first.

It was to be more than ten years before Palenque had a new ruler. Oddly, an important building was added to the palace at Palenque during this time. According to the inscription it was not intended for human occupation, but to house the royal headdress K'an Joy Chitam had left behind in Palenque. After the king was captured, the jewelry was not only a material reminder of its former wearer but the embodiment of the same. The Maya passed the headdress down as a family heirloom, and believed that it and the other signs of royalty were alive and possessed a soul. The same inscription tells us that K'an Joy Chitam's headdress was born in 598.

Not until 721 did a new ruler ascend the throne of Palenque. Recent excavations under the leadership of archeologist Alfonso Morales have revealed a temple with a platform or throne that is decorated with a long hieroglyphic text and two scenes

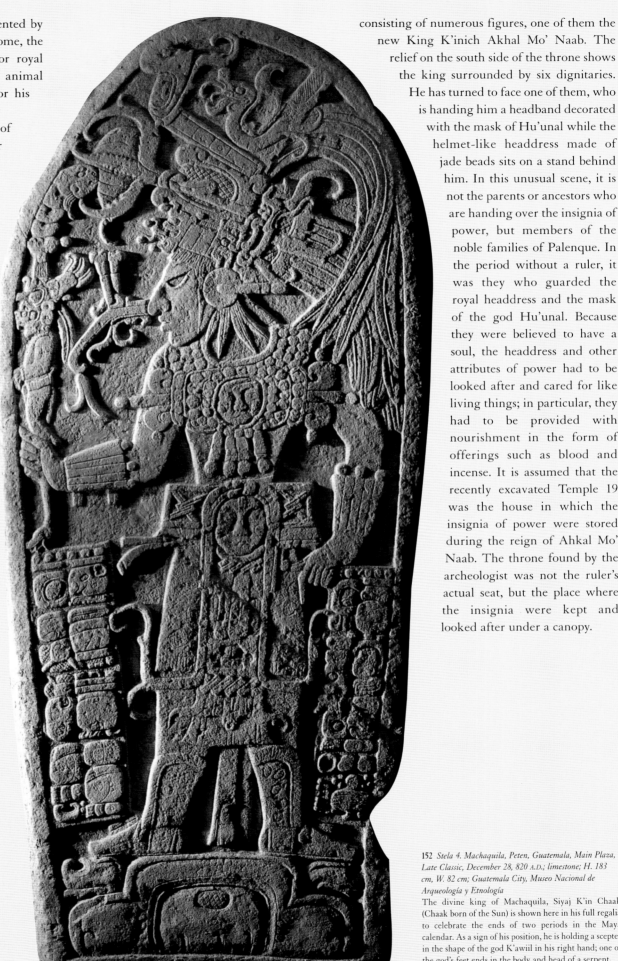

consisting of numerous figures, one of them the new King K'inich Akhal Mo' Naab. The relief on the south side of the throne shows the king surrounded by six dignitaries. He has turned to face one of them, who is handing him a headband decorated with the mask of Hu'unal while the helmet-like headdress made of jade beads sits on a stand behind him. In this unusual scene, it is not the parents or ancestors who are handing over the insignia of power, but members of the noble families of Palenque. In the period without a ruler, it was they who guarded the royal headdress and the mask of the god Hu'unal. Because they were believed to have a soul, the headdress and other attributes of power had to be looked after and cared for like living things; in particular, they had to be provided with nourishment in the form of offerings such as blood and incense. It is assumed that the recently excavated Temple 19 was the house in which the insignia of power were stored during the reign of Ahkal Mo' Naab. The throne found by the archeologist was not the ruler's actual seat, but the place where the insignia were kept and looked after under a canopy.

152 *Stela 4. Machaquila, Peten, Guatemala, Main Plaza, Late Classic, December 28, 820 A.D.; limestone; H. 183 cm, W. 82 cm; Guatemala City, Museo Nacional de Arqueología y Etnología*
The divine king of Machaquila, Siyaj K'in Chaak (Chaak born of the Sun) is shown here in his full regalia to celebrate the ends of two periods in the Maya calendar. As a sign of his position, he is holding a scepter in the shape of the god K'awiil in his right hand; one of the god's feet ends in the body and head of a serpent.

THE POWER IN THE WEST –
THE MAYA AND TEOTIHUACAN

Simon Martin

One of the more intriguing aspects of Maya culture was its relationships with its neighbors in central Mexico, most especially the great city of Teotihuacan. This vast metropolis, whose ruins lie barely 50 kilometers (30 miles) to the northeast of present-day Mexico City, was the heart of a civilization with unparalleled influence across Mesoamerica. Its distinctive art and architecture can be recognized among all the major cultures of the region and appears in the Maya area from the north of Yucatan, Mexico, to the borderlands of Honduras and the Pacific coastline of Guatemala (ill. 154).

Although we can chart the spread of Teotihuacan artifacts and building styles, their meaning is rarely self-evident. The degree to which they reflect political, cultural and economic contact is unclear; it is not easy to distinguish where the Teotihuacanos were physically involved, and where their culture was simply being emulated by others. Where we see the art of Teotihuacan in the Maya area it has, for the most part, been created and manipulated by the Maya themselves. Understanding the special role played within their own artistic

tradition is a key to unraveling Teotihuacan's wider significance during the Classic period. Conceptions of Teotihuacan as a political and cultural entity have varied to a significant degree. From a reading of its artworks there are those who envisage a benign, collective government organized on theocratic lines. Here religion is seen as the unifying force drawing people to a virtual paradise, where an awe-inspiring cosmos served as a guiding principle not only of city planning but also of social order. Teotihuacan's cultural influence is seen to flow from its busy mercantile activities, with a militaristic dimension that gained ground only in later times.

Teotihuacan – a Mesoamerican Rome

By 100 A.D., Teotihuacan had emerged as a significant city, dominating its northern branch of the Basin of Mexico. By the time of its apogee around 500

153 *Temple of Quetzalcoatl. Teotihuacan, Mexico; c. 250 A.D.*
The Temple of Quetzalcoatl, which rises up from the center of the vast citadel complex, must have been of immense importance to the rulers of Teotihuacan. As the shells make clear, the artistically sculptured façade, originally painted in brilliant red, white and green, depicted a waterworld with two specific serpent deities. One is Quetzalcoatl, the famous "Feathered Serpent." The other is shown as a headdress on its back, which is an old image for Xiuhcoatl, the "Turquoise Serpent," the fiery god of war.

154 *View of Teotihuacan before the excavation of the Street of the Dead*
The sheer size of Teotihuacan leaves a lasting impression on the visitor. However, as with any site of ruins, all we see is the framework, the empty shell of a city; the excitement lies in picturing the city as it would have been in its glory days, when it was bustling with people and activity, every house wall was plastered, and most were decorated with vast murals. The Aztecs worshipped what was left of this city, which was already in ruins during their time. It was the Aztecs who gave it its present name: Teotihuacan, the "place where people become gods." They also gave names to the most outstanding of their buildings, which they retain today: the Pyramid of the Sun, Pyramid of the Moon, and the Street of the Dead.

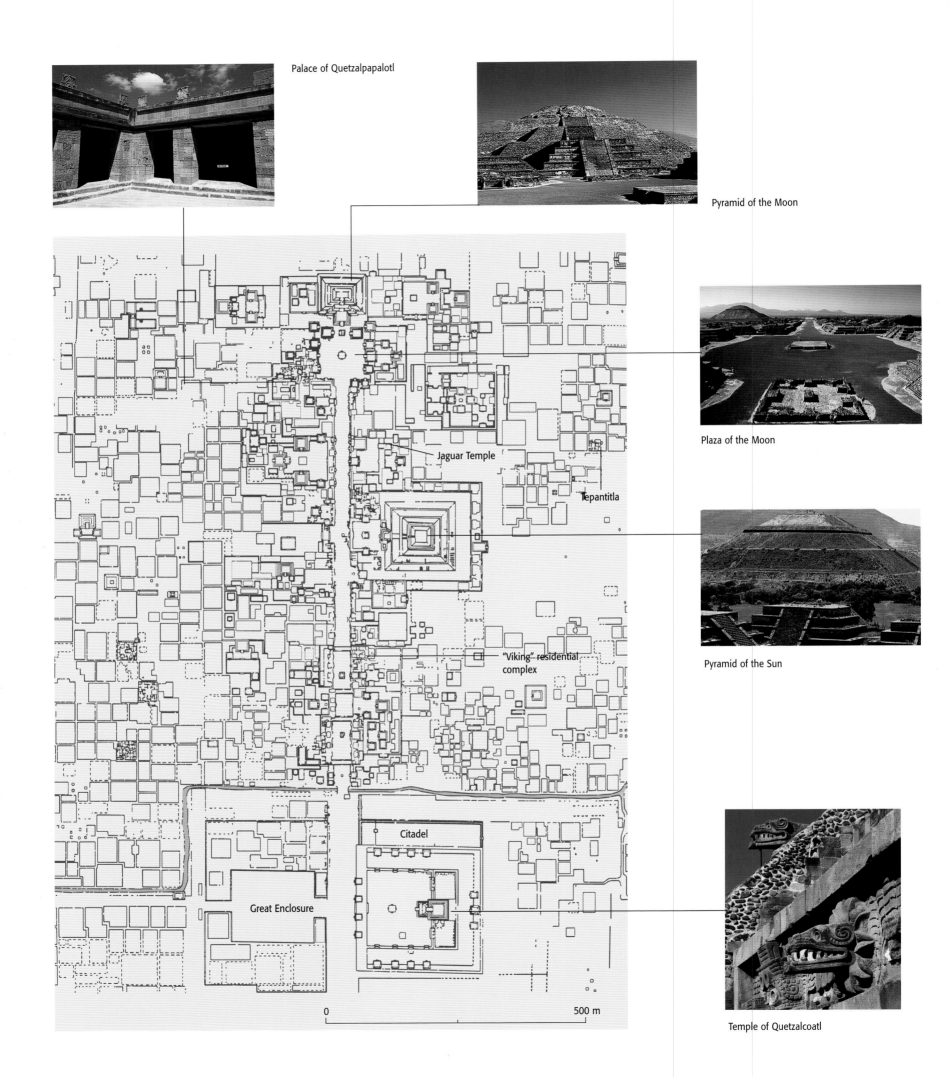

Palace of Quetzalpapalotl

Pyramid of the Moon

Plaza of the Moon

Pyramid of the Sun

Temple of Quetzalcoatl

Jaguar Temple

Tepantitla

"Viking" residential complex

Citadel

Great Enclosure

0   500 m

A.D., it boasted a population of between 125,000 and 200,000. The city was rigidly laid out in a grid pattern and even the San Juan River, that once meandered through it, was channeled into a formal canal with right-angled turns (ill. 155). Its primary, roughly north-south axis takes the form of the 2.5 kilometer (1.5 mile) long Way of the Dead, a grand processional way bordered by numerous temple platforms and palace complexes. This links Teotihuacan's two most recognizable features, the massive pyramids of the Sun and Moon – man-made mountains that interrupt the two-dimensionality of the street grid to form a third dimesion in the sky. At the southern end of the Way of the Dead there are two huge enclosures: one may have been the central market, the other, called the Ciudadela, "citadel," includes a residential compound thought to have been the governmental heart of the city. At the core of the Ciudadela lies the Temple of Quetzalcoatl or "Feathered Serpent," a pyramid lavishly decorated with sculpted serpent deities. The central buildings in the city were surrounded on all sides by some 2000 residential complexes covering an area of about 22 square kilometers (14 square miles). These single-story residences were made of roughly laid stone or adobe brick, coated in plaster and separated from each other by narrow alleyways. Inside, they consisted of connecting rooms and courtyards which were used for cooking, sleeping, and storage; they also housed communal and family shrines. One excavated complex consisted of 176 rooms.

Ceremonial architecture was dominated by a façade-style known as Talud-Tablero (ill. 156). Though not a local invention (it seems to have developed in the nearby Puebla region), this became one of Teotihuacan's most distinctive exports (see Fahsen, p. 95). Consisting of alternating levels of sloping banked walls, *talud*, over box-like projecting double ledges, *tablero*, they were built of stone blocks over a clay adobe core, finished with plaster and richly painted with figural designs such as mythical beasts, marine and flower imagery in a palette dominated by red and green. This vibrant tradition of mural painting, applied in true fresco technique, is evident throughout the city and is especially prevalent in the interiors of residential compounds. The art of Teotihuacan deals in a degree of abstraction and angularity that is more usually associated with South America than the Mesoamerican tradition of which it forms so prominent a part. This underlying aesthetic is countered and softened to some extent by florid embellishment and intricate detail. Portraits of gods and nobles are almost overwhelmed by their costumes (ill. 157), where capes, scarves, and tassels compete with feathers, pelts, and beads for the eye's attention. Most dominant are headdresses, with their sprouts of trailing plumes, which are usually based on the head of an owl, puma, coyote, or serpent, and so designed that the wearer's face emerges from the creature's jaws. In many cases we see the circular "goggle-eyes" and lightning bolt staffs of the storm god the Aztec knew as Tlaloc. Warrior figures are shown armed with a shield, darts and the wooden spear-thrower later known as the *atlatl*, sometimes brandishing flint blades with human hearts impaled on their tips. On other occasions they take the form of predatory beasts, especially owls, or – odd though it may seem to us – butterflies and moths, symbols of the ephemeral lives of warriors or, perhaps, their reincarnated souls. Characters of all kinds

155 *Map of the center of Teotihuacan*
The chessboard layout of Teotihuacan is easily recognizable on this map of the 7 square kilometers of the city center. The main axis is formed by the 2.5-km long Street of the Dead, which runs from north to south. All large buildings face this street in one way or another, from the Citadel and the Great Enclosure in the south to the huge Pyramids of the Sun and Moon, which end it at the northern and southern points. The San Juan River, which was already channeled in pre-Hispanic times, flows through the city from east to west. Only a fraction of the buildings in the center have been excavated so far.

156 *Talud-Tablero façade. Mundo Perdido, Tikal, Guatemala, Mundo Perdido Pyramid (5C-54); Early Classic, 250–500 A.D.*
Façades in the Talud-Tablero style are a characteristic feature of the architecture of Teotihuacan. They are to be found in numerous towns and cities to which the city had commercial links or which came under their direct sphere of influence, including Oxkintok in northern Yucatan and Kaminaljuyu in the Highlands of Guatemala. The alternating levels of sloping embankment walls (*talud* in Spanish) and boxlike protruding ledges (*tablero*) are evident on the main pyramid of the Early Classic Mundo Perdido group in Tikal. Talud-Tablero façades existed in Tikal before 378 A.D., a sure sign that the two cities were already linked before the arrival of Siyaj K'ak'.

are regularly shown singing or chanting, flowery "speech scrolls" curling from their lips.

Strangely for such a sophisticated society, writing at Teotihuacan reached only a rudimentary level. The names of people and places appear as hieroglyphs painted on murals or plaza floors, but there is as yet no sign that they used a complex script of the kind developed by the Maya and some other Mesoamerican cultures. As a result, any real understanding of this city's extraordinary history will forever be beyond us. In fact, we know very little about the inhabitants of Teotihuacan themselves: their origins, what language they spoke, their social and political organization, and much else besides. The lack of overtly dynastic monuments gives a rather faceless, corporate image to their government. Even so, high-status burials such as that of the Temple of Quetzalcoatl are evidence of great disparities in social rank.

Teotihuacan's great wealth stemmed from a variety of factors, including the production of craft goods and control of key minerals such as obsidian, the volcanic glass knapped into all kinds of razor-sharp blades. The distinctive, green-hued varieties quarried from nearby Tepeapulco and Pachuca found their

157 *A lord of Teotihuacan. Teotihuacan, Techinantitla district; c. 65–75 A.D.; fresco; H. 70 cm, W. 97 cm; San Francisco, The Fine Arts Museums of San Francisco*
This fragment of a mural was originally housed in a complex near the city center, and may depict one of the rulers of Teotihuacan. Footprints represent the path he is walking, a bag of offerings in his right hand which he is scattering with his left. A speech scroll is coming out of his mouth, possibly a song, and the decorations of flowers and amulets symbolize holiness. The lord is decorated with so-called "goggle-eye ornaments" and a tasseled headdress. The latter could be an indicator of social status; it is repeated in the bottom-right part of his name hieroglyph.

way to all parts of Mesoamerica. A pottery-style called "Thin Orange" is another characteristic marker of contact with Teotihuacan, and was both exported and imitated widely.

But the concentration of military imagery suggests that warfare was also a key part of its success, and it has long been conjectured that its trade routes were secured by force of arms. In Aztec times – many centuries later – there was a class of warrior-merchant called the *pochteca*, who had a major role in long-distance commerce, and a similar system has been proposed for Teotihuacan. In fact, the Aztec *pochteca* were but one element of a tribute empire, and it is reasonable to expect that much of Teotihuacan's wealth was amassed from extortion of this kind. In one way or another, a vast income would have been necessary to support Teotihuacan's populace, far too numerous for most to have been engaged in food production in the surrounding fields.

Teotihuacan was a cosmopolitan city with a sizeable number of foreign residents and special districts inhabited by peoples from the Maya, Oaxaca and Veracruz regions. Here they retained many elements of their home culture, including building techniques, burial practices, and ceramic styles (though the degree to which the latter include Teotihuacan motifs often betrays their place of manufacture). Although some of these outsiders were undoubtedly merchants, and there for commercial reasons or of their own free will, it is also highly likely that others were part of another relocation strategy related to Teotihuacan. Throughout the world, great powers have obliged representatives of subject peoples – often the offspring of rulers – to reside in their capitals, where they served as both ambassadors and de facto hostages for the good behavior of their kin.

Taken as a whole, Teotihuacan was an unparalleled phenomenon – the most complex and populous urban center of the Classic period, a cultural and economic superpower of the highest order. Its golden age lasted for over 500 years, but during the 7th century the city experienced a devastating decline. At

158 *Fragment of a mural with war owl. Teotihuacan, Techinantitla region; c. 650–750 A.D.; fresco; H. 26 cm, W. 30.5 cm; Mexico City, Instituto Nacional de Arqueología e Historia*
One of the main war motifs of Teotihuacan was an owl armed with an *atlatl* arrow or spear and a round shield. Some interpretations see it as a deity, an emblem, a particular warrior caste, or even a personal name or title. The spirals bursting forth from the beak are a frequent motif in Teotihuacan art, and represent language or song. The war owl also appears in Maya art, where it accompanies God L, who was both the god of war and the god of traders; two aspects that are closely linked to Teotihuacan's influence in the Maya region.

some point the public buildings at its heart were systematically burned and destroyed, sacked by invaders or wracked by internal revolution. By 750 A.D., its population had fallen to a fraction of its former size.

In its time, Teotihuacan was as central to the Mesoamerican world as Rome was to the Mediterranean. However, it is becoming ever clearer that the Mesoamerican style of imperialism differed from its western counterpart, and may have left few archeological traces. For want of irrefutable evidence, only a few researchers venture to speak of a "Teotihuacan Empire." Instead of the rigid control of conquered territories – epitomized by the mature Roman Empire and reflected in its vast public works throughout Europe – Mesoamericans concentrated on more "hegemonic" modes of control, looser structures which emphasized personal bonds with subject elite groups.

Crucially, it is in Teotihuacan art abroad, and specifically in the Maya area, that the themes of militarism and political order are at their most prominent. In a very real sense, information from the Maya opens a special vista on its great and influential contemporary, while supplying equally vital information about how the Maya viewed themselves.

159 *Teotihuacan war owl. Provenance unknown; c. 650–750 A.D.; fired clay, dia. 26.4 cm; Mexico City, Museo Nacional de Antropología*
This energetic representation of the Teotihuacan war owl on the lid of a black ceramic vessel shows the motif as a stylized emblem with a central shield and crossed *atlatl* spears. It is frequently seen in a similar form on murals, ceramic vessels, and stone sculptures from Teotihuacan.

Labels on image:
owl
bleeding hearts
quetzal feathers
K'uh, "god, holy one"
hair of the Great Goddess
ear plug
jade ornament hanging from the nose
hand scatters holy and precious things
holy substance (blood)

Teotihuacan and the Maya

Evidence of the impact of Teotihuacan on the Maya can be established archeologically from its art and iconography and, in recent years, also from hieroglyphic inscriptions. Each offers its own view and approach, but it is the role played by Teotihuacan in Maya art that is most conspicuous.

It is important to note the lack of any true fusion between the two styles; it is quite clear that Teotihuacan motifs are always to be viewed as "foreign" and "alien." In the grammar of Maya dress, Teotihuacan elements are absorbed in a variety of ways. At times, a single Mexican motif is incorporated into an otherwise purely Maya costume; elsewhere we see Teotihuacan from head to toe.

Throughout Mesoamerica, headgear was always a prime vehicle for symbolic information and often meant to be "read" as if it were a text. The largest and most cumbersome headdress worn by Maya kings depicts a monstrous plated serpent (ill. 162). A forerunner of the Aztec Xiuhcoatl, this deity lay at the heart of a Teotihuacan "cult of war." It was known by the Maya by the rather cryptic name of *waxaklajuun ubaah kaan* or "18-headed serpent" (ill. 161). Related items of Mexican military headgear were a rounded helmet made of shell platelets, which the Maya knew as a *ko'haw*, and a bulbous "balloon" headdress of deer hide fitted with black-tipped owl feathers. The goggle-eyed motif abounds in such contexts, whether worn as a mask or as disembodied circles fixed on the brow. Sometimes we even see the stylized

160 *The "holy fabric" of Teotihuacan. Left: section of the mural of Portico 11; Teotihuacan, Mexico, Tetitla; right: detail of Stela 3/6 at Yaxchilan; Yaxchilan, Mexico*
The stream of offerings issued by the Great Goddess of Teotihuacan is shown as divine or precious by the emblems included, such as stylized hearts, shells, eyes, hands, and flowers. The same elements are to be seen at sowing rites, which are carried out by princes who embody the deities; this we know from the symbols of special forms of vocal expressions, such as songs and poems (see ill. 157). Increasingly in the Classic period, the Maya adopted these Teotihuacan ideals and their picture language. The "holy fabric" of the Teotihuacans entered into Maya hieroglyphs for *k'uh*, "god," and *k'uhul*, "holy" (top right), and we again see Teotihuacan motifs in the representation of the Maya kings' sowing rites (bottom right).

proboscis of the butterfly war god. Completing the Mexican warrior panoply were square, war serpent-decorated shields (which contrast with the circular Maya type) and the *atlatl* spear-thrower.

Such costumes are associated with records of warfare and evidently work as special personae adopted by Maya kings to promote victory – a pointer to Teotihuacan's awesome military reputation. A second category of headgear is what we might regard as a "crown." The possession and exhibition of prestigious headdresses were vital parts of accession ceremonies, and the style of these insignia often reveals links to Teotihuacan.

One Maya ritual with very special connections to Teotihuacan is the so-called "scattering ceremony," in which the ruler sprinkled droplets or pellets either onto an altar which, for reasons which are not yet clear, was bound with knotted ropes, or into burning braziers. The bag from which these substances were drawn was suspended from a handle and always decorated with Mexican motifs.

Indeed, precisely the same ritual is pictured on murals at Teotihuacan, where this stream of the "divine horn of plenty" is identified by amulet-like objects: half and whole shells, hearts, eyes, flowers, and hands. The exact substance scattered is unclear, but blood and incense seem the likeliest metaphors for this "sacred essence." The two cultures seemed to have shared ancient ideas about this material, which the Maya knew as *k'uhlel* from the root *k'uh*, "god," and meaning literally "holy fabric." The Maya hieroglyph for these terms includes some of the same amulets, such as the half-shell seen at Teotihuacan. Given these strong connections, there seems every reason to think that this particular scattering rite was Mexican in origin (ill. 160).

This brings us to the ways in which hieroglyphic texts illuminate and interact with Mexican-style art. A sign often associated with Teotihuacan imagery has been deciphered by David Stuart as *pu* or *puh*, Mayan for "cattail reed." Significantly, sources from the Colonial period across Mesoamerica talk of Tollan or the "Place of Cattail Reeds." This legendary center was an archetype of social and religious order, but it was also attributed to a series of real centers

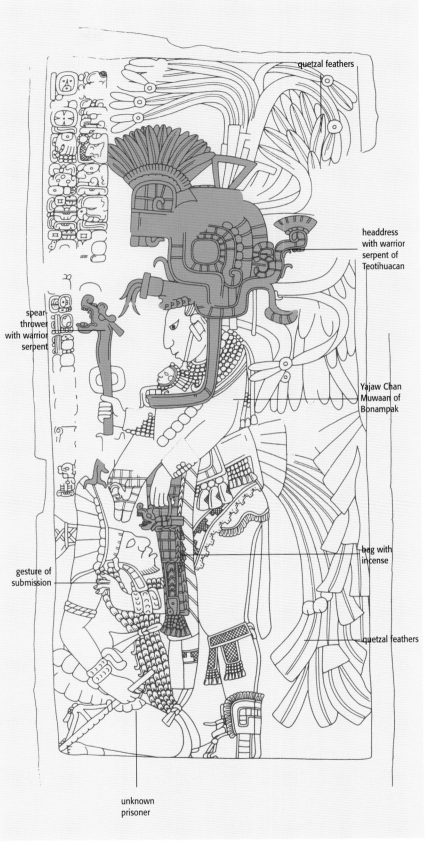

quetzal feathers

headdress with warrior serpent of Teotihuacan

spear-thrower with warrior serpent

Yajaw Chan Muwaan of Bonampak

bag with incense

gesture of submission

quetzal feathers

unknown prisoner

162 *The warrior serpent of the Maya. Bonampak, Mexico, drawing of Stela 3; 785 A.D.*
In order to participate in the power of the gods of Teotihuacan and the Teotihucans' fame as conquerors and rulers, the Classic Maya kings adopted many elements of Teotihuacan armory. This late Maya monument shows Yajaw Chan Muwaan ("lord of the heavenly falcon"), King of Bonampak, wearing the warrior serpent as a headdress and carrying an *atlatl* spear-thrower with the same motif.

161 *Maya lord in Teotihuacan robes. Painting around a bowl decorated in the Codex style; provenance unknown; c. 700 A.D.*
What is striking about this scene is the extent to which the Maya lord is surrounded by foreign symbolism which, according to need, gives him the status of a founder, conqueror, or overlord. He is riding on a warrior serpent with large "goggle eyes," wearing a balloon headdress and carrying a hook scepter.

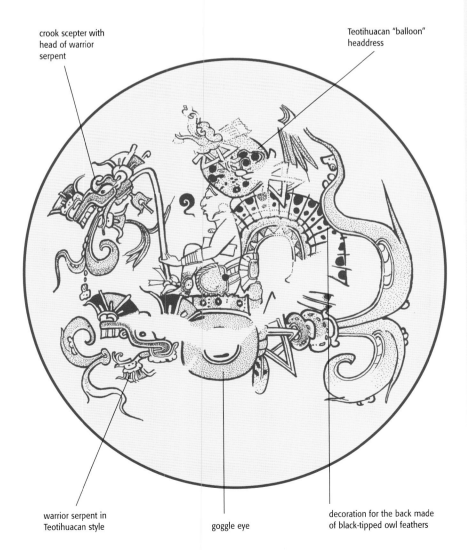

crook scepter with head of warrior serpent

Teotihuacan "balloon" headdress

warrior serpent in Teotihuacan style

goggle eye

decoration for the back made of black-tipped owl feathers

163 *Conjuring up a Teotihuacan vision. Yaxchilan, Mexico, Door lintel 25; c. 726 A.D.; limestone; H. 130.1 cm, W. 86.3 cm; London, British Museum (Kerr 2888)*

Here we see K'abal Xook, Queen of Yaxchilan, experiencing a vision after a bloodletting session. She has called up a partly decomposed monster, a mixture between a serpent and its deadly counterpart, the centipede, wearing the helmet of the Teotihuacan warrior serpent. From its mouth springs an armed warrior with the balloon headdress and "goggle-eyed" mask, which the accompanying text describes as the "flint and shield" of Yaxchilan's main patron god. It is probably a manifestation of King Itzamnaaj Balam (Shield Jaguar II) as the protector of the city.

164 *Maya hieroglyphs for Teotihuacan themes*

Maya inscriptions contain names that refer specifically to Teotihuacan terms. Thus we know, for example, that the all-present warrior serpent was known by the Maya as *waxaklajuun ubaah chan* ("18-headed serpent"). The idea of Teotihuacan as a Tollan, the "place of the reed," is illustrated by a reed symbol that means *puh*, "cattail reed." Another is the sign of the "crossed torches," which has been decoded as a kind of shrine, the birthplace and memorial of a dynasty that is linked to the great Teotihuacan. One of the highest royal titles was *kalomte'*, which means "great prince" or even "emperor." Together with *ochk'in* it forms the term "great prince of the west," a term that is linked to people who came from Teotihuacan or refers to the fact that they originated from there.

165 *The arrival of the Mexicans. Tikal, Guatemala; c. 400 A.D.; fired clay; whereabouts unknown; drawing, University of Pennsylvania, USA*

This scene from a black ceramic vessel could be an idealized description of the arrival of the Mexicans in the Maya Lowlands. To the right is a temple in the Talud-Tablero style, which possibly symbolizes Teotihuacan itself. Leaving it is a group of people in Mexican clothing. At their head are warriors armed with *atlatl*, "spear-throwers," and arrows, followed by two other people with tasseled headdresses carrying tripod vessels with lids. They are moving toward another town that is inhabited by people with typical Maya features.

of political power. When they encountered problems of legitimization, kings might claim descent from its ruling line or make pilgrimages to it to receive tokens of office. These ideas were part of a much wider Mesoamerican understanding of hierarchy that characterized not only the mortal world but that of the gods as well. For Teotihuacan to serve as a presiding Tollan of all Mesoamerica in the Classic period demonstrates the scale of its penetration into Maya concepts of politics and religion.

This is well illustrated at the city of Yaxchilan. Here on Lintel 25 we see a local queen, K'abal Xook, conjuring up a vision of a half-skeletal Mexican war serpent on the day her husband "Shield Jaguar" ascended the throne in 681 A.D. The serpent is disgorging a warrior in full Teotihuacan uniform from its mouth, apparently the king himself, manifested as the prototypical warrior and instrument of a local god named in the text. In doing so the queen became the personification of a goddess who carries the "crossed torches" glyph in her name, a mexicanized motif which had special ties to political foundations.

Waxaklajuun Ubaah Chan

reed symbol

crossed torches

Och'kin Kalomte

Teotihuacan and Tikal

No other city in Mesoamerica offers a better testimony to the comprehensive influence of Teotihuacan on art and hieroglyphic texts than Tikal. Excavations in the 1960s revealed a sudden upsurge in Mexican influence toward the end of the 4th century A.D. In Tikal (see Grube/Martin, p. 159), more than 1000 kilometers (620 miles) from Teotihuacan, monuments suddenly acquired figures in Teotihuacan attire, and a number of tombs and commemorative deposits held Teotihuacan-style lidded tripod vases. On one well-known carved vessel, a line of Mexicans, armed warriors, and other tassel-headdressed lords carrying vases, are seen to advance from a Talud-Tablero style city to one populated by the Maya. Perhaps this scene reflects a significant influx of people from Teotihuacan. Recent decipherments at Tikal suggests that this is indeed the case (ill. 165).

This event is linked to a specific date in the year 378 A.D. It marks the arrival of a certain Siyaj K'ak' ("Born of fire"). He first appeared eight days earlier, in

El Peru some 78 km due west of Tikal. However, Siyaj K'ak's arrival was not the only event on this day; it was also the day on which the ruler of Tikal, "Great Jaguar Paw," died. There is a strong sense of a political takeover or conquest having taken place. It was certainly the end of the traditional Tikal line, and it was replaced by one with claims to Mexican ancestry.

Siyaj K'ak', who carried a title that linked him to the "west," was at the center of this new political order. In 379 A.D., he installed Yax Nuun Ayiin I ("Green" or "First Crocodile") as the new Tikal ruler, and later other princes as lords of the cities of Uaxactun, Bejucal, and Rio Azul. Whether these were

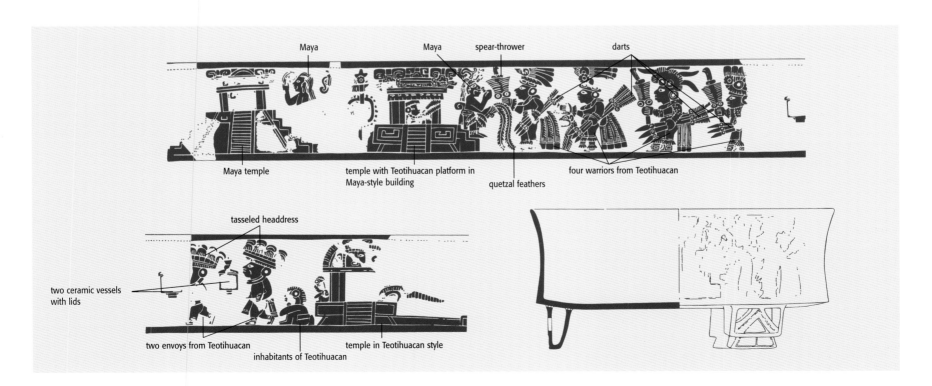

Maya   Maya   spear-thrower   darts

Maya temple   temple with Teotihuacan platform in Maya-style building   four warriors from Teotihuacan   quetzal feathers

tasseled headdress

two ceramic vessels with lids

two envoys from Teotihuacan   inhabitants of Teotihuacan   temple in Teotihuacan style

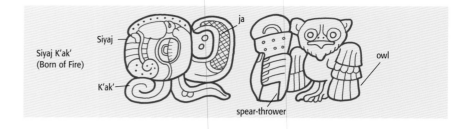

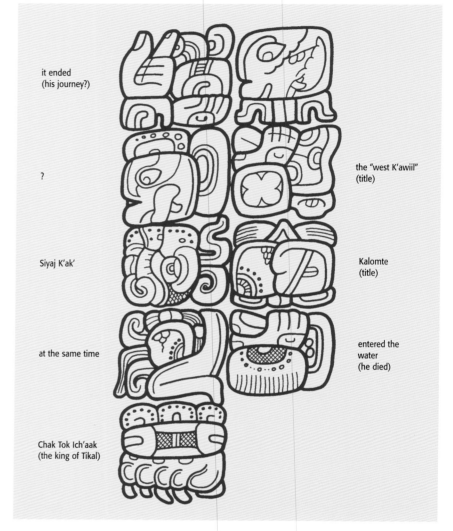

166 *The so-called Marcador of Tikal. Tikal, Guatemala; 416 A.D.; fine-grained limestone; H. 100 cm; Guatemala City, Museo Nacional de Arqueología y Etnología*
This splendid sculpture was found in a residential complex in the Mexican building style in Tikal. It represents a feather-adorned banner of the type that is also to be seen in Teotihuacan. According to the text inscribed on the shaft in 416 A.D., this banner, which is now known as "Marcador," was ceremoniously presented as a token of honor for, or a possession of, "Spear-thrower Owl." There is indeed an owl and an *atlatl*, a "spear-thrower," in the middle of the medallion. The text goes on to describe "Spear-thrower Owl's" elevation to the rank of ruler of 5-? mountain. It is possible that this was a synonym for Teotihuacan itself.

167 *The arrival of Siyaj K'ak'. Tikal, Guatemala, Stela 31 (back); 445 A.D.; limestone; H. 230 cm; Tikal, Museo Sylvanus Morley*
In 445 A.D., Siyaj Chan K'awiil, the 16th king of Tikal, had the fabulous Stela 31 erected to celebrate the completion of a ten-year period. The narrow sides and the back tell of distant events in the city's history, and also of Siyaj K'ak's arrival on January 15, 378 A.D. King Chak Tok Ich'aak died on the same day – it can safely be assumed that there was a link between the arrival of Siyaj K'ak', who was associated with the west, and the ruler's death. The event was so important that it was recorded on the adjoining "Marcador" and on two monuments in the neighboring city of Uaxactun, where the ruling dynasty was possibly replaced by vassals who were favorably inclined towards Teotihuacan.

foreign, i.e. Mexican, or compliant local lines is yet to be established. Yax Nuun Ayiin I himself is always depicted in Teotihuacan dress, while the name of his father, "Spear-thrower Owl," is that of the familiar "Warrior Owl" seen at Teotihuacan (ill. 168). On two other occasions, Spear-thrower Owl is named as the overlord of Maya rulers, and he seemed to embody the ultimate authority behind the Mexican presence in the Lowlands (ill. 166).

Other evidence demonstrates that Tikal-Teotihuacan links go back well before 378 A.D. The ubiquitous green-hued obsidian obtained from near Teotihuacan occurred in quantity much earlier, pointing to a long-lived trade relationship that once took Lowland products such as exotic feathers, pelts, and textiles to central Mexico. Tikal's original ascent in the region must be linked in part to these profitable relationships. We now know that large ceremonial complexes in the Talud-Tablero style were being erected at Tikal by 250 A.D., which could even hint at possible dynastic relationships before 378 A.D.

Under Yax Nuun Ayiin's son, Siyaj Chan K'awiil I ("God K'awiil who was born in heaven"; reigned 411–456 A.D.), these Teotihuacan features all but disappeared as the Mexican dynasty – which had now intermarried with local women – presented itself as an orthodox Maya line.

Teotihuacan's influence on the Maya cities of Kaminaljuyu and Copan

The excavation of another great Maya metropolis, Kaminaljuyu in the Southern Highlands, revealed another burst of Teotihuacan contact at the turn of the 4th century A.D. Although Kaminaljuyu enjoyed considerable wealth at one time, a severe decline left it virtually abandoned by 100 A.D. Its revitalization was characterized by major Talud-Tablero construction, with associated tombs stocked with fine Teotihuacan-style vases and prestigious offerings from as far away as the coast of the Gulf of Mexico. It is widely believed that a group of Teotihuacanos who, judging from the fine furnishing of their tombs, belonged to the nobility, had seized control of the site in order to control the rich resources of the region: jade and other minerals, including the coveted deposits of obsidian at El Chayal, as well as perishable luxuries such as quetzal feathers and cacao, the chocolate beans grown on the Pacific Coast to the south. Finds in this coastal region of Teotihuacan "incense burners" – ornate ceramic creations embellished with molded appliqué – reveal a Mexican influence.

Perhaps the clearest evidence that Teotihuacan or its Maya allies took an active part in establishing new dynasties and spreading the Classic ideal into new territories comes from Copan. Altar Q (ill. 169), the most sublime statement of dynastic power in the entire history of the Maya, is a square stone table with portraits of its kings placed in line on each side, each seated on an identifying hieroglyph. At the point where the encircling sequence meets, Yax K'uk' Mo' (First Quetzal Macaw; reigned 426–c. 437 A.D.), the "founder" of Copan, is conversing with his successor, the 16th king and commissioner of the monument. It has long been recognized that Yax K'uk' Mo' is wearing the distinctive goggle-eye ornaments and square shield of Teotihuacan.

168 *A new king in Tikal. Tikal, Guatemala, Stela 31; 445 A.D.; limestone; H. 230 cm; Tikal, Museo Sylvanus Morley*
The first king to reign in Tikal after the arrival of the Teotihuacans was Yax Nuun Ayiin I ("Green" or "First Crocodile"). His enthronement ceremony in 379 A.D. was conducted by Siyaj K'ak', the leader of the mission described above. Yax Nuun Ayiin's father was "Spear-thrower Owl," the presumed ruler of Teotihuacan. This portrait depicts the king in the full regalia of the Teotihuacan warrior with a plated headdress; he is wearing neck jewelry of shells, also an attribute of the lords of Teotihuacan.

169 *Yax K'uk' Mo' and Yax Pasaj of Copan. Copan, Honduras, Altar Q; tuff; 776 A.D.; Copan, Museo de las Esculturas*
Altar Q of Copan and its representation of the city's 16 kings is one of the key documents that helps us to understand the dynastic sequence. Each of the four sides contains four kings on their name hieroglyphs. Yax Pasaj, who commissioned the monument in 776 A.D., is seated at the point where the circle closes, opposite K'inich Yax K'uk' Mo', the founder of the royal dynasty of Copan, who arrived in the city in 426 A.D. It is not known where he came from, but the square shield and "goggle eyes" are a strong link to Teotihuacan.

Modern readings of the text on top of Altar Q tell us that Yax K'uk' Mo' rose to power and left the "House of the Crossed Torches" in 426 A.D. We now know that nearby Quirigua was involved in these same events, as part of a new hierarchy of lords set up under the aegis of Yax K'uk' Mo' who, like Siyaj K'ak', is linked by title to the "west." The crossed torches evidently mark a place of origin or royal foundation; they are a place of the "first fire," from which the flame of a dynasty was ignited.

Excavations to the lower levels of Copan's occupancy have shed light on the question of Yax K'uk' Mo's origins (ill. 171). Most early architecture at Copan reflects Tikal influence, but at the base of Temple 16 archeologists Robert Sharer and David Sedat discovered Copan's only Talud-Tablero building. Its interior

was once decorated by colorful murals, just as at Teotihuacan. Cut into the floor was the tomb of a male accompanied by rich grave offerings. The position of the tomb and the fact that it was overbuilt by at least seven temples, all dedicated to the memory of the founder, are powerful evidence that this is the body of Yax K'uk' Mo'. Chemical analysis of his bones suggest that he did not grow up in the Copan Valley and was the kind of foreigner described in the texts. Significantly, a nearby tomb held a body accompanied by *atlatl* darts, with two shell "goggle-eyes" still resting on the forehead of its skull.

As in Tikal, Copan later conducted a revival in Teotihuacan style. Again, this came in response to a political event, in this case the capture and execution of its king by a rebellious sub-king of Quirigua. Temple 26, home to the great

hieroglyphic stairway with the longest known Maya text, is dedicated to this purpose. Sculptures of six Copan kings are set into the stairway, each dressed as a Teotihuacan warrior, amidst a vast retelling of Copan's dynastic history. Its most extraordinary feature is an inscription set into the upper sanctuary of the pyramid. Dated 751 A.D., it presents a unique "bilingual" text in which Teotihuacan-style hieroglyphs are partnered by a Maya "translation."

172 *Mural from Atetelco (section). Atetelco, Teotihuacan; c. 400 A.D.; painting on stucco*
As in all large residential complexes in the center of Teotihuacan, many of the interior walls in the walled complex of Atetelco were decorated with polychrome murals. Research into these is only just beginning. Perhaps it will lead to a better understanding of objects and scenes used in the art of the Maya, who adopted symbols and motifs from Teotihuacan. The frame around these figures consists of interwoven bands of feathers, and could well have been the inspiration behind the stucco frieze at Tonina. Throughout Mesoamerica, borders such as these refer to specific mythological or historical places.

A model for Maya "Imperialism"

Teotihuacan's impact on the Maya was complex and multi-faceted in nature, a blend of true interaction and cultural resonance that endured well after the fall of the great city itself (ill. 171). On a purely ideological, religious level, Teotihuacan represented a Tollan, a distant source of prestige and authority. But its ability to intervene more directly in Maya affairs – at times exerting an overlordship over certain regions, probably achieved through actual conquest – indicates that this status was built on very real political power, sustained where necessary by military might.

The extent to which the Teotihuacan art system permeated all areas of Maya royal culture goes beyond simple appropriation and speaks of something deeper. Classic Maya kings evidently viewed Teotihuacan as a natural model and inspiration – something of a paradox if, as indicated above, we view Teotihuacan as the epitome of faceless, non-dynastic rule. In some cases, Teotihuacan was, whether directly or through the work of intermediaries, involved in the founding of Maya dynasties. To explain why, we have to look at its particular brand of "imperialism." Rather than being an all-conquering power that imposed its own political system on foreign peoples, it set out to achieve its objectives – presumably the securing of resources and trade routes – by including and utilizing local traditions and institutions. It is increasingly clear that the Classic Maya cannot be fully understood without reference to the great "power in the west." Teotihuacan's influence was an ever-present sub-text, an alien catalyst that provoked some of its most illustrious achievements.

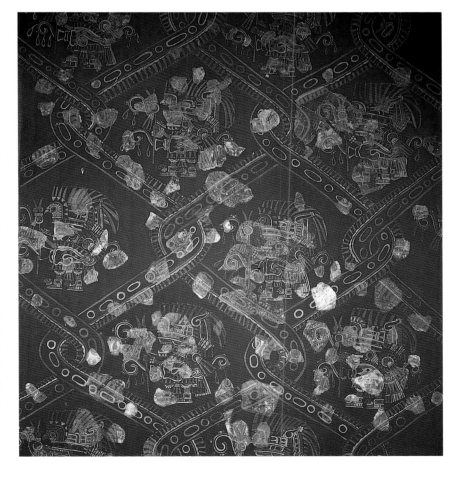

ACHIEVEMENTS

HIEROGLYPHS – THE GATEWAY TO HISTORY

Nikolai Grube

Deciphering Maya hieroglyphs rates as one of the major intellectual adventures of our time. Only fifty years ago it was inconceivable that Maya script would one day be read like any other ancient writing system. In fact, the general pessimism in the middle of the last century was such that most scholars looked on Maya writing as an "insoluble problem." Even though scholars are still unable to read some of the symbols and many of the inscriptions remain a mystery, texts from the Classic Maya period are beginning to speak to us once again (ill. 176). Deciphering hieroglyphs has done more to change our picture of the Maya in recent decades than any other research discipline.

When Spanish conquerors first trod the land of the Maya, hieroglyphs were still in full use. Convinced that Maya books and writing would hinder conquest and its Christian mission, the Spaniards did all they could to destroy every trace of native spiritual culture. Bishop Diego de Landa reported, "We found a great number of books with these letters, and because they contained nothing that was free from superstition and the devil's trickery, we burned them, which the Indians greatly lamented." Those members of the Maya nobility who were able to read and write were re-educated in Spanish monasteries and threatened with serious punishment if they used their old writing. This meant that the use and understanding of the hieroglyphs disappeared in just a few years. Although the Maya continued to record their own literature after the Spanish invasion, they now used the Roman alphabet. Hieroglyphs continued to be used only in the distant jungle regions in the south and at the center of the peninsula until at least 1697. The Franciscan Fray Andrés de Avendaño y Loyola, who visited the Itzaj Maya of these regions in 1696 to prepare them for missionary work, reported with amazement the great significance writing and books had to the Maya of Noj Peten, the capital of the Itzaj.

174 *Waldeck's drawing of the relief of the Temple of the Cross in Palenque*
The eccentric Count Waldeck was one of many travelers to visit the ruins of Palenque in the early 19th century and draw the sculptures. However, these early documents are not suitable for use as the basis of any systematic attempt to decipher the writing system. For example, Waldeck's version of the long hieroglyphic text on both sides of the central scene is incomplete, and the two individual columns on the left and right edges have been totally removed from their context to serve as decorative details.

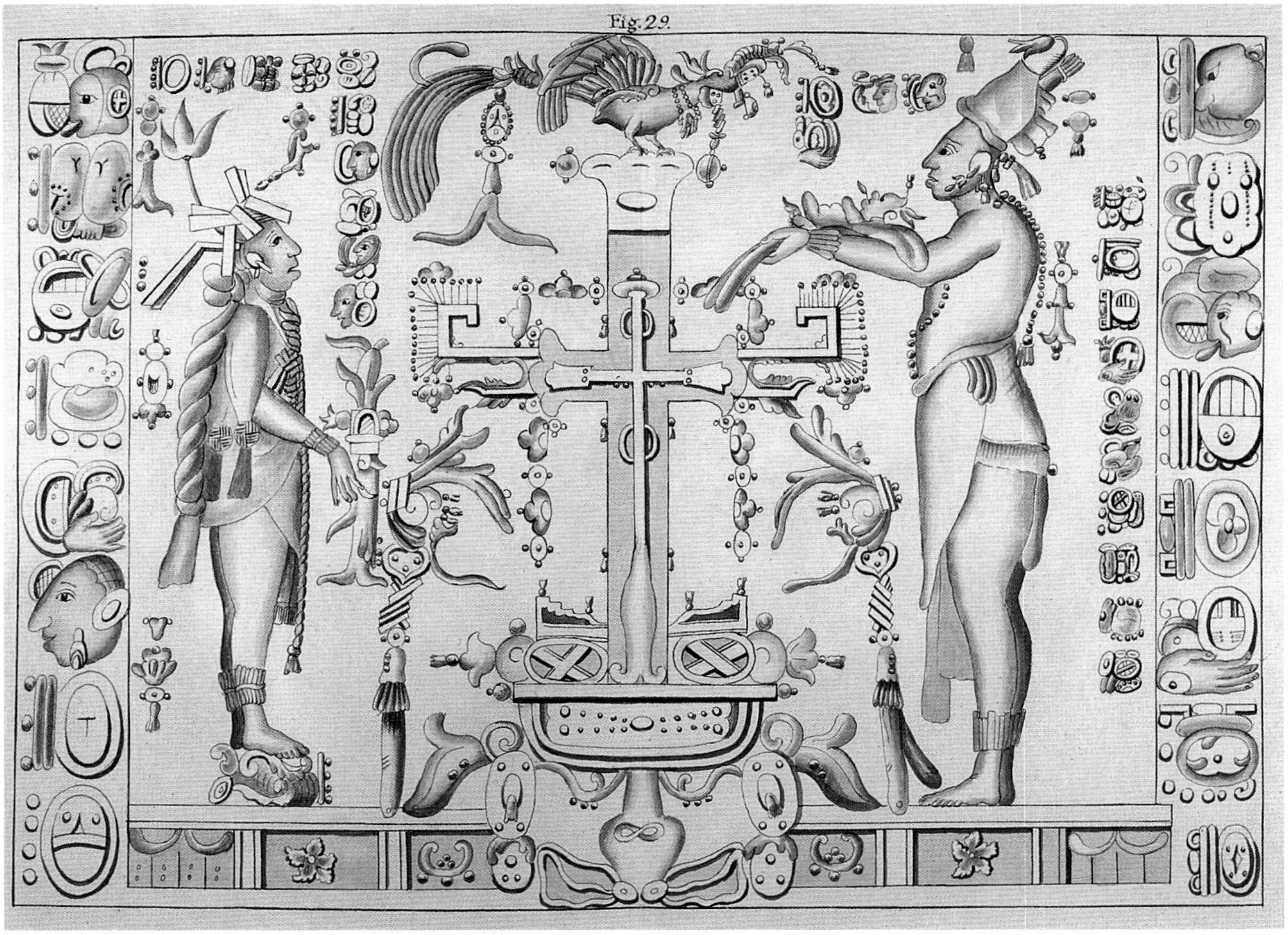

173 *Detail of the inscription on the back of Stela 31. Tikal, Guatemala; 445 A.D.; limestone; Tikal, Museo Sylvanus G. Morley*
Stela 31 was erected at Tikal in 445 A.D. by Siyaj Chan K'awiil, and contains more than 200 years of Maya history. The whole stela has been very well preserved, since it was moved from its original site and buried within Temple 33 sometime in the 6th century A.D. The extract shown here is on the back of the stela , and is an excellent example of the calligraphy of the Early Classic.

Previous double page:
Figures and hieroglyphs on a bench in Temple XIX at Palenque. Palenque, Chiapas, Mexico
This find is regarded as one of the most spectacular discoveries of recent years, and offers a clear insight into the Classic Maya mythology of creation.

Fig. 29.

Rediscovery of written records

Only four bark paper manuscripts of the Maya escaped burning by the Spanish clergy or natural decay in the humid climate of the Lowlands. Three of them were spared the fate of the other books probably because they had already been passed to the Hapsburgs as exotic gifts at the time of the first contacts between the Maya and the Spaniards, where they were soon put in cabinets of curiosities and forgotten. One of the books found its way to Vienna, then to Dresden, where it kindled the interest of Alexander von Humboldt. He copied five pages of the so-called Dresden Codex in his famous "Travels to the Cordilleras," thereby laying the foundations for the rediscovery of Maya writing (see Eggebrecht, p. 395 ff.).

Three centuries after Humboldt's report was published, books by the two researchers John Lloyd Stephens (1805–1852) and Frederick Catherwood (1799–1854) caused a tremendous amount of interest in the mysterious ruins of a people that had disappeared in the jungle. Their exquisite, highly detailed drawings of the hieroglyphs on stelae (ill. 184), door lintels, altars, walls, and stairs left no doubt that these stone witnesses must have been left by an important culture. But many of their scholarly contemporaries were unable to imagine that the impoverished Indians of the region, who could neither read nor write, could possibly be descended from so great a civilization. So they looked for alternative theories to explain the existence of a written culture in Mesoamerica. It was thought that pre-Hispanic writing on the American continent could only be the result of external stimulation through contact with the Old World. Stephens and Catherwood did not share these theories. They were the first people to refer to the builders of the old sites by the term "Maya," and see the local Indian population as the successors of the ancient inhabitants.

The few painstakingly copied examples of hieroglyphs made by Stephens and Catherwood offered no starting-point for systematically deciphering them (ill. 184). But it was soon realized that the texts seen in ruined sites such as Copan, Quirigua, and Palenque was in the same script as that in the preserved bark paper books.

Deciphering the calendar

For a long time the Dresden Codex was at the core of research interest (ill. 213). It was both the longest and the most accessible written document available at the beginning of research into the Maya. Using the dates and astronomical tables in these scripts, Saxony's royal court librarian Ernst Förstemann (1822–1906) managed to decipher the Maya numerical system and calendar in the last two decades of the 19th century (ill. 177). Förstemann discovered that the numerical system was based on the unit 20, so was a vigesimal system, and he also ascertained that the Maya used a "Long Count," whereby all the days were counted from a zero point of the calendar in the 4th millennium before the common era (B.C.). He also established that the Maya already understood the value and principle of zero.

By now, it had also been established that the hieroglyphs on the stone monuments were identical to those in the handwritten documents, and that the texts on both media were to be read in double columns. Reading started with the top-left hieroglyph, then the one to the right of that, then down to the left-hand hieroglyph a line lower, then to the one to the right of that, continuing in this way to the bottom of the text. The reader then continued with the double column to the right of the one just read.

175 *South façade of the Temple of the Inscriptions. Xcalumkin, Campeche, Mexico; photo taken in 1887 by Teobert Maler*
No other researcher discovered as many Maya sites as Teobert Maler (1842–1917), who arrived in Mexico as a follower of Emperor Maximilian and discovered his passion for archeology there. He traveled all through the Lowland jungles on arduous journeys, taking photographs of buildings and sculptures with a heavy plate camera. Xcalumkin is one of the few places in the northern Lowlands where there is a large number of well-preserved inscriptions.

176 *Extract from the hieroglyphic text on Lintel 3 in Temple 4. Tikal, Guatemala; wood from the Chicozapote tree or custard apple, (Manilkona zapota); H. 1.69 m, W. 1.90 m; Basle, Museum der Kulturen der Welt*
The wooden door lintels of the Temple of Tikal are some of our most important documents on historical events in the southern Lowlands. Lintel 3 was originally set over one of the doors in Temple 4, the highest of all Maya temples. The inscription is in two parts, one of which is shown here, and tells of a successful military campaign by King Yik'in Chan K'awiil in 743 A.D. against the city of El Peru, which was allied with Calakmul. The second part of the text is shown here, and tells of blood sacrifices and a dance to celebrate victory, and ends with the names of the parents of the successful ruler.

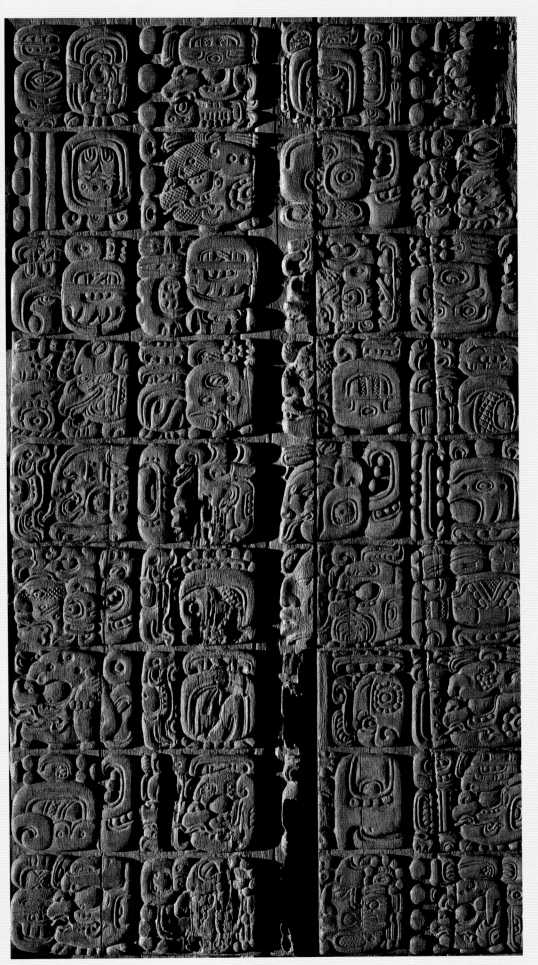

...and then he reached Tikal	three years later		Naabal K'inich (a title)	4 K'atun Emperor (in the fourth 20-year period of his life)
on the day 13 Ak'bal (July 13, 745 A.D.)	1 Ch'en		he dances	as (?)
(?) with the serpent?	Tzab Chan,		the god Akan(?)	he erects
the ruler of?	it was his first blood sacrifice (?)		Akan Haabnal (name of a temple or platform?)	in the city of Tikal
he embodies	the warrior god		he (Yik'in Chan K'awiil) is himself	the one who is cared for (the son of)
the god Akan (?)	this is the god of		Lady (?)-nal (name of the mother)	princess of Yokman
of the Emperor	the first time		Lady Twelve Macaw Tail Feathers (name or title)	he is the gift
he wore (?)	the (?)-serpent		the son of the father	Jasaw Chan K'awiil (name of the father)
Yik'in Chan K'awiil (name of the king)	Divine King of Mutal (Tikal)		Divine King of Mutal (Tikal)	4 K'atun Emperor (who lived into his fourth 20-year period of his life)

177 *Ernst Förstemann (1822–1906)*
Philologist Ernst Förstemann was one of the pioneers of Maya research; as librarian at the Royal Library of Saxony in Dresden, he had the finest Maya scripts in his care. He deciphered the entire calendar system and astronomical panels of the Dresden Codex.

178 *Tatiana Proskouriakoff (1909–1985)*
The American architect and artist Tatiana Proskouriakoff was born in Tomsk in Siberia. Her article on the historical nature of the inscriptions of Piedras Negras brought about a paradigm change in Maya research. She identified numerous words that refer to events in the lives of the rulers, such as birth, death, enthronement, and capture.

179 *Heinrich Berlin (1915–1987)*
The German-Mexican archeologist and art historian Heinrich Berlin provided the evidence that the hieroglyphic texts of the Lowlands contained hieroglyphics particular to an area which he called "emblem glyphs," a first breakthrough in the understanding of the inscriptions.

Initially there was little progress in deciphering the inscriptions on stone monuments, because up to the end of the 19th century only a few such records were known. In order to increase the database for further decipherments, the British researcher Alfred P. Maudslay (1850–1931) and the German-Austrian architect Teobert Maler (1842–1917), who arrived in Mexico as part of the retinue of Emperor Maximilian, undertook arduous expeditions through the jungles of southern Mexico and northern Central America on the backs of mules. They searched Maya ruins for inscriptions, which they photographed with cumbersome glass plate cameras (ill. 175). These two pioneers discovered numerous new sites, including important ones such as Yaxchilan, Piedras Negras, Seibal, Altar de Sacrificios, Naranjo, and Yaxha. The photographs were of excellent quality, and gave rise to a flood of new research into the meaning of these mysterious symbols. However, success was initially only achieved in the calendrical portions of the inscriptions, which took the greater part of all monumental texts. American newspaper publisher Joseph Goodman was able to convert the "zero date" of the Maya calendar to our own calendar. This conversion was based primarily on comparing Maya dates from the Colonial era with events for which the Julian dates were known. Although a number of researchers had their

doubts about Goodman's correlation, it is still used today, albeit with slight modifications, and the dates in this book are also based on it. It has now also been supported by various astronomical calculations, such as the eclipses noted by the Maya, and also by scientific dating methods such as radiocarbon analysis.

Despite the best efforts to decipher the inscriptions on stelae, altars, and door lintels, much remained enigmatic. Since everything that could be "read" consisted of calendar dates and astronomical calculations, the feeling arose in the first half of the 20th century that the remaining, as yet undeciphered, text passages concerned calendar science and the calculation of celestial cycles. This impression was neatly complemented by the prevailing picture of Maya culture as a society of peace-loving farmers, governed by priests who devoted themselves to observing the sky and pondering the phenomenon of time. As there had been no wars or power-hungry kings, it was felt that the inscriptions would not contain any historical information. Influential researchers such as Britain's Eric Thompson (1898–1975; see Grube/Martin, p. 149 ff.) regarded the inscriptions as esoteric hymns to time: Even images that seemed to represent warfare were interpreted by him and his contemporaries as confrontations between deities.

181 *Inauguration motif. Piedras Negras, Guatemala, Stela 14, outside Temple O-13; 758 A.D.; limestone; Peabody Museum, Harvard University*
Stela 14 is a beautiful example of the inauguration motif that Tatiana Proskouriakoff discovered on several different monuments in Piedras Negras. Here, it is the day of enthronement for Ruler 5 of the city, March 10, 758 A.D., and he is seated on a raised throne under a canopy of heavenly symbols with the outstretched wings of the great sky bird above them. His wife is standing in front of him, holding a knife decorated with feathers for self-sacrifice.

182 *Hieroglyphs for "birth" and "accession to the throne"*
Tatiana Proskouriakoff discovered that all of the stelae of Piedras Negras that show a seated figure in a niche also had a hieroglyph that looks like a head tied with a "toothache" bandage. Another hieroglyph in the shape of a frog looking upward occurs on these monuments with dates from about 20 years earlier. She deduced that the "upended frog glyph" meant "birth," and that the "toothache glyph" stood for "accession." Today, we can read both hieroglyphs in "Classic Maya," a precursor of the languages of the Ch'olan branch.

Discovering history

In 1960 the Russian-American art historian Tatiana Proskouriakoff (1909–1985) published her observation that the form of certain stelae from Piedras Negras reoccurred (ill. 181). She found a hieroglyph for "birth," and interpreted another as the hieroglyph for "accession" (ill. 192); she identified the last sign in a series of dates as the hieroglyph for "death." In the hieroglyphs that followed these, she recognized the names of historical people. These discoveries enabled her to prove that the inscriptions described the lives and deeds of worldly princes, and could well offer an insight into the politics and ruling systems of the big cities in the Lowlands. The German-Mexican archeologist Heinrich Berlin (1915–1987) had expressed a similar idea two years earlier (ill. 179). He had discovered hieroglyphs with basic components that were always the same but also contained an element that varied between one place and another. He called these sign combinations "emblem glyphs," terms that – in his opinion – referred to cities or their royal houses (ill. 183).

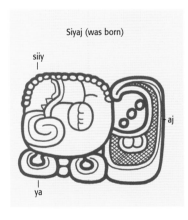

Siyaj (was born)

siiy

aj

ya

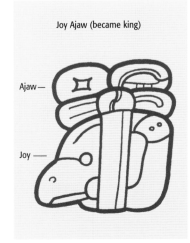

Joy Ajaw (became king)

Ajaw—

Joy—

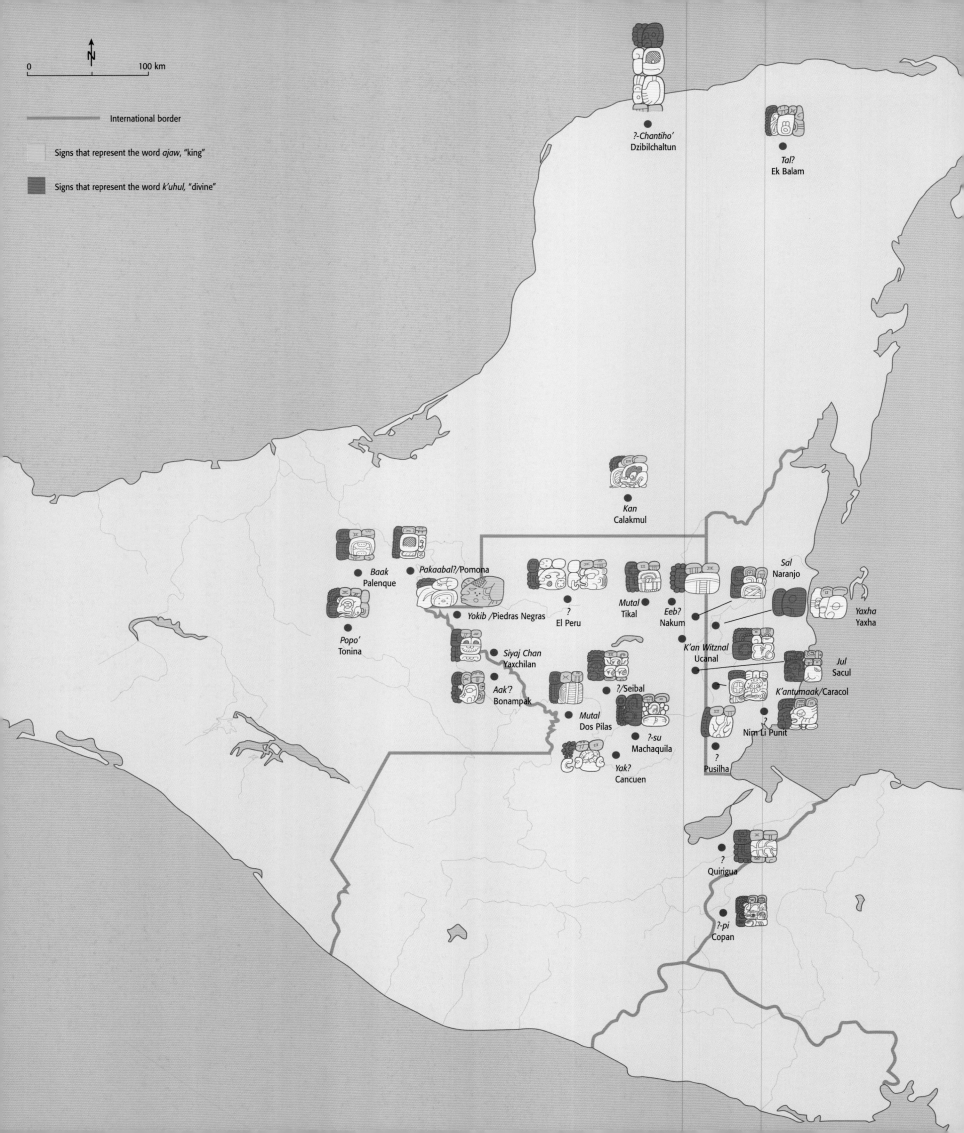

?-Chantiho'
Dzibilchaltun

Tal?
Ek Balam

Kan
Calakmul

Baak
Palenque

Pakaabal?/Pomona

Sal
Naranjo

Yokib /Piedras Negras

?
El Peru

Mutal
Tikal

Eeb?
Nakum

Yaxha
Yaxha

Popo'
Tonina

Siyaj Chan
Yaxchilan

K'an Witznal
Ucanal

Jul
Sacul

Aak?
Bonampak

?/Seibal

K'antumaak/Caracol

Mutal
Dos Pilas

?-su
Machaquila

Nim Li Punit

Yak?
Cancuen

?
Pusilha

?
Quirigua

?-pi
Copan

The key to deciphering the glyphs

Despite this paradigm shift which has revolutionized research by changing a "prehistoric" society into a people with a written history, there was still no one who could truly read Maya writing. After all, "reading" a text means being able to turn it into spoken language. In order to achieve this, one would have to understand the construction of the system and voice its signs as the Maya would have done in Classic times. But was the Maya script even a form of writing in which the signs actually represented specific spoken sounds? Until just a few decades ago, the general feeling was that the signs had little to do with sounds, but that each sign represented a word or an idea. Because of this attitude, it was felt that it was not necessary to understand the Mayan language because everyone, irrespective of nationality, would be able to understand the signs – as with today's signs for airports and rail stations.

However, the Russian archeologist and philologist Yuri Knorozov (1922–1999; ill. 180) believed differently. In 1945, as a young artillery soldier with the Red Army, he entered Berlin as it lay burning. In the streets outside the Reichsbibliothek (Imperial Library), he found boxes of books which the Germans had been unable to hide from the approaching Russians. Starved of reading matter, Knorozov fell upon the boxes, and found an edition of Diego de Landa's report on the conditions in Yucatan, and a reproduction of the three known (at the time) Maya books. Knorozov returned to Leningrad with this precious "war loot," where he completed his studies. His doctoral thesis was an annotated translation of Landa's manuscript, the most important source of information on the life of the Maya on the Yucatan peninsula on the eve of the Spanish Conquest. Landa's manuscript provided information on the writing symbols used by the Maya. Landa, who had never known any kind of writing other than alphabetical, believed that they were also some kind of alphabet. In fact, his work contains a hieroglyphic alphabet with a corresponding sign for every letter of the Latin alphabet (ill. 187). Fascinated by Landa's description of the script, Knorozov then devoted himself to systematically studying the hieroglyphs. He was already experienced in other ancient writing systems and knew that the Maya script – with about 800 written signs – could not be an alphabet in the western model. Nor could Maya writing be a purely conceptual or word form of writing, since 800 words are simply not enough to convey a full language. However, the number of symbols is similar to other ancient writing systems that are not purely word or alphabet-based. Sumerian cuneiform writing has more than 600 symbols, and the hieroglyphs of the Hittites manages with 497. These two systems, which are similarly constructed, consist of vowel-consonant combinations (a combination of words and syllables).

For established Maya scholars, and Eric Thompson in particular, it was simply unthinkable that the way Maya writing functioned was similar to other scripts of the ancient New East.

183 *The emblem glyphs of the most important Maya cities*
The emblem glyphs, which Heinrich Berlin discovered in 1958, are titles used by rulers to identify themselves as the "divine king" of a particular city or territory. The signs marked in red indicate "divine," and those in orange stand for the title *ajaw*, "king." The real core of the emblem glyphs (here in yellow) shows the name of the place or area under rule. Where we have already deciphered the name, this is given in italics next to the current name of the place.

184 *Copan, Stela A in a drawing by Catherwood*
John Lloyd Stephens and Frederick Catherwood reached Copan in 1840, and were fascinated by the abandoned monuments of a great civilization. Even then, Stephens believed that the stone stelae of the city had to be records of the history of its kings – but his theory was not to be proven for another 120 years. As we now know, Stela A, shown here in a drawing by Catherwood, was erected in 731 A.D. by Waxaklajuun Ubaah K'awiil, and it includes a list of four emblem glyphs of the four most important cities of the Maya world: Tikal, Calakmul, Palenque, and, of course, Copan itself.

Far from the major research centers on the other side of the Iron Curtain, the young Knorozov managed to prove that there was an important syllabic component to Maya writing. He recognized that the much-discussed Landa alphabet had been misunderstood and was in fact a syllabary, or listing of syllables. He realized that Landa had imposed an alphabetic model on Maya writing, and had therefore recorded, for example, the syllable symbol *be* as the alphabet symbol *b*.

Knorozov was able to confirm that his ideas were correct with the aid of books in the Dresden Codex in which most pictures were accompanied by brief hieroglyphic texts. The German researcher Paul Schellhas had already ascertained at the beginning of the 20th century that certain hieroglyphs in these accompanying texts appeared time and again with the same deities, and that there were also separate hieroglyphs for the names of animals. Knorozov established that the hieroglyph for turkey consisted of two signs, the first of which is also contained in the Landa alphabet where, unusually, it is given the value *ku* (ill. 185). Knorozov believed that this sign must stand for the syllable *ku*. The word for the wild turkey is in fact *kutz*. Knorozov deduced that the second syllable was the missing *-tz* part. He found this sign as the first component in the hieroglyph for dog, leading him to hypothesize that the second sign represented the syllable *lu*. There was a breed of dog in pre-Hispanic Yucatan called *tzul*. This offered proof that the first sign for the name of the dog had to be *tzu*. Finally, Knorozov found a date calculation in the Dresden Codex where, instead of the expected number 11, there was a three-part hieroglyph: first a weathered sign, and beneath it the signs he had deciphered as *lu* and *ku*. The Mayan word for eleven is *buluk*. This provided confirmation for his interpretations and the correctness of his methodical approach.

Using combinations such as this, Knorozov established a number of syllable signs, and was able to prove that they were always combined in the same way to write words in the Mayan language. Because almost all Mayan words are similarly constructed, and consist of consonant-vowel-consonant, such a word could be written with two syllable signs by not reading the vowel in the second syllable sign.

As logical as Knorozov's ideas appeared to be, and convincing as his decipherments were, they were at first refuted. Apart from the Marxist rhetoric

185 *Syllabic writing in the Dresden Codex*
It has been known since the turn of the last century that a combination of two symbols represented the turkey, and another the dog. However, no one was able to read these symbols as language. It was Yurii Knorozov who transferred the sound *ku* from the Landa alphabet to the first symbol in the hieroglyph for turkey. He found in dictionaries that the word *kutz* was a turkey, and deduced that the second symbol must be the syllable *tzu*. His suspicion was confirmed by the use of the second symbol in the hieroglyph for dog, *tzul*. Using this method of deduction, he was able to decipher many more symbols.

in which he was obliged to clothe his writing, there were several mistakes in the details, and this made it easy for his critics to attack his hypotheses. It was not until the 1960s that American researchers such as Floyd Lounsbury, David Kelley, and Michael Coe took up his cause and demonstrated in further decipherments that Maya writing was in fact a system that consisted of word signs (logograms) and syllable signs (syllabograms), which is why the experts refer to it as logosyllabic writing or a "mixed system."

The structure of Maya writing

Over the following years, a small group of young hieroglyphic researchers worked closely together to transfer Knorozov's approach, which was primarily restricted to painted texts in books, to the much greater body of monumental inscriptions from the Classic period. Using his method, it has now been possible to read the majority of the approximately 800 writing signs and order many of them in a syllablic grid (ill. 189). Maya syllabograms are always constructed in the same way, with one consonant and one vowel. There is at least one sign for every possible combination of consonant and vowel. Because Ch'olan – the language of the hieroglyphs – has five vowels and 22 consonants, it follows that there must have been at least 110 syllable signs. In addition, there was also a series of pure vowel signs. The number of syllabograms is actually rather more than 110, since many syllables have more than one sign to represent them. Thus the sign *bi* could be written with a symbol that consists

186 *Full figure hieroglyphs from Copan. Sculptured front of the "Harvard Bench"; Late Classic, 600–900 A.D.; tuff*
Writing signs can also be shown as living beings. Full figure texts such as this one are particularly difficult to read, but were regarded as the highest achievement of the Maya scribes. This is the name of the 15th king of Copan, who reigned from 749 to c. 764: K'ak' Yipyaj Chan K'awiil ("Fire is the strength of (the God) K'awiil").

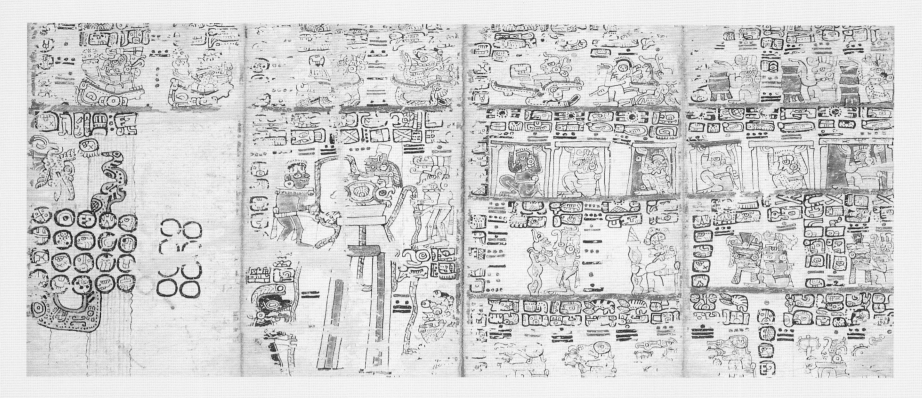

With 74 pages, the Dresden Codex is not the most extensive of the Maya books, but it is undoubtedly the most beautiful. Its contents are solely concerned with religious and ritual matters, and deal with the motion of Venus, the way in which its phases are calculated, predicting solar and lunar eclipses, and rituals for the turn of the year. It contains a chapter on the moon goddess and her influence on sickness and birth, and several others on the Rain God Chaak and his rule over the weather and harvests. The Dresden Codex seems to be a Postclassic copy of a text from the Classic period. The various styles of writing and drawing it contains indicate that at least five master scribes must have been involved in its making. Nothing is known of the place where it was created, except that it was probably somewhere in the north of Yucatan.

The 112 pages of the Madrid text, the Codex Tro Cortesiano, are not of the same aesthetic quality as the Dresden Codex. The range of subjects is more pragmatic, ranging from rituals for a successful hunt, bee keeping and the sowing of crops, to long chapters on the Rain God and his influence on the agricultural year. The Madrid Codex contains a number of sections that are identical to some in the Dresden text. They confirm that the religious ideas of the Postclassic period were strongly canonized. But the scribes of the Madrid Codex were not masters of their subject; it contains mistakes, and missing and transposed hieroglyphs have caused more than one researcher to refer to them as Maya dyslexics.

199 *Madrid Codex, pages 18 to 21. Provenance unknown; Late Postclassic, 1450–1650; fig bark paper, coated with plaster, painted; page: H. 23 cm, W. 12 cm; Madrid, Museo de las Americas*
The scribes of the Madrid Codex made many orthographic mistakes, but it remains an important document of the writing culture of the Late Postclassic period.

200 *Grolier Codex, page 6. Provenance unknown; Middle Postclassic, 1100–1350; fig bark paper, coated with plaster, painted; page: H. 19 cm, L. total 125 cm; Mexico City, Museo Nacional de Antropología e Historia, Sección de Arqueología (Kerr 4822f)*
A Mexican art collector acquired the Codex from grave robbers in 1965. In 1971 it was put on display for the first time at the Grolier Club in New York, the art gallery from which it obtained its name.

The Paris Codex, which is 22 pages long, is kept in the Bibliothèque Nationale in Paris, and it also fails to match the elegance of the Dresden book. However, it is more accurate and detailed than the Madrid Codex (ill. 199). Sadly, the wafer-thin plaster that covers the bark paper has peeled away in so many places that about 70 percent of the original artwork has been lost. Still, the remaining texts and pictures tell us enough to know that the Paris Codex deals mainly with three subjects: prophesies for the thirteen 20 years of the K'atun cycles of the Maya calendar, the description of the creation of the universe, and the 13 signs of the Maya zodiac (ill. 217).

The fourth codex was not found until thirty years ago, in Mexico. It is generally known as the Grolier Codex after the gallery in which it was first displayed (ill. 200). Stylistically, this codex differs from the others in that it does not contain hieroglyphic texts, the few hieroglyphs just represent numbers and day signs. At first, the 11 pages of the script were believed to be a fake, but it was soon established that the paper dated back to pre-Hispanic times, and that the codex – like the Dresden Codex – contained a Venus calendar, so the authenticity of this fragment can no longer be disputed.

ASTRONOMY AND MATHEMATICS

Alexander W. Voss

The Maya are the only people of Mesoamerica whose extensive mathematical and astronomical knowledge has been handed down to us. This expertise, which dates back to pre-Hispanic times, has been retained in the form of countless inscriptions on stone monuments and four folding books made of bark, which are known as codices. From colonial times it is mainly the Relación de las cosas in Yucatán ("Report on the incidents in Yucatan"), compiled from notes written by the Franciscan Diego de Landa (1524–1579,) and the native Chilam-Balam books (books of the Jaguar priest Balam) – written in Latin script but in the Yukatek Mayan language – that provide us with important information and glimpses of this knowledge. Countless ethnological studies from the Guatemalan Highlands, where elements of the pre-Hispanic calendar are still practiced, help us to understand the Mayas' ideas about time and their calendar.

The Maya used their mathematical and astronomical knowledge to design the calendar, which enabled them to predict important events in advance and also to calculate which of the omnipresent supernatural beings, with their positive or negative characteristics, would govern each individual day. These predictions helped the calendar priests *aj k'inob* (literally: "lords of the day") to prepare the ceremonies that would have a positive influence over the workings of these supernatural forces on individuals and the life of the community.

The mathematical principles

The Maya only used positive whole numbers for their calculations. They availed themselves of a system of addition and multiplication that is similar to our Arabic system of counting.

In this, the value of a digit is determined by its position in a number sequence. Thus, for example, our number "2001" can be broken down from right to left in the ascending order of ones, tens, hundreds, and thousands. The basis for this is the decimal system, which is based on the number 10. The intrinsic value of each position is indicated by the numbers 0 to 9, so in our example there is 1 one, 0 tens, 0 hundreds, and 2 thousands. But the Maya based their system on 20, *vigesima* in Latin, which is why their system is also known as the vigesimal system. It contains the values 1, 20, 400, 8000, 160,000, 3,200,000, 64,000,000, and so on.

The intrinsic value of each position in the vigesimal system is expressed by the numbers 1 to 19. As a rule, the Maya use two symbols to represent them in writing: the dot and the line. The dot has a value of 1, the line a value of 5. The Maya combined these signs to write numbers from 1 to 19. Dots and lines were not mixed, but arranged separately in groups. The dots always form

201 *Early Classic vessel with rows of day symbols. Tikal, Peten, Guatemala, Complex of the Lost World; Early Classic; 3rd century A.D.; fired clay, painted; H. 21.5 cm, dia. 10 cm; Guatemala City, Museo Nacional de Arqueología y Etnología (Kerr 5618)*
This polychrome cylindrical vase was found in the grave of a noblewoman. The hollow feet of the vessel were filled with clay pebbles to make it serve as a rattle when shaken. The handle on the lid is in the shape of a waterfowl. The day symbols of the 260-day ritual calendar are painted in black on a light yellow background on the outside.

202 *Number symbols from 0 to 20*
The Maya used either a dot and line notation or a series of individual head symbols to write numbers. The head symbols for the numbers 3 to 9 are combined with the form of the fleshless lower jaw for 10 to make numbers 13 to 19. The 0, which represents a blank, is represented by a stylized snail shell or a head whose lower jaw is replaced by a human hand. The number 20 is indicated by a moon symbol, in which only the rough outline indicates that it is a human profile.

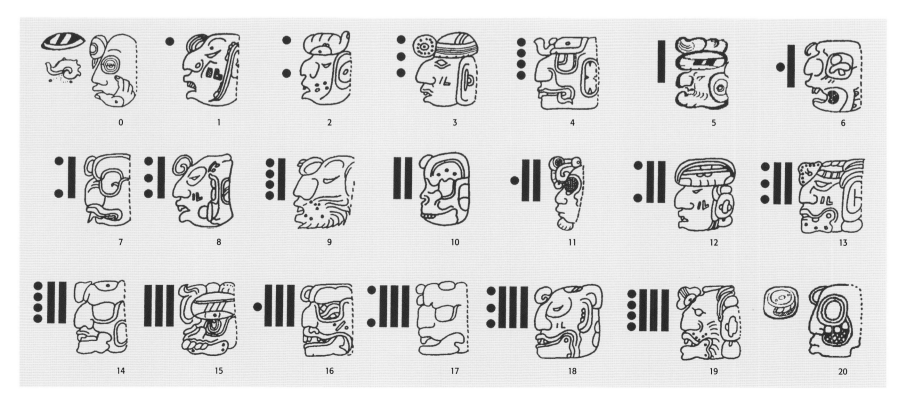

203 *The Caracol. Chichen Itza, Yucatan, Mexico; Terminal Classic, 850–1000 A.D.; limestone; H. 11.5 m, dia. 11 m*

The *Caracol* (Spanish for "snail") is one of the few circular buildings recorded in the Maya region. The name *Caracol* is derived from the spiral staircase on the inside, which leads to the top of the building. This elevated chamber contains windows that were suitable for astronomical observations. The *Caracol* is therefore regarded as the observatory of Chichen Itza, from where specific stations of the sun and moon on the horizon were noted. The hieroglyphic texts on the structure date back to the second half of the 9th century.

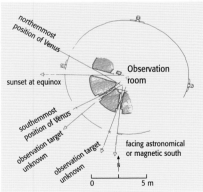

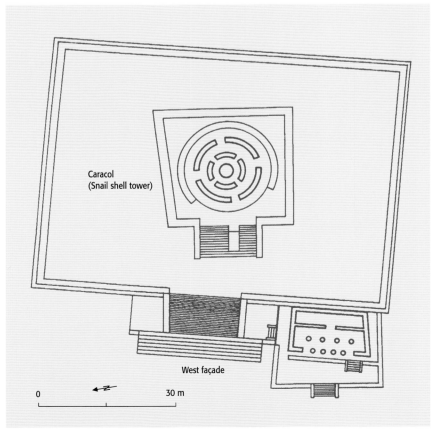

Caracol
(Snail shell tower)

West façade

0   30 m

204 *Plan of the Caracol building*
The circular building, which was used to observe the skies, was constructed on a raised rectangular platform. During the excavations of the staircase that leads up to the platform, archeologists found a number of inscriptions that recounted events in the second half of the 9th century, which is when the final building stage is believed to have been completed.

205 *The observation windows in the Caracol*
Only three windows remain in this circular building. They offer a view of various phenomena in the skies from the observation chamber. The window ledges were used to make alignments.

a row, and are parallel to the lines, which are also placed together (ill. 202). A nought required a special device. While the Arabic system uses the 0, the Maya used a stylized snail shell. As well as this 0 and the numbers 1 to 19, the number 20 also has its own symbol, which bears a certain similarity to the written symbol for the moon.

The Maya also used various other forms of pictorial representations to indicate numbers. So-called "head variants" were used to indicate the numbers 0 to 20 as pictures. Thus, for example, the number 9, called *bolon* in Yukatek Mayan, was represented by a head with the lower part of the face covered by a jaguar skin; the jaguar is called *balam* (ill. 202).

This method of writing numbers is more than a graphic and phonetic exercise, however. It indicates a fundamental aspect of how the Maya understood the world: numbers and time were not abstract entities, but living beings. They were gods with a wide range of relationships to each other, and whose good or bad characteristics had an influence on people.

The principles of astronomy

The Maya developed their calendar on the basis of astronomical observations which they made with the naked eye. They observed the horizon, especially in the mornings and evenings, from fixed locations and noted the rising and descending celestial bodies. To this end, they built a number of structures specially laid out for making astronomical observations (ill. 206). The most impressive example is the circular *Caracol*, "snail shell," in Chichen Itza in the Mexican state of Yucatan (ills. 203, 204). The top floor had a number of windows and was obviously used as an observatory to follow the paths of the celestial bodies (ill. 205): the sun (*k'in*), the moon (*uh*), the stars (*ek'ob*), and the planet Venus, the great star (*chak ek'*) (ill. 208).

206 *Diagram of the sight-lines of Group E in Uaxactun*
It is assumed that this Early Classic building complex, which is referred to in specialist literature as Group E of Uaxactun, was a simple installation used to observe the annual course of the sun. From the pyramid in the west, one looks up to a platform with three buildings. The view to the left corner of the northern building shows the point on the horizon where the sun rises at the summer equinox, and to the right corner of the building at the south of the platform one sees the position of the rising sun at the winter equinox. On the spring and fall equinoxes, by contrast, the sun appears over the center building. Similar installations have been found in many other Maya cities.

207 *Celestial bodies and phenomena in a band of the sky. Quirigia, Izabal, Guatemala, southern area of the Great Plaza, Stela 1; Late Classic, August 15, 800 A.D.; red-brown sandstone; H. 410 cm (with plinth)*
The frame on the ruler's back represents the heavens; celestial symbols and mythical creatures are suspended from it, and the bird of the heavens is seated on it with outstretched wings.

208 *The symbols for the celestial bodies*
The Maya had a separate symbol for each celestial body. The sun is shown as a four-leafed flower, and the moon as an oval surface with marks denoting the shadows on the moon. The symbol for a star is similar to the letter W, thought its full form has a more starry appearance. The word for Venus was "Great Star."

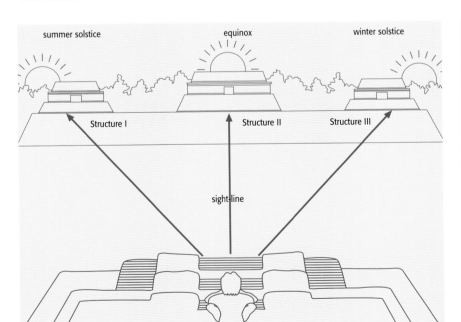

summer solstice | equinox | winter solstice

Structure I | Structure II | Structure III

sight-line

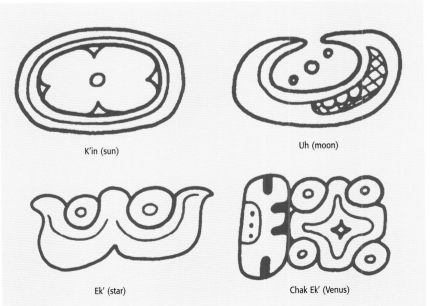

K'in (sun)

Uh (moon)

Ek' (star)

Chak Ek' (Venus)

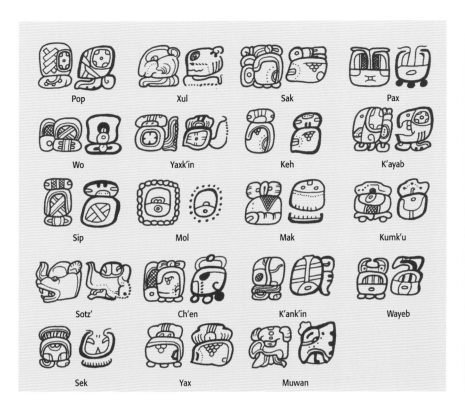

209 *The months in the 365-day Haab calendar*
The common year of the Maya contains the events in a complete agricultural cycle. It is divided into 18 Winal or Winik of 20 days, the Maya month, and there is a short month of five unlucky days at the end of the year. Each month is represented by a name hieroglyph that refers to a special feature of that section of time.

210 *Days in the 260-day Tzolk'in calendar*
The Tzolk'in ritual calendar uses 20 different symbols for days that are combined with the numbers 1 to 13. In the illustration above, the symbols have been ordered in four columns to be read from top to bottom and from left to right. It shows two forms of the symbol for a day, one from the stone inscriptions and the other from the Codices.

The Tzolk'in ritual calendar and its components

From their astronomical observations, the Maya noted sequences of days and cycles that were repeated and interlinked. The ritual calendar, the Maya's main day cycle, was 260 days long – obtained by multiplying the number 20 with the number 13. We know for a fact that the number 20 was chosen because it is the number of fingers and toes on a human body, but it is less clear what other elements were also involved. The pre-Hispanic name of the 260-day cycle is unknown. Researchers adopted the term Tzolk'in, which was introduced by the North American Maya scholar William Gates (1863–1940) and which he obtained in 1921 from the K'iche' term *Ch'ol Q'iij,* "the order of the days."

The notation of individual days in Tzolk'in consist of two parts: a number and a day symbol (ills. 204, 210). There is a total of 20 recurring day symbols, and these are always combined in the same order with the numbers 1 to 13. However, since there are only 13 numbers compared to 20 day symbols, the name of the 14th day restarts the numerical cycle with the number 1. The series of day symbols begins again on the 21st day. So the sequence for the first 20 days is: 1 Imix, 2 Ik', 3 Ak'bal, 4 K'an, 5 Chikchan, 6 Kimi, 7 Manik', 8 Lamat, 9 Muluk, 10 Ok, 11 Chuwen, 12 Eb, 13 Ben, 1 Ix, 2 Men, 3 Kib, 4 Kaban, 5 Etz'nab, 6 Kawak, 7 Ajaw.

The next unit of 20 days begins with 8 Imix, 9 Ik' and so on. Running through all of the combinations results in a complete cycle of 260 days. The series then repeats, beginning on the 261st day with 1 Imix and a new cycle.

The origins of this calendar probably lie with the Olmec culture, whose influence during the Preclassic spread across Mesoamerica. The earliest written evidence for this system is in the stone inscriptions from Monte Alban near Oaxaca, which date back to the 5th century BC. The Maya probably adopted this calendar from Mixe-Zoque peoples, their neighbors to the west and south on the Tehuantepec isthmus.

The meaning of the ritual calendar lay in the fate-determining characteristics of each day. Thus, a supernatural being was allocated to every Tzolk'in day symbol, which would define and influence every single person from the day of his or her birth onwards. This supernatural force of the day symbol was modified by the meaning of the number, and resulted in a series of 260 possibilities, from which the forecasts for the social community were determined.

The day symbol for the day of birth determined the character and fate of a newly born baby. The features of the day symbol were laid down in prediction charts, known as the "Message and art of the days" (*u mutil u chuwenil k'in*). The Chilam-Balam book of Kaua, for example, says the following for the day symbol Muluk: "The shark is its messenger. It devours offspring and wives. Children and wives will die. They are rich. He is one who kills and spoils, including food." This negative forecast is countered by the positive day symbol Chuwen: "He is the joiner. He is the carver. The army ant is the messenger of the artists. He is very wealthy. His whole [life] path is good. He will succeed in everything. He also is a person with good sense." We hear this of the day symbol Etz'nab: "He is Ah Tok' Ch'akwil, the lord of the flint for cutting. He is Etz'nabil Tok', sharp flint. The Toch bird is his messenger. He is Ah Toh Olal, the lord with an upright heart. He causes pain and deals it out. He is also a warrior."

Each of the 260 day names in turn influenced the shared lives and activities of the community. The Chilam-Balam book also contains a list of these. For example, the day 3 Chuwen was unfavorable, whereas the day 8 Kib promised a good year with plenty of rain and a rich harvest. The times for the beginning and performance of religious festivals were also determined by the day names.

The Maya retained their understanding of the fateful meaning of day symbols and day names in the Chilam-Balam books until the early 19th century, handing this knowledge down to subsequent generations. In the Highlands of Guatemala, the 260-day Ch'ol Q'iij continues to be used as a prophetic calendar, and in recent years it has found a new meaning for Maya culture as part of the rediscovery of old traditions.

The common year Haab

In addition to the ritual calendar, the Maya also had a common year with 365 days, known as Haab, which was similar to the solar year. It was divided into 18 sections of 20 days (ill. 210), known as *winal jun ek'eh* in Yucatan and which can be compared with the months in the Christian calendar. Each time division in the Haab was allocated a patron or protector, who in turn influenced each of the 20 days of the Winal with his supernatural powers. At the end of the 360 days, the remaining five days made up an independent unit forming the end of the year. Because these five days could not easily be incorporated in the vigesimal system, they were known as *u wayeb u haab*, "sleepers of the year," or *ma k'aba k'in*, "the nameless days," and were given bad prognostic features.

211 *Pawajtuun giving "math lessons." Ceramic vessel in "Codex-style"; provenance unknown; Late Classic, 600–900 A.D.; baked clay, painted; H. 9.7 cm, dia. 19.2 cm; private collection (Kerr 1196)*
The scene on this polychrome bowl shows two old men giving lessons to four young men. The net-like head coverings of the two old men are the sign of the Pawajtuun, who appear as gods of the wind and supporters of the four directions. The Pawajtuun have stuck their paint brushes into the bands of their head coverings; it is the brushes that tell us they are scribes. We know from their speech bubbles that they are instructing their pupils in the art of writing and in mathematics.

When counting the days in the Haab year, the same system of bar and dot numerals and head variants were used. Unlike the ritual calendar of the Tzolk'in, the Haab did have a "zero" day. During the Classic era this was described as the "seating" of the month, when a new patron was introduced, one whose influence would be felt over the following 19 days.

Diego de Landa gave a full description of the Haab in his report on Yucatan. He named the months and each individual day, giving the Tzolk'in name as well. The Haab begins with the Maya month Pop and ends with Kumk'u, which is followed by the five days of the Wayeb.

The common year of the Maya began in mid-July in the middle of the 16th century. Whether this was also the case in pre-Hispanic times is unknown, because it is not known whether the Maya inserted intercalary days in their common year of 365 days to allow for the tropical solar year, which was six hours longer. Although Diego de Landa wrote that Yukatek calendar priests were aware of this discrepancy and therefore introduced an extra day every four years, we do not know how the link between the common year and the ritual calendar remained unchanged.

Religious festivals

Like the Christian church year, there were a number of religious festivals in the Maya year, distributed evenly over the months of the Haab. Again, the only comprehensive representation is by Diego de Landa, according to whom New Year was the main annual festival, since it was celebrated by everybody. On this day, houses were swept clean, old household utensils replaced by new ones, and the covers for bundles of relics and images of gods renewed. This was done as a symbolic removal of the previous year's rubbish and burdens, and as a dignified welcome to the new year. In the month of Sip, which at the time of the Spanish conquest was in the months of August and September, the hunters and fishermen celebrated their festival for good hunts and catches, whereas the beekeepers celebrated their festival in the month of Tzek (October) to ask for a good honey harvest. The month of Mol (December) was seen as a particularly good time to carve new statues of gods for family and house altars. Renewing the clay statues and temples was celebrated in the month of Yax (January). In the month

of Sak (February), the hunters held a festival of thanks for the success of their endeavors. In Mak (March to April), they asked for enough water for crop growing, carrying out the fire ceremony *tup k'ak*, "extinguishing fire." The month of Muwan (April to May) was when the cacao planters said their prayers. In Pax (May), the Maya performed the *holkan ok'ot* war dance at a festival to ask for good fortune in war. Several sumptuous festivals were celebrated in the time remaining up to the five unnamed days of misfortune (mid-July), which were known as the *sabakil t'an*, "sooty days." These days of misfortune were used to prepare for the arrival of the new year. No hard physical labor was performed, and personal hygiene was neglected for fear of misfortune.

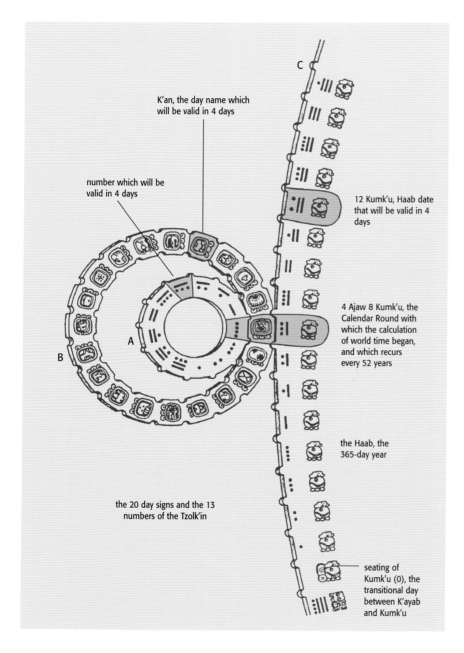

K'an, the day name which will be valid in 4 days

number which will be valid in 4 days

12 Kumk'u, Haab date that will be valid in 4 days

4 Ajaw 8 Kumk'u, the Calendar Round with which the calculation of world time began, and which recurs every 52 years

the Haab, the 365-day year

the 20 day signs and the 13 numbers of the Tzolk'in

seating of Kumk'u (0), the transitional day between K'ayab and Kumk'u

Calendar Rounds and year symbols

Although the ritual Tzolk'in and the secular Haab calendars are completely independent of each other, the Maya combined them in a greater cycle that is referred to in the literature as a the Calendar Round (ill. 212). It takes 18,980 days before any one of the 260 Tzolk'in days combines with one of the 365 Haab days. The reason behind this calculation lies in the lowest common multiple of both cycles; both numbers are used only once in working out the factors: 260 is broken down into 13 × 5 × 4, and 365 into 73 × 5 days. The lowest common multiple is obtained from 73 × 13 × 5 × 4. Thus a Tzolk'in day called 5 Imix and Haab day 9 Kumk'u will not recur until after 18,980 different combinations of all four elements, the number and the day sign of the Tzolk'in and the number and month name of the Haab – which equates to 52 Haab common years. This cycle of the calendar round was common all over Mesoamerica, and is a further basis for calendar predictions. The Maya day of world creation fell on Calendar Round 4 Ajaw 8 Kumk'u (see Wagner, p. 283).

The "year bearers" resulted from the Calendar Round which the Yukatek Maya called Bakab. These were the four Tzolk'in day symbols upon which a New Year's Day of the Haab calendar can begin. Each day symbol that appears as a year bearer is associated with a direction, a color, and particular prophecies. The Maya believed that this day was important for the entire year. The sequence of the year bearers can be calculated. Because a Haab month is always a multiple of five days, as is the cycle of 20 day symbols, each day number in the Haab can fall on only four different Tzolk'in day symbols, each of which is five days apart. At the time of Diego de Landa, only the symbols K'an, Muluk, Ix, and Kawak could fall on the first day of the month of Pop, with which the year began. The Maya common year described by Landa is a K'an year, because all Haab months begin with the Tzolk'in day symbol K'an. In the Postclassic period, by contrast, it was the day symbols Ak'bal, Lamat, Ben, and Etz'nab that influenced the year (ill. 220).

According to Maya belief, the year bearers were supernatural beings known as *bakabs* who, at the time of creation, were placed at the four cardinal points of the earth to support the sky. Each Bakab was allocated a direction, a color, and supernatural powers with which he influenced the Haab that began with his day symbol. Muluk was associated with the east (*el k'in*) and the color red; Ix with the north (*nal* or *xaman*) and the color white. Kawak was linked with the west (*oochk'in* or *chik'in*) and black, and K'an with the south (*nojool*) and yellow. By combining the year symbols with colors and directions, Maya priests tried to coordinate their ideas of time and space.

The annual changeover of the year symbols was accompanied by a huge ceremony. When it took place, the Maya stacked stones and statues of the year symbols at the entrances to towns and cities that faced the four directions. For example, if a K'an year was ending, they made a clay cult picture of the current Bakab, which was called the *k'an way u haab*, "yellow sleeper of the year," and placed it on the stack of stones at the southern entrance to the city. This was then taken to the center of the city in a festive procession. At New Year, this year symbol was taken to the east entrance to the village and left there for a common year. The next year the following year symbol was placed facing north (ill. 213).

212 How the time cycles meshed with each other
The diagram illustrates how the Tzolk'in ritual calendar linked with the Haab, the 365-day common year. The ritual calendar consists of the numbers 1 to 13 (wheel A), and the 20 day symbols (wheel B). The Haab (wheel C) consists of 18 months each of 20 days, and a five-day section at the end of the year. To make it easier to read, the month of Keh with 20 days has been represented rather than the whole wheel. The date is obtained by linking all three time wheels. A total of 18,980 days or 52 Haab years need to pass before the same date is reached again.

213 Dresden Codex, pages 25 and 26 from the chapter on the New Year. Provenance unknown; Late Postclassic, 1200–1500 A.D.; fig bark paper, coated with stucco, painted; page: H. 20.4 cm, W. 9 cm; Dresden, Sächsische Landesbibliothek
The New Year chapter is constructed so that each page contains the full course of the ceremony for one of the four possible days on which a new year can begin – Ak'bal, Lamat, Ben, and Etz'nab; and picture and text portray the important ritual actions and sacrificial gifts.

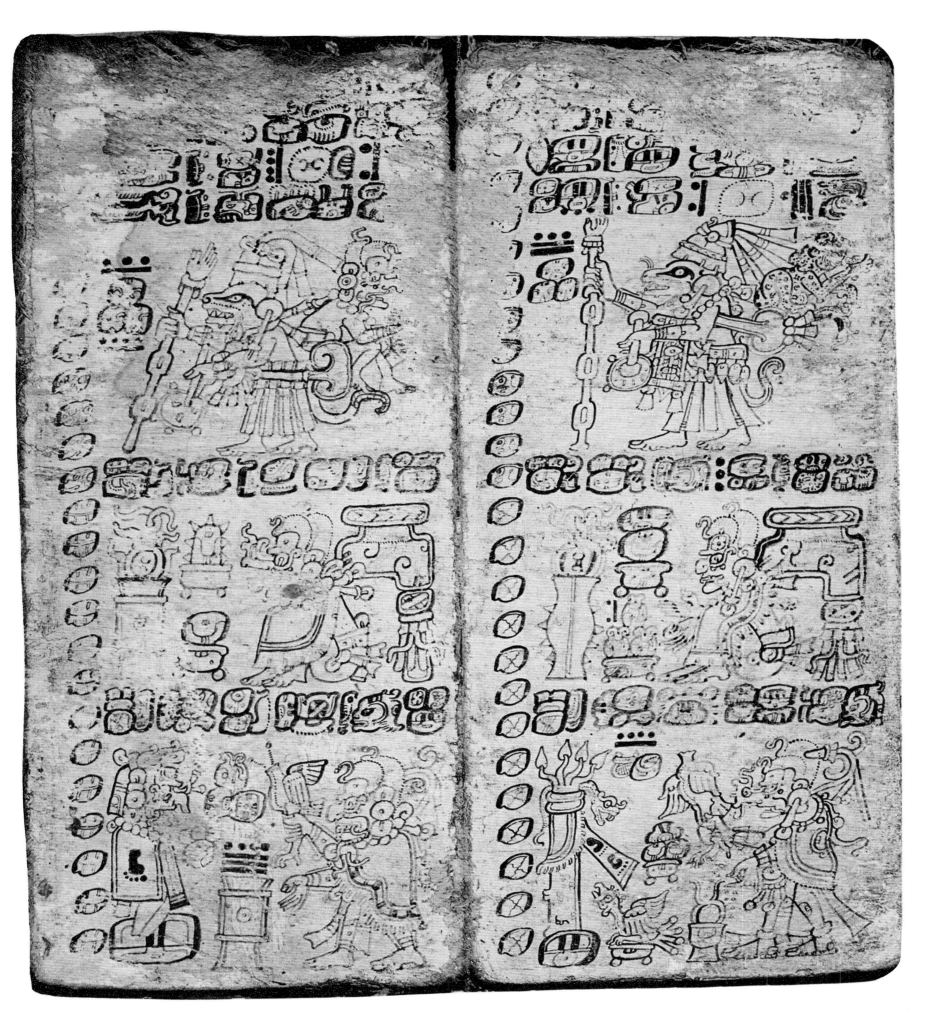

The Long Count – dividing time

The Maya counted the constantly repeating day cycles in a straight line, which gave them a clear chronological sequence. The starting point of this Long Count was the creation of the world as it is now. It is similar in principle to the Christian calendar, which counts the days, months, and years since the birth of Christ.

To calculate and represent time that had passed, the Maya developed their own process of dating, which was based on their astronomical observations and contained values that divided their calendar into ever-increasing periods of time.

The shortest period is the day, K'in. This basic unit is followed by the next highest, which lasts 20 days and is called Winal or Winik. For the third place, they switched away from the pure vigesimal system. Instead of the expected unit of 400, Winal is multiplied by the factor 18 to produce a unit of only 360 days which, depending on the region, is called Haab or Tun, i.e. year or stone. This switch was obviously introduced in order to achieve an approximation to the common year of 365 days. All following units in the Long Count increase by a factor of 20. Thus 20 Tun, with a total of 7200 days, form a K'atun, i.e. a period of about 20 years. Twenty K'atun, with a total of 144,000 days (about 395 years),

are one Bak'tun. Twenty Bak'tun, with a total of 2,880,000 days or 7890 Tun, are one Piktun (about 7,890 years), which is in turn multiplied by 20 to produce a Kalabtun with 57,600,000 days (about 157,810 years). We know the Maya continued this mathematical sequence up to 20 to the power of 21 Tun. They used these calculations in an attempt to determine by the calendar the first day of their world creation and to establish it in the cosmic order.

The terms used for the individual eras are colonial in origin and from Yukatek sources (ill. 214). Only the terms for the three lowest units, day, month, and year (Ki'n, Winal or Winik, Haab, and Tun) have so far been deciphered from inscriptions. When writing a date in the Long Count, the so-called "Introductory Glyph" comes first. This has a variable element in the middle that refers to the Haab month. This symbol represents the patron of the current Haab month, and changes every 20 days or after the five days of Wayeb.

The periods Bak'tun, K'atun, Tun, Winik, and K'in then follow in decreasing order. Thus the date on Stela 11 of Yaxchilan means that exactly 9 Bak'tun of 144,000 days, 16 K'atun of 7200 and 1 Tun of 360 days, a total of 1,411,560 days, have passed since the day of creation, and that the Calendar Round for this date is 11 Ajaw 8 Tzek (ill. 216).

With the aid of Diego de Landa's report and texts in the Mayan language found in Oxkutzcab and Yaxkukul, which were written in Latin script during the colonial period, the European method of time calculation can be tied in with the Maya calendar. Thus the Maya day of creation, 4 Ajaw 8 Kumk'u, was September 8, 3114 B.C. in the Julian Calendar, which was used in Europe until the time of Pope Gregory XIII (1502–1585) who reformed the calendar in 1582. Thus the date on Stela 11 of Yaxchilan is April 29, 752 A.D.

The Maya adopted the principle of long counting from the Mixe-Zoque peoples. The earliest evidence that this calendar existed comes from the time between 50 B.C. and 200 A.D. This means that the Long Count was the oldest method of counting that contains the number symbol 0 – older even than the Indian method of counting.

The Nine Lords of the Night

In the representation of a date, the Long Count and Tzolk'in day are followed by a hieroglyph that distinguishes between one of nine supernatural beings, each of them reigning for a day and constantly changing. These characters are erroneously called the "Nine Lords of the Night" – in fact, their

214 *Time periods used in the Long Count*
Time periods in the Long Count can be represented as abstract units or by a head variant. The Bak'tun (144,000 days) is represented by an owl with a human hand where the lower jaw should be. K'atun (7200 days) is also shown as a mythical owl-like bird. An owl with a fleshless lower jaw and an eye in the shape of the day symbol Hix represents Tun or Haab (360 days). Winal or Winik (20 days) are represented by a toad. The Sun God is used for K'in (day).

Bak'tun
20 K'atun/400 Tun
(144,000 days)

K'atun
20 Tun
(7200 days)

Tun
(year of 360 days)

Winal
(20 days)

K'in
(day)

names contain no references to the night. The starting date of the Maya calendar, 4 Ajaw 8 Kumk'u, is the hieroglyph for the ninth lord. It is followed by a hieroglyph which presumably refers to the fact that, for one day, the "Lord of the Night" wears a headband as a sign of his power. The ninth lord also ruled on the date given on Stela 11 of Yaxchilan. Sadly, nothing further is known about these "Lords of the Night," their meaning or origins (ill. 216).

The 819-day cycle

The Maya used the numbers 7, 9, and 13 to create a further cycle based on 819 days. The construction of 819 days equates to the cycle of the year bearers with the constant change between the four directions and the corresponding colors. This cycle could obviously influence the wellbeing of whole city-states. It is frequently found in conjunction with the birthday and enthronement of a ruler. The calendar zero date in the Long Count was placed on the third day of an 819-day cycle, which coincided with the direction east and the color red. Because the sun rises in the east, it symbolized the place where life originated and was therefore a favorable time for the creation of the world. It also confirmed that the creation of the world was not the origin of time, but an event that was embedded in even greater periods of time.

215 *Stela 11 from Yaxchilan with the Long Count. Yaxchilan, Chiapas, Mexico, Southern Acropolis; Stela 11 (east side); Late Classic; April 29, 752 A.D.; fine grained limestone; H. 400 cm (without plinth), W. 115 cm, D. 27 cm*

The stela depicts the ruler Yaxuun Balam (Bird Jaguar IV) from Yaxchilan and gives the date of his accession in Long Count form, a number that counts the days since the creation of the Maya world on September 8, 3114 B.C. Our picture shows an extract of the text with the long form of the date.

216 *Conversion of the date on Stela 11 from Yaxchilan* As is usual with the Long Count, the date on Stela 11 begins with an oversized hieroglyph known as the "Introductory Glyph." This is followed by the number of days, read from top to bottom as 9 Bak'tun, 16 K'atun, 1 Tun, 0 Winik and 0 K'in. The date is April 29, 752 A.D. It

is followed by the supplementary series with information on the lunar calendar and ritual cycles, then the verb for accession (not shown) and the name of the new ruler.

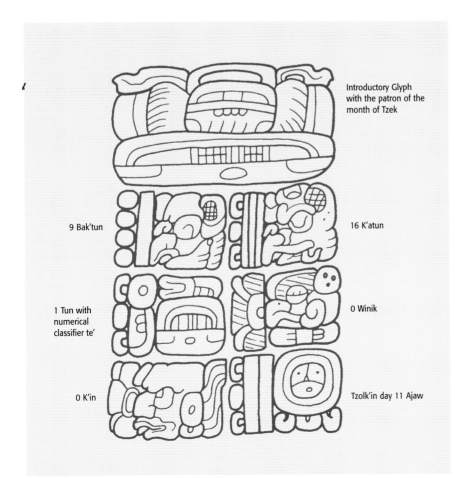

Introductory Glyph with the patron of the month of Tzek

9 Bak'tun

16 K'atun

1 Tun with numerical classifier te'

0 Winik

0 K'in

Tzolk'in day 11 Ajaw

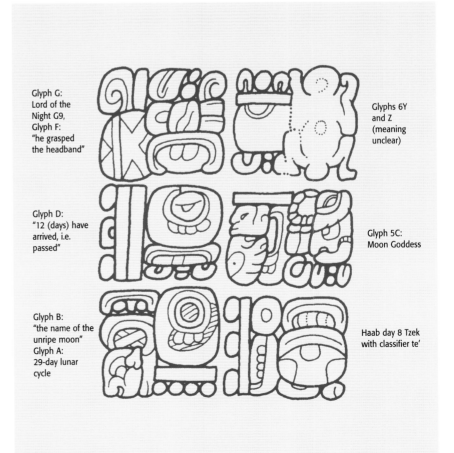

Glyph G: Lord of the Night G9, Glyph F: "he grasped the headband"

Glyph D: "12 (days) have arrived, i.e. passed"

Glyph B: "the name of the unripe moon" Glyph A: 29-day lunar cycle

Glyphs 6Y and Z (meaning unclear)

Glyph 5C: Moon Goddess

Haab day 8 Tzek with classifier te'

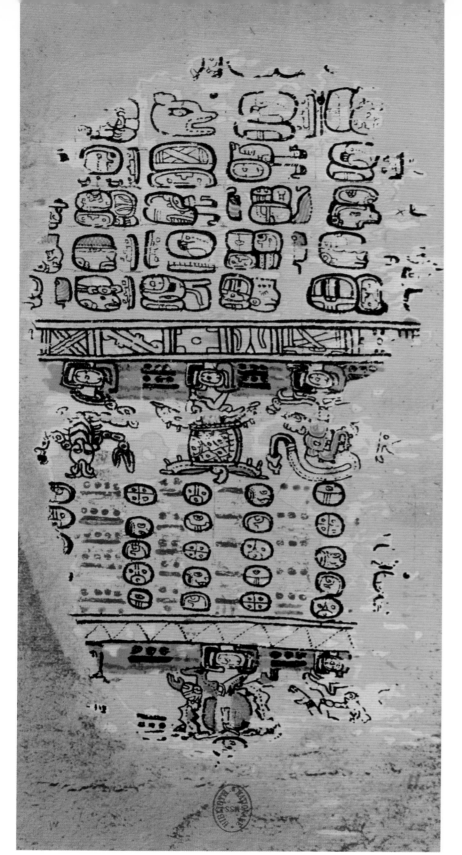

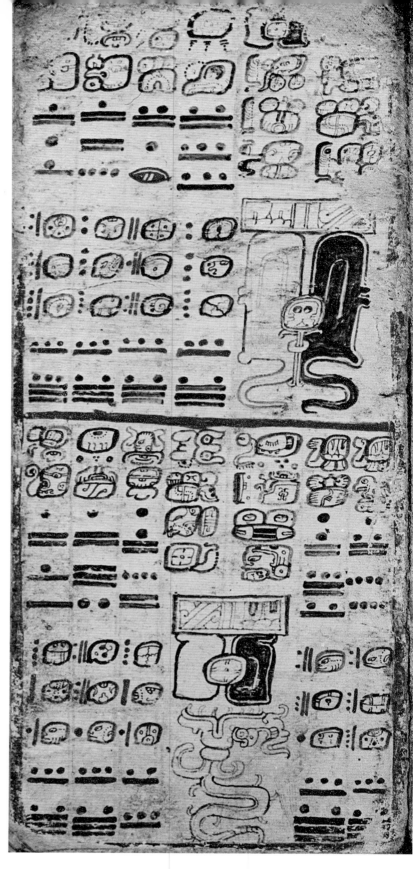

217 *The zodiac in the Paris Codex, page 23. Provenance unknown; Late Preclassic, 1200–1500 A.D.; fig bark paper, coated with limestone, painted; page: H. 23.5 cm, W. 12.5 cm; Paris, Bibliothèque Nationale*

The zodiac consists of a 364-day cycle, divided into 13 sections of 28 days. Each line contains the detailed course, and the first day a zodiac sign becomes visible is denoted by the day symbol. The 13 star signs are represented by animals and mythical creatures.

The Lunar Series

In addition to the two calendars, Tzolk'in and Haab, and the Long Count, the Maya devoted considerable attention to the Lunar Series, which is confirmed by Stela 11 from Yaxchilan (ill. 216). The Maya based their calculations on the phase between two new moons, which resulted in a lunar month of 29 or 30 days. The age of the moon was calculated from the first sighting after the new moon, and they counted the days that had passed in a separate hieroglyph. This consisted of the verb for "to arrive" preceded by a number. This meant that a certain number of days had arrived, i.e. already passed. In the case of Stela 11 from Yaxchilan, the moon had already been visible for 12 days. The next hieroglyph summarized the lunar months in three major cycles of five or six lunar months; the following one gives the name of the current moon. The name depended on the moon's position in one of the three major cycles, which in turn

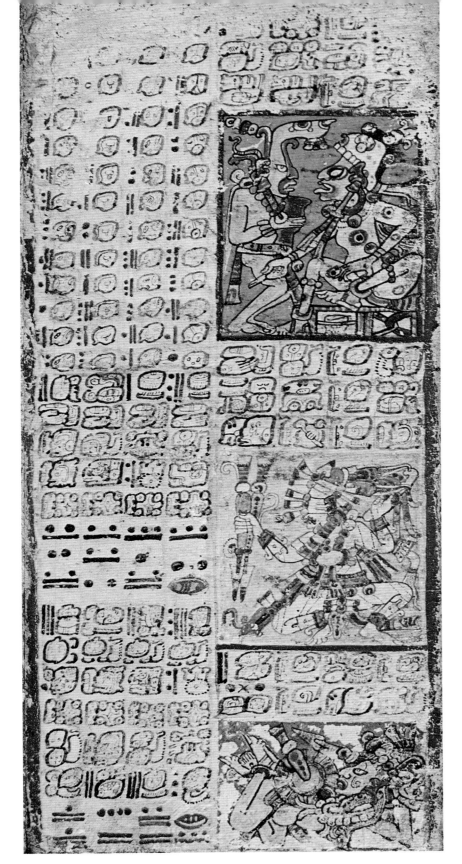

was watched over by one of three gods: the Jaguar God of the Underworld, the Death God, and the Moon Goddess. In the inscription on Stela 11 from Yaxchilan, the moon is just passing through the fifth month under the sign of the Moon Goddess.

Eclipses and the zodiac

In the chapter on eclipses in the Dresden Codex, the cycles recorded by the six lunar months are the basis for the calculation of solar and lunar eclipses (see Grube, p. 144 ff.). An eclipse is represented as a black-and-white area together with the sun or moon symbol (ill. 218). The star symbols in the zodiac also appear to be linked to the eclipse cycle. On one picture in the Paris Codex, the individual constellations are shown suspended from a sky band and biting into the symbol for a solar eclipse (ill. 217). The Maya obviously believed that the sun was devoured in a solar eclipse; in the Chilam-Balam book of Chumayel, they wrote thus of the event: "And then the face of the sun was bitten."

The Maya zodiac consists of 13 star pictures, including a bird (Libra), a tortoise (Orion's Belt), a scorpion (Scorpio), a screech owl (Gemini), a snake (Sagittarius), a parrot (Capricorn), a frog (the western part of Leo), a bat (Aquarius), a pig (the eastern part of Leo), a sign that can no longer be seen (Virgo), a skeleton (Pisces), a jaguar (Aries), and another as yet unidientified zodiac sign. This sequence of the constellations does not match the actual positions of the stars in the sky; the *aj k'inob*, "the calendar priests," put the star signs in pairs. They did this so that, as one half of a pair rose in the east in the morning the other was setting in the west, they would thus stand together in pairs. In this way they were able to establish the exact positions of the signs with no technical assistance at all.

The planet Venus

One of the most interesting chapters in the Dresden Codex is all about *chak ek'*, which is the planet Venus (ill. 219). Because the Maya believed this planet was the bringer of misfortune, bad omens and war (ill. 221), the *aj k'inob* were constantly asked to provide exact descriptions of its position so that people could avert misfortune by holding the appropriate ceremonies. To this end, the Maya divided Venus's circuit of almost 584 days into four sections: 236 days on which it was visible as the morning star in the east, 90 days as it passed behind the sun, also known as the upper conjunction, 250 days when it appeared as the evening star in the west, and eight days on which it was not visible as it passed between the earth and the sun, known as the lower conjunction. The fact that the circuits began with its first appearance in the east shows that the morning star in particular mattered to the Maya.

As far as negative effects are concerned, this was obviously the most critical section in its entire cycle. This is probably also the reason why five gods of war are dedicated to the eastern section. Only two of them, known as God L and Lajun Chan (Ten Sky) met the Maya cosmic ideals. In the Postclassic, the other three were borrowed from the pantheon of the Aztecs or their precursors, and placed by the side of their own Venus gods. These are Tlahuizcalpantecuhtli (the Lord of Dawn), Xiuhtecuhtli (Beautiful Lord of the Year), and Kaktonal (Sandals Day) or Ce Acatonal (One Reed); all brought death and destruction. They pierced other cosmic beings with arrows, thereby robbing people of the positive characteristics embodied by their victims.

218 Dresden Codex, page 57 of the chapter on eclipses. Provenance unknown; Late Postclassic, 1200–1500 A.D.; fig bark paper, painted; page: H. 20,4 cm, W. 9 cm; Dresden, Sächsische Landesbibliothek
The chapter on solar and lunar eclipses provides tables for predicting their occurrence. Columns with three day symbols always refer to a three-day period in which an eclipse may take place. Because the Maya did not use fractions, periods of less than a complete day were added together and inserted in the cycle at the appropriate places to balance their calculations. A solar or lunar eclipse is shown as a black-and-white area around the symbol for the moon or sun.

219 Dresden Codex, page 49 of the chapter on Venus. Provenance unknown; Late Postclassic, 1200–1500 A.D.; fig bark paper, painted; page: H. 20.4 cm, W. 9 cm; Dresden, Sächsische Landesbibliothek
The chapter on Venus is used to calculate the stations through which Venus passes on the 584 days of its circuit. Any period in which Venus appeared as the morning star was considered to be calamitous. The lords of the morning star are depicted with their negative features on the right half of the page. In the middle is the god of the morning star, shown as a warrior with a spear thrower and arrows. His mortally wounded opponent is shown beneath him, writhing on the ground with an arrow through his body.

THE LAST MANIFESTATIONS OF THE MAYA CALENDAR IN COLONIAL TIMES

The Annals of Oxkutzcab are a short document, written in Latin script but in the Yukatek language, from the year 1685. The style of this unique text reveals that it is second-generation copy of a text originally written in hieroglyphs. The Annals tell of important events in connection with the Spanish invasion of the Yucatan peninsula. The dates of historical events are given in both the Christian-Julian calendar and in the Maya calendar.

Passage taken from the annals of Oxkutzcab, 1685, Tozzer Library, Harvard University (translated from Yukatek Mayan into German by Nikolai Grube):

... in the year 1542, 1 Pop fell on 13 K'an, and the Spanish established a settlement in Tiho [now Merida]. They settled there, and for the first time the people of Mani and its province began to pay tribute ...

... in the year 1543, 1 Pop fell on 1 Muluk, and the people of Dzidzantun were killed by an army of Spaniards, whose captain was Alonso Lopez ..."

It was information such as this, obtained from sources dating back to colonial times, that enabled researchers to understand the Maya calendar for the first time. The writer of the annals was obviously not interested in recording the exact day and month of a particular event, but only with giving the year, naming it first in the then more usual Julian calendar and continuing with the years according to the Maya calendar. In both he refers to the day 1 Pop, the first day in the 365-day year, which the Maya called Haab. The number 1 means that it is the first day of the month (each month had 20 days with the exception of the 19th, which had only five). Pop is the name of the first month. So it can be said that, for the Maya, 1 Pop was New Year's Day. The Maya had a 260-day calendar as well as the 365-day version, the former running parallel to the latter (see Voss, p. 134–135). Thus the author of the annals refers to the days 13 K'an and 1 Muluk. These are the days in the 260-day calendar on which, according to the 365-day calendar, New Year's Day fell in 1542 and 1543. There were exactly 365 days between day 1 Pop in 1542 and 1 Pop in 1543. The name of a day in the 260-day calendar is a combination of one of the numbers between 1 and 13, and one of 20 different day names. So one 260-day cycle and the first 105 days of a second one were combined in one 365-day period. If a day in the 260-day calendar had the number 13 in its name, then the next New Year's Day would fall on a day with the number 1, because 365 is 28×13, with a remainder of 1. Since they counted only from 1 to 13 in the 260-day calendar, there was no day with the number 14; instead they began again from the beginning.

The day names moved forward by five, as 265 is 18×20 (the number of day names), with a remainder of 5. A calendar priest could now count the days, K'an, Chikchan, Kimi, Manik, Lamat, Muluk, and then knew the name of the relevant day. Thus it came about that the first New Year's Day after 13 K'an fell on day 1 Muluk. New Year's Day of the following year would fall on 2 Ix. In the 260-day calendar, the days that coincided with day 1 Pop were referred to by the calendar priests as the "year bearers." Some Maya groups in the Highlands of Guatemala still calculate and celebrate them today.

220 *The foundation year of Merida (Yucatan, Mexico) as calculated by the Maya*
The diagram shows the foundation year of Merida as calculated by the Maya and recorded in the annals of Oxkutzcab. The period encompasses the year 1542 of the Julian Calendar. Here, the 365-day Haab is combined with the Tzolk'in cycle of 260 days. The year with 365 days begins on 1 Pop, the first day of the month Pop, which in the Julian year of 1542 fell on Tzolk'in day 13 K'an. In 1543, 365 days later, New Year's Day 1 Pop of Haab fell on Tzolk'in day 1 Muluk. The name of the Tzolk'in day on which the Haab year began was also the name of its year symbol. In this example, the year symbols are K'an and Muluk.

New Year	2nd day	3rd day	259th day	260th day	261st day	363rd day	364th day	365th day	New Year
1 Pop	2 Pop	3 Pop	19 Mak	K'ank'in seated	1 K'ank'in	3 Wayeb	4 Wayeb	Pop seated	1 Pop
13 K'an	1 Chikchan	2 Kimi	11 Ik'	12 Ak'bal	13 K'an	11 Kimi	12 Manik'	13 Lamat	1 Muluk

221 *Door lintel showing the ruler Yaxuun Balam. Yaxchilan, Chiapas, Mexico, West Acropolis, door lintel 41; Late Classic, May 5, 755 A.D.; fine-grained limestone; L. overall more than 120 cm (section 60 cm), W. 93 cm, D. 10 cm; London, British Museum*
This scene shows the ruler Yaxuun Balam (Bird Jaguar IV), in full war regalia, with his wife Wak Jalam Chan Ajaw. The text at the top left edge of the picture gives the date 7 Imix 14 Tzek (May 5, 755 A.D.). This is followed by the so-called star-war verb, which consists of half of the sign for star and flowing water droplets, and a place name. The text tells us that Yaxchilan went to war against a neighboring place. The current view is that Venus' position as the morning star would have played an important part in determining auspicious days for military activities. However, we still cannot be certain of the exact connection between Venus and the days on which military campaigns took place.

For precise calculations, Venus' circuit was noted a total of 65 times, which equates to exactly 104 common years, 146 Tzolk'in circuits or two Calendar Rounds. However, there was one small problem in the form of five extra days that had accumulated after these 65 Venus circuits. Because the calendar preceded the actual movement of the planets, the appropriate adjustment was made to set it back. The reverse correction procedure was applied with the zodiac which, at 364 days, was already six days behind after just five sequences. Despite this mathematical inaccuracy, the Venus chapter in the Dresden Codex contains references to Venus' first appearance as the morning star on November 20, 934 A.D. (10.5.6.4.0 in Long Count notation, 1 Ajaw 18 K'ayab in the Calendar Round), an event that was actually observed and used to confirm the conversion method for the Maya and Christian calendars.

How the Maya understood time

This section on Maya mathematics and astronomy can only offer a brief look at the complex understanding of the calendar accumulated by the priesthood over generations. Their interest in a comprehensive reckoning of time would probably fill books. The calendar arose from the observation of a number of astronomical phenomena, but also from their efforts to find formulae that bound or summarized the various seasonal and ritual cycles. Another reason why the Maya continued to develop new calendars was their desire to look into the future and recognize and predetermine the powers and movements of celestial bodies.

The calendar was never intended as an end in itself or merely as a means of dividing time. Lifelike sculptural representations and descriptions show that time was not an abstract physical phenomenon to the Maya, but was manifest in supernatural beings on the far side of the human world. These beings also lived, loved, ate and drank, ruled, and killed. In a never-ending cycle they were born, developed their powers and then died, only to be born again at a precisely determined time and start a new cycle.

To the Maya, these supernatural entities represented time and were responsible for maintaining cosmic order. Their features and actions determined the way of the world. The calendar priests, the *aj k'inob*, believed they could see the effects of these cosmic beings in astronomical phenomena. They recorded these in laws, which people had to obey, and from them derived prognoses which they used to forecast the effects of supernatural forces and prepare people for coming events.

The arrival of the Spaniards and resulting conversion to Christianity gradually superseded the ancient Maya knowledge. However, Western ideas of cosmic order and healing did not penetrate every Maya region to the same extent. While the powerful presence of the Catholic church in northern Yucatan contributed to the destruction of the traditional social order, thereby hastening the demise of ancient ideas of belief and the calendar, the gods (especially in the Highlands of Guatemala) were subject to a number of changes before they took up their allocated places, dressed in western robes and under new names, by the side of Jesus, Mary, and the various Catholic saints. The ancient astronomical and calendar knowledge has been preserved, especially in less accessible areas.

In the last century in particular, western science has also contributed to the rediscovery and interpretation of written documents left by the pre-Hispanic Maya culture, and has been invaluable in helping us to regain some of our understanding of the Maya cosmos.

SOLAR ECLIPSES – FEARING THE END OF THE WORLD

Nikolai Grube

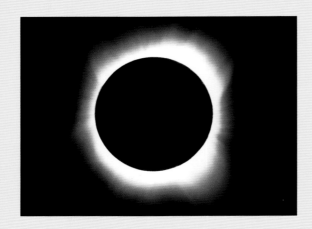

One day a great excitement broke out in Señor, a remote Maya village in Quintana Roo where I was staying to learn the language of Yukatek Mayan. According to the newspapers, there was going to be a total lunar eclipse during the night. Only a few of the Yukatek Maya in the village could read, but the young people who had been to school in the next town soon spread the news. The Mayan language radio station also referred to the imminent event in its news programs. It would have been easy to miss the news about the impending lunar eclipse, with the softly spoken reporters presenting international items and the expected outcome of the governor's elections taking place in the state of Quintana Roo. But in Señor, everyone was concerned about the impending lunar eclipse. "Will Señora Luna, Lady Moon, ever come back? Why is she leaving us?" an anxious old lady asked me as she prepared to seek refuge in a nearby church.

The Maya do not consider the moon to be a lifeless celestial body wandering through the universe, but a lady, the ancient Moon Goddess. An eclipse can only be interpreted as a serious misfortune experienced by the Moon Goddess or the Sun God. If the sun disappears in broad daylight giving way to darkness, or a black segment suddenly covers the full moon, there is no doubt in the Maya's minds that serious trouble is on the way. They still live in fear and dread of eclipses of the sun and moon and, because the Moon Goddess also watches over pregnancies and births, they believe that pregnant women are particularly at risk during an eclipse. In pre-Hispanic times, people also believed that eclipses heralded wars or major disasters for the whole community.

If an eclipse occurs, the women and children gather together in the church, whilst the men fire shots with their rifles to try to drive away the giant ants, which they fear will eat away the sun or the moon. The word for "eclipse of the sun" is *u chibal k'in*, which means "the swallowing of the sun" (ill. 224). In Señor, the Maya priest rang the bells of his church, while the children banged on saucepans with spoons. The din from the church in the middle of the night was terrible. In front of the church, the men fired shots from ancient shotguns, while inside the women called upon their ancient gods.

222 Total Eclipse of the Sun
Total eclipses of the sun, when the sun is completely covered by the moon, are very seldom observed. All over the world they are considered to be signs of foreboding, terror and misfortune as they turn day into night and, at the darkest point, even render the starry sky visible.

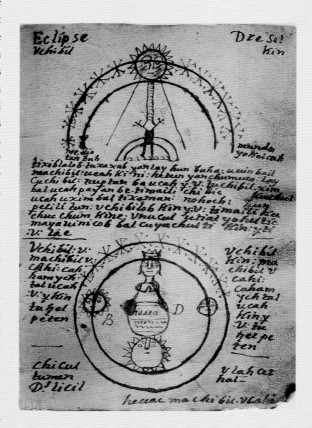

223 Explanation of the eclipse phenomenon in the Chilam-Balam book of Chumayel. Handwritten, page 27; 2nd half of the 18th century; Philadelphia, University Museum
Spanish missionaries during the colonial period tried to introduce the Maya to the European explanation of eclipses. This text refutes the idea that the moon was being eaten up.

The fear of eclipses was no less marked in pre-Hispanic times and the priests were able to predict the dangerous days when the eclipses of the sun or moon were likely to occur (see Voss, p. 141). Seven pages of the Dresden Codex contain a table, which enabled the calendar priests to determine the days on which the moon's path would intersect with the sun's visible route across the sky (ill. 225). The calendar priests knew that an eclipse of the sun or moon could only occur within a period of 18 days before or after such a "nodal crossing," the astronomical term used to describe the intersection of the sun and the moon's paths. They had observed that eclipses of both the sun and the moon actually occurred approximately 148 days (five lunar months) or 177 days (six lunar months) from one another. Even though many, if not most, eclipses could not be observed because they were not visible in the Maya region, the Maya astronomers were nevertheless able to refer to the data recorded in books over several centuries to help them to understand and predict the cycles of the eclipses.

The two intervals of 148 and 177 days are at the center of the eclipse table on pages 51 to 58 of the Dresden Codex (ill. 225). The main part of the table begins in the top half of page 52 with the initial data on the basis of which the table can be calculated. The figure 177 is written in Maya numerals (a red 8 above a black 17, giving $8 \times 20 + 17 \times 1 = 177$) in the lower section of the top half of page 53. This represents the number of days between one eclipse and the next. However, the people did not expect to see an actual eclipse every 177 days. Another 177 is written to the right, with the figure 148 in the third column. After the figure 148, the columns of figures are interrupted by a picture of the god of death seated on a throne of bones, indicating that the people actually observed an eclipse or expected one to be visible on this occasion. The question of whether the eclipse table was used to predict eclipses of the sun and the moon or whether it represents eclipses that were actually observed in the Yucatan region has not yet been solved by research. The eight-page table covers 405 lunar months or 11,960 days, a period which was also significant for the Maya because it corresponded to 46 cycles of 260 days.

The astronomical knowledge of the Maya was lost after the Spanish invasion. However, the idea that eclipses signify the end of the world, misfortune and disease is still widespread. This is surprising when we consider that Spanish missionaries and teachers have been striving since the earliest colonial times to explain to the Maya that an eclipse is caused by the earth's shadow over the moon or a segment of the moon covering the sun (ill. 223). Even the daily paper read by some of the young people of Señor patiently described to its readers what would happen during the impending lunar eclipse. But even so, traditional beliefs triumphed over all the well-meant scientific explanations. Here, as in other fields, 500 years of contact with European thinking have not been able to replace Maya beliefs.

Jubilation reigned at daybreak in Señor, when the first pale light of the crescent moon appeared, gradually intensifying to reveal that the Moon

Goddess had survived. The world had once again been saved from disaster.

224 *Serpent with wide-open jaws causing an eclipse. Paris Codex, p. 23; provenance unknown; fig bark paper, covered with layer of limestone, painted; Late Preclassic, 1350–1500 A.D.; H. 24.8 cm; L. 145 cm in total; Paris, Bibliothèque Nationale*
The serpent is one of the 13 animal symbols. Here it indicates the place where an eclipse will be visible in the sky. Its wide-open jaws depict the idea that the sun or moon is eaten up when an eclipse occurs.

225 *Page of the eclipse table (diagram and photograph). Dresden Codex, p. 53; provenance unknown; Late Postclassic, 1200–1500 A.D.; fig bark paper, covered with layer of limestone, painted; page H. 20.4 cm; W. 9 cm; Dresden, Sächsische Landesbibliothek*
The eclipse table consists of eight pages and begins on page 53 shown here (upper half). The bottom halves of the pages are read after the top halves of pages 51–58.

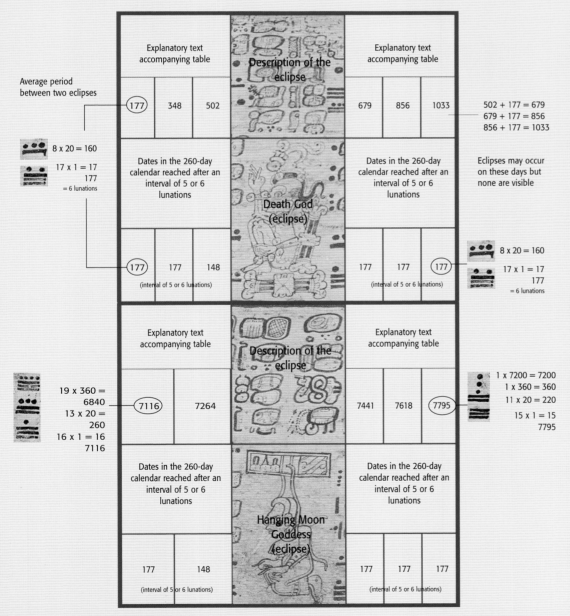

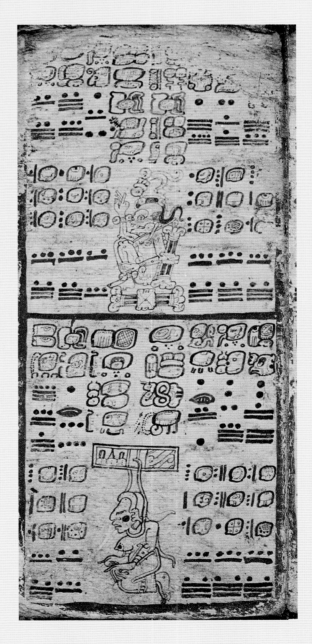

POLITICS AND DYNASTY

THE DYNASTIC HISTORY OF THE MAYA

Nikolai Grube and Simon Martin

The use of hieroglyphic script is the main cultural trait that differentiates the Classic Maya period (250–909 A.D.) from the earlier Preclassic period. The development of hieroglyphic script in the Maya Lowlands was a result of far-reaching social change occurring after the collapse of the large Preclassic cities (see Hansen, p. 51 ff.). It is still not known for certain what finally led to the decline of most of these settlements. It has emerged, however, that some cities survived this major process of transformation to form the nucleus of the Classic Maya culture. Particularly in the central parts of the southern Lowlands, places such as Tikal, Uaxactun, Yaxha and Xultun came out of these radical changes in an even stronger position.

A new political institution, hereditary kingship, developed during the early Classic period at the same time as the hieroglyphic script. While Preclassic art had been impersonal and expressed itself through masks of the gods and cosmic symbols, the early Classic period brought representations of historical figures into prominence, each with their own individually designated characteristics. The task of hieroglyphic scripts and artistic works during the Classic period was to establish the real claims to power of the godlike kings and justify their position at the center of the cosmos and as mediators between man and the gods.

The establishment of royal dynasties

The earliest written texts go back to the time the first royal dynasties were founded in the 1st century A.D., and give a retrospective view of this event. The lack of contemporary inscriptions created by the founders of the dynasty themselves may on the one hand be partly explained by the fact that they did not consider themselves as such, and that this role was attributed to them by later generations. On the other hand, it could be that the contemporary texts were written on impermanent materials such as wood and bark, or painted on the stuccoed walls of buildings which no longer exist.

The founders of the dynasties were extremely important in terms of the way later rulers saw themselves. Successive kings linked themselves to their founding fathers with titles which often used the formula "nth ruler in succession to the founder," which created a kind of census of rulers.

One of the first royal dynasties of the Maya Lowlands was the Tikal dynasty. Although the dates of Yax Eeb Xook, the first ruler of this royal family, have not survived, the census of rulers indicates that he lived and reigned in the second half of the 1st century. He is probably buried in the first royal grave, which was discovered in the North Acropolis of Tikal, and features characteristic royal burial objects such as a life-size mask with a royal *hu'un*, a headband decorated with three stylized flowers. During the Classic period, the *hu'un* headdress itself was venerated as a god and patron of the royal dynasties (see Grube, p. 96 ff.).

Rival divine kingdoms

The founders of royal dynasties and their successors assumed the position of *ajaw*, "leader," "priest" and "king," after their enthronement. After 400 A.D., the highest rulers were given the title of *k'uhul ajaw*, "divine king," in order to differentiate them from a growing category of lesser nobility and emphasize their divine origins. Although the title *k'uhul ajaw* was originally limited to the most important kingdoms, such as Tikal and Calakmul, it was soon granted to many other rulers wishing to express their divine status. By around 450 A.D. there were several dozen kings in the Lowlands who had laid claim to this title, asserting their links with dynasty founders and regarding themselves as the focal point of the small states they ruled.

This small state structure remained unchanged throughout the Classic period. The Lowlands never gained political unity and there was never a unified Maya kingdom, as was previously assumed. The political division of the Lowlands is depicted in the large number of so-called emblem glyphs (see Grube p. 120). These sign combinations represent royal titles, which identified their bearers as *k'uhul ajaw*, "divine kings," in a particular territory. They consist of three main elements, two of which represent the title *k'uhul ajaw*. The third and largest element refers to the name of the state in question. The kings of Tikal, which was called Mutal during the Classic period, was referred to as *k'uhul mutal ajaw*, "divine king of Mutal/Tikal," and the rulers of the city of Piedras Negras were given the title of *k'uhul yokib ajaw*, "divine king of the land of ravines" (ill. 183).

By examining all these titles, it can be deduced that around 50 small states existed in the course of Classic history, each with its own *ajaw*, who as its leader claimed divine origins. The fact that these states never formed a political union could be linked to the particular form of hegemonic rule in force throughout Meso-America. According to this system, conquered areas were not integrated entirely into the victorious state, but continued to exist as autonomous states. The conquered kings were forced to pay tribute and show loyalty to their vanquishers, however. A network of personal and family relationships between the royal families, such as marriages involving a king's daughter, bound subjugated states to their conquerors and made them into vassals.

Tributes were paid in the form of quetzal feathers, cacao beans, expensive ceramics, and finely woven cloth.

Previous double page:
Palace scene. Late Classic, 600-900 A.D.; fired clay, painted; H. 16.0 cm, dia. 16.4 cm; private collection (Kerr 5943)
A nobleman kneels before a Maya ruler seated on a jaguar throne, in awe and with his arms crossed as a sign of respect. Behind the ruler's back, two servants carrying a fan and a cloth await their master's instructions.

226 *Top of an incense burner. Copan, Honduras, Temple 26 in front of Burial XXXVII-4, Late Classic, 7th century A.D.; clay, painted; H. 58 cm, Dia. 26.5 cm; Copan, Instituto Hondureño de Antropología e Historia*
Eleven broken incense burners were found at the entrance to the burial of the 12th King of Copan under Temple 26. The enthroned clay figures on the lids of the cylindrical incense burners probably represent the 11 predecessors of the deceased.

Hierarchies between Maya states

The longstanding idea that these small states had been totally autonomous and independent from one another can be seen to be unfounded if we compare the architecture of the various capital cities. Had they been autonomous, a city of the size of Tikal would have had the same political power as the comparatively small Dos Pilas, which was also home to a *k'uhul ajaw*. In actual fact, hieroglyphic inscriptions point to a political system in which power and wealth were distributed unevenly between the states, with a few states controlling a large number of others. Variations in power and influence are also reflected in the hieroglyphic inscriptions. They describe how a few states intervened in the domestic matters of others and manipulated their political systems, conduct of war and dynastic succession. The inscriptions include accounts which state that the leader of a particular place gained his position "under the supervision" of the king of another area (ill. 228). Such references provide concrete proof of a hierarchical system. The title of *yajaw*, from the word *ajaw*, "king" or "leader," provides an even clearer indication of the existence of hierarchies between the different kingdoms. The literal translation of the title is "... the king of ...," implying that the holder of the title was subject to another king and considered his property. The title is followed by the name of a second king, who is always the more powerful of the two and for whom the holder of the title *yajaw* is no more than a vassal, forever at his disposal. If we consider these allusions to hierarchical links and a system of subordination in the context of other political events, military campaigns and diplomatic relations, a surprising network of relationships between the various Maya states emerges. The two most important kings, who enthroned the rulers of other states and were appointed leaders of the feudal princes, were the rulers of Tikal and Calakmul. There were a number of powerful, influential states in the Lowlands whose kings also enthroned feudal leaders, but none had as much power and diplomatic skill as Calakmul and Tikal.

Tikal and Calakmul were real superpowers in the Maya Lowlands, and ruled over their own networks of feudal states (ill. 243). Although the relationships between different states occasionally changed and there were repeated revolts in which the vassals tried to shake off their dependent status and obligation to pay tributes, the two superpowers were surprisingly stable throughout most of the Classic period, their success founded above all on personal and family connections.

The royal court culture

Although the dynasties of the small states and superpowers enjoyed varying degrees of power, the Maya nobility shared a common court culture. During the Classic period, the kings and their families had a privileged existence, surrounded by wealth and personal luxury (ill. 227).

Young princes, and possibly all members of the nobility with no regal status were given the symbolic title of *ch'ok*, "child." The future heir to the throne was referred to as *bah ch'ok*, "first child," and had to prove that he was fit for his future position by partaking in a number of rituals, which generally included making the first blood sacrifice at the age of five (ill. 229). The line of succession usually followed the paternal line, which meant that first-born sons generally became heirs to the throne. Although this was the ideal scenario, it did not always occur. If a designated heir to the throne was killed in battle, his brother took his place and, in cases where there was no male successor, women

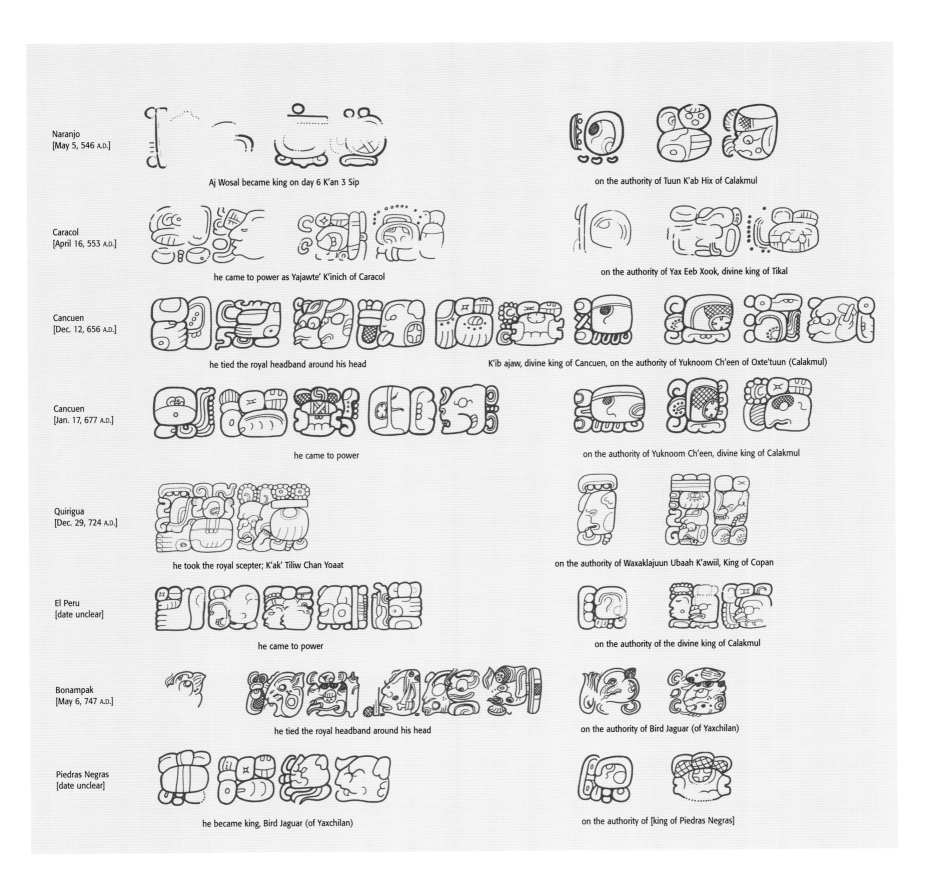

Naranjo [May 5, 546 A.D.]	Aj Wosal became king on day 6 K'an 3 Sip	on the authority of Tuun K'ab Hix of Calakmul
Caracol [April 16, 553 A.D.]	he came to power as Yajawte' K'inich of Caracol	on the authority of Yax Eeb Xook, divine king of Tikal
Cancuen [Dec. 12, 656 A.D.]	he tied the royal headband around his head	K'ib ajaw, divine king of Cancuen, on the authority of Yuknoom Ch'een of Oxte'tuun (Calakmul)
Cancuen [Jan. 17, 677 A.D.]	he came to power	on the authority of Yuknoom Ch'een, divine king of Calakmul
Quirigua [Dec. 29, 724 A.D.]	he took the royal scepter; K'ak' Tiliw Chan Yoaat	on the authority of Waxaklajuun Ubaah K'awiil, King of Copan
El Peru [date unclear]	he came to power	on the authority of the divine king of Calakmul
Bonampak [May 6, 747 A.D.]	he tied the royal headband around his head	on the authority of Bird Jaguar (of Yaxchilan)
Piedras Negras [date unclear]	he became king, Bird Jaguar (of Yaxchilan)	on the authority of [king of Piedras Negras]

227 *Scene at the royal court. Provenance unknown; Late Classic, 600–900 A.D.; clay, painted; H. 24.0 cm, dia. 17.0 cm; rollout of a polychrome painted earthenware vessel; private collection (Kerr 1453)*

Life in the royal court was characterized by pomp and luxury. A large royal household was responsible for looking after and entertaining the royal family. This vessel depicts the King of Motul de San Jose seated on a throne and leaning against a cushion held by a servant. His overlong fingernails and portly stature indicate that he did not have to carry out any physical work and was looked after with the utmost care. Court dwarfs and hunchbacks crouch before him. One of the dwarfs is standing on the throne holding an obsidian mirror. Two clay trumpets and a triton shell dominate the picture. The musicians of the royal court chapel remain hidden behind a pillar or curtain.

228 *Ascension to the throne under the supervision of foreign rulers*

Some of the most important events recorded in hieroglyphic texts are the accessions of Maya kings to the throne. Many kings did not attain royal dignity simply because of their charisma or their position as heirs to the throne in a royal dynasty, but because they were supported and promoted by other, more powerful rulers. The latter required their favorites to offer loyalty and support for their political decisions. The illustration shows royal accessions in different places and at different times in which kings acceded to the throne by offering favors to more powerful potentates. The left half of the illustration shows accessions to the throne and the right side the names of the supporting rulers, introduced by the hieroglyph *u kabjiiy*, "under the supervision of." It is clear that the kings of Tikal and Calakmul were particularly accustomed to overseeing the enthronement of foreign leaders.

229 *Panel 19. Dos Pilas, Peten, Guatemala; between 727 and 735 A.D.; limestone; H. 64 cm; Guatemala City, Museo Nacional de Arqueología y Etnología*
The first blood sacrifice of a royal heir was seldom depicted in such detail as in Panel 19 of Dos Pilas. The extraordinarily explicit representation of the first blood sacrifice of a child, who is named *ch'ok mutal ajaw*, "Prince of Dos Pilas," in the accompanying text and was probably the young K'awiil Chan K'inich, shows that his predecessor, Ruler 3, who commissioned this relief, was very concerned about his successor. In the center of the scene we see a richly clothed youth, whose penis is being pierced by a kneeling priest. The blood is dripping into a bowl. The scene is observed by Ruler 3 and his wife from Cancuen on the left. Two dignitaries stand on the right, one of whom is an ambassador from Calakmul.

230 *Two sides of a scepter. Provenance unknown; Late Classic period, 600–900 A.D.; slate; H. 24.4 cm. W. 8.75 cm; private collection (Kerr 3409)*
This carved slate scepter was a valued sign of rank and power. It is made in the form of an axe, with both its broad sides bearing representations of figures. One side depicts one of the divine twins, Hun Ajaw, who is represented here as a hunter with a blowgun, while the other shows a ruler seated on a low throne, possibly the former owner of this splendid piece. A finely carved hieroglyphic text on the narrow side names the owner as the "captor of the ruler of Pusilha." As Pusilha lies in the south of Belize in a region where slate is found, it can be assumed that the place where the scepter was produced, is to be found in the border region between Guatemala and Belize.

could also gain positions of power. Numerous conflicts developed within royal dynasties as well as between states when the rightful succession was at issue. A designated heir to the throne therefore did his best to prove that he was a capable leader in battle before being appointed. Many military campaigns in fact only served to enable future rulers to make their mark. Kings who took prisoners before acceding to the throne were often granted the lifelong title "possessor of ...," followed by the name of their captive.

When the time came for the new king to accede to the throne (usually between ten days and several months after the death of his predecessor), the accession ceremonies began. These ceremonies were seldom represented in art, and even hieroglyphic texts only describe key episodes with stereotyped expressions, such as *chumlaj ti ajawlel*, "he acceded to the throne," *u ch'amaw k'awiil,* "he took the scepter in the form of the god K'awiil" and *k'alaj hu'un tu baah,* "he tied the royal headdress firmly around his head"; ill. 228).

The kings changed their names upon accession to the throne. Some kept their own name, but the acceptance of an additional *k'uhul k'aba*, "a divine name," was an expression of their new role and identity. The chosen names often referred to gods and their activities, objects with a special sacred significance, or animals which played an important role as manifestations or assistants of the gods. Royal heirs often chose the name of their grandfather or another famous forebear in order to maintain links with a long chain of tradition. A king who assumed a divine name finally became a *k'uhul ajaw*, a "divine king," and was thus elevated to a different sphere of existence.

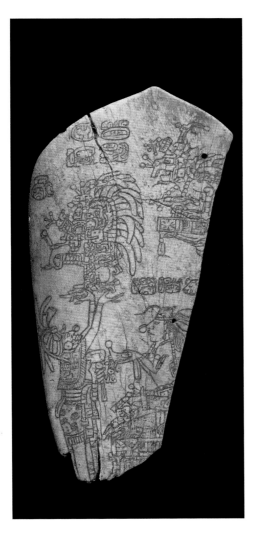

231 *Enthronement scene. Provenance unknown; Late Classic, 600–900 A.D.; engraved bone; H. 6.2 cm; Dallas, Dallas Museum of Art*
An enthronement scene is depicted here in firmly drawn lines on a piece of bone only a few inches long. The heir is seated on a throne under a canopy (only partly preserved), which is crowned with a depiction of the god Itzamnaaj in the form of a bird. The old Jaguar God, one aspect of the Sun God, holds the royal headdress in the air, ready to place it on the head of the successor.

232 *Bird Jaguar disguised as Chaak capturing prisoners. Yaxchilan, Chiapas, Mexico, in front of Temple 40; Late Classic, April 29, 752; limestone*
By putting on divine masks, kings assumed the identity of gods, as on Stela 1 at Yaxchilan, in which Bird Jaguar IV appears wearing a mask of the god Chaak. Maya artists nevertheless made sure that the dual identity of the king was still visible. The sovereign's human face can therefore still be seen underneath the mask.

Mediators between men and gods

Kings were godly beings and stood outside society. They lived in a different world from their fellow men. This position was expressed in all courtly culture, and also in the expectations that the city state dwellers had of their king. The proximity of the king to the gods obliged him to act as a mediator and advocate for society before the gods and to deliver their divine messages to the people.

The role of the king as a connecting link between the two worlds was also apparent in his clothing. Many representations show kings with the attributes of the gods (ill. 232). Such images made it clear to the observer that the kings not only disguised themselves as gods, but also assumed their identity. As gods, the kings carried out many public rituals intended to have a positive effect on the fate of the whole community (ill. 233). In their divine roles, they performed dance dramas whose central episodes not only depicted and publicly staged the story of creation, but in the minds of spectators were regularly repeated and re-enacted. These royal dances were the subject of many artistic representations (ill. 237).

One of the most important rituals was the royal blood sacrifice (ill. 233). While male rulers drained blood from their earlobes, tongues or (the holiest blood) genitalia using stingray spines, bone needles or obsidian spikes, other blood sacrifice scenes show women at the center of the action, drawing barbed cords through a hole in their tongue. The precious royal blood dripped into baskets lined with strips of paper. When the strips were soaked, they were placed

in incense burners and thus merged with the noble aromas of the incense to create food for the gods.

This type of royal blood sacrifice is likely to have been the high point of rituals that lasted for several days. They were apparently so important for the community that they were performed in public. The layout of the cities, with their numerous squares and flights of steps, was very well suited to creating stages on which to present such spectacles. Artistic pieces from the Classic period, such as the famous lintel from Yaxchilan (ill. 233), associated blood sacrifices with visionary experiences. It is not known whether the visions were provoked by the rapid loss of blood or by hallucinogenic substances taken beforehand. In any event, one of the important functions of the kings was to call forth visionary manifestations and make contact with the gods and their ancestors. Such visions are always depicted in art in the form of snakes, with the head of a god or ancestor emerging from their wide-open jaws.

Of the many divine roles embodied by the Maya kings, that of the young Maize God was probably the most important. Many artistic representations and hieroglyphic inscriptions depict kings as the embodiment of the fertility and wealth brought by the Maize God (see Taube, p. 271). The birth of a king was compared with the bursting forth of maize (corn) from the underworld, whilst the death of a king corresponded to the descent of the Maize God into the underworld. Similarly, when a grain of maize was reborn in the soil, the deceased sovereign was reincarnated in the form of his heir. The maize cycle, corresponding to the life and death of the Maize God, thus became a metaphor for the royal life cycle. The roots of this metaphor lie in the culture of simple maize farmers. It bound Maya society together from the lowest to the highest ranks in a form that was accessible and understandable to everyone.

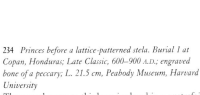

233 Lintel 24. Yaxchilan, Chiapas, Mexico, Temple 23; Late Classic, c. 726 A.D.; limestone; H. 110.5 cm, W. 80.6 cm, D. 10.1 cm; London, The British Museum
This Maya masterpiece depicts the queen K'abal Xook sacrificing blood from her tongue with a barbed cord, while her husband Itzamnaaj Balam holds out a torch to offer her light. The scene is obviously taking place in a dark temple room or at nighttime. A basket at the woman's feet contains strips of paper to catch the sacrificial blood.

234 Princes before a lattice-patterned stela. Burial 1 at Copan, Honduras; Late Classic, 600–900 A.D.; engraved bone of a peccary; L. 21.5 cm, Peabody Museum, Harvard University
The central scene on this bone is placed in a quatrefoil frame, which in Maya art defines the portal between the human world and the underworld. Through the portal we see an altar in front of a lattice-patterned stela, to the left and right of which stand two dignitaries, possibly unidentified early kings of Copan. The lace or lattice patterns found on stelae and other stones was part of the ritual used to celebrate the end of a time period.

235 Royal ball game. La Corona, Peten, Guatemala; September 13, 726; limestone; H. 26.7 cm, W. 43.2 cm. D. 6.7 cm; Chicago, Chicago Art Institute (Kerr 2882)
One of the many titles conferred on the kings was that of *aj pitz*, "ballplayer." Public monuments depict kings as ball players dressed in thick, protective leather clothing and crowned with an extravagant headdress. Here a subject lord of Calakmul has thrown himself on the ground, reaching out his arm to hit the ball. An unknown opponent stands opposite him; two steps in the background indicate that the scene is taking place in a ball game court.

236 *Stela E. Quirigua, Guatemala, Main Plaza; January 20, 771; sandstone; H. 7.25 m*
Stela E is the highest stela in the whole of the Maya region, standing 7.25 m high. The erection of this 30-ton monolith must have been a major technical and logistical feat. The gigantic proportions of the Late Classic Quirigua monument reflect the importance of the city after its king, K'ak' Tiliw Chan Yoaat, had raided Copan in 738 A.D. and beheaded the local king, Waxaklajuun Ubaah K'awiil. Ironically, the ruler of Copan had actually helped K'ak Tiliw to gain power 14 years earlier, so this belligerent act in Quirigua was actually a betrayal of a former supporter. Stela E, seen here in a historic photograph by Alfred Maudslay, is a monumental portrait of K'ak Tiliw as a proud victor displaying all the signs of his power.

237 *Bird Jaguar dancing. Yaxchilan, Chiapas, Mexico, Lintel 3, Structure 33; c. 760 A.D.; limestone; H. 94 cm, W. 83 cm, D. 40 cm; in situ*
The king's activities included performing dances in opulent clothing on the occasion of important festivals and anniversaries of historical events. Many lintels, particularly in the city of Yaxchilan, depict royal dances featuring Itzamnaaj Balam and his successor, Bird Jaguar IV, in divine clothing and with numerous attributes after which these dances were named. This lintel shows Bird Jaguar IV on the day of his enthronement, April 29, 752. One of his wives, Great Skull, holds out a holy bundle to him while he prepares for the dance with the K'awiil scepter.

238 *Traders and translators at the court. Provenance unknown; Late Classic, 700–750 A.D.; clay, painted; H. 17.1 cm. dia. 14.3 cm; private collection (Kerr 1728)*
The subjects depicted on polychrome painted vessels often included palace scenes. The rolled-up curtain above the scene and the throne indicate that we are inside a palace. Two traders have come and are offering bundles of their wares. A scribe and a *chilam*, "interpreter," squat on the floor in front of the traders from afar. King K'inich Laman Ek' of Motul de San Jose is seated on the throne. Behind him stands one of his courtiers in a relaxed pose with a cigar in his mouth and a torch for lighting it in his right hand. The text indicates that the people gathered here are negotiating the price of the goods.

There were many occasions when the kings appeared as gods, sacrificed blood and performed rituals. The end of the major time periods, such as the 20-year K'atun, and also the five and ten year periods, were celebrated with great feasts. In most cities, at the end of a K'atun the kings erected a stela with an altar before it (ill. 236). The erection of the stela (*tz'apaj u lakamtuunil*), a ritual described as *k'al tuun*, "binding the stone" (ill. 234), and the shedding of blood or burning of incense on an altar (*chokwaj ch'aaj*) were rituals which reenacted mythical episodes, in which the gods set the universe in motion.

Life at court

The king spent most of his life in the palace. Although it is difficult to establish the former function of buildings from their remains, finds of polychrome painted pottery do give an insight into life at court (ills. 227, 238). Many of the items were made in palace workshops for the court and illustrated scenes such as the paying of tributes, the arrival of vassals, preparations for dances and the activities of court staff, including dwarfs and jesters (see Prager, p. 278 ff.), whose task was to entertain the king and his important guests. Tribute scenes show the king seated on a sumptuous throne covered with jaguar skin. Vassals kneel before him holding out bundles of fine materials, feathers and bags of cacao beans (ill. 238). The employees of the court also included *aj tz'ib*, "scribes," who compared the goods being handed over with their list of tributes. Such scenes give a rare insight into the economics of the Maya states and show that one of the king's most important activities was that of increasing his personal wealth as well as that of society as a whole. To this end wars were waged and neighboring states overthrown. The rulers of besieged states were taken prisoner and, in many cases, kept as hostages. They were occasionally released, sent back to their homes and obliged to pay regular tributes (ill. 239). A subtle form of hostage taking was the establishment of residences for the sons and other family members of overthrown rulers in the victor's capital. Officially, the foreign nobility were used as messengers and envoys of the overthrown city-states, but in reality they guaranteed their lives to prevent further rebellion and to make sure that tributes were regularly paid. Some of the large palaces in cities such as Tikal and Calakmul are thought to have served as residences for conquered royal families. It is possible that the offspring of foreign nobility were brought up in the victor's court so that, when an heir to the throne was required in the vassal state, they could be sent back to their birthplace but would still maintain their links.

The royal palaces were also used for gatherings and celebrations, such as the sealing of marriage contracts between children from different royal houses,

239 *Panel 3. Piedras Negras, Peten, Guatemala, Structure O-13; 782 A.D.; limestone; Guatemala City, Museo Nacional de Arqueología y Ethnología (Kerr 4892)*
This panel, set into the wall of Temple O-13 at Piedras Negras, was a tribute from Ruler 7 to Ruler 4. The inscription ends with the description of a fire ritual, carried out in 782 at the latter's tomb. The scene shows the celebration of the K'atun anniversary of the accession to the throne of Ruler 4 in 749. The king is seated on a

decorated throne surrounded by dignitaries and visitors. One of the visitors is King Yoaat Balam II of Yaxchilan, who seems to have been a vassal of Piedras Negras and for that reason was modestly concealed in later Yaxchilan inscriptions. Provincial governors, scribes and scholars are seated on the floor in front of the king. The pottery vessels standing between them probably contained cacao which was offered in celebration of the event.

240 *Text from the Tablet of the 96 Hieroglyphs at Palenque*
Our knowledge of the dynastic history of the Maya, and the birth and enthronement of their kings, has been obtained from hieroglyphic inscriptions. However, not all the texts are as easy to understand as the inscription on the so-called Tablet of the 96 Hieroglyphs, which was found at the foot of the tower of the palace in Palenque. It tells of the opening of a wing of the palace in Palenque (the "house with the white skin") under K'inich Janaab

Pakal I and the enthronement of three of his successors on a throne installed in this wing. The inscription ends as usual with a dedication, which also quotes the name of the artist who carved the relief for King K'inich K'uk' Balam in 783 A.D.

on day 12 Ajaw/
8 Keh [on the day 9.11.0.0.0 in the Long Count, on October 11, 652 in the Julian Calendar]

completed/
the 11th K'atun (20-year) period

under the supervision of/
K'inich Janaab Pakal I

He of the five pyramids/
divine King of Palenque

11 days, 1 Winal/
and 2 Tun later

it was on/
day 9 Chuwen

9 Mak [on the day 9.11.2.1.11 in the Long Count, on November 1, 654 in the Julian Calendar]/
fire entered

[into] the house with the white skin [House E of the palace]/
in the building of

K'inich Janaab Pakal I/
the king, who was five 20 year periods old

And then/
17 days, 4 Winal

8 Tun/
and 2 K'atun later,

it was on/
day 5 Lamat

6 Xul [on the day 9.13.10.6.8 in the Long Count or May 30, 702 in the Julian Calendar]/
he was seated

into kingship, Ox-?/
K'inich K'an Joy Chitam II

divine king of Palenque./
He acceded to the throne

[in the] house with the white skin./
And then,

14 days, 15 Winal/
and 19 Tun later,

it was on/
day 9 Ik'

5 K'ayab [on the day 9.14.10.4.2 in the Long Count, on December 30, 721 in the Julian Calendar]/
he acceded to the office of king,

the lord of the family(?)
K'inich Ahkal

Mo Naab III,/
divine king of Palenque.

He acceded to the throne/
[in the] house with the white skin.

And then/
5 days, 14 Winal,

2 Tun/
and 2 K'atun later,

wedding celebrations, receiving state visits and supplicants, and convening meetings between the leaders of groups of noble origin. As administrative centers, it is likely that the palaces were also the headquarters of officials, military commanders, stock-keepers and other subordinates.

The rise of Tikal

We do not need to examine each of the 50 or so small states in detail in order to gain an impression of the history of the Lowlands. It is sufficient to focus on the two superpowers, Tikal and Calakmul, whose politics and power network influenced the fate of the entire Lowlands a great deal more than any other kingdom.

A great deal of research has been carried out on the dynastic history of Tikal, which confirms that it was already one of the leading powers in the Lowlands by the end of the Preclassic period. The founder of the royal dynasty of Tikal, Yax Eeb Xook, lived in the second half of the 1st century and was buried in a richly decorated grave in the North Acropolis. His immediate successors are unknown and did not leave any inscriptions behind. The oldest stela in Tikal, Stela 29, is dated 292 A.D. and shows a ruler in full regalia on the front (ill. 241). Although the inscription following the date can no longer be deciphered, the depicted king is probably the ruler Siyaj Chan K'awiil I. He is associated with another, smaller stela in nearby El Encanto, which is dated just a few years later. An inscription on a piece of pottery, which was made at least two centuries later, names Siyaj Chan K'awiil I as "the 11th successor" of Yax Eeb Xook. This indicates that there must have been nine rulers between the first king and Siyaj Chan K'awiil. So far, researchers have been unable to discover the names and histories of these rulers.

In 317 A.D., it looked as though the male line had been interrupted, as the celebrations at the end of the *K'atun* 8.14.0.0.0 were organized by a woman. Her name, Une Balam, Baby Jaguar, was the same as that of a local goddess. The 13th ruler of Tikal was K'inich Muwaan Jol. Very little is known about his rule, except that he was the father of the next king of Tikal and probably died

in 359 A.D. His son and successor, Chak Tok Ich'aak I, is the best known of the early rulers of Tikal. After coming to the throne in 360 A.D., he ordered a number of important building projects to be carried out in Tikal. As well as considerably expanding the Mundo Perdido complex, one of the two ritual centers in the area, he also oversaw the construction of a large palace (see. Harrison, p. 222 ff.), from which the Central Acropolis later developed. The stelae in relief originating from the time of Chak Tok Ich'aak I are sculptural masterpieces, and the pottery from the same period reflects the skills of the artists and the wealth of Tikal during his reign. Chak Tok Ich'aak I ruled over the largest and most advanced of all the Maya cities. Part of the great success of Tikal can certainly be attributed to its trade relations with the highlands of Guatemala and central Mexico.

The takeover by Teotihuacan

Links between Tikal and central Mexico changed suddenly, however, when in 378 A.D. a group of people from Teotihuacan "arrived" in Tikal under the military leadership of a nobleman from Teotihuacan, always referred to in Maya inscriptions as Siyaj K'ak', "Born of fire." This arrival is depicted on Stela 31 at Tikal alongside the death of King Chak Tok Ich'aak I, indicating that it must have been a violent event. As a result of these dynastic changes, a new dynasty was established in Tikal inspired by Teotihuacan (see Martin p. 99 ff.).

The new ruler, Yax Nuun Ayiin, is believed to have been the son of a leading dignitary of Teotihuacan and a woman from the Tikal nobility. The artistic works from this period in Tikal, particularly pottery and architecture, reflect the enormous influence of Teotihuacan on the community. During the years following the takeover of Tikal, the city initiated far-reaching changes, which also affected other parts of the Lowlands, such as Uaxactun, situated just 20 kilometers (12 miles) north of Tikal. The local rulers were apparently superseded on the same day as those from Tikal by a dynasty having friendly relations with Teotihuacan. New rulers also came to power in more distant places such as Rio Azul, Bejucal and possibly Copan. Control

it was on/
day 9 Manik'

15 Wo [9.16.13.0.7 in the Long Count or March 4, 764 in the Julian Calendar]/
he was seated into kingship,

who with the bone spirit companion,/
he, a player of ballgames,

K'inich K'uk' Balam II/
divine king of Palenque.

He acceded to the throne/
[in] house with the white skin.

An then,/
1 K'atun later,

it was on/
day 7 Manik'

during the month of Pax [9.17.13.0.7 in the Long Count or November 20, 783 in the Julian Calendar]/
an end came

to his first K'atun/
as king,

he with the bone spirit companion,/
the player of ballgames

Head of the family (?)/
K'inich K'uk' Balam I

Head of a K'atun,/
the first in the world

He is the son of/
(?)

K'inich Ahkal/
Mo'Naab III

divine king of Palenque;/
he himself is

the child looked after/
by (?) lady – the

Lady Saj Hu./it was 7 days

after day 13 ajaw/
13 Muwan [on day 9.17.13.0.0 in the Long Count or November 13, 783 in the Julian Calendar]

[when the] 13 Tun [had ended]/
an end came to

his first K'atun as king./
He sculpted the precious stone,

Uut ajaw/
k'uhul-(?)-(?)-tan [name of the artist?]

It [the hieroglyphic relief] was erected under the supervision of/
in the 5th K'atun of

K'inich Janaab Pakal./
This

marked the end of one K'atun/
in the office of king.

of these outlying areas was placed under the supervision of Siyaj K'ak and the Teotihuacanos.

The two stelae erected during Yax Nuun Ayiin's lifetime are very different from earlier rulers' representations. They show the king from the front, seated and dressed in robes and a headdress of Mexican design. Yax Nuun Ayiin was the representative of Teotihuacan's important influence up until his death around 410 A.D. Even the adornments of his burial chamber, which was comparatively large even for a ruler, reflected his origins outside the Lowlands.

This form of self-portrait changed when his son Siyaj Chan K'awiil II came to power. He tried to re-establish links with the Maya traditions of earlier rulers. As he was only related to the founder of the dynasty on his mother's side, he gave special importance to sculptures to depict this line of his forebears. One of his politically most important projects is the erection of Stela 31, which summarizes the entire history of Tikal and portrays him in full regalia on the front, while his father is depicted on the side in the uniform of a Teotihuacan warrior.

Turbulent times – wars and dynastic crises in Tikal

Siyaj Chan K'awiil II ruled Tikal from 411 to 456 A.D. and was succeeded by his son K'an Chitam in 458 A.D. Little is known about K'an Chitam's rule, apart from the fact that one of the first military campaigns to be recorded in inscriptions was probably conducted under his aegis. Military conflicts had been waged prior to this time, but they were now more intense and politically explosive and so became a subject to be recorded in written inscriptions. This military campaign could have been a reaction to the far-reaching changes taking place in Tikal and a large part of the Lowlands in the second half of the 5th century in terms of power structures and their economic causes. The changing size and quality of the Tikal stelae indicate that after the erection of the final monument of the Preclassic period, Stela 40 from 468 A.D. (ill. 242), there were no more resources to realize any really ambitious projects involving self-portraiture. The son of K'an Chitam, Chak Tok Ich'aak II, erected comparatively small, poorly executed stelae. His rule ended with the unmistakeable sign that Tikal no longer held uncontested supremacy in the

241 *Stela 29, the oldest known stela in the Lowlands. North of Temple III, Tikal, Peten, Guatemala; July 8, 292 A.D.; limestone; H. 205 cm, W. 64 cm, D. 32 cm; Tikal, Museo Sylvanus G. Morley*
Stela 29 bears the oldest date of all the inscriptions found in controlled excavations in the Lowlands. Older inscriptions have been found on other objects, but their precise origin and archeological context are unknown because they were plundered. The front portrays an unknown king, perhaps King Siyaj Chan K'awiil I, looking to the right with a lavish headdress and a divine mask in his left hand. The back bears the dates, reading from top to bottom, 8 Bak'tun, 12 K'atun, 14 Tun, 8 Winal and 15 K'in which correspond to July 8, 292 A.D. This could have been the date on which the ruler came to the throne.

242 *Stela 40. Tikal, Peten, Guatemala, west of the front of Structure 5D-29; June 19, 468 A.D.; limestone; Tikal, Museo lítico*
Stela 40, discovered in August, 1996 in Tikal, is the most recent monument found in Tikal in the highly detailed, baroque style of the Early Classic period. The front depicts the 17th king of Tikal, K'an Chitam, clasping a ceremonial staff, symbol of his royal authority, in his left hand. The two narrow sides of the stela portray his parents: his father, Siyaj Chan K'awiil, on the left and his mother, Lady Ayiin, on the right. On the back (not shown here) is a long hieroglyphic text describing the birth of K'an Chitam in 415, his accession to the throne in 458 and the erection of the stela in 468 A.D.

Lowlands. One of the kings of the aspiring kingdom of Yaxchilan on the Usumacinta river waged a war against Tikal in 508 A.D., during which Yaxchilan took a member of the royal house prisoner. The King of Tikal died a few days later, and this is described on an altar in Tonina.

The death of the king marked a dramatic turning point for Tikal as there was clearly no suitable male heir. In 511 A.D. a girl, probably the daughter of Chak Tok Ich'aak II, was therefore appointed regent at the age of only six. The fact that the ruling dynasty decided to take this unusual step shows how desperately they wanted to maintain the dynastic line. Using the girl as a façade, members of the nobility maintained power during this period, one of whom was a military leader called Kalomte Balam. He had already made his mark in 486

A.D., during the previous king's lifetime, in a campaign against the ruler of Maasal (probably the archeological site of Naachtun). Kalomte Balam, whose family origins are unclear, portrays himself on Stela 12 of 527 A.D. as the "19th descendant," indicating that he had seized power in Tikal and forced the young woman, then aged 22, into the background.

However, Chak Tok Ich'aak also had a son, Wak Chan K'awiil. He was born in 508 A.D., the year of his father's death, and because of his tender age was at first not considered as heir to the throne. It was not until much later that he became king of Tikal, in quite an unusual way. Wak Chan K'awiil had been living in exile during his elder sister's reign and did not return to his birthplace until 537 to seize the power to which he was entitled as part of the male line.

Conflict with Caracol

In spite of this dynastic turmoil, Tikal remained a powerful player on the political stage. In 553 A.D., Wak Chan K'awiil appointed a new king to reign over the city of Caracol situated 60 kilometers (37 miles) south-east in modern-day Belize (ill. 244). Caracol had been occupied since the Late Preclassic period and had its own dynasty, whose founder Te K'ab Chaak had acceded to the throne in 331 A.D. Situated on a high plateau in the Maya Mountains, Caracol had access to valuable resources such as granite, slate, hematite and pine wood, which made it into a strategic, economically significant center. The new king, Yajaw Te K'inich, was the son of the previous ruler, K'an I. The declaration on Stela 6 and Altar 21 that his accession to the throne was the work of Wak Chan K'awiil of Tikal, indicates the strong political influence that Tikal wielded over domestic matters in Caracol. However, the bond between Caracol and Tikal was to be shortlived. During the same period, another kingdom situated between Tikal and Caracol, Naranjo, entered the sphere of influence of the important developing power of Calakmul, situated approximately 100 kilometers (62 miles) north-west of Tikal. It looked as though Caracol would soon not be able to prevent the powerful King of Calakmul from gaining power. A conflict developed in 556 A.D. between Tikal and its vassal-state Caracol when Wak Chan K'awiil ordered a nobleman from Caracol to be beheaded. A similar fate befell Wak Chan K'awiil just a few years later. The inscription on Altar 21 of Caracol tells of a war waged against Tikal in 562. Although the inscription has been largely destroyed, sufficient details remain to indicate that this war was sparked by Calakmul, the new superpower in the Lowlands. The war against Tikal was probably a reaction to the conflicts between Tikal and Caracol in which Calakmul had intervened as Caracol's new protecting power. This military defeat interrupted Tikal's dominating role in the central Lowlands for

at least 130 years, and marked the start of a gloomy period for the city during which neither stelae nor buildings were erected.

The rise of Calakmul

The defeat of Tikal marked the start of a new period in the Lowlands, during which Calakmul became the center of an important network of dependent states (ill. 243). Situated just a few miles north of El Mirador, Calakmul saw itself as belonging to the traditions and heritage of the major Preclassic cities. Calakmul was a Preclassic center of considerable size; a city which, like Tikal, had survived the political turmoil that had marked the transition between the Preclassic and Classic periods (ill. 246). From a structural point of view, Calakmul differed from other states in the Lowlands in that it seems to have controlled a larger territory and had a more complex administration. The present-day ruined city of Calakmul was probably not the only, nor the oldest, capital of this state. The earliest references to the divine kings of Calakmul are to be found not in Calakmul itself, but in the recently explored city of Dzibanche, situated 150 kilometers (93 miles) north-east of Calakmul, where a hieroglyphic staircase depicts the campaign of conquest led by King Yuknoom Ch'een I towards the end of the 5th century (ill. 245).

The rulers of other cities made numerous references to the rapid rise of Calakmul to become Tikal's opponent. These references also mention the former's involvement in the domestic affairs of Tikal. The earliest indication of Calakmul's expansion is to be found in an inscription from the city of Naranjo, which gives an account of the enthronement in 546 A.D. of the local ruler, Aj Wosal, under the supervision of Tuun K'ab Hix of Calakmul. This intervention by one of Tikal's neighboring states in the line of succession must have been seen

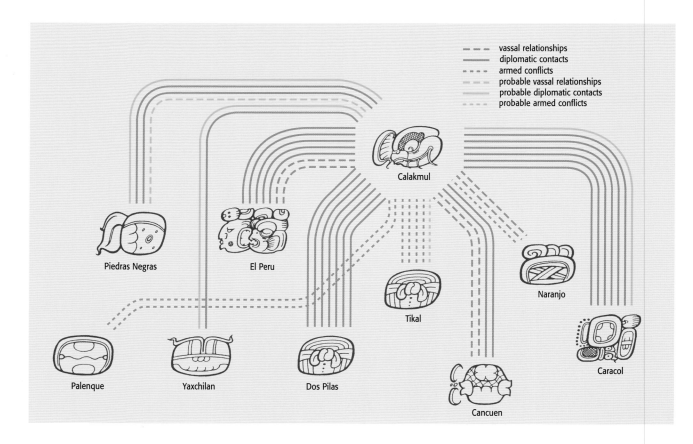

legend:
- – – – vassal relationships
- ——— diplomatic contacts
- - - - - armed conflicts
- ———— probable vassal relationships
- ———— probable diplomatic contacts
- - - - - probable armed conflicts

Piedras Negras

El Peru

Calakmul

Naranjo

Tikal

Palenque

Yaxchilan

Dos Pilas

Cancuen

Caracol

243 *The influence of the superpower Calakmul on other cities*
The diagram shows that Calakmul was involved in a network of relationships, which helped it to influence the entire Lowlands. No other Maya city in the Lowlands conducted such active international politics as Calakmul. While the relationships between most cities and Calakmul were of a peaceful, diplomatic nature, antagonistic relations existed with Palenque and Tikal which culminated in wars. Punitive campaigns were initiated against other cities that came into armed conflict with Calakmul, as Calakmul strove to prevent these cities from escaping from its sphere of influence.

244 *View of the excavation site of the Caana Pyramid in Caracol, Belize*
The city of Caracol lies on a limestone plateau in the south of the Cayo district of Belize. The 43 m high Caana Pyramid dominates one of the two central squares in the city, from which raised causeways extend over distances of up to 12 km into the surrounding countryside. Long rows of rooms on the different levels of the pyramid may serve as dwelling places for the royal family and their household. The buildings on the highest platform were adorned with stucco decorations with hieroglyphic texts telling of a war between Caracol and Naranjo.

245 *View of the Temple of the Owl (Structure 1) in Dzibanche, Quintana Roo, Mexico*
The earliest references to the kings of Kaan, as the rulers of Calakamul called themselves, were not found in the city of Calakamul itself but in Dzibanche, located far to the north-east. Excavations of the main building in Dzibanche, led by the Mexican archeologist Enrique Nalda, have unearthed a hieroglyphic staircase, which tells of the conquests of the ruler Yuknoom Ch'een I, possibly during the period from 479 to 490 A.D. Dzibanche may have been the seat of the so-called Kaan Dynasty during the Early Classic period.

as provocation by Tikal and marked the first of a series of conflicts over political supremacy in the Lowlands.

Under the rule of the king known as "Sky Witness" Los Alacranes also entered the political sphere of Calakmul when a local king was appointed in 561 A.D. by the ruler of Calakmul. "Sky Witness" also led Calakmul's successful campaign against Tikal in the following year, as a result of which Tikal was eliminated as a serious rival of Calakmul for the next 130 years. Further attacks on Tikal's allies helped Calakmul to extend its sphere of influence over subsequent years (ill. 247). References to an attack by Calakmul in 599 A.D. have been found in the city of Palenque, situated on the western border of Maya territory and linked with Tikal, as a result of which the city was sacked.

246 *Aerial photograph of Structure 2 at Calakmul, Mexico*
More than 6,000 buildings have been discovered and mapped by archeologists to date, making Calakmul the largest of all the Mayan cities. Structure 2, an enormous Preclassic platform, each side measuring over 120 m and standing 45 m high, is situated in the center of the city. Excavations in 1999 and 2000 unearthed the remains of a building in the innermost part of Structure 2 which dates from the early part of the Late Classic period; its lavishly decorated stucco façade is completely preserved. An extension was built onto the Preclassic pyramid in the Early Classic period to house three temple buildings. Further extensions took place in the Late Classic period.

Palenque was attacked a second time in 611 A.D. under the leadership of "Scroll Serpent," the ruler of Calakmul. The city's ruling class were killed off and links with the paternal line thus broken. This campaign clearly demonstrated the political ambition and efforts made by Calakmul to win supremacy in the Lowlands.

An alliance against Naranjo

Whilst Calakmul secured its influence in the western Lowlands by means of military campaigns and clever diplomacy, the death of King Aj Wosal, whom it had appointed in the east, marked the loss of a faithful ally. After Aj Wosal's death, a new ruler came to power in Naranjo who clearly wanted to sever links with Calakmul and break free from its hegemony. Caracol, which had become Calakmul's partner in the eastern Lowlands, began to initiate punitive campaigns in 626 A.D. The origins of Caracol's ruler, K'an II, meant that he already had close links with the royal family of Calakmul. He was the son of the ruler Yajawte K'inich, under whose aegis Caracol had severed links with Tikal and formed an alliance with Calakmul, and a princess who had married Yajawte K'inich in 584 at the age of 18. Although the princess' birthplace is not known, we have reason to believe that she came from the royal family of Calakmul, or at least a closely related family. In 626 A.D., K'an II attacked two settlements in the region of Naranjo. These attacks were only a foretaste, however, of the conquest that was to be waged five years later by Calakmul, as a result of which the rebellious King of Naranjo was taken to Calakmul and tortured.

Over the next few years, Naranjo faded into political insignificance. The lack of stelae and other monuments from this period indicates that the throne remained vacant or that the ruler did not possess sufficient power

247 *Major military campaigns in the southern Lowlands during the Late Classic period*
During the Late Classic period, Tikal was involved in military conflict with places which were all vassals of Calakmul. In 556 A.D., Tikal attacked Caracol, and subsequently Tikal was invaded by Calakmul in 562 A.D. Dos Pilas, whose ruling dynasty had severed links with Tikal, claimed power over Tikal. The rulers of Dos Pilas used the same emblem glyphs as those of Tikal. After Tikal's victory over Calakmul in 695 A.D., the network of states linked to Calakmul gradually disintegrated and, in order to secure his supremacy, Yik'in Chan K'awiil of Tikal attacked the cities of El Peru and Naranjo, former vassals of Calakmul, in 743 and 744 A.D.

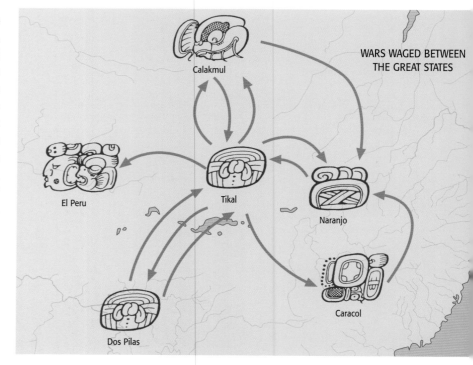

WARS WAGED BETWEEN THE GREAT STATES

Calakmul

El Peru

Tikal

Naranjo

Dos Pilas

Caracol

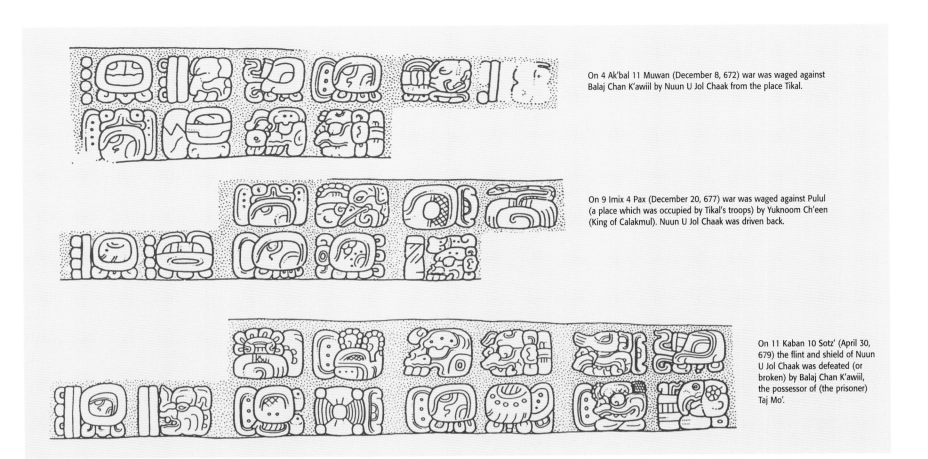

On 4 Ak'bal 11 Muwan (December 8, 672) war was waged against Balaj Chan K'awiil by Nuun U Jol Chaak from the place Tikal.

On 9 Imix 4 Pax (December 20, 677) war was waged against Pulul (a place which was occupied by Tikal's troops) by Yuknoom Ch'een (King of Calakmul). Nuun U Jol Chaak was driven back.

On 11 Kaban 10 Sotz' (April 30, 679) the flint and shield of Nuun U Jol Chaak was defeated (or broken) by Balaj Chan K'awiil, the possessor of (the prisoner) Taj Mo'.

and resources to immortalize his image on monuments. Naranjo's political ambitions were not completely eradicated, however. A stucco inscription from Caracol indicates that an unnamed ruler of Naranjo took revenge in 680 A.D., attacking Caracol and forcing the King of Caracol, a successor of K'an II, called K'ak' U Jol K'inich, into exile. This inscription proves that Naranjo had managed to shake off the yoke of Calakmul over the previous decades. If a city reported that it had been attacked by enemies, the aim was generally to justify a military attack of its own. The above-mentioned fragment has not been fully excavated, but it can be assumed that it ends with the victory of Caracol over Naranjo, as was customary in such cases. The fact that Naranjo did not enjoy a lasting victory is indicated by the lack of inscriptions and references on buildings.

248 *Description of the war between Calakmul, Tikal and Dos Pilas on Hieroglyphic Stairway 3 in Dos Pilas*
The five steps of Hieroglyphic Stairway 3 in Dos Pilas, completely covered with hieroglyphic inscriptions, were not excavated until 1990. They describe the different episodes in the conflict between the cities of Dos Pilas, Tikal and Calakmul. The chronicle of military campaigns ends predictably with the victory of Balaj Chan K'awiil of Dos Pilos over Nuun U Jol Chaak of Tikal in 679. Even though these accounts of wars seldom admit to defeats by the host state, this is done to make the final triumph seem even greater and to justify the annihilation of the opponent.

Dos Pilas – a second Tikal

The fate of Tikal during the 130 years after the defeat against Calakmul remains largely unclear. What we know about Tikal during this period has been obtained from inscriptions on pots and plates found in graves. These inscriptions indicate that kings continued to rule over Tikal. A ruler with the name of "Animal Skull" succeeded the defeated Wak Chan K'awiil. There are indications, however, that "Animal Skull" was not connected with the former Tikal dynasty, but was a puppet of the conqueror. "Animal Skull" could even have been a member of the royal family of Calakmul, and had been dispatched to Tikal. Although no details are known about Calakmul's authority over Tikal, it can be assumed that Calakmul succeeded in dividing the remaining members of Tikal's former royal family. The nobility of Tikal formed themselves into two groups, the first cooperating with the new hegemonic power and the second remaining loyal to the old royal dynasty. In the middle of the 7th century, the group connected with the former King of Tikal appears to have gained the upper hand in an internal power struggle, when in 648 A.D. a discontented or exiled branch of the ruling family settled in Dos Pilas, establishing it as the capital city of a new state. The new kings of Dos Pilas bore the title of "divine king of Mutal," like the kings of Tikal. The exiled challengers for authority over the state of Mutal sought protection from Calakmul, which had clearly lost control over Tikal, conquered 86 years earlier. They were probably hoping that Calakmul would also help them to regain power over Tikal.

In the middle of the 7th century, Nuun U Jol Chaak, a ruler who fought for independence from Calakmul, acceded to the throne in Tikal. Tikal was thus the victim of another attack by Calakmul at this time (ill. 248) resulting in the expulsion of Nuun U Jol Chaak from Tikal. Hieroglyphic texts from far-away Palenque refer to him in 659 A.D. as the companion of the powerful ruler K'inich Janaab Pakal. It is not known how long Nuun U Jol Chaak remained in

165

Palenque, but he appears to have reconquered Tikal and taken his revenge, and in 672 A.D. he even led a campaign of revenge against Dos Pilas. The course of history was thus reversed for a short time, and during the five-year period in which Nuun U Jol Chaak occupied Dos Pilas, the sovereign Balaj Chan K'awiil was driven out of the city. In 677 A.D., Calakmul came to the aid of the exiled Balaj Chan K'awiil and liberated Don Pilas. The final decisive battle took place two years later, during which Nuun U Jol Chaak was defeated by Dos Pilas and its protecting power, Calakmul. The fate of the King of Tikal is unclear, but the lack of later indications in the form of victory monuments and other images and texts indicates that he was either killed in battle or returned to the defeated state of Tikal as an inglorious loser.

Calakmul at the height of its power

The new victory over Tikal marked the high point of Calakmul's power. Under the rule of King Yuknoom the Great, who came to the throne in 636 A.D., Calakmul extended its influence to all parts of the Lowlands. The victory over Tikal was thus helpful in all respects. On the one hand, it meant that the main opponent for supremacy in the Lowlands had been removed and, on the other, the victory over Tikal was a clear sign of Calakmul's military prowess. Calakmul no longer needed to use military force to achieve its goals. It managed to make states into submissive, faithful vassals simply by threatening to use force.

One of the few states that dared to free itself from the yoke of Calakmul's supremacy was Naranjo, situated approximately 120 kilometers (75 miles) south-east of Calakmul. However, the lack of evidence of a separate ruling dynasty indicates that Naranjo's attempt to overthrow Caracol in 680 A.D. was unsuccessful and was followed by a punitive campaign. Then Calakmul sought to establish a new, independent dynasty in Naranjo which would pose no threat of rebellion. In 682 A.D., Balaj Chan K'awiil, the King of Dos Pilas and vassal of Calakmul, sent his daughter "Six Sky" to Naranjo where she married into one

of the noble families (ill. 250). In spite of his noble origins, her husband had no political influence. "Six Sky" ruled over Naranjo more or less on her own and even waged wars. Her son K'ak' Tiliw Chan Chaak was appointed heir to the throne at the age of six, thus establishing a male heir who also had links with Dos Pilas, a state loyal to Calakmul, through his mother. The new ruler was known as "Vassal of Calakmul" and his subsequent military campaigns were waged against many of the cities which had previously been owned by Tikal, including the city of Yaxha and the region of Ucancal, which had maintained links with Tikal since the Early Classic period.

The influence of Calakmul in these areas is clear and was accepted as normal. Yuknoom the Great supervised the enthronement of the ruler of the city of El Peru to the west of Tikal. In Cancuen, situated 250 kilometers (155 miles) south of Cakalmul, three successive generations of kings came to the throne as vassals of Calakmul. Yuknoom the Great also supervised the succession of the local ruler to the throne in Moral, approximately 100 kilometers (62 miles) east of Palenque, and there are even indications that Calakmul was recognized as a superpower in Piedras Negras, the largest settlement on the Usumacinta River (ill. 249). In 686 A.D., when Yuknoom the Great died, Tikal was thus practically surrounded by Calakmul's vassals and allies. However, Calakmul never actually managed to subjugate Tikal for any significant period.

249 *Panel 2. Piedras Negras, Peten, Guatemala; July 25, 667; limestone; H. 91.5 cm. W. 122 cm; Cambridge, Peabody Museum, Harvard University*
For a long time Piedras Negras was the most powerful city on the Usumacinta River, the most important trading route between the Gulf of Mexico and the central Lowlands. Towards the end of the Early Classic and at the beginning of the Late Classic period, Piedras Negras dominated the entire Usumacinta region. Panel 2, a sculpture dating from the reign of Ruler 2 (639–686 A.D.), shows the king with his young heir behind him and in front of him six kneeling vassals in military uniform. They are young Ajaws from Yaxchilan, Bonampak and Lacanha. The hieroglyphic inscription also refers to an event that occurred in 510 A.D., 150 years before the depicted scene, when one of the previous kings of Piedras Negras received the *kohaw*, "war helmet," from a foreign king.

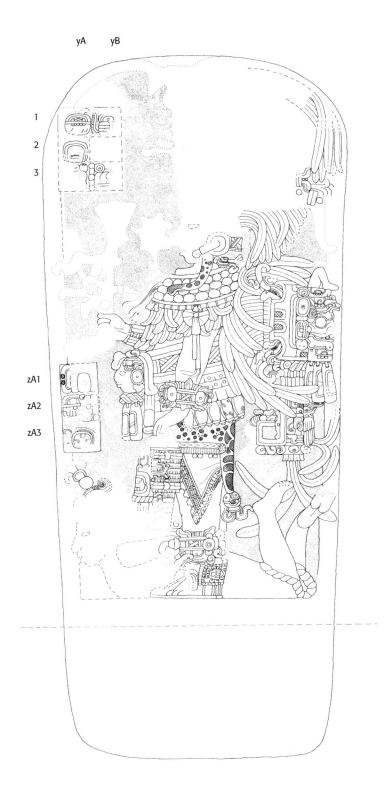

250 *Stela 24. Naranjo, Peten, Guatemala, in front of Structure C-7; January 22, 702; limestone; H. 192 cm, W. 87 cm; Guatemala City, Museo Nacional de Arqueología y Etnología*

This stela from the city of Naranjo is one of the few monuments depicting a woman, in the pose of a victorious warrior, standing on a prisoner's back. The woman is "Six Sky"; born in Dos Pilas, the daughter of the ruler Balaj Chan K'awiil, she was sent to Naranjo in 682 to marry one of the local noblemen and to establish a new vassal dynasty that would be loyal to Calakmul. She bore a son, who acceded to the throne when he was still a child, while she continued to pursue her political affairs in the background.

251 *Drawing of Stela 5. Tikal, Peten, Guatemala, north platform of the main plaza; June 10, 744; limestone*

Tikal's resumption of power began with the victory over Calakmul in 695 A.D. King Yik'in Chan K'awiil (734–c. 746 A.D.) successfully strengthened Tikal's sphere of influence, waging wars against former vassal states of Calakmul, including the city of Naranjo located in the east. On February 4, 744, he besieged Naranjo and took its king, Yax Mayuy Chan Chaak, prisoner. The defeated ruler is depicted here as a prisoner tied up at the feet of the richly adorned King of Tikal, who carries a large shield depicting a tutelary god or a god of war.

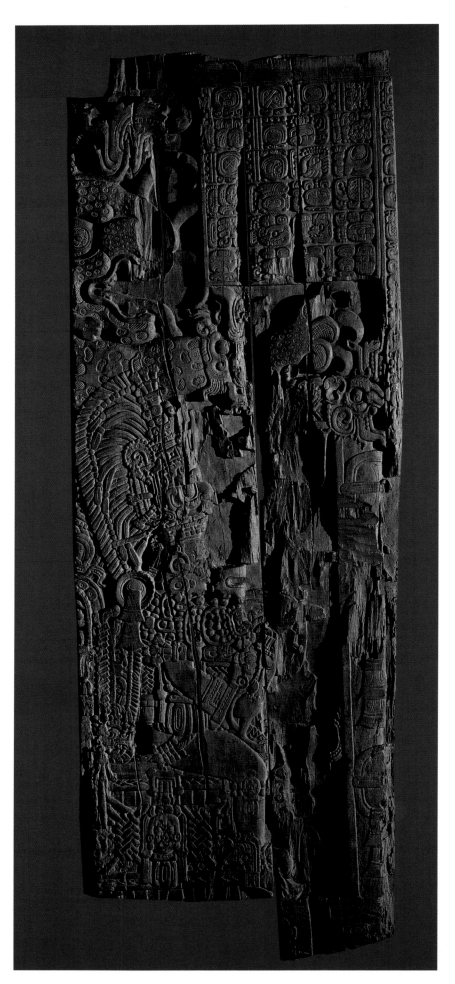

The renewed influence of Tikal

Neither Tikal nor Calakmul were able to integrate their conquests into their political sphere of influence in a really stable manner. Although the two superpowers were able to mobilize considerable armies, their infrastructures did not allow them to subjugate conquered states completely or to remove or change their rulers and bureaucratic systems. Instead, the conquering states tried to keep the costs of these operations to a minimum by taking over the local power structures and ensuring the cooperation of local representatives either by force or by clever diplomacy. However, this strategy proved to be fatally flawed for Calakmul's relations with Tikal. Jasaw Chan K'awiil, the son of Nuun U Jol Chaak, defeated by Calakmul in 679 A.D., was appointed King of Tikal in May, 682, apparently without opposition from Calakmul. He successfully defeated the successor of Yuknoom the Great, King Yich'aak K'ak' of Calakmul. The battle, laconically described on the wooden lintel of Temple 1 in Tikal as the "Defeat of the flint and shield of Yich'aak K'ak," marked a turning point in the history of the entire Lowlands.

During the years that followed, Jasaw Chan K'awiil organized a major building project in Tikal, the aim of which was to demonstrate the greatness of Tikal to the people. Many of the buildings were deliberately designed with elements taken from the art and architecture of Teotihuacan. Jasaw Chan K'awiil wanted his rule and his works to reflect the former Golden Age that has been shaped by Teotihuacan.

The consolidation of Tikal's authority

It is not clear what happened after the victory of Tikal against Calakmul. It is presumed that the city was ruled for several years by a new king, this time appointed by Tikal. While Tikal's victory did not lead to the complete decline of Calakmul, the latter was significantly weakened. The fact that Calakmul was referred to less and less in the hieroglyphic texts of other cities is evidence of this.

Jasaw Chan K'awiil had conclusively freed Tikal from the hegemony of Calakmul, but it was his son, Yik'in Chan K'awiil, the 27th ruler of Tikal, who brought Tikal's expansionist policy to its peak. Under his rule, Calakmul was once again the target of an attack in about 736 A.D. His aim, however, was not simply to defeat Calakmul, but also to conquer its allies. Two major campaigns during the following years were thus waged against the two main former allies of Calakmul, El Peru and Naranjo. The king of El Peru, "Jaguar Throne," was captured and his magnificent litter, with the statue of the city's god of protection, taken to Tikal (ill. 273). Six months later, Yik'in Chan K'awiil turned his attention to the east and attacked Naranjo. The ruler of Naranjo, Yax Mayuy Chan Chaak, was also carried off to Tikal. On one of the stelae dating from Yik'in Chan K'awiil's rule, the king is shown standing on his prisoner, with the latter crouching beneath him – a sign of extreme humiliation (ill. 251).

These two victories enabled Tikal to break away from encirclement by Calakmul's allies. No new stelae were erected in the city-states captured by Tikal for several centuries, indicating that Tikal was firmly in control of these areas. Tikal's new supremacy over the Lowlands was also displayed in its wealth and an unprecedented building boom. Many of the large temples and palaces of Tikal were built or completed under the rule of Yik'in Chan K'awiil, including the 65 meter (213 ft.) high Temple IV, the tallest building of the Classic period. This phase of expansion continued under the next two kings: the 28th ruler, whose name is unknown, and Nuun Yax Ayiin II, who was enthroned in 768.

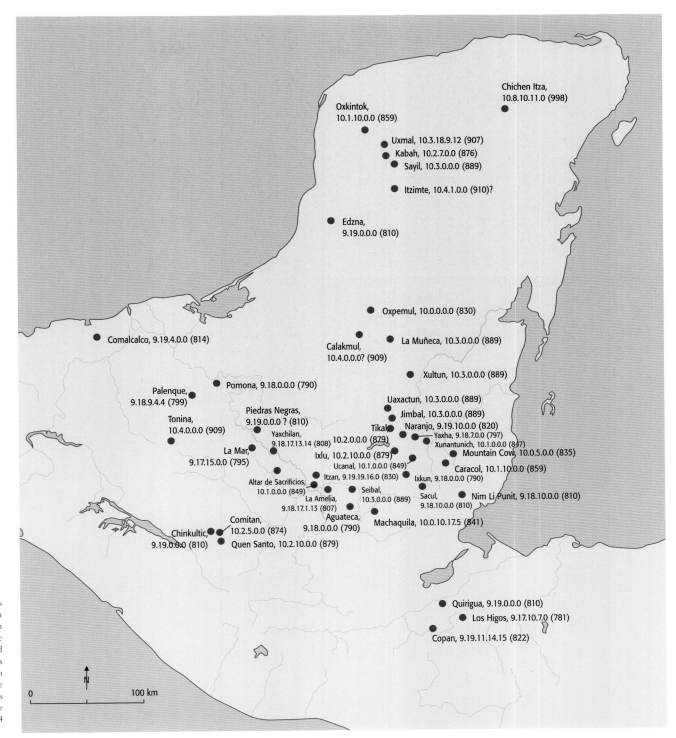

252 *Lintel 3 from Temple 1, Tikal, Peten, Guatemala; c. 735 A.D.; wood from the sapodilla tree (Manilkara zapote); H. 183 cm, W. 126 cm; Basel, Museum der Kulturen der Welt*
One of the key events in the history of the Lowlands was the victory of Tikal over Calakmul in 695 A.D. It marked the end of Calakmul's military supremacy and influence over other states. This wooden lintel from Temple 1 in Tikal shows Jasaw Chan K'awiil on a richly decorated throne covered with jaguar skin. The throne is placed on a portable wooden palanquin, a kind of outsize litter. A large jaguar figure is positioned behind the proudly posing king. This is probably a stuffed figure or one made from wood and animal skin depicting Calakmul's patron god. The litter probably belonged to the conquered King Yich'aak K'ak of Calakmul and was put on show in Tikal as valuable war booty.

253 *Map of the last dates recorded in different cities*
The last dates to be recorded in inscriptions in the cities of the Lowlands gives an impression of the period when Classical Maya culture collapsed. The end of the erection of dated monuments reflects the breakdown of the divine kingdom and its institutions. After the kings had disappeared, the cities were populated by a few families who lived like "squatters" in the broken-down buildings. The dates reveal that the collapse began in the west and that the cities in the center and on the outskirts of the Lowlands lasted the longest. The last date to be written in the Classic style was found on Monument 104 in Tonina in Chiapas (909 A.D.).

The role of the cities in the final phases of the Classic period

Despite recovering its reputation and strengthening its power, and despite a phase of internal stability and organized succession under its rulers, the beginning of the 9th century marked the beginning of a crisis in Tikal which would eventually lead to the city being abandoned. The last four rulers of Tikal were unknown princes who did not launch any significant building projects and only erected a few stelae. While the former kings had celebrated the end of each K'atun by building a stela, no monument was erected at the end of the 10th Bak'tun, which was an even more important cycle in the Maya calendar. The last

stela originating from Tikal is Stela 11, dating from 869 A.D. It contains the city's very last inscriptions and thus marks the end of the royal dynasty. Nearly all the cities of the Lowlands met with the same fate in the 8th and 9th centuries (ill. 253). The last inscription from Palenque dates from 799 A.D. Yaxchilan erected its last lintel a good ten years later, Dos Pilas was destroyed in 761 A.D., and Caracol's last monument is a rough stela dating from 859 A.D. A sculptor in Copal left behind an unfinished altar which had been commissioned in around 822 A.D. (ill. 255). The decline of Classic Maya culture spanned more than two centuries. The final inscription for a Classic Maya king was produced in 909 A.D. in the city of Tonina, situated in the extreme south-west of the Maya region. And

254 *Stela 12 depicting military triumph. Piedras Negras, Peten, Guatemala; September 11, 795 A.D.; limestone; H. 404 cm, W. 103 cm, D. 42 cm; Guatemala City; Museo Nacional de Arqueología y Etnología*

Stela 12 is a fine example of the late sculptural style of Piedras Negras. It is decorated on three sides. The narrow sides bear a long hieroglyphic inscription telling of several military campaigns conducted by Piedras Negras against the little known site of Pomona, also located on the Usumacinta River. The front portrays the prisoners from the conquered area of Pomona. The bound prisoners crouch at the feet of Ruler 7 of Piedras Negras, who is seated on a throne with his field marshal from La Mar on the left. The names of the bound prisoners, robbed of their insignia, are written in hieroglyphs. The leader of the defeated side, the Prince of Pomona, crouches beneath the throne of the king of Piedras Negras and touches his right shoulder with his left hand – a sign of submission and respect. This was the final victory of the ruler of Piedras Negras. In 808 A.D., the city was the victim of an attack by the ruler of Yaxchilan, K'inich Tatbu Skull III, from which it never recovered.

255 *Altar L, front. Copan, Honduras, northern end of Ball Court A-III; February 6, 822 A.D.; tuff*

Altar L in Copan is one of the last, if not the last, monument to be erected in Copan and documents the sudden collapse of the community. The front depicts the last ruler of Copan, U Kit Took', on the left seated on the hieroglyph of his name. His predecessor, Yax Pasaj, sits opposite him, also on the hieroglyph of his name. The hieroglyphic text between the two gives the date of the accession of U Kit Took' as February 6, 822. The combination of the portrait of a ruler with a depiction of his predecessor is frequently found in the art of Copan.

256 *Altar L, back. Copan, Honduras*

The back of the altar shows that it was never completed. The authority of the newly appointed ruler was so meager, it did not even last long enough for the carving of the altar to be completed. Only the outlines of the figures and a few isolated hieroglyphs were done before the artist abandoned his tools and disappeared. For a place like Copan, which had such a passion for sculptures, this is clear evidence of its decline.

so the political system of the Classic Maya culture, which had been successful for centuries, finally collapsed. The theories surrounding this spectacular fall fascinate researchers and laypeople alike. It is still not clear, however, what actually happened during the last 200 years of the Classic period in the Maya Lowlands.

The population increased steadily throughout the entire Classic period and a real population explosion occurred in the Late Classic period. For a time it was possible to provide for a population that had doubled, but there came a point when the environmental effects were so drastic that dry periods inevitably led to famine. The increasing erosion of the thin tropical soil, the clearing of the last remaining forests and the subsequent climate changes resulting in the depletion of the water table presented risks which made huge demands on all Maya society. The divine kings were unable to deal with these new ecological and logistical problems. Remains of skeletons show that deficiency diseases and infant mortality increased during the final phase of the Classic period.

The collapse of political order

More recent research places more emphasis on internal political factors. The collapse of the two antagonistic hegemonic blocs led to the dissolution of the entire political and social structure of Classic Maya society. As long as the major power blocs maintained a political balance, wars could be limited and calculated by the dominant powers. The weakening of the balance between the two power blocs led to a decline in interaction between different states. The Late Classic period was a time when the Maya states enjoyed greater independence, but they were also more isolated from one another. This is linked to the phenomenon whereby more and more cities which had previously been ruled by subordinate princes became the capitals of new small states. The political division in the Lowlands is also depicted in art which often portrays the king stepping down in favor of other princes and officials. The kings were no longer the only ones to immortalize their image in stone and some researchers have even referred to the rise of a middle class which laid claim to royal privileges.

Although a few states, such as Caracol and the city of Seibal on the Rio de la Pasion, benefited for a short time from the transformations of the Late Classic period (ill. 260), Maya society had changed so dramatically that it would have been impossible to return to the organizational structure of the Classic period. The tendency towards division and large-scale dissolution could no longer be prevented.

One of the events that may have triggered the collapse of the political system was the victory of Tikal over Calakmul in 695 A.D. Although it appeared to be just another military campaign, this victory could have undermined the hegemonic power system, which was based on the representation and acknowledgment of supremacy. Independent and allied states interpreted the attack as a sign of the vulnerability of the powers that dominated them and took advantage of the situation. This date can be seen as a turning point in the political structure of the Lowlands, as it marked the beginning of the political decline of Calakmul and a period of escalating wars. The victorious state of Tikal does not appear to have been able to create a new infrastructure to replace the one established by Calakmul. This led to the creation of a political vacuum which a number of competing states attempted to fill. It is not surprising that the last written records found in many places tell of wars between previously friendly neighbors. The collapse of the hegemonic system was probably accelerated by population pressure, ecological crises and climatic changes, resulting in the depopulation of outlying parts of the Lowlands at the end of the 9th century. A few years after the last kings had abandoned their palaces, the cities were once again absorbed by the jungle.

257 *Stela 10. Seibal, Peten, Guatemala, Southern Plaza north of Structure A-3; April 26, 849 A.D.; fine limestone; H. 217 cm, W. 129 cm, D. 35 cm; in situ*
Between 830 and 889 A.D., while cities were being abandoned throughout the rest of the Lowlands, Seibal became a center of great significance. Various researchers believe that the short-lived boom of Seibal was due to foreign influence, which was apparent not only in the pottery of this period but also in the features of the princes depicted on the stelae. However, the rulers of Seibal saw themselves as part of the Classic tradition and strove to create a political restoration. Stela 10 tells of the attempt by the ruler Wat'ul K'atel to establish a political group in 849 by inviting the kings of Tikal, Calakmul and Motul de San Jose to a celebration of the end of a time-period.

MARRIAGE DIPLOMACY – WOMEN AT THE ROYAL COURT

Stefanie Teufel

The most important contribution so far to research into the role of women in Maya society was provided in the 1960s by Tatiana Proskouriakoff (1909–1985), a Russian emigrant living in the USA who was the first to study the representation of women in Maya inscriptions. She discovered a sign in the form of a woman's head in hieroglyphic texts and identified it as an indication of a woman's name, which was sometimes connected with a designation of origin (ill. 259).

This fundamental research and subsequent deciphering of the hieroglyphs eventually provided insights into the position of women in the Maya royal courts.

For the Maya, the role of the woman corresponded to the traditional image of a society dominated by men. The women represented in images are usually portrayed as being subordinate to the sovereign and are depicted above all in their function as mother of the heir to the throne. The only traces of women considered as sovereigns in Maya history have been found in Palenque and Tikal. The fact that their position was unusual and challenging is reflected in the problems faced by their successors when trying to justify the throne inherited from their mothers. However, the position of women in this patriarchal society should not be underestimated. Monuments were often erected in their honor, they bore important titles and even held office. In depictions of the affiliation of their ruling sons, the mother's name featured alongside that of the father.

Women from the ruling classes played a particularly important role in the politics of marriage alliances. Not only did they establish family links beyond political boundaries, they also brought prestige, particularly if the bride originated from a

258 *Lintel depicting the ruler Yaxuun Balam. Yaxchilan, Chiapas, Mexico, Structure 21, Lintel 17; Late Classic, 770 A.D.; limestone, previously in color; H. 69.2 cm, W. 76.2 cm, D. 5 cm; London, The British Museum (Kerr 2886)*
As justification of his power and following the way his father had been portrayed, Yaxuun Balam (Bird Jaguar IV) had himself depicted in a self-sacrificial scene. He is seated on the right of the image on a seat decorated with feathers, attending a sacrifice. A woman, Mut Balam of Hix Witz, kneels on the left pulling a cord through her tongue. The reason for this mortification of the flesh is explained in the accompanying text, which tells of the birth of the son, Shield Jaguar, on 18.2.752 A.D. Although the woman depicted is not the child's birth mother, she supports her husband's right to succession as a representative of her place of origin.

more powerful place than the bridegroom. Very few inscriptions describe the actual marriage ceremony. The only hieroglyphic reference to marriage is generally in the form of "wife of" or the description of the ruling son's origins.

The well-preserved inscriptions from places in Yaxchilan on the banks of the Usumacinta River and Naranjo in eastern Peten give an exemplary insight into the strategically planned marriage politics of the Late Classic period.

Before the middle of the 7th century, a marriage marked the coming together of two previously autonomous powers on the banks of the Usumacinta River, which have become known as Yaxchilan. The region developed considerably under the rule of

Itzamnaaj Balam II, the son born of this alliance. This is reflected above all in the extensive building program with depictions of his victorious acts. This sovereign was involved with several women, including a noblewoman from the once influential city of Calakmul. They had a son, Yaxuun Balam IV, who only acceded to the throne 11 years after his father's death in 751. Various hypotheses have been put forward to explain this late accession, such as conflicts with Dos Pilas and domestic disputes. It is likely that his origins prevented him from becoming king earlier, as his mother was never mentioned during his father's lifetime and her place of birth was closely connected with Dos Pilas.

| first divine woman | Lady Ik'-Skull | Lady of the divine headdress | princess of Calakmul | eastern empress of war |

259 *Hieroglyphs representing the name of the woman called Uh-Chanil. Detail of Stela 10 at Yaxchilan, Chiapas, Mexico; Late Classic, 766 A.D.*
The series of names depicted here shows a woman's head, which indicates that it is a woman's name, and the word *ixik*, woman. The second hieroglyph gives her personal name. The nickname Ik-Skull was given to her by researchers, but her real name was probably *Ixik Uh-Chanil*. These are followed by various titles such as *aj k'uhul hu'un*, "possessor of the royal headband," and indications of her origin as the female *ajaw*, "queen" or "princess," of Calakmul. Lady Ik-Skull is recorded in the annals of Yaxchilan as the mother of the famous ruler Yaxuun Balam or Bird Jaguar IV.

Yaxuun Balam IV therefore had to act cleverly in order to gain power. He married a woman from Yaxchilan and appointed the son born of this marriage as his successor. However, he increased his power not only with the help of influential people within his own state, but extended it further through victorious wars and marriages with women from other regions. Yaxuun Balam IV insured that he would be confirmed as the legitimate successor and upholder of the dynastic line, even outside his own state, by having a woman from Hix Witz depicted as conducting a blood sacrifice while his son was being born. This made it clear to the outside world that Yaxuun Balam IV was connected with women from other royal dynasties who assisted him during important family and religious events (ill. 258). He gained another ally by marrying a noblewoman from Motul de San Jose, the capital of a small state in the immediate vicinity of the great power of Tikal, which had once been involved in a war with Dos Pilas. When he died, his son Itzamnaaj Balam III used the same marriage policy to form alliances. He married a noblewoman from Bonampak in order to strengthen old friendships and obtain support in his numerous military campaigns.

Naranjo was the capital of an influential state to the east of the Peten. In 642, the city was opposed by Caracol and became involved in a war with this powerful city. Some researchers believe that it was sparked by the marriage between a noblewoman from Naranjo and an important figure from Tikal, the arch enemy of Caracol, as Naranjo eventually became one of Tikal's allies. This war overshadowed the history of Naranjo to such an extent that hardly any monuments were erected during this period. It was not until 40 years later that the city regained its former standing, when the ruler of Dos Pilas took advantage of the opportunity presented by the defeat of Naranjo. He married a woman from the immediate vicinity, thereby establishing his supremacy in the region. In

682 A.D., he sent his daughter Wak Chan Ajaw from his second marriage to Naranjo to revitalize the dynasty. This was a remarkable strategy as it enabled him to establish a new base and demonstrate his power over his arch enemy Tikal. His daughter's name not only contained her noble origins but also the title of ruler over her hometown of Dos Pilas.

Her son became ruler of Naranjo at the age of five. The young boy was obviously not the actual ruler; it was his mother who dealt with all political affairs. The father appears to have been an unknown nobleman, who is barely mentioned in inscriptions. The ancestors of the rulers of Dos Pilas, and therefore also of Wak Chan Ajaw, were from Calakmul and it was they who eventually brought Naranjo under the influence of this great power which was constantly in conflict with Tikal. It was therefore only natural that her son saw himself as a "vassal of the king of Calakmul." In the 4th decade of the 8th century, Tikal prepared to retaliate and waged a war against Calakmul and Naranjo. Naranjo, which had blossomed under the reign of Wak Chan Ajaw and her son, who by this time had been ruling for several decades, declined in power and standing during the subsequent period.

As these examples show, marriage diplomacy was an important strategy for the aristocracy (as it is in contemporary Europe) in terms of pursuing political aims. It created domestic stability as well as securing new diplomatic allies.

260 *The so-called Yomop stela. Provenance unknown; Late Classic, c. 700 A.D.; limestone; H. 178 cm, W. 82 cm, D. 8.5 cm; private collection; © Galerie Mermoz*
It is often difficult to identify marriages and alliances between royal houses, because the exact provenance of a stela or inscription is unknown. This stela, in excellent condition, shows a woman dressed as the Goddess of Creation or the Moon Goddess, standing in the watery underworld surrounded by water lilies. According to the inscription, she is a noblewoman from Yomop, a place which was probably situated between Tortuguero and Tonina. The artist who created the monument came frtom Oxte K'uh, also mentioned in the inscriptions of Palenque. This confirms the assumption that the stela and the portrayed Lady Ix Ook Ayiin ("Lady Alligator Foot") stem from the western Maya Lowlands.

UNDER A DEADLY STAR – WARFARE AMONG THE CLASSIC MAYA

Simon Martin

Of all the misconceptions about the ancient Maya that dominated the first half of the 20th century, one of the hardest to understand today is their supposedly harmonious, peaceful nature. Maya monuments abound with displays of militarism, from the weaponry brandished by kings to the trussed bodies of the captives shown trampled beneath their feet. Painted murals and cylinder vases depict both panoramas of battles and the bloody reckonings that followed, the torture and execution of hapless prisoners (ill. 272). The idea that these were minor "raids," designed to seize captives for ritual sacrifice, has been swept away by a modern understanding that they are expressions of bitter inter-kingdom rivalry, with major implications for how we view Maya kingship and society.

Although these images provide an essential window into Maya conflict, it is only through the historicism of the inscriptions that we can recover its political context: the on-going power struggles, shifting alliances, treacheries, and misfortunes that characterize war the world over. If we are ultimately to understand Maya conflict, we must reach some view about its causes and objectives: why kings went to war and what they hoped to gain.

With the development of a political landscape crowded by distinct, territorially-restricted kingdoms, each directly abutting its neighbor and each ruled by a *k'uhul ajaw*, "divine lord," it is perhaps little wonder that Maya society saw frequent conflict. But we now know that in addition to simple neighborly

disputes, there were more complex regional processes at work. Powerful rulers sought to achieve "over-king" status, to expand their control over other kingdoms and turn rival kings into their vassals, sometimes at great geographic distance. Tikal and Calakmul were, if not the only, then certainly the most successful states involved in this wider geo-political game. There is good reason to believe that material enrichment was a key goal of these dynamic, but nevertheless enduring, political hegemonies. We know that tribute had a central role throughout recorded Maya history, with numerous scenes painted on vases showing the reception and accounting of bundled levies (see Reents-Budet, p. 252). While we must look for governing processes such as this wherever possible, we should keep in mind that the spark for individual wars might often be more emotional: personal insults, jealousies, or grudges that reached back through generations.

Some scholars believe that the Maya respected a certain code of conflict, at least during the Classic period (300–900 A.D.), and that commonly-agreed ethics prevented wholesale destruction of people and property. But with the onset of the calamitous 9th century, these chivalrous understandings are seen to evaporate, casting the Maya into the chaos of unlimited war. Manifested in a complex mix of ecological decline, demographic collapse and disintegration of royal authority, there is good reason to think that the drastically changed circumstances of this collapse period did indeed see violent times in the

261 *Lintel depicting the presentation of prisoners. Provenance unknown, probably Laxtunich, Chiapas, Mexico or La Pasadita, Peten, Guatemala; 783 A.D.; limestone with remnants of paint; H. 115.3 cm, W. 88.9 cm; Fort Worth, Kimbell Art Museum (Kerr 2823)*
King Itzamnaaj Balam III of Yaxchilan (769–c. 800 A.D.), seated on a throne inscribed with his name, receives a warlord, Aj Chak Maax, who presents him with three captives on the steps leading to the throne room. Their earrings have been removed and replaced with strips of paper as a sign of humiliation. This may be referred to in the text, which states that the prisoners were "adorned" for three days after their capture.

262 *The warrior king. Ucanal, Peten, Guatemala, Stela 4; November 26, 849 A.D.; limestone; Guatemala City; Museo Nacional de Arqueología y Etnología*
The archetypal pose of victory in Maya warfare showed the trampling of captives underfoot – the Maya equivalent to the Egyptian Pharaoh's smiting of his enemies. In this detail from a stela at Ucanal we see the feet of the successful king standing on his victim's body, meanwhile a lieutenant stands on the victim's head.

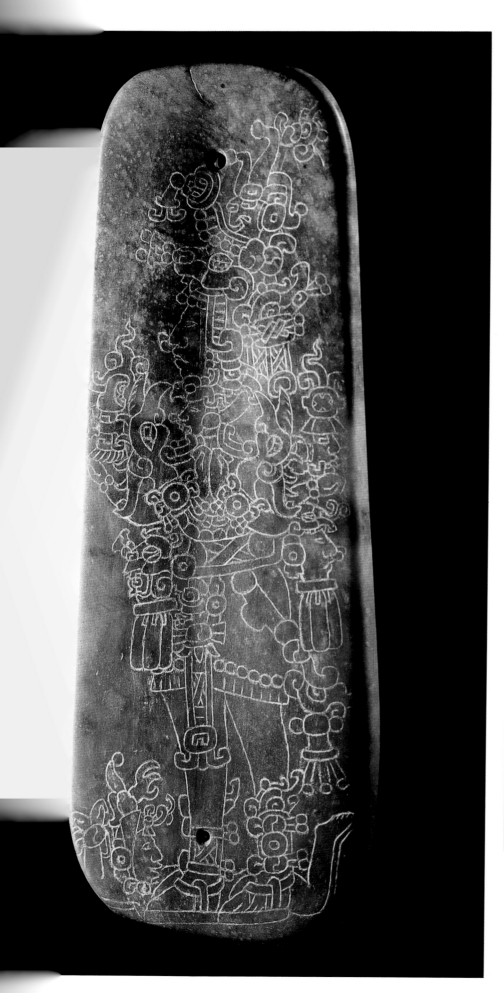

southern Lowlands. But this should not distract us from viewing the conflict of the Classic period as anything other than appropriate to its environment, as determined and ruthless as was necessary to achieve its aims. It may well be that vengeful dynastic vendettas, total destruction of cities and the enslavement of whole populations occurred throughout Maya history.

War depicted in Maya art

The earliest representations of captured prisoners date to the Late Preclassic, and we can take it that conflict played a role in the creation of the huge political centers of this era, cities such as El Mirador and Nakbe. By the time of the first pictorial representations of such conflicts in the Maya Lowlands, c. 300 A.D., a common pattern had emerged. While the public art of the Preclassic had concentrated on impersonal gods and cosmic themes, the shift to individual personality in the Classic period saw the ruler assume the idealized role of "warrior king." He is shown standing above or on top of his bound enemy, who is often identified by name glyphs in his headdress, or later by associated captions (ill. 263).

It was not until the 6th century that warfare finds a regular place within longer hieroglyphic inscriptions. This marks an important development in royal

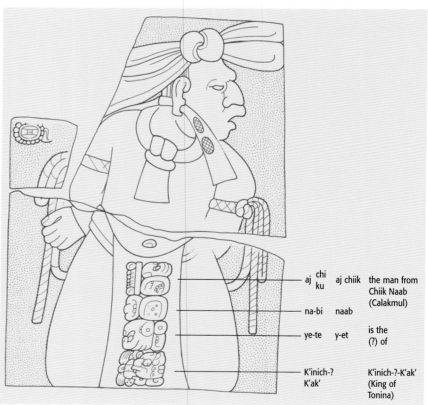

		the man from
aj chi ku	aj chiik	Chiik Naab (Calakmul)
na-bi	naab	is the
ye-te	y-et	(?) of
K'inich-? K'ak'		K'inich-?-K'ak' (King of Tonina)

263 *Humiliation of a prisoner. Region of Puerto Barrios, Izabal, Guatemala; September 17, 320 A.D.; jade; H. 21.7 cm; Leiden, Rijksmuseum voor Volkenkunde (Kerr 2909)*
With the emergence of the first dynastic monuments in the Maya Lowlands, around 300 A.D., we quickly see rulers cast themselves in the role of "warrior kings." Depictions of trussed prisoners at the ruler's feet, as seen on this famous "Leiden Plaque," become commonplace in the Classic era.

264 *Identification of prisoners. Sketch; Tonina, Chiapas, Mexico, Monument 153; Late Classic, 716–723 A.D.; limestone; H. 81 cm, W. 55 cm, dia. 7.5 cm; Tonina, Museo del Sitio*
It was important for the Maya to establish the identity of their prisoners. They usually inscribed the name, origin, position, and date of a prisoner offered as a sacrifice. These references can even be found on public sculptures.

THE GREAT WARLORD KIQ'AB' CONQUERS ENEMY PEOPLES

The Popol Wuj not only contains extracts on mythology and religion; it also deals with historical events from the point of view of the K'iche'. The passage below describes their military expansion and hegemonic strategies.

They hated Kiq'ab' and waged wars against him. He completely crushed and destroyed the valleys and areas of Rab'inal, Kaqchikel and Saquleew until they collapsed and gave in to him. If they refused to serve him, King Kiq'ab' had them killed. If one or two communities failed to pay tributes, he attacked them. They were forced to bring their tributes to Kiq'ab' and Qawisimaj. They were then incorporated into the lineage but were

an extremely powerful man to whom all cities paid tribute. The rulers fortified the exits to the gorges and the cities of all the other defeated peoples, and the guards served as soldiers' lookouts. Teams of guards were formed to watch these peoples "in case they returned to their former rulers."

When the people had finished their discussions, they marched to their posts declaring, "You are like our shield, like our proud line. Our walls and defenses, our courage and manhood will be likewise."

They then went to their posts, each among his people, as soldiers against the enemy.

They separated and set out as watchmen living in the mountains among the [conquered] peoples. "Go forth! This is now our land! Do not be afraid!

with bows and spear-throwers set out and the grandfathers and fathers of all the K'iche' dispersed throughout the mountains. Watchmen were positioned on every mountain and every hill armed with spear-throwers and arrows. They served as watchmen and soldiers. They were awake at dawn and did not even think of the gods. They blocked the exits to all the towns [...]

Each one set out for his mountain. Prisoners were captured and brought before Kiq'ab' and Qawisimaj and the princes and noblemen. The warriors continued to wage war armed with their bows and spear-throwers. They had become heroes and were esteemed and respected by their rulers when they surrendered their prisoners.

violently beaten and tied to trees where they were left inglorious and powerless. Cities were destroyed and razed to the ground within minutes.

Nobody was able to kill or defeat him. He was

If [enemy] soldiers come to kill you, inform me immediately and I will eliminate them." Thus spoke Kiq'ab' when he gave them orders in the presence of princes and noblemen. Warriors armed

265 *Meeting between a king of Naranjo and his vassal lords. Rollout of a polychrome pot; provenance unknown; Early Classic, 520–580 A.D.; clay, painted; H. 20.5 cm, dia. 19.0 cm; private collection (Kerr 7716)*
The King of Naranjo, Aj Wosal, is shown seated on a litter bedecked in jaguar skin. He is attended by lords carrying battle standards and, to the right, an effigy of Naranjo's patron god.

rhetoric, clearly fulfilling some new political need. Such records serve to fix conflicts in time and expand what can be said about the identity of the enemy. As one would expect, the great majority describe success (ill. 269), but just occasionally we are told of humiliating defeats. These always appear within a greater narrative, either as a means of highlighting success over adversity, or justifying aggression, or as part of wider histories explaining dynastic rupture.

How war was portrayed in hieroglyphic texts

Like most Maya texts, these references are formulaic in style, lacking overt color or descriptive detail. The type of military action involved, however, with the victim always clearly identified whether by personal name or specific locality, is precisely described.

One of the most enigmatic hieroglyphs is the "star war" (ill. 267). For all Mesoamerican cultures the celestial patron of war was not Mars but Venus, which the Maya knew as Chak Ek' or "Great Star." We get a strong impression of its malevolence in the Dresden Codex. Here various helical risings of the planet are depicted as varied personae of Venus, each spearing a victim below. In the Classic period, battles associated with stellar phenomena are marked by a hieroglyph showing a star from which a stream of liquid, water or perhaps blood, falls onto the earth below (ill. 267). Such actions mark the most dramatic of attacks, resulting in the deaths of kings and the fall of dynasties.

Another war glyph, *ch'ak*, meaning literally "to chop," appears in some texts as a reference to decapitation: *ch'ak ub'aah*, "his head was chopped." On other occasions, *ch'ak* describes an action against a place, and here it must have a wider

226 *Venus as the god of war. Dresden Codex, extract from page 49; provenance unknown, Late Postclassic period, 1200–1500 A.D.; fig bark paper coated with whitewash, painted; page: H. 20.4 cm, W. 9 cm; Dresden, Sächsische Landesbibliothek*
Venus was a frightening phenomenon for all Meso-american peoples. The appearance of this god in the heavens could signify death and destruction. The Postclassic Dresden Codex contains a table with calculations of the helical rising of Venus as the morning star, in which she is depicted as a divinity armed with a spear-thrower (note the hook-like object in the left hand) and spearing victims down on Earth with arrows.

"star war"   ch'akaj

och ch'een   puluy

jubuy u took' pakal   chukaj

267 *War hieroglyphs*
A number of different glyphic terms were used to specify the type of military actions that had taken place. Some refer to attacks on locations, like the famous but still undeciphered "star war." Others refer to the seizure of individuals or their defeat in field battles fought outside urban settlements.

meaning of "attack" or "destruction." In one such assault on Palenque, we are told that the patron gods of the city were *yalej*, "thrown down," suggesting a desecration of idols in the core of the city. A relatively uncommon form is *och ch'een*, "entered the cave." The word *ch'een*, "cave," is a recent decipherment, and seems to have a derived meaning of "town/city," either because settlements were symbolically, or literally, associated with particular caves; or because the word simply abbreviated the metaphorical couplet *chan ch'een*, "sky-cave," which referred to key population centers. One of the most descriptive forms of attack is based on the verb root *pul*, "to burn" (ill. 267). The iconic representation of conquest for Mexican cultures was a temple in flames, though it is unclear whether the Maya term referred to a similar destruction of elite shrines and palaces, or to a more general conflagration of the predominately thatched-roofed towns.

The most common war expression involves the term *chukaj*, based on the Mayan verb "to seize." The term *jub'uy*, to "bring down," seems to be the main description of field battles away from population centers. Here it is often applied to the *took' pakal*, "the flint and shield". While on one level this was clearly an emblematic device – a symbolic standard if you will – elsewhere in Mesoamerica this kind of paired form serves as a literary metaphor, and success over the enemy king's *took' pakal* may allude more directly to the defeat of his army.

The fate of prisoners

Like most pre-Columbian societies, the Maya placed stress on the capture of live enemies, their display and humiliation in the victor's city (ill. 275), followed in many cases by their torture and death (ills. 268, 269). Prisoner sacrifice can be said to have had its own temple – the stone ball courts found in the heart of all major Maya cities (see Colas/Voss, p. 186 ff.). These were always much more than arenas for sport, they replicated the ball court of the underworld, the setting for the central struggle between life and death in Maya myth. We might imagine that the defeated team symbolized the vanquished foe in the way that most team sports can be seen to mimic combat. In one rather macabre form of sacrifice, prisoners are shown bound into giant balls, then bounced down flights of steps to their death or grievous injury. Another fate that might await them was *k'uxaj*, "to be tortured or perhaps eaten." Ritual cannibalism is not

lance with point made of chert (*took'*)

strips of paper in place of jade jewelry: a form of humiliation

prisoner

report on the defeat of the King of Tonina

"war serpent" of Teotihuacan

unknown king of Palenque

flexible cotton shield

268 *The mythology of sacrifice. Tonina, Chiapas, Mexico, Monument 155; 688–715 A.D.; limestone*
On quite a number of occasions prisoners are said to have been *nawaj*, "adorned." This probably refers to the rags of strips of paper drawn through their earlobes, replacing their fine jade jewelry. However, sometimes this may refer to a more elaborate dressing of the victim. The captive shown here comes from the site of Anaite close by the Usumacinta River, and was probably seized by the Tonina king K'inich Baaknal Chaak around the year 700. He is bound at the arms and wearing eye decoration and flame-marked ear of a well-known jaguar deity. Although Maya lords regularly went into battle dressed as gods, the prominence of a myth that climaxes in the sacrifice of this same jaguar deity suggests that the captive has been specially prepared to re-enact his story.

269 *King and prisoner. Sketch of a wall relief; Palenque, Chiapas, Mexico, Temple XVII, c. 687 A.D.; limestone; Palenque, Museo del Sitio Palenque*
The depiction of prisoners being trampled by their conquerors is generally confined to the narrow format of monolithic stelae. Wider reliefs depict more naturalistic scenes and more sensitive portraits of the misery of prisoners. This relief represents a king of Palenque holding a serrated spear in one hand and a flexible shield, probably made of cotton, in the other. The Mexican war serpent forms part of his headdress, alluding to the great military prestige of distant Teotihuacan. The small text on the top right appears to refer to the defeat of the great rival of Palenque, the kingdom of Tonina, in 687 A.D.

unknown in Mesoamerica, though here it may have been reserved for the most heinous of offences (of which rebellion against one's "over-king" seems to have been one). In one text at Yaxchilan prisoners are said to be the "food" of local deities. In this way, war captives can be seen as necessary nourishment for the gods, who might wither and lose their protective powers without a steady supply of blood victims.

Arms and armor

Away from the grand strategies of divine kings, how were battles actually fought? We know next to nothing about the tactics of Classic Maya engagements, though both contemporary depictions and later sources suggest little in the way of formal organization (ills. 270, 271). Evidently the main weapon used was the thrusting spear. This consisted of a heavy shaft, seldom more than two meters (six feet) in length, topped by a large flint blade (ill. 271). This was a close-quarter, jabbing weapon not meant to be thrown. Sometimes the upper shaft is shown with a serrated edge, clearly designed to inflict additional saw-like injuries. Longer-range, projectile armory came with the *atlatl*, a spear-thrower that worked rather like a wooden sling. It was equipped with two finger holes for added grip and a notch that fitted the ends of long darts (somewhere between an arrow and a javelin in length). Modern studies have confirmed its impressive range and high degree of accuracy.

In Maya art the *atlatl* is most often associated with Mexican dress and seems to have been regarded as a specific import from there. The Maya depicted a variety of axes and clubs, and, while seldom actually shown, stone blades hafted onto wooden handles were clearly used in battle. A few images indicate that the Maya possessed "swords," wooden shafts edged with flint or obsidian flakes, much like those later used by the Aztec.

For protection, warriors were routinely equipped with either circular or square shields (the latter usually seen as Mexican in inspiration). They were evidently made of wood with coverings that included animal hide, their faces usually decorated with heraldic devices or the portraits of gods. Maya warriors wore protective clothing, though the highly decorative form often makes it hard to discern. Heavy rope bibs, perhaps made from twisted cotton or fibrous palm leaves, protected the chest, while close-fitting cuirasses of cotton or hide were also worn. Little of the headgear we see in Maya art seems overtly protective in function, concentrating as it does on elaborate visual displays that included animals in effigy or stuffed form, often spotted felines, deer and snakes, as well as ubiquitous splays of feathers. We know that the Aztec wore such encumbering garb in combat and that is certainly how Maya warriors are shown in narrative scenes of fighting.

Many rulers' portraits show them outfitted with Mexican, specifically Teotihuacan, costume and weaponry (ill. 269). They sought to cloak themselves in the symbolism of a foreign power whose military reputation deeply impressed the whole region. Most of all, Maya kings hoped to enlist the aid of Teotihuacan

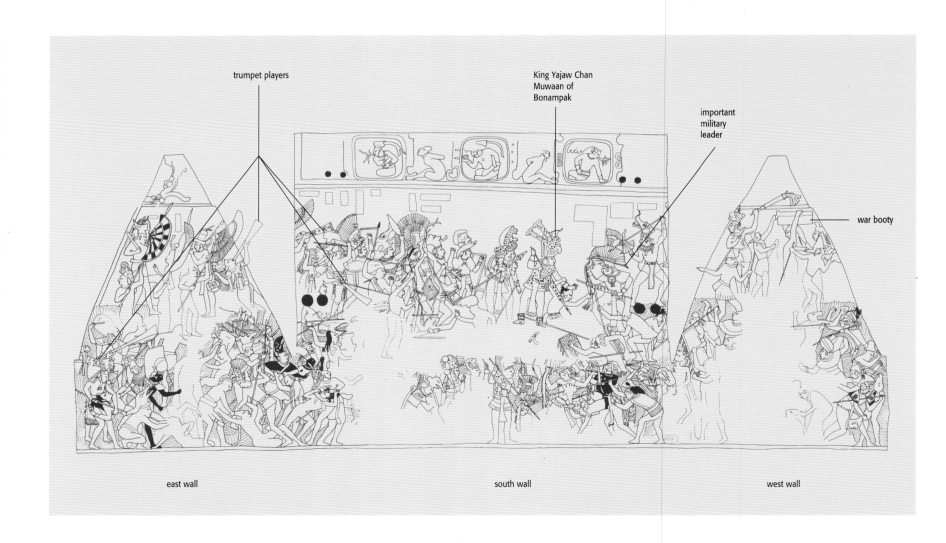

trumpet players

King Yajaw Chan Muwaan of Bonampak

important military leader

war booty

east wall

south wall

west wall

gods such as the war serpent *waxaklajuun ub'aah kaan*, a patron that had become linked to ideals of pan-Mesoamerican conquest and hegemony (see Martin p. 98–111).

Throughout human history, armed groups have used sound and image to boost the morale of their own fighters and intimidate those of the enemy.

271 *Battle scene. Rollout of a painted cylindrical vessel; region of Nebaj, Guatemala; Late Classic, 600–800 A.D.; clay, painted, H. 17 cm, W. 46,8 cm (Kerr 2352)*
Some of the most evocative scenes of a Maya battle are represented on cylindrical vessels from the region of Nebaj in Guatemala. They depict the splendor of the feathers and sumptuous textiles adorning the warriors as well as their practical accessories, such as protective leather or cotton jackets. Here we see warriors holding their spears downward in both hands so that they can attack their victims with maximum force.

270 *Battle painting from Bonampak. Drawing of the east, south and west walls of Room 2, Bonampak, Chiapas, Mexico; Late Classic, c. 790 A.D.*
A dense throng of warriors crowd this scene of battle painted over three walls of a room interior at the site of Bonampak. The conflict concerned is not securely dated, but took place around 790 A.D. At the extreme left we see three men carrying parasol-style banners, while others provide the necessary sound accompaniment, the blowing of trumpets and the shaking of rattles. Near the center we see the Bonampak King Yajaw Chan Muwaan taking a captive, while looking down from the sky is a collection of his ancestors and their own bound victims.

272 *The King triumphant. Extract from the south wall of Room 2 (digitally reconstructed), Bonampak, Chiapas, Mexico, Late Classic, c. 790 A.D.*
The capture of a high-ranking opponent was the climatic act of Maya war, whether depicted on carved monuments, painted vases or, as here, wall murals. We seen Yajaw Chan Muwaan, the victorious king, dressed in a jaguar skin jerkin with a "trophy head" (a decorative jade mosaic mark on this occasion) slung around his neck. A faint outline in front of his face is a cutaway view of his mask, demonstrating that he went into battle in the guise of a deity or ancestor. His prisoner has already had his fine costume stripped from him and his spear broken in two as he is brusquely grabbed by his hair and thrown to the ground.

From accounts of the Spanish conquest we know that Maya armies went into battle accompanied by the blowing of conch-shell trumpets and the beating of wooden drums and turtle carapaces (ills. 271, 272). The visual dimension was fulfilled by means of bodypaint, costumes and banners. Only a few images of the latter have survived, but in some we clearly see the use of cloth flags, boldly painted with gaudy colours and emblems. Occasionally, rather than being held, banks of square pennants were fixed into the rear belts of warriors, like those of samurai lords. Especially important were the feathered standards, clearly developed from the form of a parasol. Smaller parasols, when held in a downward position, were often symbolic of submission or defeat.

Divine protection

The Maya carried effigies of their gods, borne on elaborate litters, into battle. These patrons were essential participants in the action, part of an understanding of war that pitted divine powers against one another in just the same way as mortal warriors. The seizure of an opposing god's image led to its parading through the victor's capital in the style of human captives (ills. 273, 274). This is reminiscent of the Aztec, who are known to have held captive god effigies in a special temple. Here they were revered as sacred beings, now subordinated to the greater power of Aztec gods.

Cosmological phenomena provided a religious and conceptual underpinning to organized violence in Mesoamerica, yet we need not believe that it had a determining role; the relationship between ideology and pragmatism was always that of slave to master. When "star war" events are examined in detail, we find that only a few fall on truly relevant nodes of the Venus cycle. This suggests that whatever auguries were consulted or elaborate planetary motions charted, war was timed primarily to meet tactical rather than esoteric criteria.

The Maya conduct of war as reflected by archeology

The archeological remains of warfare are scanty and often equivocal. The bodies of common people, including slain warriors, are often poorly preserved in the tropical environment of the Maya region, leaving little information about casualties. Evidence for burning can be detected, but its cause is seldom apparent

273 *Festive war processions. Tikal, Peten, Guatemala, Temple IV, Lintel 3, after 746 A.D.; sapodilla wood; H. 176 cm, L. 205 cm; Basel, Museum der Kulturen*
A second lintel from Tikal Temple IV shows Yik'in Chan K'awiil seated on another processional litter, dwarfed by a giant god effigy that rises above him (whose face can be seen at top right). This throne and god image were seized from the rival kingdom of Naranjo in a "star war" battle described in the text as happened in 744 A.D. This war saw the capture of the Naranjo capital and the fall of its then King Yax Mayuy Chan Chaak.

274 *Warrior gods and ceremonial litters. Tikal, Peten, Guatemala, Temple IV, Lintel 2; after 747 A.D.; sapodilla wood; H. 216 cm, W. 186 cm; Basel, Museum der Kulturen*
The images and texts carved into the remarkable wooden lintels of Tikal Temple IV supply valuable information about the relationship between religion and warfare. The scene on Lintel 2 shows the ruler Yiki'in Chan K'awiil (Ruler B) seated on a processional litter and surrounded by the effigy of a giant supernatural serpent. The text records his victory against the King of El Peru, which occurred at the place called Yaxa' in 743 A.D. The personal god of the El Peru king was captured as booty and returned to Tikal the next day. The scene shows a celebratory commemoration with dancing and god impersonation that took place three years later.

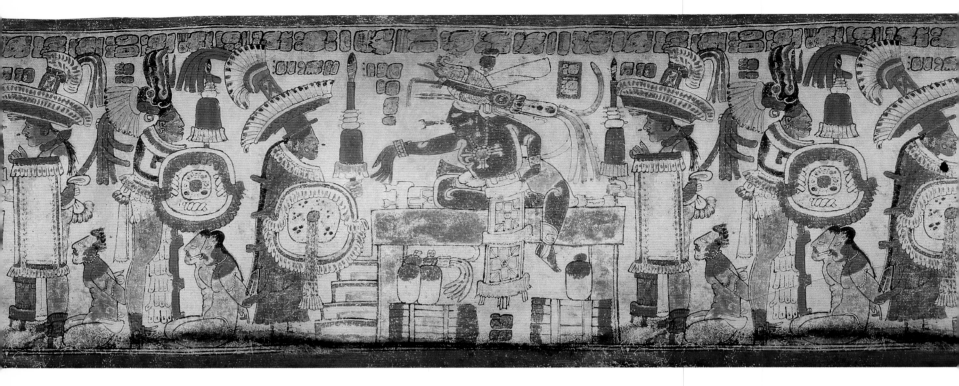

275 *Exhibition of prisoners. Rollout of a painted cylindrical vessel; provenance unknown; clay, painted; H. 28.1 cm, L. 45 cm; private collection*
After the battle, the prisoners were taken to the victor's capital where various fates awaited them. Some were clearly sacrificed, but others may have become slaves or simple vassals. Heaps of valuable objects are often portrayed in presentation scenes such as the one on this painted vessel. Presumably they represent captured booty or enforced tribute.

276 *Warrior statuette in Jaina style. Provenance unknown; Late Classic, 600–800 A.D.; fired clay; H. 26 cm; Cleveland, Cleveland Museum of Art, James Albert and Mary Gardiner Ford Memorial Fund*
This warrior is wearing a garment made of blue feathers with a broad protective collar and an imposing helmet that seems to offer genuine head protection. His spear and shield have been lost.

and we know that most war damage was repaired. Normally, fortifications provide some of the best physical information, though in the Maya region these are rather limited. In later times we know that northern Maya towns were surrounded by double rings of stone walls or wooden palisades, but only a few such structures have been identified in the Classic Lowlands (ills. 278, 277).

In the 1960s, a deeply cut ditch and embankment running over 9 km (5.6 miles) was discovered 4.5 km (2.8 miles) to the north of Tikal. Fragments of a similar barrier to the south of the city indicate that it once formed part of a massive fortification, presumably once topped by a parapet, that linked flanking swamps to the west and east. Tikal stands out alone in this regard, but too little research has been done in the far hinterland of Maya cities to be sure that other centers did not have similar works, especially if their dominant form was the wooden palisade with only a modest ditch construction. A rather impressive moat is known from Becan, built at quite an early date, while low wall systems have been found in the Petexbatun region, where they were hurriedly built at the very end of the Classic period, as the great social collapse of the southern Lowlands was underway. There is ample evidence that these obstacles were overwhelmed and their settlements, most notably Aguateca, abandoned in haste and burned.

Few, if any, such barriers can repel an attacker without an active human defense, and works such as those of Tikal would have required large numbers of people to man them or to concentrate quickly at the site of an assault. The vast area they enclose (around 125 square kilometers/78 square miles) shows that a rural heartland, rather than the urban core, was the primary object of this defense. It is tempting to think that it was operated only seasonally, when particular crops were at their most vulnerable to burning, ravaging or theft, and little human labor was required – leaving men free to defend their fields, or conversely attack those of others.

The extent and meaning of wars

This directly addresses the question of how many warriors took part in these conflicts, and whether battle was reserved for a noble few or mass armies were employed. We have sources for the Postclassic that describe a military elite, yet one that led bands of peasant-warriors seasonally drawn from their work in the fields. Those scholars who have worked on the statistical incidence of war through the calendar year have found signs that it peaked in dry periods. This would have eased the transport of armies but also adds weight to the idea that most wars were fought when the harvest was in and the number of men available to fight was at its maximum. This is our best clue yet that Maya armies could, on at least some occasions, have been sizeable. It is clear that some conflicts led to the seizure of foreign capitals, the capture and death of defeated kings. It is hard to conceive that such desperate encounters would have been restricted to a professional minority, rather than consuming the efforts of many royal subjects defending their city and "divine" ruler (ill. 272).

While the role of warfare in the earliest development of Maya civilization is still unclear, it remains likely that conflict had a significant role in the formation of complex Preclassic societies and the great cities that controlled them. By the dawn of the Classic period, by at least 300 A.D., militarism had taken a key place in the art of the Lowlands and the ideal of the "warrior king" had emerged as a crucial component of Maya rulership. From the 6th century onwards, a developed political landscape of numerous, highly competitive kingdoms led to important innovations. Conflicts were increasingly recorded in glyphic inscriptions throughout the Late Classic and their role in dynastic narratives emphasized over more generic images of military prowess.

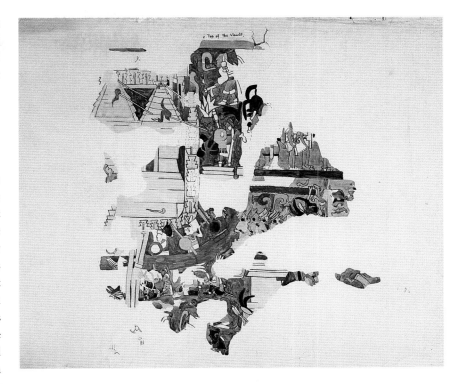

277 *Attack on a city fortified by two walls. Chichen Itza, Yucatan, Mexico, Nunnery, Room 22; Late Classic or Early Postclassic, 800–1200 A.D.; wall painting (copy)*
Although only fragments have survived, this wall painting is an unusual illustration of a double wall system in action. At top left we see temples encircled by a wall covered with diamond-shaped patterns. This in turn is surrounded by a second wall painted red. A shower of burning arrows rains down on the temples. They have probably been fired from the attackers' *atlatl*, "spear-throwers." Other warriors in this zone seem to belong to the defenders, and the figures to their right could be prisoners.

For the Maya, warfare had a strong spiritual component, in which deities were thought to have a decisive influence on events. By appealing to pan-Mesoamerican gods of Mexican origin, Maya kings hoped to stack the odds in their favor and provide a governing paradigm for conquest and subjugation. Nevertheless, we can discern that practical goals, specifically political expansion through the control of vassal kings and resulting material enrichment, had primacy. While wars were fought at every level of intensity, and doubtless for numerous different reasons, the influence of a few powerful kingdoms and their assertive "over-kings" had a major impact on Classic Maya patterns of warfare.

This situation persisted in the flourishing southern Lowlands until the wider disintegration of Classic society there in the 9th century. The collapse of royal dynastic rule seems to have led to an even more fractured landscape populated by petty warlords, each struggling to control ever-diminishing resources. Where Maya civilization survived in any cohesive form, in the northern Lowlands and southern Highlands, political conflict continued much as before.

Pre-Hispanic Maya civilization in no way resembles the peaceful utopia once imagined for it. But in its militaristic character – no more brutal that any comparable society – we at least, and at last, find a fuller and more convincing picture of one of the world's most spectacular cultural achievements.

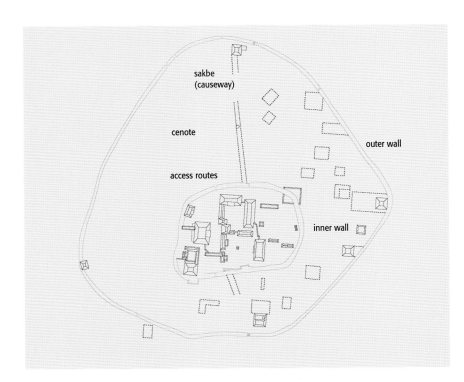

278 *A site in Yucatan fortified by double walls. Map of the archeological site of Cuca, Yucatan, Mexico*
This map of Cuca shows concentric city walls which are very similar to those depicted in the murals at Chichen Itza. The outer ring is low but up to 4 m thick and may once have been protected by palisades or thorny hedges. The inner wall is 10–12 m thick and much more solid, standing 3 m high in places.

A GAME OF LIFE AND DEATH – THE MAYA BALL GAME

Pierre R. Colas and Alexander Voss

The ball game was a central part of the social life for the Precolumbian Maya. Remains of ball courts and representations of the players have been found not only throughout the Maya territory, but also among all the other peoples of Mesoamerica. What is more, the ball game even extended as far as the south-western part of the modern-day United States, and can therefore be seen as a cross-cultural phenomenon.

Not only did the ball game extend over a large geographical area, it was also practiced over a surprisingly long period of time. Archeological traces have been found dating as far back as the 5th century B.C. The oldest ball courts have been discovered at the middle course of the Grijalva River in Chiapas, and finds from the Olmec settlement of San Lorenzo may also date from this period.

Most of the ball courts in the Maya region were built in the Classic period between the 3rd and 9th centuries A.D. Shortly before the arrival of the Spaniards, however, Maya ball courts were only to be found in the Highlands of Guatemala among the K'iche' and Kaqchikel, and in Utatlan and Iximche. Variants of the ball game are still played in the Mexican states of Sinaloa and Michoacan.

The fact that the ball game survived for several centuries even in the face of radical historical changes shows its great cultural significance in Mesoamerica.

279 Central marker stone of the Great Ball Court. Copan, Honduras, Ball Court A-II; Late Classic, after 695 A.D.; green tuff; dia. 74 cm; Copan Ruinas, Museo de Arqueología
Three marker stones were set in the ground at the center and at the ends of a ball court. This center stone belongs to a previous version of the present ball court. The relief portrays the king playing the ball game against a god from the underworld. Another indication that the game is taking place in the underworld is the stylized representation of a gateway to it which appears at the edge.

280 Scene from a ball game. Provenance unknown; Late Classic, 600–900 A.D.; fired clay, painted; H. 23 cm, dia. 17.7 cm; St. Louis, St. Louis Art Museum (Kerr 5345)
The scene is like a snapshot of a passage of play between two players in a ball game. All the players are wearing protective belts and kneepads as well as headdresses which clearly indicate which team they belong to. Thus the two players on the left of the ball are wearing a bird's head, and those on the right a deer's head. On a flight of steps which serves as a stand for spectators, two men are involved in a heated conversation, while a third, holding a conch shell, appears to be encouraging the players. The black wavy lines and hieroglyphs in the background depict the players' cries.

The myth of the ball game

The key to understanding the significance of the ball game in Maya culture lies in the tales of the Popol Wuj, the "Book of Council," which describes the myth surrounding the origins of the K'iche' people. Although this document is from colonial times, the similarities between the different tales and details from inscriptions and images are so great that the myths of the Popol Wuj seem like a Postclassic version of the myth of creation in Classic times.

The first part of the Popol Wuj tells of the two brothers Jun Junajpu (1 blowgun) and Wuqub' Junajpu (7 blowgun) playing the ball game before entering the underworld. The rulers of the underworld were disturbed by the noise and ordered the brothers to descend to the underworld to test their skills against them in a ball game. This was in fact a trap. The brothers were deceived, killed, and Jun Junajpu's head was hung from a tree. A girl by the name of Xkik' (woman of blood) saw the strange tree and approached it, whereupon the head spat into the palm of her hand. Xkik' magically became pregnant as a result. The young woman feared the revenge of her father, one of the rulers of the underworld, and fled to the dead brothers' mother in the upper world. There she gave birth to twins, Junajpu (blowgun) and Xb'alanke (young jaguar), who found their father's ball game equipment, started to play with it and were also summoned to

the underworld. Here the ballplayers, usually called the Hero Twins, had to undergo all kinds of tests. During one of these tests, Junajpu's head was torn off by a bat. The rulers of the underworld thought they were bound to win, but Xb'alanke replaced his brother's head with a pumpkin. Junajpu invited the rulers of the underworld to play ball with his head. Xb'alanke played a trick on the rulers, distracting their attention by having a rabbit hop across the ball court like a ball. He managed to recover his brother's head and brought Junajpu back to life. Nevertheless, the twins were eventually killed after being subjected to all the tests and their remains were scattered in the river of the underworld. After five days they returned, however, and worked a series of great miracles, killing many creatures and bringing them back to life. When the rulers of the underworld begged the twins to do the same to them, the twins killed the rulers but did not resuscitate them. The rulers of the underworld were thus defeated and the twins ascended to the heavens as the sun and the moon.

The depiction of this myth is particularly impressive on the reliefs of the Great Ball Court of Chichen Itza (ill. 283). They portray a kneeling headless player whose blood is spurting out from his neck in the form of a snake. The player opposite him holds the severed head in his left hand and a flint knife in his right. These scenes are pictorial renditions of the myth of the Hero Twins, and give no indication that the players were sacrificed at the end of a game. Stories such as this really belong in the realm of fantasy but, because of their strange exoticism, are adopted time and again without criticism.

The rules of the game

Today, the rules of the ball game played in the Classic period can only be pieced together in a fragmentary way through representations on painted vessels, clay sculptures, and stone monuments. A few eyewitness accounts by Europeans in the 16th century have also led to conclusions being drawn about the way the Maya ball game was played. We know little more than the fact that the ball was thrown by hand onto the ball court at the start of the game, but could then only be hit with the hip or the thigh after that. Any other contact was against the rules. We do not know how scores were made or how the winner was decided. There were probably different regional variants of the game. It is also unclear whether the game was played in teams and how many players made up a team.

281 *Ballplayer with protective belt. Provenance unknown; Late Classic, 600–900 A.D.; fired clay, painted; private collection*
This small clay sculpture clearly shows the different pieces of equipment worn by a ballplayer. A large protective belt is fastened around the hips, which the players used to hit the ball. The kneepads offered protection when the players had to support themselves on the hard ground to play the ball.

Statements in the Popol Wuj suggest that the game was played one against one as well as in pairs and by groups of unequal strength (ill. 280). Nearly all representations of the ball game depict the players as men. Only on the Hieroglyphic Stairway 2 at Yaxchilan does there seem to be two women playing the ball game. Most players are shown kneeling or lying almost flat on the ground, sometimes propping themselves up with an arm (ill. 282), while others stand upright and hold the ball in their hand. The different positions of the players clearly show different stages and situations in the game.

The players' equipment

Because the players were often hit by the massive rubber ball and frequently threw themselves to the ground, they had to protect themselves against injuries. The most important part of their protective clothing was the belt, referred to in Spanish as the *yugo*, "yoke." It was shaped like a horseshoe and was worn around the stomach (ill. 281). Numerous stone *yugos* have been found. The actual purpose of these heavy stone yokes is disputed, however. According to one theory, the stone yokes served as a kind of mold, which was covered with damp leather to form an imprint of the motif for the belt. When they were dry, the leather pieces were removed for further processing. The players also wore kneepads, hand and elbow protection, and special footwear (ill. 281). The kneepads were in the form of small shields and were fastened behind the knee. The players' backside and thighs were protected by a leather skirt and a loincloth. The players rarely wore sandals and generally played barefoot. The greatest variety of designs was reserved for the ballplayers' headdress. Representations depict deer heads (ill. 280), broad-brimmed hats and net cloths, such as those worn by the ancient God N. It is interesting to note that these headdresses were worn both by ballplayers and hunters. Although it has been known for many years, this parallel is still difficult to interpret.

282 *Ruler playing the ball game. Presumably from La Corona, Peten, Guatemala; Late Classic, 600–900 A.D.; limestone; H. 38.1 cm, W. 27.6 cm, D. 2 cm; New York, National Museum of the American Indian*
This relief belongs to a group of monuments, whose similarity in terms of materials and style indicates that they come from the same area. It portrays a player kneeling on the ground preparing to hit the ball with his hip. The hieroglyphs in front of his face give his title *pitzil*, "ballplayer," and his name.

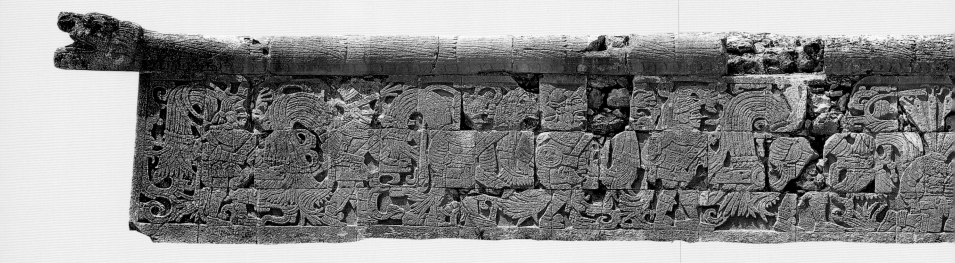

283 *Relief at the Great Ball Court. Chichen Itza, Yucatan, Mexico; Late Classic, 900–1000 A.D.; limestone*
This ball court relief depicts processions of groups of 14 players gathered around a central stage. It combines two episodes which have come down to us from the Popol Wuj. The skull on the ball stands for the spitting skull of Jun Junajpu, who is passing on his life force to the next generation. At the same time it refers to the decapitation and death of the twins. The motif is therefore a symbol of the eternal cycle of birth and death.

The balls

The balls were made from liquid latex obtained from local rubber trees. This resin forms threads when it is heated, which were wound into a round ball and kneaded with the hands or pressed in a mold. These balls weighed between three and eight kilograms (seven and 18 pounds). Because of their weight, the balls easily went out of shape and had to be suspended in a sling in order to regain their original form. It seems that each player had his own ball, since balls formed part of their personal equipment. A scene in the Popol Wuj describes how the rulers of the underworld argued with the twins before the game over which ball to use (ill. 280).

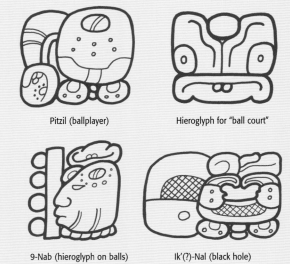

Pitzil (ballplayer)   Hieroglyph for "ball court"

9-Nab (hieroglyph on balls)   Ik'(?)-Nal (black hole)

284 *Hieroglyphs for a) ballplayer, b) ball court, c) ball, d) underworld*
a) The hieroglyph for ballplayer reads as *pitzil*. It often appears in inscriptions as the title in a ruler's name. b) The hieroglyph for ball court is a pictogram which shows the outline of a ball court with a ball in the center between the embankments. c) The balls were often inscribed with the hieroglyph which reads as *nab*. This is preceded by a number; so far the numbers 7, 9, 12, 13, and 14 have been documented. The meaning of this hieroglyph has not yet been fully established. d) Some inscriptions refer to mythical ball games which were played in the underworld, the name of which translates as "black hole."

Depictions of the balls show them varying in size between about the size of a hand and that of a modern-day medicine ball.

The ball game as religious drama

Basing their efforts on the mythical ball game episodes in the Popol Wuj, Maya artists sometimes depicted the skull of Jun Junajpu, the head of Junajpu or the rabbit on the ball, and sometimes prisoners in chains (ill. 285). These helpless prisoners were obviously thrown down the em-

285 *Winners and losers in a ball game. Yaxchilan, Chiapas, Mexico, Structure 33; Late Classic, before 771 A.D.; limestone; W. 165 cm*
The relief shows the ruler Bird Jaguar IV taking part in a ball game in front of a flight of steps down which a ball is rolling. The scene refers to the killing of a prisoner of war from Lakamtuun who was bound and thrown down the steps like the ball. The two dwarfs on the right of Bird Jaguar IV represent messengers from the underworld. The hieroglyphic text on the right relates the event to a ball game that took place on 9.15.13.6.9 or in 744 A.D. The text on the left describes three decapitations which took place on a ball court in the underworld.

bankments of ball courts or staircases with the idea of killing them (ill. 285). These depictions reflect the gruesome aspect of the ball game. The rulers presented themselves as relentless victors in the political power struggle, and put their opponents on public show to humiliate them. This scenario also had a parallel in mythology, of course, and even though we only have fragmentary evidence from the Classic inscriptions, these correspond to the Popol Wuj to a considerable extent. The text on Hieroglyphic Stairway 2 in Yaxchilan (ill. 285) refers to the beheading *(ch'ak baah)* of three gods in the mythical past. Each of the three suicides is described as a victory *(ahal)*. Because the event took place on a ball court, the place in which the drama was played out was named Ox Ahal Eeb, "staircase of the three victories." The inscription also states that the three mythological beings set out for the underworld *(ooch bih)* after their death on the ball court. This ball court is located in a place known as "black hole," which indicates that it stands at the entrance to the underworld. The three decapitated gods seemed to represent different aspects of the Maize God. According to Maya beliefs, only this death in the underworld could allow for the rebirth of the maize and the completion of the life cycle.

The ball courts

The ball courts retained a similar design in every period. The long sides of the rectangular playing field are between 20 and 30 meters (22 and 33 yd.) long and are surrounded by embankments measuring between three and four meters (10 and 13 ft.) in height (ill. 287). On the platforms around the playing area are buildings which would have been used by selected spectators as recreation rooms. At each end of the main playing strip there were

286 *Drawn reconstruction of the ball court in Copan*
This reconstruction by the architect and art historian Tatiana Proskouriakoff gives an impression of the structure of the Copan ball court in its final phase. The ball court was rebuilt several times. The first version was built at the beginning of the 5th century by Yax K'uk' Mo', the founder of the royal dynasty, while the final building work was undertaken by Waxaklajuun Ubaah K'awiil, who was taken prisoner by the rival city Quirigua and beheaded shortly afterwards.

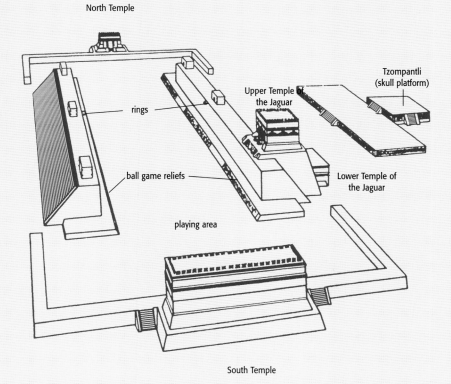

North Temple

rings

ball game reliefs

Upper Temple the Jaguar

Tzompantli (skull platform)

Lower Temple of the Jaguar

playing area

South Temple

287 *The Great Ball Court. Chichen Itza, Yucatan, Mexico; Terminal Classic, 900–1000 A.D.; L. 138 m, W. 40 m, H. 8 m*
The largest ball court in the Maya region and throughout the whole of Mesoamerica is in Chichen Itza. Its size and shape differ considerably from those of other ball courts. The ground plan resembles a stretched-out "H," surrounded by high, perpendicular walls. The lateral slopes are extremely low compared with the width of the court and are very steep; they are decorated with bas-reliefs (ill. 283).

additional open spaces which could be used, giving the ball court the appearance of a Roman "I." A good example of this is the Copan ball court (ills. 286, 292), which is considered to be one of the finest in Mesoamerica. Three marker stones were generally positioned at equal intervals down the length of the court. In some cases, there is only one stone, positioned in the middle of the court. Additional markers in the form of sculpted macaws' heads were placed on the outer edges of the embankments at the Copan court (illus. 290). On some ball courts, complete sculptures or stone rings were placed halfway along the court. No complete representations of ball courts have been discovered so far on Maya sculptures or painted pottery. For the most part, only a side view or, less frequently, a cross section, is depicted. The sides are usually portrayed in the form of steps down which the ball is rolled. The inscriptions contain words such as *eeb* which stands for "staircase," *pitz*, "to play ball," and *aj pitz*, "ballplayer," a title which was also conferred on many rulers (ill. 284).

Continuity and transformation – the Great Ball Court of Chichen Itza

The most impressive ball court in the Maya region is situated in Chichen Itza. With an overall length of 138 meters (151 yd.) and a width of 40 meters (44 yd.), it is the largest ever built in Mesoamerica (ill. 289). It differs from the usual Maya ball courts both in size and design. The side slopes are low and could not be used to throw

288 *Stone ring on the Great Ball Court. Chichen Itza, Yucatan, Mexico; Terminal Classic, 900–1000 A.D.*
Stone rings were set vertically into the upper part of the court's boundary walls. The ball had to be hit through them in the game. This ring is decorated with a relief of two intertwined serpents. The size of the ball court and the use of rings as targets show that the game was obviously played with different techniques and rules in Chichen Itza from those used in the southern Maya region.

289 *View of the southern end of the Great Ball Court. Chichen Itza, Yucatan, Mexico; Terminal Classic, 900–1000 A.D.*
Small temples stand at the southern end of the Great Ball Court (and at the northern end which is not shown here). Their vaulted inner sides were once richly decorated with mythological scenes.

prisoners to their death. In contrast, the court's perpendicular walls stand eight meters (26 ft.) high. Possible predecessors of this type of structure have been found in north-west Mexico. Stone rings with openings 50 centimeters (20 in.) in diameter are set at a height of seven meters (23 ft.) in the center of the walls (ill. 288). In order to get the ball through these rings, the players seem to have used a kind of bat with a handle, decorated at the top of the shaft with a lizard's head.

Even the players' equipment was different from that used in other places. To protect themselves against high-flying balls, the players wore a special guard fixed to their belt to protect the chest and face. This spoon-shaped object is called a *palma* or *palmeta* and is now only found in Veracruz, Puebla, and the Highlands of Guatemala. The immense size of the playing strip indicates that large teams were put together, which could be distinguished from one another by their headdresses and the decorations on their chests.

The life cycle and the ball game

The sporting side of the ball games is described in Spanish reports on the Aztecs, but its religious dimension remained unclear for a long time. It is certain that the meaning of the game is connected with the ball-playing twins of the Popol Wuj who defeated the rulers of the underworld. The close association between the ball game and contact with the underworld is also reflected in a painting of Junajpu as a ballplayer in the cave of Naj Tunich (ill. 291). Caves were considered to be natural entrances to the underworld and were used as ritual sites. The ball courts were laid out in the form of artificial gorges and, like caves, symbolized entrances to the underworld. They were a stage for playing out one of the central myths on which the godlike supremacy of the lords was based. Here the rulers

could present themselves as heroes who descended to the underworld to conquer death. The notion that kings, by playing the ball game, symbolically entered the underworld to match themselves against its leaders is also shown on the three marker stones of the Copan ball court. Each scene is set in a frame, which is meant to represent the entrance to the underworld. Each of the three marker stones depicts two players next to a ball. The northern stone may represent the twins Junajpu and Xb'alanke, with the southern one depicting their father and uncle at the ball game. The central stone represents the creator of the ball court, the ruler Waxaklajuun Ubaah K'awiil (672–738) of Copan, in conflict with a lord of the underworld. Ball courts were therefore not simply symbolic entrances to the underworld, but also places in which death could be overcome. The concept of the ball game in the Highland epics of the K'iche'-Maya is closely linked

291 *Junajpu as a ballplayer. Naj Tunich, Peten, Guatemala, Drawing 21; Late Classic, 600–900 A.D.; charcoal on limestone rock; H. 22 cm, W. 19 cm*
This drawing from the Naj Tunich cave shows a ballplayer before a flight of three steps. The player's equipment can be clearly distinguished and consists of a kneepad on the left leg and a protective belt around the upper body to which a long apron is attached. There is a ball on the middle step. The significance of the number nine on the top of the ball has not yet been fully explained, but it probably links the game with a mythical ballgame in the underworld. The figure probably represents the Classic depiction of Junajpu, one of the mythical heroes of the Popol Wuj.

to death and resurrection. The cycle of living and dying is here explained in one of the great mytho-logical tales of human history.

292 *The ball court. Copan, Honduras, Ball Court A-III, Structure 10L-9/10; Late Classic, 738 A.D.; L. 36 m, W. 10 m*
This ball court, one of the finest in the whole Maya region, is typical of the southern Lowlands. The court, in the form of an extended "I," is bordered by two embankments. Marker stones have been set in the ground in the center and at both ends of the court along the longitudinal axis. They stand opposite more marker stones on the outer edge of the embankments, which in Copan were sculpted in the form of macaws' heads. The ball court is surrounded on both sides by buildings.

290 *Ball court façade sculpture. Copan, Honduras, Structure 10L-10; Late Classic, 738 A.D.*
Like all the buildings in the center of Copan, the architecture surrounding the ball court was originally richly decorated on the upper part of the façade. In general, the sculptural decoration is linked to the mythical place symbolized by a building. This ball court façade sculpture depicts a bird-like being with the head of a macaw combined with motifs referring to a holy mountain. The ball court is therefore associated with an underworld counterpart at the heart of the mythical Mo' Witz mountain ("Macaw Mountain"), which is frequently referred to in Copan inscriptions.

ARCHITECTURE AND ART

UNITY IN SPACE AND TIME – THE MAYA ARCHITECTURE

Annegrete Hohmann-Vogrin

Of all the evidence that we have of Maya culture, architecture is the most impressive and well known. The buildings are in the form of agglomerations of terraces, platforms, courtyards, and squares with retaining walls, stairways, terracing, and buildings with inner rooms, which are relatively small and present in small numbers compared with the structured open spaces. Interpretations of Maya architecture have left many aspects unresolved. Scholars venture plainly and without hesitation to speak of "Maya cities." To refer to the tall, terraced solitary buildings as "pyramids" is too great a simplification in terms of form, and the division of most other buildings into "temples" and "palaces" is often arbitrary, because their functions and significance have not yet been fully clarified. Only ball courts can be clearly identified by their characteristic boundaries consisting of two parallel walls.

The building materials available in the different regions, particularly the various types of stone, were clearly one of the factors which determined the architectural style. Although limestone is predominant in many regions, there were certainly other materials in particular areas which were suitable for building. In Copan, for example, tuff was used, as it was easy to work, whilst sandstone was favored in Quirigua. In Comalcalco flat, fired bricks were used as building materials (ill. 295).

The changes in building techniques and styles observed over the centuries in particular regions were linked to the varying availability of the flint and obsidian tools used to work the rock, or wood to burn the lime. The obsidian and flint supplies may no longer have been accessible or may have been depleted and the forests may have been cleared. The introduction of other building materials and tools brought a change in building styles. Stylistic differences in architecture were, however, initially attributed to changes in cultural influence.

For as long as a region was populated and prospered, it was subject to constant change. New building procedures were not only introduced after large-scale demolition of existing structures, as is customary in our culture, but often as a result of repeated overbuilding on existing sites. The previous structures were generally integrated into the new ones and used as foundations for taller buildings (ill. 294). The final versions of great platform systems in regions with a long history thus consist of numerous layers of stucco floors, terraces, platforms, huge steps, and stairways. Fortunately for current archeological research, great care was taken in some cases to protect the original building

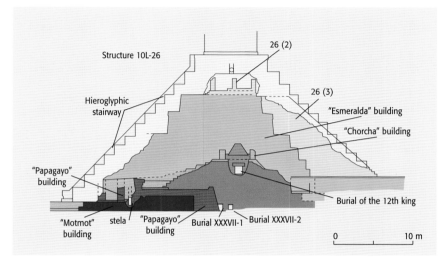

294 *Cross section of Temple 26 in Copan, Honduras*
The acropolis of Copan is an example of how architectural complexes could develop and change over time. The oldest building in Temple 26 shown here is the so-called Papagayo. This temple, which was probably commissioned by the second king of the city, was partly destroyed by the fourth king and replaced with a newer, larger structure. The 12th king erected a building on top of this one at the beginning of the 7th century, which has been named Chorcha by archeologists and in which he is buried. His burial chamber was later overbuilt by the Esmeralda building. Temple 26 was altered and extended several times under subsequent kings, including the addition of the hieroglyphic stairway, for which it is famous today.

when the superstructure was erected. The façade decorations were carefully filled in before being overlaid by the new shell. These building activities were often closely linked with burials of noblemen, whose burial chambers were laid out in these buildings.

Buildings made from perishable materials

Many of the buildings constructed through the ages were made from perishable materials. There are indications that simple houses erected on base platforms, such as those still found in the Maya region, have always formed part of the housing pattern (ill. 296). Posts were driven into the base of carefully constructed platforms. They supported the roof, which was tied into a system of horizontal beams secured by lianas (ill. 297). The roof was made from palm leaves or other natural materials (ill. 298). Walls were built in various ways according to the thickness required. They were either made from loosely interwoven sticks of wood or from half-timbering filled with clay or woven material and coated with clay and plastered. The lower part of the walls consisted of several layers of stonewalling, such as can still be seen today in the populated regions of Copan and in the ruins of the old town. It is not unusual to find houses with walls going up to the base of the roof.

Previous double page:
Daybreak at the Central Acropolis of Tikal, Guatemala
View of the so-called Central Acropolis on the southern side of the main plaza in Tikal. Long houses on layered terraces with rooms on all sides, covered with false vaults, form intimate courtyards. The Central Acropolis was probably the main residence of the nobility of Tikal.

293 *The Castillo. Chichen Itza, Yucatan, Mexico*
With 91 steps on each side, the Castillo pyramid on the main plaza of Chichen Itza unifies time and space. The total number of steps, including the ledge at the entrance to the temple, corresponds to the number of days in the solar year. Like many other Maya buildings, the Castillo (Spanish for "castle"), was given its misleading name in colonial times. For the Maya, it represented the mountain on which corn was grown.

295 *Building made of fired bricks. Comalcalco, Tabasco, Mexico*
While the architecture of nearly all Maya cities was made from local stone, the building material used here is flat, fired brick. It was even used for the vaults, as shown in this illustration of the ruins of such a building. The brick walls were coated with a layer of limestone plaster to protect them against storms.

299 *Pyramid N10-43 at Lamanai, Belize*
Early constructions maintained their shape even when built over many times. The stairways flanked by meter-high stucco surrounds were a characteristic part of the structure. These wide terraced platforms from the Late Preclassic reached a height of 33 m (108 ft.). Three buildings made from wood and palm leaves were erected on the platforms in the typical Preclassic triad form.

296 *Main platform. Uaxactun, Peten, Guatemala, Group A-5*
The excavations conducted by the Carnegie Institution of Washington at Group A in Uaxactun unearthed an oval base platform from the Early Classic period underneath a large Classic palace. The four holes in the stucco base mark the former positions of the wooden posts which carried a roof structure made from wood and palm leaves.

297 *Roof construction of a new Maya house*
The photograph shows a construction detail from the roof of a Maya house. The knot binds the vertical posts to the horizontal circular timbers to which a tie is attached. This holds together the rafters to which long canes were fastened, between which the palm leaves were then plaited to form the roof covering.

298 *Modern house on a base platform*
Simple houses on different types of base are common in the Maya region even today. This construction is made from intertwined circular timber poles coated with clay. The roof is made from leaves of the Guano palm (*Sabal mexicana*).

The typical courtyard group

The basic elements of a typical courtyard group consisted of a house, a platform, and a forecourt. Several of these were grouped together around a common courtyard. This layout was characteristic not only of simple buildings, but also formed the basic principle underpinning monumental architecture (ill. 299). The erection of huge platforms, which framed massive plazas and courtyards, was one of the earliest building methods used in Mesoamerica and throughout the Maya region as a whole. In the Highlands of Guatemala, in Kaminaljuyu, for example, these platforms were raised to a height of 20 meters (66 ft.) and covered with clay mixed with volcanic ash. The use of stone was still very limited among the Maya on the Pacific coast. Only in the central karst-layered Lowlands, in the tropical rain forests where many places had to manage without surface water, were huge platforms built, using stone and mortar to make them resistant to tropical downpours. This was done as early as the first millennium B.C., for example in Nakbe and later on in El Mirador. Even at this early period, many of these platforms were connected to each other over all kinds of terrain by broad causeways, which were reinforced with a thick layer of mortar like the plazas themselves. Numerous further platforms were erected in layers on these plazas, with the top level forming a terrace; typically at the time, further sets of layered platforms could be built around three sides of this terrace. The central platform facing the stairway was significantly larger than the others. The construction consisted of walls surrounding a central core made of rubble. This area was divided into separate chambers, probably for structural reasons. The outer surfaces were coated with thick layers of mortar, which were smoothed and painted and decorated with bas-reliefs in the same material (see Hansen, p. 51 ff).

300 *Diagram of a pyramid*
Temples generally stood on terraced foundation buildings with open staircases, which were often erected on top of burial chambers. The core of the structure was stabilized with rough stone walls covered with stones and mortar. These pyramids were then clad with carved stone and a stairway was built at the entrance. The final stage was the construction of the temple itself from wood or palm leaves.

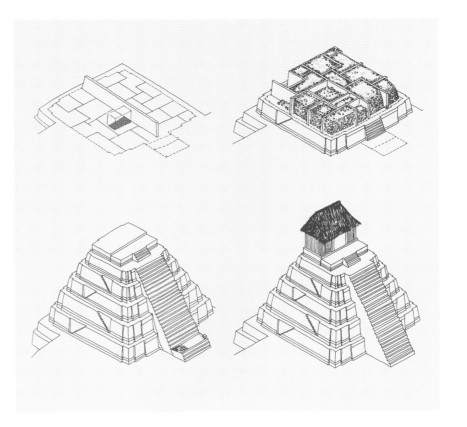

301 *Stucco relief from the palace of Palenque (detail). Palenque, Chiapas, Mexico, underground passage beneath the palace*
Stucco work was carried out with great skill in Palenque. Reliefs made from this frequently used material decorated façades as well as building interiors. They were attached to the walls with stone tenons. Occasionally, basic shapes were made of stone and then decorated with stucco. The depiction of the monster of the heavens on this relief, which shows one of its two heads, is positioned at the entrance to one of the rooms of the acropolis.

302 *Stucco relief from Balamku (detail). Balamku Campeche, Mexico*
Balamku, in the south of the federal Mexican state, was not discovered until 1990. Grave robbers had found part of an Early Classic stucco frieze. When archeologists from the Mexican antiquities authority INAH unearthed the whole frieze, it emerged that it had decorated the upper part of a façade. It showed three frogs with human forms emerging from their wide-open jaws. The animals are seated on three masks which represent *witz*, the god of the mountains.

Stucco work

In the Middle and Late Preclassic, most of the reliefs on the outer walls of buildings were formed and modeled in stucco (ill. 301). Characteristic of this early period of Maya architecture are the stucco masks, measuring up to four meters (13 ft.) high and representing gods, which decorated the façades of platforms. Very few examples of Preclassic stucco sculptures remain. Only in Late Classic buildings, where broad solitary terraced pyramids enclose an earlier Preclassic central section, have the stucco decorations escaped ruin. One example of this is the main pyramid in the Mundo Perdido group in Tikal, which after being built over several times stands at around 30 meters (98 ft.) high. In Caracol, before the city's defeat, a similar structure was the most important building. It resembles the main pyramid in Calakmul, of a city which was considered one of the leading Late Classic Maya centers. Some of these buildings decorated with stucco masks, such as the ones in Kohunich and Balamku (ill. 302) date back to the Early Classic period (6th century A.D. or earlier). Later stuccowork is more intricate, however, with more varied motifs and designs. Stucco continued to be used in the Late Classic period. It was used less frequently, however, and its purpose was to add a protective layer or painting surface to buildings.

Bridging techniques and vault construction

Changes between the Preclassic and Early Classic periods can also be seen in the improvement of building techniques. The walls tended to be made from more precisely cut stones, which meant that the layer of mortar could be thinner.

Becan – false towers of the Rio Bec style

In the north of the Peten lies a region named after, and therefore, not clearly distinguishable from an archeological site discovered earlier. Early relics have been found all over this region, but the latest buildings and versions of most structures date from the Late or Terminal Classic periods. This is true of Kohunlich, with its Early Classic stucco masks, and Becan, with its circular wall enclosing numerous burial places, which dates back to the Late Preclassic period. Palatial structures with many rooms and isolated buildings set on high terraced substructures combine in a strange symbiosis. The latter are integrated into the symmetrical palace buildings as towers, their façades showing traces of staircases and high temple reliefs. In addition to these, there are many other building types with one or many stories. For example, Structure IV in Becan in its current form is seen from the south as a high, several-story base structure with a broad staircase entrance, crowned with richly decorated buildings enclosing a courtyard (ill. 323–326). False staircases have been attached to the sides and a narrow staircase entrance is concealed underneath the one on the west side. From the north side, the building looks like a four-story palace. The technique and decorations used are more consistent than in other areas. The inner and outer walls and vaults are faced and coated with stone and mortar. The main motif of the mosaic-like façades is the mask. Some are located in the vertical vaulted areas on the façades, while others are positioned above one another as decorative elements, either flush with the wall or protruding at the corners of the building. However, the most spectacular mask motifs are to be found in the entrances, where they sometimes depict terrifying serpent jaws. Stone mosaics were generally coated with thin limestone mortar and painted. Some façade decorations were extensively reworked in stucco later.

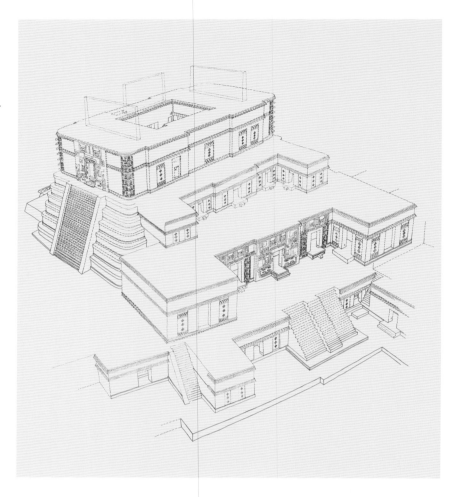

323 *Perspective reconstruction of Structure IV at Becan, Campeche, Mexico*
The broad staircase entrance on the north side leads up to an architectural complex, which encloses an inner courtyard and forms the highest level of a palace built on four levels on the north side. A false staircase, characteristic of the Rio Bec style, can be seen on the east side. The main entrances to the building are in the form of wide-open jaws.

324 *View of the platform in front of Structure IV at Becan*
Structure IV stands on a monumental terraced platform on top of an earlier acropolis, which was begun in the middle of the Preclassic period. Different structures stand on the plateau, including a cylindrical platform from the Terminal Classic period. The south side is bordered by a building with two towers in the Rio Bec style.

325 *View of Structure IV at Becan*
From the south, Structure IV is a high, terraced base structure with a broad staircase entrance. It is crowned with a richly decorated structure enclosing a courtyard. Becan was discovered in 1934 by archeologists from the American Carnegie Institute, but excavations did not begin until 1969–1971. It was revealed that the city had been an important center during the Preclassic period but declined in importance in the Early Classic. It was not until the Late Classic that new building projects were initiated and Structure IV stems from this late period.

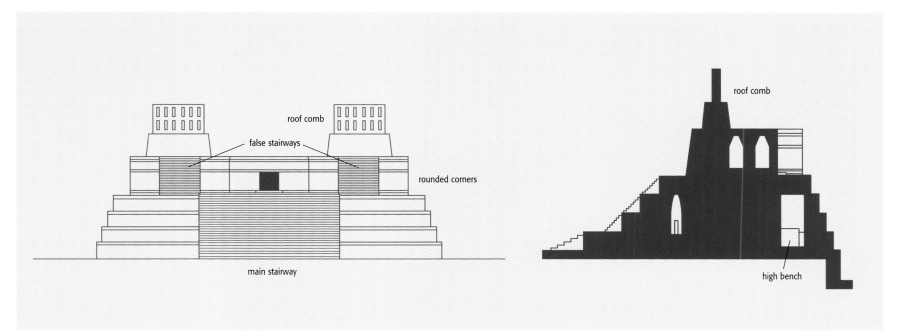

326a *Perspective drawing of the west side of Structure I at Becan*
Structure I is an example of the Rio Bec style which was widespread in the center of the Yucatan peninsula. It stands on a high platform accessed by a broad open stairway. It has only one entrance and is flanked by two false towers. The staircases are too steep to climb.

326b *Section of Structure I at Becan*
Judging by the temple towers in the Rio Bec style, it can be assumed that they represent the large pyramids in central Peten, particularly the ones in Tikal, in a reduced, symbolic form. The stairways with steps and stringboards at the front are too steep to climb. The temples on the upper platform with their closed doors are examples of illusory architecture.

Uxmal – The Terminal Classic in the Puuc region

In the northern part of the Yucatan peninsula, mainly in the hills of the Puuc region, more austere motifs dominate building façades. The lower wall areas between the entrances, many of which have been extended with pillars and columns, tend to have smooth surfaces. The bases, and above all the vaulted areas of the buildings, are often richly decorated (ill. 329). Some façades extend further and take the form of front-facing roof combs. Masks, serpents, and other motifs from the animal world are represented in geometric form. The façades are extremely varied, with their ledges, pillars, and interwoven motifs (ill. 327; see Dunning, p. 325 ff.).

Uxmal, possibly the most important archeological site in the region, is dominated by impressive burial complexes. The so-called Magician's Pyramid, a structure which has been reworked numerous times, features broad stairway entrances on the east and west sides. This pyramid is connected to the so-called Nunnery, a four-sided courtyard enclosed by extended buildings on a low platform. It was completed between 906 A.D. and 909 by King Chan Chaak K'ak'nal Ajaw, who ruled over Uxmal when it was at its height. Each of the four sides of the convent is built in a completely different form (ill. 328). A terrace with a ballcourt, build by this same king, separates this group from an even wider platform, which dominates the 100 meter (328 ft.) long building known as the Governor's Palace. This building, which stands on a separate base structure, consists of two rows of high vaulted rooms, and is traversed by two "transepts." The exposed position and overall display of splendor set this building apart from other palaces at the site.

Other complexes in this same elaborate style surround the spectacular main structure together with enclosed courtyards and plazas and a few high, terraced base platforms. Modest ramparts, which enclose the center of the city, have also

been revealed. A causeway connects Uxmal to Kabah and leads to a freestanding gate, whose vault is approximately four meters (13 ft.) wide and eight meters (26 ft.) high. Several groups of palaces, including a building whose west side is decorated with a mask mosaic, determine the architecture of this region, as also seen at Labna, Sayil and Oxkintok.

Causeways, *sakbe*, have been identified in many areas connecting groups of building or settlements. One of the longest is between Coba and Yaxuna and covers a distance of 100 kilometers (62 miles). A large number of these causeways can be found between several lakes in Cabo on the east coast of Yucatan.

327 *Detail of the façade decoration of the Monjas complex in Uxmal, Yucatan, Mexico*
The façade decorations of the Puuc region, the hilly area in northern Yucatan, are generally more austere and less decorative than the Chenes and Rio Bec architecture in the south. The sculptors of Uxmal nevertheless knew how to combine smooth wall surfaces with sections which were richly decorated with ornaments. This decoration is composed of ready-cut stone elements, like a mosaic. On the right of the picture one can see a simple farmhouse with a roof made from palm leaves. It is incorporated like a setpiece in the grand architecture of the Monjas complex in Uxmal.

328 *View of the east wing of the Monjas complex in Uxmal. Historic photograph taken by Augustus Le Plongeon in 1857/59*
This early archeological photograph shows the east wing of the Monjas complex before it was excavated and consolidated. The façade decoration is limited to the upper section. The lower wall area is smooth, closed and undecorated and is only punctuated by the doorways. The optical attraction of the frieze, framed with heavy ledges, lies in its combination of simple geometric motifs and realistic representations of houses above the doors.

329 *Structure I at Xlapak, Yucatan, Mexico; Late Classic period*
The richly decorated vault area is typical of the architecture of the Terminal Classic period. It consists mainly of geometric motifs interspersed with abstract groups of masks. Apart from the pillars at the corners, the lower wall area is not decorated.

THE BUILDINGS OF YUCATAN

330 *View of the east side of the east wing of the Monjas building. Chichen Itza, Yucatan, Mexico. Historic photograph; c. 1857/59 by Augustus Le Plongeon*
This early archæological photograph shows the façade before it was restored. The dragon mouth portal and the building's decorations covering the entire façade resemble buildings in the Chenes style.

When Diego de Landa came to Yucatan in the middle of the 16th century, he was surprised to find a large number of urban settlements with huge impressive temples and palaces. His admiration is reflected in the following text:

Translated from: Diego de Landa, "Relación de las cosas de Yucatán" (Report on the incidents in Yucatan), Mexico, 1938.

If Yucatan had made its name and become famous for the range, size, and beauty of its buildings, as is the case with other Indian settlements with their gold, silver, and [other] treasures, its reputation would have become as widespread as that of Peru and modern Spain, since such a range of buildings has never been discovered in any other Indian settlement. It is amazing that there are so many buildings in so many different places in their distinctive square stone style. I will try to explain why this country is not in the same position, even though it is a thriving country, as it was when it reached its height, when so many splendid buildings were erected even though there was no metal with which to work the stone. My theories are based on the ideas of those who have studied these buildings. The reason is that these people must have been subjugated to rulers who were happy to keep them occupied and allocate work to them. And because they appear to have been deeply involved in idolatry, they built common temples for their idols. In addition, settlements were transferred for various reasons and it was their custom to build new temples, chapels, and wooden houses with straw roofs for their chieftains wherever they went. Or it may have been that their large supplies of stone, limestone, and a kind of white soil, which was excellent for building, inspired them to construct so many. Unless we actually see these buildings for ourselves, we may think that the person describing them is joking. It could be that the country holds some kind of secret which, since it has not been discovered by the inhabitants of the area, is unlikely to be fathomed in our time.

Postclassic architecture in Chichen Itza

Maya architecture underwent further changes at Chichen Itza. Until the Terminal Classic, splendid building complexes had been created in this region in the Puuc style, including a circular building with an interior spiral entrance referred to as a *caracol*, "snail," which is thought to have been an observatory (ill. 331). In subsequent periods, huge plazas and terraces were established and monumental buildings erected, including a large ball court with steep side walls and target rings. Long columned halls (ills. 332, 333), which had never been part of this culture, developed and can be seen in the original Early Classic building in Ake. Later temples strongly resemble similar ones from the central Highlands of Mexico and are therefore often referred to as evidence of the close links between Central Mexico and Chichen Itza.

The buildings' sculptures show changes in the motifs used and in their meaning. A terraced pyramid, which has been reconstructed several times and features staircases on all four sides, the so-called El Castillo, stands in the center of the "new" part of Chichen Itza (ills. 293, 334, 335).

The development of this city stagnated during the 13th century. Smaller, more densely populated areas, often surrounded by walls, were a typical feature of this period. But although the overall appearance of the settlements became simpler and less decorative, the old, traditional architectural concepts still remained.

A number of changes were made in the building style of the Postclassic period. More flat roofs were built with wooden substructures and a stone and mortar coating, a method probably also used for the roof constructions of the columned halls in Chichen Itza. Rubble vaults were still common, however. On the east coast of Yucatan, there are many areas with small buildings and vaults created using the rubble technique. Examples include El Meco, San Gervasio on Cozumel Island, Tancah, Xelha, Tulum and Santa Rita Corozal. The vaulted sections of the façades often tend to point outwards. The wall structure is rougher and the mortar layer thicker. The buildings were decorated once again with stucco and multi-colored wall paintings, often with complex mythological motifs. Areas marked by the Postclassic style are located not only in Yucatan, but also in the southern Lowlands (Topoxte and Lamanai, for example) and in the Highlands of Guatemala in Q'umarkaj, Iximche', and Mixco Viejo, capitals of the Postclassic Highland states.

331 *The Caracol of Chichen Itza. Colored lithograph based on a drawing by Frederick Catherwood; 1844*
The Caracol of Chichen Itza is a monumental circular building standing on a large, rectangular platform accessed by a broad open staircase. Because only very few circular buildings exist in Yucatan, the Caracol attracted the attention of scholars and travelers very early on. It was not scientifically examined, however, until the 1920s by the Carnegie Institute in Washington. The inscriptions date from the final building phase in around 906 A.D.

332 *The Temple of the Warriors at Chichen Itza, Yucatan, Mexico*
Long columned halls and avenues are a typical feature of the hybrid architecture of Chichen Itza, where elements of Maya architecture merge with forms from Central Mexico and other regions of Mesoamerica. The layout and structure of the Temple of the Warriors correspond to the so-called Morning Star Temple in the small pre-Hispanic settlement of Tula in the federal Mexican state of Hidalgo. By using columns and pillars as supports, it was possible to create large, airy halls. The tall pillars consist of several stone slabs and their capitals are topped with square covering stones.

333 *View of the Temple of the Warriors at Chichen Itza*
The entrance to the Temple of the Warriors is guarded by a stone figure lying on its back holding a circular bowl over its stomach and looking sideways as though observing the main plaza of Chichen Itza. This type of sculpture is called a Chacmool and they were common throughout the Postclassic period, and particularly so in Chichen Itza. The two erect serpents' bodies once supported the Temple of the Warriors' roof structure. An altar stands by the rear wall supported by small atlanteans.

334 *View of the El Castillo of Chichen Itza from the Temple of the Warriors*
The monumental buildings of the Postclassic period, whose form differed considerably from earlier architecture, were linked together in huge plazas. On the left of the picture is the so-called Group of the Thousand Columns with the El Castillo pyramid in the center and on the left the large ball court, one of the 13 ball courts in this metropolis. All the buildings in this area are in the same style, which is very similar to that found in Central Mexico.

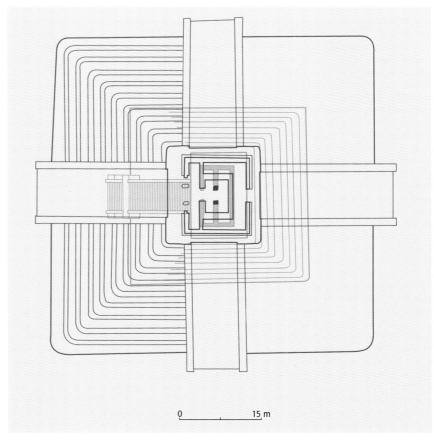

335 *Ground plan of the El Castillo of Chichen Itza*
The El Castillo is a temple building on a nine-stepped pyramid base. It is accessed by four stairways, each of which has 91 steps. The total number of steps including the platform therefore corresponds to the number of days in the year. Archeologists from the Carnegie Institute discovered an old building inside the El Castillo, where, in a well-preserved temple, a Chacmool figure and a red painted throne in the form of a jaguar were found. The jaguar's eyes and spots are made from pieces of jade.

0   15 m

THE HISTORY OF A MAYA SETTLEMENT – RESEARCH RESULTS FROM THE EXCAVATIONS AT XKIPCHE

Michael Vallo

About 1200 years ago, the Puuc area inhabited by the Maya south of the Sierrita de Ticul in the south-west part of the federal Mexican state of Yucatan formed a relatively unified cultural area. Some of the most impressive archeological relics from this once densely populated zone are its elaborately decorated stone buildings. The German/Austrian architect and photographer Teobert Maler produced important pioneering work in researching and documenting these pre-Hispanic settlements with his detailed building sketches, descriptions, and photographs. On one of his expeditions, in December, 1883, he visited the archeological site of Xkipche, approximately nine kilometers (5.5. miles) south of Uxmal, accompanied by two Indian helpers. His detailed account, which can be consulted at the Ibero-American Institute in Berlin, includes a brief description, pencil sketch, and photograph of the largest preserved building in Xkipche.

Questions concerning the origins and dates of the Puuc settlements remain largely unanswered even today, mainly because scientific research into the region's architecture and ceramics has only just begun. In order to establish reliable data relating to the Puuc region and its architecture, the Institute of Ancient American Studies and Ethnology at Bonn

University conducted six excavations spanning several months between 1991 and 1997 in cooperation with Mexican institutions.

An important part of the archeological research conducted in Xkipche, in addition to dating individual building sections and architectural styles, was concerned with the wider area covered by settlements in the Puuc region, the way they were divided, supplied themselves with basic necessities. The initial stages involved meticulous documentation of visible remains. According to the maps drawn up of the region, the buildings in Xkipche covered an area of approximately 0.7 square kilometers (0.4 square miles), and show a

total of 278 buildings in eight groups. The settlement is thought to have been inhabited by between 2000 and 3000 people when it was at its height. Cruciform groups of buildings built according to the points of the compass, which are separated from the central settlement by less densely built areas, surround the palace and ceremonial groups which appear to have formed the center.

The excavation work focused above all on the structure documented by Teobert Maler, which is now referred to as A1 (ill. 337) and the buildings in its immediate vicinity. Compared with the overall construction volume, Structure A1 (the so-called palace) is the largest in Xkipche and, with its 45 rooms, the

336 Structure A1 at Xkipche, west side of south wing. Xkipche, Yucatan, Mexico; 750–900 A.D. Structure A1 at Xkipche is a two-story palace which was repeatedly overbuilt, extended and added to over a long period. The aim of the excavation project was to investigate the founding of this large palace structure and to date its building phases.

337 Central area of Structure A showing Palace Structure A1 and the adjoining courtyards, Xkipche Structure A1, with 40 rooms, lies at the center of the largest archeological group in Xkipche. The two levels are connected by numerous stairway entrances and passages between the monumental structure and the other buildings. As is the case with nearly all the settlements in the Puuc area, the larger stone buildings surround smaller ones made from perishable materials. The latter were probably used for the preparation of food and for supplying the palace inhabitants with water from the numerous underground wells. The building phases of Structure A are indicated by the numbers 0 to 6 in the diagram, the earliest phase being 0 and the latest 6.

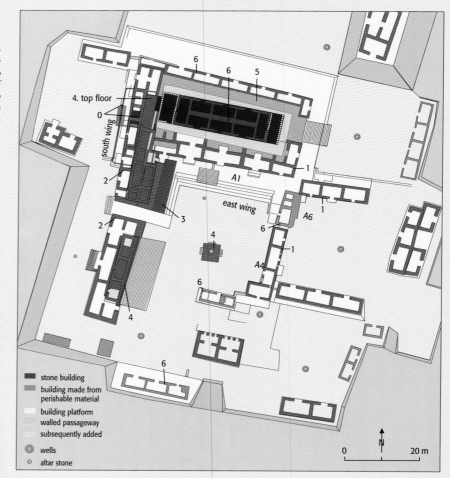

stone building
building made from perishable material
building platform
walled passageway
subsequently added
wells
altar stone

0   20 m

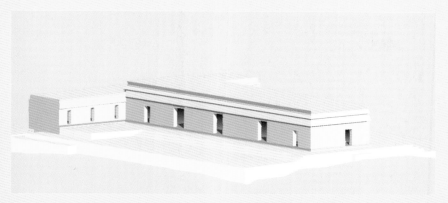

338 *CAD reconstruction of Structure A1 at Xkipche after the completion of the east and south wings*
Using CAD reconstructions based on precise measurements of visible remains, it is possible to trace the history of the building. Two building phases can be identified here. Most of the buildings in the Puuc region reached their final form after the addition of further sections over a long period of time.

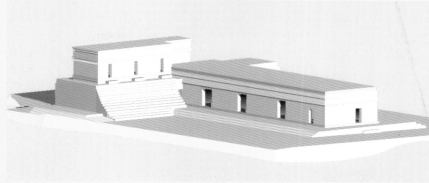

339 *CAD reconstruction of Structure A1 at Xkipche after the completion of the top floor on the south wing*
During the third building phase, another level was added to the south wing. Some of the lower rooms had to be strengthened with undressed stones in order to ensure stability. The open staircases built to the east and west of the south wing eventually granted access to the top floor.

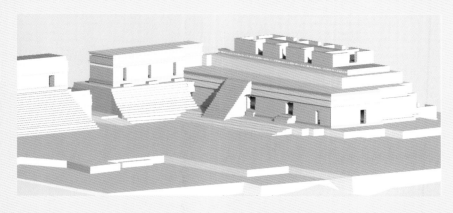

340 *CAD reconstruction of Structure A1 at Xkipche after the completion of the top floor on the west wing*
A further level was finally added to the east wing. Here too some of the lower rooms had to be strengthened with undressed stones in order to bear the weight. The top floor was accessed by an open staircase built in front of the east wing.

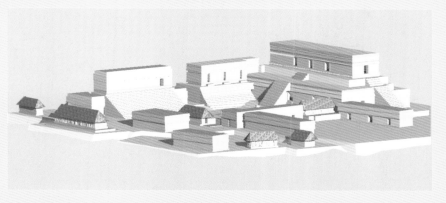

341 *CAD reconstruction of Structure A1 at Xkipche with surrounding stone buildings and constructions made from perishable material*
The illustration shows the incomplete layout of Structure A1. The work was suddenly interrupted. Further incomplete buildings indicate that the settlement was abandoned unexpectedly for reasons which are as yet unknown.

third largest building in the entire Puuc region. It consists of two two-story buildings, the east wing running from left to right, and the L-shaped south wing. According to current research, the settlement was established between 650 and 1050 A.D. in several phases on a large, artificially designed platform.

Ancient ceramic fragments discovered underneath the large platform structure in excavations of Structures A4 and A6 are extremely early traces of dense settlements in the Puuc region. Although the remains from this period are isolated and relatively inaccessible, wall sections have been discovered underneath Structure A4, which indicate the presence of an earlier buiding. This previous construction was almost completely destroyed in around 500 A.D., however, and an L-shaped building featuring a richly decorated stucco frieze was erected on top (ill. 338).

Remains of walls of a previous smaller building have also been found underneath the south wing of Structure A1, with colorfully painted stucco remains which were almost completely destroyed between c. 650 and 700 A.D. A building running from east to west with 12 rooms was erected in its place. Because of its huge stone doorposts and wooden and stone lintels, its façade divided into two or three sections and its characteristic rubble wall construction, this is a good example of the Classic Puuc architectural style. The ground floor of the current south wing was built shortly afterwards. During the period between c. 800 and 900 A.D., this L-shaped section of Structure A1 was extended into a monumental structure (ill. 339). An enormous open staircase was built to the west of the current south wing to access the rooms on the top floor which were built soon after.

The final phase in the construction of Structure A1 demonstrates the skills and general concepts used at the time. In around 950–1050 A.D., a platform measuring barely one and an half meters (five feet) high was added to the east wing of Structure A1. It was designed as a base for the ten rooms on the top floor. The building reached a height of approximately 1.8 meters (6 ft.) before suddenly being abandoned (ill. 340). A similar thing occurred during the extension of the northern section of Structure A1. The incomplete stone door reveals show that construction work came to an abrupt end in this period.

The reasons for this sudden halt in building work have so far not been explained. There is no evidence in the settlement areas examined either of fires occurring as a result of political conflict or indications of sudden upheavals which could have led to the overthrow of the nobility in the area. However, recent research results from the examination of pollen in the northern part of the Yucatan peninsula point to a general decline in climatic conditions toward the end of the 10th century. Reduced rainfall, coupled with an excessive strain on the soil, could have led to a dramatic decline in food supplies, which could account for the deterioration of this settlement area.

MAYA ARCHITECTURE AT TIKAL, GUATEMALA

Peter D. Harrison

Tikal was one of the largest cities in the Maya Lowlands (ill. 342). It gained huge political significance in the Early Classic period and therefore had an enormous influence not only on the politics but also on the art and architecture of many other Maya states in the Lowlands. The geographical location of Tikal favored its development into a Maya metropolis which spanned a large area and was characterized by outstanding architecture (ill. 344). Tikal is set among a series of broken hills that formed part of the watershed divide of the Yukatek peninsula. The fact that Tikal was established in this strategic position, through which one of the region's principal routes passed, linking the major river system of the Usumacinta River in the west to the Caribbean in the east, enabled the inhabitants to gain control over international trade.

The lifespan of Tikal is shorter than that of many Maya sites, extending from 800 B.C. to 950 A.D. Within this relatively short period, important cultural developments reached fruition, and these are reflected both in the architecture and in population numbers. Growth in the latter leads to an expansion in the numbers of buildings through time and hence a greater diversity in the types of architecture. Therefore, more is known about the later end of the spectrum than the earlier one. While we have a picture of Preclassic architecture at Tikal, we know a very great deal more about the Late Classic, where the style had been become peculiar to the city. During the earliest phases of Tikal's growth, the architecture bears greater similarity to that of other sites, and the diversion into a local style increases until the apogee of the Late Classic in the 8th and 9th centuries A.D. (ill. 343).

The roots of Maya architecture

The basis for most Maya architecture is derived from the form of the earliest farmhouses, built mostly of perishable materials, but which from the earliest times were set upon a more durable base (ill. 343).

A rock platform was prepared first and supporting posts were set into this platform. The walls were built of vertical poles with horizontal binders for support. This structure of bound poles (or wattles) was then covered with a rough plaster similar to the daub used in early European houses. The horizontal binders protrude, dividing the wall into two visible zones. The roof structure is held together by a single gable with connected supporting beams. The roof was covered with leaves of the guano (fan palm). Like the ancient agricultural techniques, the simplest version of the Maya hut has survived up to modern times. From this simple structure come all of the elements of the later, vaulted "palace" buildings and the temple structures which sit atop stepped pyramids (ill. 343).

Apart from those monumental buildings which derive from the vernacular architecture of the people, there is one other basic form, the pyramid, which is believed to be derived from the shape of mountain peaks. In the highlands of Guatemala and Mexico, Maya groups such as the Tzotzil of Zinacantan and Chamula still observe ceremonies to celebrate the gods which live in certain peaks. These stepped pyramids were seen as the dwelling place of gods, as is further confirmed by many sculptures at the base of these buildings, which describe the *witz*, the sacred mountain, of the Maya.

The early pyramids were the image of the holy mountain rendered in stone, but we do not know whether the top level contained a permanent building as the stone equivalent of the traditional palm-roofed huts. As the Maya were continually overbuilding, and in the process removed the highest parts of their old buildings (ill. 343), such traces are hard to find.

Late Classic Maya architecture at Tikal is mainly characterized by two elements: the representation in stone of a sacred mountain, and the representation in stone of the early house form. A great temple is, pictorially speaking, a house on a mountain, though this is a gross oversimplification of what could be done and was done in reality in the field of symbolic representation.

342 *View of Temples I and II. Tikal, Peten, Guatemala 734 A.D.*
Temples I and II soar above a sea of vegetation like towers. The actual temple buildings are positioned on solid, pyramid-shaped bases and crowned by a cresteria or "roof comb," a structure whose only function is to decorate the building and make its appearance even more imposing. These roof ridges were once covered with stucco and painted. Temple I, the rear temple in this drawing, was built in around 734 A.D. as a burial monument for King Jasaw Chan K'awiil.

343 *Section of the North Acropolis of Tikal*
During the excavations conducted by the University of Pennsylvania between 1956 and 1969, different phases in the construction of the North Acropolis were documented. The acropolis stood at the heart of the city and was the burial place of many early kings. This section gives a simplified overview of the buildings' history from the Preclassic to the Late Classic period.

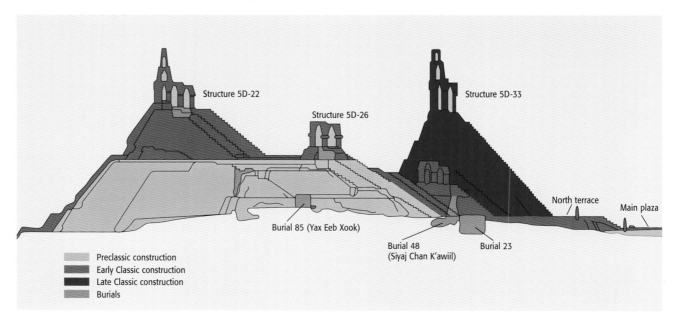

Structure 5D-22
Structure 5D-26
Structure 5D-33
North terrace
Main plaza
Burial 85 (Yax Eeb Xook)
Burial 48 (Siyaj Chan K'awiil)
Burial 23

Preclassic construction
Early Classic construction
Late Classic construction
Burials

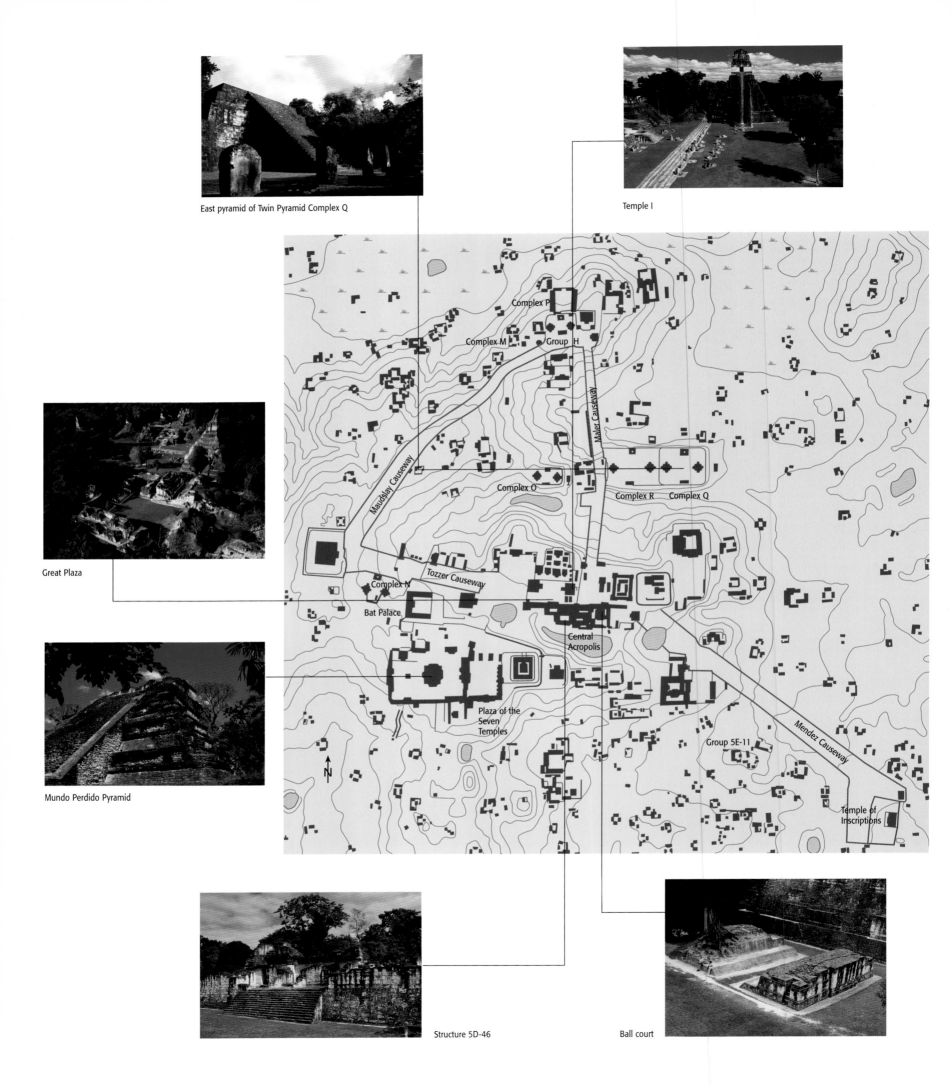

East pyramid of Twin Pyramid Complex Q

Temple I

Great Plaza

Mundo Perdido Pyramid

Structure 5D-46

Ball court

Complex P

Complex M

Group H

Maler Causeway

Maudslay Causeway

Complex O

Complex R

Complex Q

Tozzer Causeway

Complex N

Bat Palace

Central Acropolis

Plaza of the Seven Temples

Group 5E-11

Mendez Causeway

Temple of Inscriptions

N

344 *Map of Tikal*
This map (covering 4 square kilometers) shows the center of Tikal. The labeled buildings bear witness to over 1500 years of settlement and building activities. Four causeways, *sakbe*, link the main groups of buildings. The temples on either side of the Great Plaza in the center of the city were inaugurated in 734 A.D. Over the years, different cosmographic structures were created, the most important of which were Group H, Temple IV, and Temple VI, built toward the end of the 7th century. Smaller groups of house platforms are also marked.

345 *View from the North Acropolis of Temple I and the Central Acropolis. Tikal, Peten, Guatemala*
The photograph shows one of the most important buildings in the city center. The view is from the North Acropolis over the Great Plaza, bordered by Temple I on its east side, and the Central Acropolis, which the author of this chapter excavated. The Great Plaza marked the center of Tikal. The Central Acropolis probably served as an extended palace in which members of the nobility and the royal family lived.

The Great Plaza – the center point of the city and the universe

The cosmological orientation toward the four points of the compass, with their various specific associations, can be found in the Great Plaza of Tikal, the physical and cultic center point of the city. In all Maya cities, large public plazas formed the center of social and religious life. The highest temple pyramids were grouped around the central plazas together with the living quarters of the nobility. These plazas were often abandoned in the course of a city's life and re-established in another place. In general, however, the pavement of the plazas were made up of many layers of white stucco placed on top of each other. They were continually renewed and formed the center point of the community for several decades and often even lasted for several centuries.

The architectural elements which surround the Great Plaza were the longest used buildings in the city (ill. 345). Some of the oldest buildings rose on the so-called North Acropolis, which forms the northern border of the plaza. None of the Preclassic buildings has been preserved above ground level, having been pulled down or built over later. By the time of the Early Classic (250–550 A.D.), most of the existing buildings had been erected. These were all temples, and while not every one has been excavated, sufficient archeological information has been retrieved to establish that the site must have been a necropolis, the burial place of kings. The north-south axis of the Acropolis was favored during the Early Classic, but soon became too architecturally crowded to allow for further mortuary structures. New temples were built across the front of the Acropolis on the North Terrace.

On the south side of the Great Plaza is the Central Acropolis, already mentioned as a seat of the royal court and partly used as a royal residence. This group also has its beginnings in the Late Preclassic (150–250 A.D.), then flourished during the Early Classic and completely exploded with new constructions during the Late Classic under the influence of Tikal's peak of wealth and success under the aegis of three successive rulers.

King Jasaw Chan K'awiil was responsible for the remainder of the Great Plaza as we see it today. It included Structure 5D-33-1, the earliest of the tall temples that characterize the Tikal style of temple architecture. Temples I and II, facing each across the square on its east and west sides, were erected under the aegis of his son Yik'in Chan K'awiil (734–736 A.D.; ill. 346). With the erection of these last two mighty temples, Yik'in Chan K'awiil created a new cosmic space for the city. Whereas the North Acropolis had served as one of Tikal's cosmic realms during the Early Classic (the other was in the Mundo Perdido pyramid group; see ill. 354), now the whole complex surrounding the Great Plaza served as a new cosmic zone, replicating in many ways the configuration of the twin pyramid complex (ill. 359). Temples I and II are not identical twins, but both are ceremonial pyramidal structures which bound the east and west sides of a defined platform. The North Acropolis, once itself a cosmic group, now represented the heavens, the resting place of kings. To symbolize the underworld there is a nine-doorway palace (5D-120) on the south side, which is more elaborate than those found in similarly conceived twin pyramid buildings. It is raised on several platforms and originally had a pair of galleries situated one behind the other. It does not lie on the central north-south axis of the Plaza of the North Acropolis and this is probably because an earlier building, Structure 5D-71, was considered too important to remove. This building, with its three doorways, lies exactly on the sacred north-south axis.

Palaces – the dwelling places of kings and their royal households

For Maya scholars, the palace concept comprises a wide range of forms and functions. It is the palace that most emulates the shapes of normal houses made of non-durable materials. The term "range-type structure" rather awkwardly describes the fact that the majority of palaces contain several rooms arranged next to each other. However, as a single group study in the Central Acropolis demonstrated, the variety from simplest to most complex includes single room (unconnected), and every possible variety of rooms placed beside and behind one another (ill. 349–351). The term "acropolis" has been used by Maya scholars to refer to the large platforms on which several building complexes stand. A functional description is not implied, but in the case of the Central Acropolis it can be assumed that the building did indeed serve as a royal palace (ill. 351). Palaces often consisted of several stories, each one (ill. 351) being a later addition with access to an outdoor staircase. In a few isolated cases, however, they were also equipped with inner staircases (ills. 346, 347).

Extensive groups of buildings such as the Central Acropolis had a range of complex functions and were probably the seat of the royal court. A major question is whether some or all of the palaces served as residences and, again, there is no single answer. There are many clues to suggest that some of the larger structures of the Central Acropolis served as dwelling places for the rulers of Tikal. For example, Structure 5D-46 is accepted as the permanent residence built by the ruler Great Jaguar Paw (A.D. 359–378; ill. 348).

There are other Late Classic palace groupings at Tikal such as Group G, Group F, and the Bat Palace. Examination of the masonry styles and interior features, together with some excavations for all but F Group, dates these palaces as firmly Late Classic (roughly 730–830 A.D.). These groups could well have served multiple functions for successive rulers as both residences and the seat of various offices of their royal courts. The core location of the Central Acropolis, adjacent to the Great Plaza, suggests that at least some functions of the royal court took place here from its first construction in the Late Preclassic (350 B.C.) until the abandonment of Tikal (c. 950 A.D.).

346 *Aerial view of the center of Tikal*

This aerial photograph taken by Nicholas Hellmuth shows the center of the Maya city of Tikal in its present state. In the foreground we see the multi-story palace building dating back to the 4th–9th century A.D. The large Temples I and II are in the center of the picture in front of part of the North Acropolis, which was the necropolis of the rulers of Tikal and the shrine of the dynastic nobility during the Early Classic period. Most of this large city in central Peten, Guatemala, was later reclaimed by the forest.

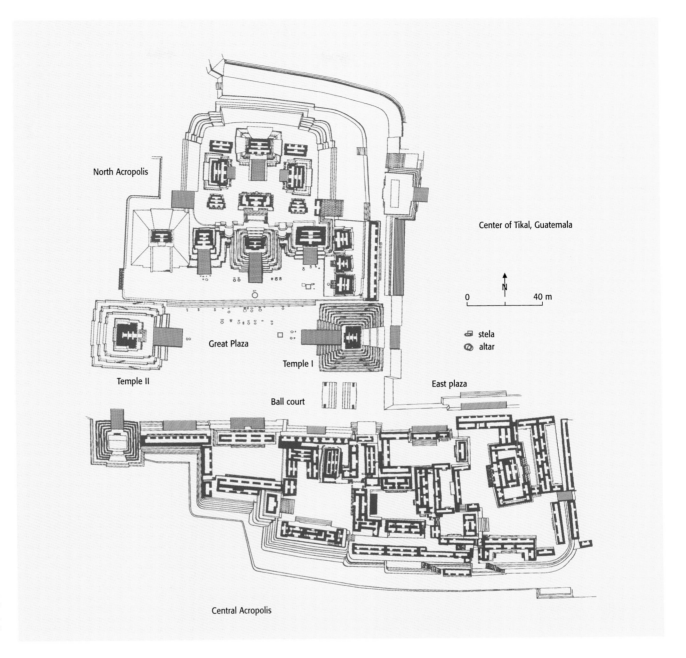

North Acropolis

Center of Tikal, Guatemala

N

0   40 m

stela
altar

Great Plaza

Temple I

Temple II

East plaza

Ball court

Central Acropolis

347 *The holy center of Tikal*

The center of Tikal grew up around the North Acropolis in around 800 B.C. The area now known as the Great Plaza was completed between 695 and 734 A.D., when the ruler Jasaw Chan K'awiil established a "Three Stone Place." This image of the hearthstones, which represented the center of the universe in Maya cosmology, consisted of Temples 5D-33-1, I and II. The Central Acropolis was located south of this point and, in contrast to the temples further north, served as the residence of Tikal's ruling dynasty.

348 *Structure 5D-46, a royal residence from the Early Classic period. Tikal, Peten, Guatemala; Early Classic, middle of 4th century A.D.*

Some of the buildings in the Central Acropolis housed the royal living chambers. Structure 5D-46 was erected in the middle of the 4th century A.D. by the ruler "Great Jaguar Paw." The original palace, which had been spared repeated attacks on the city, was extended several centuries later. The inscription on a devotional vessel found under the western staircase refers to the building as *yotoot*, "dwelling," of King Great Jaguar Paw. The palace served for five hundred years, from 350–850 A.D., as a residence and was still inhabited during the city's decline (850–950 A.D.).

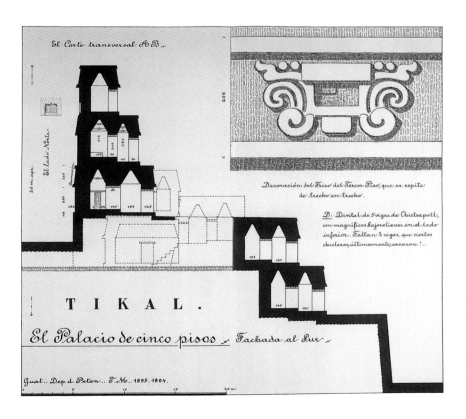

349 *Inner room of Structure 5D-52. Tikal, Peten, Guatemala; A.D. 741*
The interior of this building, erected in 741 A.D. by the 27th ruler, Yik'in Chan K'awiil, features vaults with the original wooden beams made from Campeche wood (*Haematoxilum campechianum*) from the nearby marshes. Walled, plastered benches can also be seen, which may have been used for resting or receiving visitors. The building consists of three different stories from different periods. The building is situated close to the older building erected by Yikin Chan K'awiil's ancestors and the family seat of the ruler Chak Tok Yich'aak, shown in ill. 348.

350 *A room in the Central Acropolis*
The crumbling vault in a room in the Central Acropolis reveals the high vaults that were characteristic of Tikal, and a bench placed along the narrow side of the room. A typical feature of Tikal architecture was the discrepancy between the size of the buildings and the space available inside.

351 *Section of the "Five Story Palace" in Tikal. Drawing by Teobert Maler, 1904*
Teobert Maler traveled to Tikal in 1895 and 1904 to measure and draw the city's architecture and to capture its hieroglyphic inscriptions on glass with a camera. He was particularly impressed by the "Five Story Palace," a building consisting of two sections, the top three stories and lower two-story structure added later on. The top level was reached via a complicated staircase system.

353 *The ball court. Tikal, Peten, Guatemala, Building 5D-74; Late Classic, 600–900 A.D.*
The three most well-known ball courts in Tikal are fairly small in comparison with those in other locations. The ball court shown here was in a particularly exposed location between Temple I (in the background) and the Central Acropolis, from where this photograph was taken.

Ball courts – the coming together of sport and religion

Ball courts were used by the Maya right up to the Spanish Conquest when games were witnessed in action. The game was highly ceremonial and played an important role in the ritual training of young men, probably with a focus on learning the arts of competition and physical confrontational skills. Ball courts can be recognized by their characteristic form – a playing field in the form of a stretched-out "I" surrounded on either side by banked walls (see Colas/Voss, p. 186 ff.).

There were few ballcourts at Tikal. The one located in the East Plaza, behind Temple I, is quite elaborate with a roofed building atop each of the sloping embankments which bordered the playing area. This is probably the work of King Jasaw Chan Kawiil (A.D. 682–734).

A second much smaller ball court is located prominently in the Great Plaza just south of Temple I (ills. 352, 353). The court can be clearly seen from some of the tall palaces bordering the central acropolis as well as from Temple I. The court also contained staircases leading to small platforms on the embankments.

The third example is a building complex, so far not excavated, which lies east of the Mundo Perdido Group in an area known as the Plaza of the Seven Temples. Here, the configuration suggests three adjacent playing courts. The hills of rubble are quite large and could be hiding elaborate structures.

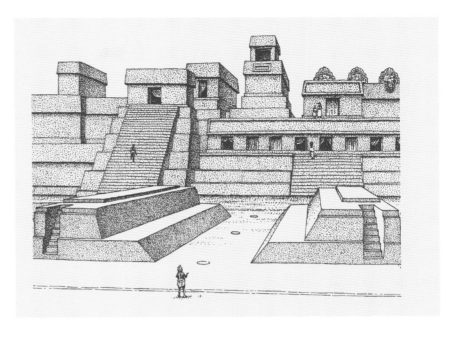

352 *Drawing reconstructing the ball court and the Central Acropolis in Tikal*
This reconstruction shows the ball court to the south of Temple I on the Great Plaza. The view of the Central Acropolis behind shows the complexity of this palace complex and the different superstructures, beneath which the earlier architecture has been retained. A room at the northern end of Structure 5D-62 in the center of the upper building group has a large window opening directly onto the central axis of the ball court. It probably served as the royal box during ball games.

Temples – dwelling places for the gods and the nobility

A temple is defined as a structure with a primarily ceremonial function, devoted to a god or gods, which may also include human ancestors. Evidence of ceremonial activities, such as sacrificial fires on the floors, the presence of votive offerings and occasional associated middens of the ceramics of ceremony (censers, figurines, musical instruments). Temples were also built as monumental tombs over the burial of a king (ill. 343). There are six large temples erected on pyramids in Tikal. They were all built in the Late Classic period, probably in the 8th century during the reign of King Jasaw Chan K'awiil and his sons. Temple I was built in around 735 A.D. as a burial chamber for Jasaw Chan K'awiil (ills. 355, 356). It is not known whether the other temple pyramids also contained burials. Temple IV, built in around 745 A.D. to the west of the city center, is the highest building ever erected by the Maya, standing 65 meters (213 ft.) high. The temple building and attic of Temple 6 are completely covered with a hieroglyphic inscription which recounts the entire history of Tikal.

353 *Temple I at Tikal, plan and cross section. Drawing by Teobert Maler, 1904*
The obvious inconsistency between the usable space and the mass of a building, which were typical of the Temple of Tikal and many other cities in the southern Lowlands, can be seen in the plan of the 47 m high Temple I and above all in the cross section of the building. The entire nine-step pyramid base consists of banked-up rocks and

mortar and only the outer façade of the pyramid is covered with cut stones. The actual temple building consisted of three small, narrow rooms. Each door was topped with a lintel made from the hard wood of the sapodilla or chicozapote tree. The recessed roof structure served simply as decoration and had no practical function. It contained two empty rooms, which reduced the weight resting on the vaults.

354 *The Mundo Perdido Pyramid. Tikal, Petem, Guatemala; Early Classic period*
The Mundo Perdido Pyramid (Structure 5C-54), excavated by Guatemalan architects under the leadership of Juan Pedro Laporte in the 1980s, and the highest building in Tikal from the Early Classic, consists of a long building with a symmetrical radial layout. A staircase rose on all four sides and this structure was later maintained in superstructures and extensions.

The different building stages extended from the beginning of the Late Preclassic to the Early Classic. The version from the latter period is still in existence and was never built over. The layout and orientation of the building are similar to those of Structure E-VII-sub in nearby Uaxactun. Like the latter building, the Mundo Perdido Pyramid may have been used as a kind of solar observatory.

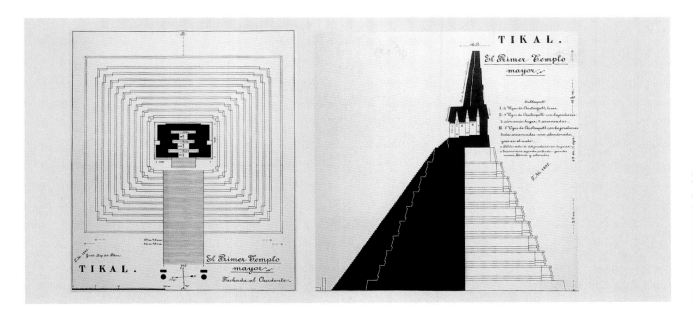

356 *Temple I. Tikal, Peten, Guatemala; c. 732 A.D.*
This building, erected for Jasaw Chan K'awiil, is typical
of the Tikal style and has become a symbol of the city
and its 26th ruler. The latter is thought to have died in
732 A.D. and his burial temple was built during the
following two years. Temple II opposite, from where
this photograph was taken, was dedicated to the wife of
Jasaw Chan K'awiil and was begun before his death. It
was probably completed, however, at the same time as
Temple I. The relief depiction of the ruler and his wife
on the lintel of the burial temple will overlook the Great
Plaza for eternity.

357 *The east pyramid of Twin Pyramid Complex Q. Tikal, Peten, Guatemala; 771 A.D.*

Complex Q was erected on the east of the Great Plaza by Yax Ayiin, the 29th ruler of Tikal, in 771 A.D. to mark the end of the 17th K'atun. A symmetrical radial pyramid forms the eastern part of a group of two identical buildings. Being a rare example of a so-called twin pyramid complex, Complex Q was partly reconstructed to give observers an impression of this type of building. A row of smooth stelae stands in front of the east pyramid, whilst others depicting the royal clients of the buildings stand within an enclosure on the north side.

358 *Stela 16 and Altar 5. Tikal, Twin Pyramid Complex N; 711 A.D.; Stela 16: H. 352 cm, W. 128 cm; Altar 5: dia. 167 cm*

Stela 16 was built at the same time as Altar 5 in 711 A.D. to celebrate the end of a K'atun period in the Twin Pyramid Complex N on Tozzer Way. Whilst the stela depicts King Jasaw Chan K'awiil in his full official regalia, Altar 5 presents a historical scene whose interpretation is still unclear. Two people – probably the king of Tikal and a distant relative – exhume the bones of a noble person, probably the wife of Jasaw Chan K'awiil. The altar originally lay in front of Stela 16.

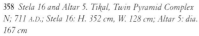

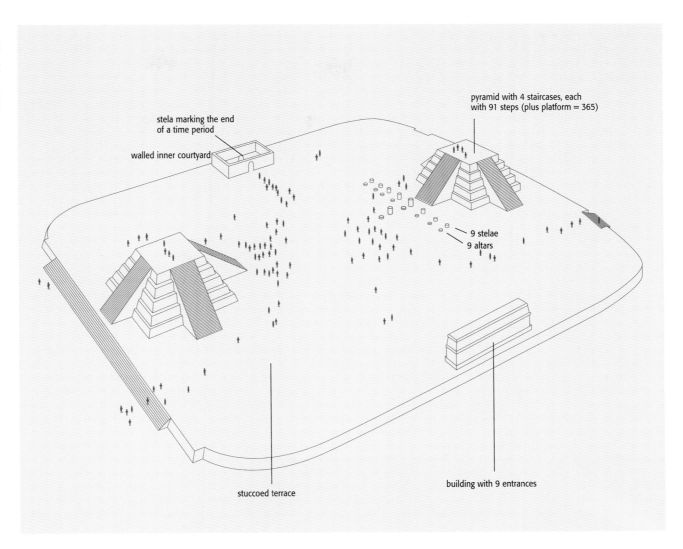

359 *Diagram of a twin pyramid complex*
Twin pyramid complexes were large temple pyramids which were erected every 20 years to celebrate the end of a K'atun period. The date marking the event is preserved on the stela, which stands at the north end of the square in an enclosure. The large pyramids stand on an east/west axis and mark the course followed by the sun, while the building at the south represents the underworld.

stela marking the end of a time period

pyramid with 4 staircases, each with 91 steps (plus platform = 365)

walled inner courtyard

9 stelae
9 altars

stuccoed terrace

building with 9 entrances

Twin pyramid groups – celebrating the 20 year cycle

The twin pyramid is seen as the typical form for building groups in Tikal. It is gradually becoming clear, though, that this same type of grouping is to be found in the surrounding area at much smaller "satellite" sites such as Ixlu, Zacpeten, and Yaxha. The complex consists of a pair of matching stepped pyramids on the east and west sides of a raised platform (ill. 359).

The pyramids are radially symmetric, with a staircase on each of the four sides (ill. 357). The whole group is oriented to the cardinal points, representing the world view of the Maya. The east and west represent the direction of the sun's movement as it rises and sets each day. The number of stairs at all buildings in the group adds up to 365, corresponding to one calendar year. The buildings on the north and south sides of the plaza represent the heavens and the underworld. A row of nine non-sculpted stelae stands in front of the buildings on the west side of the plaza. The significance of these monuments is still unclear.

Each of these building complexes was constructed at the end of a 20-year K'atun of the Maya calendar by the ruling leader to announce to his subjects that he had successfully completed this 20-year ruling period, even if it had not begun under his rule. The ceremonial purpose, therefore, was a dual celebration of the passage of time without catastrophe, and also a celebration of the ruler himself.

Accordingly, on the north side, representing the heavens, there was an open-topped enclosure containing a carved stone stela depicting the ruler in triumph, accompanied by a round stone altar in front, usually depicting a subjugated, conquered ruler from another city state.

Group N is located close to Temple IV and contains Stela 16 dating from 711 A.D. and Altar 5 from the same period (ill. 358). Altar 5 does not depict a vanquished opponent, but rather shows two lords in conference over a pile of bones and a skull. The long inscription describes how the ruler of Tikal, Jasaw Chan K'awiil, met with a distant relative to retrieve the bones of his deceased wife from another city where she had been buried, prior to an invasion of that city which threatened desecration of her grave. It is a remarkable and unique story of diplomacy and love – something which is seldom found in hieroglyphic inscriptions.

The building of twin pyramid groups as ceremonial time markers began in Tikal in the Early Classic period and continued until 790 A.D. when the last one was erected. It has been speculated that the flat-topped pyramids were used for dance ceremonies that occurred, perhaps each new year, to mark the passing of time, until a new grouping was constructed.

The south side of the complex was marked by a single room, a long "palace" structure with nine doorways facing north. This building is seen as representing the underworld, while the nine doorways are the nine lords of the underworld who figure largely in Maya mythology.

Architectural geometry and the three great kings of Tikal

In a period of a little more than a century (692–800 A.D.), three rulers in father-son-grandson succession changed the face of Tikal. Nearly all of the great temples were constructed during this period, but not all can be attributed precisely to a ruler by name (ill. 360). Structure 5D-33-1 was built under the rule of Jasaw Chan K'awiil. Temples I, II, and IV, and probably Temple VI, were built by his son Yik'in Chan K'awiil as well as numerous other palaces and a twin pyramid group. Finally, the grandson, Nun Yax Ayiin II, is thought to have constructed Temple V along with other major palaces and twin pyramid groups. Temple III is later in date (A.D. 810) and represents the last major monumental effort to be completed at Tikal. Other large projects such as the remains of the East Acropolis may be the unfinished attempt of a nearly bankrupt king to build his own glorious temple.

Although they did not initiate a particular form of geometric layout, it was through the efforts of the three major rulers that we find examples of city planning using a triangular configuration based upon earlier structures. There

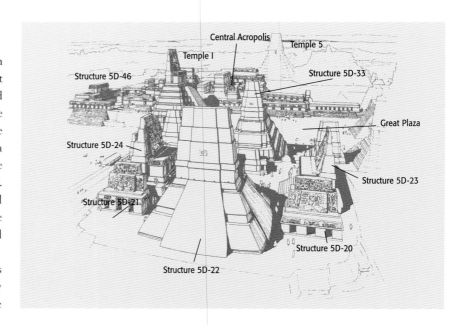

360 *City plan*
Right-angled triangles were often used in Tikal to link new buildings with existing ones. In the constellation shown here, Temple 43 of the northern group (Group H) is connected with Altar V in Twin Pyramid Complex N and Temple I. The former originates from the Early Classic period and is the oldest element. This triangular configuration must already have been planned when Group N and Altar V were erected in 711 A.D. The same constructor built Temples I and II on the connecting axis, forming a perfect right-angle on the threshold of Temple I.

361 *Drawing reconstructing the North Acropolis and the Main plaza*
The North Acropolis, whose construction spanned several centuries, is the burial place of the kings of Tikal. This reconstruction gives an impression of its condition in 800 A.D. The highest building at the North Acropolis, Temple 22, is in the foreground. The view stretches from the Great Plaza, past Temple V in the background and the gigantic, non-excavated South Acropolis, an enormous platform on which another temple stands.

exist literally dozens of examples of the use of right-angled triangles to plan new buildings at Tikal, but the most spectacular examples date to the reigns of Yik'in Chan K'awiil and Nuun Yax Ayiin II. They created Group N, a twin pyramid group that now lies close to Temple IV, not yet built at the time, and Temples I and II, which stand directly opposite each other.

The central axis of the two temples leads directly to Altar V described above, in the northern enclosure of Group N. The significance is that Temple II was dedicated to the deceased wife of Jasaw, who planned his own mortuary structure at Temple I, and commemorated his wife's death at Altar V. As if this feat were not enough, a right-angle from the doorway of Temple I, the easternmost point of the above-cited alignment, leads to the doorway of Temple 3D-43 in the North Acropolis. The latter is an Early Classic mortuary structure, and it is not known who it was erected for. It was considered sufficiently important by King Yik'in Chan K'awiil to use it as a reference point for his ancestral triangulation. The three points of the triangle are the doorway of Temple I, Altar V, and the doorway of 3D-43. They form a perfect right-angled triangle (ill. 360).

A further example is the connection between Great Temples I, V, and IV. This also is a right-angled triangle with the added feature of an alignment through a palace window in Structure 5D-65. The room in the palace is laid out asymmetrically, and looks directly at the doorway of Temple V. As the latest of these three Great Temples, it follows that Temple V and Palace 5D-65 were built together as a unified project. In all cases of such precise triangulation, one ruler is paying physical tribute to one or more of his direct ancestors. While this feature of city planning is known at other major sites (for example Palenque), it is best demonstrated at Tikal where excavations have revealed a chronological ordering, and indicate that each new monumental building project paid homage in some carefully planned spatial relationship to two earlier structures.

The influence of Tikal's architecture on other cities

The architecture of Tikal is similar to that of the surrounding regions in many respects, especially at the early end of the occupational scale. However, it was during the Late Classic that the city flourished and developed a style of its own. This style was introduced by a single ruler, Jasaw Chan K'awiil, and was continued and expanded by his own direct descendants. The tall, single-doorway temple raised to the heavens on an artificial mountain was a style that Tikal began and was imitated in the region immediately surrounding it, and is called the Central Peten style. Decades later, in the Rio Bec region to the north, range-structure palaces appeared with a façade of two flanking false fronts, imitating the style of Temple I at Tikal (ill. 362). This suggests that the Tikal style influenced a large area of the Maya Lowlands over a long period.

The influence of its architecture can also be seen further north in the buildings of the city of Oxkintok. The main pyramid features a façade decoration in which the end wall of a pyramid step is connected to an upper sloping area with a staggered area underneath. This type of structure is known as "apron molding" and is characteristic of Tikal architecture. It is an impressive example of the extent to which Tikal influenced the architectural style of the Maya.

362 *The Palace at Rio Bec Bin Campeche, Mexico; c.600–900 A.D.*
A palace with false façades resembling copies of Temple I at Tikal was erected in Rio Bec, situated far to the north of Tikal. It is assumed that this building was created after the downfall of Tikal, but it was nevertheless influenced by the style of the architecture from the period of the 26th ruler of Tikal. This "cultural remembrance" of a different period may relate to political relationships which were re-established at this time after a long phase of enmity between Tikal and this northern region.

PROCESSIONS, PILGRIMS AND LOAD-CARRIERS – THE CEREMONIAL ROADS

Markus Eberl

The Maya Lowlands are an extremely diverse cultural area. Besides the agricultural terraces, it was above all the ceremonial causeways, with which the Maya shaped their natural environment according to their own ideas. Because of their pale limestone layer, they were referred to as *sakbe*, which in Yukatek Maya means white causeway. These causeways were designed to resist adverse weather and erosion and their networks came together in the center of Maya cities from where they radiated out into the surrounding areas. However, there is no archeological evidence so far of extensive causeway networks connecting the main centers.

The causeways were between a few dozen and 100 meters (110 yd.) long and five to ten meters (16 to 33 ft.) wide. They were created in the form of causeways (generally only around 50 centimeters/20 inches high), which made them stand out in the surrounding countryside (ill. 363). Only a small

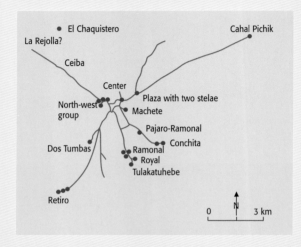

363 *The causeway network in Caracol*
With a total length of at least 70 km, Caracol in Belize possesses one of the largest known regional causeway networks in the Maya Lowlands. It radiates out from the city and connects small surrounding areas with the center. By means of the streets, an area of over 300 square kilometers was developed, and was probably directly controlled by Caracol.

number of cities, such as Caracol for example, had actual networks which linked the separate *sakbe* together and covered several kilometers. The most extensive causeway network is the one in the area of Coba in the north-eastern part of the Yucatan peninsula (ill. 364) with around 50 *sakbe* covering a total length of over 150 kilometers (93 miles).

The Maya built their streets according to a standard principle. They cleared the ground of vegetation, laid the side walls and filled the area in between with rubble. A thin layer of lime cement or mortar was added to make the streets resistant to water and deterioration. The top layer was sometimes slightly vaulted, allowing water that accumulated during the rainy season to drain off easily.

The *sakbe* tended to be built in straight lines rather than following the natural course of the landscape. Turnings and corners were rare, and gentle bends generally marked changes in direction. Uneven ground was leveled out with appropriate

364 *The ceremonial causeway in the center of Labna, Yucatan, Mexico*
The causeway connected the area of the Puuc settlement of Labna used for ceremonies with the distant palace, the residence of the ruling classes. The elevation and light stucco coating are typical of the ceremonial pathways, which were referred to by the Yukatek Maya as "white causeways."

he is (?)

(the god)
Chaak

dry
tortillas

on the
causeway

goods
(he brings)

are his
sacrificial
food

365 *The Rain God as a wanderer on a causeway. Detail from the Dresden Codex, p. 65; provenance unknown; Late Postclassic, 1200–1500 A.D.; fig bark paper coated with lime, painted; side: H. 20.4 cm, W. 9.0 cm; Dresden, Sächsische Landesbibliothek*
With a gnarled walking stick in his left hand and a bundle on his back, the Rain God Chaak is walking on a causeway depicted here as a band with footprints. The inscription, consisting of six hieroglyphs on the upper edge, relates to the picture: the Rain God Chaak is on a journey. The simple, unseasoned food, typical of what was taken on journeys at the time, is to be given as a sacrifice for Chaak.

foundations and filling materials. Very few bridges were built, however.

The causeways, some of which covered several kilometers, revealed a high level of organizational skill and technical expertise. The extent of the building activities is reflected in the fact that far more earth and rubble was required for certain causeways than for a pyramid standing dozens of meters high. A great deal of effort must have been required simply to organize the workforce involved. The famous *sakbe* have been well preserved in many

areas despite being more than 1,000 years old, which is clear proof of their solid construction. Only a few *sakbe* were constructed between distant settlements. Above all they were a typical feature of the cities themselves. They connected different quarters together, as well as individual temple and palace complexes within these quarters.

In addition to these connections, there were also regional causeways which began in the center of the city and on which arches or special buildings were erected. The finest examples are to be found in northern Yucatan. In Kabah, a square platform was erected in the place where the causeway from Uxmal arrives in the center of Kabah. Two ramps lead up to the platform. A single arch creates a link between the city center and the surrounding area. The *sakbe* were not designed for caravans or oxcarts. There were no pack animals in the Yucatan region and, although the Mayas were familiar with the wheel (the *sakbe* were leveled with large stone rollers), they never made wheeled vehicles. From the Preclassic period until the arrival of the Spaniards, most goods were transported on people's backs (ills. 365, 366). A considerable weight of goods was carried on waterways and coastal routes, however. In contrast to the Roman Empire, military and administrative aspects were not considered important with regard to the Maya causeway systems, as they had no standing army and no extensive military organization.

The missionaries who arrived in the country when Yucatan was conquered by the Spaniards refer repeatedly to the solid causeway structure in their reports. In 1688, the Spanish author Fray Diego López de Cogolludo described the religious significance of the island of Cozumel in north-west Yucatan and the associated pilgrimage:

"The causeways (which like the major [Spanish] roads could be trusted to lead to the desired destination) enabled them [the pilgrims] to reach Cozumel: to keep their vows, to present their sacrifices, to beg for help for their troubles and their misplaced adoration of false gods."

This and other reports tell of the pilgrims and processions that used the *sakbe*. Evidence of their ceremonial function can be found not only in colonial documents, which describe the actual use of the *sakbe* or at least memories of such uses, but also in the structure and features of these streets. They culminated in the centers of cities, which were dominated by temple pyramids and residential complexes for the nobility where the most important rituals were held. With a little imagination we can almost see the celebratory processions and pilgrimages that covered these streets more than 1,000 years ago.

The ceremonial nature of the *sakbe* did not preclude other functions, however. It seems likely that the Maya causeways were also used for economic purposes even though they did not form extensive networks. The ruling nobility were dependent on the paying of tributes. Colorful representations on painted vessels depict gifts of food, beans, material and luxury items such as jaguar pelts and codices being presented to the ruler. Tributes collected by underlings may have been brought to the court of the divine ruler in the center of the city via the ceremonial causeways. The political symbolism of these causeways may also have been significant. The urban *sakbe* not only linked the temple areas with the residences of the upper social level, they also made them stand out in the surrounding area. In this way the ruling elites could be sure that the simple maize farmers were aware of their special status and ubiquitous divine standing.

366 *On the way to market*
In Guatemala people still carry goods on their backs. The load tied to the wooden frame is held in place with a headband, known in local Spanish as a *mecapal*. Because of the rough ground and the lack of pack animals, this was the only way of carrying heavy items over long distances. This photograph, taken in the Highlands of Guatemala in the 1930s, shows a Maya carrying clay jugs on his way to market. To this day, traders still carry packs on foot over distances of up to 30 km.

UNDERSTANDING THE MURALS OF BONAMPAK

Mary Miller

From the end of the first millennium B.C. until the time of the Spanish invasion, the Maya frequently decorated the walls of their buildings with colored paintings (ill. 367). Most of these paintings are found in tombs, but particularly in the western Maya region and toward the end of the Late Classic period, at the same time that sculpture was also painted, artists worked to cover entire walls with elaborate programs executed in dry stucco.

The most remarkable example of Maya mural painting came to light in 1946, when Lacandon Maya led the American film-maker Giles Healey to a site that they had long known themselves but which they had showed to no outsider until then (ill. 369). Rumors of such a place had reached Teobert Maler during his late 19th-century exploration of the region, but Maler took the wrong direction and ended up at Budsilha, along the Usumacinta River. Healey, who was making a movie about the ancient ruins and the life of the modern Maya, immediately recognized the importance of the painted buildings. Within days he had reported their existence to leading Maya scholars. Sylvanus Morley, the most senior Mayanist at the Carnegie Institution, called the site "Bonampak," meaning "painted walls" in Yukatek Mayan. Scientists soon began to refer to the Bonampak images to illustrate and support their ideas about Maya culture. Although fragments of other painted walls have survived, the pictures at Bonampak are distinguished by a number of features, not least of which is their almost intact condition.

Depictions of daily court life and dynastic history

The paintings give a clear depiction of the lives of the pre-Hispanic Maya, touching on themes such as social hierarchy, wars and court life. Within the three-chambered building now known as Structure 1 (ill. 371), hundreds of individual Maya lords can be seen together. The paintings are scaled at one-half to two-thirds life size, and they create a life-like environment for the viewer. The paintings reveal emotion, particularly in the rendering of the captives in

Room 2. Emotion and humor feature in the painting of ceramic vessels, but no other monumental work captures so well the spirit of agony and victory in ancient America. Although several artists worked on the paintings, some of them, particularly the masters of the north walls of Rooms 1 and 2, were extraordinary in their ability to render the contours and movements of the human body (ill. 368). The three rooms can be read in sequence, although Room 2 is the largest and its bench the highest, so it would surely have served as the throne room from which the most important lord would have presided. By placing the room celebrating war and battle between rooms celebrating other events from the history of the dynasty, the paintings also provide a united, harmonious narration of a world that seems simultaneously fractured by war and sacrifice.

Just 26 kilometers (16 miles) from Yaxchilan, the Bonampak lords had affiliated themselves with both the major Maya city of Yaxchilan and another smaller nearby town, Lacanha, by the end of the 8th century, when the great paintings were made. The paintings celebrate the relationship between these centers and the victories they shared.

The rulers of Bonampak had adopted the Early Classic Tikal manner of constructing their important ceremonial buildings in one acropolis complex. Stelae lined the plaza and the lower levels of the acropolis; wall panels studded the recessed façades. Beyond the plaza, at both the Burned Group and the Frey Group, Bonampak lords may have had palatial dwellings, as well as communal dwellings for warriors and priests (ill. 370).

The huge building of Structure 1, built c. 790, was certainly the single most elaborate building ever constructed at the site. In its attention to the larger world

367 *View of the west wall of Room1. Bonampak, Chiapas, Mexico, Structure 1; Late Classic, c. 790 A.D.; wall painting*
The inner walls of the three rooms in Structure 1 in Bonampak are covered with paintings of historical scenes to form a kind of stone codex. Unfortunately there are no other buildings in the Maya region in which the wall paintings have been so well preserved.

368 *Musicians' procession. Copy of a wall painting (detail); Bonampak, Chiapas, Mexico, Structure 1, Room 1, west wall; Late Classic, c. 790 A.D.*
This painting in the lower part of the west wall shows part of a musicians' procession (ill. 367). The central figure beats the large slit drum and looks at two men who are hitting a tortoise shell with a deer's antlers. Two other figures hold large pumpkin rattles in their hands.

369 *The acropolis of Bonampak deep in the jungle*
Bonampak was hidden in the jungle for many years and was only known to a group of Lacandon Maya. In 1946, they led the American film-maker Giles Healey to the ruins, which he then made known to scientists. This illustration only shows the acropolis emerging from the woodland. Numerous other groups of buildings still lie buried beneath thick layers of vegetation.

Painters began to map out the large color areas, particularly the blue and red backgrounds, and then painted the human figures over these. Finally, once all the pigments had been applied, master calligraphers painted the final black outline (although using red for much of the Room 3 outline), enhancing faces and hands, providing flourishes for details throughout the scheme. In many cases, the subtle layering of color, which would subsequently be articulated by black line, suggests that the painters of the final outline also painted the color.

Room 1 features the "Initial Series" or standard introduction for a Maya text, indicating this room's primacy in the reading order. Elaborate lunar data follow the first date (9.18.0.3.4, in 790 A.D.), and presumably this date, painted on the same red background as the scene above, relates to that scene. Above this text, lords in white mantles – some of whom are explicitly titled *ajaw*, lord – approach a royal family assembled on a large throne, including a small child who is held up to the lords by a servant. A bundle to the right of the throne bears a few glyphs painted directly on it that identify the contents as five 8,000-bean counts of cacao, in what would have been a substantial tribute or tax payment in a world where the cacao bean was one of the few standard means of exchange (ill. 374). The lords, then, are presumably paying their taxes and cementing their loyalty to the royal family at the same time. The text below notes an installation in office on the date of the initial series, possibly of the child presented above, under the supervision of the Yaxchilan royal family. Unfortunately, the name has been eroded. Whether a Bonampak or Yaxchilan king is sitting on the throne remains unknown: the caption frames overhead were never filled in. Nevertheless, given the prominent position of this enthroned lord and his conspicuous wealth, he may well be Yajaw Chan Muwaan.

In this scene, the 14 lords in attendance all wear a standard costume: the white mantle, seen relatively rarely in Maya art. These white mantles feature on a few ceramics from Tikal, a throne from Palenque and the "Sculpted Stone 1" from Bonampak. Maya dignitaries wore them when they paid tribute to their king and presented him with gifts as a sign of their devotion. Although the garment may signal an inferior status vis à vis the reigning monarch, the *ajaws* of Room 1 dominate the scene and so may reveal their growing power (ill. 371). One wonders, in fact, if they have not been the ones to commission the scene: although rendered with remarkable attention to detail and to the space each figure occupies, it is as a group that they are most distinctive. Additionally, the *ajaws* are painted with attention to physiognomy and dress – a master calligrapher has rendered their features – whereas the royal family is painted clumsily in comparison. One need only consider their awkward grouping on the throne, or the feeble workmanship evident in the hands and feet of the child being presented, to see that a less adept artist has completed this section of the painting.

of Bonampak nobles and aristocrats, it may have had as a goal the incorporation of the many strata of the upper classes – although the text of Room 1 explicitly states that the building itself belong to the king of Bonampak, Yajaw Chan Muwaan, who had come to power in 776.

Structure 1 was painted inside and out, although little remains of the exterior ornament. Just below the cornice runs a long text, probably once consisting of nearly a hundred glyphs, framing the outside of the building in the way a Maya vase's rim text frames the vessel. The unusual architectural design of the building emphasizes the intensely colored war scenes depicted in the paintings.

A masterpiece of the painter's art

After the interior walls were prepared with white stucco, a master artist probably sketched out the entire pictorial scheme with red wash or chalk.

The quetzal dance in a narrative scene

Only a viewer seated on the built-in bench could have studied the north wall over the doorway. This wall shows three principal lords preparing for celebrations and dancing, which they subsequently perform on the south wall, once their matching costumes of jaguar pelt, quetzal feathers, and boa constrictors are completely in place. These sequential scenes relate to a single event, where dancing is the culminating action, and this action is in fact named in caption 42, which explains that "this is the quetzal dance."

370 *Perspective drawing reconstructing the Bonampak acropolis*
On the steps of the acropolis stand several buildings from which the main plaza in front of the acropolis can be seen. A few had simple roofs made from palm leaves, whilst others featured richly decorated stone vaults and were crowned with extravagant ornamental crests. The large building on the central ledge is Structure 1, decorated with wall paintings.

371 *Lengthways section of Structure 1 at Bonampak*
This lengthways section of Structure 1 shows the three painted rooms. Each one contains a stone bench seat. The bench in the middle room is slightly higher than the other two.

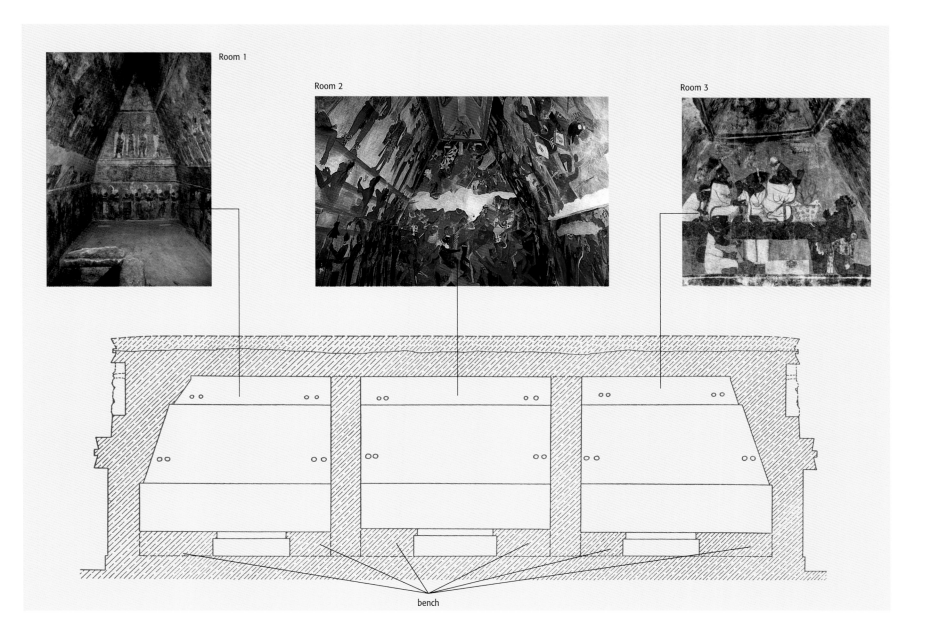

Room 1

Room 2

Room 3

bench

372 *Dressing the Lord. Photograph of the wall painting on the north wall of Structure 1, Room 1 in Bonampak, Chiapas, Mexico; Late Classic, c. 790 A.D.*
The photograph shows the present state of the paintings and will help to demonstrate the poor condition of many parts of these murals. Especially in the lower register, the color has flaked off and been badly damaged by humidity and mildew.

373 *Dressing the Lord. Copy of a wall painting, by Antonio Tejeda; Bonampak, Chiapas, Mexico, Structure 1, Room 1, North wall; Late Classic, c. 790 A.D.*
The paintings above the entrance on the north wall of Room 1 can be studied from the bench seat. The central scene depicts a lord being dressed. Two servants stand beside him, one of whom is dabbing his master's body with paint.

In preparation, on the north wall, a servant to the right of the lord at center daubs his master with red paint, and the artist has added drops of paint or pigment to his hand. Those who stand farther to the right may be waiting their turn to adorn the lords (ills. 372, 373). Another servant strains to secure a feather backrack in the frame of the lord on the left. With the assistance of their servants, the principal lords don a uniform with only the slightest of variation for their leader. Identical feather backracks fit into what appear to be leather hip pouches; their elaborate woven headdresses appear to be made from finely woven palm fiber, like a panama hat today. In the register below, attendants with packs wrapped in jaguar pelts display whole jaguar pelts like those worn above. They may unwrap them from their packs, or perhaps the point is the conspicuous display of such luxury goods.

Recent infra-red photography has unmasked the long-invisible skill of the painters, who applied a lively final black outline over the blocked-out colors, especially on the north wall. Body contours and the articulation of limbs reveal a deep understanding of human form and foreshortened perspective. The hands are painted with the utmost care, but the sculptural detail is more in keeping with the sculptural tradition of Yaxchilan rather than the miniature paintings on Maya vases.

The principal lords of the dressing scene on the north wall, who one sees upon stepping into the room, are then represented a second time, as dancers. The sequence is clear: dressing precedes performance. In making such sequences specific, the Maya painters emphasize the narrative that threads its way through the rooms. Protagonists reappear from scene to scene, providing a sense that the story moves both backward and forward in time. In this regard, the paintings are more visually narrative than any other pre-Columbian work of art. If we were to describe this in linguistic terms, we might say that the paintings are like a series of verbal events, and in this they differ from the more typical stelae of the Maya, and almost all other pre-Columbian works. The Bonampak murals may be the only works of Maya art that visually surpass the narrative complexity of Maya writing. On the lowest tableau in Room 1, Maya musicians and regional governors flank the dancers at center. Parasols flank the text above and feature reversed iconography left and right, as if they were modern quotation marks. Thirteen regional governors, or *sajals*, as they are explicitly named in their captions, file in to the right of the dancers. Their number is probably significant, as are their costumes and their attributes. The first stands close to the smallest dancer; he bears a short-handled parasol in his hands, and this may be a broken parasol of the sort carried by captives at Yaxchilan, a clear indication of political subjection. Yet the subjection may be at this point symbolic, since all these people appear as individuals of some privilege.

At least one is explicitly named as a singer, *k'ayoom*, while the figures represented across the room play instruments. At least one of these *sajals* also smokes a thin cigar, and exhales tobacco smoke.

Musicians and actors

From the perspective of the dancers themselves, or for a very important spectator who might sit on the bench right in front of them, the *sajals* and musicians would seem to be entering the doorway in pairs and then dividing as they flow across the walls. Musicians lead the way, with gourd rattle players at the front, followed by the large stationary drum *huehuetl*, "player," with the turtleshell players behind (ill. 368). Performers in masks pause at the north-east corner; trumpeters and a small ceramic drum player bring up the rear (ill. 375). Moving here in what would seem to be clockwise formation, the musicians may in fact be moving in a circle, around the stationary drum player and perhaps the performers, as was commonly the case among the Aztecs.

Maya musicians are a common subject matter for ceramic vessels, where of course they also follow a circle. They also appear in a consistent order, whether on ceramic vessels or in the Bonampak paintings. Musicians were highly trained professionals in Mesoamerican society, and just as one knows where to find the violins in a modern orchestra, one can spot the trumpets or turtle shells of the Maya musical band. The beauty of their music may have been linked to the beauty of the human form, for these players are rendered with special attention to the elegance of their profiles.

Wedged in between the musicians is a group of performers, all masked except for a single handsome young man. He can be identified as the Maize God, and it may be that these actors are shown preparing to perform the story of the rebirth of the Maize God. Behind him, two hooded figures examine an ear of

tender maize and wear simple ball game costumes. In the Popol Wuj, the Maize God's resurrection takes place in a ball court.

Battle scenes

The vividness of the scene in Room 2 sets it apart from Room 1: a single battle scene encompasses all three walls surrounding the viewer upon his or her entrance into the space, seemingly drawing any viewer into the fray (ill. 240). Dozens of combatants charge into battle from the east wall, banners and

374 *Infra-red photograph of a so-called microtext. Bonampak, Chiapas, Mexico, Structure 1, Room 3, north wall*
Infra-red photography highlights numerous details in paintings which cannot be seen by the human eye as a result of significant weather damage affecting certain sections. These details include the two hieroglyphs on a bundle positioned between the seated dignitaries, which refer to its valuable contents, *pik kakaw*, or 40,000 cacao beans.

375 *Musicians and dancers. Digitalized reconstruction of a wall painting; Bonampak, Chiapas, Mexico, Structure 1, Room 1, west wall; Late Classic, c. 790 A.D.*
At the end of the long procession of dancers and musicians depicted on the west wall is a man with rattles and two trumpet players, who hold their instruments probably made from wood or clay in the air. Four masked actors dance in front of them, with two men dressed as ball players seated between their feet. One of the actors is disguised as a giant crab. In Maya symbolism, water creatures represented inhabitants of the underworld.

weapons held high. They converge under a large angled text on the south wall, where jaguar-attired warriors, including Yajaw Chan Muwaan, strike their enemy with such energy that his body almost seems to fly right out of the picture plane.

The accompanying hieroglyphic text offers only an enigmatic date, probably to be located a few years before the Maya equivalent of 790 A.D. inscribed in Room 1. In the upper west vault, defenders try to protect a wooden box, perhaps the same one that then appears under the throne in Room 3. Damage along the join of the walls and bench may conceal scenes of captive taking and dismemberment. Unusual dark pigments used in the background indicate that the violence takes place in the dark. Sketchy depictions of vegetation suggest that the battle also takes place well away from any city center, and such may well have been the case for much Maya warfare.

Encoded into the battle painting is a different rendering of time and duration. On the upper east wall, the battle has just started, and although some warriors hold weapons high, others let loose the blare of trumpets, in prelude to the dominant scene of the south wall, where Yajaw Chan Muwaan smites his enemy. The sense of movement through time for the duration of the battle continues on the west wall and the lower tableaux, as captives are seized by victorious teams of two or three, with the final scene showing nearly naked captives being dragged off the field. Only one of the defeated reveals serious wounds; although the battle suggests the noise and chaos of a real fight, the depiction under-represents the blood and pain of such conflict.

The narration presumably ends on the lower east wall, where capture is complete. In other words, time is shown in sequence, with preliminaries followed by the climax of conflict, and ending with the mopping up of the defeated. Some individuals are rendered more than once, providing evidence of the Maya ability to create a narrative that was to be seen at once but embedded within a sequence.

Prisoners and human sacrifices

On the north wall, Yajaw Chan Muwaan, accompanied by warriors and ladies of the court, including his wife from Yaxchilan, receives prisoners led before him on a staircase seven tiers high; a staircase was the preferred setting for such an event (ills. 376, 377). In all likelihood, these seven massive steps are those at the north end of the Bonampak plaza, the steps that lead into the acropolis. In the painting, Maya constellations oversee the sacrifice, including the turtle at right (Orion) and the Peccaries (Gemini?), probably identifying that the sacrifice begins at dawn. Elegantly drawn, with sweeping, continuous lines defining body outline, eyes, hands, and hair, the prisoners are among the most beautiful figures of Maya art. Prisoners on the right reach out, as if to protest their treatment at the hands of the warrior at far left, his figure partly truncated by crosstie holes. Bending over, this warrior grabs a captive by the wrist, and either pulls out the fingernails or trims off the final finger joint. Blood arcs and spurts from the hands of captives sitting in a row, most of whom also seem to have lost their teeth, and one howls in agony.

In front of Yajaw Chan Muwaan, an officer extends his arm, presumably presenting the captives to the powerful lord. Strikingly, in one hand he grasps what would seem to be a jade bead; in the other he holds out a bundle of quetzal feathers.

These two materials, jade and quetzal feathers, embodied all that was precious in ancient Mesoamerica. At the time of the Spanish invasion, they were linked in metaphorical speech by Aztec poets to represent all things of value.

Victory at Bonampak may have meant that the victor won the loser's maize crop and hauled off the other's skilled workers, as well as victims for sacrifice. But not to be forgotten was the valuable loot, especially the jade and feathers stripped from the defeated.

A single captive presented on the upper tier appeals to Yajaw Chan Muwaan, who stares over his head. At his feet, a dead prisoner sprawls, cuts visible across

376 *The presentation of the prisoners. Drawing reconstructing a wall painting, by Antonio Tejeda; Bonampak, Chiapas, Mexico, Structure 1, Room 2, north wall; Late Classic, c. 790 A.D.*
This scene in Room 2, depicting the presentation of prisoners, is one of the finest paintings from the Classic period. There are few paintings which combine courtly ceremonies, deep emotion and terrible suffering with such tense realism. The visitor entering the room is immediately drawn into the scene.

377 *The presentation of the prisoners (detail)*
Yajaw Chan Muwaan, the victorious king of Bonampak, proudly looks down at the pleading subject sprawled before him on the highest step. Blood drips from his fingers and those of the other prisoners, whose nakedness represents extreme humility. Robbed of their jewelry, particularly their headdresses and earrings, the supposed noblemen can no longer be distinguished from simple peasants. A severed head at the feet of the outstretched man seems to indicate their fate.

his body; his foot leads to a decapitated head, gray brains dribbling from the open cranium. No figure in Maya art is painted with greater understanding of the human anatomy or with more attention to the effects of naked flesh than this dead captive of Room 2. The powerful line of the diagonal body both leads to the comparatively wooden rendering of the king but also subverts his image: for any individual seated on the bench, the captive's body is in the center of what one can see. In making this visual statement, the artists of Bonampak pushed their skills to the limit, making sensuality out of sacrifice and death: the eroticized body of the dead captive of Room 2, sprawled on the diagonal, dominates the scene altogether and undermines the representation of victory (ill. 377).

Below, on the lowest level, lunging warriors assault the open doorway or what appears to be a void, however one may wish to interpret the scene. But if we repopulate that space and imagine a captive delivered through the doorway, then the warriors would seem to be attacking this person. In other words, the wall only operates fully when living figures inhabit the spaces created by the painting.

Ritualistic and symbolic significance of the painted rooms

One of the questions always asked of the Bonampak paintings is what these rooms were used for. Certainly, they may well have functioned as storage places, especially safe and relatively fireproof spaces for valued goods, from jade and feathers to maize seed for the coming season. Additionally, it is worth noting that the Room 2 bench is 10 cm (4 in.) higher than those of the adjacent rooms and slightly larger; although the initial series indicates that the beginning of the narrative occurs in Room 1, Room 2, at the center, may well be the most important.

When lords occupied these rooms, those who occupied Room 2 dominated the scene. And in dominating the scene, the occupants of Room 2 may also have dominated their fellow men. The articulation of the doorway suggests that captives were presented for humiliation, and that humiliation may have included sexual intimidation and rape. The beauty of the prisoners may have enhanced their desirability, and violence upon that beauty may have been a Maya aesthetic.

In Room 3, the lords of Bonampak don great "dancer's wings" for a final orgy of self-sacrifice and captive dismemberment (ill. 379), all arrayed against a large pyramid that wraps around the east, south, and west walls. Whirling lords have pierced their penises, and blood collects on the white diaper-like cloth at the groin while captives led in from the side are slaughtered at the center of the south wall. Despite the severe weather damage affecting the figure of the dead captive at the start of the vault, one can still recognize jaguar fur on his feet and hands, and so the sacrifice may re-enact a mythic event for the Maya, in which the god Chaak sacrificed a jaguar god.

Small texts about 2 cm (0.75 in.) high – that is, the size of many a pot inscription – are painted in several locations, but a particularly fine one at the center of the south wall, where it would easily be noticed, names Itzamnaaj Balam III, the King of Yaxchilan at the end of the 8th century. What is unusual about the positioning of this small text is that it appears to be on a banner that has been unfurled between two lords in "wings." If this were indeed a large unfurled cloth, then it would be a unique representation in Maya art of the sort of painting on cloth known as a *lienzo* in Central Mexico at the time of the Spanish invasion.

Atop the pyramid, the three principal dancers are the same principal dancers from Room 1, as indicated by the captions. Strikingly, the figure at the very top wears a prominent Sun God headdress. The second event of the initial series in Room 1 named a dedication event, either performed by or in honor of Yajaw Chan Muwaan, who is named there as the Sun God.

This may relate to the second date, in 791, and celebrate the dedication of the building or the construction program. However, one should bear in mind that the caption accompanying this figure does not name Yajaw Chan Muwaan but

378 *Self-castigation of noblewomen. Digitalized reconstruction of a wall painting; Bonampak, Chiapas, Mexico, Structure 1, Room 3, rollout of all four wall; Late Classic, c. 790 A.D.*
Ladies of the court, seated before and on a throne in white clothing, are depicted here in a self-castigation scene. They pierce their tongues with thorns and collect the blood in a vessel on the right of the throne. A man kneels in front of them with a thorn in his hand. He is probably a servant who is helping the women with the blood sacrifice.

379 *Dance on the pyramids. Drawing reconstructing a wall painting, by Antonio Tejeda; Bonampak, Chiapas, Mexico, Structure 1, Room 3, rollout of all four walls; Late Classic, c. 790 A.D.*
A group of figures in strange costumes dances in front of a staircase, which may represent the entrance to the acropolis of Bonampak. A tiny hieroglyphic text refers to one of the figures as Itzamnaaj Balam III, who was the king of the neighboring state of Yaxchilan during the wall painting period. The three main dancers on the highest step are identical to the princes depicted on the south wall of Room 1.

rather one of the dancing trio. Yajaw Chan Muwaan may have died prior to completion of the mural scheme.

In the upper vault, scenes that flank the dance on the pyramid, Maya artists have rendered other intimate views of palace life. A band of deformed musicians performs on the west vault, perhaps to be read as moving in a circle, like the musicians of Room 1. In a particularly beautifully painted scene, the ladies of the court gather in the throne room depicted in the upper east vault (ill. 378), to pierce their tongues and instruct a little child, presumably the same one featured in Room 1, who holds out a hand for piercing. Rendered only in the first and final scenes of the scheme, the small heir may have been the ostensible motivation for the entire sequence of events, whose more important purpose may have been to represent Yajaw Chan Muwaan. Under the throne rests a mat-covered box, perhaps the box claimed in the battle, and it may well have held the sacred objects forcibly taken from another town or city. As if to pay final witness, the white-mantled lords of Room 1 also return, lining the north wall of Room 3.

Perhaps the single greatest achievements of Maya art, the Bonampak murals are also undoubtedly the finest paintings of the indigenous New World. They are also the most extensive window on life at the end of the 8th century, when the Maya struggled to survive against the obstacles of environmental disaster and constant warfare. But the scale of warfare on this occasion may show an elite world out of control: if this battle is just one of many carried out by Bonampak, and perhaps indirectly to serve Yaxchilan as well, then the Bonampak murals reveal a world convulsed by war and chaos, beyond the reach of order and control that human sacrifice sought to reinstate.

Over the years since the discovery of the paintings in 1946, time has taken its toll, and today the in situ paintings are a shadow of their former selves. Fortunately, new technology, particularly in the form of digital infra-red imaging, is contributing to the study of the Bonampak murals, constantly revealing new details and helping to bring secrets to light.

GRAVE LOOTERS IN THE JUNGLE

Nikolai Grube

On the afternoon of the third day of our jungle trek, we reached our resting place, exhausted. It was one of the few waterholes in this rough, uninhabited area on the northern high ground of the Peten province in Guatemala. A group in search of rubber had stumbled upon an archeological site where they had discovered inscribed stelae. They wanted to lead our small expedition to this forgotten city. To our surprise, when we reached the marshy banks of the waterhole, we found not only fresh traces of animals, but also of people. Antonio, our leader, told us to be extremely careful, released the safety catch on his rifle and set out in search of these unknown people with collectors of chicle. We wondered whether we could have disturbed soldiers, guerrilla fighters, bandits or illegal Mexican immigrants in this godforsaken part of the forest. The group soon returned. In the thickets just behind the part of the forest they had discovered two grave looters, who were luckily not armed. They had heard us coming and had hidden. Only when they were sure that we were not soldiers did they dare to come out. Two ragged figures, who had been living in a primitive plastic shed for months, emerged from the thicket. They had run out of food and their water supply was being depleted due to a lack of rain. They became more talkative after we had given them some of our rice and beans. They both lived in the city of San Benito, 120 kilometers (75 miles) further south, where they had wives and children. They had never been to school, had not learnt a trade and were unemployed. They saw the plundering of archeological sites in the border area between Mexico and Guatemala as their only chance of keeping their families alive. They had been digging with bush knives, shovels and their battered hands for months amongst the overgrown ruins, channeling out deep tunnels in the hope of discovering a rich burial (ills. 380, 381). They constantly feared that the tunnels might cave in over them and they would be buried alive like so many looters before them. They had found very little: a painted plate (ills. 382) and a few broken, unpainted vessels but nothing that a trader in the provincial capital of Flores would have bought.

The plundering of archeological sites is illegal in all modern states on ancient Maya territory. A country like Guatemala, one of the poorest countries

380 *Grave looters in action. Northern Peten, Guatemala; photograph from 1998*
Armed only with machetes, pick-axes and shovels, the plunderers dig a meter-deep tunnel inside an overgrown building in the hope of finding a burial. They have opened one burial, which only contains the disintegrated bones of the corpse and a few ceramic vessels.

381 *Grave looters with their tools. Northern Peten, Guatemala; photograph from 1998*
Grave looters are generally only equipped with simple tools. They usually work in small groups. While one digs the tunnel, the others get rid of the debris. In an unknown number of cases, the underground tunnels collapse and one or more looters are buried.

382 *Grave looters showing their wares. Campamento El Aguacate, Peten, Guatemala; photograph from 1997*
One of the plunderers gives Nikolai Grube a painted plate. Plates are sold for less than vases in art markets and are therefore often left behind by the robbers. In this case, they were prepared to present the piece to a private museum in the village of Uaxactun.

of the continent, is not however in a position to provide proper protection for its many thousands of archeological sites. In the seclusion of the jungle, grave robbers can operate undisturbed. Only a small number of archeological sites have not yet been struck by plunderers and it is likely that the last remaining ones will fall prey to illegal excavations over the next few years. The looters sometimes work alone but usually they are in groups, sent by men behind the scenes in the capital to plunder particular Classic cities. They set out in search of graves containing jade and painted ceramics which can be sold in international art markets for five or six-figure amounts and sometimes even use heavy machinery and bulldozers. The stolen goods are transported from the site with the help of drug dealers operating in the region. They use their own airplanes and runways to transport marijuana and cocaine from Colombia to the United States. The grave looters destroy entire buildings, and even entire archeological sites, in order to reach the burials (ill. 383). The city of Naranjo, for example, one of the most important Maya cities of the Classic period, was almost razed to the ground in this way in 1997.

The plundering of archeological treasures will continue for as long as there is a market for Maya art in the United States and Europe and for as long as collectors are prepared to pay high prices for the stolen goods. But it is also the extreme poverty of the population which drives more and more people to seek their fortune in the jungle. The construction of new roads, even in protected areas like the "Maya Biosphere," by woodcutting and oil companies is making it even easier for looters to access the archeological sites in northern Guatemala which were previously so isolated.

The plundering and selling of goods to the United States and Europe have catastrophic consequences not only for archeology but also for the region itself. Once a stolen ceramic object has been removed from its archeological context, we no longer know in which city or in which burial it was found. Valuable information about Maya society is therefore lost forever. A further consequence is the obliteration of the cultural heritage of an entire people. There are barely any valuable painted ceramics left in Guatemala and Mexico, for example. Painted pottery masterpieces can now only be admired in private collections and museums in New York, Geneva, and Brussels.

THE ART OF CLASSIC VASE PAINTING

Dorie Reents-Budet

Ancient Maya art is renowned for its aesthetic beauty and narrative content. Of all the media in which Maya artists worked, their paintings on pottery are among the most impressive because of their technical and aesthetic sophistication. These complex pictorial scenes accompanied by hieroglyphic texts recount historic events of the Classic period and reveal the religious ideology upon which the Maya built a great civilization. Maya ceramics were used for many different purposes during this period. They were used, among other things, as serving wares and were given by members of the upper strata as gifts, or were buried with honored figures. Their symbolic and hieroglyphic representations reveal important details about Maya history and religion and provide an insight into courtly life (ill. 384), the aesthetic splendor of the Classic period, and the sacredness whose philosophical depth is reflected in these vessels. They were created as models and ceramic metaphors of central religious beliefs and myths (ill. 385) and in particular cosmic creation. The artistry of these ceramics reflects the technical skills, aesthetic creativity, intellectual achievements, and sensitivity of the Maya ceramic artists of the Classic period, whose mastery of this art has not been matched anywhere in the world.

The slip painted pottery technique

Classic Maya polychrome ceramics are one of the world's most advanced forms of low-fire slip painted pottery, surpassing even the famous ancient Greek ceramics in their technical and artistic finesse. Maya ceramic artists developed a remarkably glossy and hard-surfaced slip paint called *terra sigillata* in modern ceramic terminology. *Terra sigillata* is made by separating out the tiniest particles of clay through levitation of finely ground clay mixed with large amounts of water in a settling basin. Modern potters add such alkalis as sodium silicates or soda ash to this slurry which causes the clay particles to deflocculate or repel each other. The larger particles settle to the bottom and the tiniest ones remain in suspension. The resulting *terra sigillata* can be concentrated by evaporation which allows a high degree of flexibility in creating a wide range of densely opaque to very translucent slip paints.

384 *Polychrome cylindrical vase. Provenance unknown; Late Classic, 8th century A.D.; fired clay, painted*
Court life was one of the most frequently depicted subjects on Classic Maya ceramics. Most of these valuable vessels were probably created for use in the court. Precious vases like these were presented by kings and noblemen to subordinate princes to secure their loyalty.

385 *Bowl depicting one of the Hero Twins. Provenance unknown; Late Classic, c. 700–750 A.D.; fired clay, painted; H. 13 cm, dia. 15 cm; Boston, Museum of Fine Arts (MS1837)*
This extract shows one of the Hero Twins holding a bowl containing the jewels of his father, the Maize God.

The surface clay used by Maya potters was applied to the vessels in a bath before firing. It contains considerable amounts of iron and free alkalis, which are difficult to process into a fine-grained clay product such as *terra sigillata*. In addition, if the clay contains illites or montmorillonites, as do many of the clays from the Maya regions, these cause the clay particles to group together rather than to float freely. During firing, the tiny clay particles in the *terra sigillata* become evenly dispersed on the surface of the vessel. They form an overlapping fish-scale structure that creates a glossy, hard surface which is resistant to chemical attack and makes the vessel impervious to liquids. *Terra sigillata* is used today in the manufacture of drain tiles to make them leak-proof, a quality needed for any pottery used as food service wares, as were Classic Maya vessels. An important characteristic of slip paints which was fully exploited by Maya painters is that, unlike glazes, slip paints create well-defined lines because the slips do not fuse and run during firing (ills. 384, 385).

Creating the colors

To create colors, small amounts of coloring oxides are added to the *terra sigillata*. The most common pigments used by the Classic Maya were iron oxides, especially red iron oxide and black iron oxide. These oxides provide a wide color range from yellow to red, brown and black. The range can be increased by adding other metallic oxides (e.g. manganese, cobalt) to produce such colors as pink and maroon (ill. 387), as well as by processing the iron oxides through a pre-firing treatment called calcining which darkens the hue of the original oxide.

The firing process

Classic Maya pottery was fired at temperatures ranging between 500–700°C, a low temperature range easily reached in open bonfires and pit fires. There is little evidence for the use of kilns in pottery production among the Maya and other contemporaneous cultures of Mesoamerica. No true kilns have been found at Classic period Maya sites, although Heather McKillop may have recently found such constructions in northern Belize. Arguing against the need for kilns to create Classic Maya polychrome pottery is the fact that the high temperatures usually achieved in kiln firings would have significantly lowered the glossiness of *terra sigillata* slip paints. Outside the Maya region, ancient kilns have been found in Highland Mexico.

The kinds of adobe bricks used by most potters to construct kilns easily disintegrate into small particles of fired clay. If the Maya were using similar adobe bricks to make kilns, they may not be readily identifiable in the archeological record. Maya potters today bake their wares in open bonfires as well as in pits dug into the ground, and it is believed that these were the two primary ancient firing techniques. Although open firings would leave little evidence in the archeological record, what may be fire pits have been found by archeologists such as the "group of twelve" discovered on the outskirts of the Classic period site of Emal, Yucatan.

386 *Palace scene at the court of a ruler of Maan. Rollout of a ceramic object; provenance unknown; Late Classic, c. 8th century A.D.; fired clay, painted; H. 20.2 cm, dia. 16.5 cm; Washington, Dumbarton Oaks, Harvard University (Kerr 2784/MS0445)*
The scene shows a gathering in the 8th century A.D. in a palace of the ruler of Maan, one of the sites in the Lowlands which has not yet been located. Underneath the hieroglyphic band with the standard sequence and the reference to the owner of the vessel, the prince sits on a throne, surrounded by servants, officials, and noblemen. The names and titles of the different individuals are indicated in the field to the left of or above the figures. The artist has signed his work on the far right. The walls of the room are red with decorated jaguar heads and other multi-colored paintings interrupting the red background.

387 *Cylinder vase with watercolor effect. Provenance unknown; Late Classic, 600–900 A.D.; fired clay, painted; H. 23 cm, dia. 8.4 cm; private collection (Kerr 5850/MS1688)*
The Classic ceramic painters developed many different colors within the typical range used for mineral paints, including black, brown, red, and yellow and extended their palette with numerous shades of light and dark. The unusual pink tone used in the hieroglyphs is difficult to obtain, not only in terms of producing the color, but also in terms of the watercolor effect.

388 *Gathering at the ruler's court. Rollout of a vase; provenance unknown; Late Classic, 600–900 A.D.; fired clay, painted; H. 18.2 cm, dia. 13 cm; private collection (Kerr 1599/MS0651)*
The scene is a state banquet or ritual meal which is taking place at a palace gathering. The celebratory nature of the food is reflected in the crockery used. Beside the throne stand a vase, which probably contains a chocolate drink, a bowl whose content is unknown, and a plate of tamales coated with a red sauce.

Expensive tableware

The elaborately painted pottery played many important roles during the Classic period. Foremost among these was their function as food service ware among the elite. Scenes on the pottery depict the vessels in use during "state banquets" (ills. 386, 388), which were an important component of the pageantry of the royal court. Many vessels' upper rims are painted with a hieroglyphic text (ill. 397). Its recent decipherment has identified five constituent parts, the third and fourth sections confirming the vessels' food service function. Cylinder vases are called "drinking vessels" for *kakaw* or cacao-based beverages. *Kakaw*-based drinks include those made from the roasted and ground bean as well as from the sweet-tasting pulp surrounding the bean. Bowls are also "drinking vessels" and held *ul*, a corn-based liquid cereal usually consumed as a drink, but also as a

more solid substance eaten with a spoon. Plates were used to serve *noj waaj*, "big bread," a tamale-like solid food composed of cooked corn dough seasoned with spices, sauces, and meats.

The first two and final sections of the hieroglyphic sequences are concerned with the social role of these painted vessels. The glyphs comprise a blessing statement which makes the vessel "worthy" for its intended functions. Of interest is the verbal structure of this two-part section which suggests that it is the act of painting that blesses and makes the vase worthy. The final section names the vessel's owner or patron and occasionally ends with the name or titles of the artist who painted the vessel (ills. 395, 396, 397).

Vessels for the dead

In addition to their food service function, many vessels found their way into the tombs and burials of the elite and sometimes the not-so-elite of the Classic period. Many probably held foods for the souls of the dead. Interestingly, a small hole was drilled into the centers of some plates shortly before they were placed in the burial (ill. 389). As a ritual act, perhaps these holes served to release the spirit of the vessel prior to its interment. This same practice was common among other Native American peoples such as the ancestors of the modern Hopi of the US Southwest.

401 *Vessel with lid symbolizing a royal court. Provenance unknown; Late Classic period, 600–900; fired clay, painted; H. 22.5 cm, dia. 17 cm; private collection (Kerr 5943/MS1719)*

This vessel is in the form of a miniature palace from the Classic period, in which princes and courtiers meet, and could be a model of the royal court. The lid represents the roof.

402 *Mythological palace scene. Provenance unknown; Late Classic, 600–900 A.D.; fired clay, painted; H. 30 cm, dia. 12 cm; private collection (Kerr 631)*
The modeled, painted section on the upper part of this

vase represents the straw-covered roof of a building, indicating that the vessel represents a built structure. The scene shows a gathering of animals and mythological figures on the steps leading up to a palace.

The Ik' vase in the woman's tomb at Altar de Sacrificios may indicate her family affiliation with the Ik' site and her marriage into an elite lineage at Altar de Sacrificios.

Ceramics as cosmic models

Classic painted ceramics were more than high status serving vessels, funerary offerings, and social currency. Some are modeled and painted with imagery that transforms them into ceramic expressions of other materials and objects as well as locales both natural and supernatural. Some low cylinder vessels from Yucatan are painted with diagonal stripes in a dark brown slip that replicates the grain of carved wooden vessels (ill. 398). Wood was a primary medium for Classic Maya sculptors although most of their creations have not survived the wet tropical environment and human destructive forces. Other vessels are modeled and painted in imitation of gourds, calabashes, and baskets (ill. 399). Many tall cylinder vases are painted with scenes taking place inside court buildings, and a few have lids with decorated knobs. Together, the painted

scene and vessel form become an abstract cylindrical model of a Classic Maya court building (ill. 401). Although rare, square vessels are particularly reminiscent of Classic architecture such as court buildings and palace complexes. The scenes incised on these vases depict a lord seated on a bench inside a building. The lids have modeled knobs which recall the decorated roof comb characteristic of court buildings. A few rare examples have a modeled and painted flange just below the vase's rim that replicates the building's palm-covered roof (ills. 402, 406).

Other vessels represent supernatural locales and the entrances to them. For example, one plate is painted with a black background in which float red catfish and water lilies. They surround a red quatrefoil-shaped opening painted in the plate's center which recalls the quadripartite portal between the earth and the underworld and its black waters. This plate reverses the usual human viewpoint looking from the surface of the earth down into the underworld; instead, the view is from the underworld looking up through its black water "sky" and out through the cave opening into the (red) earthly realm.

Hieroglyphs naming supernatural locales are occasionally painted on both the interior and exterior bottoms of dishes and plates, transforming them into

403 *Plate depicting the dancing Maize God. Provenance unknown; Late Classic, 600–900 A.D.; fired clay, painted; H. 14 cm, dia. 33 cm; (Kerr 5723/MS0605)*

This plate is a model of the Three Stone Place in cosmic creation. The three feet on which it stands symbolize the hearth made from three stones at the center of every Maya house. According to mythology, it was made on the day the universe was created by the gods.

ceramic models of these sacred places. The most common is a place designated by the glyph compound *wuk-ha-nal* or Seven Water Place (ill. 400). Plates and low-sided dishes symbolizing this supernatural place are frequently found in the Codex-style ceramics made at sites in the Mirador Basin of northern Guatemala. Although the identification of this mythological place remains obscure, its representation in glyphic and ceramic forms is often accompanied by iconography associated with the sky and the underworld.

One of the most important mythological locales is the Three-Stone-Place which is mentioned in Classic period inscriptions and in the 16th-century Popol Wuj. This is the place of generative force, the place where the gods brought the

universe into being, and where they erected the World Tree which sustains the physical structure of the universe. The representation on a tripod plate from central Peten with a cream-colored background relates to the Three Stone Place. The stones are presented here as a cross in the form of the K'an glyph and arranged to correspond to the cosmic hearth of creation. The K'an cross is associated with the celestial realm, creation, and the birthplace of the Maize God. It too is a central icon found on Early Classic lip-to-lip lidded vessels, some of which contain natural materials whose arrangements inside the vessels recall cosmic structural and generative themes. The plate also has three supports arrayed in the same equilateral triangular pattern and its entire exterior bottom is painted red, a rare feature for Classic Maya plates whose bottom surfaces usually lack slip painting. The three supports and red slip paint underscore the metaphorical nature of the plate as the Three Stone Place cosmic hearth.

404 *Plate depicting the dancing Maize God. Provenance unknown; Late Classic, 600–900 A.D.; fired clay, painted; H. 14 cm, dia. 33 cm; (Kerr 5723/MS0605)*
The circular hieroglyphic texts consist of the so-called primary standard sequence, a devotional phrase that states the type of vessel and the name of this bowl's owner. The inner side of the plate depicts the dance of the Maize God as a ritualistic element in the creation of the world. The god carries an enormous decoration on his back beneath which he is barely recognizable. The three bowls depicted on the plate probably symbolize the place of creation, as do the feet.

405 *The feet of the plate representing the three hearthstones*
The feet represent the three hearthstones in a Maya house. The unusual painting on this type of vessel reflects its special meaning. The base of the vessel shows the unusual form of the bowl. The outer edge of the bowl features three large areas containing repeated painted motifs.

406 *Palace scene. Provenance unknown; Late Classic, 600–900 A.D.; fired clay, painted; H. 30 cm, dia. 14 cm; private collection*
The vessel is thought to represent the presentation of a tribute or gift on a staircase in front of a building. A ruler is seated on the top step and is being presented with a strip of white cloth by an underling. A painting on the upper part of the vase represents the lower edge of a palm-covered roof.

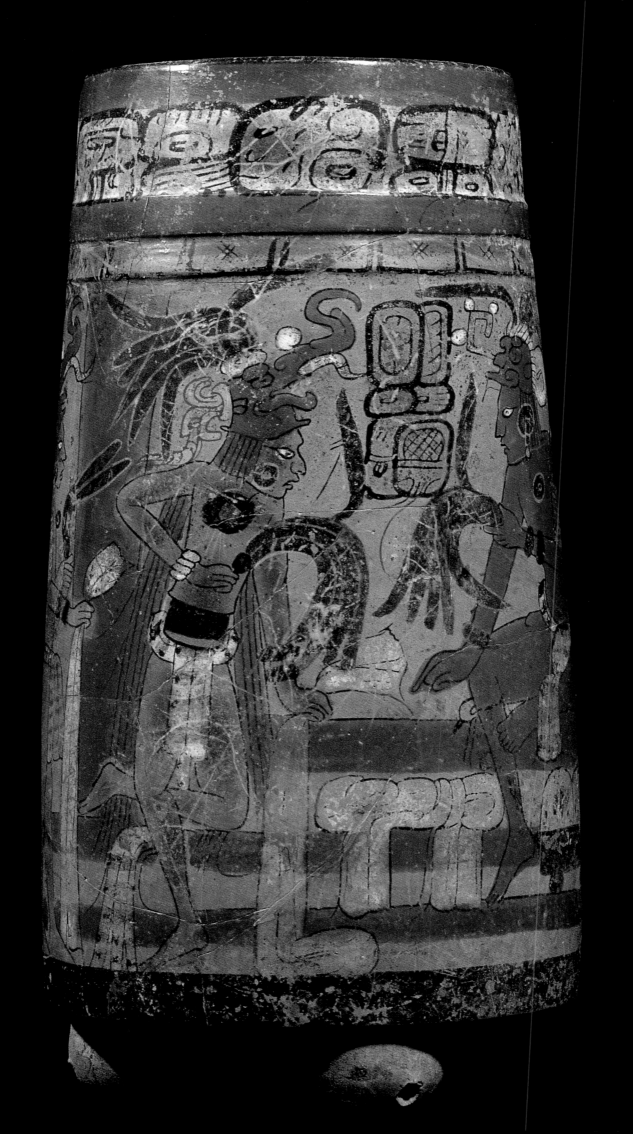

Similar to the red-painted exterior of this plate, a circle of red pigment or paint is found on the bottoms of other tripod plates. A feasible explanation of this unusual decorative feature is that these red circles refer to the cosmic hearth, the plate being a ceramic model of this mythological place.

One Late Classic tripod plate from the region of Holmul, Guatemala, includes all constituent elements of the cosmic hearth (ills. 403, 404, 405). This plate's tall supports are painted white with black stripes and are arranged in the expected equilateral triangular form. The black-and-white striped supports could signify stone in the symbolic language of central Mexico. The three legs surround a red circle painted in the center of the plate's bottom. The form and painting of this plate combine to suggest the Three Stone Place where the gods created the world.

407 *The Vase of the Seven Gods. Provenance unknown; Late Classic period, 600–900 A.D.; fired clay, painted; H. 27.3 cm, dia. 11.5 cm; Chicago, Chicago Art Institute (Kerr 2796/MS1763)*

The vase, painted by the famous artist Aj Maxam, depicts the gods of creation meeting in the darkness to create the universe. They are being instructed by God L, the ruler of the underworld, who is seated on a jaguar throne.

408 *The dance of the Maize God. Provenance unknown; Late Classic period, 600–900 A.D.; fired clay, painted; H. 24 cm, dia. 16 cm; private collection (Kerr 633/MS1744)*

Three paintings on ceramics by Aj Maxam have been found. This one represents the dance of the Maize God as a ritualistic element in the creation of the world.

Three vases (ills. 407, 408, 409) painted by Aj Maxam, a regal artist from Naranjo, Guatemala, comprise a rare set of metaphorical vessels. Their individual narratives depict three key events of cosmic creation, and together they become a three-dimensional ceramic model of the Three Stone Place and embody the central aspects of creation and universal life. Each vase is painted with one color as its primary hue. The first in the series, the vessel with the black background, depicts the meeting in the primordial darkness of the gods of creation on 4 Ajaw 8 Kumk'u (Ill. 407). God L, the ruler of the underworld, faces a gathering of six other gods among whom is the Maize God.

The second vessel, mainly in white, is painted with a few black flower motifs (ill. 409). In Maya symbolism, flowers and blossom stood for the life-force or spirit-breath, brought into the world by the creator gods.

The main images on the red-painted vase show three versions of the dancing Maize God in the guise of Jun Junajpu, the father of the Hero Twins of the Popol Wuj (ill. 408). He dances during the process of creation at the Three Stone Place. On the vase, each dancer wears a backrack which is a model of the Maya cosmos. Sitting within this cosmogram are three divine animals related to cosmic forces including a jaguar holding a mask of K'awiil, a long-snouted lizard, and an anthropomorphic howler monkey as the patron of Maya artists, here holding a paintbrush or carving tool.

The same cosmic event depicted on this vase is recorded on Stela C in Quirigua which recounts the placing of the three stones of the cosmic hearth. The Jaguar Paddler placed the jaguar-throne-stone, Black-House placed the serpent-throne-stone, and Itzamnaaj placed the waterlily-throne-stone. All was overseen by the Maize God, who like nearly all Maya gods can appear in different forms, in his manifestation as Jun Ye Nal. On the red vase, these stones are symbolized by the animal fate-doubles seated within the backracks worn by Jun Ye Nal. Here, however, the artist substituted Jun Chuwen, one of the supernatural simian patrons of Maya artists, for the water-throne-stone. This substitution underscores the like-in-kind relationship of Classic Maya artists with the gods of creation. Each of these three vessels recounts a portion of the creation myth. Together they function as a three-dimensional metaphor for the Classic creation story.

Of particular interest are the three different hues chosen by the painter as the dominant color for each vase; red, black, and white. The black vase depicts the cosmos before the beginning of time, when all was in darkness. The red vase evokes the original dance and sacrifice by the gods of creation whose red blood infused the newly-formed world with life-force or spirit-breath. The white vase evokes the light brought into the world when these gods infused it with life-force.

A second motivation behind the artist's choice of these three colors is tied to the like-in-kind relationship between Maya artists and their gods of creation. Throughout Mesoamerica, the "red and the black" is a verbal metaphor referring to books, to the artists who made the books, and to the esoteric and often cosmological knowledge contained therein. The Maya painter Aj Maxam aptly chose the three colors of sacred knowledge for his ceramic metaphor of creation.

409 *Vase with the signature of the artist Aj Maxam. Provenance unknown; Late Classic period, 600–900 A.D.; fired clay, painted; H. 23.5 cm, dia. 14.5 cm; Chicago, Chicago Art Institute (Kerr 635/MS1375)*

The third vessel created by Aj Maxam is decorated with fleur-de-lys motifs, symbolizing the divine breath blown onto the world by the gods of creation. Aj Maxam signed this vase as his only work (third hieroglyph from the right in the bottom row).

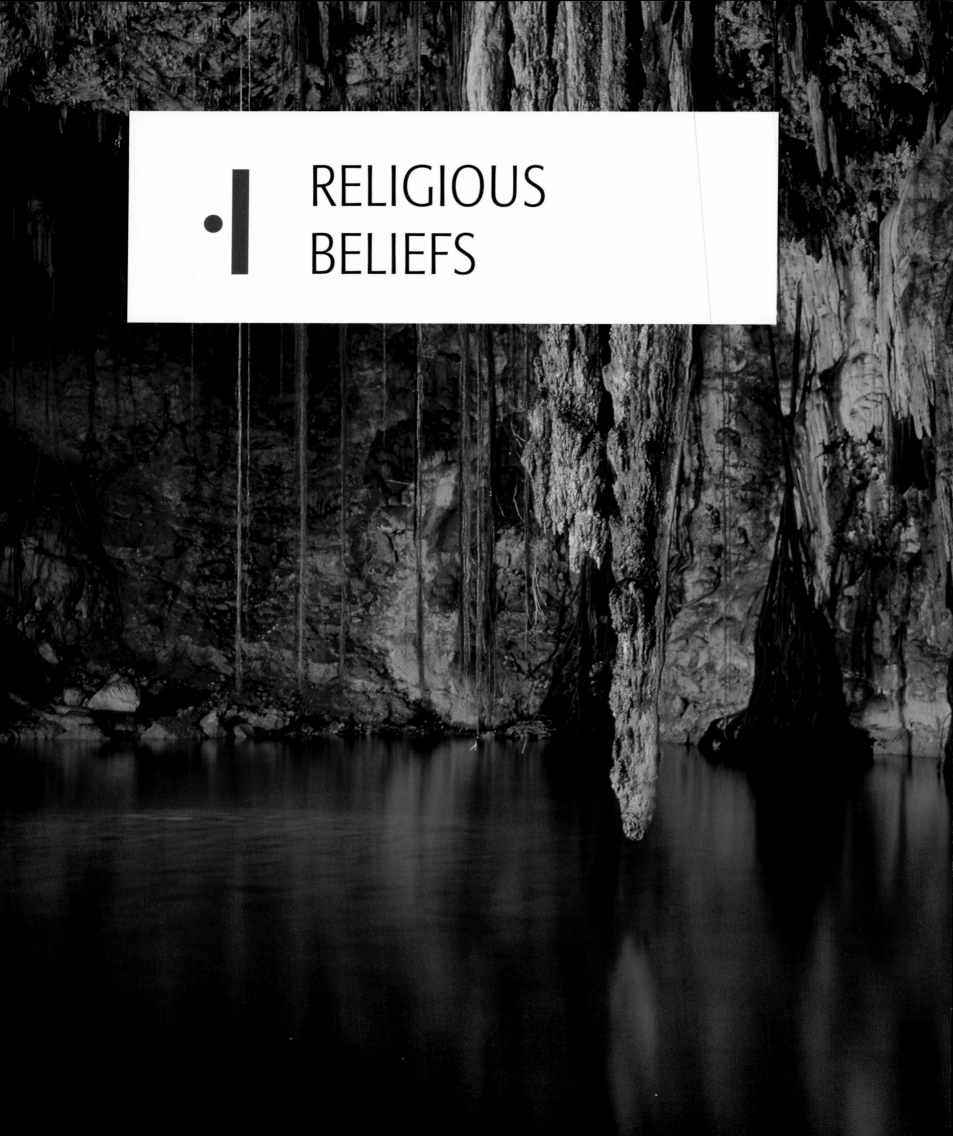

RELIGIOUS
BELIEFS

THE CLASSIC MAYA GODS

Karl Taube

One of the more striking traits of ancient Maya religion is the varied and complex array of gods and other supernatural beings. Among the first Europeans to describe the Maya deities was Fray Diego de Landa (1524–1579), in his encyclopedic study of the 16th-century Yucatec Maya, "Relación de las cosas de Yucatán" (Report on the incidents in Yucatan). In this work, Landa describes in detail the names and attributes of particular gods, along with their roles in particular time-specific calendar rituals. Landa, however, was little interested in Maya mythology, the dynamic interaction of the gods in sacred narrative. He was more concerned with the parallels between the Maya religion and Christianity.

By far the most important source for ancient Maya mythology derives from the Highland Maya Popol Wuj, an early colonial K'iche' Maya document tran-

scribed by the Dominican Francisco Ximenez near the end of the 17th century. Along with being an invaluable fount of information concerning particular gods and creation mythology (see Eberl, p. 315 ff.), this document also reveals how the ancient Maya viewed themselves in relation to both their gods and ancestors.

First investigations of the Maya pantheon

During the late 19th century, scholars began to study the ancient gods appearing in pre-Columbian Maya writing and art. In this pioneering era, Paul Schellhas (1854–1945) was the first to systematically identify and label the many gods appearing in the Dresden, Paris, and Madrid codices (ill. 411). Along with

Previous double page:
Cave in Dzitnup (near Valladolid), Yucatan, Mexico
The limestone karst cave systems symbolized entrances to the underworld for the Maya, and also supplied drinking water to the population of the northern part of the peninsula, which was poorly supplied with surface water.

410 *Incense burner, Tikal, Peten, Guatemala, Structure 5D-34, Burial 10; Early Classic, 300–600 A.D.; fired clay, painted; H. 35 cm, Tikal, Museo Sylvanus G. Morley*
When incense was burned in this incense burner in the form of a god of the underworld, smoke came out through the mouth and openings in the center of the forehead.

411 *The list of gods drawn up by Paul Schellhas*
Paul Schellhas, made the first attempt to identify the gods referred to in Postclassic Maya books. He published his results in 1886 and 1887. He identified a total of 15 different gods on the basis of their characteristics as well as their name glyphs. He did not manage to decipher

these hieroglyphs, however, and therefore referred to the gods using letters of our alphabet.

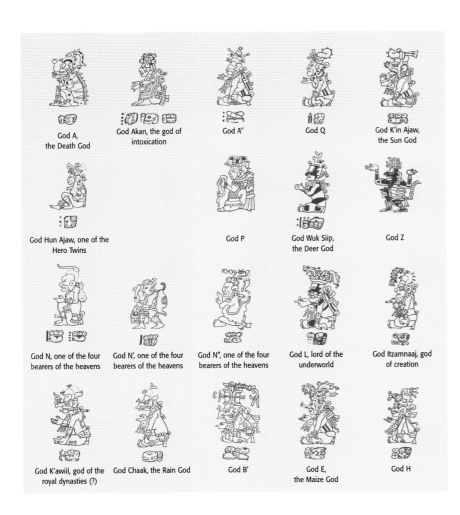

God A,
the Death God

God Akan, the god of intoxication

God A''

God Q

God K'in Ajaw,
the Sun God

God Hun Ajaw, one of the Hero Twins

God P

God Wuk Siip,
the Deer God

God Z

God N, one of the four bearers of the heavens

God N', one of the four bearers of the heavens

God N'', one of the four bearers of the heavens

God L, lord of the underworld

God Itzamnaaj, god of creation

God K'awiil, god of the royal dynasties (?)

God Chaak, the Rain God

God B'

God E,
the Maize God

God H

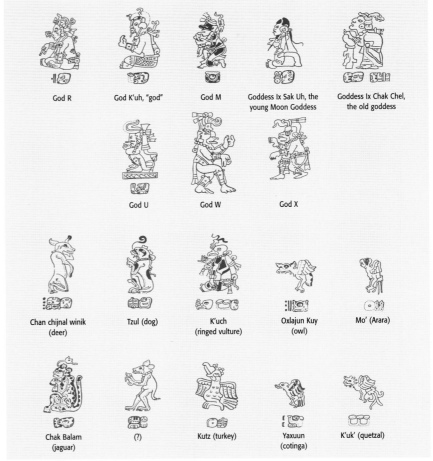

God R

God K'uh, "god"

God M

Goddess Ix Sak Uh, the young Moon Goddess

Goddess Ix Chak Chel, the old goddess

God U

God W

God X

Chan chijnal winik
(deer)

Tzul (dog)

K'uch
(ringed vulture)

Oxlajun Kuy
(owl)

Mo' (Arara)

Chak Balam
(jaguar)

(?)

Kutz (turkey)

Yaxuun
(cotinga)

K'uk' (quetzal)

describing the costumes, physical attributes, and magical powers of some fifteen deities, Schellhas also identified their name glyphs. Because the people at the time were unable to read the name glyphs of the gods and their significance was unclear in many cases, Schellhas arbitrarily designated each god by a letter from the Roman alphabet. Some of these terms, such as God L or God N, are still commonly used by scholars today. Schellhas focused his research upon the deities appearing in the three known codices; these gods also appear in other Late Postclassic media, including ceramics, mural paintings, and monuments. In addition, virtually all of them are present in Classic Maya art and writing. Indeed, one of the most striking traits of Maya gods and religion is the extraordinary degree of cultural continuity.

Themes in the research of Maya religion

Thanks to the meticulous iconographic research carried out, it is now possible to discuss Classic Maya mythology, particularity deities and episodes that correspond to the later K'iche' Popol Wuj. Such Popol Wuj characters as the monster bird Wuqub' Kak'ix, the Hero Twins and their arrogant half-brothers, Jun B'atz' and Jun Chuwen, occupied a significant position in Maya religion and its pictorial representations. Above all, they featured in highly narrative ceramic vessel scenes. One of the primary characters in these scenes is the young Maize God, the Classic version of the K'iche' Jun Junajpu, the father of the Hero Twins (ill. 412). In addition, recent research by the art historian Linda Schele (1942–1998) has identified some of the major gods and events involved in the creation of the world according to Maya mythology at 13.0.0.0.0.4 Ajaw 8 Kumk'u (corresponding to August 13, 3113 B.C. in the Julian Calendar).

Maya epigraphic studies are producing a great deal of information concerning gods and their attributes. One particular glyph, the head of a god, serves as the logographic sign for *k'uh*, the Maya term for god (ill. 413). This glyph frequently introduces a god or series of gods, including the pairing of gods of sky and earth (ill. 414).

Another important development has been the identification of the *way* beings, a fascinating sub-class of divinities with strong ties to the dark

413 *The k'uh hieroglyph*
The k'uh hieroglyph symbolizes the essence within all holy things. *K'uh* is personified in the form of a man whose head forms the hieroglyph.

414 *Hieroglyphs for the divine pair of the heavens and earth*
The inscription on the back of Stela 31 in Tikal not only tells of the founding of the dynasty and its early rulers, but also of the different gods who were called up by Siyaj Chan K'awiil when the monument was consecrated. They included Chan K'uh and Kab K'uh, the gods of the heaven and earth.

k'uh

Chan K'uh (god of the heavens)   Kab K'uh (god of the Earth)

412 *The young Maize God. Copan, Honduras, Structure 10L-22; Late Classic, 715 A.D.; green tuff, H. 89.7 cm; London, British Museum (Kerr 2889)*
This bust was originally part of the frieze in Structure 22 in Copan. This temple was erected by Waxaklajuun Ubaah K'awiil for the first jubilee of his reign on the northern side of the east courtyard of the acropolis. It represents the mythical Yaxhal Witz mountain, "green mountain," where the first maize grew, personified in the young Maize God Jun Ye Nal, "first corn cob." This sculpture of a handsome young boy with maize growing out of his head, referred to by Paul Schellhas as God E, relates to this mythical event.

underworld. These divinities were doppelgängers in the form of fantastic animals. It was believed that these *ways* were connected with a human spirit but lived in the underworld.

Groups of gods

Thanks to over one hundred years of research, a great deal can now be said concerning the qualities and natures of ancient Maya gods. Firstly, there is remarkable degree of consistency in the portrayal of specific deities in Classic Maya writing and art. In addition, particular beings and their mythological

BLOODLETTING FOR THE DEVIL

From: Diego de Landa, "Relación de las cosas de Yucatán" (Report on the incidents in Yucatan), Mexico, 1938.

They offered sacrifices with their own blood, sometimes cutting round sections from their ears. Their scarred ears remained as a symbol. On other occasions, they pierced holes in their cheeks and lower lips and sometimes made incisions in specific parts of their body or made holes in their tongues from one side to the other. The most painful ritual consisted of pulling straw through the holes before tearing the skin from their penises so that they resembled ears. The author of the General History of the Indians [Gonzalo Fernández de Oviedo] was thus mistaken when he said that these people were generally circumcised.

Sometimes they also made painful, sordid sacrifices. Those who were conducting the ritual met at the temple where they stood in a line and pierced holes through the width of their penises before pulling a large piece of string through the holes so that were linked together in a line. They smeared the devil [the divine image] with the blood

from their penises and the person who did this the most was considered the bravest. Their sons began at a very early age to sacrifice themselves in this way with terrifying enthusiasm.

For women this kind of bloodletting was not as common, although they were fairly pious. They frequently smeared the face of the devil [the divine image] with the blood of birds, animals, and fish or whatever creature they could find. They also sacrificed their possessions. In some cases

415 *Blood sacrifice from the tongue. Madrid Codex, page 96b; Late Postclassic, 1450–1650 A.D.; fig bark paper coated with lime, painted; page: H. 23 cm, W. 12 cm, Madrid, Museo de América*
One of the valuable gifts offered by people to the gods was their own blood, which was often obtained by piercing a hole in the tongue.

they cut the hearts out of certain animals and sacrificed them and in others they sacrificed the whole animal, living or dead, cooked or raw. They also sacrificed large quantities of [maize] bread and wine and all kinds of common food and drink.

In order to ensure the dignity of their celebrations, human sacrifices were made. In desperate or urgent circumstances, the priests or *Chilanes*, "magicians," sometimes demanded human sacrifices. Great efforts were made so that slaves could be bought and young children offered with great piety. They were looked after lovingly and with great care and attention up until the day of the sacrifice so that they would not run away or be sullied by carnal sin. While they were taken dancing from place to place, the priests fasted with the *Chilanes* and their official helpers.

416 *Blood sacrifice from the earlobes. Madrid Codex, page 95a*
The custom of sacrificing blood from the earlobes dates only from the Postclassic period. This illustration from the Madrid Codex shows earlobes being pierced with fine obsidian spears.

episodes are to be found recurring in various places such as Palenque, Copan and Calakmul. The specific roles of these gods could, however, vary greatly according to the prevailing policies of the dynasty and local ideology.

The rulers of Palenque are particularly drawn to the idea of a trinity of gods as the protective overlords of their dynasty. Other city-states such as Tikal and Caracol were clearly under the protection of their own divine trinity. Beside the trinity groups, we also find groups of four gods, each one of whom presides over a heavenly aspect, corresponding to a cardinal direction.

The fusion of the deities

At times, two or more gods can be merged into a single being. This merging directly links related beings, such as the fiery Lightning God K'awiil with the Rain God Chaak. Fusion can also be, however, a means of further specifying the characteristics or personality traits of individual gods.

A particularly complex example of deity fusion appears on the Early Classic Tikal Stela 31, dedicated to Siyaj Chan K'awiil, meaning "Born of the sky K'awiil" (ill. 417). Here the frontal belt mask worn by the king represents three merged gods, who appear also separately as the head variants of the numbers 3, 4, and 7 (ill. 418). Whereas the deities of the numbers 4 and 7 represent the day and night sun respectively, the god of the number 3 is a wind god. Although the head displays the typical pupil of the day sun, the eye is surrounded by the twisted "cruller" form of the night sun. The flower woven headband and cheek markings of the Stela 31 head are diagnostic characteristics of the Wind God, who formed an important part of Maya beliefs about life, death, and resurrection. In the Stela 31 text, the same three gods appear directly underneath the "divine gods" hieroglyph, which represents the gods of heaven and earth mentioned above. The merged divine being is seen, like the latter, as the mask of a heavenly being. In fact, the belt to which the mask is fastened is a celestial band, a common convention in Classic Maya iconography.

The same linking of celestial band and mask occurs on Stela 40, excavated in Tikal in 1996. The front portrays King K'an Joy Chitam, whilst the sides portray his parents, Siyaj Chan K'awiil and his consort. In this case, the belt is not worn by Siyaj Chan K'awiil

417 *Stela 31. Tikal, Peten, Guatemala, Structure 5D-33-1; Early Classic, 445 A.D.; limestone; H. 245 cm, W. 70 cm, D. 53 cm; Tikal, Museo Sylvanus G. Morley*
The stela shows the ruler Sijay ChanK'awiil (411-456 A.D.) at the moment of his coronation. He presents the royal headdress with his right hand. The heads of the patron gods of his dynasty and the city are visable on his belt, his left arm, and his headdress. Above the king's head we see the head of his dead father Yax Nuun Ayiin. A long inscription on the back of the monument describes the founding of the royal house and the predecessors of Siyaj Chan K'awiil.

420 *Early Classic vessel decorated with stucco. Tikal, Peten, Guatemala, Structure 5D-34, Burial 10; Early Classic, 300–600 A.D.; wood, painted stucco*
This vessel decorated with stucco was found in the burial of the ruler Siyaj Chan K'inich. It portrays beings from the underworld standing up to their chest in a river decked with waterlilies. Two of them have name glyphs on their heads, which distinguish them from the others and indicate that they are important gods of the underworld. The young Wind God rises up from the ocean of the underworld, while another god holds a serpent in his hands, a symbol of night and darkness.

418 *Fusion of three gods into one. Tikal, Peten, Guatemala, Structure 5D-33-1, Stela 31 (detail); Early Classic, 445 A.D.; limestone; Tikal, Museo Sylvanus G. Morley*
The attributes of different gods were often combined in the depiction of Maya gods. The mask on the belt of Siyaj Chan K'awiil on Stela 31 at Tikal combines features of the Sun God, the Fire God, and the Wind God. These three deities, and others, are also mentioned in the inscription on the back of the stela. Part of this deity's name glyph is on his head and reads *ikal ajaw*.

419 *Statue of an actor with rattle. Copan, Honduras, west courtyard, Structure 10L-11; Late Classic, 769 A.D.; green tuff*
In the lower part of the south side of this temple, which is thought to be a representation of the cosmos, the central staircase and terrace depict a mythical under-world ball court that lies under the waters of the underworld. An actor in the guise of a monkey rises out of these waters, symbolized by stone conch shells on the edge of the terrace. The rattle in his left hand bears the sign *Ik'*, "wind," further evidence of the connection between music and sounds and the wind.

but by his wife. Not only does the frontal belt piece unite the same three gods, but they also appear in consecutive order in the text on the back of the stela.

An Early Classic stucco painted vessel from Tikal portrays the same three beings waist deep in water. The youthful Wind God, with his bound flower headband and long locks, stands in the center of the scene (ill. 420). This divine triad was of special importance for the naming of the kings. The Maya rulers gave themselves names of gods in order to emphasize their divine authority. They sometimes used a combination of different divine names. These fusions are important in terms of understanding religious symbolism, as they help us to identify and understand the main attributes of specific deities.

Birth places

It is something of a truism that people make gods in their own image, that is, gods are direct and profound expressions of human social constructs and values. The Maya believed that gods were born like humans and that their lives were

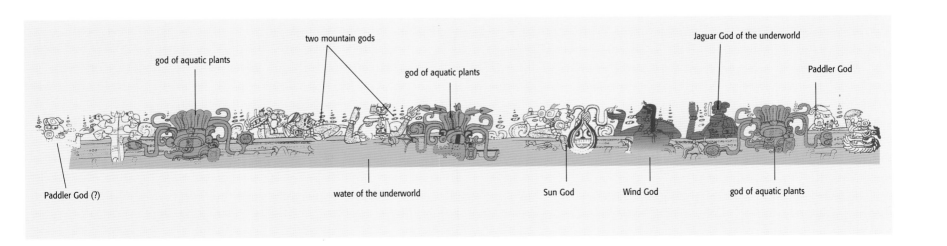

god of aquatic plants

two mountain gods

god of aquatic plants

Jaguar God of the underworld

Paddler God

Paddler God (?)

water of the underworld

Sun God

Wind God

god of aquatic plants

421 *K'awiil. Provenance unknown; Late Classic, 600–900 A.D.; fired clay, painted; H. 14 cm, dia. 13 cm; private collection (Kerr 3150)*
The name of the being referred to in the list drawn up by Paul Schellhas as God K, is recorded in many pre- Columbian Maya inscriptions as K'awiil. K'awiil is often portrayed as a figurative scepter, which is a sign of supreme power. In this depiction of his birth, the god emerges from the jaws of a visionary serpent in the form of a cylindrical ceremonial staff.

marked by the same kinds of events and conflicts, friendships and intrigues, joy and pain.

The Palenque triad provides specific information about these ideas, as separate temples were erected in Palenque for each of the three gods. The small shrines within the temples, which on the inscriptions are labeled as *pib naah*, "sweat baths," represent structures not only widely identified with birthing in the Maya region, but Mesoamerica as whole.

A vase painting from the Late Classic period contains elaborate references to a godly birth in the distant past (ill. 421). The god K'awiil is shown being brought into the world by a serpent, and passing through the ceremonial staff, which is decorated with flowers and jade at both ends; the newborn god is seen grasping one of the jeweled flowers with his left hand. A lightning god truly born of the sky, K'awiil is closely related to the celestial serpent.

Sacrifices for the rebirth of the gods

The ritualistic resurrection of gods and ancestors conducted by the Maya in the form of blood sacrifices represented a kind of symbolic birth. As a burning, celestial lightning being, K'awiil and his serpent foot embody the manifestation and rebirth of gods and ancestors (ill. 423). At the center of the sacrificial ritual stands the god Tojil, who represents the god K'awiil according to the Popol Wuj. The Maya scholars Nikolai Grube and Werner Nahm discovered that the verbal hieroglyph *tzak* found in the inscriptions corresponds to a word meaning "to conjure clouds or wind" in colonial Yukatek Maya. In texts accompanying "vision serpent" scenes, K'awiil is commonly the conjured deity, much as if the serpent constituted one of his aspects.

The deities often enter their heavenly world as small children resembling human infants. In Classic Maya art, gods frequently appear as small children held in the arms of rulers. Often the deities lie on their backs, a convention for newborn children featuring in Maya art, and at times they even appear to be struggling and squirming. The portrayal of rulers carrying these beings obviously underlined their spiritual power and unique bond to their gods, but the meaning of this convention remains to be explained. Even if the Classic Maya gods could be reborn as children, they were nevertheless ancient, primeval beings. Using this model of the divine world, the Classic elites were able to trace and understand their dynastic history over several centuries.

The act of blood sacrifice, a metaphor mentioned in the Popol Wuj, was tantamount to nurturing the gods. The texts in the holy Maya books pair the term "suckle" with the word for "embrace," recalling how, in Classic Maya scenes, the gods are held by the rulers like babies pressed against the breast. The Maya kings saw themselves as caring parents of the gods. The gods were looked after and kept alive thanks to the religious activities of the elites. The Popol Wuj also mentions that the stone images of Tojil and two other deities were revived as living, child-like beings through blood sacrifice.

> They [...] pierced holes in their ears and elbows,
> Collected the blood and anointed the mouths of the stone images.
> But the images were stone no more: each one revealed itself as a boy
> Feasting on the blood of the faithful sacrificing priests.

In Classic Maya art, the conjuring and rebirth of gods and ancestors are expressed through the so-called "vision serpent" rising out of burning offerings. Another common image in Maya art is the ceremonial staff carried by the kings, with the reborn being emerging from its tip.

Paying tribute to the gods

The Maya gods were therefore associated with two different aspects. On the one hand, they were considered as children cherished by the princes and, on the other, as powerful lords who exact tribute through ritual offerings.

Ritual tribute to gods is also expressed by the three elements typically contained in the offering bowl marked with the sun sign *k'in* (ill. 422). The two flanking elements are a conch shell and a bound feather bundle, both esteemed items of Classic Maya courtly tribute. These rare goods qualify the precious nature of the central element, a stingray spine, the basic tool by which penitential blood was offered to the gods and ancestors. The offering bowl is actually a censer, a means by which blood and other sacrificial offerings were burned.

Although the ritual offering of blood and other precious items can be construed as acts of piety, they are also political statements. Tribute paid to the gods of a community is much the same as tribute paid to the state; both are public statements of fealty and dependence. In the Popol Wuj, other Highland Maya groups agreed to nourish Tojil with their blood and hearts in exchange for fire. Only the Kaqchikel Maya avoided this religious and political subjugation:

He demanded no fire for the Kaqchikels. They did not give
themselves up. But all the other tribes surrendered
when they agreed to rest their shoulders on their ribs.

422 *Sacrificial bowl. Provenance unknown; Late Classic, 600–900 A.D.; fired clay, painted; dia. 30 cm; private collection (Kerr 1270)*
The bottom of this sacrificial bowl portrays a visionary serpent with the young Maize God emerging from its jaws. This is one of the sacrificial bowls which bears the *k'in* ("day," "sun") sign symbolizing the sunrise and the east. As well as depicting the rebirth of the Maize God, the hieroglyph stands for the renewal brought about by the sacrifice.

423 *K'awiil. Provenance unknown; Late Classic, 600–900 A.D.; limestone; Cleveland, Cleveland Museum of Art (Kerr 2879)*
This extract of a relief shows K'awiil in an unusually lively pose. He is not depicted as a scepter as usual, but as a small being sitting on a lady's hand, looking up at her with his head back. The typical characteristics of the god are a long nose, a smoking torch on his forehead and feet in the form of serpents. The scepter accompanying his image was one of the rulers' insignia.

In Classic Maya art, there are many examples of gods presiding in palace temples, but of course this was not their condition in the natural, everyday world of living humans. Instead, they were much like honored ancestors, distant beings to be conjured and contacted through specific rituals of petition and supplication. Classic Maya texts refer to shrines as *waybil*, "place of sleep," suggesting not only the residences of the gods and ancestors but also places where they must be woken and summoned (ills. 425, 426). According to the Popol Wuj, the lineage gods Tojil, Awilix and Jakawitz initially spoke, but were turned to inert stone at the first dawning.

The transfiguration of the ancestors

The borders between Classic Maya gods and deceased ancestors of the nobility are fluid. Respected ancestors were honored like gods. The common Classic Maya theme of gods or ancestors hovering in the sky over historical figures originates in Late Preclassic Maya monumental art. On Stela 4 of Early Classic Tikal, K'awiil hovers in the sky as a generic ancestor, and quite frequently elite ancestors have a burning torch or axe in their forehead, which in Maya art are attributes of K'awiil. Another Early Classic Tikal monument, Stela 31, portrays King Yax Nuun Ayiin apotheosized as the Sun God, and although the king bears his name in this headdress, his portrayal is markedly similar to the Sun God appearing on the much earlier Late Preclassic Abaj Takalik Stela 2, probably dating to the 1st century B.C. The celebrated founder of the Copan dynasty, K'inich Yax K'uk' Mo', appears apotheosized as an avian Sun God on the Early Classic building known as the Rosa-lila (Pink-purple) temple. A major sculpture from a later building overlaid on Temple 16 again portrays the founder as the Sun God, here performing a war dance in a "solar mirror shield" (ill. 424).

Yet another deity commonly identified with elite ancestors is the Maize God, who symbolically dies at the beginning of the sowing season and is reborn as new, sprouting growth.

424 *Yax K'uk' Mo' performing a war dance in the sunlight. Copan, Honduras, Structure 10L-16; Late Classic, after 763 A.D.; green tuff; Copán Ruinas, Museo de Escultura*
Temple 16, the shrine of the ancestors of Copan, is situated in the center of the city. It was erected over several previous structures and, like the first shrine, stands on top of the grave of the founder of the dynasty, K'inich Yax K'uk' Mo'. One of the altars of the staircase of Temple 16 portrays him as the Sun God performing a war dance in the solar disk. He emerges from the underworld like the rising sun. The portrait statue of Yax K'uk' Mo' stands in a niche surrounded by fused solar disks and a square shield. The statue's headdress and features recall those of the quetzal, the macaw and the Sun God and thus symbolize the name K'inich Yax K'uk' Mo', "Great-Sun Green Quetzal Macaw."

425/426 *Small shrines in the form of houses. Copan, Honduras, Structure 10L-29; Late Classic, after 763 A.D.; green tuff; Copan Ruinas, Museo de Escultura*
To the south of the Copan acropolis with the central dynastic shrine Temple 16 lies the family residence of the 16th king of Copan, Yax Pasaj. Structure 10L-29 on the north-west side of this complex was the ancestral shrine of other members of the royal family. Stone copies of simple houses with roofs made from palm leaves have been discovered in the vicinity. The inscriptions on the walls indicate that they were shrines, *waybil*, of the divine essence of a particular person, and so, at the entrance to each of these houses sits the personification of the hieroglyph for the divine essence, *k'uh*. The hieroglyph for the breath soul features on the roofs. In addition to details relating to the owner and type of shrines, one of the roofs bears another inscription which cannot be totally deciphered due to deterioration. It is probably a consecration inscription. Similar inscriptions have been discovered on different kinds of stone monuments in Copan. In addition to the consecration date, indications are often given of the type of object concerned and its owner or patron.

A carved Early Classic vessel from Tikal portrays King "Great Jaguar Paw" as this being, and the accompanying text gives him titles associating him with the Maize God as a protective deity. An Early Classic figured incense burner, a basic means of invoking gods and ancestors, also portrays this ruler as the Maize God. Two Late Classic kings, K'inich Janaab Pakal of Palenque and Yax Pasaj of Copan, were also rendered as the Maize God, although in this case displaying the burning torch of K'awiil on their forehead.

Gods and ancestors hovering in the sky or emerging from celestial serpents are frequently portrayed with swirling volutes of water-filled clouds or smoke, two inextricably linked concepts in Mesoamerican ritual and thought. Whereas such beings can appear with explicit cloud signs, the clouds are ritually manifested by fire offerings. It is becoming increasingly clear that fire ritual was a central focus of ancient Maya ceremonialism and features prominently in temple texts and iconography. The smoke rising from the sacrificial offerings constituted both the food and essence of the supernatural beings. For the Tzotzil Maya, this meant that rain-laden clouds harbored sweet incense smoke, k'uhlel, the spiritual essence of the living universe. Clearly related to the Classic Mayan

word for divinity, k'uh, the term k'uhlel is the Tzotzil Mayan word for the inner soul, and is specifically located in the heart and, by extension, the blood of people.

Concepts of godliness and the soul

Recent discussions of ancient Maya concepts of godliness and the soul tend to focus on the importance and sacredness of blood. However, as an ethereal soul centered in the heart, the k'uhlel is more than blood. The immaterial aspect of the k'uhlel among the Tzotzil of Chenalho is described as follows: "It is as air; it is in the image of the body ... it is the impalpable essence of the individual ..." The Tzotzil k'uhlel is comparable to the concept of the inner soul, or áanma among the Mam Maya of Chimaltenango. Deriving from the Spanish term for soul, ánima, the Mam inner soul is based in the heart, like the k'uhlel.

However, breath constitutes the soul essence, which continues after death as an ethereal soul of the dead. Rather than eating actual food, the spirits consume the breath or aroma, whether this be of food, flowers, incense, or blood.

Reports of the period prior to the Spanish invasion and illustrations from pre-Columbian times indicate that sacrifices typically involved burning blood-soaked paper, as well as copal, the sweet-smelling "blood" or sap of trees. Maya priests still burn other precious aromatic substances such as dried blossom, alcohol, tobacco, and the blood of sacrificed animals together with copal resin. For the ancient Maya, it was not blood per se, but the rarefied essence or "breath" of the inner soul that formed the conduit of contact between the world of the living and the supernatural.

The breath soul

The concept of the breath soul is extremely widespread in both ancient and contemporary Mesoamerica. This breath soul is closely related to both smell, such as the pungent aromas of flowers and copal, and sound, especially music, ethereal qualities carried by wind or air. From the Olmec art of the Middle Preclassic period to the Late Postclassic codices, the breath soul is conveyed by a flower or jade placed to or in the nose, or hovering before the face. The ritual capture of this soul at the death of the Poqom Maya kings is described as follows:

[...] they had ready a precious stone which they placed to his mouth when he appeared to expire, in which they believe he took the spirit, and on expiring, they very lightly rubbed his face with it. It takes up the breath, soul, or spirit into it [...].

In Early Classic Maya art, swirls forming a serpent face frequently accompany the breath element. This "breath serpent" is nothing more than a form of the "Bearded Dragon," a celestial conduit for gods and ancestors. The Bearded Dragon is often portrayed in Late Classic art as a serpent exhaling swirling flames from its wide-open mouth. In Cacaxtla, an archeological site in Central America which is famous for its Maya wall paintings, Quetzalcoatl is depicted as the Wind God in the form of a bearded feathered fire-breathing serpent (ill. 427). The swirls of flames, clouds and smoke surrounding celestial beings contain wind and it is this wind that both feeds the fire and conveys burnt offerings into the sky. The T-shaped sign *ik'*, "wind," as well as flower elements commonly issue from the mouth of the celestial Bearded Dragon. In one instance, the serpent breathes out the head of the floral Wind God, the personification of the breath soul. The innumerable scenes of figures emerging from serpents and other reptilian heads in ancient Maya art represent divine beings breathed and conjured into existence.

Incense offerings as soul sacrifices

Breath or wind is not simply the food of gods and ancestors, but also constitutes their spiritual nature, like the perfume of flowers and incense. This concept is vividly illustrated by the two-part effigy censers of the Maya (ill. 410) and other peoples of ancient Mesoamerica. Early Classic examples from

Kaminaljuyu, Tikal, and other Maya sites portray gods and rulers with exit holes through their mouths. One of these censers portrays King "Great Jaguar Paw" seated atop a bound flower, essentially the floral wreath form found at the ends of many ceremonial staffs.

Among the Maya in pre-Columbian times, copal balls commonly symbolized the heart, the seat of the inner soul. In the Popol Wuj, the maiden Xkik' substitutes a ball of copal for her heart and thereby deceives the gods of death. The copal balls recovered from the Sacred Well at Chichen Itza resemble hearts with the severed aortas at the top. Placed within the two-part censer, the burning copal heart creates the spirit "breath" illustrated on the censer and now awakens it to life.

The most impressive representation of the calling up of the breath soul with incense is on Stela 40 at Piedras Negras. It shows Ruler 4 of Piedras Negras scattering incense into his mother's cavernous burial chamber. A twisted rope extends from the grave to the heavens, where it culminates in a stylized serpent's head. The rope is decorated with triple knots and feathers, which occur in Maya iconography alongside blood sacrifice instruments. These instruments were often engraved with faces which gave the impression that they were alive. Stela 40 portrays the soul of the mother of Ruler 4 rising up from her burial to heaven in a fire sacrifice. The twisted rope in geometrical form recalls the famous "psychoduct," the channel of souls leading to the burial chamber in the Temple of Inscriptions at Palenque where K'inich Janaab' Pakal is buried (see Eberl, p. 314).

The Wind God as the embodiment of the breath soul

The Wind God, referred to by academics as God H, was the embodiment of the breath soul and in the Classic period was also the god of the number 3 and patron of the month Mak (ill. 429). Both Classic and Postclassic representations portray him as a handsome young man with a splendid headdress and flower motif in relief on his brow. Images from the Classic period show him with the clearly recognisable sign for *ik'*, "wind," on his cheek or ear.

428 *Incense burner. Palenque, Chiapas, Mexico; Late Classic, 600–900 A.D.; fired clay, painted; H. 114 cm, W. 60.5 cm; Mexico City, Museo Nacional de Antropología*
The burning of incense was an essential part of most rituals. Numerous incense burners have been found in the excavations in Palenque near the Cross-group temple. These clay cylinders were placed on the terraces and platforms, and the bowls bearing incense and other sacrificial gifts were laid on top. Most of these incense burners feature the face of the Fire God as the night-time and underworld aspect of the Sun God. The kindling and extinguishing of fire associated with certain gods, including the Sun God depicted, were also important parts of the ceremonies referred to in hieroglyphic texts. This may be explained by the fact that the creation of fire was a central theme in archaic reincarnation myths.

Classical hieroglyphs portraying the Wind God generally show markings on the cheeks which are otherwise only found in depictions of women. In this context, they probably indicate the handsomeness of the god. The flowers on his brow generally form two curved lines. In Maya art, this is a visual convention for the portrayal of scents and aromas. However, the Wind God is not only associated with sweetly scented flowers; he is also linked with musical sounds. On the relief in Palenque palace, the Wind God is depicted as the patron of the month Mak, holding a rattle and singing. In the above-mentioned representation from Tikal, which depicts three deities standing up to their hips in water, the Wind God also appears to be singing. His head is turned towards the Sun God, who is holding up a water container. This scene probably represents a natural phenomenon, namely the vaporization by the sun and the wind of the dampness brought by the rain.

During the Classic period, the Wind God was not simply limited to numbers and the calendar. He also appeared in numerous mythological scenes. In Tikal, he is not only referred to in the inscriptions on the Early Classic Stelae 31 and 40, but also in two texts engraved on bones from Burial 116. One of the texts relates to two calendrical episodes which describe his burning and death.

The Wind God was the god of the number 3. In some Maya languages, the word denoting the number 3 is very similar to the words for breath, steam, scent, and spirit. A very common expression for "death" in the classical inscriptions describes the obliteration of two elements: the white flower, *sak nik*, and the wind, *ik'*. The white flower is also associated with the breath of the soul, as Maya art includes representations of skulls which breathe out both the *ik'* sign and flowers (see "white flowery breath" in the article by Eberl, p. 311 ff.).

The divine creator Itzamnaaj

The ancient god known as Itzamnaaj is one of the high gods of the Maya pantheon. He is often depicted on Classic pottery paintings seated on a heavenly throne ruling over other gods (ill. 430). Sources from Yucatan dating from the colonial period describe him as the highest ruler of the heavens. Itzamnaaj and the Wind God are related beings and their names are even interchanged in Postclassic scripts. Itzamnaaj is portrayed as an ancient, wise god with a hooked

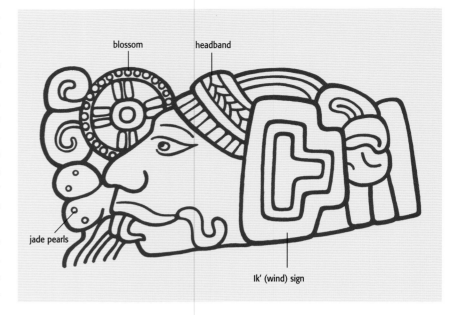

blossom   headband

jade pearls

Ik' (wind) sign

nose and large, square eyes like the Sun God. His headdress decoration appears to be made from a shell, which protrudes from the top of his head, and a headband with a mirror in the shape of a flower resting on his brow. The pearl-studded strip hanging from this flower motif is referred to as *itz*, a Maya word meaning both "nectar" and "dew." According to a text from the colonial period, Itzamnaaj was the dew of the clouds and the heaven. The Maya collected dew from leaves and used this holy water in a number of rituals. Representations

430 *Itzamnaaj and the Hero Twins. Provenance unknown; Late Classic, 600–900 A.D.; fired clay, painted; H. 20 cm, dia. 17 cm; private collection (Kerr 1183)*
Itzamnaaj is holding an audience in his human form in heaven, which is symbolized by a throne with a celestial band. Opposite him are the mythical Hero Twins from the Popol Wuj, Hun Ajpu and Xb'alanke, shown here in the Classic version. A basket with a bundle on top stands before him. It is open, showing its contents, a skull decorated with ear pegs and flowers thought to be that of Jun Junajpu, the father of the twins. The hieroglyph *ik*, standing for breath, wind, and life, decorates the basket and indicates that Itzamnaaj can bring the dead back to life with his magical powers.

from the Postclassic period portray Itzamnaaj as a priest scattering the dew with the help of a rattlesnake's rattle.

Itzamnaaj was also associated with the World Tree, the central axis which links together heaven, earth, and the underworld. Certain scenes portray the metamorphosis of Itzamnaaj as Wuqub' Kaqix, the giant bird of the Popol Wuj (ill. 341). A number of precise representations of this episode show different forest animals, such as deer, jaguars, squirrels, and armadillos, offering dishes of food and drink to the victorious Hero Twins as if they were paying tribute to conquering warrior kings. In another scene, Itzamnaaj, in the form of a bird, and a deer are looking at a figure covered with jaguar spots. This was the Classic representation of the Hero Twin Xb'alanke of the Popol Wuj. Xb'alanke is believed to have been the god of hunting during the Classic period. The shooting of the giant bird may perhaps be interpreted as the victory of Xb'alanke over the animal kingdom (ill. 432). Like Xb'alanke's twin brother, Junajpu or One Ajaw

who ruled over humans as the embodiment of the instituion of kingdom, *ajaw*, Xb'alanke was the ruler of the forest. Considering the victory of the Hero Twins over the giant bird, the close relationship between this creature and Itzamnaaj may seem surprising. But as heavenly inhabitants of the earth, both Itzamnaaj and the giant bird are responsible for granting access to the divine world and bringing their forebears back to life.

The Sun God K'inich Ajaw

With Itzamnaaj, the Sun God K'inich Ajaw was one of the most important divine entities (ill. 433). As his name suggests, he was a powerful, royal figure who was associated with the authority of the nobility and the institution of kingdom. The Sun God was also connected with war and sacrifice.

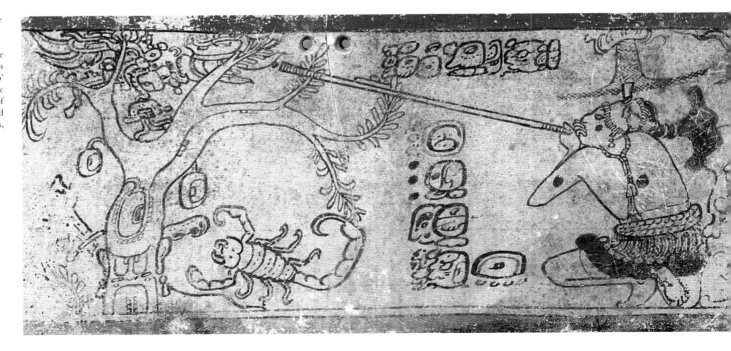

Diego de Landa described how the Yukatek Maya performed war dances and offered blood sacrifices for K'inich Ajaw at one of the New Year ceremonies. A similar event is portrayed in Room 3 of Structure 1 in Bonampak, where axe-bearing dancers perform a blood sacrifice dance directly beneath the image of the Sun God. The same dance is shown on the above-mentioned sculpture of K'inich Yax K'uk' Mo' in Temple 16 in Copan. This monument portrays the founder of the Copan dynasty as the Sun God performing a blood sacrifice war dance in front of a kind of large mirror, which is meant to represent the sun. The skeletal heads in the corners of this sun mirror have been identified by the hieroglyphic researchers Werner Nahm and Nikolai Grube as belonging to centipedes. Grube has also stated that the Yukatek Maya believed that the sun's rays could be transformed into centipedes. Skeletal centipedes are also depicted alongside the Sun God because they represented death and darkness and therefore accompany the first rays of the sun as it rises from the underworld.

The Death God Kimi

One of the most important divine figures inhabiting the underworld was the Death God Kimi (ill. 434). Sources from the Late Postclassic period refer to him as Kimi, but it is not known whether he also used this name during the Classic period. In Classic representations he is depicted both as a comical, grotesque figure and as a terrifying god. He is sometimes seen with his huge stomach performing wild dances, which contrast sharply with the dignified dances that the noble classes apparently preferred. The Maya appear to have seen the Death God as a disgusting, not particularly spiritual being who could be deceived with rituals and clever tricks. In the Popol Wuj, the Hero Twins manage to deceive the naïve Death Gods and eventually defeat them.

433 *The Sun God K'inich Ajaw. Copan, Honduras, Structure 8N-66; Late Classic, 600–900 A.D.; green tuff; Copán Ruinas, Museo de Escultura*
The throne in the central room of structure 8N-66 is decorated with a relief. It depicts four gods, who are associated with the celestial quadrants *tzuk*, symbolized here by masks. This detail shows the Sun God K'inich Ajaw emerging from the solar disk. As the rising sun, he is associated with the east. This iconography defines the place as an illustration of the cosmos with the ruler at its center.

434 *The Death God. Provenance unknown; Late Classic, 600–900 A.D.; fired clay, painted; H. 18.3 cm, dia. 18 cm; private collection (Kerr 7287)*
The Death God, referred to by Schellhas as God A, is one of the most important deities in the Maya pantheon. Artistic representations show him with numerous attributes, but always in the form of a totally or partially skeletal human corpse. Here he stands in the waters of the underworld in which waterlilies are growing. He holds an object, probably a bundle of bones, in both hands above his head.

The *k'ex* sacrifice

One of these rituals is the *k'ex* sacrifice, which is described in the Popol Wuj and is still practiced by the Maya today. In the Popol Wuj the pregnant Xkik' replaces her heart with a copal resin ball, which enables her to escape from the underworld and give birth to the Hero Twins on earth. Contemporary Maya often offer chickens and other sacrifices to the gods and demons of death and disease in exchange for sick patients. A scene depicted in Classic Maya art indicates that children were sacrificed in the *k'ex* ceremonies for members of the noble class. Remains of children's bones found in caves seem to confirm this practice, which may even stem from Preclassic Olmec beliefs. Olmec jade and clay figures represented sacrifices of children with jaguar features. Many Olmec jade objects in the form of so-called jaguar babies were probably used as expensive replacements for children whom the people were not prepared to sacrifice. Many of the sacrificial scenes depicted on Codex-style ceramics, showing jaguar babies disappearing into the jaws of the underworld, probably relate to these *k'ex* sacrifices. It is interesting to note that these sacrifices were generally buried rather than burned.

In contrast to the Wind God, with his sweet-smelling breath soul, the Death God is characterized as spreading stench and putrefication. This explains why one of the names given to the Death God by the Yukatek Maya is *kisin*, a word which literally means "the farter."

The sacrifices and food associated with the above-mentioned *way* beings were also objects of death and decline. Many scenes depict the *way* beings holding bowls containing eyeballs, bones, and severed hands and heads. As for many contemporary Maya, the *way* beings of the Classic period were probably also associated with witchcraft, healing rituals, and disease. Like the Death God, they were creatures of darkness, night, and the deadly underworld. A study of *way* hieroglyphs has established that a symbol in the form of our percentage sign not only stands for death, but can also be used to replace the *way* sign. It also reveals that a bony figure in the hieroglyphic text of Temple 14 at Palenque is described as the *way* of the god K'awiil. This being is the *sak baak naah chapaat*, the "white bone house centipede," a creature of darkness and the underworld. The jaws of this being form part of the hieroglyph for the last five-day month of the year, Wayeb, when the old year dies. The entrance to the underworld is often depicted in Maya art by the jaws of a centipede. In contrast to the Bearded Dragon, this *way* of K'awiil does not encourage heavenly resurrection, but descent into the deadly underworld.

435 *Jaguar baby sacrifice. Provenance unknown; Late Classic, 600–900 A.D.; fired clay, painted; H. 16.3 cm, dia. 10 cm; New York, Metropolitan Museum of Art (Kerr 521)* Vase painting reflects the rich mythology of the Pre-Columbian Maya. A popular episode is the sacrifice of the jaguar baby. The axe-wielding Rain God Chaak throws this being, half human half animal, into the jaws of the underworld where the Death God and a dog-like creature await their prey with open arms. A glowworm lights up the darkness with a torch.

COURT DWARFS – THE COMPANIONS OF RULERS AND ENVOYS OF THE UNDERWORLD

Christian Prager

Many of the colorful painted clay vessels found in burial chambers dating from the Classic period depict the daily court life of the Maya princes. These ceramics feature hieroglyphic texts, indicating that they were mainly produced for the upper political and social strata, because only the elites and not the ordinary Maya people could read.

These representations provide us with insight into daily court life. The people employed to look after the physical and spiritual well being of the royal family and their guests included "human curiosities" such as court dwarfs (ill. 438) and hunchbacks, who entertained the nobility with comical dances and burlesque performances, as was the case in royal courts in Europe. Culinary services were also part of the duties of court dwarfs. They served exquisite dishes and sampled the quality of the drinks.

A colorful piece of pottery of unknown origin shows a scene at the residence of the ruler Siyaj K'awiil (ill. 437). He is receiving gifts in his function

as k'uhul ajaw, "divine ruler," of Motul de San Jose. His dark complexion, position, elegant clothing, and impressive headdress clearly distinguish him from the other people. On the right-hand side of the picture, a corpulent court official is seated at the foot of the throne holding a fan, with the hieroglyphic folders for which he was responsible laid out in front of him. The gesticulating ruler looks at his profile in a mirror which is held by a kneeling court dwarf. A second dwarf appears to be testing the quality of the drinks in the calabashes and clay jugs. The hunchback next to the two dwarfs can be identified as an official of the royal court by his characteristic headband. Illustrated vase and hieroglyphic texts show that the court dwarfs also carried out administrative duties. They offered gifts to guests, dowries for weddings (ill. 439), accepted tributes, and checked the quality of products. These included fans, bundles of feathers, tripod plates, calabashes containing cacao or beans, mirrors, and other prestigious objects. As the ruler's

servants, they often carried a scepter with the image of K'awiil, one of the most important gods for the ruling classes of the Classic period.

The dwarfs were not only employed to entertain the court, they also helped to create stone monuments. The signature cartouches on a sculpted stela of unknown origin show that the artist must have been a dwarf.

According to Spanish sources, dwarfs, hunchbacks, cripples, and albinos also lived at the Aztec courts, where they entertained and looked after the physical well-being of their rulers as well as serving as mirror bearers (ill. 436). Dwarfs also acted as servants and underlings for the Inca princes of South America.

The divine Maya kings represented the center of the universe and could even be personified as gods and achieve contact with them through rituals (see Grube/Martin, p. 153). Because of their physical shape, dwarfs, hunchbacks, and other malformed figures were seen as supernatural beings in a human form. They were also considered, like the Maya kings, as messengers and contacts with the transcendental world of the gods, and for that reason rulers often chose these people to be their companions. The Maya may have associated this idea with the belief that the presence of a superhuman being could call forth a medium through which the gods could participate in earthly

436 Back of a mirror depicting a dancing dwarf. Provenance unknown; Late Classic, 600–900 A.D.; slate; dia. 9 cm; Cologne, Rautenstrauch-Joest Museum
The sculpted back of this slate mirror shows a dwarf in a feather costume performing a ceremonial dance. Spanish chroniclers reported that dwarfs and hunchbacks were often appointed to entertain the court, often as actors wearing costumes in which they were able to imitate the flapping of wings and other movements of birds, particularly herons.

437 Dwarfs at court. Photograph of a colorful painted ceramic vessel (detail); provenance unknown; Late Classic, 600–900 A.D.; private collection (Kerr 1453)
Court dwarfs had a range of functions. Here one is shown kneeling before the king holding a mirror, whilst another tests the quality of the food in the calabashes and jugs.

life. This also explains the numerous represent-ations found on vases and stone monuments which depict court dwarfs as spectators of profane, ritualistic acts. In order to emphasize their absolute social power and religious authority, rulers were portrayed in the company of low-ranking groups such as vassals, court officials, and prisoners, but also in the company of gods and other supernatural beings, including court dwarfs.

Dwarfs were also associated with the underworld, which was seen as a kind of parallel world. The Maya believed that they came from beyond the natural world and embodied the lives and manifestations of divine beings and other supernatural figures. For the Maya, the boundaries and entrances to this world were to be found in holes in the forests and in dark caves and deep ravines. Shimmering water surfaces covered with dark green waterlilies or dark cenotes (under-ground water courses) were also believed to be entrances to the underworld. This kingdom between the real and supernatural worlds was inhabited by frogs, water-serpents, and scorpions, and also by gnomes, forest spirits, and small people. This explains why dwarfs appear in the iconography in scenes relating to the underworld.

Dwarfs also played an important role in Maya mythology. According to Classic Maya beliefs, four dwarfs were given the task of raising the vault of heaven. The Olmecs also believed that the heavens were held up by four dwarfs. This belief survived

438 *Clay figure representing a dwarf. Jaina, Campeche, Mexico; Late Classic, 600–900 A.D.; fired clay, painted; H. 11.1 cm; Mexico City, Museo Nacional de Antropología*
This clay figurine represents a dwarf with the typical characteristics of chondrodysplasia, the most common variation of over 200 types of microsomia: short, thick extremities, a large stomach, a disproportionately large head, thick drooping lower lip, and a flat nose. The dwarf wears a headdress in the form of a bird's head and a wrap-around apron. A shell hangs by a string at his chest, probably symbolizing the underworld.

until the Postclassic period, when dwarf-like stone figures with raised arms served as supports for altar structures, which may have represented the vault of heaven. The Maya even saw two dwarfs in the firmament representing an undiscovered constella-tion. Dwarfs are often depicted as companions and servants of the Sun and Maize Gods. Numerous stelae show the ruler with a decorative waistband on which the face of the Sun God is portrayed. This also explains why regents were often surrounded by dwarfs, who were depicted with them in stone sculptures. It appears that by being accompanied by court dwarfs and wearing a specific costume, the king was able to slip into the role of the Sun God and thus embody both the center of the real world and the world beyond.

439 *Carved ceramics depicting dwarfs. Provenance unknown; Late Classic, 600–900 A.D.; clay, incised; H. 16.5 cm, dia. 15.4 cm; private collection (Kerr 8076)*
The left-hand scene in the sequence shows a *coati* or hog-nosed coon accompanying a ruler as his animal spirit or alter ego. The hieroglyphic text states that "few tributes are paid." The dwarf standing on the right of a nobleman is saying: "Receive the visit, beautiful lady!" This may be an appeal for her to marry the young man. The animal spirit may be advising against marriage for material reasons.

MAYA CREATION MYTHS AND COSMOGRAPHY

Elizabeth Wagner

Maya mythology was a highly developed, rich world of ideas and imagery that has been preserved for us on numerous painted ceramic vessels and stone monuments. A number of these depictions revolve, as do many of the hieroglyphic texts, around the most important myth of all, that of the creation of the cosmos. According to inscriptions from the Classic, the world as it exists today was created on the day 4 Ajaw 8 Kumk'u, which in the Julian Calendar used in astronomical calculation falls on September 8, 3114 B.C. In the view of the Maya this world was not, however, the first world to have existed. The present era follows at least one previous creation and Maya texts refer to a number of events that took place in this long distant epoch. Research in comparative iconography has revealed that the Maya conception of their origins belongs to an older tradition, which can be traced back to the period of the La Venta culture of the Olmec (1000–800 B.C.), the predecessors of the Maya.

Our knowledge of the mythology and religious beliefs of the Maya remains fragmentary, with many key concepts still shrouded in uncertainty. Nonetheless, advances in deciphering Maya hieroglyphic inscriptions have provided new insights into an ancient world view and the ritual practices that were inspired by it.

The birth of the first pair of gods

Information concerning the era before the creation of the present world is provided largely by inscriptions from the three temples of the Cross Group in Palenque, in particular, the relief panel set at the heart of the Temple of the Cross (ill. 442). The text begins with the birth of the First Mother, about six years before the beginning of the present era. This was preceded by the birth of the First Father, approximately eight years before the Day of Creation. But this prehistoric period stretches back much further into the past. In a throne inscription recently discovered in Temple XIX at Palenque, not only the birth of the First Father is recorded, but also his enthronement under the supervision of Itzamnaaj, who must thus have lived long before the original pair of gods. Itzamnaaj was evidently the supreme being in the Maya pantheon (ill. 443).

440 *The World Tree*
This ceiba tree (*Ceiba pentranda*), almost 40 m high, stands at the entrance to the Tikal archeological site (Peten, Guatemala). The Maya regarded the ceiba tree as sacred because it embodied the common axis that linked the various levels of the universe. The Maya name for the tree is Yaxche or "green tree," not only because of its green leaves, but also because green was the color that signified the center of the cosmos. Ceiba trees are, to this day, treated with respect and are not cut down when areas of jungle are cleared in order to plant maize fields.

441 *Stela C. Quirigua, Izabal, Guatemala: in front of Structure 1A-3; Late Classic, 775 A.D., reddish brown sandstone; H. 400 cm*
The inscription on the sides of this monument tell of the creation of the world and the placing of three stones at the center of the cosmos. The text also contains details of how the stela was erected in the year 775 A.D. by K'ak' Tiliw Chan Yoaat. The front shows this ruler playing the role of the god who set up the "Jaguar-throne-stone" on the Day of Creation. The brief inscription on the plinth describes the monument as *wak ajaw tuun*, "6 Ajaw stone." This name refers to the day when it was erected, day 6 Ajaw in the 260-day calendar.

442 *Relief panel of the Temple of the Cross. Palenque, Chiapas, Mexico; Late Classic, 692 A.D.; limestone; H. 190 cm, W. 325 cm, D. 13.5 cm; Mexico City, Museo Nacional de Antropología e Historia*

The Temple of the Cross is the largest and most northernly of the three shrines of the Cross Group. It takes its name from the cross-shaped central motif on the relief panel on the rear wall of the sanctuary inside the temple. It is, in fact, a highly stylized representation of the World Tree, which grows out of a sacrificial bowl and has the bird aspect of Itzamnaaj sitting at the top. This tree marks the center of the sky, as indicated by the band of heaven on which it stands. The location of the Temple of the Cross marks the northern quadrant of the cosmos, which is assigned to the sky.

443 *Relief panel on the south side of the throne dais of Temple XIX. Palenque, Chiapas, Mexico; late Classic, 736 A.D.; limestone; H. 45 cm, W. 248 cm, D. 5–6 cm.*

The inscription on the south side of the dais tells of the enthronement of the god Jun Ye Nal Chaak by Itzamnaaj on day 12.10.1.13.2 9 Ik 5 Mol, a date falling in 3310 B.C., long before the beginning of the present era. The central scene of the relief appears to illustrate this mythical event but, in fact, it depicts its re-staging on the occasion of the ascent to the throne of K'inich Ahkal Mo' Naab III in 721 A.D., with mortals assuming the roles of the gods. The ruler of Palenque has taken on the part of Jun Ye Nal Chaak, and a nobleman appears as Itzamnaaj. The latter point is noteworthy inasmuch as it reveals the great importance of the nobility during the regency of K'inich Ahkal Mo' Naab III.

The creation of the present world

The birth of the First Pair of Gods and the inauguration of their rule was followed by the Day of Creation, 4 Ajaw 8 Kumk'u. On this day, with the completion of the 13th Bak'tun (1 Bak'tun = 400 years), the preceding era came to an end and the present age began.

Monuments such as Altar 1 of Piedras Negras, Stela 1 of Coba, Stela 23 from Copan, and above all the lengthy inscription on the west side of Stela C from Quirigua, not only describe the transition from the old era to the new, but also often use the formulaic expression "the image manifested itself" or "the hearth was set up" (ill. 444). These are some of the most frequently used phrases when describing how the cosmos came into being. But the account given in the inscription on Stela C from Quirigua goes into much more detail.

After the world had been created, three stones were placed in a mythological location named Na Ho Chan, "the first of five heavens." Two divinities described as "paddler gods" placed the first stone, the "Jaguar-throne-stone." Then a god, whose name has not as yet been deciphered with certainty, placed the "Serpent-throne-stone" in a location associated with the Earth. The third and last stone was the "Water-throne-stone," which Itzamnaaj, the supreme divinity, placed at the mythological location "first three-stone-place."

These three stones play a central part in Maya mythology. They correspond to the three hearthstones that, for thousands of years, have been at the center of every Maya house. For the Maya, the house is a metaphor of the entire universe. Just as the three hearth stones are the center of the house, the three stones that were placed during the creation are the center of the cosmos. They alone made it possible for the sky to be raised up out of the primeval ocean.

The creation myth, as it is described on Stela C from Quirigua (ill. 441), ends with the completion of the 13th Bak'tun by Wak Chan Ajaw, the "Lord of the sixth heaven." We know from other hieroglyphic inscriptions that this was an epithet of the Maize God.

There is an obvious relationship between the stone placings mentioned on Stela C and the scene on the "Vase of the Seven Gods," painted on a black background, from Naranjo (ill. 445). One of the old rulers of the underworld sits on a jaguar throne facing six other divine beings. The jaguar throne is synonymous with the "Jaguar-throne-stone." The inscription relating to the

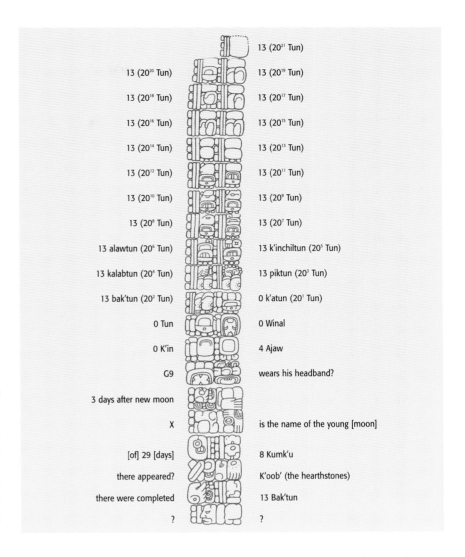

	13 (20²¹ Tun)
13 (20²⁰ Tun)	13 (20¹⁹ Tun)
13 (20¹⁸ Tun)	13 (20¹⁷ Tun)
13 (20¹⁶ Tun)	13 (20¹⁵ Tun)
13 (20¹⁴ Tun)	13 (20¹³ Tun)
13 (20¹² Tun)	13 (20¹¹ Tun)
13 (20¹⁰ Tun)	13 (20⁹ Tun)
13 (20⁸ Tun)	13 (20⁷ Tun)
13 alawtun (20⁶ Tun)	13 k'inchiltun (20⁵ Tun)
13 kalabtun (20⁴ Tun)	13 piktun (20³ Tun)
13 bak'tun (20² Tun)	0 k'atun (20¹ Tun)
0 Tun	0 Winal
0 K'in	4 Ajaw
G9	wears his headband?
3 days after new moon	
X	is the name of the young [moon]
[of] 29 [days]	8 Kumk'u
there appeared?	K'oob' (the hearthstones)
there were completed	13 Bak'tun
?	?

444 *Stela 1. Coba, Quintana Roo, Mexico, Structure A-9; Late Classic, 680–750 A.D.; limestone; H. 292 cm, W. 143 cm, D. 36 cm*
The inscription begins with the Day of Creation, 4 Ajaw 8 Kumk'u. It is linked with *halaj k'oob'* ("the hearthstones appeared") and *tzutzaj oxlajun pih* ("13 Bak'tun were completed"). Instead of the usual form of this date in the Long Count, viz. 13.0.0.0.0, 20 further positions appear here with signs preceded by the coefficient 13. This corresponds to a period of time of 20²¹x13x360 days. Evidently the beginning of the present creation did not mark an absolute zero point of time.

445 *The Vase of the Seven Gods. Provenance unknown; Late Classic, 600–900 A.D., fired clay, painted; H. 27.3 cm, dia. 11.5 cm; private collection (Kerr 2796)*
The black painting on a beige ground shows six gods who have assembled on the Day of Creation, 4 Ajaw 8 Kumk'u, before God L, the ruler of the underworld. The latter is seated on a jaguar throne in a cave. The scene is evidently set in the night world or the underworld. The inscription, telling how the universe was arranged on that day, also gives the names of the six gods. They form three pairs of opposites with different spheres of authority within the upper world, the heavenly realm, and the underworld. (see also ill. 407)

scene depicted gives the date 4 Ajaw 8 Kumk'u, leaving no doubt that it is an episode from the creation myth. The event is described using the hieroglyphs "they put the black center in order," followed by the names of the six divinities, who have assembled for the occasion of the imminent act of creation. "The black center" denotes the condition of the universe at the moment of creation, when the sky was dark and had not yet been separated from the primeval ocean.

Inscriptions in Palenque record, in three sections, the act of raising the sky, about a year and a half after the placing of the three stones. The first section begins with the entry of the First Father, the Maize God Jun Ye Nal ("One Revealed Maize"), into heaven and ends with the consecration of the "North House" at the "Place of the Maize God." The "North House" is a metaphor for the sky and its stars, which revolve around the north pole of the sky, with its four cardinal points and four subsidiary directions, the latter marking the corners of the sky. In order to set up this place, Jun Ye Nal raised the sky and supported it by putting the tree Wakah Chan at the center of the universe. The illustration on a vessel from a sacrificial cache in Tikal depicts this episode in a simplified form (ills. 446, 447). The Maize God, Jun Ye Nal, together with two paddler gods, raises up the sky, here represented as a two-headed, serpentlike creature. Two hieroglyphs adjoining the Maize God's face identify him as Wak Chan Winik, "Six Skies Man." They thus confirm the account of the creation in Palenque, in which Jun Ye Nal is mentioned, concealed behind the title Wak Chan Ajaw, "Lord of the Raised Sky."

Name of the ———— Tikal King Chak Tok Yich'aak

Paddler God   Maize God   Maize God   Paddler God

vision serpent   vision serpent

The sky was now raised up and separated from the Earth, and the universe had been created by setting up the World Tree at its center. But it was only after two further Bak'tun cycles that the creation was complete, when the First Father had made the "heart of the raised sky," the center of the sky, revolve. In a geocentric conception of the universe, this meant that the starry sky was made to spin about its center. By this act of creation, the hitherto rigid order of the universe was imbued with life. The rotation of the sky around its axis, the paths taken by the stars in the firmament, and the trajectory of the sun and moon were the basis of the astronomical cycles, whose regularity the Maya observed with great fascination and accuracy, and which they were eventually also able to calculate and explain in mythic terms.

The birth of the patron deities

In Palenque, this creation myth is linked to the later birth of three divine beings, the "Palenque Triad," as the patron deities for that place and their ruling dynasty (ill. 448). They are the descendants of the First Pair of Gods and were first identified as patron deities of Palenque by Heinrich Berlin in 1963. Eight hundred years after the arrival of these three beings at a mythological location

446/447 *Ritual cache vessel, Rollout, drawing (above), photograph (below); Tikal, Peten, Guatemala, Structure 5D-46, Early Classic, 350–378 A.D.; fired clay; Tikal, Museo Sylvanus G. Morley.*

The inscription on the lid records the consecration of the house of the progenitor of the dynasty of Tikal, Yax Eeb Xook and his descendant Chak Tok Yich'aak. It is worth noting that the name of the former here includes the epithet *wak chan te*, which denotes the World Tree. Thus, the most significant event of the creation is linked to the foundation of the ruling house of Tikal. The engraved scene shows the evocation of the paddler gods by the Maize God *wak chan winik*, "6th heaven man."

called Matawil, the First Mother performed an incantatory rite, which took place on the "first greening mountain," the birthplace of the "first maize plant." This rite probably refers to the origin of maize, from which the first humans were later created. The creation of humans is not, however, explicitly recorded in the inscriptions that are known at present; it is mentioned only in sources dating from the colonial era. The question of the origin of maize is, to this day, a central topic of Maya folklore. In Palenque the mythical narrative ends when the reign of the First Mother begins, 809 years after the creation of the universe. The connection between the First Mother and the Earth is clear from her epithet: Jemnal Ixik, "Woman of the Valley Site," as it appears in the inscription of the Temple of the Foliated Cross.

the first pair of gods

Father: Jun Ye Nal Chaak I   Mother: Jemnal Ixik Matan

God 1 (Jun Ye Nal Chaak II)   God 2 (K'awiil)   God 3 (K'inich Ajaw)

448 *The gods of the Palenque Triad and their parents. Reconstruction of the family relationships based on the Palenque inscriptions*

The three patron deities of Palenque (the hieroglyphs for their names are shown in the illustration) are the children of the first pair of gods. The three shrines of the Cross Group (ill. 442) are dedicated to them.

Allusions to the creation of humans appear over and over again in the art of the Classic. For example, the Rain God Chaak split the mountain Yax Hal Witz with his lightning ax so that the first maize could grow from it, from which, in their turn, the first people were created. Other beings symbolizing the Earth, such as the peccary and the turtle, are often substituted for the mountain. The maize then grows out of them in the guise of the young Maize God (ill. 449).

The structure of the cosmos

Maya cosmography can be reconstructed from the extant fragments of myth and representations of rituals. The structure of their worldview accords, to a large extent, with the shamanistic model of the world described by the well-known historian of religions Mircea Eliade (1907–1986): it is divided into four parts, and a central axis links the cosmic levels of heaven, Earth, and the underworld (ill. 450).

In most Maya legends the surface of the Earth is described as a square with a clearly marked center. It floats in a large pool of water, which forms the boundary with the underworld. In Classic art, the Earth often appears as a turtle, a crocodile, or a peccary. The sides of this quadripartite world face towards the four cardinal points, the corners of which are determined by the points where the sun rises and sets at the summer and winter solstices. At the center of each side there is a mythical mountain with a cave, and a tree standing at its entrance. It is here that the entrances to the underworld, and to the mythical primeval ocean that lies above it, are to be found. Deceased ancestors and other supernatural beings also live there. Four paths lead into these caves from the center of the world, linking the center with the four cardinal points.

449 *The birth of the Maize God. Provenance unknown; Late Classic, 600–900 A.D.; fired clay, painted; Boston, Museum of Fine Arts (Kerr 1892)*
The bottom of the bowl shows maize, in the form of the young Maize God Jun Ye Nal, sprouting from the Earth, which is symbolized by a turtle drifting in the primeval ocean, indicated here by the signs for water and waterlilies. A water deity looks out from the rear opening of the turtle's shell. The twins Hun Ajaw and Yax Balam are present at the birth of the Maize God. The inscription above the scene indicates the type of vessel and its owner: *u lak Tojam K'awiil Sak Way*, "the bowl of the Tojam K'awiil Sak Way."

Creation myths in monuments from the colonial era

Mythical events, including the creation of the world, are also recorded in a number of documents from the colonial era, written in the Latin alphabet but in the Mayan language. Some of these documents are based on hieroglyphic manuscripts.

These include, among others, the Popol Wuj, the "Book of the Council," which was written down from oral evidence c. 1530. It combines the story of the ruling K'iche' Maya dynasty with the myth of the battle of the Hero Twins, the sons of the founding fathers of the K'iche' Maya, against the lords of the underworld. It also begins with an account of the creation of the world. Episodes from the Popol Wuj appear in some early images from the site of protoclassic ruins at Izapa in the Mexican state of Chiapas, and are later to be found in Classic Maya art.

The Popol Wuj tells of the repeated creation and destruction of earlier worlds that preceded our own. One striking feature of these accounts is that the measuring out of the universe is described using the same words as the layout of a maize field (*milpa*) or the building of a house. The creating deities laid out a square using a measuring cord to determine the dimensions of the firmament and the Earth. After the world, and the animals and plants that live on it, had been created, the First Father and the First Mother created humans out of maize dough. All earlier attempts to create humans using other materials, such as mud and wood, had failed. Hence, to this day, the Maya call themselves "maize people" in their own literature.

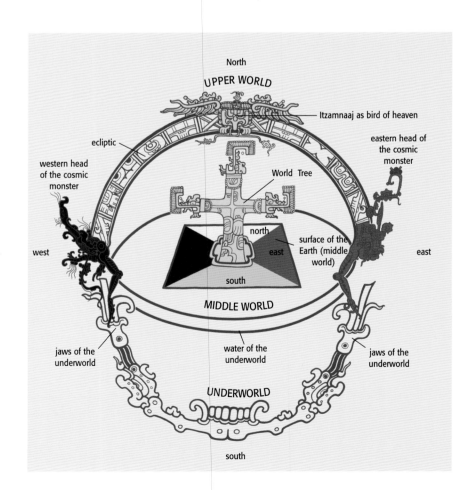

450 *A shamanistic model of the world. Reconstruction drawing based on the Palenque inscriptions and the Dresden Codex*
Shamanistic religions the world over have in common the idea of a multi-tiered universe, with sides assigned to the four cardinal points and associated with particular colors, and with a World Tree at its center.

451 *The "Cosmic Plate." Provenance unknown; Late Classic, 600–900 A.D.; fired clay, painted; dia. 31cm; private collection (Kerr 1609)*
The tripod "Cosmic Plate," a ceramic in "codex style," is one of the undisputed masterpieces of Classic Maya vessel painting. The unknown master, from the Nakbe region in Guatemala, has executed the black and brown lines on the cream-colored background with a sure hand. Around the rim of the plate there is a striking red stripe. On the outside, stylized water lilies are intended to symbolize the watery surface of the underworld. Few pictures of the cosmos in Maya art are as vivid as this painting.

452 *Two-dimensional drawing of the painting at the bottom of the plate*
Around the rim of the plate there is a two-headed monster representing the sky. Signs symbolizing the firmament form its body, with Itzamnaaj sitting at the center as a bird of heaven. The Rain God Chaak rises up from the primeval ocean as a World Tree, marking the boundary with the underworld and represented by parallel black stripes. The "place of the black water" is situated in the wide open jaws of Sak Baak Chapaat, the "white bone centipede," at the entrance to the underworld.

Itzamnaaj as bird of heaven

symbol for "star"

jaguar

top of the World Tree

eastern head of the cosmic monster

western head of the cosmic monster

branch of the World Tree, in the form of a vision serpent

jaws of the underworld

symbol for water

jaws of the underworld, symbol for Ik'?-nal, the "black hole place"

the Rain God Chaak as the World Tree

Ik' Naabnal, the "black ocean place," the waters of the underworld

aquatic plants

Like the surface of the Earth, the primeval ocean, and the underworld, the sky is also divided into four parts. It was imagined, similarly to the underworld, to consist of several levels. The boundaries of the eastern and the western cosmic region are formed by the solstice points. The quadripartite firmament is held up by four gods, the Bakab, or Pawajtuun.

In Maya art, the sky appears as a two-headed being with a body like a crocodile. A sky band with star and planet symbols, or spirals symbolizing clouds, is frequently substituted for the body. A pool of water filled with waterlilies, fish, shells, and other marine creatures represents the ocean in which the Earth floats. At the center of the cosmos stands a huge ceiba tree. In iconography it is occasionally replaced by a maize plant. At the top of this World Tree, at its highest point, sits the bird of heaven Itzam Ye, one of the symbolic forms of the supreme deity Itzamnaaj or Yax Itzam, the "First Magician," as one Classic text calls him. It was only through his art that the universe was imbued with a soul.

Each main direction or cosmic region was assigned a color. Red stood for the east, white for the north, black for the west, and yellow for the south. The central point of reference, as regards the continuation of the universe and all its creatures, is the path of the sun. This is also the reason for the prominence given

THE CREATION OF THE WORLD IN THE CHILAM BALAM BOOK OF CHUMAYEL

The books of Chilam Balam are collections of texts written in the Yukatek Mayan language but using the Roman alphabet. They were compiled by village scribes in the 17th and 18th centuries from a wide range of sources, including texts whose origins were pre-Hispanic. Only ten or so of the many Chilam Balam books that once existed have survived. They are named after the villages where the manuscripts were found or last kept. The Chilam Balam of Chumayel is one of the most comprehensive and important of them. In addition to numerous passages of a historical or prophetic nature, there is also an account of the creation of the universe. The actual act of creation was preceded by the destruction of the previous world by flood. The re-creation of the cosmos was achieved by setting up trees at the corners and center of the universe. The trees are associated with the colors for the cardinal points, and birds sit in them, as they also do in depictions of the World Tree in Palenque. Despite intensive research, however, many of the symbols and metaphors in this account of the creation have yet to be interpreted.

Introduction by E. Wagner; text and source anonymous (from the German translation of the Mayan by Nikolai Grube):

"There was a sudden rise of the waters when the theft of the insignia of Oxlahun-Ti-K'u occurred.

Then the sky fell down. It fell onto the Earth, at which point the four gods, the four Bacabs, who brought about the destruction of the world, were set up. Then, when the destruction of the world was complete, a tree was set up in order to put the yellow Yuyum bird in its place. Next, the white Imix tree was planted. One pillar of the sky was then set up, with the white Imix tree in the north as a sign of the destruction of the world. Then the black Imix tree was erected in the west, so that the black-breasted Pixoy bird could sit on it, followed by the yellow Imix tree, which was set up in the south as a symbol of the destruction of the world, so that the yellow-breasted Pixoy bird could sit on it – the yellow Yuyum bird, the yellow bird of courage. Then the green Imix tree was placed at the center of the Earth as a reminder of the destruction of the world.

The bowl of another K'atun was set down in position by messengers, the servants of their master. The red Piltek was set in the east of the world to

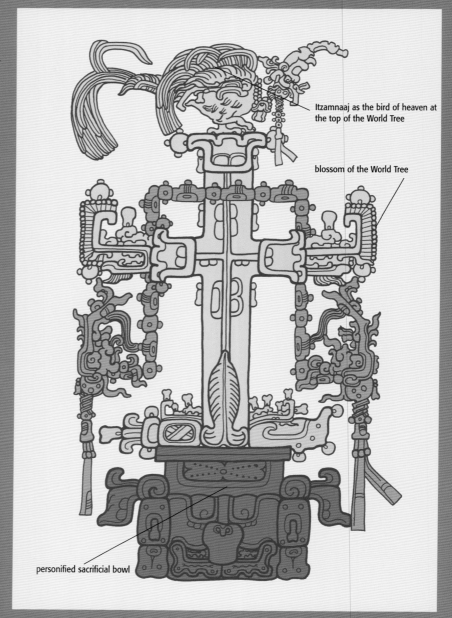

Itzamnaaj as the bird of heaven at the top of the World Tree

blossom of the World Tree

personified sacrificial bowl

453 *Representation of the World Tree, drawing taken from a relief panel (detail). Palenque, Chiapas, Mexico, Temple of the Cross; Late Classic, A.D. 692; limestone; H. 190 cm, W. 325 cm; Mexico City, Museo Nacional de Antropologia e Historia* The central motif of this relief panel in the sanctuary of the Temple of the Cross is a symbolic representation of the World Tree rising up from a sacrificial bowl. From both sides of the trunk, a branch with a large blossom rises up. A double-headed serpent with a body consisting of jade beads, and a continuous sequence of the hieroglyph "yax," symbolizes the fresh green of the tree and the color of the center of the cosmos. On the blossom at the top of the tree, Itzamnaaj sits enthroned in the guise of the bird of heaven.

lead men to their master, and the white Piltek was placed in the north, to lead men to their master. Lahun Chaan was set in the west to lead men to their master, and the yellow Piltek was put in the south to lead men to their master. Aj Wuk Chek'nal ("who fertilizes the maize seven times over") was set over the entire world. He came from the seventh level of the Earth, he descended to fertilize Itzam-Kab-Ayiin ("Itzam, the earth-crocodile"). There, he vigorously descended between the four corners of Earth and heaven, roaming between the four candles, between the four levels of the stars. The world was not yet illuminated; there was neither day nor night, nor the moon. Then they perceived that the world was awakened. The world awoke".

to the east-west axis. In the worldview of the Maya, the east is associated with the sun and daylight, the west with darkness and nighttime. The south is the direction of the planet Venus, or the night sky in general, while the north is associated with the moon. These motifs also appear, among other places, on the "glyphic sky bands." In art, they are used to make up the simplest form of the cosmogram such as we find on the edge of the relief on the Palenque sarcophagus lid. The sky bands often appear on thrones, as on a sculpted bench from Structure 8N-66, one of the residences of the nobility from the eastern sector of Copan. In this case, the cosmogram is complemented by its arrangement, highlighting the north-south axis of the cosmos, each separated from the next by a mask symbolizing *tzuk*, "the cosmic quadrants."

One of the finest representations of the cosmos has been preserved for us on a painted vessel, the "Cosmic Plate" (ills. 451, 452). Heaven is embodied by a double-headed monster painted around the upper rim of the plate, whose body is formed from signs that symbolize the stars in the sky. In the middle of heaven sits the great sky bird Itzam Ye. At the center of the entire scene, the Rain God Chaak rises up from the primeval ocean as a World Tree. Beings from the underworld can be seen below this band of water. On the eastern side, the head of the young Maize God can be discerned, putting out green leaves that evoke ideas of fertility and renewal. The ocean, the "place of the black water," as it called in the hieroglyphs on the band of water, is held in the gaping jaws of a monster. This is Sak Baak Chapaat, the "white bone centipede" at the entrance to the underworld.

The basic features of these cosmogram can be found in all Maya communities and elsewhere in Mesoamerica, and can be traced back to the Preclassic. Fundamental ideas of creation and the structure of the universe have survived, not only the demise of Classic Maya culture, but also the upheavals that followed the Spanish invasion. In many communities, they continue to this day, and form the basis of religious belief and its associated rituals. Ceremonies that accompany the building of a house, the laying out of a *milpa*, and sowing time are still derived from these ancient ideas.

Cosmography as a principle of spatial organization

Whenever the Maya made incursions into natural space – by laying out a settlement, erecting a building or an altar, or clearing jungle to create land for cultivation – they copied the quadripartite model of the world. Plazas, pyramids, temples, and palaces imitate in symbolic form the mythical landscape that was given its shape by the gods on the Day of Creation. From *milpa* to entire settlements, regardless of whether it was a simple peasant's house or the cultic buildings at the center of a city, all were modeled on the cosmos.

The Maya also believed that tombs should be modeled on the universe. The painted burial chambers of Rio Azul in the north-east of Guatemala are particularly fine examples; their walls depict the sides and corners of the quadripartite world with the hieroglyphs for their names (ills. 454, 455), and also

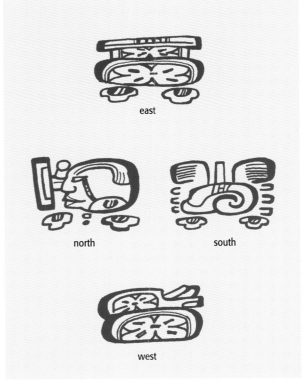

east

north   south

west

454 *Burial 12. Rio Azul, Peten, Guatemala, Structure A-4, Burial 12; Early Classic, 450 A.D.; mural painting*
The hieroglyphs denoting the four cardinal points have been written on the corresponding walls of the burial chamber. The four quadrants of the cosmos are assigned the names of their markers, which are designated here as prophetic stones. The names of the corner points of the quadrants also appear at the corners of the tomb, probably referring to the solstice points on the horizon. Thus, the tomb becomes a reflection of the cosmos, with the dead ruler at its center. An inscription on the north wall gives an account of his funeral.

455 *Hieroglyphs for the four cardinal points, copied from the lower hieroglyphs on the side walls of Burial 12 of Rio Azul*
The hieroglyphs for the four cardinal points are painted on the walls of the tomb. The manner in which east and west are denoted is derived from the course of the sun, but the significance of the hieroglyphs for north and south has not as yet been established with certainty. The east is called *el k'in* ("where the sun emerges"), and the west is *och k'in* ("where the sun goes in [the underworld]"). The hieroglyph for south can be translated as *nojol,* "right," because the south lies in that direction when one looks towards the east.

show the mythical mountains at the sides of the cosmos and the primeval ocean. The body of the deceased ruler was placed at the center of this cosmogram. It thus lay in the uppermost tier of the underworld.

The Maya city as a symbolic landscape

Pyramids, crowned with temples and with tombs inside them, were built to reflect the mythical mountains and caves where deceased ancestors and beings from the underworld reside (ill. 457). The sites where pyramids were built often symbolized a mythical place on Earth or on the surface of the primordial waters. The terms used to describe various types of building reveal how the parts of a city also represented elements of the cosmos; *Naab* ("plaza") also means "ocean," "lake," or "standing water." Similarly, the sacred mountains (*witz*) were imitated by people, who embodied them in the pyramidal temples.

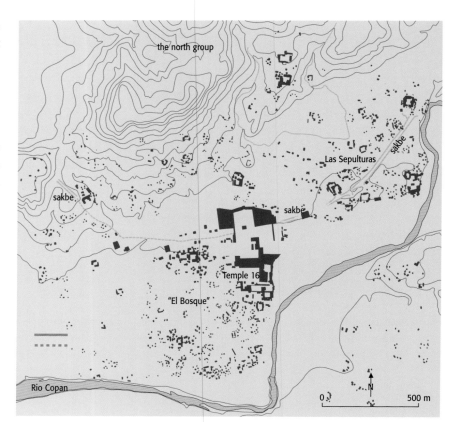

456 *Map of the city center at Copan, Honduras*
The map shows the main group at the center, surrounded by four large residential areas about a kilometer apart. At the center, above the tomb of the founder of the dynasty Yax K'uk Mo', is the central ancestral shrine along with the residence of the ruling family. The residential districts face in the four main directions and were residences of noble families, their artisans, and their courtiers. Those in the east and west are each linked to the center by means of a *sakbe*, or "causeway." Embedded in the landscape, with its watercourses and mountains, the city of Copan is an ideal model of the Maya cosmos.

It was not only the design of plazas and buildings that was based on the quadripartite model of the world. Cities in their entirety were also laid out as reflections of the universe, in order to identify them as the seat of political and religious power. Cities were built to symbolize the mythical landscape shaped and inhabited by gods – the layout of a Maya city was the image of a cosmogram projected onto a horizontal surface (ill. 456). The city not only reproduced the divine order of the cosmos, it also represented the structure of the secular world. The ruler's residence and the shrines of his ancestors were located there, and the ruler himself represented and sustained the harmony of both macrocosm and microcosm.

In the layout of a city, the axes of the cosmos were often represented by spacious causeways called *sakbe,* leading outwards from the center and linking it with outlying districts. The east-west axis was often given particular emphasis. Shrines located in caves, on mountain peaks, and at the foot of mountains marked the boundaries of a city in the surrounding countryside. Other shrines took the form of stelae and altars set up on the outskirts of the city. Occasionally, these were explicitly denoted, in their inscriptions, as marker points for the particular cosmic quadrant (ill. 458). The sites of monuments such as these were also regarded as openings or connecting paths giving access to the various cosmic levels. The layout of settlements in the vicinity of particular mountains, caves, rivers, or springs was not based exclusively on practical considerations, but also took into account the traditional cosmographic model of an ideal landscape. Mountains with caves in the area surrounding a settlement were, and still are, seen as the equivalents of the mythical mountains and caves in which ancestors and local patron deities resided (see Brady, p. 298).

The aim of the cosmographic layout of a city, embedding it in mythical geography, was to create a harmony between the earthly world and the divine order. The basic model can be seen throughout the entire Maya area, albeit with local and regional variants. The properties of sacred sites, and the beings associated with them, were also reproduced in the iconography of exterior ornamentation, usually carried out in stucco or in stone sculpture. This created a sacred area, like a map of sacral geography.

Cosmography and social structure

The fundamental design of the cosmogram was the basis of all levels of spatial organization in a city, from an individual house, via the central group of courtyards in a residential area, to the layout of the entire city. The spatial

457 *Entrance to the sanctuary of Temple 22. Copan, Honduras, Structure 10L-22; Late Classic, 715 A.D.; green tuff*
Erected by Waxaklajuun Ubaah K'awiil to mark the 1st K'atun anniversary of his rule, Temple 22, at the northern edge of the eastern courtyard of the acropolis, represents the image of the mythical mountain Mo' Witz, the seat of a patron deity of the Copan dynasty. The sculptures at the inner entrance to the sanctuary symbolize the cosmos in its east-west axis, the ecliptic. This section of the sky is represented by a two-headed reptilian being with a body of spiral cloud, held up by two Atlanteans. These *Bakab,* or *Pawajtuun,* crouch on skulls, which symbolize the underworld.

458 *Stela 19. Copan, Honduras, 5.5 km west of the center; Late Classic, 652 A.D.; green tuff, H. 317 c., W. 63 cm, D. 43 cm*
In 652 A.D., "Smoke Imix," the 12th ruler of Copan, put up a series of stelae at remote locations in the valley of Copan, as marker stones for the east and west quadrants of his city. One of them is Stela 19, which, together with an altar, constitutes the western boundary shrine. The inscription, which has been severely eroded by the weather in places, tells, among other things, of the erection of the monument by the king.

hierarchy seen here reflected a ranking order among the nobility within society, as can also be learned from inscriptions. The ruler, the *k'uhul ajaw*, "Divine Lord," stands at the center of this cosmos. Maya rulers saw themselves as the *axis mundi*, and many had themselves portrayed as the embodiment of this axis on monuments. These portrayals often show the ruler in a costume that symbolizes the World Tree, Wakah Chan, with the *tzuk* face of the tree trunk at the center of the loincloth, often flanked by serpents' heads representing branches or blossoms. The headdress frequently shows the head and feathers of the bird of heaven, Itzam Ye, sitting at the top of the tree.

The ruler saw himself both in the role of the person who maintained order on Earth, and in that of the god who created cosmic order, including meteorological, astronomical, and other natural phenomena, which were of major importance for the agricultural cycle (ills. 459, 460). The rulers resided at the center of the cities and also acted as high priests and mediators. By means of their rituals, they transferred divine power to the earthly community, thereby legitimizing their own status. The center of secular and religious power was equated with the center of the universe.

Every family head from the lesser nobility, when laying out his residence and on ritual occasions, used the same cosmographic symbols as the ruler, thereby perpetuating divine order in the latter's sphere of power. Maya cities exemplify the type of "regal-ritual" city that is widespread in preindustrial cultures. Such a city was a symbolic cosmos, comprising all the social units involved in the government of the kingdom. It was both the ruler's residence and the residential area of the nobility. Each lower unit, which was dependent on the unit above it, reproduced the cosmographic order.

Cosmography and ritual

The act of creation was of great significance when compiling the calendar and the ritual activities laid down in it. Rituals often marked the ends of periods, particularly the end of a K'atun, with the erection of stelae and altars as symbolic reenactments of the setting up of the stones at the beginning of the creation. Architectural alterations to plazas and other buildings occasionally accompanied such rituals to underline their role as renewal ceremonies. The ruler symbolically destroyed the world and created it anew. Temples and palaces of former rulers had to be demolished to make way for the buildings that subsequent rulers built over them.

A further example of such ritual reenactment of the destruction and re-creation of the world are the New Year rites, which were described both in the Dresden Codex and by the Spanish chronicler Diego de Landa (1524–1579). The central acts in these rituals included erecting trees or images of the gods and setting stones facing the four cardinal points.

Thus, a figure of the god K'awiil was set up every 819 days. After each cycle of 819 days, the god entered a new cosmic quadrant, thereby changing his color by taking on that assigned to the corresponding direction.

By creating the world, the gods not only created the material basis for human existence, but marked the beginning of time and of all order. It was a model for social life. The rituals ensured that people did not destroy the balance of creation, but kept it alive with symbolic re-creation and sacrifice.

459 *Stela H at Copan, Honduras. Hand-colored Lithograph by Frederick Catherwood, 1844*
The artist Frederick Catherwood was not only attracted to the magic of the place, which he visited with John Lloyd Stephens in 1840, but also created the first reliable drawings of Maya stone monuments such as Stela H shown here. The plate is one of 26 hand-colored lithographs which Catherwood published, together with detailed commentary, in his work *Views of Ancient Monuments in Central America, Chiapas and Yucatan*. The stela depicts the ruler Waxaklajuun Ub'aah Chan K'awiil of Copan in the year 731 A.D.

460 *Stela B. Copan, Honduras, Great Plaza; Late Classic, 721 A.D., green tuff; H. 373 cm, W. 118 cm, D. 100 cm*
The monument was erected by Waxaklajuun Ubaah K'awiil, the 13th ruler of Copan, and shows him as the personification of various gods in a cave of Mo' Witz, "Macaw Mountain," one of the mountains on the four sides of the Copan cosmos, and the seat of the patron deity of the ruling dynasty. Mo' Witz was probably the name of the great massif to the north of the city. The face on the prince's loincloth signifies *tzuk*, "section," indicating that the person portrayed stands in the central axis of a cosmic quadrant.

INTOXICATION AND ECSTASY

Nikolai Grube

An aspect of Maya culture that caused great revulsion to the Spanish priests was what they regarded as excessive indulgence in alcohol and drugs during religious festivals. Missionary Diego de Landa (1524–1579) discovered that there was scarcely a single solemn occasion that did not end in a bout of heavy drinking: "The Indios were extremely uninhibited when drinking or drunk, which had many ill effects; it led them, for example, to kill one another ... They made wine from honey, water, and the root of a certain tree which they grew for this purpose, which made the wine strong and foul

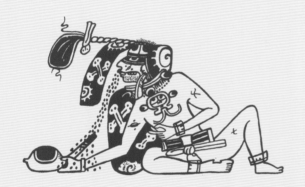

smelling. They would dance, make merry, and eat in pairs or groups of four. After they had eaten, their cupbearers, who as a rule did not get drunk, brought out large tubs for them to drink from, which led in the end to a general uproar. The women were very concerned when their husbands came home drunk."

The drink described by Landa was probably balche', an alcoholic brew of water, wild bees' honey, and the bark of the balche' tree (*Lonchocarpus longistylus*), which was grown for this purpose in many domestic gardens. Balche' has a very low alcohol content, which means that large quantities must have been imbibed for any intoxicating effect to be achieved. Balche' is, to this day, produced and drunk on ceremonial occasions throughout the entire Yucatan peninsula. The Lakandons of Naha' make an infusion from the bark in a hollow tree trunk in the early morning. By the following morning, the balche' ritual can begin: a bout of drinking that lasts the whole day and which takes place in the presence of images of the gods.

In the Classic, in addition to balche', there was another alcoholic drink brewed from the fermented sap of agaves. The Maya called the drink *chi*, which was their name for the agave itself. Depictions of bouts of drinking on Classic Maya ceramics often show large vessels bearing the hieroglyphic inscription *chi* (ill. 463). Drinking scenes such as these also shed light on another aspect of Maya consumption of alcohol. Since the drinks contained no more alcohol than a light ale, large quantities had to be consumed in order to experience the desired state of intoxication. It is evident that the brew was drunk until it led to vomiting. The vomit was caught in special ceremonial bags worn on the chest like bibs. But in order to introduce more alcohol into the body more quickly, enema syringes made

462 *Smoker. Provenance unknown; Late Classic, 700–720 A.D.; clay, painted; H. 21.3 cm, dia. 11.5 cm; private collection (Kerr 5453)*

This depiction of a smoker is one of the few frontal representations of a face in Maya art. The unusual hat, in the shape of an animal's head, gives the scene an additional aspect of humor.

461 *Akan, the god of intoxication. Two-dimensional drawing of a painting on a polychrome ceramic vessel*
Black spots around the eyes and "percentage signs" on the body are the attributes of Akan, the god of intoxication, seen here vomiting while holding an enema syringe.

463 *Drinking bout. Rollout of a polychrome painted vessel; provenance unknown; Early Late Classic; 550–700 A.D.; clay, painted (Kerr 1092)*
The scene shows an orgiastic feast with intensive consumption of alcohol. Two of the clay jugs bear the hieroglyphic inscription *chi* (fermented agave sap). The two figures in the middle are wearing bags to catch their vomit.

of pumpkins and clay, were used (ill. 464). This procedure enabled the person concerned to become extremely inebriated. Thus, many depictions of scenes of intoxication show men dancing, staggering, and falling down (ill. 463). Toxic substances were often added to the drinks; they were intended to enhance the effect still further, but were also highly detrimental to the taste. This was presumably another reason for administering enemas, because they allowed liquids to be introduced into the body that, if taken orally, would have imposed an excessive strain on the taste buds. There was even a god who watched over the ritual enemas and had special "authority" with regard to drinking bouts. This god, Akan, was described by the Spaniards as the "Bacchus" of the Maya (ill. 461).

These orgiastic bouts of drinking seem often to have taken place in caves, which were regarded as entrances to the underworld. As places of eternal darkness, they were not only timeless, but were also beyond the rules of social living that held sway in the daytime world. In this alternative world without light, the eyes as sensory organs played very little part. By way of compensation, people were able, with the help of stimulants, to indulge in hallucinations and visions. Indeed, in some caves, large-bellied vessels have been found that can be recognized from vase paintings as the containers used to hold the fermented agave sap *chi*.

Alcoholic drinks were, however, only one of the many kinds of drug that the Maya took in order to leave the visible world and gain access to a different reality by means of visions and fantasies. An entire menu, so to speak, of psychoactive drugs was available to them. Combined with fasting for days on end, monotonous music, and ecstatic dancing they made it possible to exchange one world for another. Most drugs were of vegetable origin and affected the central nervous system directly by altering perception, consciousness, and general state of being. One of the oldest psychotropic plants from the New World is tobacco, more than 35 varieties of which occur naturally in the Maya area (ills. 462, 465).

Tobacco was not only smoked, it was also taken as snuff or chewed, and a decoction produced from the plant was taken as a drink. The Maya rarely took tobacco by itself. To enhance its many and varied effects, they mixed it with the leaves of the rafflesia (a species of *Brugmansia*) and the seeds of the thorn apple (a species of *Datura*), which contain numerous alkaloids with hallucinogenic and stimulating effects.

Mushrooms that produce the alkaloid psilocybin also thrive in the Highlands. To this day, shamans

464 *Depiction of an enema being administered. Provenance unknown; Late Classic, 600–900 A.D.; black clay; H. 17.5 cm, dia. 13.3.cm (Kerr 1550)*
The protagonist in the scene, lying on the ground with one leg drawn up at an angle, is receiving an enema using an unusually large enema syringe. While supporting his head with one hand, a sign of great relaxation, he is helping, with his other hand, to insert the end of the syringe into his rectum.

465 *Smoker. Provenance unknown; Late Classic, 600–900 A.D.; mussel shell; H. 26.5 cm; Cleveland, The Cleveland Museum of Art, The Norweb Collection*
The prince, wearing only a loincloth and a headdress in the form of a stag's head, sits in front of a triton shell, from which a serpent is emerging.

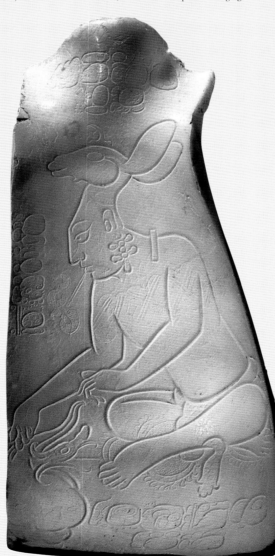

dry them and grind them to a powder using grindstones, enhancing their strongly hallucinogenic effect. These mushrooms were probably used as far back as the late Preclassic, because stone sculptures shaped like mushrooms have been found in Kaminaljuyu and throughout the entire Highlands of Guatemala.

In addition to drugs obtained from plants, the Maya also obtained psychoactive substances from the poisonous secretions of the bullfrog (*buffo marinus*). This toad's poison contains the substance bufotenine, which is related to LSD, and if taken in large doses, can even cause death. Depictions of toads are widespread in the Preclassic, with the glands situated behind their ears always given particular prominence. Recent research by the Californian ethnologist Johannes Wilbert suggests that a mollusc (a species of *spondylus*), often found in graves and sacrificial depositories, also had hallucinogenic effects. This helps to explain the great importance attached throughout the Maya area to this mollusc, which is also an important attribute of the Rain God Chaak.

Most drugs, when taken, cause immediate reactions, such as vomiting, increased sensitivity to light, and numbness in the limbs. But these are followed by the desired effects. The soul seems to leave the body and set out on a journey to the ancestors and gods, mythical animals appear, the dead begin to speak, and distant places seem to be within reach. These visions are not random phenomena, but are rooted in traditional mythological themes, cultural experience, and the concrete expectations of those involved. In the art of the Classic, visions are always represented as serpents. From their wide open jaws, the ancestors and gods, who can be spoken to and heard, emerge. The taking of drugs was, therefore, a fixed element in rituals used by shamanistic healers, as well as by godlike kings, in order to receive council and help from their gods and ancestors.

UNCOVERING THE DARK SECRETS OF THE MAYA – THE ARCHEOLOGY OF MAYA CAVES

James E. Brady

The great Mayanist, J. Eric Thompson notes that caves were one of the three major focuses of ancient Maya religious life, along with mountains and temple pyramids. Despite this testimony to their importance, until recently, caves were ignored and poorly understood features of the ancient landscape. Why this should be is not altogether clear. At the inception of Maya studies in the 1840s, caves were well represented in the work of John Lloyd Stephens and Fredrick Catherwood. Catherwood's famous lithograph of the huge wooden stairway at Bolanchen dramatically illustrated the scale of indigenous construction surrounding cave utilization (ill. 467). In some cases, the conditions – strenuous climbing, and crawling in oppressively hot and humid conditions – contributed to keeping the richness of Maya caves a secret. At the Gruta de Chac, it appears that the descent was so arduous that Stephens, and another early archeologist Henry C. Mercer, were too exhausted to explore or record the large deposit of archeological material at the bottom of the cave.

The crux of the problem, however, was the failure to understand that caves were essentially religious, rather than habitational, sites, and also to appreciate the central importance of these features in Mesoamerican religion (ill. 469). For instance, at the ruins of Quen Santo, Eduard Seler rejected the translation of the site's name as a straightforward combination of Maya and Spanish meaning "Holy Cave," and in doing so missed the significance of the three caves located beneath the site. This was particularly unfortunate because the caves contained both impressive architecture and monumental sculpture. Rather than seeing the caves as the religious heart of this pre-Columbian city, Seler considered the passages simply as a place where sculptures were stored when the site was abandoned.

Without a clear understanding of the significance of caves, archeologists had little incentive to investigate them. The first attempt to synthesize what was known did not come until 1959, and the systematic study of caves began only in the 1980s. During the 1990s, there was a rapid expansion in cave studies, with new discoveries bringing new insights.

Maya religion and the physical landscape

It is not possible to appreciate the importance of caves to the ancient Maya without understanding the role of landscape in their religion. It appears that, unlike Western people, all native American groups have an orientation to the Earth as a sacred and animate entity (ills. 470, 471). This orientation to the Earth is still a strong element in the worldview of many modern Maya. Anthropologists have found that the personage called the Earth lord (Tzuultaq'a in Q'eqchi' Mayan) is the single most important figure in indigenous religion. The word *tzuultaq'a* means "hill-valley," and carries strong supernatural significance even when used in everyday contexts to indicate a geographic area. A number of different Mayan languages address the Earth lord by a name that translates as "hill-valley," so this should be seen as a general Maya pattern. Thus, the landscape itself is being personified and deified. In many Mayan languages, the word for cave means "stone house," because it is believed that the Earth lord resides in a cave within the mountain sacred to him or her.

There has been a tendency in the past to treat mountains and caves as opposites representing up versus down, or sky versus underworld, but this does

466 *The Loltun cave, Yucatan, Mexico*
The photograph shows one of the larger chambers of the Loltun Cave. The roof has caved in, allowing sunlight to penetrate. Debris is gathered in the center. The Maya believed that such openings in the Earth's surface connected the upper world with the underworld.

467 *The Bolonchen Well. Lithograph by Frederick Catherwood, early 19th century*
In the northern Yucatan, where there are no rivers or lakes, cenotes and underground cave water, along with cisterns, provided the people who lived there with water. Water from the caves was also used for ritual purposes. The lithograph shows the impressive well site at Bolonchen in the early 19th century. A huge wooden stairway leads from a side entrance down to a small lake at the bottom of the cenote.

cave   "jaws of the Earth monster"   altepetl (city-state)   witz (mountain)

468 *Maya hieroglyphs for cave, "jaws of the Earth monster," mountain, and the Aztec hieroglyph for city*
Place names in Maya inscriptions often include hieroglyphs for the particular form of landscape. An ideal landscape in Mesoamerican thinking, widespread for a long time, is the sacred mountain that rises up from the waters of the underworld. The Aztec concept of "city," *altepetl*, is based on this ideal; literally translated it means "water mountain."

not appear to be the case in Maya mythology. The term "hill-valley" actually unifies both dimensions in a single entity. Furthermore, mountains and caves are clearly linked conceptually, in that the Maya believe mountains to be hollow. Their interior is variously conceived of as containing the Earth lord's home, their corrals where they keep all types of wild animals, or to be filled with maize, water, or treasure. In actual practice, it is clear that for modern Maya, mountains and caves are closely related. The Q'eqchi' recognize 13 major sacred mountains, each being the home of an important Tzuultaq'a. Each mountain also has its cave, which is the most sacred spot and the location for the performance of rites to the Tzuultaq'a. When the Q'eqchi' speak of going to Xucaneb', the most important sacred mountain, their destination is actually the cave.

The consolidation of mountains and caves, the two most important features in the sacred landscape, to form a single sacred symbol has further implications. David Stuart has produced epigraphic evidence that Maya pyramids were called *witz*, "hills" or "mountains" (ill. 468). In identifying Maya hieroglyphic place names, Stuart and Stephen Houston remark that what "is perhaps most striking is that ... the idiom for referring to manmade construction is often a metaphor for 'hill.'" This suggests that ancient temple pyramids represented sacred mountains. The doorways of the temples, built on top of these pyramids, are commonly considered to be entrances to symbolic caves. This is often made explicit by façades representing the open mouth of the Earth monster, a common

cave symbol, surrounding the doorway. Returning to the idea that caves, mountains, and temple pyramids formed the three focuses of Maya religious life, it should now be clear that these are not three distinct and separate cults or areas of worship. Rather, they are all part of a single, all-important theme – Earth.

Caves, landscape, and Maya settlement

If the Earth was so important that a site's public monuments were models of natural features, then the selection of a settlement location within the landscape must have been a matter of great significance. We know, cross-culturally, that reasons for the choice of location are always recorded, justified, and celebrated in local mythology. In many cases, these important points have to be divinely revealed or discovered through signs. The most famous Mesoamerican example is the founding of Tenochtitlan on the spot where the Aztec discovered an eagle sitting on a cactus, holding a serpent. What is less well known is that the cactus was growing on top of a cave, from which two springs issued.

Ethnohistorical documents recording foundation rituals from communities in all parts of Mesoamerica found that people sought very specific geographical features when founding settlements. These were of such importance that groups would bypass areas that were better endowed ecologically but lacked these features. García-Zenbrano has noted that they "searched for an environment with specific characteristics. ... Such a place had to recall the mythical moment when the Earth was created: an aquatic universe framed by four mountains, with a fifth elevation protruding in the middle of the water.

469 *Longitudinal section of the Loltun Cave, Yucatan, Mexico*
The Loltun Cave had been archeologically explored by the end of the 19th century. Henry C. Mercer investigated it in the 1890s with the aim of obtaining information about its early use as a place of settlement and ritual. He measured and drew the cave, and also made several archeological cuts there.

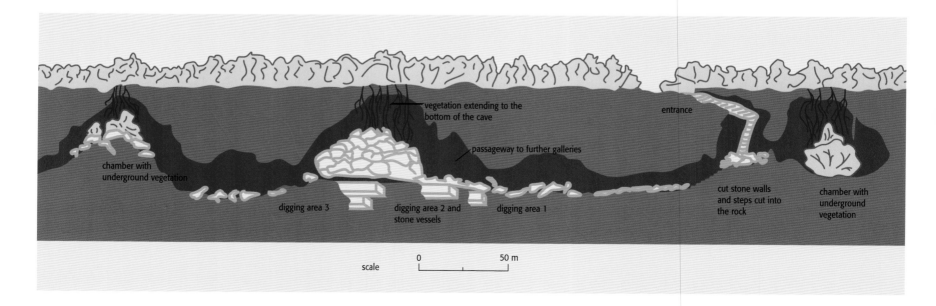

chamber with underground vegetation

vegetation extending to the bottom of the cave

entrance

passageway to further galleries

digging area 3   digging area 2 and stone vessels   digging area 1

cut stone walls and steps cut into the rock

chamber with underground vegetation

scale   0   50 m

The mountain at the core had to be dotted with caves and springs, and sometimes be surrounded by smaller hills. A setting like this duplicated, and forever would freeze, the primordial scene when the waters and the sky separated and the earth sprouted upward."

The selection of a location that replicates the setting for the world's creation is not unexpected: groups cross-culturally present the founding of their city as a repetition of the creation of the world. It must also be recognized that great acts of creation always occur at the very center of the cosmos, so the new settlement was appropriating for itself this place of power and prestige. The connection with sacred and mythic landscape was carried further in Mesoamerica. According to García-Zenbrano, "a natural cave [in the center of the area] had to contain water or be surrounded by it (ill. 478). Many times, the grotto was manually excavated to approximate its shape to that of the mythological place of origin ... Chicomoztoc, Apoala, Tulan Zuyua, and Chalchiuitlapazco. These cavities, when ritually dedicated to the divinities, became the pulsing heart of the new town, providing the cosmogonic referents that legitimized the settlers' rights to occupy that space, and the ruler's authority over that site."

The fact that foundation rituals in all parts of Mesoamerica draw on the same symbols suggests that the mountain-cave-water complex lies at the heart of the Mesoamerican system of ideology. The cave, along with its mountain, is associated with ancestors, the place of group origin, and even with ethnic identity. Thus, they are strongly charged features. In Central Mexico, the close relationship between community and landscape is reflected in the Nahuatl term for community, *altépetl*, which literally means "water-filled mountain," and the glyphic rendering is a mountain with a cave at its base (ill. 468). Vestiges of this strong settlement orientation to caves can still be found among the modern Maya. The location of one Lakandon Maya village in the Lowlands was

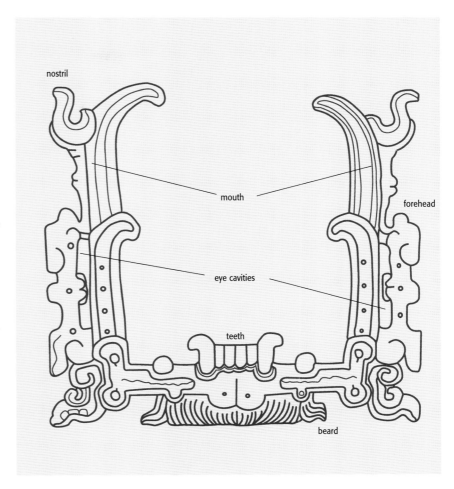

470 *The jaws of the underworld*
In Maya art, landscape forms, such as mountains, caves, and cenotes, are often represented as mythical beings. The wide open jaws of the Sak Baak Chapaat (white bone centipede) in Maya inscriptions symbolize a cenote as the "jaws of the underworld holding the waters of the underworld." The natural models for this mythical place are not only cenotes but also underground cave lakes.

471 *Altar in the shape of a mountain with a cave entrance.* Tonina, Chiapas, Mexico, Structure E5-5; Early Classic, 300–600 A.D.; modeled stucco on masonry; H. 150 cm, W. 250 cm
Maya buildings, especially cultic buildings, are often copies of locations that play an important part in mythology. Temples and their associated pyramid-like buildings symbolize sacred mountains. In art, these are portrayed as reptilian beings containing, by way of architectural sculpture, artificial copies of mythical locations. At symbolic cave entrances, the Maya set up altars, on which they performed the same sacrificial acts as in real caves, burning incense and laying down gifts.

472 *Chalcatzingo, the "El Rey" rock relief. Chalcatzingo, Morelos, Mexico; Olmec, Middle Preclassic, 700–500 B.C.*
A richly adorned human figure, presumably a ruler or the ancestor of a ruler of Chalcatzingo, seated on a low throne in the jaws of the Earth monster, signifying a cave entrance. Spirals symbolize the wind issuing from the cave, bringing clouds from which rain falls. The figure holds the symbol for "cloud" in his arms, and is presented as a rain god. This relief is evidently based on the notion, which to this day is widespread in Mesoamerica, that clouds, above all life-giving rain clouds, are formed in caves and rise up from them.

determined by the desire of the villagers to be close to a sacred cave, despite poor soil in the area. Tzotzil Maya communities in the Chiapas Highlands settled near named caves, which gave their names to the community. Community members inherit the responsibility for venerating and caring for the cave that is thought to be the home of the the owner of the community's land, the Earth lord. A similar practice was noted in the Tzotzil Maya community of Larrainzar. The village was founded near a large cave formed in white rock, giving the community the name *Zacanch'en*, "White Cave." With Aztec domination, the name was translated into Nahuatl Istacostoc, and the Spaniards added a saints name to make it San Andres Istacostoc, which it kept until the 1930s. Tzotzil Maya settlements often take their names from cave features. Caves are associated with different social units and are thought to be the home of ancestral deities.

Until recently, archeologists had not begun to investigate whether ancient Maya sites were laid out with the same considerations as those mentioned in

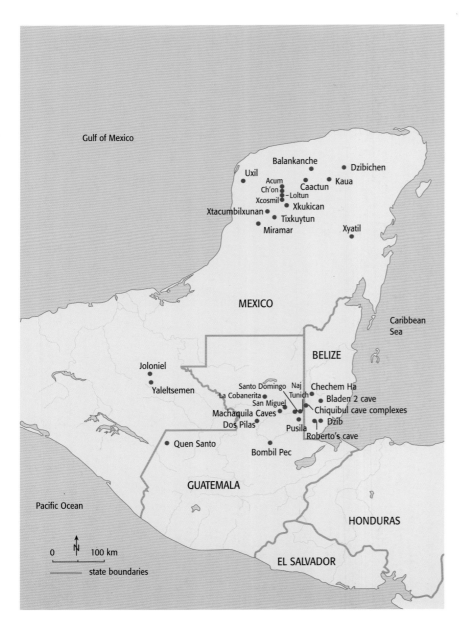

historical documents. A project carried out at Dos Pilas in Lowland Guatemala, however, documented that all three of the site's major architectural complexes were aligned with large and important caves. The largest and most impressive is the El Duende Pyramid, the highest natural hill in the area, which was modified to form a massive pyramidal base, on which a stone temple was built. From stelae set up on the pyramid we know that this complex was called *K'inalha'* in ancient times, which is a reference to water. The temple at the top of El Duende is oriented to a resurgent spring, and excavation of a sinkhole near the western edge of the complex discovered a one-and-a-half kilometer- (one-mile-) long cave, which passes beneath the temple at the top of the hill. The part of the passage directly beneath the pyramid contains an underground lake, the largest body of contained water in the Dos Pilas vicinity. The abundance of artifacts and human bone in the cave show that ancient inhabitants of Dos Pilas were using this cave (ills. 474, 475), so there is little doubt that the entire complex took its name from this feature. The second major complex, the main plaza, is also aligned with springs, and a cave may possibly extend beneath the architecture.

Approximately half a kilometer (one-third of a mile) west of the El Duende Pyramid, the Bat Palace is the third largest architectural complex at the site, and was the residence of the last two rulers of Dos Pilas. Just below the palace's platform lies the entrance to the Cave of the Bats, which is the discharge point for a subterranean river system more than ten kilometers (six miles) in length. Although the cave was relatively dry when mapped, after heavy rains, water pours from the mouth with such force that the roar can be heard clearly in the central plaza. To the Maya, this was undoubtedly an awe-inspiring display of the Earth's sacred power. Such events signaled the onset of the rainy season, and hence, the beginning of the agricultural cycle. Identifying the royal palace with this dramatic water source loudly proclaimed the king's control over water, rainmaking, and fertility. Interestingly, exactly the same claim was made by the non-Maya king of the first millennium B.C. on Chalcatzingo's "El Rey" panel. In this scene, carved in rock at the entrance to a cave, a ruler is depicted seated

473 *The best-known caves in the Maya area.*
There are innumerable caves in the karstic areas of the Yucatan peninsula. Many of them are, to this day, still used by the Maya as ritual locations. Again and again, however, one encounters unknown caves, in some cases with spectacular finds. Especially in the inaccessible regions of the Peten jungle and to the west of Belize, some further discoveries may be expected in the future.

inside a stylized cave symbol. Wind issues from the cave entrance and rain is shown falling from above (ill. 472).

The layout of Dos Pilas's architectural complexes around cave mouths did not stop with these great public monuments. A number of secondary public structures and other palaces were also constructed in relation to the two dozen caves located at the site. What is most surprising is that even humble domestic compounds and individual house structures are associated with very small caves, all of which have been found to contain artifacts. In the cases investigated, the cave entrances were located just behind the platforms, and tunnels then extended beneath the structures. This pattern of utilization reflects patterns seen across the entire population, from king to commoner. Sacred landmarks and symbols colored perception of all spaces at Dos Pilas, from the great to the mundane.

The archeological and historical context of cave utilization is also of interest. Hieroglyphic inscriptions suggest that Dos Pilas began to become a major site very late in Maya history, in about 640 A.D. Archeological excavations in surface architecture seem to confirm this because very little evidence of Preclassic (300 B.C. – 250 A.D.) or Early Classic (A.D. 250–550) settlement was found. In contrast, every one of the large caves held significant Preclassic artifact assemblages, indicating that they were important features in the sacred landscape centuries before the Dos Pilas polity began its rapid expansion. When the massive Late Classic construction program began, it respected, utilized, and incorporated a pattern of sacred landmarks that may have been established for as long as 1,000 years. Indeed, one has to suspect that the first kings of Dos Pilas were particularly anxious to appropriate symbols with which to lay claim to a more ancient past for their newly established capital.

474 *Ceramic vessels as offerings in the Cueva del Sangre. Dos Pilas, Peten, Guatemala; fired clay*
Like most Maya caves, the Cueva del Sangre (Spanish: "Cave of Blood") in Dos Pilas was regarded as a secret and sacred place. It was visited only for the performance of rituals and the laying down of offerings.

475 *The Cueva del Sangre, Dos Pilas, Peten, Guatemala*
Caves were regarded as sacred by the Maya, and were often a deciding factor when settlements were laid out. Dos Pilas is no exception in this respect, being located near the Cueva del Sangre, an important cult site for the Maya.

476 *An artificial underworld. Tonina, Chiapas, Mexico, second terrace of the acropolis; Late Classic, 600–900 A.D.*
The mythical landscape in which, long ago, the gods were active, was copied by the Maya. In this model of an artificial mythical landscape, they ritually re-enacted the story of the creation and other significant religious episodes. In addition to sacred mountains and waters, caves, with their often complex ramifications, were also copied. An example of this is the labyrinth on one of the terraces of the Tonina acropolis. Such massive buildings, with convoluted narrow passageways and dark rooms, can also be found at many other sites of Maya culture.

Artificial caves

In our earlier discussion of the role of caves in foundation rituals, we noted that the rituals appear to draw on pan-Mesoamerican symbols at the core of the ideological system. What is interesting is that the ideology spans radically different geological zones. Caves are usually formed in karstic terrain, where water dissolves the bedrock (usually limestone) to create caverns and sinkholes. But much of Mesoamerica consists of non-karstic, volcanic regions where caves do not normally occur. If the cave is the ritual heart of the community and legitimates the people's claim to the land, how did the system function in areas without naturally occurring caves?

Archeological literature contains a few mentions of artificial caves, but they were not considered significant until about 1990, when a number of them came to light and they became recognized as an architectural form in their own right. They seem to occur in two contexts, one associated with sites and the other associated with sacred places. One of the best examples of an artificial cave associated with a site was reported by French archeologist Alain Ichon at the site of La Lagunita in the Department of Quiche in the Guatemalan Highlands. The tunnel ran from the stairway of one of the four principal pyramids surrounding the central plaza, and terminated in the middle of the plaza. A spectacular cache of more than four hundred ceramic vessels and other artifacts had been left in the cave, but there were no human bones to suggest that they were burial offerings. Ichon feels that the cave, located in the heart of the ceremonial center, represents the mythological cave of origin.

An even more spectacular example is found at the site of Q'umarkaj (Utatlan), the 16th century capital of the K'iche' Maya conquered by the Spaniards under Pedro de Alvarado. At least three caves existed, the longest of which had more than 125 meters (410 feet) of passageways, and terminated beneath the central plaza. The pattern of side passages suggests that the cave represented the seven-chambered cave from where the K'iche' emerged and their kings received the right to rule from the high god Tojil. The caves remain an important pilgrimage spot today for the K'iche' Maya.

It now appears that the Maya Highlands contain many more of these features. Another in the Quiche area, mentioned in passing by Fray Francisco Ximénez, is located near San Sebastian Lomoa. The German anthropologist Franz Termer reported artificial caves under the central plazas at both Mixco and Chinautla Viejo, and two are recorded at Mixco Viejo. Artificial caves extend as far east as Honduras, where one is described in the Bay Islands and another at the site of Tenampua.

In addition to the artificial caves found within sites, a number seem to mark sacred spots and are still used as places of worship by the Maya. Two such caves are found at Esquipulas, the largest pilgrimage center in Central America dedicated to the cult of the Black Christ. The caves are located along the Rio Milagro (Miraculous River) but, interestingly, the water from the river is felt to have miraculous power only in front of the entrance to the larger cave. The walls of the cave are covered with a thick, black grease from the constant stream of visitors burning copal incense within the cave. It appears that the caves

477 *The labyrinth. Yaxchilan, Chiapas, Mexico, Structure 19*
The Yaxchilan labyrinth is just one of a large number of similar buildings throughout the entire Maya area. There is also the Satunsaat building at Oxkintok in Yucatan, and the vaulted passageways beneath the palace at Palenque. The absolute darkness inside them suggests that they were artificial underworlds, in which ceremonies that were relevant to the location took place.

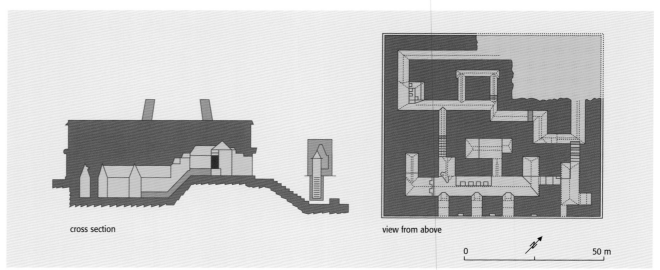

cross section

view from above

0   50 m

may have been the focus of pre-Columbian worship before the Christian cult appropriated the location.

Another pair of artificial caves are located on a high ridge near the site of Xab'aj, Quiche, Guatemala. In the 1950s, the caves attracted pilgrims from a wide area, and more recently, a case has been made for this being the location of one of the "dawning places" where, according to the Popol Wuj, the K'iche' Maya observed the first sunrise.

The recognition of artificial caves has taken on new importance with the recent revelation that the cave beneath the Pyramid of the Sun at Teotihuacan is artificial. When the cave, which begins under the central stairway and terminates beneath the center of the structure, was discovered in 1971, it was thought to be a natural feature. It appears instead that both the huge pyramid and its cave were part of a single constructed cosmogram. The famous caves at Xochicalco, also in Central Mexico, were also constructed, making it clear that artificial caves are pan-Mesoamerican in distribution.

478 *Underground cave lake. Xtacumbilxunan, Yucatan, Mexico*
In Maya cosmography, a dark, stagnant pool in a large hole in the Earth formed the boundary between the upper world and the underworld. This idea was derived from the water-filled cenotes and the numerous caves with lakes, such as that at Xtacumbilxunan.

The practice of constructing caves seems to be derived from the tradition of incorporating natural caves into site architecture, as we have seen at Dos Pilas. The artificial caves that have so far been discovered appear to date back to at least as early as the Late Preclassic (300 B.C. – 250 A.D.), making it likely that the basic model for weaving sites into the natural landscape must be still more ancient. Furthermore, the importance of caves is, ironically, most eloquently demonstrated in non-karstic areas, where caves do not naturally occur. Rather than finding that caves are considered unimportant in these regions, it would appear that they were such an indispensable element of the sacred geography that pre-Columbian peoples felt the need to construct caves of their own.

Pilgrimage

It is well known that, in all parts of the world, there are religious landmarks that so perfectly epitomize the cultural ideal of the sacred that they become widely recognized as having such special significance and power that large numbers of people travel to visit them. These are pilgrimage centers. It would be difficult to overestimate the importance of such centers because the largest known human gatherings have occurred in connection with pilgrimages.

This is relevant to our discussion of caves because Mesoamerican pilgrimage centers tend to be associated with rain and water deities. Because rain gods, without exception, are believed to live in caves, and rain itself is thought to be formed in caves, it is not surprising that caves count for a large percentage of the known centers. One of the most famous of these cave sites is the Cenote of Sacrifice at Chichen Itza. Bishop Diego de Landa described pilgrims in the 16th century throwing offerings, including human sacrifices, into the cenote. At the turn of the 20th century, Edward Thompson dredged part of the cenote in an attempt to verify Landa's account, and recovered large quantities of artifacts, including gold, jade, and human bone. Another cult center mentioned by Landa was located on Cozumel Island and was dedicated to the Moon Goddess, Ixchel, who is also associated with water. Many idols and incense burners were recovered from caves on the island, indicating that these were important focuses of ritual activity. In Central Mexico, the famed Christian pilgrimage shrine at Chalma simply took over a pre-Columbian center dedicated to Oztoteotl, the Lord of the Caves.

Archeologists have only begun to address the question of pilgrimage in the last few years, so there is no consensus even on what a pilgrimage center will look like archeologically. One of the characteristics of pilgrimage locations noted throughout the world is their association with impressive physical settings. Several of the known Maya pilgrimage caves (such as Naj Tunich, Seamay in Alta Verapaz, perhaps Santo Domingo and the Cueva de las Pinturas in the Peten, and Loltun in Yucatan) have enormous entrances and entrance chambers. In addition to this, Naj Tunich, Cueva de las Pinturas, Loltun (ills. 466, 480), and Seamay show signs of extensive modification. Many of the caves appear to have been modified to restrict access to inner chambers, which suggests that only important visitors were allowed into the most remote and sacred locations. All of the above caves also conform to the general Mesoamerican pattern in which pilgrimage sites tend to be located away from population centers.

Three of the caves (Naj Tunich, Santo Domingo and Cueva de las Pinturas) contain hieroglyphic inscriptions. The inscriptions at both Naj Tunich (ills. 481, 482) and Cueva de las Pinturas contain the glyph *il*, which means "to visit" or "witness," and is generally interpreted in these contexts to be related to pilgrimage visits. It is possible that hieroglyphic inscriptions in caves are often records of visits by important individuals. In this respect, these three caves conform to what little we know of ancient Mesoamerican pilgrimage sites.

The identification of these caves as pilgrimage centers raises the question of what induced Maya communities to invest so heavily in the architectural elaboration of a cave. Religion is one of the most powerful institutions in human society, and the presence of a major pilgrimage shrine within a polity's border is always considered a sign of supernatural favor and a matter of enormous pride. Political leaders throughout the world covet the prestige and moral authority connected with such centers. This, in itself, could explain the huge investment made by the Maya at the sites noted above.

Caves and ritual

Discussions in the preceding sections have focused on the largest and most important types of cave. They have been located in the ceremonial cores of Maya centers, and so were the focus of entire polities and public rituals (ill. 473). In other cases, the caves were pilgrimage centers that attracted believers from far and wide. For every such great cave there must have been several, perhaps hundreds, of smaller, more humble caverns that entertained the rituals of ordinary people. At Dos Pilas, we have already seen that some houses were built over very small caves. These probably served as shrines for the religious activities of only those who lived directly above. Most caves were not even located within centers, but were scattered throughout the countryside and received offerings only from peasant farmers in the immediate area. The vast majority of caves so far explored, regardless of location, show evidence of ancient use. This strongly suggests that these features, both natural and artificial, and no matter how small or remote, were never overlooked.

What types of activities went on in these ordinary caves? First and foremost, they were connected to rituals revolving around the agricultural cycle (ill. 479). If there was a cave located in the a farmer's field, it was probably used to ask the Earth god's permission to clear and burn the forest in preparation for planting. If no cave was present, the ritual would have been carried out in the field itself.

479 *Offerings in the Balankanche cave, Yucatan, Mexico.*
Late Classic and Early Postclassic, 800–1150 A.D.
Only a few kilometers south-east of Chichen Itza is the Balankanche cave. The offerings found there are evidence that is was a symbolic creation site. The *incensarios* bear the face of the Mexican Rain God Tlaloc, who was associated by the Maya with the foundation of royal dynasties. The small maize grinding-stones arise from the belief that the previous creation was inhabited by dwarfs. The intention was evidently to pay tribute to them in this way.

480 *Rock relief at the entrance to the Loltun cave,*
Yucatan, Mexico. Late Preclassic, 300 B.C.–100 A.D.
The rock face to the right of the entrance to the Loltun cave bears one of the earliest representations in the Maya area of a ruler with the attributes of the Rain God Chaak. There is an almost illegible inscription above the figure's head. It probably represents a deceased ruler who, as a divine ancestor, guarantees, in the role of the rain god, water and fertility. Both the relief and its position anticipate later Maya works, which show both ancestors and the rain god inside caves.

481 *Painting in the Naj Tunic cave, Peten, Guatemala. Drawing 68; Late Classic, 600–900 A.D.; charcoal on limestone rock*
One of the largest rock drawings in the Naj Tunic cave shows a noble master together with a dwarf, during a drinking bout. The inscription between the two figures evidently gives the name of a prince from Ixtutz, who was visiting the cave as a pilgrim. This is clear from the hieroglyph inscribed beneath, which gives the title Ho Kab Ajaw. This also appears as an emblem glyph on the monuments of an archeological site 40 km north-west of Naj Tunich that is known today by the name of Ixtutz.

483 *The Rain God Chaak at the entrance to a cave. Provenance unknown; Late Classic, 600–900 A.D.; fired clay, painted, H. 24 cm, dia. 16.7 cm; Ethnolog. Museum, Berlin (Kerr 530)*
This part of a scene on a painted ceramic vessel shows the Rain God Chaak seated at the entrance to a cave. The cave is symbolized by the wide open jaws of a being that, both in iconography and hieroglyphic writing, stands for the word *witz*, "mountain." In front of it, people have gathered for a feast and have taken intoxicating liquids in the form of enemas. This latter fact is indicated by the two jugs and the enema funnels. The cultic rituals that took place in the caves were probably accompanied by excessive festivity.

482 *Inscription in the Naj Tunich cave, Peten, Guatemala. Drawing 82; Late Classic; 600–900 A.D.; charcoal on limestone rock*
In a number of caves, there are inscriptions on the rock walls that were evidently left by high-ranking dignitaries in order to immortalize their visits as pilgrims. One of the finest inscriptions was discovered in the Naj Tunich cave. It does not, however, document a visit, but gives an account of an event, not as yet completely understood, involving the "carrying of fire." A certain Tum Yool K'inich of Caracol and a ruler from Ixkun, was involved, perhaps along with the ruler of the distant Calakmul.

The most important Maya ceremony, which is still performed all over Mesoamerica, occurs at the beginning of May, just before the onset of the rainy season. Whole villages go to their local cave to petition their Earth god, or the Rain God Chaak (ill. 483), for rain and a bountiful harvest. Additional ceremonies may also be undertaken on an emergency basis if there is a drought or pestilence because these events are believed to be indications of supernatural displeasure. The planting of maize has religious connections throughout Mesoamerica, and the annual process involves a whole range of rituals. All areas of Mesoamerica also have some type of harvest ritual, and these vary from place to place.

The discovery of small corncobs, four to five centimeters (one-and-a-half to two inches) long, at sites such as Naj Tunich and Grodon's Cave at Copan, suggests that, during the Classic period (250–900 A.D.), there may have been an offering of the first young ears soon after they appeared. In ways like this, caves participated in every aspect of agricultural ritual.

Concepts of good and evil are not as sharply dichotomized in Mesoamerican cosmology as they are in Western religions. Thus, the Earth is considered a source of rain, fertility, and life itself, but is a major source of disease as well. In Yucatan, disease is thought to be caused by breezes that emanate from caves and cenotes. Offerings are made to caves located near settlements in an attempt to prevent the disease-spreading gusts from escaping (ill. 484). Once a person has fallen ill, the curing ceremony often involves rituals held in a cave. In many cases, the disease-causing agent can be removed by a shaman passing an egg over the person's body or sucking out a poisonous intrusion. The disease-bearing object will then be deposited in a cave, returning the evil to its source.

Shamans are frequently associated with caves, because they are often thought to draw their supernatural powers from the Earth. Prognosis of an illness, and

484 *Pilgrims in a cave in the Chama hills, Alta Verapaz, Guatemala*
Inside a cave, in the "belly of the mountain," a group of pilgrims light hundreds of candles in the darkness, to prepare this holy place for the celebration of the Waxaqib' B'atz' Feast. This feast counts as the "New Year Festival" in the 260-day Maya calendar and is celebrated on Day 8 Monkey, with which this calendar begins. Incense, sugar-cane brandy, flowers, tobacco, and animals will be offered as sacrifices on the rocks. The recipients of these sacrifices are the gods of the mountains, who watch over the souls of the dead but can also bring earthquakes and bad luck.

both the diagnosis and treatment, are often done with the help of crystals. In recent years, archeologists have begun reporting large numbers of crystals discovered in caves, which are likely to have been left by ritual specialists. Shamans are often shadowy and mysterious figures who are respected for their power, but also feared because they are suspected of witchcraft and sorcery. It is commonly believed that a shaman will go to a small cave in the countryside to perform dark arts. Among the Tzotzil Maya, this sorcerous behavior may involve making a pact to sell another person's soul to the Earth god.

Beyond these common and widespread types of ritual, anthropological literature abounds with cave ceremonies tied both to the cycle of life and death, and to the calendar. Archeology has found that ancient cave rituals were even more highly developed than they are today. As proof, just three seasons of fieldwork at Dos Pilas produced tens of thousands of cave artifacts. These offerings and tools of ritual are gradually changing our appreciation of ancient Maya religion. They have certainly raised our admiration for the dedication of the Maya, who ventured as far as 16 kilometers (ten miles) into the Earth, using only the light of wooden torches to guide their way.

JAINA – THE ISLAND NECROPOLIS

Christian Prager

Today, the islet of Jaina, 40 kilometers (25 miles) north of Campeche City, is overgrown with dense vegetation consisting of mangroves, fan palms, grasses, and other plants. With an area of less than one square kilometer (just over half a square mile), it seems to be no more than an unremarkable dot on the map (ill. 485).

In pre-Hispanic times, the island served, for more than five centuries, as the most important necropolis (burial place) on the west coast of Yucatan. Jaina owes its fame to a vast number of terracotta grave figurines, modeled with masterly skill, which have been discovered during recent decades. Their realism has aroused the interest of scholars because they provide important insights into the life of the pre-Hispanic Maya.

The word Jaina is derived either from *ja'ilnah*, "house of water" or *ja'nal*, "place of water." There is a narrow channel about 60 meters (197 feet) wide between the island and the marshy banks of the mainland, which, during the Late Classic, was crossed at its narrowest point (ill. 486) by an artificially created embankment. At that time, inhabitants and visitors were able to reach the site without wetting their feet. Because Jaina is situated at sea level, the variable groundwater level on the island creates small watercourses and swampbelts, making the subsoil marshy and soft. In order to

make the island habitable, and to be able to use it as a burial ground, the inhabitants in the Classic fetched and piled up large quantities of rubble to form raised terraces, so creating a site for ceremonial purposes and for residential settlements.

In the central area, there is a rectangular plaza extending across the island, bounded to the west and the east by massive pyramid-shaped platforms and other edifices. This was the location of the ritual and administrative center of Jaina's ruling elite, whose domain and sphere of influence very probably extended far into the mainland at the beginning of the 7th century.

Most of the burials were not, however, positioned along this religious-administrative axis, but in zones around the ceremonial center, where the settlement area of the common people lay. It is estimated that, during the period between 500 and 1000 A.D., some 20,000 earthen graves were laid out, about a thousand of which have so far been archeologically investigated, and some of the findings have been published. The dead were buried in body-shaped graves and burial urns. In the case of an adult body, jade pearls were placed in the mouth as part of a funeral ritual, the details of which are still a mystery. Then the deceased was wrapped in a shroud and was buried in a crouched posture along with offerings. Prior to the actual

486 *View of the channel separating the island of Jaina from the mainland*
A channel about 60 m wide separates the island of Jaina from the mangrove coast of Campeche. It was once joined to the mainland by an artificial embankment, which made it possible to reach the site without getting wet. Jaina is only one of many islands off the west coast of Mexico where magnificent graves containing ceramic figurines as funerary offerings have been found.

burial, mineral dyes, such as cinnabar and hematite, were used to color the corpse bundle red. This symbolized the blood of life, and was a widespread practice during the Classic. Small children were buried as bundles, crouched and with folded arms, in clay vessels which were sealed with flat tripod ceramic plates and buried in the calcareous subsoil.

To arm the dead for the dangerous journey through the underworld, their graves were furnished with provisions, things from everyday life, and sacred objects. Thus, alongside the famous clay figures, whose purpose was to lead the dead through the underworld, and which were mainly placed next to the head or on the chest of the deceased, objects such as jewelry, metates and pestles, flint points and blades, as well as tools made of stone and shells are also to be found.

The Jaina terracotta figurines are masterpieces of sculpture. The artists succeeded in creating figures that are faithful to nature and that vividly portray the complexity of the human body, and also a range of human feelings. In these clay sculptures, art has transcended, as in painting, the usual static

485 *Map of the island of Jaina*
The island of Jaina rises only a few meters above sea level. Large belts of swampland are criss-crossed by small watercourses. The highest pyramid on Jaina is that of the Zacpool complex. However, the elaborate burials were found, not in the immediate area of the ceremonial buildings, but in the residential areas of the common people. They lie between 60 cm and several meters beneath the surface.

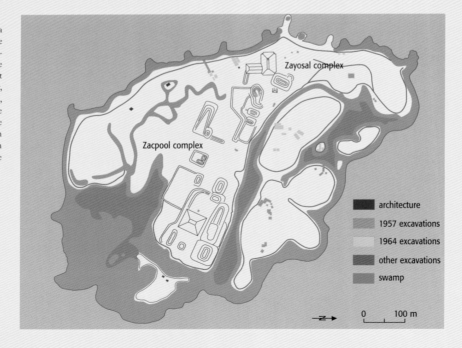

Zayosal complex

Zacpool complex

architecture
1957 excavations
1964 excavations
other excavations
swamp

0   100 m

nature of the main characters, and has breathed life into the figures. Rooted in the multifaceted world of their lives, the figures reveal emotional states and physical charm, and also show signs of illness, degeneration, or ugliness.

When creating their figures, the artists of Jaina employed two main techniques. Between 500 and 800 A.D., the sculptures they created were massive. The head, torso, and limbs of the clay figures were built up by hand and given individual shapes. Although the artistic motifs of Jaina figures were frequently repeated, the figures that have survived from this period are unique works that radiate emotion, individuality, and grace.

Between 800 and 1000 A.D., a demand for more mass-produced works arose. In order to meet this increased demand, artists switched to a more productive method. They used negative molds, from which a large number of statuettes could be produced in a very short time. With their hollow body, they could also be used as rattles, by putting small clay beads inside them. This more economical method of production did, however, lead to a loss of individuality and expressive power in the figurines.

For present-day scholars, it is above all the carefully hand-modeled figurines that yield insights into the daily lives of the Late Classic Maya elite. Apart from rare cases of motifs derived from animals, gods, and architecture, it is people in their social environment who stand at the center of the portraits. Noble lords frequently appear as warriors equipped with weapons and in full battledress (ills. 487, 489), adroit dancers, or audacious ball game players. They wear the ceremonial finery of headdress, breastplate, and decorative girdle. The ladies of Maya nobility, who were portrayed much less frequently, are dressed in magnificent gowns and adorned with rich jewelry, lavish headdresses, and fashion accessories such as fans and bags. Some statuettes have adornments to the face, which were affixed either temporarily or permanently, in the shape of artificial extensions of the nose, masks, or ornaments on the forehead and cheeks.

With their wide variety of splendid items of clothing, jewelry, and other details, the Jaina figurines reflect one section of society. In addition to the rulers, who appear as warriors or ball game players, priests and certain classes of servants are also featured in the sculptures. The artists' interest in human anatomy can be seen in the vivid presentation of extreme physical situations, such as old age (ill. 488) and sickness. Artistic portrayals of faces grimacing with pain, and the maltreated bodies of prisoners of war, were just as common as representations of the blind or the physically stunted. Among the Maya, as in other civilizations, death was surrounded by a number of rituals. The figurines found in the Jaina graves are part of a complex rite of passage, which is, at present, still shrouded in mystery. The question of the specific role assigned to the numerous clay figurines, as regards the afterlife, continues to pose one of the many riddles of Maya research.

487 *Noble warrior in full armour. Jaina, Campeche, Mexico; Late Classic, 600–900 A.D.; fired clay, painted; H. 20.6 cm; Yale, Yale University Art Gallery, Stephen Carlton Clark*
Knee-length armor, made of feathers and tightly pressed cotton, protects the body of this gallant warrior from the arrows and blows of his adversaries. In his right hand he holds a blue-painted shield, in his left hand he probably had a long spear, which has, however, been lost. A substantial ruff adorned with pieces of jade protects the man's neck and chest, on which he wears a decorative pyrite mirror.

488 *Statuette of an old man. Jaina, Campeche, Mexico; Late Classic, 600–900 A.D.; fired clay; H. 36.4 cm, W. 14 cm; New York, National Museum of the American Indian, Heye Foundation*
Ritual acts and ceremonies were often associated with carnal abstinence, euphoric dancing, and drinking bouts. This clay figurine shows a drunken man. He is holding two clay vessels under his left arm and is stroking his chin. The vessels probably contain an intoxicating liquid, which was either imbibed or administered as an enema.

489 *Figure of a warrior. Jaina, Campeche, Mexico; Late Classic, 600–900 A.D.; fired clay; H. 18 cm, W. 12.7 cm; Mexico City, Museo Nacional de Antropología*
Dressed in cotton armor and adorned with imposing feathers on his back, this warrior is prepared to face his enemy. In his left hand he holds a large oblong shield, while in his right hand he once held a wooden spear, which has not been preserved. A chain hangs from his upper body, which probably consisted of heavy jade beads, and an opened spondylus shell.

DEATH AND CONCEPTIONS OF THE SOUL

Markus Eberl

On August 28, 683 A.D., K'inich Janaab Pakal, the man who, for almost three generations, ruled over the Maya state Baak with its capital Palenque, died. To adopt the poetic language of one of the inscriptions, at the age of just over 81, the "white flowery breath" of K'inich Janaab Pakal was extinguished.

Lakamha is the old name of the city in the south-west of the Maya Lowlands, now known as Palenque. The fact that Palenque is well known today is, to a large extent, due to the building activities of K'inich Janaab Pakal. One of the inscriptions recording his death explicitly points out that he was the lord and builder of five temple pyramids.

K'inich Janaab Pakal did not, however, go down in the history of Palenque merely as a builder. It was thanks to his ideas that the settlement, which before his accession at the beginning of the 7th century had suffered a series of devastating and humiliating defeats, regained its former eminence. K'inich Janaab Pakal was responsible for the renewal of Palenque's political influence, military strength, and ceremonial dignity. For his descendants and successors, his death was an important event in history.

The burial of a ruler in pre-Hispanic times

The death of K'inich Janaab Pakal is recounted a number of times in stone inscriptions, but always expressed in a highly abbreviated and formulaic form. On August 28, A.D. 683, as is recorded twice in the Temple of the Inscriptions, he "entered the road." The Maya formulae used to express death focus on two aspects of death. On the one hand, when a person died, the various souls – in this case the "white flowery breath" – were detached from the body. On the other hand, the deceased set out on the path into the next world.

Both notions are still visible in the design and elaboration of K'inich Janaab Pakal's tomb, as in those of other rulers. His body was buried in the Temple of Inscriptions, which he had designed and built as his personal shrine during his own lifetime. A spiral stairway leads from the temple at the top of a pyramid to K'inich Janaab Pakal's tomb in the interior of the pyramid (ill. 491). As regards its layout and positioning, the burial chamber resembles a place in the underworld (ill. 497). A small tube leads from the tomb back up to the temple. This tube is called the "psychoduct," meaning that it allowed the soul to detach itself from the dead body and climb upwards.

Conceptions of the Soul

The "white flowery breath" that was extinguished with the death of K'inich Janaab Pakal, is one of a small group of elements or notions that are best paraphrased by the concept of "the soul." The ideas of the Classic, as well as the modern, Maya concerning the soul are based on a particular perception of humans and their relationship with the environment. In contrast to European ideas, people see themselves not so much as independent individuals (with the opposition of soul and body), but rather as an integral part of their surroundings, with which they feel connected in numerous ways. The term "soul" can be used to denote those powers and ideas which act as links and mediators between humans and their environment, being rooted in both spheres. For the Maya, souls are by no means intangible and invisible, but can take on concrete form and materialize in special rituals, such as blood sacrifices and dancing (ill. 495).

490 *The Berlin tripod vessel. Provenance unknown; Early Classic, 300–600 A.D.; clay, engraved; H. 12.9 cm, dia. 17.3 cm; Berlin, Museum für Völkerkunde*

The Museum für Völkerkunde in Berlin acquired this Early Classic tripod vessel, which is made out of grey clay and worked using engraving techniques. Its precise origin is unknown. However, it probably came from a location in central Peten (in the north of present-day Guatemala), and was probably the funerary offering of the Maya noble who is named as its owner on the feet.

491 *Stairs leading to the burial chamber in the Temple of the Inscriptions. Palenque, Chiapas, Mexico; Late Classic*

It was not until 1949 that the Mexican archeologist Alberto Ruiz Lhuillier discovered, in the Temple of Inscriptions, the top of the stairs leading down to the burial chamber of K'inich Janaab Pakal, which the Maya had carefully covered up. It took three years to clear the stairway. To the right of the picture, the remains of a stone tube can be seen – the psychoduct, or "canal of the soul," which linked the deceased with the human world.

The "white flowery breath" describes the part of the soul that transfers the natural cycle – the growth and death of plants – to people. "White flowery breath" is a literal translation of the phrase *sak nik nahal*. Comparison of the inscriptions in which this phrase occurs shows that "white flowery breath" is implanted in every person at birth. The course of human life is equated with the growth and death of a plant: what begins at birth when the *sak nik nahal* is implanted, ends when a person dies and the *sak nik nahal* is extinguished.

To represent the "white flowery breath," (ill. 494) the Maya used the sign for "ruler," which also means "blossom" because kings indicated their status by threading blossoms into their headbands. Shoots grow out of this sign, often in the form of stylized representations of young maize plants. The special significance of maize to the Maya is revealed in the creation myth of the K'iche'

in the Highlands of Guatemala: after attempts to create humans from clay and from wood had failed, the gods finally formed them from maize dough. Only these maize people proved viable, and all present-day humans are descended from them. The Maya were dependent on maize in many respects: directly, for their livelihood – a good harvest promised a superabundance, whereas a bad crop meant hunger – and also mentally, because they regarded themselves as having been born of maize. The growth and death of the "white flowery breath" thus appears as a logical symbol of the intimate connection between maize and people.

In addition to the "white flowery breath," the Classic Maya also had the *way* soul (ill. 494). The *way* is a protective spirit that accompanies humans. It can assume very different forms, but in most cases it appears in the form of an animal. The *way* soul covers the entire spectrum of Yucatan fauna, from

492 *Drawing showing the scene on the Berlin tripod vessel.* The thurible shown in the opened out photograph below is a unique masterpiece of Early Classic Maya art. It is rare for mourning of the dead to be portrayed so realistically. We do not know the identity of the almost naked mourners. Are they the sons of the deceased, or even vassal princes, weeping here for their chieftain in an act of collective mourning? In the right-hand scene, the deceased has become a tree and, in this guise, joins his parents, who are likewise fruit-bearing trees – trees such as these grow in Maya domestic gardens, and accompany the living every day.

493 *Rollout photograph of the Berlin tripod vessel. Provenance unknown; Early Classic, 300–600 A.D.; clay, engraved; H. 12.9 cm, dia. 17.3 cm; Berlin, Museum für Völkerkunde (Kerr 6547)*
The images can be divided into two scenes, which relate to the funeral ritual and to a Maya conception of the afterlife respectively. On the left, the funeral of a Maya noble is reproduced. The deceased, wrapped in a shroud with nine knots, lies on a stone bier and is mourned by three men to his right and three to his left. Above him hovers his flower soul, and his spirit companions (a monkey on the left and a jaguar on the right) crouch by his sides. In the right-hand scene, the deceased, who has by now become a skeleton, lies at the foot of a stepped pyramid and is being transformed into a respected ancestor, i.e. into an anthropomorphic tree that is growing out of his bones. He is flanked by his parents, likewise in the guise of ancestor-trees.

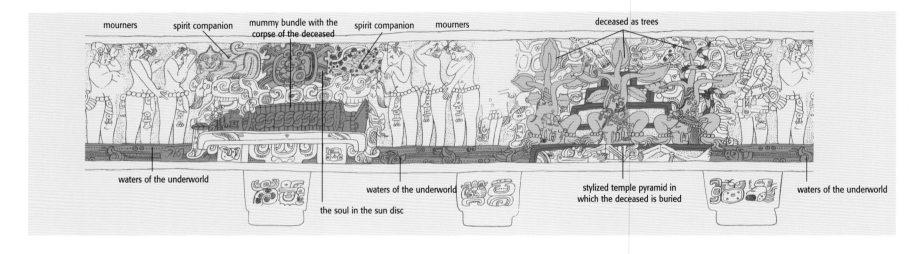

mourners · spirit companion · mummy bundle with the corpse of the deceased · spirit companion · mourners · deceased as trees

waters of the underworld · the soul in the sun disc · waters of the underworld · stylized temple pyramid in which the deceased is buried · waters of the underworld

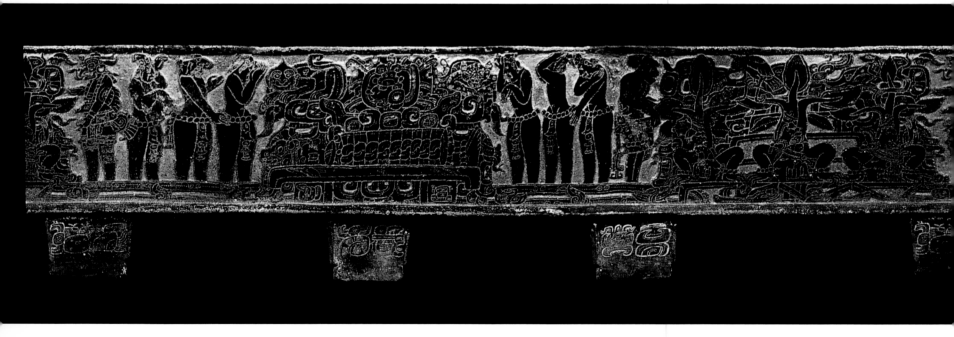

u way/"his spirit companion"

"his white flowery breath"

494 *Hieroglyphs for two forms of the soul*
The hieroglyph for the *way* soul, i.e. the soul in the guise of an animal double with a shared fate, takes the form of a stylized head, half covered with jaguar skin. It is usually preceded by the pronoun *u* and is sometimes followed by the name of the deceased. The hieroglyph *u sak nik nahal*, "his white flowery breath," means the soul that is implanted in every person at birth and leaves his body after death.

mammals (such as stags, monkeys, and dogs) to reptiles and insects. Maya rulers were fond of assigning the jaguar, the most powerful and dangerous animal in the Lowlands, to themselves as their *way* soul. *Way* animals were subtly subdivided in terms of different attributes and characteristics. Some 15 *way* varieties of the jaguar, the most common *way* animal, are known, including a "fire-jaguar," a "water-jaguar," and a "cloud-jaguar." Hybrid animals also occur as *way* souls. A "stag-serpent" combines the characteristics of both animals. Fantastic, mythological, and divine beings (including deities of death and sacrifice), along with natural phenomena such as comets and lightning, make up the last kinds of *way* soul.

A *way* exists as an *alter ego*. Their fates are inseparably connected. All changes in the life of the *way* or the person (including, in particular, injuries, sicknesses, or in the worst possible case, death) immediately affect both of them in the same way. If the man is sick, then his *way* also falls ill, and a mortally wounded *way* entails the death of its human partner. A person's date of birth is regarded as a decisive attribute for identifying his or her accompanying *way*. But special events or coincidences can work to the benefit of a *way*, or may reveal an animal double hitherto unknown to the person, so that some people can possess several very different animal doubles. It is believed that individual character and personal qualities accord with the characteristics of a person's accompanying animal.

Animal doubles are, by no means, the exclusive preserve of humans. On the contrary, in the eyes of the Maya, *way* souls are a phenomenon occurring throughout and beyond the natural world, also affecting animals and even plants. Deities and supernatural beings also have a *way* of their own. K'awiil, for example, one of the most important Maya deities, has as his *way* the deity Yax Loot Jun Winik Na Kan, who is invoked during blood sacrifices.

495 *Front side of Stela 40. Piedras Negras, Peten, Guatemala, Structure J-3; Late Classic, A.D. 746; limestone; H. 485 cm, W. 118 cm, D. 46 cm; Guatemala City, Museo Nacional de Arqueología y Etnografía*
The stela, erected c. 746 A.D., has a top section showing Ruler 4 of Piedras Negras during a sacrificial ceremony in honor of a deceased ancestor. Kneeling, he lets drops of blood or grains of incense fall from his right hand into a shaft that leads to a vaulted tomb, the elevation of which is suggested at the bottom. On a bier lie the remains of a bundled dead person. The erect bust, lavishly adorned with jade, is particularly conspicuous.

It is not by chance that *way* entities associated with blood sacrifice and death are named as accompanying spirits, because the belief in *way* has a further dimension that transcends the existence of animal or supernatural doubles. In the Lowland languages, *way* means on the one hand "to sleep" or "to dream," meanings which are appropriate for beings that live alongside people and are invisible but permanently present. On the other hand, *way* also means "to be transformed" or "to cast a spell" on somebody. Some people, shamans for example, were thought to possess the ability to change into an animal by means of ecstatic rituals and drugtaking, and to take on its attributes for a brief period (in the case of birds, for instance, the ability to fly). The ability to undergo transformation of this kind was also attributed to Classic Maya rulers. Ceremonies to mark the end of important periods of time, for example, were taken as occasions to change into an animal or supernatural being, to the accompaniment of blood sacrifice and ecstatic dancing. To this end, the rulers wore appropriate animal or god masks, and designated themselves, using glyph inscriptions, as embodiments of the particular animal or god.

Walking the path of death

The death of K'inich Janaab Pakal of Palenque is described, not only as a process by which his souls are detached and extinguished, but also as treading a path into the afterlife, and the two notions were evidently not mutually exclusive. For the Classic Maya, the afterlife was a subterranean world of water, linked to the world of the living by real stretches of water, or by caves. K'inich Janaab Pakal's funeral re-enacted his walk into the afterlife. His dead body was laid to rest in the burial chamber at the center of the Temple of the Inscriptions, a symbolic descent into the interior of the Earth via the stairway into the subterranean world.

The inscription on the cover of K'inich Janaab Pakal's sarcophagus (ill. 496) gives a powerful account of what awaited him after death: following the call of his ancestors and forbears, he walked the path into the underworld, which his predecessors had walked before him. For the Maya, dead ancestors were not passive beings, but intervened in everyday life and manifested themselves in ceremonies and rituals.

496 *The sarcophagus cover in the tomb of K'inich Janaab Pakal. Palenque, Chiapas, Mexico, Temple of the Inscriptions; Late Classic, 683 A.D.; limestone; L. 379 cm, W. 220 cm* The sarcophagus cover records a decisive moment on the path to the other world, which K'inich Janaab Pakal had to walk. The ruler climbs out from the skeletal jaws of the underworld in the guise of the young Maize God. The cross-shaped tree of the worlds grows out of him, indicating the path of the deceased into the other world and symbolizing his transformation into an ancestor.

On their way into the afterlife, a dead person had to surmount many and various obstacles. The members of the family strove to ease this path. The burning of aromatic or consecrated plants was intended to keep evil spirits at bay; modern Maya have a particular fear of the *okol-pixan*, the "soul-robbers," who can capture a dying person's soul in its ascent. Special apertures in the roofs of houses – or the "psychoduct" in the Temple of the Inscriptions at Palenque – served as a hiding place and an escape route for souls.

From ruler to god

The most impressive description of the descent into the underworld comes from the Highlands of Guatemala. Among the central themes of the early colonial Popol Wuj are the experiences of the Hero Twins Junajpu and Xb'alanke. The description of their descent into the underworld, their disputes with the lords of the underworld, and their death and triumphant return, is considered to be the most profound and detailed account of the conceptions of the pre-Hispanic Maya regarding death and the afterlife. The story begins with the sad fate of the forbears of Junajpu and Xb'alanke – two brothers named Jun Junajpu (one blowgun) and Wuqub' Junajpu (seven blowgun). One of the favorite occupations of these two brothers was the ball game. During one of their ball games – they were playing against the sons of Jun Junapu – the lords of the

497 *View of K'inich Janaab Pakal's burial chamber. Palenque, Chiapas, Mexico, Temple of the Inscriptions; Late Classic; H. 7 m, L. 10 m, W. 4 m.*
The way to K'inich Janaab Pakal's burial chamber leads first to the nine-step pyramid of the Temple of the

Inscriptions. At the rear, an interior stairway leads to the crypt. This is dominated by the sarcophagus, which holds K'inich Janaab Pakal's mortal remains. Its cover, with an ornamental relief, is probably the most famous work of Maya art.

The layout of a burial chamber

A burial chamber was usually not laid out until after the death of a nobleman. However, in a few cases elderly kings had begun to plan their own burial chambers themselves.

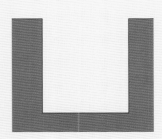

First, a trench 3 to 4.3 m deep was dug in the plaza.

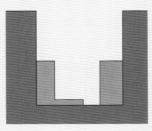

After this, the floor of the burial chamber, the bench, and the walls were laid out and rendered with lime plaster. Ladders made of wood or uncut stones gave the workers access to the burial chamber.

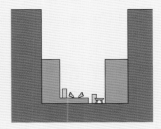

The deceased was buried with offerings comprising numerous ceramic vessels, plates filled with food, a variety of household goods, clothing, and his personal possessions. Since this burial was laid out in the middle of a courtyard, it may be assumed that the funeral ceremony was not secret but was held with great pomp and ostentation.

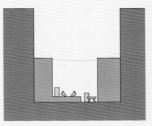

A cotton cloth was stretched across the opening of the tomb, possibly in order to protect the corpse and the sacred offerings from falling plaster, and to shield it from the workers' profane gaze. During excavations, the mark left by such a cloth around the tomb opening has been found.

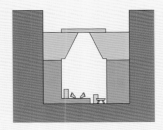

Three layers of corbeled vaulting masonry were piled on top of each other. The burial chamber was closed off with beams made from "tinto" (*hematoxylum campechianum*), the logwood from Campeche. This made it possible to complete the tomb quickly. Some of these wooden beams have survived.

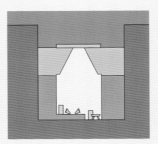

bedrock

stuccoed masonry

ceiling made of "tinto" (logwood)

filling

Over these beams, priests sprinkled thousands of black obsidian chips mixed with rubble. Then the erection of the temple was started, leaving the burial chamber completely closed off beneath the massive construction. There was no access to the tomb from outside either by windows, doors, or subterranean passageways. Excavation of Burial 196 of Structure 5D-73 in Tikal lasted for months and yielded precise and specific information concerning the building of the temple and, in particular, the burial of the corpse. Following the 1965–67 digs, archeologists realized that it was only after the death of the nobleman that the temples were built by his successors, in order to uphold the prestige of the dynasty.

underworld became annoyed by the unaccustomed noise on the surface of the Earth. The lords of the underworld probably thought that Jun Junajpu and Wuqub' Junajpu were lacking in respect towards them. The lords of the underworld, therefore, decided to invite the two of them to a ball game in the underworld, in order to test them. Unsuspectingly, the two men accepted the invitation. Messengers took them into the underworld – an arduous and dangerous journey of steep steps, torrential rivers, and narrow ravines. The lords of the underworld received Jun Junajpu and Wuqub' Junajpu in a quarrelsome manner, confident of victory. The brothers were greeted by being assigned a red-hot stone as a bench to sit on. When the brothers tried to sit down and jumped up with their faces distorted with pain, the lords of the underworld doubled up with laughter.

Since the ball game was not due to take place until the following morning, the brothers were offered the "house of darkness" to sleep in. Because it was so dark inside they were given a burning wood chip, and one lighted cigar each, but with the demand that the (pine) torch and both cigars should be given back unused the next morning. During the night, the (pine) torch and the cigars burned out. The following morning, when the brothers were asked what had happened to the (pine) torch and the cigars, they had to admit that they had used them up. The lords of the underworld unhesitatingly sacrificed Jun Junajpu and Waqub' Junajpu. Jun Junajpu was beheaded (ill. 500), and his head was hung in a tree overhanging the side of a road.

One day, the daughter of one of the lords of the underworld passed by the tree, which was bearing fruit, and stepped up to it in order to pick some fruit. Then Jun Junajpu's skull spoke to her, spat into her outstretched right hand, and made her pregnant with his saliva. Fearing that her pregnancy would be discovered, the girl fled from the underworld. In time, she gave birth to the two Hero Twins, Junajpu and Xb'alanke. They grew up to be accomplished hunters. A mouse that they caught revealed to them where Jun Junajpu and Wuqub' Junajpu had hidden their ball game equipment before descending into the underworld. They tried out the equipment and practised the ball game.

498 *Early Classic panel. Precise provenance unknown, Usumacinta region; Early Classic, 521 A.D.; limestone; private collection*
On both sides of the central hieroglyphic text, in which the consecration of this lintel (also known as "Po Throne Panel") is dated as June 30, 521 A.D. , a Maya nobleman is represented. Seated on the right is the then ruler of Bonampak, who commissioned the lintel for his grandfather's burial place and had it fitted there. The ancestor, from Lacanja, who was honored in this way can be seen on the left; his tufted beard indicates that he was long since deceased.

When the lords of the underworld became annoyed once more by the noise, the two ball game players again received an invitation to display their art in the underworld. Junajpu and Xb'alanke accepted the invitation and climbed down the dangerous path into the underworld. When they arrived there, Junajpu and Xb'alanke were more successful than their predecessors had been in passing the tests set by the lords of the underworld. They too were given the "house of darkness" as a place to sleep, but the Hero Twins substituted the gleaming tail feather of a parrot for the (pine) torch , which they were required to give back unused, and attached glowworms to the ends of their cigars. The following morning, the lords of the underworld were surprised when they gave back the wood chip and cigars unused.

Their surprise increased with each further test, which the Hero Twins cunningly dealt with. They successfully passed the "house of the obsidian knives," the "house of frost," and the "house of fire." Only the final test, in the "house of bats," took an unfortunate course. Forced to spend the night among bats with razor-sharp teeth, the twins, in wondrous fashion, climbed into their blowguns. But when Junajpu wanted to check whether it was daybreak yet, he was careless and incautiously stretched his head out of his blowgun. One of the bats immediately bit off his head. The next morning, in the ball game with the lords of the underworld, Xb'alanke was able to substitute a pumpkin for Junajpu's head, but he was no longer able to avert defeat and sacrifice. The lords of the underworld killed the Hero Twins (ill. 501), ground up their bodies, and scattered their bones in a river.

But at the bottom of the river, the bones gathered and grew together again to make bodies. On the fifth day after being sacrificed, the Hero Twins emerged

HOW THE JEALOUS HALF-BROTHERS WERE TRANSFORMED INTO MONKEYS

The Popol Wuj examines the question of how the existence of the world and its inhabitants is to be explained. The following extract describes the origins of the spider monkeys.

And that is their birth; we shall tell of it. When she found out the day of the birth, the girl, Xk'ik as she is called, was confined. But the grandmother did not see their birth. They appeared suddenly; both were born, Junajpu and Xb'alanke were their names. They appeared on the mountain, and from there they went home. But they did not sleep. "You ought to get rid of them, for truly they are noisy," said the grandmother.

So they were laid in a bed of ants, but they slept peacefully there. Then they went away and were laid on a bed of thorns, for that was what Jun B'atz' and Jun Chuwen (their elder half brothers) wanted: for them to die among the ants, for them to die in the thorns. They wanted this because of their jealousy and their anger, which made the faces of Jun B'atz' and Jun Chuwen red. At first they would not even allow their younger brothers into the house, they did not even know them.

For Jun B'atz' and Jun Chuwen had grown up in the mountains. They were great flautists and singers. They had grown up in great poverty. They had suffered pain, they had been tormented. Thus they became great and wise men. Now they were flautists and singers, painters and woodcarvers. Everything came easily to them. They truly knew their destiny.

. . .

One day Junajpu and Xb'alanke went to the foot of the tree that is called the yellow tree, accompanied by their elder brothers. When they arrived, they began to shoot. There were countless birds in the tree. They chirped and cackled, and the elder brothers were amazed when they saw the birds. But as regards the birds, not one fell from the tree. "These are our birds, but they will not fall. Go on, climb up," they said to their elder brothers. "Alright," the latter replied. So they climbed the tree, but the tree grew and the root swelled up, so that Jun B'atz' and Jun Chuwen could no longer climb back down when they tried. So they called down from the tree: "How shall we be rescued, oh our younger brothers? Have pity on us, this tree

frightens us, so it seems, oh our younger brothers!" Thus they called down from the tree, and then Junajpu and Xb'alanke said: "Take off your loincloths and tie them below your stomachs with a long end hanging down behind you like a tail, then you will be able to run better." That is what the younger brothers told them. "Alright," they said and pulled out the ends from their loincloths. These immediately turned into tails; they changed into spider monkeys. They disappeared across the trees on the low hills, on the great mountains, and then they vanished in the forest. They shrieked and swung hand over hand between the branches of the trees. So that was the victory of Junajpu and Xb'alanke over Jun Chuwen and Jun B'atz'.

499 *The Classic version of Jun B'atz' and Jun Chuwen. Provenance unknown; Late Classic; 600–900 A.D.; fired clay, painted; H. 16.2 cm, dia. 16 cm; private collection (Kerr 2220)*
In the art of Classic Maya culture, we have already found representations of mythical beings very similar to the characters in the myths preserved in the Popol Wuj. They include two monkey-faced divine beings who clearly correspond to Jun B'atz' and Jun Chuwen, the half-brothers of the Hero Twins Junjapu and Xb'alanke.

The continued existence of the deceased in the afterlife was (and still is) seen as dependent on the satisfaction of basic needs such as hunger and thirst. The Maya regarded making regular provision for the dead as a yardstick for assessing the relationships between the living and their dead family members. If the dead were "hungry," the living could expect little in the way of good fortune. Offerings of money or pieces of jade, as in Diego de Landa's account, show that the afterlife was not an abstract idea but, like the real world, was determined by needs and rules.

The grave – designated *muknal,* "place of burial," in the inscriptions – symbolizes, without doubt, the end of a person's physical existence. But their survival as an ancestor is unaffected by this (ills. 491, 492). The description of the journey into the next world illustrates the complex and multifaceted notions that, for the Maya, were associated with that place. Outstanding individuals, such as rulers, inhabited, in both life and death, the border zone between this world and the next, and could pass to and fro between them. When they died, they were of course compelled, like any normal mortal, to undergo the journey into the underworld, but they had the opportunity, as handed down in the myth of the Hero Twins, to overcome death and become gods.

500 *Frieze from the fifth tier of the acropolis of Tonina, Chiapas, Mexico; stucco.*
The presence of death is most directly expressed in the stuccoed frieze from Tonina. It was created following a victory by the rulers of Tonina, and integrates the sacrifice of the prisoners of war that had been taken, into

the view of death and the underworld held by the Classic Maya. The severed heads of the prisoners mark the crossing points of the fields of images. Skeletal deities associated with sacrifice and death, or deities in the shape of animals, repeat the ritual killing of the vanquished.

502 *Noble's tomb. Rio Azul, Peten, Guatemala, Burial 23; Early Classic, 5th century A.D.*
The Maya nobleman who was buried in Burial 23 in the 5th century A.D. belonged to the ruling class of Rio Azul. This is indicated in particular by the many

ceramic burial offerings – plates, bowls, and cylindrical vessels with covers. The crypt was painted in red. The Moon Goddess, and possibly a monster from the underworld, are depicted on the cone of rock that protrudes into the tomb.

from the river. They immediately proceeded to take their revenge on the lords of the underworld. Disguised as beggars, they made a name for themselves by dancing and performing miracles. When the lords of the underworld heard about them, they invited them to appear at the court of the underworld. The lords were so enthusiastic about their performance that they asked the Hero Twins to show proof of all their skills. The twins killed a dog and brought it back to life. They set fire to the residence of the rulers of the underworld without causing any damage to the house. In their enthusiasm, the lords of the underworld asked them to sacrifice each other and bring each other back to life again. When Xb'alanke had done this with Junajpu, the lords of the underworld finally asked to be sacrificed and brought back to life themselves. The Hero Twins cut open their chests and tore out their hearts, and left the bodies of the lords of the underworld without bringing them back to life. In this way, they took their revenge on the lords of the underworld and broke their power. Finally the Hero Twins transformed themselves into the sun and the moon.

When Classic Maya rulers died, they re-enacted the fate of the Hero Twins, and were taken by death into the underworld by a route involving many obstacles and adventures. In contrast to ordinary people, rulers like Junajpu and Xb'alanke, could use cunning to pass the tests of the underworld, break the power of the underworld (and thus of death), and rise up as deified beings.

The presence of death

Belief in a continuation of life after death was an integral part of pre-Hispanic Maya religion. This is expressed in the custom of putting food and drink into the grave with the deceased (ill. 502). Diego de Landa (1524–1579) documented this in the 16th century: "They wrap the dead in a shroud. The mouth of the corpse is filled with ground maize, known as *k'oyem,* which is food and drink to them, so that they will not be left without food in the afterlife."

501 *Tzompantli (skull platform). Chichen Itza, Yucatan, Mexico, Great Plaza; Terminal Classic/Early Postclassic, 850–1100 A.D.; limestone*
The *Tzompantli,* also found in other cities of Mesoamerica, especially in central Mexico, is a stone

platform on which, according to Spanish sources, the severed heads of sacrificed humans were impaled and exhibited. The sides of the platform are adorned with representations of impaled skulls.

:| FROM THE CLASSIC TO THE POSTCLASSIC

LONG TWILIGHT OR NEW DAWN?
TRANSFORMATIONS OF MAYA CIVILIZATION
IN THE PUUC REGION

Nicholas P. Dunning

Hills rose around us on every side, and, for that country, the scene was picturesque, but all waste and silent. The stillness of the grave rested upon the ruins, and the notes of a little flycatcher were the only sounds we heard ... farther on we reached an edifice, which Mr. Catherwood afterward drew.

Thus wrote John Lloyd Stephens about the ancient Maya ruins of Xculoc, Campeche, in 1842. Since the stirring 19th century accounts of Stephens, Waldeck, Charnay, Maler, and others, the world has been aware of the extraordinary architectural remains created by the Maya in the Puuc region, or hill country, of southern Yucatan and the northern Campeche states of Mexico. A few buildings erected in the Puuc, such as the Governor's Palace at Uxmal (ill. 523), rank among the world's greatest architectural achievements. Such constructions are products and symbols of transformations occurring in Maya civilization in the Puuc during the Late and Terminal Classic periods (600–950 A.D.). In the hill country, Classic Maya civilization experienced a long twilight, with many Puuc cities and dynasties surviving and retaining old traditions into the early 10th century A.D. – a century longer than in many parts of the Maya Lowlands. Nevertheless, by the end of the 10th century, large portions of the region had been virtually abandoned. The Late and Terminal Classic periods were marked by great growth and then horrendous decline, but the Puuc people produced significant political changes in Maya society, transformations that helped set the stage for the dawn of the Postclassic.

504 *The "Palace of Figures" in Xculoc. Engraving by Frederick Catherwood, 1842; from John L. Stephens,* Incidents of Travel in Yucatan, *1843*
During the rainy period of 1842, Stephens and Catherwood reached Xculoc in Campeche, led by a boy who wore only a straw hat and sandals. Frederick Catherwood drew the "Palace of Figures," the name referring to the three stone sculptures in the frieze which support the roof like Atlases, between two attacks of malaria. The figures were later stolen and a few years ago turned up on the international art market.

503 *Masks from the north wing of the Monjas building. Uxmal, Yucatan, Mexico; Terminal Classic, 900–910 A.D.*
Mosaic masks, laid one on top of the other, several at a time, are typical of architectural sculpture in the Puuc style. At the Monjas building in Uxmal, these towers of masks have reached their greatest perfection. The entire façade of the north wing, which constitutes the main area of the four-part site, is adorned with symbols referring to war. The four masks are also crowned by a stylized depiction of the Mexican god Tlaloc. The strikingly large, round eyes are a typical feature of this god of war.

page 320–321
The pyramid of Kukulcan in Chichen Itza, Yucatan. Mexico
View from the Venus platform of the north side of the Kukulcan pyramid, which is also known as Castillo. The sculpture in the foreground depicts the stylized head of a serpent, which occupies a dominant position in the iconography of Chichen Itza.

layer of weathered, softer limestone marl, which could be excavated with relative ease. Virtually every group of residential buildings in the Puuc has at least one *chultun*, and often several *chultunes,* as a vital part of its makeup. A typical *chultun* would hold about 30,000 liters (6,625 gallons) of water.

While the scarcity of water posed certain problems for the Maya in occupation of the Puuc, the abundance of another resource, good agricultural soil, provided a great attraction for settlement. Large tracts of fertile soils, with Maya names like *puslu'um,* "soft earth," *ek'lu'um,* "black earth," and *k'ankab,* "yellow earth," make the Puuc one of the richest agricultural areas in the Maya Lowlands. Such tracts of soil are especially abundant along the interior margins of the Santa Elena Valley. Thus, it is not surprising that many of the region's largest centers, such as Kabah, were located along the escarpments defining the valley's edge, in order to take advantage of the tremendous local agricultural potential. In the Bolonchen Hills, large tracts of good soil are less common, occurring irregularly in the limestone solution valleys among the hills. Maya communities were often positioned in these locations to take advantage of the limited fertile valley soils, with settlements also spreading up onto surrounding hills, such as at Balche' (ill. 507).

505 *The wild witz-landscape (cone karst) of the Bolonchen Hills near Balche', Campeche, Mexico. Photo dated 1989* The small Structure A-6 can be seen in the foreground. In the Bolonchen karst landscape, sites were, in most cases, located in the valleys, but individual groups of buildings could often be found on the tops of hills. They were an essential element of many settlements, whether marking their official boundaries or emphasizing lines of sight that ran from a central plaza in the city to the main cardinal points or other cosmologically significant points.

506 *Diagram of a typical small residential site in the Puuc region* In addition to the dwelling house, the site includes a *chultun* (cistern) dug from the *saskab* (layer of limestone marl). Rainwater gathered there during the wet season. Such reservoirs were vitally important for the survival of the Maya in the Puuc region, where year-round natural sources of water are rare and lengthy dry periods have to be reckoned with. Water was always used sparingly, in accordance with a household's various needs.

Physical geography and cultural adaptation

In order to understand fully the nature of ancient Maya civilization in the Puuc region, it is necessary to begin with the bedrock. The Puuc region derives its name from a range of fault-block hills that separate the hill country from the relatively flat land of the Northern Plains (ill. 505). The region includes the Puuc Ridge (or Sierrita de Ticul), the rolling terrain of the Santa Elena Valley, and the rugged cone karst landscape of the Bolonchen Hills. Importantly, within the Puuc region, the permanent groundwater table lies about 65 meters (213 feet) below the surface and is only accessible through a very few deep cave systems. In contrast, on the neighboring plains to the west and north of the Puuc, groundwater lies much nearer to the surface and can be reached by many natural breaks in the surface rock (*cenotes*) and through hand-dug wells. The absence of year-round surface and underground water sources was a serious constraint to Maya occupation of the Puuc, particularly because of the highly seasonal nature of rainfall. Like all of the Maya Lowlands, the climate of the Puuc is tropical/subtropical, with pronounced wet and dry seasons. The Puuc receives about 1,100 millimeters (43 inches) of rainfall a year, with more than 90 percent arriving during the late-May to November wet season.

In order to survive the winter to spring dry season in the Puuc area, the Maya had to devise a way to capture and store large quantities of rainwater. In some of their larger towns and cities, the Puuc Maya modified natural depressions called *ak'alche* to serve as reservoirs. However, the more prevalent means of storing water was in a *chultun*: an underground cistern into which rainwater was funneled from a paved, sloping catchment surface (ill. 506). The construction of the necessarily vast numbers of these *chultunes* was facilitated by nature. Underlying the very hard caprock layer in many areas of the Puuc is a

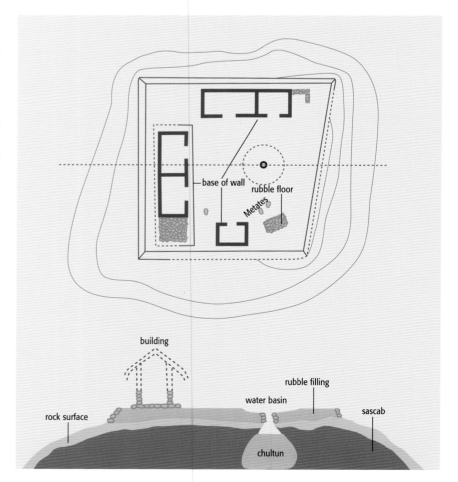

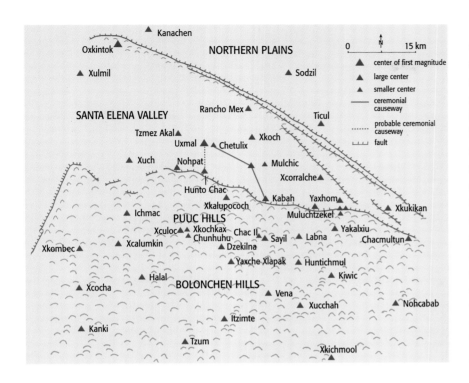

Among the masons of the Puuc region, a new technology was developing that would liberate the Maya from several traditional constraints in the construction of stone buildings. Sometime around 600 A.D., a new kind of stone architecture, now referred to as early Puuc style, began to spread across the region. Increasing quantities of more durable cement were used to anchor stone in place, greatly improving the stability of structures. The large slabs and stone blocks used in earlier architecture were replaced with thin veneer stones tied by tenons into a core of cemented stone rubble. Although the shape of the traditional corbeled vault was retained, the vault was no longer supported by cantilevered stone slabs. Instead, the strength of the cement wall core alone held the arch in place. This liberation from the physical constraints imposed by true corbeled arches allowed the Puuc masons to create larger interior room spaces (ill. 512). The new concrete-cored building method was also more efficient than earlier techniques. Consequently, the spread of early Puuc architecture was accompanied by an explosion in the quantity of stone architecture being built. In earlier times, and in other regions of the Maya Lowlands, vaulted stone masonry was largely reserved for monumental stone architecture and the residences of the uppermost levels of society. In contrast, in the Puuc, vaulted stone construction became part of a wide range of residential and non-residential architecture. At Sayil, for example, a third of all dwellings were vaulted stone buildings.

507 *Map of the Puuc region with the most important centers of settlement*
The Sierrita de Ticul, the Puuc mountain range, separates the region from the Lowlands that adjoin it to the north. The wide Santa Elena Valley probably has the most fertile soil in the entire region. The low-lying areas of the mountainous landscape of Bolonchen are also agriculturally productive. A network of paved causeways criss-crosses the central area of the regional state; in about 900 A.D., its capital city was Uxmal.

508 *Talud-tablero architecture. Oxkintok, Yucatan, Mexico, Structure CA-4; early Oxkintok style. 300–500 A.D.*
This pyramid in the city center of Oxkintok shows the strength of the Teotihuacan influence on the early architecture in the north-west of the peninsula. The question of whether this influence was exercised directly by the metropolis, or whether it reached the north by way of Tikal or some other location in the Maya area, is still being investigated. Oxkintok was an important center in the Early Classic, and because of its proximity to the coastal salt deposits, it may possibly have been a center for the salt trade.

Cultural history and architectural innovation

Although earlier non-architectural deposits have been found in the Puuc, principally in caves, the first stone architecture known to have been built in the region dates to the Late Preclassic (400 B.C. – 250 A.D.). This is a relatively late date compared with other regions of the Maya Lowlands. Furthermore, stone constructions in the Puuc remained modest in size and few in number until well into the Early Classic. By about 400 A.D., however, larger and more elaborate monumental architecture began to appear in the region. By far the largest center in the Puuc region during the Early Classic was Oxkintok. Between 400 and 600 A.D., the city center of Oxkintok grew both outward and upward, with several large pyramid temples dominating the skyline. Teotihuacan-related materials, culture, and symbolism, including distinctive talud-tablero architecture, were clearly influential at Oxkintok during this time, as they were elsewhere in the Maya Lowlands. Distinctive regional styles of stone masonry architecture were also evolving at Oxkintok and other western Puuc sites, such as Kanki and Ichmac at this time. Known as the early Oxkintok and proto-Puuc styles (ill. 508), the corbeled vaulting, using cantilevered stone slabs rising to a bridge-able gap, and roughly cut stone wall blocks covered with heavy coats of painted stucco were stylistically similar to contemporary architecture at Palenque.

509 *Chenes architecture. Dzibilnocac, Campeche, Mexico, Structure A-1; Late Classic, 600–900 A.D.*
The Chenes style is closely related to the Rio Bec style, which is characteristic of the architecture further south and at the center of the peninsula. False towers are an example of a shared feature. But entrances in the shape of wide open mouths are a feature of the Chenes style that is not shared. Those at Dzibilnocac are particularly lavish, forming the jaws of masks representing personified mountains and serpents. With their baroque exuberance of detail, they cover the entire temple building, which stands on a pyramid platform.

During the Late Classic and Terminal Classic, when early Puuc style, then Classic Puuc style architecture was being constructed, Maya potters of the Puuc region were producing a range of distinctive "slateware," and other ceramics known to archeologists as the Cehpech complex. Unlike in most parts of the Maya Lowlands, these ceramics included almost no polychrome painted vessels, a fact that may have helped to preserve many Maya ruins in the Puuc. In comparison to other regions, looting has been relatively light, probably because the polychrome ceramics prized by illegal art traffickers are rarely found.

The heyday of early Puuc architecture was from about 600 to 770 A.D. While the stonework and masonry employed in early Puuc buildings represented significant advances over earlier styles, the primary form of ornamentation continued to be the decoration of upper façades with painted stucco patterns and figures. In some cases, the decorated zone was further extended with the use of towering roof combs, allowing artisans to create more elaborate scenes (ill. 509). Gradually, more elaborate decorative stonework came to be included on the façades of masonry buildings, and the Classic Puuc architectural style evolved (ill. 515).

Classic Puuc architecture was constructed during the period from about 770 to 950 A.D., and can be divided into two phases (Classic Colonnette and Classic Mosaic) that overlapped in time to an unknown extent. Classic Colonnette style structures feature rows of columns, often divided by medial "spool" elements (ill. 516). The combination of columns and spools is generally believed to represent poles bound together with rope, such as would be found in a typical pole and thatch dwelling. We know from inscriptions that the Maya referred to even huge stone palaces as *naah*, "house," the same term as was used for a small pole and thatch hut. Colonnettes are also a common element in Classic mosaic-style ornamentations, and complex "mosaic" façades featured elaborate decoration (ills. 515, 516). Using hundreds of precut stones, masons assembled the complex mosaic façades. These included geometric designs found in late Classic elite architecture extending from Oaxaca and Veracruz to Yucatan, indicating that the Puuc Maya were part of the wide-reaching Mesoamerican trade and exchange networks. However, many Classic Mosaic decorative forms were rooted in traditional Classic Maya symbolism, reproducing patterns found on late Classic Maya textiles, perhaps reflecting the strong regional economic importance of woven cotton cloth products known from later periods in Yucatan. Long-nosed deity masks were often placed over doorways or at building corners. Distinctive symbols identify many of these masks as Chaak, the Rain God, but other deities were also frequently portrayed, including the Witz or Earth/cave/mountain "monster," the two-headed celestial or sky serpent, and K'awiil, the spirit of statues and an important royal patron. Some façades also included woven mat designs, apparently designating them as "worthy of the lords of the mat," that is, worthy of royalty or high-status nobility. The elements of mosaic façades often made powerful statements about the status of a building's occupants.

During the heyday of Classic Puuc architecture, the population of the region grew, older communities expanded, and new centers appeared. While the early 10th century witnessed peak population and construction in the Puuc, the latter part of the century saw drastic depopulation and virtual abandonment of many areas. Nevertheless, some centers continued to be occupied in to the Postclassic and beyond 1000 A.D.

510 *The Codz-Poop building. Kabah, Yucatan, Mexico, Structure 2C-6; Terminal Classic, 800–900 A.D.*
The Codz-Poop building, also known as the "Palace of Masks," is the best known building in the city of Kabah, and at the same time one of the most famous examples of the late Puuc style. It is 46 m (150 ft) long and has ten rooms arranged in pairs. Whereas in most Puuc buildings the lower section of the outside walls was left undecorated, in this case, all the surfaces are covered with mosaic masks that are, to a large extent, identical. The palace is crowned with a high roof comb. In front of it, on the side not included in the illustration, five life-sized stone figures once stood.

511 *Entrance to the interior courtyard of the Monjas building. Uxmal, Yucatan, Mexico, Monjas building, south wing; Terminal Classic, 900–910 A.D.*
The great Monjas building was probably built by King Chan Chaak K'ak'nal Ajaw of Uxmal. The interior courtyard was generally entered by the monumental vaulted portal of the south wing. The entrance divides the south wing, the lowest of the four wings of the Monjas complex, into two symmetrical parts, thereby creating an optical counterweight to the otherwise dominant north wing. If, from the inner courtyard, one looks in the opposite direction, one can see the central axis of the ball court.

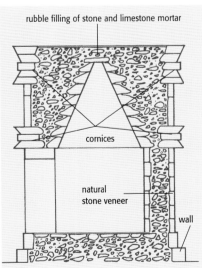

512 *Cross section of a wing of the Monjas building. Uxmal, Yucatan, Mexico; Terminal Classic, 900–910 A.D.*
The vaulting and the walls of Puuc buildings have a core of rubble and mortar. Only the façades are faced with cut stone. They divide into two planes at the height where the vaulting begins.

Urban and rural settlement

Urban populations in the Puuc regions were more nucleated than in many other areas of the Maya Lowlands, resulting in comparatively high urban population densities. Nevertheless, within Puuc communities, more than 70 percent of the available land was left open and was not built upon. This land was used for a variety of economic activities, including agriculture, food processing, storage, and pottery making. Intensively cultivated domestic gardens and "infields" were a vital part of the urban landscape and of Maya subsistence. Puuc centers can be described as true garden cities, with large portions of urban space devoted to orchards of fruit trees, care-intensive vegetables, herbs, ornamental plants, and even fields of maize, beans, and squashes.

The city of Sayil in the Bolonchen Hills has been the subject of extensive mapping and excavation work. The urban settlement zone of Sayil covered about five square kilometers (two square miles) and had a population of about 7,000 or 8,000. The urban layout of Sayil included several groups of monumental

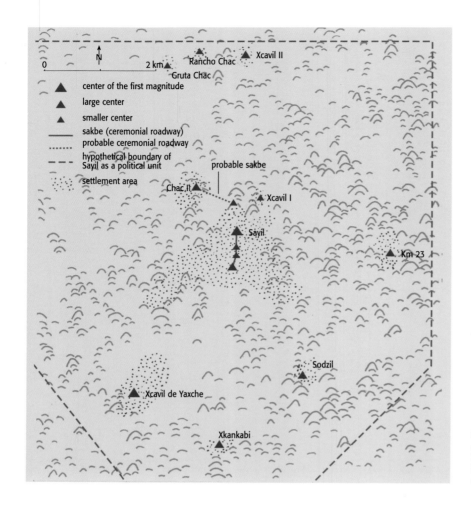

513 *Map of Sayil and the centers within its sphere of influence*
The more important centers of the north-east of the Puuc region were, in general, some six to eight kilometers apart. The smaller locations in their vicinity were probably satellite settlements under the control of larger cities such as Sayil. They were often located at the outer perimeter of a small state, possibly in order to secure the border area. Other villages appear to have been of a purely agricultural nature.

514 *The Great Palace of Sayil, seen from the south-west. Sayil, Yucatan, Mexico; Late Classic, 650–900 A.D.*
Like the Governor's Palace at Uxmal, this splendid building was both a residence and an administrative center in one – it had a dual function. It seems to have been built in several stages between 650 and 900 A.D. New wings and platforms were added piecemeal, when, for reasons relating to statics, inside rooms on existing levels were filled with rubble and sealed off.

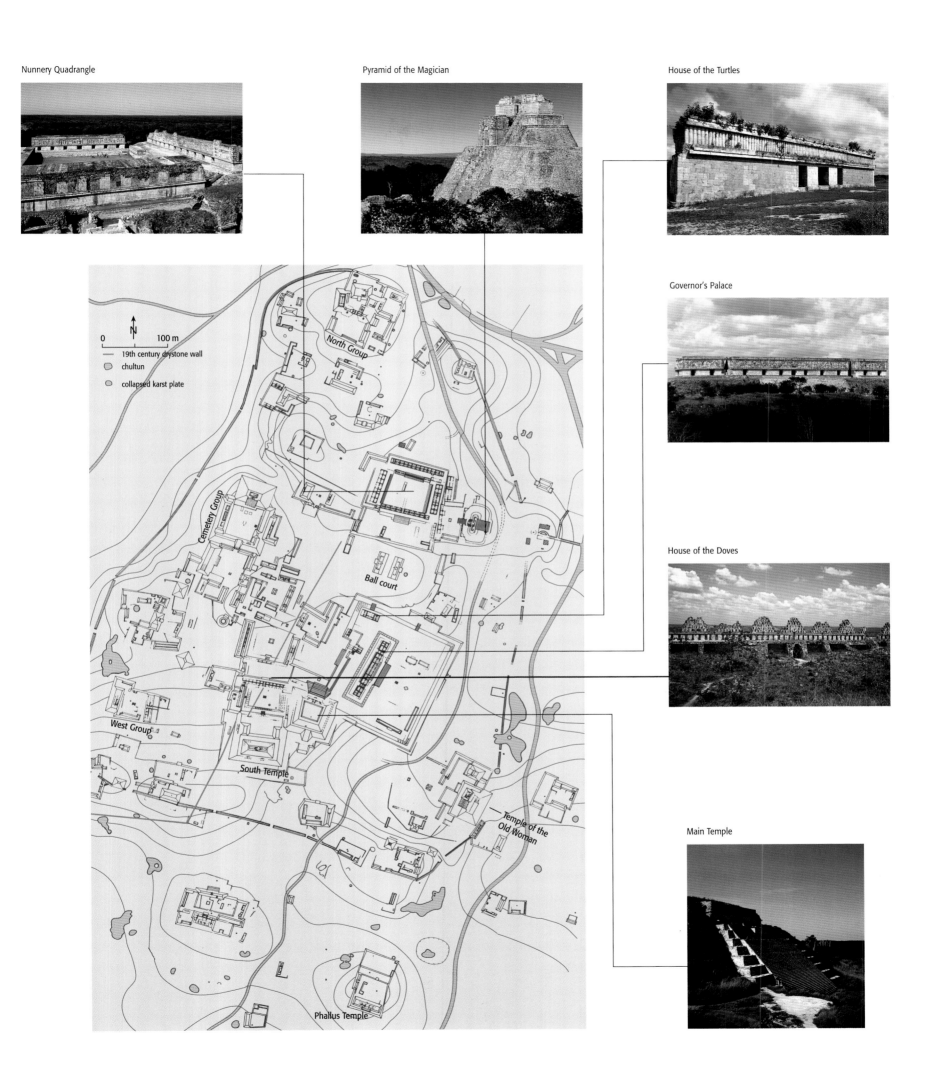

Nunnery Quadrangle

Pyramid of the Magician

House of the Turtles

Governor's Palace

House of the Doves

Main Temple

North Group

Cemetery Group

Ball court

West Group

South Temple

Temple of the Old Woman

Phallus Temple

0   100 m

N

— 19th century drystone wall

⬭ chultun

⬭ collapsed karst plate

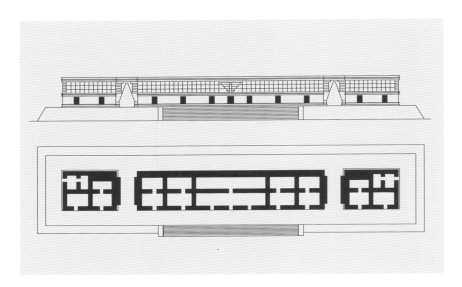

The Nunnery Quadrangle is a potent symbol of the political power of Uxmal and its ruler (ill. 520). In essence, the buildings of the quadrangle make up a huge cosmogram of the Maya universe. The ranges of the quadrangle are erected on three elevated levels. The southern range is the lowest, and is decorated with underworld symbolism and named *itzam nah*, or "conjuring house." This building is linked architecturally with Ball Court 1, a symbolic portal to Xibalba, the underworld in Maya cosmology. In contrast, the northern range – elevated above the rest of the quadrangle – was ornamented with celestial symbolism, and was referred to as *chan-nah*, "sky house," *itzam nah*, "conjuring house," or *ch'ok-te-nah*, "sprout-tree-house" or "lineage house." The eastern and western ranges of the Nunnery Quadrangle were built at an intermediate elevation, corresponding to the middle world of the Maya cosmos. Ornamentation on the eastern range focuses on themes of world creation, whereas the western range emphasizes war, sacrifice, death, and rebirth. At the center of the quadrangle was a huge columnar stone representing the *wakaj-chan*, the World Tree, and a jaguar throne or altar, representing the mythical first stone of the cosmic hearth. Taken together, the elements of the Nunnery Quadrangle represent an enormous and elaborate diagram of the Maya cosmos, centered on the World Tree and the cosmic hearth (see Wagner p. 283 ff.). This visually stunning architectural complex was also a powerful political statement, proclaiming that the ruler of Uxmal was enthroned at the center of the universe.

The creation of a regional state at Uxmal was probably a fairly violent process. Military themes are pervasive in much of the art and architectural ornamentation at Uxmal, Kabah, Oxkintok, and other sites from about A.D. 900. The vanquished, bound, and naked captives below Lord Chaak on

522 *Plan and elevation of the Governor's Palace in Uxmal*
The American architect Frank Lloyd Wright described the Governor's Palace in Uxmal as one of the most outstanding works of architecture on the entire American continent. He was particularly impressed by the treatment of the façade, which is marked by the contrast between the lavishly decorated upper part and the bare lower part. The building stands on a three-level platform, 15 m high and of monumental proportions. The 24 rooms are divided between three units, separated from one another by high, pointed, arched gateways.

523 *The Governor's Palace. Uxmal, Yucatan, Mexico; Terminal Classic, 900–910 A.D.*
The building, on its massive pyramid base, was built for Chan Chaak K'ak'nal Ajaw, who ruled in Uxmal in about 900 A.D. The great stone sculpture above the main entrance shows him surrounded by sky serpents and seated on a throne. His palace combines elements of a royal residence and an administrative complex, and is in the Classic Mosaic style. In the upper part of the façade, some 20,000 pre-shaped stones have been used to form geometrical ornaments, masks, and figures.

524 *View of the center of Uxmal*
The view across the center shows some of the most important buildings of Uxmal, including, on the left, part of the Governor's Palace. In the center is the Pyramid of the Magician, one of the few pyramids with an oval goundplan. It was rebuilt at least four times, with parts of the previous temples in the Chenes style being integrated. Existing buildings set limits to the dimensions of the pyramid base, so it expanded upward instead. As a result, the steps leading upward are particularly steep.

525 *Plan and elevation of the Pyramid of the Magician. Uxmal, Yucatan, Mexico; Late Classic, 600–900 A.D.*
The elevation of the Pyramid of the Magician shows that it was built by Maya architects on top of an older temple. The entrance of the previous building, in the Chenes style, is situated directly at the end of the western open stairway. The actual temple building from Uxmal's final building phase was reached via the eastern stairway that was added somewhat later.

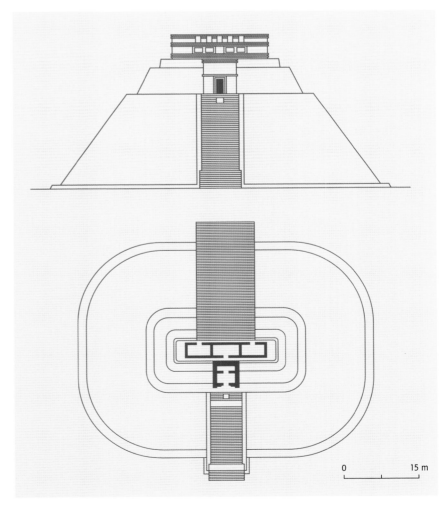

Stela 14 at Uxmal is one of many such examples (ill. 526). Perhaps the most graphic portrayal of the violent expansion of the Uxmal state is found on murals at the small site of Mulchic near Nohpat (ill. 527). These murals depict elaborately costumed warriors, one of whom may well be Lord Chaak of Uxmal, attacking and capturing people who were subsequently sacrificed. Some of the warriors bear a striking resemblance to those portrayed in contemporary art at Chichen Itza. Several important individuals known from Chichen Itza are also named in the inscriptions of Uxmal. This information suggests that Lord Chaak, and other Uxmal rulers, may have formed an alliance with Chichen Itza that allowed the use of Itza warriors in Uxmal's military campaigns.

If Uxmal was allied with Chichen Itza, the relationship appears to have soured. Certainly by 950 A.D., and possibly as early as 925 A.D., the Puuc regional capital of Uxmal had been reduced to a shadow of its former self. Sotuta complex ceramics, identified archeologically with Chichen Itza, appear along with small C-shaped buildings constructed in and around the Nunnery Quadrangle, on the platform of the Governor's Palace, and in other prominent places in central Uxmal. No more monumental architecture would be erected at Uxmal. The late construction of a defensive wall around the central part of Uxmal suggests that the city was violently subjugated by the Itza, or that the Itza occupation of Uxmal was violently resisted by the Puuc Maya (ill. 527).

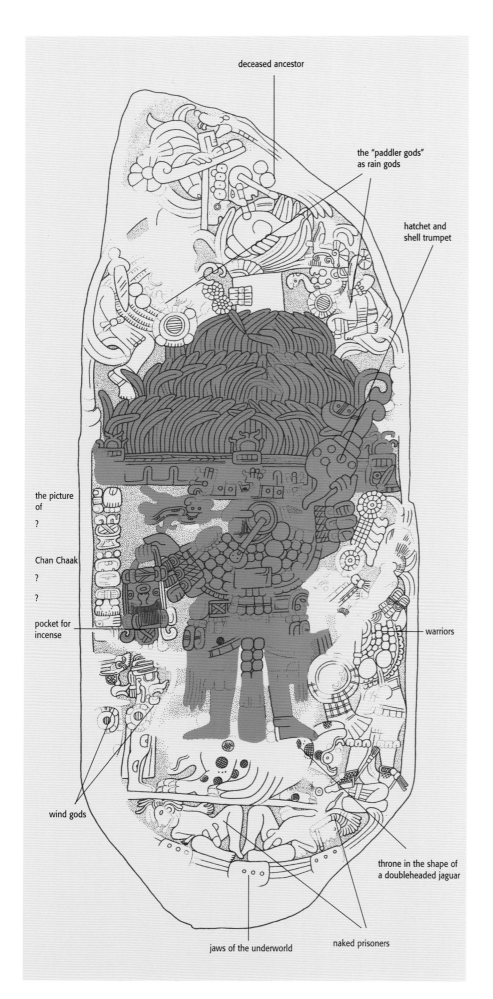

deceased ancestor

the "paddler gods"
as rain gods

hatchet and
shell trumpet

the picture
of

?

Chan Chaak

?

?

pocket for
incense

warriors

wind gods

throne in the shape of
a doubleheaded jaguar

jaws of the underworld

naked prisoners

Around the time that the Uxmal state was overthrown or collapsed, the eastern Puuc region was largely depopulated. However, this depopulation does not appear to have been particularly rapid. At Kabah, a reduced urban population appears to have constructed monumental architecture on a modest scale, perhaps continuing as late as 1050 A.D. At Xkipche, the small, remaining population occupied parts of the site center, sometimes pulling down and reusing cut stones from older buildings. Nevertheless, by sometime early in the 11th century, the eastern Puuc had been abandoned. The dramatic nature of this regional depopulation strongly suggests that the eastern Puuc had become virtually uninhabitable. Given the total dependence of the Puuc's inhabitants on rainfall for their survival, a prolonged drought is the most likely explanation for the region's abandonment. Indeed, a growing body of paleoenvironmental data suggests that several persistent regional droughts may have laid waste to portions of the Maya Lowlands during the Terminal Classic.

Intriguingly, while the eastern Puuc was being abandoned, at least a few centers in the western Puuc continued to be occupied into the Postclassic, surviving as important towns until the 16th century. Many western Puuc centers also had political histories that differed markedly from those of the eastern Puuc.

Classic and Postclassic transformations in western Puuc

A significant environmental factor that sets some areas of the western Puuc apart from the rest of the region is the greater availability of groundwater. Where hill country merges with the coastal plains of Campeche, the permanent groundwater table is much closer to the surface, and is occasionally accessible in cenotes. This environmental factor helps to explain why the western Puuc was the location of much of both the earliest and latest settlement in the region.

The western Puuc region, including Oxkintok, was the focus of Early Classic settlement, and the probable birthplace of the distinctive Puuc architectural tradition. The western Puuc was also home to significant changes in political organization. At Xcalumkin, inscriptions from about A.D. 652 onward record a ruling system apparently headed by a group of equally ranked individuals or *sajaloob*. This system is suggestive of an early form of *mul tepal*, the joint or conciliar form of government used later in the Terminal Classic and in the Postclassic periods at Chichen Itza and Mayapan (see Masson, p. 343 ff.). In the 16th century, much of western Puuc was part of the Aj Canul polity, a *kuuchkabal* or council government dominated by the Kanul lineage. It is interesting to speculate whether this type of government, developed at Xcalumkin and in other western Puuc sites in the 7th century, persisted in the region until the time of the Spanish conquest.

Settlement patterns in the Xculoc area suggest that, at least in parts of the western Puuc, dominant major centers did not emerge as they did in

526 *Representation of Chan Chaak K'ak'nal Ajaw, drawing taken from Stela 14. Uxmal, Yucatan, Mexico; Stela 14; Terminal Classic, c. 900 A.D.; limestone; H. 271 cm, W. 111 cm; Uxmal, Museo del Sitio*
This monument, along with 15 other stelae, stood on a special platform to the west of the Monjas building. Chaak appears, accompanied by his subordinates, as victor over the prisoners beneath him. This type of representation accords with the Classic style, and the lavish attire of the princes is also characteristic of this period. This applies, for example, to the girdles with *Ajaw* masks and mussel shells, and the headband that shows Sak Hu'unal, the god of regal dignity. The expansive broad-brimmed feather headdress also shows that the ruler is wearing the costume of Chaak, the ritual embodiment of the Rain God. His assistants, the wind gods, are to be seen at the front. Lord Chaak is standing on a throne in the shape of the doubleheaded spotted jaguar.

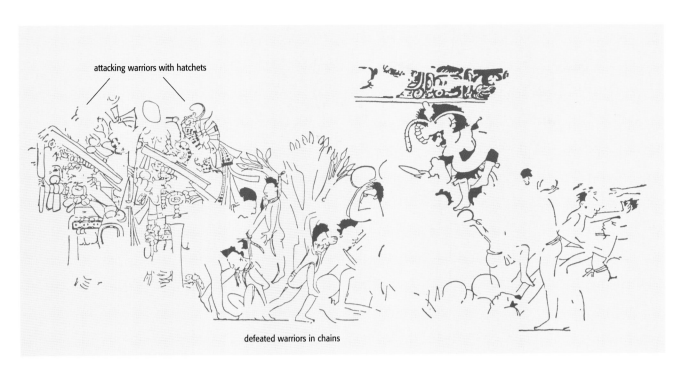

attacking warriors with hatchets

defeated warriors in chains

527 *Drawing copied from a mural painting. Mulchic, Yucatan, Mexico; Late Classic, 770–925 A.D.*
The picture shows a ceremonial human sacrifice. A ruler is seated on a high dais holding a sacrificial knife. Prisoners are being stoned and hanged, some of them spit blood in their death throes. The two figures with hatchets on the left embody the Rain God Chaak, and are part of a larger scene showing a ritual dance to mark a military victory. A fierce battle, with many prisoners being taken, is a secondary theme.

the east, suggesting that Maya territory control was less hierarchical here. With the exception of Oxkintok, stelae are absent in western Puuc centers, which indicates that the ruler-centric political organization that characterized the eastern Puuc did not exist in the west. At Oxkintok, the Classic motif stelae that were erected during the mid 8th to early 9th centuries. were replaced by "panel-style" stelae from the mid 9th century onward. These "panel-style" monuments de-emphasize individual protagonists, are narrative in composition, and seem to include multiple rulers or individuals of approximately equal status. At the same time that this transformation of stela style was taking place, the pattern of building activity at Oxkintok was changing, de-emphasizing centralized monuments in favor of smaller buildings in multiple locations.

The western Puuc was also home to a highly distinctive decorated ceramic tradition known as the Chochola style. These ceramics were carved with unique images and inscriptions. Some of the same artists who carved these ceramics also sculpted stone monuments at Xcalumkin, Oxkintok, and other western Puuc centers.

While the giant center of Oxkintok was apparently abandoned by 1050, a few western Puuc centers survived the Classic to Postclassic transition. Research at Xuch, for example, has revealed monumental building activity up until the 16th century. This supports the idea that new forms of political government, developed in the western Puuc during the Classic, may have helped shape the nature of Postclassic Maya civilization (see Masson, p. 346 ff.).

During the 16th and 17th centuries, the decimation of the Maya population by Old World diseases and the economic needs of the Spanish colonists led to the implementation of a program of relocations, in which populations were forcibly moved to a smaller number of towns. The entire region was abandoned, until resettlement began in the late 18th century.

Aftermath

Today, the Puuc is a land of striking contrasts. Tourism has, in some respects, resurrected certain ancient Maya centers. Tens of thousands of visitors flock to Uxmal each year to experience the grandeur of its ancient architecture and the

tragedy of its demise. Maya people are also returning to the Puuc in growing numbers, putting more and more of the region's rich soils back into production. Irrigation agriculture, using deep wells and modern pumps, now allows two or even three crops annually in many areas. Yet for large parts of the Puuc, the shroud of the forest and the song of birds still prevail over the ever crumbling ruins built by those who dwelt there long ago (ill. 505).

528 *Ceramic vessel in the Chochola style. Provenance unknown; Late Classic, 600–900 A.D.; fired clay; H. 10.6 cm, dia. 15 cm; New York, American Museum of Natural History (Kerr 4022)*
These relief ceramics, displaying great artistry, were produced during the Late Classic. Carved inscriptions identify some of the unmistakable vessels as the work of specific artists and workshops in Xcalumkin (Campeche, Mexico). Chochola ceramics are the only ceramics in the Puuc region that have figurative motifs. Here, a young man is depicted painting with a brush the body of a woman seated in front of him.

... AND THEN IT WAS SCULPTED, THE PRECIOUS STONE – THE MAYA STONEMASONS AND SCULPTORS

Elizabeth Wagner

Among the great artistic achievements bequeathed to us by the Maya are their numerous stone monuments. The tradition of cutting monuments from stone, and erecting stelae and altars, goes back to the Preclassic. Its golden age came during the Classic, so by the Late Classic, a wide variety of regional styles had evolved.

As regards material, in most cities local limestone was quarried (ill. 529), but in the southern Maya area (the Highlands of Guatemala and Chiapas, the Maya Mountains of Belize, and the region around Copan in western Honduras), other kinds of stone were predominant. In Quirigua, Tonina, and Pusilha, the local sandstone was used. In Copan, the particularly soft volcanic tuff, being easy to work, not only made possible the development of three-dimensional sculpture on stelae and altars, but also produced architectural sculpture of unique diversity and quality (ill. 530). In the cities of the Highlands, volcanic material such as basalt was generally used.

The sites where stone for sculpture and building work was quarried and prepared, were situated close to cities, sometimes even within the city limits.

It is likely that the stone in question was cut roughly to shape at the quarry using simple tools, then transported to where it was needed, where the sculptor began his work. As can still be seen on the incomplete reliefs on the side walls of Pakal's sarcophagus in Palenque, images or inscriptions were then sketched on the dressed stone.

Since metal tools were unknown, tools made from stone and wood were used. At the quarry, the material was usually broken up using axes and chisels made of flint. For more delicate dressing work and for sculpture, chisels of various sizes made from ground and polished hardrock were used, along with drills. Hammer stones and wooden tools were used as mallets. Particularly delicate and soft stone, such as the limestone from the region around Palenque, was also worked with knives. A tool of this kind is illustrated on a relief panel of unknown origin (ill. 531).

The Maya artists had mastered all the techniques of sculpture, but favored bas-relief for most of their work. In the Late Classic, a style of three-dimensional sculpture developed in places, such as Copan and Tonina, where the newly

530 *Head of the god Chaak. Copan, Honduras, Structure 10L-26-sub ("Hijole"); Late Classic, 600–900 A.D.; green tuff; H. 90 cm, D. 47 cm; Copan Ruinas, Museo de Escultura*
During the reign of Waxaklajuun Ubaah K'awiil, a sculptural style, remarkable for its plasticity and wealth of detail, developed in Copan. It was not limited to stelae and altars, but also generated a unique diversity and quality of architectural sculpture. The head of a long-nosed being, shown in the illustration, with the protruding neck and head of a cormorant, probably depicts one aspect of the god Chaak. A freshly caught fish wriggles in the bird's beak. The almost filigree work and the carefully smoothed surface bear witness to the sculptor's absolute mastery of his material.

529 *Modern quarry near Tikal, Peten, Guatemala*
Stone for sculptures and building work was quarried in the vicinity of the cities, often even within city limits. In Tikal, some of these quarries are still in use to this day. They provide the material for current restoration work. Apart from the use of modern metal tools, working techniques are not essentially different from those of the pre-Hispanic era. Grooves are first cut into the working face of soft limestone close to the surface, then continued to a depth at which the rough-hewn blocks can be removed using levers and wedges.

quarried soft stone was easy to work. Techniques less frequently adopted included recessed relief, in which the relief image is not above, but below the surface. Intaglio, a technique similar to engraving, in which an image is formed from incised lines, also became popular in certain areas.

On a number of monuments from the Classic, short texts can be found carved on the relief surface, all displaying the same structure (ill. 532). At the beginning, there is a hieroglyph with a particularly conspicuous main sign – a bat's head. The same hieroglyph appears on ceramics with decorative carving or reliefs, near to the spot where, on colored ceramics, *u tz'ibal*, "his writing" or "the painting of," can be seen. It is therefore supposed that the hieroglyph with the bat's head signifies "engraving" or "sculpture." Because the hieroglyphic text often contains a possessive pronoun and is followed by a person's name, it can be inferred that the short texts with the bat hieroglyph are sculptors' signatures. In the inscription on the illustrated relief panel from the museum in Emiliano Zapata (ill. 531), this hieroglyph is used to describe the act of sculpting: *i uxulji k'an tuun*, "… and then it was sculpted, the precious stone."

The great majority of such signatures are known to us from sites in the upper Usumacinta region, especially from Yaxchilan and Piedras Negras, where a relief style marked by scenic depiction and particular realism developed during the Late Classic. In particular, there are an extraordinarily large number of signed works by the sculptors who worked under "Ruler 7" of Piedras Negras, who reigned from 785 to 795 A.D. This ruler evidently employed a large number of talented sculptors. They developed a regional school of their own, with a dynamic and realistic style that was not limited to Piedras Negras, but also appeared to have some stylistic influence in the surrounding provinces.

As many as nine signatures can be found on a single monument. This suggests that a group of sculptors worked together on one piece of sculpture. In some cases, the signature of the same artist appears on several dated monuments spread over a lengthy period of time. Because stylistic consistency can also be observed, it is possible, to a certain extent, to trace the development in an artist's work. Occasionally, signatures also yield information regarding a sculptor's social status, or the internal organization of a workshop. The artist indicates not only his name, but also his relationship to his patron or to another sculptor, presumably of higher rank than himself. No biographical details are given,

however, and there are still many unanswered questions regarding the training of craftsmen, the structure and organization of workshop activity, and the organization of labor in the planning and execution of sculptural projects.

In addition to proper names, various titles or indications of occupation, such as engraver, carver, or sculptor, also feature in the signatures. The extent to which these titles indicate a fixed hierarchy of occupations within the division of labor in a workshop cannot yet be ascertained from entries in colonial Spanish dictionaries, or from translations based on concepts from Classic Maya inscriptions. By leaving their signatures, the artists have emerged from anonymity and provided us with information regarding their social status within Maya society. Their high social standing is clear from their titles, which show them to have been members of the nobility: *ch'ok*, "child" or "young noble." Occasionally, this title is also preceded by the epithet *chak*, meaning "great," possibly identifying the *chak ch'ok* as a member of the ruling family.

Hierarchy within the workshop is suggested by the title *ba uxul*, "first sculptor." It can be assumed that the Maya had sculpture workshops with divisions of labor, employing assistants under the direction of one or several master sculptors. This is also suggested by the signatures of several sculptors appearing on a single piece of sculpture. A master sculptor was probably responsible for designing the monument and coordinating work. Further evidence of a hierarchy within the workshop can be found on a relief panel portrait of a woman of unknown origin, from a hitherto unidentified

532 *Sculptor's signature. Yaxchilan, Chiapas, Mexico, Structure 44, Lintel 46 (detail); Late Classic, 713 A.D.; limestone*
The sculptor has left his signature on the lintel relief. It begins with a hieroglyph with the head of a bat as its main sign. This is an expression meaning "engraving" or "sculpting." The hieroglyph components probably produce the word *y-uxul*, which is based on the verb root *uxul*, "to carve or scrape." This is followed by the artist's name: Tz'ib Chaak.

site known as Yomop. It was signed by two artists, one of whom uses the expression *yanabil*, "he is the sculptor of …" followed by a noble's name thereby identifying himself as a craftsman under the patronage of the person who commissioned the monument. The other sculpter mentions his rank, as an artist of evidently higher standing.

It may be assumed that Maya sculptors would also have worked with materials other than stone. For example, the consummate use of line in many inscriptions, especially notable in the panel of the 96 inscriptions from Palenque, suggests that their creator may also have worked as a scribe or painter, or at least that someone trained in calligraphy was responsible for the master drawing.

Monuments from the Usumacinta region in particular provide evidence that sculptural traditions spread from the major Maya centers to smaller, subordinate locations. Probably because of dynastic relationships, or in return for military or other services rendered to the central ruling house, provincial governors would have been able to claim privileges to which only the ruling dynasty was normally entitled. This may have included the right to commission monuments and inscriptions.

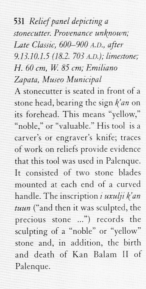

531 *Relief panel depicting a stonecutter. Provenance unknown; Late Classic, 600–900 A.D., after 9.13.10.1.5 (18.2. 703 A.D.); limestone; H. 60 cm, W. 85 cm; Emiliano Zapata, Museo Municipal*
A stonecutter is seated in front of a stone head, bearing the sign *k'an* on its forehead. This means "yellow," "noble," or "valuable." His tool is a carver's or engraver's knife; traces of work on reliefs provide evidence that this tool was used in Palenque. It consisted of two stone blades mounted at each end of a curved handle. The inscription *i uxulji k'an tuun* ("and then it was sculpted, the precious stone …") records the sculpting of a "noble" or "yellow" stone and, in addition, the birth and death of Kan Balam II of Palenque.

THE DYNAMICS OF MATURING STATEHOOD IN POSTCLASSIC MAYA CIVILIZATION

Marilyn Masson

Traditional perceptions of Postclassic Maya society

The Postclassic in the Maya Lowlands extends from about 900 or 1000 A.D. to the time of Spanish contact in 1517. The very term "Postclassic" implies that Maya culture during this period was an aftermath of former glory. The assessment and unfortunate naming of this period was primarily based on the disappearance, in the southern Lowlands, of carved stone monuments, the cessation of massive, well-preserved architectural constructions, and the abandonment of many urban centers. Postclassic artifacts that have been found in the surface deposits of southern architecture built in earlier times have been interpreted as evidence of "pilgrims," "squatters," or "refugees," based on the questionable assumption that stable local populations are represented primarily by architectural construction, rather than scattered household debris located in surface topsoil.

These perceptions of Postclassic Maya society are being challenged by recent archeological investigations. While the beginning of the Postclassic marks a time of social upheaval and transformation, the nature and direction of social change varied considerably across the Lowland Maya landscape. Part of the problem is that the fate of Postclassic Maya populations has been largely ascertained from their scattered representation at former political centers. There is little question that these populations abandoned their urban cores, and are found in new locations often unmarked by conspicuous monumental architecture, buried in layers of tropical jungle vegetation. The southern and northern Lowland Maya areas have very different histories, but these histories are closely related. Viewing these subregions as a whole, more than five centuries of Postclassic cultural development are documented across the Lowlands from 900 to 1500 A.D., which reflect a pattern of long term economic growth, population increase in coastal areas, and increased north-south integration over time. By the time the Spaniards arrived, a sophisticated, affluent, literate society with a vast and complex international economic network had been well established for several hundred years (ill. 534).

Postclassic literary traditions

There is ample evidence that the erection of hieroglyphic monuments did not actually disappear in the Postclassic. Although the use of the Long Count calendrical system was no longer observed, the Postclassic Maya at many sites, in the Peten Lakes, northern Belize, Quintana Roo, and northern Yucatan, erected uncarved stelae, which are thought to have been covered in stucco and painted because remnants of these coverings are occasionally found. Some of these monuments were also carved, as observed at Mayapan and Tayasal, with Postclassic K'atun ending dates. Unfortunately, the medium of stucco and paint has not survived on most of these monuments, and the information has been lost. The penchant for mural painting during the Postclassic has also resulted in problematic preservation of Maya political art and writing for this period. Codex books of Postclassic age reveal that hieroglyphic writing and calendrical tradi-

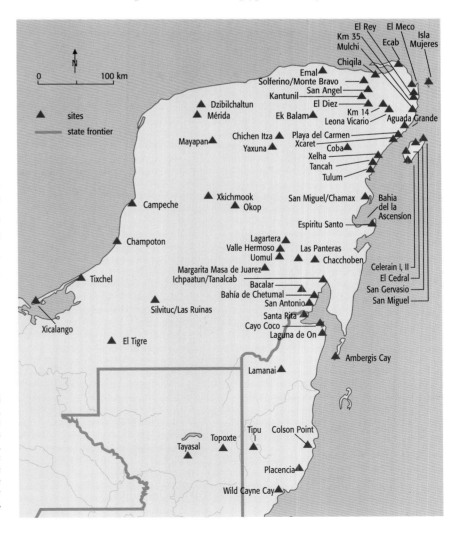

533 *View of the Caracol of Mayapan, Yukatan, Mexico*
The center of the city of Mayapan covers an area of 5km², with a high density of buildings that can be seen to be copies, on a smaller and less spectacular scale, of the buildings at Chichen Itza. For example, Mayapan has a circular building called "Caracol," like the predecessor on which it is based. The Caracol at Mayapan is much lower, however, without the interior stairway leading upward. The plaza in front of the building is dominated by platforms that echo the Skull Platform and the Venus Platform on the Grand Plaza of Chichen Itza.

534 *Map of Postclassic Maya sites and provinces*
The ethnohistorian Ralph Roys reconstructed 16 provinces, or territories, designated as *kuchkabalo'ob*, that existed at the time of the Spanish conquest. Their boundaries often changed, however. Politically, the areas were integrated to varying degrees as regional sub-units, and their hierarchic structures had reached different stages of development. Chichen Itza and Mayapan were the most powerful centers of their time, but were repeatedly compelled to assert their claim to power against distant territories in which they had an interest, either as allies or as trading partners.

tions were intact, and continued until Spanish contact. Although the use of the Long Count system was discontinued after the early 10th century, this probably reflects a conscious rejection of the convention, rather than a decline in scientific knowledge. The use of the convention was mainly to legitimize Classic kings and to boast of their exploits. The rejection of the institution of kingship may have included rejection of the method of recording dynastic histories.

Because the Postclassic immediately precedes Spanish colonial times, many European and indigenous historic documents are available to assist in reconstructing models of Maya society prior to Spanish arrival. Primary sources of information include Friar Diego de Landa's "Relación de las cosas in Yucatán," and the mythohistorical chronicles of native priests, known as the books of the Chilam Balam (ill. 535). Landa's account provides details of Maya history from the memories of 16th century colonial indigenous informants, as well as the priest's own observations about political, social, and ideological institutions of Maya culture. The books of the Chilam Balam reflect oral histories from several northern Yucatan towns, recorded in print many generations after Spanish arrival. These books provide references to migrations of northern Itza rulers, the foundation of the centers of Chichen Itza and Mayapan, the role of foreign warriors and traders in the affairs of Postclassic Maya states, and centuries of K'atun cycles of prophecies and events. Unfortunately, myths and actual historic events are often difficult to distinguish from one another in the poetic narrative of these works.

Postclassic Maya chronology

The temptation to rely on historic works has been irresistible for most Postclassic archeologists. Early attempts to graft the chronology of site occupations and the ethnic affiliation of these sites from cryptic historical accounts, has resulted in confusion. While historical accounts have to be considered, the works are limited in scope and written according to the agendas of their time. Conclusions should be tempered with evaluation of archeological evidence.

535 *Chilam-Balam book of Chumayel, page 87. c. 1780–1790; paper; H. 30 cm, W. 21 cm; Philadelphia, Pennsylvania University Museum*
We know of ten Chilam Balam books from the Spanish colonial era that are named after the places where they were preserved. They are manuscript collections giving accounts of events in pre-Hispanic times and of the history of the conquest. But they also deal with religious themes, the old calendar, and prophecies referring to the 20-year K'atun periods. The most famous, and perhaps also the most important, of these Chilam Balam books is the one from Chumayel. It has 107 pages and was probably copied and compiled in this form from older sources by Juan José Hoil. The page illustrated shows the master of one K'atun period; it bears the head of a king because such a unit of time could only end on an *ajaw,* "lord" or "king," day.

536 *Mural painting in Structure 16. Tulum, Quintana Roo, Mexico; Late Postclassic*
The section illustrated shows groups of figures separated by intertwined snakes with "Venus Star eyes." Bands of snakes are often a link with the world of the supernatural, symbolizing umbilical cords and the connection between humans and gods in general. The figures, carrying staffs and other insignia, bring tamales as offerings. The mural paintings combine elements from Oaxaca with features that recall the Postclassic Maya codices.

Northern Yucatan was dominated by the existence of powerful political centers throughout the Postclassic. The collapse of Classic centers of the central Peten and affiliated sites in the south by 900 A.D. was accompanied by the rise in power of the northern center of Chichen Itza (ill. 537). This political center consolidated its power over much of the northern Lowlands, and became one of the most powerful states in Maya history. Chichen Itza was succeeded by a northern rival, Mayapan. This site inherited much of Chichen's economic empire, and dominated political and economic affairs in the Lowlands until about 1517.

Dating issues are complicated in the north by the fact that site deposits are shallow, and occupations spanning several hundred years can be mixed together in a few centimeters of soil. The proximity to the surface of late deposits results in them being eroded more seriously than earlier deposits. The majority of scholars now believe that Chichen Itza was established during the Terminal Classic period (by the 9th century), and that it became the dominant northern Maya power during the Early Postclassic (1000 to 1200). This center was succeeded in its position of power by Mayapan soon after 1200. Mayapan went on to dominate much of the northern region during most of the Late Postclassic (1200 to 1500), but was overthrown, according to ethnohistoric documents, in 1441. The role that this center took after this period is still being evaluated archeologically.

537 *View of the Castillo pyramid from the Temple of the Warriors, Chichen Itza, Yucatan, Mexico*
The Castillo pyramid is the central point of the northern district of the city. It has a radially symmetrical layout, with open stairways at all four corners, as is typical of Postclassic Maya sites. The serpent-shaped balustrades may be connected with the ruling family, underlining its legitimacy by referring back to the creation myths of the *K'uk'ulkan*, "feathered serpent."

The rise of the Itza polity

The ethnic identity of ruling elites at Chichen Itza is hotly debated, because historical accounts refer repeatedly to "foreign" rulers. Similarities in architecture observed at Chichen Itza and the contemporary central Mexican site of Tula have led some scholars to support the idea of foreign invasion. The rise of a new ruling elite is often legitimized by claims of exotic or foreign origins. It is important to evaluate whether such claims represent true foreign invasion or more moderate circumstances, where foreigners enforce their ties by marriage or other forms of alliance to another power. Evidence supporting both types of takeover are found in the architectural styles at Chichen Itza (ill. 538). The southern area of the site exhibits "Puuc" styles similar to those of conventional northern Yucatan (ills. 539, 540), and the northern area exhibits more international styles, as observed in the "Atlantean" figures found in the Temple

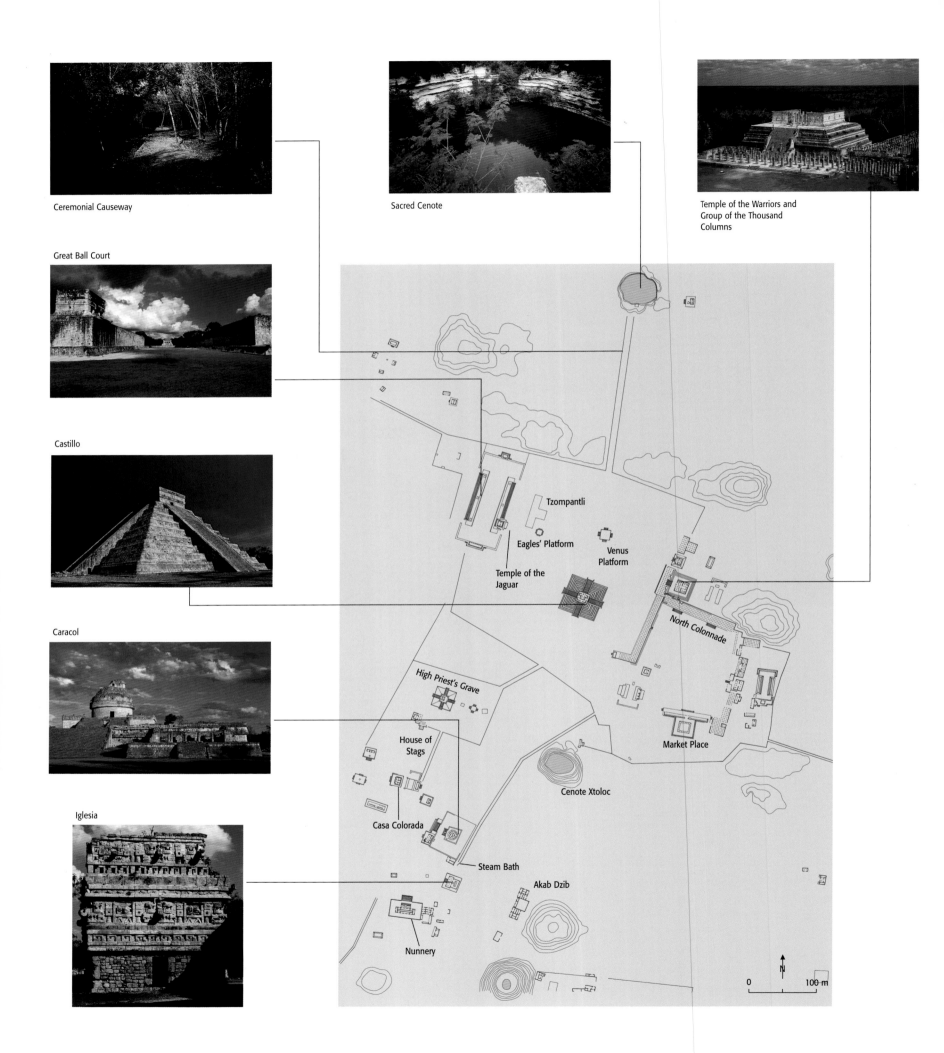

Ceremonial Causeway

Sacred Cenote

Temple of the Warriors and Group of the Thousand Columns

Great Ball Court

Castillo

Caracol

Iglesia

Tzompantli

Eagles' Platform

Venus Platform

Temple of the Jaguar

North Colonnade

High Priest's Grave

House of Stags

Market Place

Cenote Xtoloc

Casa Colorada

Steam Bath

Akab Dzib

Nunnery

0 100 m

N

of the Jaguar, the Chacmool altars, and the colonnaded Temple of the Warriors. The Castillo, a four-sided pyramid, dominates a large plaza in this portion of the site (ill. 537), and one of the largest ball courts in all of Mesoamerica is found to the north-west of this structure.

Most scholars agree that Chichen Itza was established as a center by the Late Classic, and that a military intrusion of an elite ruling faction not local to northern Yucatan is corroborated by the archeological, artistic, and hieroglyphic record. This intrusion had occurred by the dawn of the 11th century and marks the beginning of the Postclassic. Large, powerful centers that had ruled the north prior to the advent of Chichen Itza, such as Ek Balam and Yaxuna, appear to have been defeated by the military operations of this powerful and aggressive new state at about this time. Evidence of the destruction of buildings and defensive works at these sites is associated with the military conquest of the invading Itza polity.

Scholars differ in their views on the identification of the place of origin of this ruling elite, the Itza. Locations that have been suggested include Highland Mexico (the Toltec of Tula), the Gulf Coast, "Mexicanized" Putun Maya, and emigrating elites of the fallen southern centers of the Peten region of Guatemala. A number of migrations are referred to in documents, and it is probable that people arrived in northern Yucatan from different regions at different times. It is also probable that long distance multiethnic alliances and migrations had their origins in earlier times and were not unique to the Postclassic. Regardless of the ethnic origins of the Itza, it is clear that the political faction responsible for the rise of Chichen Itza to a dominant world power during the Early Postclassic was a cosmopolitan, revisionist, aggressive, highly organized group, with an outwardly economic and stylistic focus. Recent examinations of their historic traditions in art, writing, and architecture by Schele and Matthews reveal that the Itza did not ignore fundamental earlier religious institutions of the Maya Lowlands. Instead, they skilfully incorporated important traditions, such as creation mythology, in support of the new political regime. The Classic to Postclassic transition was characterized by the appearance of a renewed internationalism for many Mesoamerican societies, and far-flung trade networks among both Highland and Lowland societies accelerated interaction and the spread of what Smith and Heath-Smith have termed "international styles." It can, therefore, be difficult in this context to evaluate the ethnicity of a ruling elite based on style of dress, religious symbols, military weapons, or architectural forms alone.

538 *Map of Chichen Itza*
Chichen Itza consisted of a north and a south city, as can be seen from the distribution and arrangement of the various buildings, and the existence of similar sites (pyramids with square groundplans, Venus platforms, and cenotes) in both parts of the city. Buildings in the Puuc style are concentrated in the southern center, and can be clearly distinguished from the buildings in the other areas. These follow innovative, panregional stylistic trends and are comparable to contemporary architecture in Mexico. Chichen Itza was unmistakably a cosmopolitan and multiethnic city.

539 *The "Iglesia." Puuc architecture in Chichen Itza, Yucatan, Mexico; Terminal Classic*
The "Iglesia" (church) is located at the southern edge of the site and is one of a group of Puuc monuments (along with the nunnery and the Akab Dzib). It is covered with long-nosed gods' masks and shows the recessed friezes that were typical of Late Classic architecture in the Puuc region in the north-west of Yucatan, for example in Uxmal.

540 *Mosaic mask in the Puuc style. Chichen Itza, Yucatan, Mexico, nunnery; Terminal Classic, 800-900 A.D.*
Larger-than-life gods' masks made, like mosaics, from a large number of preworked stones, are one of the characteristic features of the Puuc style. Because of their long noses, the masks were, for a long time, thought to represent the god Chaak. But it has now been established that there are numerous differences between them, and that they probably portray many different gods.

541 *View of Structure Q-80 in the center of Mayapan, Yucatan, Mexico*
The structure to which archeologists gave the technical name Q-80 lies in the center of Mayapan, directly north of the Castillo pyramid (ill. 543). The actual building stands on a platform and had 6 small rooms. The main room was excavated only a few years ago. At that time the Mexican archeologists discovered that the back wall of this room was adorned with spectacular wall paintings. The building probably had a timber-frame roof held up by stone or wooden supports. Due to the poor quality of the masonry the roof and a large part of the side walls caved in. The function of this presumably once very important building is as yet unknown.

The legacy of Mayapan

Historical sources suggest Mayapan rose to power as a result of intrigue, treachery, and an alliance of political factions against the center of Chichen Itza. Military assistance from Gulf coast Maya allies from Xicalango is recognized in historical accounts.

Architecture at Mayapan is neither as large, well-preserved, nor extensively distributed as that observed at Chichen Itza (ill. 541). Despite the importance of this center, the analysis of the architecture and artifacts led scholars of the Carnegie Project, published in 1962, to dismiss late Postclassic Maya society as "decadent" and "degenerate." Since these early investigations, a contrasting interpretation has emerged. Late Postclassic Maya society has instead been characterized as "efficient" and "mercantile," and the shift in focus away from elaborate architecture reflects an important reorientation in political and economic organization. Social energies were invested into economic production and exchange, and market systems encouraged participation from all members of society in economic affairs, providing them with the opportunity to profit from the fruits of their labor. This open economic system rewarded entrepreneurs, and decreased social distances between elites and commoners, allowing more people to enjoy an affluent lifestyle. The less elaborate public and residential architecture is viewed, not as a "devolution" of former Classic practices, but a reflection of new social norms and economic priorities. This shift is observed in maturing state societies throughout world history, and may represent an inevitable aspect of long term cultural development. The need for monumentality dwindles as bureaucratic organizations become more sophisticated.

The method of construction at Mayapan, Cozumel, and other Late Postclassic sites was highly efficient. Buildings would have had wooden walls covered in stucco and plaster, with thatched roofs. Public structures at Postclassic centers had elaborate murals and stucco decorations, as observed at Tulum and Santa Rita, of which only fragments have survived.

Lords of the Mayapan confederacy are said to have resided within the city. Archeological studies reveal that settlement was tightly packed within the city walls, as well as outside them. The range of house sizes suggests that elites and commoners lived in close proximity. A four-sided temple (El Castillo) dominates the central plaza (ill. 543). The Castillo is located to the immediate west of a cenote or well, and is surrounded by colonnaded halls (ill. 541), elite residences, temples, shrines, oratories, and round structures. Beyond the plaza, elite and nonelite houses and courtyards extend in all directions. Small sculptures of turtles and diving figures found in these domestic zones indicate that some rituals took place outside the central precinct. Turtles are inscribed with ajaw dates, and were probably related to celebrations of calendrical period endings.

There is some indication that the people of Mayapan revived practices that had long since been abandoned, such as stela erection. A stela platform is located at this site's center. In a number of contemporary southern Lowlands sites stelae were either re-erected stelae from earlier times or new ones were erected, possibly covered in stucco and paint. Although the chronology and extent of this phenomenon remains to be fully documented, this pattern may reflect an important revivalistic strategy promoted by the leaders of this late center.

East coast sites

Along the east coast of the Yucatan peninsula, a densely settled Late Postclassic occupation zone has been identified. Political centers are located at key coastal locations along this vast strip (ill. 534), including El Meco, San Gervasio, Buenavista, Tulum, Ichpaatun, Santa Rita, and others. Each of these sites has a unique combination of temples, residences, and shrines. Tulum and Ichpaatun are walled communities, and Tulum and Santa Rita are known for their well-preserved late murals (ills. 536, 547). All of these coastal communities are thought to have served as trading centers. Local products made in their affiliated provinces were exchanged for commodities from Lowland Maya provinces. Products were circulated with the help of maritime merchants.

542 *Map of Mayapan*

Mayapan was a densely settled city-state, surrounded by a defensive wall, and extending over an area of 3 × 2 km². In the middle of the ceremonial center, which measures 2.5 hectares, is the Castillo pyramid (Structure 162), built to a square groundplan and surrounded by an observatory, a stela platform, temples, oratories, and shrines. The largest columned halls are also to be found in this area, where the ruling families lived. Like Chichen Itza, Mayapan was also multiethnic, and its princes had important trade links from the Gulf of Mexico to the Gulf of Honduras.

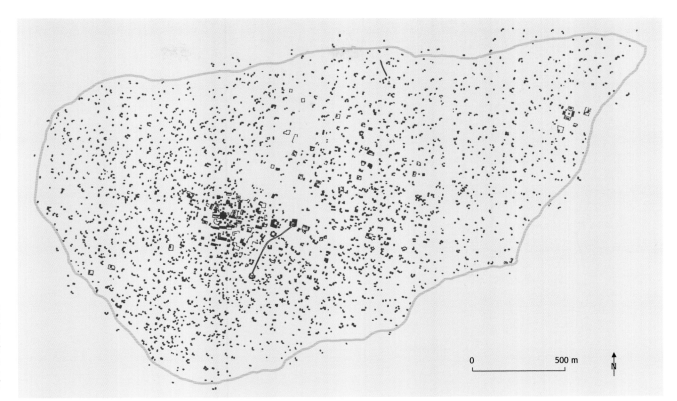

543 *The Castillo pyramid. Mayapan, Yucatan, Mexico; Middle or Late Postclassic, 1200-1500 A.D.*

In the foreground on the right is the Castillo pyramid, sometimes also called the K'uk'ulkan pyramid, which dominates the center of Mayapan and is a smaller copy of the famous original in Chichen Itza. On the left is the Caracol, likewise a smaller imitation of the building of the same name in Chichen Itza. By copying models in this way, the inhabitants of Mayapan were evidently attempting to share in the greatness and importance of Chichen Itza.

0   500 m

N

Population dynamics of the southern Lowlands

In the southern Lowlands, archeologists have documented substantial depopulation in the inland core region of Classic Peten. Specific studies in the Tikal and Petexbatun regions, in the south-west Lowlands, show a virtual absence of Postclassic settlement at earlier monumental centers. In the Tikal region, a settlement shift is noted, with Postclassic minor occupations appearing along aquatic zones like the Peten Lakes. The Peten was densely populated and politically dominant during the Late Classic, when a number of political centers and associated settlements existed in close proximity to one another. Many of these sites had been abandoned by 900 A.D. Did individuals perish in wars, famines, or epidemics of this region?

One possibility is that populations simply moved to new locations. Some appear to have founded agricultural hamlets and villages along lake shores or on islands, while others may have migrated to welcoming territories. Population movement was endemic throughout the southern Lowlands during Spanish colonial times.

Areas to the east of the Peten core, like northern Belize, show evidence of substantial population during the Early Postclassic. The northern Belize center of Lamanai, located along an inland lagoon with access to the Caribbean Sea, shows no signs of political collapse. Remarkably, it sustained its role as an important center from Classic through to Postclassic times. The discovery of many sites in the fertile, aquatic zones of Belize and Quintana Roo suggests that the eastern coastal Lowlands provided a home for substantial Postclassic populations. A concentration on island and peninsular occupation is a form of waterside settlement shared in many areas; this pattern is found at the Peten Lake sites of Tayasal, Macanche, Zacpeten, and others, the northern Belize sites of Laguna de On, Caye Muerto, and Caye Coco, the Campeche site of Isla Civiltuk, multiple coastal settlements on Cozumel Island, and the Yucatan site of Isla Cerritos. Coastal settlements were much more significant during the Postclassic. Some inland sites are found at locations not dominated by water features, but they appear to capitalize on key local resources, as observed at the Postclassic settlement of Colha, which is located at one of the finest chert outcrops in the Maya area. Influence from both the Peten and from Chichen Itza is reflected in the decorated ceramic traditions of the Early Postclassic in northern Belize, which exhibit characteristics of Chichen paste technology and decorative motifs shared with Peten vessel forms and slip characteristics. This influence is probably attributed to a combination of population movement and the establishment of important north-south trading ties during this period.

During the Late Postclassic (1200 to 1500), population levels appear to have remained high in northern Belize. In both the Peten region and northern Belize, the ceramic technology reflects greater standardization and proficiency in manufacturing techniques compared to earlier periods, as new patterns of production took hold. These trends indicate the presence of long-term, stable populations in these regions from the 10th through to the 16th century – ceramic traditions reflect long term unbroken social development. The emergence of a new set of regional centers is documented after the mid 13th century in zones such as northern Belize, and this pattern suggests that political restructuring in this area accompanied the rise of Mayapan in northern Yucatan. The addition of Mayapan-style utilitarian and ritual ceramic forms to the wares produced locally indicates the far-reaching influence of this northern center. Spanish documents indicate that the Chetumal province region of northern Belize was closely allied with Mayapan, and that this area continued to be extremely affluent and influential after the northern center fell from power during the mid 15th century. Sites like Lamanai were occupied into the 17th century.

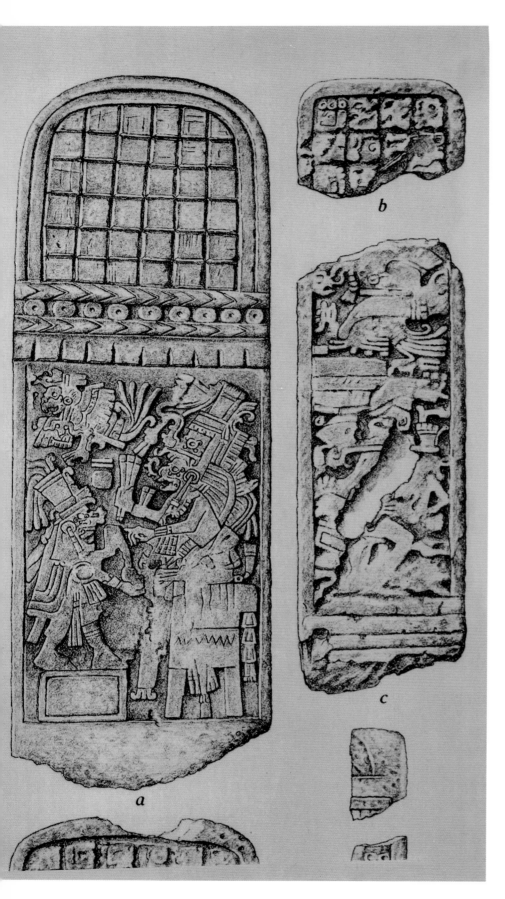

544 *Stelae. Mayapan, Yucatan, Mexico; Middle Postclassic, 1185 (?); limestone; measurements of Stela 1 (a): H. 175 cm, W. 59 cm, D. 20 cm*
The stelae typify the cultural revival of Classic symbolism by the rulers of Mayapan. Virtually no stelae had been erected in the Maya area during the preceding 200 years. Those illustrated here bear dates, but these do not readily accord with our calendar. Three of them probably refer to the period when Mayapan flourished.

by a confederation of territories and lineages controlling them, referred to as the "League of Mayapan." The presence of multiple elite residences and long structures or colonnaded (open) halls, around the centers of Mayapan and other Postclassic sites throughout the Lowlands, implies the co-residence of several powerful families at political centers. Some political offices may have been occupied on a rotating basis, as suggested by appointment records of 20 year "K'atun lords" in the Paris codex, identified by Bruce Love. This sharing of power would have had a highly integrative effect on regional organization. Modern Maya communities in the Highlands have similar councils, or assemblies, in a system that operates on a rotational basis. Individuals vie for positions in these councils through years of community service before they are ultimately elected to the councils. While this modern system was partly shaped by procedures imposed during the Spanish colonial era, earlier pre-Columbian societies may have functioned in a similar way. Systems such as *mul tepal*, and their extensive associated bureaucracies of officials, represent an important opposition to the unchecked rise to power of highly ambitious individuals.

This form of government was a major departure from institutions of leadership that dominated the Maya world during the Classic. Then the fate of communities hinged on the successes of charismatic monarch warriors claiming to be descended from the gods, and imbued with supernatural powers. A recent examination of the various political systems in Mesoamerica, by Richard Blanton and colleagues, has identified a "corporate" political strategy among the Postclassic Maya. It emphasized rule by assembly and promoted more "egalitarian behavior" in political action and related cognitive codes, to which society was compelled to conform. As these authors point out, such strategies may have their historical origin in opposition to earlier tyrannical reigns. It is possible that this may have been the case for the Postclassic Maya, as they redefined their society in the aftermath of Classic kingship.

545 *The ruler's residence. Tulum, Quintana Roo, Mexico, Structure 25; Postclassic*
The columned hall was, at one time, probably either a temple or the residence of one of the ruling families of Tulum. Inside, above a doorway, there is a niche with a stucco sculpture of a god dropping from the sky, a frequent motif in Postclassic art.

Political geography and regional organization

The political organization of Postclassic society has been analyzed on both regional and local scales. Relying on historical sources, the ethnohistorian Ralph Roys identified the boundaries of 16 political territories (*kuuchkabalo'ob*), which he termed provinces, at the time of Spanish contact. These territories varied in their internal organization. Some were hierarchical, governed by a ruler known as the *jalach winik*, who lived at the political center. Intermediary officials, known as *batab*, represented individual communities and performed organizational functions on behalf of the *jalach winik*. Other territories were less stratified, and recognized only *batab* community leadership without a *jalach winik*. Others still were loosely organized, consisting of peripheral, less populated confederacies of villages that lacked both of these offices. Archeological research suggests that the east coast provinces of Ecab, Uaymil, and Chetumal were allied with Mayapan. It has also been suggested that the provinces from Ah Canul west to Cupul, Tazes, and Cochuah were aligned with this center. Chikinchel, Canpech, and Chanputun do not reflect a close relationship to Mayapan, according to archeological and historical evidence.

The political organization of the Late Postclassic Maya has been the subject of much recent scholastic attention. Although documents indicate that regional rulers and tiers of specialized supporting political offices existed at the time of Spanish contact, the permanence of these offices and their prevalence across the peninsula are not well understood. Documents indicate that Mayapan was ruled by a form of assembly government, known as *mul tepal*. This state was formed

546 *Columned hall. Mayapan, Yucatan, Mexico, Structure 163*
Columned halls, such as Structure 163, due west of the Castillo, are a typical feature of the architecture of the rulers of Mayapan and other sites in Yucatan. The architect Tatiana Proskouriakoff, who took part in the excavations at Mayapan, interpreted them as being young men's houses, others saw them as council buildings where representatives of the influential families would meet. Some of these columned halls were probably also palaces.

The multiple factions governing Postclassic Maya society are reflected in the type of architecture found at political centers of this period. Multiple elite residences, family temples or shrines, and open halls cluster near the central plazas of these sites (ill. 546). At Tulum, a number of family temples and colonnaded halls are present (ill. 545). Public architecture at the sites of Chichen Itza, Mayapan, and Utatlan feature quadripartite pyramids. Quadripartite temples, notable for having staircases on all four slopes, represent a materialization of four directions, symbolism that is prevalent in Maya art throughout many periods. As such, the construction of temples of this nature are powerful symbols of integration of the divisions within communities and regions. The territory around Lake Peten Itza was occupied by four primary lineage groups, a pattern present in Highland K'iche' centers as well.

Staircases of four-sided temples and doorways in other types of temple often feature serpent balustrades or pillars. The *chan* glyph for "four" translates in hieroglyphic Mayan as the words for "sky" and "snake." Serpent imagery is farther related to themes of centrality among geographic and social partitions. Images of snakes in Maya art represent these creatures as conduits that connect the sky with the Earth, or this world with the supernatural. Serpent cords, known as the *k'uxa'an suum*, also connect lineage groups, and have been represented as a sort of umbilicus binding related individuals together. Snake imagery on murals at Tulum connect individuals who are probably genealogically related. The serpent murals at Structure 16 at Tulum connect

the celestial realm in the ceiling to other scenes shown below on the temple walls (ill. 536).

Murals at Santa Rita show processions of individuals, probably important lords in the Chetumal province during the late 14th or 15th centuries. Many of these lords are associated with a year glyph, and one pair of lords is shown leaving and entering a temple. This mural may reflect the involvement of individuals in assembly rule or rotating offices. The themes of art and architecture at Postclassic sites thus emphasize multiplicity of political officials, their associated lineages, and their integration into the community or regional level through ritual.

It is known from the documents that conflict was common among Postclassic territories, that boundaries were fluid, and that social disputes required continual negotiation. Some territories were more highly integrated with their neighbors than others at the time of Spanish contact. Mayapan, Cozumel, Tulum, and Santa Rita appear to represent an alliance that linked Mayapan to the east coast of Yucatan.

In the Guatemalan Highlands, a Late Postclassic military invasion is documented in archeological and ethnohistoric records. Lowland Maya groups are thought to have conquered the K'iche' region. The architectural similarity of highland sites like Utatlan and Iximche to those in Mayapan and the Peten lakes region reflects relationships between the Highlands and Lowlands. This conquest provided economic advantage for the rulers of sites like Utatlan. During the Late Postclassic, most of the obsidian blades found at Lowland sites came from Ixtepeque in the Guatemalan Highlands. Prior to this, they came from diverse sources in Mexico as well as from the Maya Highlands. These alternative sources dwindled in favor of Highland Maya obsidian during the Late Postclassic. K'iche' power was maintained in part by its involvement in circum-Yukatek trade networks (see Sachse, p. 360 ff.).

547 *Part of the mural paintings in Structure 1 at Santa Rita Corozal. Copy by Thomas Gann; Santa Rita Corozal, Belize, Structure 1; Late Postclassic, 1440-1500*
The mural paintings in Structure 1 at Santa Rita, which was probably the most important place in the province of Uaymil during the Postclassic, are among the most important examples of all Postclassic art. Unfortunately, they were destroyed immediately following their discovery, so that today they can be reconstructed only with the help of the drawings made by Thomas Gann, who discovered them. Gods were portrayed standing guard over Tun periods. Stylistic influences from central Mexico and Oaxaca can be discerned.

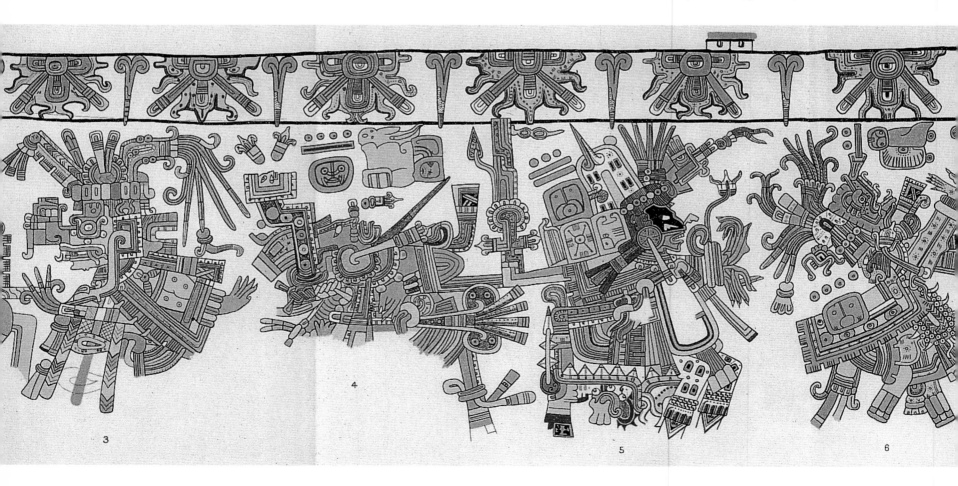

548 *Decorated tripod vessel. Lamanai, Belize, cache N.10-43/1; Middle to Late Postclassic, 1150-1300 A.D.; clay with orange-colored coating, H. 11.6 cm, dia. 18.9 cm; Belmopan, Department of Archeology*
This engobed tripod bowl with figurative decoration is a prime example – as regards mass, form, and color – of the special kind of ceramics that were produced in Lamanai at the beginning of the Postclassic. Reliefed and modeled,

they are assembled from several parts, and they have an orange-red coating. Such composite pottery was, however, already being produced in Belize by the Terminal Classic. The manufacturing techniques remained in use, for other vessels too (with or without engobing), up until the Spanish invasion.

Social structure, households, and communities

Documentary and archeological sources indicate that lineage-based power was a critical element of community rule in Postclassic societies. Mayapan was, at one point, ruled by a confederation of powerful lineages, and founding lineage migrations, such as the Aj Kanul, established their own communities. Recent research by Sergio Quezada emphasizes the importance of lineage-based political structure for some territories. The exact relationship between individuals in such lineage groups is not well understood. It is likely that they included individuals related by blood and marriage, as well as other important allies who chose to affiliate themselves. Robert Carmack and John Fox have demonstrated that the organization of Postclassic Highland communities reflected the governing coalitions among the Quiche of Utatlan and other sites.

Some aspects of Postclassic architecture reflect the multiplicity of lineage factions among the governing elite. These include the multiple palace and temple or shrine complexes around site centers, and the presence of long houses or halls, which are found at Mayapan (ill. 546), at Peten Lakes island sites, in the K'iche' Highlands, and at many other centers. These structures are thought to have been constructed by multiple elite factions of Postclassic centers, and would have been used for convening and conferring over matters of state, much like the council houses at sites like Copan, Ek Balam, and Chichen Itza.

Communities may have varied in the degree to which lineage ties predominated in negotiating community affairs. Rotating offices, urging negotiation and integration among the multiple groups, were also in place.

Burial patterns at Postclassic sites indicate that most community members received comparable treatment in terms of funerary features and grave offerings. It can be difficult to distinguish elites from commoners, with a couple

of exceptions at Santa Rita and Lamanai. Burials took place in and around family residences, and a view emerges of a largely affluent population with moderate status distinctions (that appear as gradations along a continuum) in individual communities. Drastic class differences are not observed, and it is probable that upward social mobility was common in this society.

Religion

Much information about Postclassic Maya religion is preserved through the accounts of Spanish friars, who struggled to convert Lowland populations between 1517 and 1697. Accounts are ripe with descriptions of "idolatry." Bishop Landa describes rituals observed at the time of contact, and the friars who journeyed deep into the jungles of Belize and Guatemala discuss the persistence of indigenous rituals. Many of the described rituals reflect the celebration of calendrical festivities throughout the year, as well as end of year and K'atun ending rituals. At occasions such as New Year's *wayeb* ceremonies, effigies were constructed, old ones were discarded, and offerings of incense and game were made. Such festivities took place in the homes of community leaders, and were often accompanied by processions through the towns.

The archeological remains of such ceremonies include incense burners (ill. 549), figurines, food and water vessels, sacrificed animal carcasses, obsidian blades, shell objects, and stone tools. Diane Chase has identified calendrical offerings at the site of Santa Rita in northern Belize, where figurine caches have been found in the courtyards of prominent residences. At other Postclassic centers, incense burners are concentrated in greater numbers in temples and shrines. Their use in the codices reflects the custom of burning incense at a great

549 *Hourglass incense burners from central Belize. Provenance unknown; Late Postclassic, 1200-1500 A.D.; fired clay; Belmopan, Department of Archeology*
These two ceramics are prime examples of incense burners that were manufactured and used throughout the entire cultural area of the Postclassic Lowlands. Their widespread use shows that the rulers of different

city-states performed almost identical calendrical ceremonies and religious rituals, which probably originated in Chichen Itza and later in Mayapan. Shared ritual practises were an important integrating factor. They helped to sustain the coherence of the particular political elites, and also to consolidate the economic links between the Lowland provinces.

550 *Incense burner in the shape of the god Itzamnaaj. Mayapan, Yucatan, Mexico; Late Postclassic. 1200-1500; fired clay, painted; H. 60 cm, W. 34 cm, D. 34 cm; Mexico City, Museo Nacional de Antropología*
The old face with the hooked nose and prominent canine teeth protruding at the corners of the mouth, strongly suggest that the deity portrayed is Itzamnaaj. He is only one of a number of gods to be portrayed on incense burners in the Chen Mul style. In his hands, he holds a special maize loaf or pressed resin for incense as an offering.

551 *Incense burner portraying an unknown god. Dzibanche, Quintana Roo, Mexico; Late Postclassic, 1300-1400; fired clay*
The figure is typical of modeled Chen Mul ceramics. These portrayals of various gods, which were sometimes also manufactured from other materials, were developed in Mayapan, and are most frequently to be found there. They were at the center of many religious calendrical ceremonies in the Postclassic and during colonial times, and were probably linked to an ancient religious cult that was encouraged by the city princes. Many of these sculptures, such as the example illustrated, show the gods bringing offerings of food or incense. Incense was burned in the burner at the back of the figure.

number of ceremonial events which marked calendrical passages in particular. These celebrations would have integrated participants. Fragments of incense burners are also found in domestic contexts, but in smaller quantities than at ritual locations. These distributions suggest symbolic links between household members and community or lineage shrines. Censers were also sometimes used as burial offerings for important individuals, as observed at Lamanai, Caye Coco, and Mayapan.

Two forms of ceramic incense burners are identified in mural art, codices, and from archeological sites: noneffigy and effigy censers. Noneffigy censers were often fashioned in an hourglass shape with a pedestal base (ill. 549). Other forms include censer jars or *ollas*, which stood on three legs. Decorations on noneffigy censers include rosettes or round "buttons" of clay, cone-shaped spikes, and filleted bands of finger-impressed clay. Elaborate noneffigy censers can also have flanges that project downward from the base or upward from the neck in the form of step-terraced trefoil motifs. Effigy censers are "bucket" pedestal vessels attached to modeled anthropomorphic figures (ills. 550, 551). At Mayapan, a few of these effigies are identified as specific deities, but most lack identifying characteristics. They are associated with the end of the Postclassic, and are most numerous at Mayapan, which appears to be the place where rituals involving these objects originated. Their appearance at virtually all Late Postclassic Lowland sites points to widespread participation in Mayapan-inspired ritual practices.

Economy

Chichen Itza created a powerful economic empire based on maritime trade, which connected the Maya Yucatan peninsula to lower Central America, the Maya Highlands, the Mexican Gulf Coast, and the Mexican Highlands. The site of Isla Cerritos served as a place for merchant canoes to exchange commodities (ill. 552). Items traded included salt, grinding stones, textiles, hides, honey, wax, chocolate, obsidian, incense, feathers, copper ornaments and bells, and exotic lapidary ornaments. Most essential everyday items were made by communities located throughout the peninsula, and non-local obsidian, jade, ground stone, and metals were imported from the Highland Maya area or from central Mexico and southern Central America. This trade benefited the economies of communities located around the coast, such as Chikinchel, where the scale of salt production was increased to an industrial level in the face of newly expanded markets in Mesoamerica. After Mayapan replaced Chichen Itza as the dominant political center in northern Yucatan during the 13th century, it assumed control of this circum-Yukatek maritime trade, and Postclassic Maya polities allied with Mayapan prospered. Sites like Tulum, El Meco, a number of communities on Cozumel Island, Santa Rita, and others served as trading centers for associated Maya territories along the east coast. All these sites have elaborate ritual facilities, so it is possible that transethnic religious pilgrimage was linked to trading activity at these sites. Their sacred facilities provided a neutral ground for potentially conflictive economic exchanges with merchants from foreign territories. The use of "international styles" at these sites would have assisted in interethnic communication, and transcended subregional differences.

Most members of society participated directly in market production and exchange. The "rise of the Maya merchant class" had an important effect on the transformation of Postclassic society. Upward mobility was possible, and substantial wealth differences did not distinguish commoners from most of the nobility. Although elites sponsored important integrative ritual activities, negotiated trading partnerships, and oversaw political and military matters, it appears that they encouraged, rather than controlled the production and exchange of commodities. Archeological data indicates that valuables are found in substantial quantities among households of all different sizes and social statuses, and that the differences between elites and commoners are hard to distinguish by their possessions.

The maturation of Maya society

The new social order that emerged during the Late Postclassic functioned through the broad geographic integration of largely autonomous local polities, linked through exchange. The rise of early states is often centered on massive monumental construction and the support of "divine" kings. This orientation later gives way to more mature political formations that exhibit the following characteristics: 1) increasing technological innovation and efficiency, 2) increasing size of political units, 3) universality in ideological concepts, 4) increasing political stability, 5) increasing capacity for large scale warfare, 6) less investment of surplus into religious architecture ("secularization"), and 7) increasing amount of intersocietal trade, which breaks down social barriers.

In applying these criteria to the Postclassic Maya, scholars have documented the technological innovation and efficiency of building styles of this period, the decreased investment in religious architecture, and the acceleration of international trade. Universality in ideological concepts is indicated by the use of international styles at trading ports and similarities in ritual objects and architecture, observed from Mayapan to the Maya Highlands. The increase in size of political units may be reflected in the greater integration of northern and southern Lowland populations through shared utilitarian and ritual styles and a vast, interconnected regional economy. However, this Maya Lowlands regional unit was comprised of many semiautonomous polities, which may have been the key to the stability and flexibility of Postclassic society over time. Increased political stability is reflected in the flourishing economies and long-term developmental sequences of Postclassic ceramics, and growth trends in population levels and site complexity within many regions over time.

The emergence of Postclassic Maya civilization reflects the evolution of a new social order. No longer perceived as the age of "decadence," the cultural institutions of this period are now seen as the cumulative products of the long-term development of a highly successful, geographically vast, and ethnically diverse people. Although they rejected massive architectural monuments and the tyranny of ambitious dynasts, these populations created an economically flourishing system that minimized social differences within individual communities and reinterpreted historical traditions in innovative and contemporary ways. The result of these transformations was a strikingly stable, long-term trend of growth for numerous Lowland communities. Geographical shifts in prosperity are noted among territories allied with Chichen Itza and Mayapan, but the overall pattern for the Lowland peninsula represents a cycle of upward development from the beginning to the end of the Postclassic. Military expansion and economic consolidation in the Guatemalan Highlands no doubt contributed to the trend of economic integration within the Maya area, which culminated at the time of Mayapan's rise to power.

552 *Gold ear spools. Santa Rita Corozal, Belize, Structure 216; Late Postclassic, 1200–1500 A.D.; gold, turquoise, obsidian; H. 6.4 cm, W. 3.9 cm, D. 4.1 cm; Belmopan, Department of Archeology*
At the tail end of the Postclassic, Maya centers, such as Santa Rita, were centers of extensive international trade networks, with an importance and influence supported by the allied seaports around the Yucatan peninsula. Via these routes, artifacts made of gold, copper, bronze, and other metal alloys reached the ruling houses of the southern Lowlands. These ear pegs are encrusted with turquoise from north Mexico and attached to cylindrical rods of black obsidian, probably from the Highlands of Guatemala.

THE ART OF WEAVING

Stefanie Teufel

The Maya art of weaving has a tradition going back well over a thousand years (ill. 554). As the domain of women, it enjoyed the patronage of the goddess Chak Chel, and was linked with the gift of childbirth. Unfortunately, because of the humid climate, only a few examples of textiles from pre-Hispanic times have survived; we therefore have only a very limited view of the diversity of weaving techniques involved. Most of the examples that have survived – totaling about 600 – come from the sacrificial well at Chichen Itza, where they were found buried in mud, and not exposed to oxygen. These items date from the Postclassic. The oldest textile fragments so far found are from Rio Azul in the southern Maya Lowlands. They have been dated, by chemical analysis, as belonging to the period 250 to 550 A.D. These finds show that the Maya at that time practiced not only simple weaving techniques, but also complex procedures, such as mull weaving, brocading, and embroidery.

Archeological finds and sources from the colonial era tell us that the material used was either fiber from the henequén agave, or white and brown cotton (ill. 557). Pollen analysis proves that these were grown from at least 1500 B.C. onward.

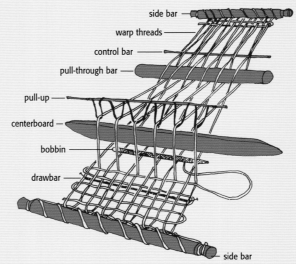

553 *Diagram illustrating a back-belt loom*
Back-belt looms, such as this, have probably been used by the Maya for several thousand years. They are light, portable, and can be taken on journeys. They do not, however, enable very broad cloth to be woven, which means that many items of clothing have to be sewn together using several widths.

554 *Woman from San Antonio Polopo, Solola, Guatemala, weaving with a traditional loom*
San Antonio Polopo is situated directly beside Lake Atitlan, in a region well known for the production and sale of woven fabrics. Here, the traditional techniques are, to this day, passed down from mother to daughter.

Though more laborious to cultivate than the agave, cotton has distinct advantages. It is soft yet tough and takes dye very well. Furthermore, the fibres can be worked immediately after being plucked, cleaned, and sorted. Finds in simple graves have confirmed that cotton was by no means reserved exclusively for the upper classes, as had been previously supposed. The cotton was spun using spinning wharves on a spindle bar. One hand was used to prepare the fiber for twisting, the other to turn the spindle. After spinning, the yarns could be dyed, but the Maya were probably also familiar with the "tie-dye technique" of tying the threads before dying. Blue dye was derived from plants of the *Indigofera* species, carmine from the cochineal beetle, and dark violet from the *purpura* snail. There must have been a wide range of available colors, as can be seen today from the remaining colors on ancient ceramics and mural paintings.

555 *Woman with a loom. Jaina, Campeche, Mexico; Late Classic, 600-900 A.D.; fired clay; H. 17 cm, L. 16 cm, W. 10 cm; Mexico City, Museo Nacional de Antropología e Historia*
This clay figurine from the island of Jaina shows a young woman wearing a *huipil* and skirt. The traditional belt loom goes around her body. The other end is tied to a tree, with a bird sitting on it.

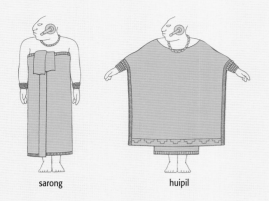

sarong   huipil

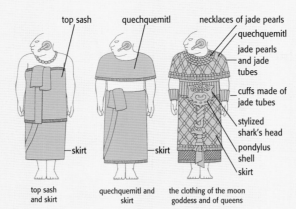

top sash   quechquemitl   necklaces of jade pearls

quechquemitl

jade pearls
and jade
tubes

cuffs made of
jade tubes

stylized
shark's head

pondylus
shell

skirt

skirt   skirt

top sash
and skirt   quechquemitl and
skirt   the clothing of the moon
goddess and of queens

556 *The cut of womens' clothes*
There was wide variety in women's clothing. The basic item was always a wraparound skirt, which could be combined with various shawls, sashes, and items of jewelry. A queen's clothing included a wrap of jade necklaces and symbolic jewelry, intended to show that she was created in the image of the Moon Goddess.

Weaving was preceded by warping – sorting the threads by color, length, and crossovers – and by mounting the threads onto the loom. The maximum width of the cloth was determined by the length of the weaver's arm. A figurine from Jaina (ill. 555) shows the old weaving technique using a back belt, a method still used to this day (ill. 553). The warp threads are stretched lengthwise and fixed to bars at the top and bottom. The upper part of the loom has a cord for attaching it to a fixed point, such as a tree. The lower part has a belt, which the weaver passes around her hips. By means of two bars, the separator bar and the heddle bar, to which the straight threads are tied, a shed is produced, through which the weft thread is passed. The weaver guides the weft by means of a bar, to which a bundle of threads are tied, after each pull and push with the separator bar. A close weave is achieved with the aid of the centerboard. The finished cloth can then be embroidered, dyed, or stamped with a pattern, then used to produce items of clothing.

Textiles were produced for trade, as payment of tribute, or for personal use. Many illustrations in works of art show us what was worn at that time and which fashions were highly regarded by the Maya. Fabrics were usually not cut to shape but loosely draped around the body. The principal item of clothing in all social classes was the loincloth for men and the *huipil* for women, a sleeveless top garment, which at that time was always worn long (ill. 556). Clothing varied according to circumstance and social standing. Probably only persons of elevated rank owned a short or long apron, or a coat and cape. For protection when at war, a short coat, a padded jacket, and a kind of cotton shawl were worn. For the ball game, a broad belt was worn over the clothing. Additional adornments to the head indicated the wearer's social standing: a sheaf of papers or a paintbrush, for example, indicated the occupation of scribe. After the Spanish invasion, Maya clothing changed drastically. Not only were there new materials, such as silk and wool, there

were also new tools, and techniques such as personalized tailoring and working with the pedal loom, which became an occupation for men. But it was not so much technical innovations as regulations concerning clothing during the colonial era that brought about the disappearance of many traditional items of clothing. Missionaries thought the native attire indecent because it often left women's breasts uncovered. They were obliged to cover the upper part of the body, and eventually to wear a headscarf or a veil in church. Men, for their part, were made to wear wide trousers over the loincloth. Anyone who aspired to public office had to wear shoes, long trousers, a jacket, and a hat. Men were compelled, partly or even wholly, to

abandon their traditional costume. The efforts by the Spaniards to restrict the indigenous population to specific areas encouraged the development of local costumes, which was intended to make it easier to control individual communities.

Modern Maya clothing evolved, in time, from this mingling of cultures. Today, it is predominantly women who still wear traditional dress, for example, a wide, long blouse, the *huipil*, a wraparound skirt, and a sash. Colors and patterns are subject to fashion, and it is often impossible to say whether a particular feature has been taken from Maya tradition or from the world of European fashion. The significance of any kind of costume – what it tells us about the age and social position of the wearer, and the circumstances under which it is worn – applies only within the community, because clothing is village-specific, and even the village next door may prefer other colors and patterns. Every Maya community has created, in its textiles, its own unmistakable means of identification, a visual code, so to speak. Today, women in particular make a display of a kind of overall Maya movement by combining features taken from different regions. For many young people today, wearing traditional clothing also signifies that they are rediscovering, and putting on display, their cultural identity.

557 *Textile fragment. Chichen Itza, Yucatan, Mexico; Late Classic or Early Postclassic, 600-1200 A.D.; cotton, dyed; W. 11.5 cm; Cambridge, Peabody Museum of Archeology and Ethnology, Harvard University*
Many artifacts made from organic materials, such as this brocaded fabric woven from cotton, were preserved in the sacrificial well at Chichen Itza.

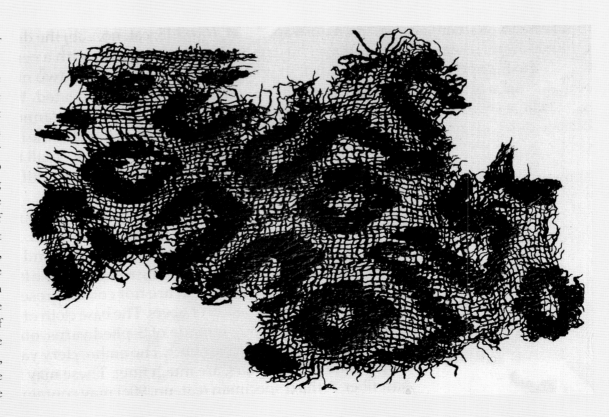

THE MARTIAL DYNASTIES – THE POSTCLASSIC IN THE MAYA HIGHLANDS

Frauke Sachse

With the end of the Classic, an era began in Mesoamerica which, seen from the vantage point of present-day scholarship, seems like a Dark Age lying between the golden era of the Maya as documented in archeology and inscriptions, and the Amerindian culture of the colonial era, as described by the Spaniards. There is no other period in the evolution of Maya culture whose import is as difficult to grasp and interpret as the Postclassic (c. 900-1520 A.D.).

This period was marked by wars, migrations, and profound changes affecting almost all aspects of Maya culture. The typical features that characterize the Postclassic are very much the same throughout the entire Maya area, despite the fact that developments in the Lowlands and the Highlands should be treated separately. The cultural change in question began considerably earlier in the Maya Lowlands than in the Highlands, with many elements of the Classic Maya culture being retained. The Maya of the Postclassic Highlands had only slight contact with the people of the Classic Lowland culture. It is, however, common to both regions that, in all areas of culture (art, architecture, weaponry, religion, etc.) influences from central Mexico made themselves felt, and can be regarded as the most definitive feature of Postclassic Maya culture.

In the Highlands, a form of Maya culture emerged during the Postclassic with cultural patterns that are today relatively unified, although even since pre-Hispanic times, the region has been fragmented into many language groups and cannot be regarded as an ethnically homogenous area (ill. 559). At present, 18 different Mayan languages are spoken in the Highlands, by speakers belonging, to some extent, to different ethnic groups. The most important language groups are the closely related K'iche' languages: K'iche', Kaqchikel and Tz'utujil, along with Q'eqchi', Poqom, Mam, and Ixil. The present-day ethnic and territorial makeup of the Highlands is, on the one hand, the result of multiple resettlement of the indigenous population by the Spanish colonial administration, and on the other hand, the result of regional developments in the Postclassic.

The Postclassic as a radical new beginning

In many respects, the Postclassic stands out from the preceding Classic as a new era. Throughout the entire Maya area, one is struck by features that indicate a central Mexican influence. Changed forms in ceramics and architecture clearly show a fundamental change in the intellectual culture and religion of the

558 *Early Postclassic burial urn. Precise provenance unknown, Guatemalan Highlands; Early Postclassic, c. 900 A.D.; fired clay, painted; H. 115 cm, W. 60 cm, Guatemala City. Museo Popol Wuj*
The carefully worked burial urn is painted in a number of colors and has a detachable, conical cover in the form of a seated jaguar. The frontal view of the body of the vessel itself shows the face of a deity looking out from the jaws of a serpent, a common motif in connection with the offering of incense.

559 *Map of Postclassic archeological sites in the Guatemalan Highlands*
The map shows the most important archeological sites in the Highlands of Guatemala, with an approximate indication of the distribution of the most important language groups. The density of settlement was, however, greater, because many sites from this period have yet to be investigated and are not shown on this map. Their visible legacy is not spectacular, indeed in many cases it is scarcely discernible.

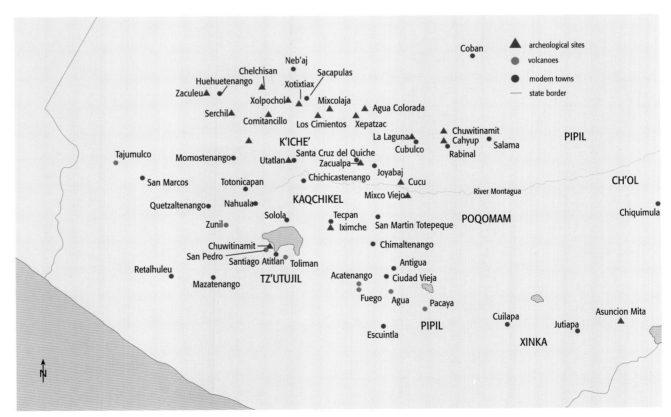

Highlands. Postclassic architecture of buildings made of solid stone and mortar was an innovation in this area, replacing the clay brick buildings that predominated in the Highlands during the Classic. With the new materials, building techniques and styles also changed. Increasingly, types of building following central Mexican models became generally established; there are also some examples of these from the Postclassic Lowlands.

Architectural forms of a new kind, from the Late Postclassic, are to be found in many places. They include palaces (ill. 575), columned temples on pyramidal platforms, columned halls, circular temples, platforms for dancing, I-shaped ball courts, and stone platforms where the skulls of sacrificed captives were put on show (ills. 561–562). Twin temples, (not to be confused with twin pyramids; see Harrison, p. 229), comprising two temple buildings built parallel to each other on the same platform (ills. 562, 576), are a form widespread in the Highlands, but otherwise found only in central Mexico.

Developments in the architecture of temple buildings and the new ball courts and skull platforms are suggestive of a religion that was practised in public and a cult of warfare of a central Mexican stamp that ousted and replaced earlier spiritual practices. Ceramic artifacts from the Postclassic Highlands also point to a change in religious beliefs. One is struck by the large incense burners with modeled representations of gods, including deities that are clearly of Mexican origin, such as Xipe Totec, with whom the practice of human sacrifice by flaying is associated. Furthermore, the increased use of urn vessels in the Postclassic seems to indicate that there was a change in the mortuary practices of the Maya from burial to cremation (ill. 558). Ceramic finds also provide a good deal of information regarding the cultural development of the Postclassic Highlands. For example, vessels with new shapes can indicate changed nutritional habits. Large, flat clay plates (*comales*), which to this day are used to make tortillas, and

560 *Incense burner. Nebaj, El Quiche, Guatemala; Late Postclassic, 1200-1500 A.D.; clay, painted; H. 24.8 cm, dia. 23 cm; Guatemala City; Museo Nacional de Arqueología y Etnografía*

This Late Postclassic incense burner is painted in the "Maya blue" characteristic of the period and shows, at the front, a modeled figure wearing a diadem, ear spools, and a disc-shaped pendant around the neck. Realistic depictions of this kind on ceramics are typical of the Postclassic period in the Maya Highlands.

561 *The center of Cahyup', Baja Verapaz, Guatemala. Perspective reconstructiom drawing by Tatiana Proskouriakoff (1946)*
Situated on the eastern outskirts of the K'iche' sphere of influence, Cahyup' was the capital of the Rab'inal. The settlements, with twin temples and longhouses on the north and south sides of the central plaza, can be demarcated clearly from those of the K'iche'. Shortly before the Spaniards arrived, Cahyup' was the target of a Kaqchikel campaign of conquest.

562 *Chuwitinamit, Baja Verapaz, Guatemala. Perspective reconstructiom drawing by Tatiana Proskouriakoff (1946)*
The center is situated, as at many other archeological sites with finds from the Postclassic period, on a hill that can be defended easily. Along with the twin temple and the longhouses, the I-shaped ball court in the background is also characteristic of Late Postclassic architecture in the Highlands.

chili graters (*molcajetes*) remained unknown in the Highlands well into the Postclassic, and did not begin to appear until they were adopted as innovations of central Mexican origin. Whether or not the tortilla was eaten in the Maya area during the Classic is a moot point. Ceramic depictions from the Classic suggest, rather, that the Maya used maize to make small loaves of bread (*tamales*).

All Postclassic ceramics from the Maya Highlands are of local or regional origin (ill. 560). In the Early Postclassic, a new ceramic product was added, in the form of lead glaze pottery, which derives from the coastal area inhabited by the Nahua-speaking Pipil in the south-east of present-day Guatemala (ills. 566, 564). Central Mexican stylistic influences can be seen in occasional finds of vessels of bright orange-colored clay, delicately decorated with slip – the so-called fine orange ware – and in ceramics in the Mixteca-Puebla style (ill. 565).

Metalworking gave the Maya of the Postclassic a new skill that they had not had during the Classic. Gold and copper were worked, along with silver, zinc, and tin. The Maya used copper and gold to make jewelry such as necklaces (ill. 567), rings, ear flares, diadems, and lip plugs, which often deviate from Classic forms and are more like the jewelry that is common in central Mexico. Metal was also used to manufacture figurines, axes, discs, needles, and wire. A further innovation in the sphere of ritual artifacts was the use of small copper bells as adornments for dancers, and probably also for ornamenting figures of deities. The Postclassic was a time of conflict. Artistic depictions of warriors and gods of war, along with the skulls of sacrificed enemies displayed on wooden scaffolds, illustrate the importance of armed conflict. Finds of weapons of central Mexican origin suggest greater efficiency on the battlefield.

The spear-thrower (*atlatl*) first appeared in the Maya area during the Early Classic, but warriors now seem to have made greater use of it. They also used bows and arrows and wore combat clothing made of several layers of cotton steeped in brine to make it stronger, as protection against the enemy's arrows.

The Postclassic Maya Highlands were marked by persistent warfare and displacement. This can be deduced not only from the decline and temporary

563 *Zaculeu, Huehuetenango, Guatemala. View of the plaza with the main temple*
Zaculeu was the center of the Mam Maya in the Late Postclassic. It is situated in a high valley not far from the modern city of Huehuetenango. The site was excavated and lavishly reconstructed in the 1940s, with funds provided by the United Fruit Company.

absence of imported goods in the area, which in places wasn't very safe, but can also be seen in a new pattern of settlement, which was determined by considerations of defense. In the course of the Early Postclassic, the large Classic ceremonial centers, such as Kaminaljuyu in the Valley of Guatemala, or Chujuyub' in central Quiche, were abandoned everywhere in favor of smaller, fortress-like settlements located, with a view to defence on hills and elevated plateaus. In places such as Baja Verapaz, smaller valley settlements from the Classic continued to exist. They are characterized by the fact that, although they are located in valleys, their locations are strategically advantageous. Political centers on the other hand are, without exception, to be found on hill tops.

Wars brought the displacements of populations or the political integration of conquered regions by the victorious group. Many sites were abandoned, and in other areas, the patterns of settlement changed significantly.

The supremacy of the K'iche'

At the beginning of the Late Postclassic, the K'iche' people became the strongest of the Highland groups, and with their aggressive policy of expansion brought first the territories of their immediate neighbors, and subsequently almost the entire Highlands under their sway. In the Popol Wuj (the written source from the colonial era that describes, in the language of the K'iche', the creation of the world, the origins of the humans, and the history of the K'iche') the emerging power of the K'iche' and the appearance of central Mexican elements in their culture are given a mythological explanation. Like many other Mesoamerican ruling elites, the families of the K'iche' nobility justified their dominance in terms of the fact that their ancestors came from Tollan. Tollan was thought of as the mythological place of origin, where the gods were said to have created the founding fathers of the ruling dynasties. In central Mexican mythology, Tollan is the area settled by the Toltecs, who were revered as the bringers of culture, an ethnic group that probably actually existed and that was associated with economic prosperity and cultural wealth. To what extent distant ancestors of the K'iche' nobility really were of central Mexican descent is not known. The Popol Wuj also gives an account of new customs and religious ideas that the immigrant ancestors brought with them and, by means of war and conquest, forced on the indigenous population of the Highlands. The account goes on to say that they intermarried with local women and thus became the founders of the K'iche', Kaqchikel, Rab'inal, and Tz'utujil ethnic groups.

564 *Jug in the shape of a bird. Asuncion Mita, Jutiapa, Guatemala; Early Postclassic, 900-1150 A.D.; clay with lead glaze; H. 15.8 cm; Guatemala City, Museo Nacional de Arqueología y Etnografía*

The site at Asuncion Mita in south-west Guatemala was one of the centers for the manufacture of lead glaze ceramics, the only pottery in the whole of pre-Hispanic America with a genuine glaze. They are made from clays containing lead, and baked in closed kilns at extremely high temperatures.

565 *Jug from Mixco Viejo. Mixco Viejo, Chimaltenango, Guatemala; Late Postclassic, 1300-1500 A.D.; ceramic, painted; H. 27.5 cm; Guatemala City, Museo Nacional de Arqueología y Etnografía*

Mixco Viejo, a Postclassic center of a group of Kaqchikel Maya, is located in the immediate vicinity of modern Chinautla in Guatemala, where pottery is produced to this day. As regards color and decoration, the modern city differs hardly at all from its predecessors found at the neighboring Postclassic site.

According to this account, a confederacy of the three K'iche'-speaking groups Nimak'iche' (Great or Old K'iche'), Ilokab' (Watchman), and Tamub' (Drummer), were taken by the four founding fathers of the Nimak'iche' – B'alam Kitze', B'alam Aq'ab', Majukutaj, and Ik'i B'alam – to the Chujuyub' mountains in the central Highlands, where they fought and won the first battles for the K'iche' political supremacy. According to legend, the most important of these conflicts was the battle of Jakawitz – the legendary mountain that was believed to be the first place settled by the K'iche'. This battle, in which the three confederate K'iche' groups – Nimak'iche', Tamub', and Ilokab' – subjugated the previous population (described as "stag people"), served as a powerful and evocative myth. With their new weapons (bows and arrows, spear-throwers, and battle-axes), the K'iche' were superior to the indigenous population; bees and wasps helped them to defeat the enemy with their stings. Finally, the "stag people" surrendered and payed tribute to their new masters.

This mythological first K'iche' settlement at Jakawitz was believed to be the place from which K'iche' campaigns were launched by the ruler Tz'ikin against the Rab'inal in the east of the Chujuyub' and the Iqomaq'i in the Cubulco region. The K'iche' gradually evolved into a military power that aimed to subjugate other groups and exact tribute from them as vassals.

In the Popol Wuj, the success of the K'iche' in war is attributed to the superiority of their gods – Tojil, Awilix, and Jakawitz – in comparison with the deities of other Highland peoples. Prisoners and members of the defeated groups were sacrificed to Tojil, the god of thunder and lightning.

Once their supremacy in the Chujuyub' mountains seemed assured, the K'iche', four generations after the battle at Jakawitz, transferred their center of government some 15 kilometers (nine miles) south-west to Ismachi, not far from

567 *Gold necklace from a lord's tomb. Iximche, Chimaltenango, Guatemala, Burial 27-A; Late Postclassic, 1200-1500; L. 27 cm; Guatemala City, Museo Nacional de Arqueología y Etnografía*
Metalworking is a typical feature of the Postclassic. This goldsmith's piece of work, with jaguar heads and pearls, comes from the most elaborate lord's tomb at Iximiche. In addition to this necklace, the attire of the deceased included a diadem and a disc, also made of gold. The lord died of a fractured skull, possibly sustained in battle. Three of his servants were buried with him.

their later capital Q'umarkaj (Utatlan), near presentday Santa Cruz del Quiche. The three confederate groups of the K'iche' initially lived together in this strategically advantageous site. They steadily extended their area of rule under the leadership of the Nimak'iche', who came to the fore by means of a skilful alliance policy. But the dominance of the Nimak'iche' became a bone of contention between the confederate groups, and under the K'iche' leader Q'uq'kumatz, the community broke up. The Nimak'iche' took up residence in Qu'markaj, and proceeded to evolve into the most powerful of the K'iche' groups (ills. 570, 571). Traditional accounts suggest that the K'iche' rulers who exercised political power and military control within this area were descended from the ranks of the Nimak'iche'. Three of their ruling royal houses claimed to draw their authority from the K'iche' founding fathers: the Kaweq' from B'alam Kitze', the Nijaib' from B'alam Aq'ab', and the Ajaw K'iche' from Majukutaj. Qu'markaj, as the seat of the Nimak'iche', became the political center of an expanding sphere of influence. Situated on a plateau that was difficult to reach and accessible by only two paths (which were easy to defend), Qu'markaj was an near-impregnable fortress, where the members of the K'iche' royal houses, provided with food and goods by their vassals in the surrounding countryside, were safe from attack by their enemies (ill. 569).

THE SYMBOLS OF POWER THAT WERE GIVEN TO THE K'ICHE' IN CHIISMACHI

The following quotation lists a number of venerable ancient rulers' insignias belonging to the K'iche' royal houses. The text also records how the K'iche' royal houses originated when their forefathers departed from Tulan and finally settled in the Highlands.

Translated from: "El Titulo de Totonicapan" (Land Title of Totonicapan). Text, translation and comments by Robert M. Carmack and James L. Mondloch, Universidad Nacional Autónoma de México, Mexico, D.F. 1983, pp. 189f.

These are the symbols of power that came from where the sun rises, from the other side of the lake, from the other side of the sea: a small gourd, a drinking vessel, the eagle's talons, the jaguar's claws, the stag's head and legs, the flute, the drum, the great shawm, the bones of the eagle's wing, the finger bones of the jaguar, the snail, the wad of tobacco, the stag's tail, the bracelet, the heron's feathers, the black and yellow stones.

The lords used these symbols of rule, which came from where the sun rises, to pierce and cut up their bodies (for the blood sacrifice). There were nine mushroom stones for the Ajpop and the Ajpop Q'amja, and in each case four, three, two, and one staffs with the Quetzal's feathers and green feathers, together with garlands, the Chalchihuites precious stones, with the sagging lower jaw and the bundle of fire for the Temazcal steam bath.

There were 360 arrows and 540 lances.

When the four forefathers discharged their duties, their staffs of office were adorned with chopped armadillos.

All this occurred in Chiismachi at that time. And when they received their offices, they inaugurated the small power and created the small fame for themselves. The power of the four forefathers was less than that of the three great noble houses. Power was received and praised. Even so, the rule was still small here in Chiismachi, when the symbols of power were revealed, when K'okaib went to take these symbols to Jakawitz, the first place ....

The three groups of the K'iche' were united with one another: the Tamub', Ilokab', and Saqajib'. They were united because they all came from where the sun rises, from Tulan Siwan.

When this occurred in Chiismachi, there was as yet no copal resin or blood, copal of the child, blood of the child, mushrooms, green twigs, nor were there any burnt offerings. Nor were there as yet any slaves, nor the mother of the Xkakaq'ix bird, nor great burnt offerings, nor the Poq'ob' Chanal dance.

568 *Mushroom stones in the shapes of a man and a jaguar. L.h. figurine: provenance unknown, r.h. figurine: Kaminaljuyu, Guatemala City, Guatemala; Late Preclassic, 400 B.C.-250 A.D.; volcanic rock; r.h. stone: H. 36.9 cm, W. 16.2 cm; Guatemala City, Museo Nacional de Arqueología y Etnología*
As a means of intoxication, the Maya used selected species of mushroom containing hallucinogenic substances to produce pain and ecstasy when particular rituals were performed – for example when blood was drawn from sensitive parts of the body, or during ecstatic dancing. Mushroom stones in the shapes of men and animals were widespread in the Guatemalan Highlands during the Classic. The passage quoted from the "Titulo de Totonicapan" mentions the fact that, prior to the arrival of the Spaniards, mushroom stones were used by the K'iche' princes as insignias of power.

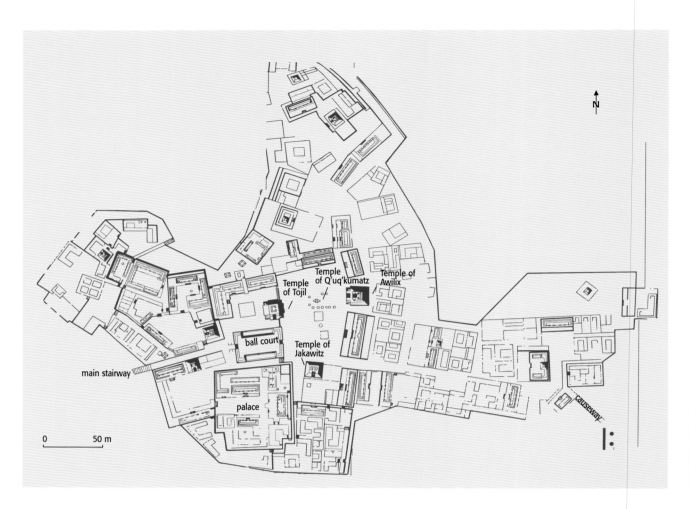

569 *Plan of Q'umarkaj. Utalan, El Quiche, Guatemala*
Situated on an almost inaccessible plateau, the Nimak'iche' center of government has a new impregnable fortress. The complexes of courts – consisting of a temple, a palace, and administrative buildings – are a typical feature. The site is known by both its K'iche' name Q'umarkaj, and its Aztec name Utalan, which it was given when the Spanish conquerors arrived with their Aztec-speaking auxiliary troops.

Temple of Q'uq'kumatz

Temple of Awilix

Temple of Tojil

ball court

Temple of Jakawitz

main stairway

palace

causeway

0   50 m

570 *The Temple of Tojil at Q'umarkaj. Steel engraving by Frederick Catherwood, 1841*
The engraving shows the remains of the temple of the god Tojil at the center of Q'umarkaj. When Catherwood and Stephens visited the former Nimak'iche' metropolis, close to the modern city of Santa Cruz del Quiche, it was the only building still standing.

In the first quarter of the 15th century, Q'uq'kumatz, the founder of Q'umarkaj and the eighth K'iche' ruler, launched a radical expansionist policy and subjugated all the neighboring population. He was succeeded as ruler by K'iq'ab, whose conquests, with the military support of the allied Kaqchickel, expanded the area of K'iche' rule to its fullest extent in the mid 15th century. By the end of his reign, the K'iche' controlled almost the entire Guatemalan Highlands and the western Pacific seaboard.

Collapse of power

K'iq'ab's program of colonization, and the sending of representatives of the royal houses to the conquered regions, necessitated the reorganization of society in Q'umarkaj. Being the greatest military power in the K'iche' bloc, the Kaqchikel were relieved of their vassal status, integrated as a social group into the power system, and given a capital city of their own at Chiawar Tz'upitaq'aj. Two sources from the colonial era, the "Land Title of Totonicapan" and the "Kaqchikel Annals," written in K'iche' and Kaqchikel respectively, record that by about 1470 certain vassals rose up in revolt against K'iq'ab' and had attempted to kill him. As a result of this revolt, the Kaqchikel left Q'umarkaj and Chiawar Tz'upitaq'aj to establish a political center of their own at Iximche (ill. 573).

After K'iq'ab's death, a period of permanent warfare and violent invasions began, the details of which can be discerned using sources from the colonial era. The K'iche' tried to put down the Kaqchikel in Iximche but were defeated by their former vassals – experienced fighters who killed many K'iche' and stole

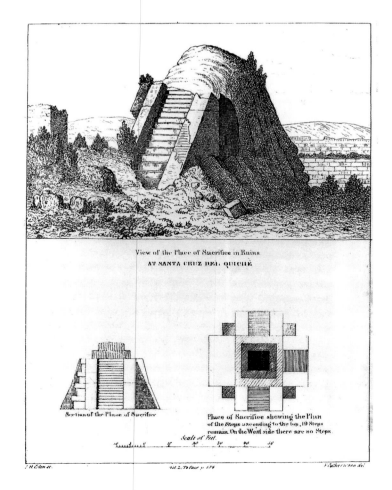

View of the Place of Sacrifice in Ruins
AT SANTA CRUZ DEL QUICHE

Section of the Place of Sacrifice

Place of Sacrifice showing the Plan of the Steps ascending to the top, 19 Steps remain On the West side there are no Steps
Scale of Feet

571 *The Temple of Tojil. Q'umarkaj, Utatlan, El Quiche, Guatemala; Late Postclassic, c.1250 A.D.*
The Temple of Tojil is still one of the few striking buildings in the Nimak'iche' capital. Hardly any archeological work has been carried out so far. For the K'iche' who live in the neigborhood, the place, which was built over a number of natural caves, is sacred. Ajq'ijaab (calendrical priests) make offerings in the caves and before the temples.

from them the divine image of Tojil. Deprived of their divine power, the K'iche' did not dare to attack the Kaqchikel again on their home ground. Hostilities also broke out between the K'iche' and Tz'utujil, culminating in a series of wars, in the course of which, at the end of the 15th century, the K'iche' regent Tekum, Ki'q'ab's son, was killed. More and more regions ruled by Q'umarkaj attempted to withhold payment of tribute, thereby compelling the K'iche' to obtain the commodities themselves by way of military expeditions.

One of these expeditions was launched against the inhabitants of Rab'inal – situated about 40 kilometers (25 miles) east of Q'umarkaj – and Cubulco. The people of Rab'inal had been the victims of numerous attacks by the K'iche' during the late Postclassic. The "Rab'inal Achi," a dance-drama from Rab'inal written in K'iche' tells of a pre-colonial territorial dispute between the Rab'inal and the K'iche'. (Charles Etienne Brasseur de Bourbourg (1814–1874), a Catholic priest and eminent collector of written records from the colonial era, wrote down the story in 1862 and published it in the same year). The issue in dispute was the illicit incursion of a warrior from the K'iche' royal house of Kaweq' into Rab'inal territory. He was taken prisoner, condemned, and finally executed. In an impressive speech, a Rab'inal warrior accuses the Kaweq' warrior of having made vassals and tribute-payers of his brothers and fellow K'iche' speakers:

Brave warrior of the Kaweq'-K'iche':
Then it is only you that I follow, only you
are my brother.
Indeed I lost my soul when I looked at you
in the great fortress.
But now you are the one
who howls like a coyote, a wildcat, an agouti, and a jaguar
in the great fortress.
You are the one who frightened the white children,
the one who drove us out of the great fortress,
so that they collect yellow and green honey,
food for my people and my revered Lord Job' Toj.

To what extent concrete historical events are recorded in this drama, and which of the disputes between K'iche' and Rab'inal is described here, remain questions for ethnohistorical research. It is, however, obvious that the theme is associated with this period of collapse of K'iche' supremacy.

K'iq'ab's advance to the border of Soconusco brought the K'iche' into contact with the area of Aztec rule. In the Postclassic, the Aztecs ruled over Soconusco and used it as a center of trade with the regions of southern Mesoamerica. In this way, elements of central Mexican culture spread far into the south of Mesoamerica. In 1510, as a result of the unstable political situation and the weakened position of the K'iche', Q'umarkaj was ordered to pay tribute to the Aztecs. The superior power of Tenochtitlan and the presence of Aztec traders, and perhaps also diplomats, in Q'umarkaj brought an end to the ongoing warfare in the Highlands, until the Spanish conquest.

The social system

The system of social and political organization of the region in the Postclassic (ill. 574) provides a key to understanding the developments that led the K'iche' first to achieve and then to lose supremacy over the Highlands. The smallest political unit in the Postclassic Highlands was the *chinamit* (Nahuatl: "bounded location"), that is to say a district along with its inhabitants. They were all subjects of the same royal house, and defined themselves as a community in these terms. Their relationship with the royal house, whose name they used, was one of fictitious kinship. Within the *chinamit*, society was divided into two social strata: nobles or princes (*ajaw*), and the common people or vassals (*al k'ajol*).

The nobles made up the actual royal house, which constituted itself by reference to the paternal line of descent. They occupied the political and religious offices and acted as military leaders. In Q'umarkaj, the members of the highest royal houses of the Nimak'iche' held the most important political offices. The ruler (*ajpop*) and his chosen successor (*ajpop k'amja*) came from the ranks of the Kaweq', the supreme judges (*q'alel*) were provided by the Nijaib' and the Saqik, and the speaker (*atzij winaq*) was a member of the royal house of Ajaw K'iche'. The chronicler Zorita records that the officials of the K'iche' were

572 *Sculpture in the shape of a serpent's open jaws. Mixco Viejo, Chimaltenango, Guatemala, ball court;* Postclassic Central Mexican stylistic elements, such as this sculpture in the shape of a serpent's open jaws at the ball court in Mixco Viejo, are regarded as characteristic innovations in the Postclassic architecture of the Maya Highlands. This architectural sculpture is built into the side wall level with the middle of the ball court, and probably marked a line that was important for the game.

573 *View of the palace of Ahpo Sotz'il. Iximche Chimaltenango, Guatemala*
The palace of Ahpo Sotz'il was the seat of the ruling house of the Kaqchikel. The original court complex with the central altar was built in three stages. A residence comprising several groups of courts was later built over it. This may possibly reflect the splitting up of the Sotz'il dynasty into several *chinamit* (lines of descent).

chosen according to ability, and that parentage was not the sole decisive factor. The princes lived at a fortified location with stone architecture (*tinamit*) and received tribute from their vassals. The social rank of a warrior was initially reserved for the nobility, but in the course of time, due to the need for increased military capacity, it was also granted to vassals. In addition to the two strata mentioned, the sources give information concerning other social groups: slaves (*munib'*), agricultural serfs (*nima'q achi*), traders (*ajb'eyom*), and craftsmen (*ajtoltekat*).

While the social strata within the *chinamit* cannot be identified with certainty, the fortified locations with their particular patterns of settlement shed some light on the interrelationships of the various royal houses. Their designation as *nimja*, "great house," is derived from the large administrative buildings that can be identified as a basic component of typical K'iche' groups of courts. This is based on the assumption that a group of courts – comprising a temple, a palace, and a longhouse used as an administrative building – was the seat of a royal house. Accordingly, settlements such as Ismachi or Q'umarkaj, where there are a large numbers of such groups of courts, must have been the seat of various royal houses allied by marriage, constituting a political unit to which the *chinamit* was subordinate.

Again and again in the history of the K'iche', new groupings emerged within the royal houses. As a result of splits and political divisions between the four mighty houses of Q'umarkaj, Kaweq', Nijaib', Ajaw K'iche', and Saqik, 24 principalities had come into being by the beginning of the colonial era. As political representatives of a *chinamit*, the royal houses were more likely to be linked with other *chinamit* groups by way of marriage and military alliances than by common settlement with a confederate *nimja*. Using sources from the colonial era and the descriptions of buildings that they contain, it is possible to assign particular districts in the city of Q'umarkaj to the four highest Nimak'iche' royal houses. For example, the only ball court for the ritual ball

game in Q'umarkaj is located in the sector of the Kaweq', who are described as the most important of the Nimak'iche' rulers.

Allied royal houses not only constituted, as *chinamit* alliances, a united sphere of power, but also joined together in an *amaq'*, which is variously translated as either "tribe" or "people." The confederate groups of the Nimak'iche', Ilokab', and Tamub' each formed an *amaq'*, and were called K'iche *winak*, "K'iche' people." It appears that in the Postclassic, ethnic and linguistic boundaries were not identical to the boundaries of political units. People identified themselves primarily on the level of the *amaq'*, not in terms of a common language. The political landscape of the time thus presents a picture of extensive fragmentation.

The social system described here provides an explanation for both the origins and the collapse of K'iche' rule. With the *chinamit* as the smallest political unit, with a royal house able to enter flexibly into alliances with another *chinamit* in order to exercise military and territorial control, the Postclassic Maya Highlands show a social organization that enabled the Nimak'iche' to expand their own political power steadily throughout the Highlands. Relationships by marriage between the royal families of the K'iche' and the houses of conquered or allied *amaq'*, along with the dispatch of representatives of the K'iche' royal houses to subjugated territories, created a system of hegemonic rule. Notwithstanding the rebellions and the secessions at the end of the 15th century the system remained, for large parts of the Highlands, an integrating force that lasted well into the colonial era.

574 *Diagram showing the social and political organization of the K'iche' as reconstructed by Robert Carmack*
This reconstruction of the still little-known political and social structure of the K'iche' is based primarily on ethnohistoric documents. The smallest political unit was the *chinamit*, "bounded location." A royal house descended from one of the K'iche' groups ruled over a number of *chinamit*. Together, these groups made up the K'iche' people. But there was also direct contact at *chinamit* level with the royal houses of the Kaqchikel.

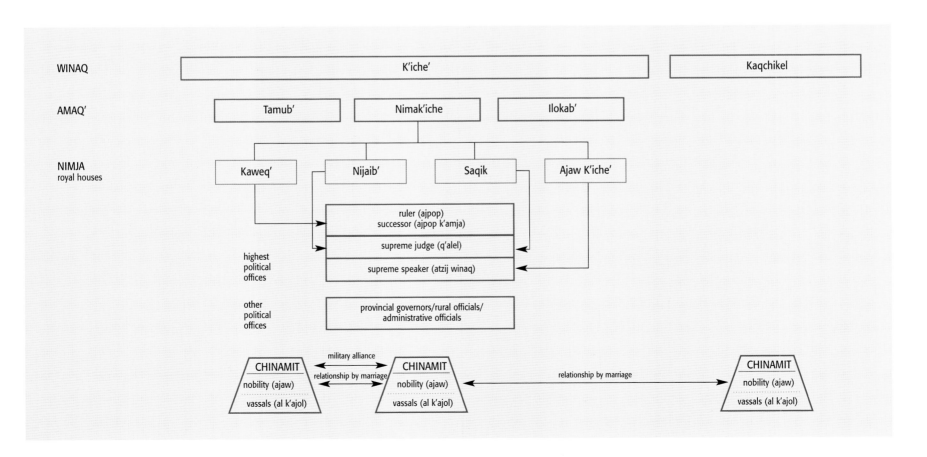

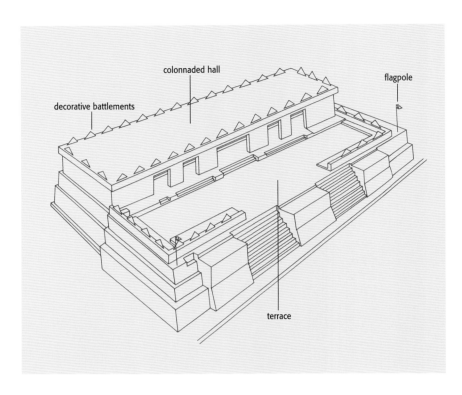

decorative battlements

colonnaded hall

flagpole

terrace

575 *A palace at Q'umarkaj. Perspective reconstruction drawing*
The palaces at Q'umarkaj, and probably many other locations in the Guatemalan Highlands, were built on raised platforms reached by open stairways. On the platform there was a forecourt adjoined to the actual living quarters. Wide entrances are characteristic of late Postclassic buildings. There appear to have been battlements on many of the roofs, which had a decorative function but also indicated that the occupants belonged to a particular line of descent.

577 *The first page of the Popol Wuj. c. 1700; H. 26 cm, W. 16 cm; paper, Chicago, Newberry Library*
The two-column copy of the sacred book of the K'iche', with a Spanish translation, was compiled by Father Francisco Ximénez in Chichicastenango at the beginning of the 18th century. The original text in the K'iche' language is no longer extant.

576 *Twin temples. Mixco Viejo, Chimaltenango, Guatemala; Postclassic*
Twin temples were one of the architectural innovations of the Postclassic. The idea of erecting two parallel buildings on the same platform originated in central Mexico. The best known example is the Templo Mayor in Mexico City, the central temple site of the Aztec capital Tenochtitlan. It was dedicated to two deities, the Aztec chief god Huitzilpochtli, and the regent god Tlaloc.

The issue of outside influences on the culture of the Highland Maya

The issue of the central Mexican influence, as seen in the cultural innovations of the Postclassic (ill. 572), is crucial to the evaluation of Postclassic Maya culture. This influence is particularly strong in architecture and the production of ceramics. Curiously, it is ceramics, along with some architectural features specific to the Highlands, that show a clear cultural continuity with the Classic. If Postclassic changes were triggered off by immigration, as the Popol Wuj tells us, it can only have been a matter of a few small groups settling in the Highlands introducing cultural innovations, but to a large extent conforming to the indigenous culture. An influx of foreign groups, speaking foreign languages, would inevitably be reflected in some way in the languages of the Highlands. If the K'iche' languages – K'iche', Kaqchikel, and Tz'utujil – are considered from a philological point of view, there are about 80 words that were taken from Nahua back in the pre-Hispanic era. Most of these terms relate to matters of political organization: religion, warfare, food and fruit growing (*chocola*, "cacao"), household goods, and animal species. To what extent these borrowed terms did in fact arise from an influx of other groups, or whether they were merely adopted as a result of contact with Nahua-speaking peoples, is a controversial issue. If there had been an influx by a new ruling class, one would have to suppose either that a larger number of Nahua terms would have been borrowed than happened in this case, or that the royal houses retained their own language and did not abandon it in favor of the languages of the vassals they had subjugated. If this is taken into account, and bearing in mind the close affinity of the K'iche', Kaqchikel, and Tz'utujil languages, it would appear more realistic to assume that new terms were taken over from Nahua by the Maya, than to imagine the migration of an entire linguistic community.

According to sources from the colonial era, it was small groups of warrior princes who migrated into the Highlands in the 10th and 11th centuries and founded the K'iche' branch of the Maya peoples. Migration sagas, such these, are nowadays seen by scholars as mythological narratives and cultural conventions rather than as historical chronicles in the western sense.

Outside influences on religion

As regards the religion of the Postclassic Highland Maya, the appearance of new kinds of temple building, skull scaffolds, and the increased practise of cremation, suggest changes in religious ideas. But these changes are not so radical that they need to be explained as the result of an influx of foreign groups importing the pantheon of central Mexican gods. In fact, as far as the realm of religious ideas of the Postclassic Highland Maya is concerned, a clear continuity with the Classic can be demonstrated. Some artifacts used in religious ritual, such as incense burners for example, changed their outward form but continued to be used in the same contexts.

The principal source concerning religion in the Postclassic Highlands is the Popol Wuj, the first part of which gives an account of the creation of the world and the human race (ill. 577). Elements of creation mythology, and accounts of the adventures of the Hero Twins Junajpu and Xb'alanke in their struggle against the underworld, are some of the themes that appear in the artistry of Classic vase painting. Other topics, such as the cult of the sacred bundles – in which ancestors' bones are kept and revered – and the wearing of heads as trophies, have often been categorized as Postclassic Highland innovations. But there is evidence that they may date back as far as the Classic accounts of the Lowland Maya. The god Tojil, who according to the Popol Wuj was worshipped by the Postclassic K'iche', occupied a similar position at the end of the Classic and in Postclassic Yucatan, where masks of the Rain God Chaak adorned the façades of buildings everywhere.

It can now be stated that although the Postclassic Highland Maya did indeed adopt some features of central Mexican religion, such as their accounts of Xipe Totec (a god of human sacrifice) and Quetzlcoatl (Q'uq'kumatz, the "feathered serpent"), their religious ideas and myths were, to a large extent, the same as those of the Classic, and have survived to the present day.

This continuity in many cultural spheres clearly indicates that the foreign influences, of which there is some evidence, were a cultural reorientation of Highland society rather than an influx of Nahua-speaking groups. The Postclassic in the Maya Highlands was an era of change, not of cultural hiatus brought about by an influx of alien groups.

THE COLONIAL ERA

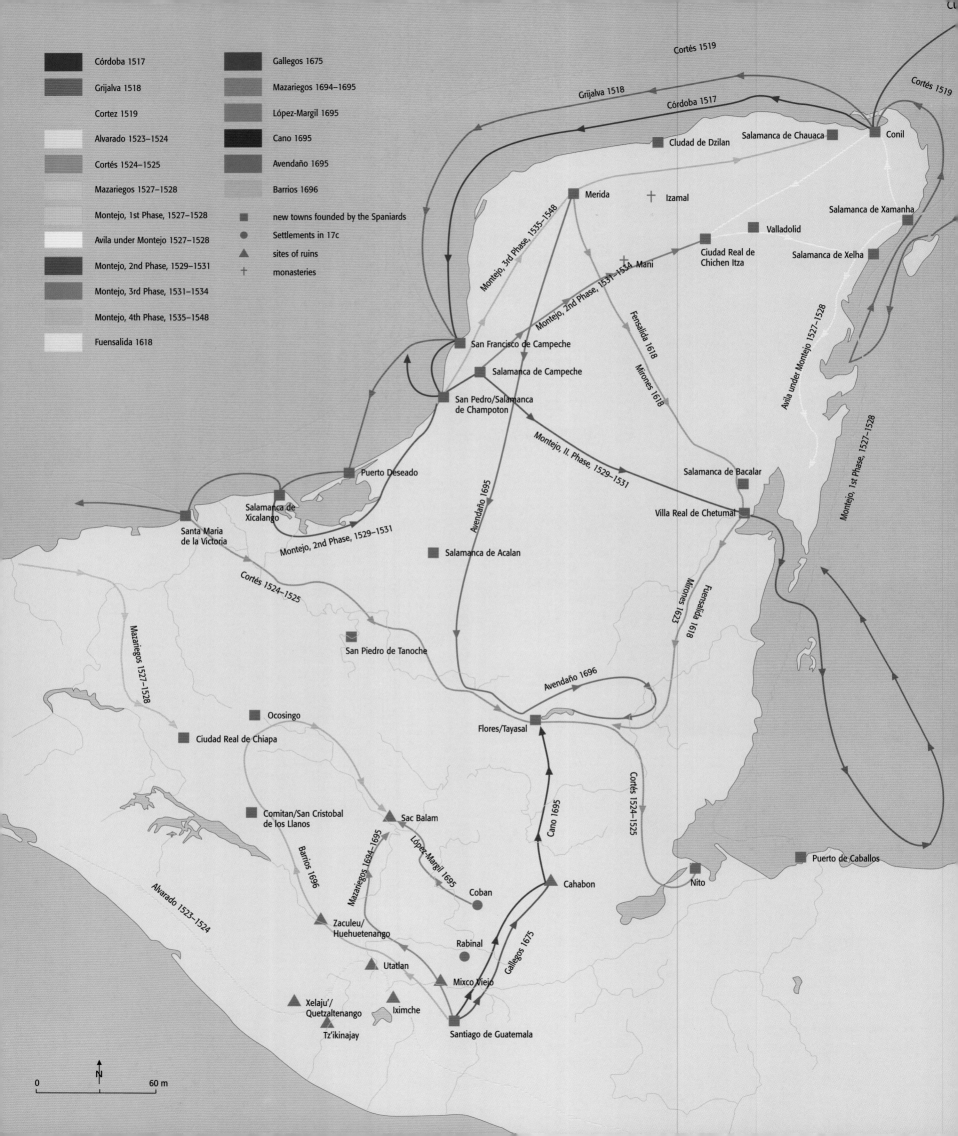

Legend:

Córdoba 1517
Grijalva 1518
Cortez 1519
Alvarado 1523–1524
Cortés 1524–1525
Mazariegos 1527–1528
Montejo, 1st Phase, 1527–1528
Avila under Montejo 1527–1528
Montejo, 2nd Phase, 1529–1531
Montejo, 3rd Phase, 1531–1534
Montejo, 4th Phase, 1535–1548
Fuensalida 1618

Gallegos 1675
Mazariegos 1694–1695
López-Margil 1695
Cano 1695
Avendaño 1695
Barrios 1696

■ new towns founded by the Spaniards
● Settlements in 17c
▲ sites of ruins
† monasteries

Map labels:

Cortés 1519
Grijalva 1518
Córdoba 1517
Conil
Cortés 1519
Cortés 1519
Salamanca de Chauaca
Ciudad de Dzilan
Salamanca de Xamanha
Merida
† Izamal
Valladolid
Ciudad Real de Chichen Itza
Salamanca de Xelha
Montejo, 3rd Phase, 1535–1548
Montejo, 2nd Phase, 1531–1534
† Mani
Fensalida 1618
Mirones 1618
Avila under Montejo 1527–1528
Montejo, 1st Phase, 1527–1528
San Francisco de Campeche
Salamanca de Campeche
San Pedro/Salamanca de Champoton
Montejo, II. Phase, 1529–1531
Salamanca de Bacalar
Avendaño 1695
Puerto Deseado
Villa Real de Chetumal
Salamanca de Xicalango
Santa Maria de la Victoria
Montejo, 2nd Phase, 1529–1531
Cortés 1524–1525
Salamanca de Acalan
Mirones 1623
Fuensalida 1618
Mazariegos 1527–1528
San Piedro de Tanoche
Avendaño 1696
Cortés 1524–1525
Ocosingo
Flores/Tayasal
Ciudad Real de Chiapa
Comitan/San Cristobal de los Llanos
Sac Balam
Cano 1695
Puerto de Caballos
Barrios 1696
Mazariegos 1694–1695
López-Margil 1695
Nito
Coban
Cahabon
Alvarado 1523–1524
Zaculeu/Huehuetenango
Rabinal
Gallegos 1675
Utatlan
Mixco Viejo
Xelaju'/Quetzaltenango
Iximche
Tz'ikinajay
Santiago de Guatemala

0   N   60 m

THE SPANISH CONQUEST OF YUCATAN AND GUATEMALA IN THE 16TH AND 17TH CENTURIES

Christian Prager

The discovery, conquest, and colonization of the American continent from the 16th to the 18th century and the conversion of its original inhabitants to Christianity by missionaries of the European great powers Spain, Portugal, England, and France, had a distinct influence on the modern view of the world, and have for centuries stimulated the imagination of artists and scholars alike (ill. 579). The history of the conquest of Latin America shows that political and economic preconditions were similar in all regions and that occupation followed, to a large extent, the same patterns. Charters granted by the queens of Spain and Portugal, giving full authority to conquer and colonize unknown countries, allowed the conquistadors to equip military expeditions, which were for the most part financed by private funds and loans. Individual conquistadors often turned to groups of wealthy people, asking them to meet a large part of the costs of a voyage of exploration and conquest. As a rule, the wealth of the conquistadors was increased by sharing out booty and territory, exploiting unpaid labor, and accumulating the wealth thus obtained, so that in most cases the debts could be speedily repaid.

Even if the initial contact between the indigenous population and the Spaniards was often peaceable and marked by curiosity and mutual interest, the conquistadors' expeditions generally led to war, looting, the destruction of towns and villages, and the enslavement and massacre of the indigenous population. The conquerors' success did not depend solely on the soldiers' iron resolve and technological superiority, but also on the level of civilization of the subjugated culture. Only the colonization of people at a high level of cultural development promised real spoils.

The members of the indigenous ruling houses were obliged, in the end, to yield to military force and they gave up the role of leadership to the Spaniards. This control was then imposed on the indigenous peoples with extreme ruthlessness by the introduction of profitable economic systems, as in the case of the *encomienda*. Countless names of people and their experiences during the conquest of the New World fill thousands of pages in books. The following account can therefore give only a brief survey of the occupation of the Yucatan peninsula and Guatemala by the Spaniards in the 16th century.

577 *The ruins of Tulum on the east coast of Yucatan*
By virtue of its strategically advantageous location directly by the sea, the Maya city of Tulum on the east coast of Yucatan attained great importance in the Postclassic as an entrepôt and port of call for the numerous traders who plied vigorous long-distance trade in Mesoamerica. To this day, lavish buildings and numerous mural paintings bear witness to the former splendor and wealth of this site.

578 *The most important expeditions of conquest in the 16th and 17th centuries*
The map of the Yucatan peninsula shows the routes taken by the Spaniards along the coast and on the mainland in their journeys of exploration and conquest in the 16th and 17th centuries. Control of the northwest of the peninsula was an important goal, which was pursued from 1527 onward but not formally achieved before 1548. The almost inaccessible regions in the center of Yucatan were not brought under their rule until the mid or late 17th century. Parts of Chiapas and the Highlands of Guatemala, in contrast, were "pacified" by around 1530.

579 *Map dating from 1587. From: Abraham Ortel, Ortelius Theatrum Orbis Terrarum. 1587*
This map from the atlas compiled by the Flemish cartographer Abraham Ortel (1527–1598), who was famous in his day, shows the New World as it was thought to be about 100 years after its discovery by Columbus.

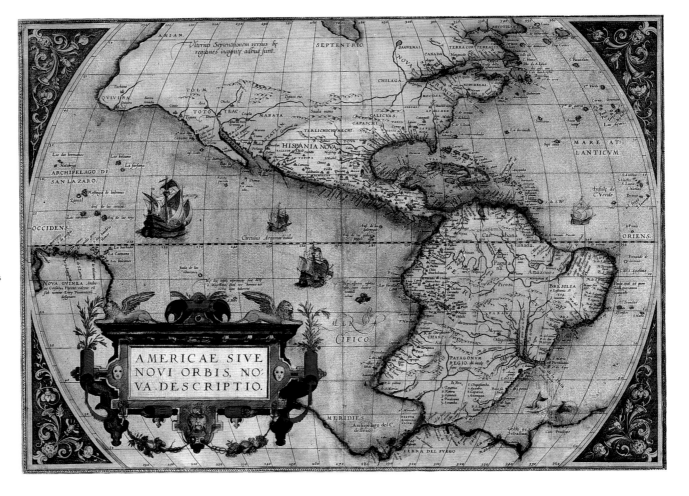

580 *Christopher Columbus (1451–1506)*
The seafarer who was born as Cristofero Colombo in the Italian port of Genoa in 1451, is regarded by historians as the discoverer of America. Between 1492 and 1506, he made four journeys by ship, during which time he kept a diary. His notes have been lost, but extracts are contained in the detailed biography written by his son Fernando in 1537–1539. Columbus was the first European to make contact, in 1502, with the Maya of Yucatan.

581 *Juan de Grijalva (1480–1527)*
Grijalva took part in the conquest of Cuba in 1511 with his uncle Diego Velázquez. Following the initial exploration of Yucatan by Francisco Hernández de Córdoba in 1517, colonialists in Cuba organized a second expedition to the same destination and commissioned the 38-year-old Grijalva to lead it. Grijalva returned to Cuba without much gold, but was able to report that there was an empire further to the north that was said to possess large quantities of the coveted metal.

Period of contact and the first phase of conquest (1502–1529)

One of the earliest contacts between Europeans and the people of Yucatan was the meeting between Christopher Columbus (1451–1506) (ill. 580) and a group of traders from the province of Maia. According to Hernando Columbus, Christopher's son, the meeting took place in 1502 off the coast of Yucatan, which at the time had not been discovered.

A few years later, in 1511, a Spanish expeditionary ship in search of slaves and gold capsized off the east coast of Yucatan. Only a few of the those on board survived, two of them being Gerónimo de Aguilar (1489–1531) and Gonzalo de Guerrero (died 1536). Together with the other survivors from the ship, they were captured by a Maya ruler and destined to be sacrificed. The two men managed to escape shortly before the sacrificial ritual, but were captured and enslaved by another Maya cacique, "village chief." In the years that followed, they became integrated into the indigenous society. In 1519, Aguilar joined Hérnan Cortés (1485–1547), who was exploring Yucatan and searching for the seamen from the shipwreck at the same time. Aguilar entered Cortés' service as an interpreter and informant, but Guerrero remained with the Maya, became the leader of their army, and successfully directed insurrections and battles against the advancing Spaniards.

Credit for discovering the Yucatan peninsula for the Spanish crown must go to the Spanish seafarer Francisco Hernández de Córdoba (1475–1518), who in 1517, coming from Cuba in search of precious metals and slaves, was driven off course by a severe storm and landed on its north-east coast. There, while exploring the north coast in the direction of Campeche, he encountered a hitherto unknown civilization. Córdoba's expedition took him beyond Campeche to Champoton, where he was ferociously attacked by the Maya people, badly wounded, and compelled to flee.

Rich colonialists in Cuba, among them Pedro de Alvarado (1485–1541) (ill. 583), the later conqueror of Guatemala, heard of the newly discovered country called Yucatan and put up money from their own pockets for a second expedition under Juan de Grijalva (1480–1527) (ill. 581) in the hope of acquiring great wealth. Grijalva explored the east coast of the country as far as Bahia de Ascension, and led his expedition back as far as the Laguna de Terminos on the west coast of Yucatan, where jewelry made of gold and turquoise was presented to the Spaniards – merchandize from the empire of the Aztecs (ill. 584), which was as yet still unknown but which promised great treasures.

Fired by Grijalva's enticing reports, a series of wealthy colonialists in Cuba financed a third expedition to Yucatan. In February 1519, 11 caravels with 500 men on board set sail for Yucatan under the command of Hernán Cortés

Spaniards in the empire of Mexico, and now hoped to benefit from the presence of the Spaniards in their struggle against the K'iche', by accepting the rule of the Europeans and agreeing to support them in the conquest of Guatemala. In 1522, Cortés sent reconnaissance detachments of his Mexican allies to the southern frontiers of the Maya area in the province of Soconusco (the present-day Mexican federal state of Chiapas), and learned of revolts and unrest. Thereupon, he sent his lieutenant, Pedro de Alavrado, to Guatemala with orders to pacify the region and make it subject to the Spanish crown. Alvarado set out from Tenochtitlan on December 6, 1523, with a large number of Spanish and indigenous troops. Following an old indigenous trade route, he arrived on January 12, 1524, in Tehuantepec in the province of Soconusco, where he encountered resistance for the first time in the region around Tonala. Alvarado managed to defeat the Mam Maya attackers and he pressed onward with his troops along the coast in a south-easterly direction. The Spaniards, with their central Mexican allies, crossed a mountain pass to the north of Zapotitlan, and finally reached the K'iche' city of Xelaju'. The city had been abandoned by its inhabitants, enabling the Spaniards to take it without a struggle. But in the meantime, thousands of K'iche' warriors assembled and attacked the Spanish and Mexican troops from all sides. Alvarado succeeded in repelling the Maya attack and killing or capturing many of the leaders.

The K'iche' did not, however, immediately accept defeat, despite the fact that one of their most important leaders, Tekum Umam, had been killed by the Spaniards in the clashes. Cunningly, the K'iche' secretly incited other Maya tribes to fight against the Spanish conquistadors. At the same time, the rulers of Xelaju' and other cities offered themselves up as loyal subjects and friends of the Spanish, and invited them to Utatlan, the present-day Santa Cruz del Quiche.

589 *Portrait of Bartolomé de Las Casas (1474–1566), Bishop of Chiapas*
Las Casas denounced the brutal treatment of the indigenous population by the conquistadors. This priest demanded that an end be put to the physical and material exploitation of the indigenous peoples by the Spanish colonial masters, and that slaves from black Africa be used as labor. His intervention resulted in an expansion of the slave trade.

590 *Spanish troops under Pedro de Alvarado attack and massacre the Maya population. Colored copperplate engraving; from: Theodorus de Bry, "America pars quinta", Frankfurt 1594*
There are documents to show that Pedro de Alvarado (1485–1541) was twice called to account before a court of law in Spain because of his brutality toward the indigenous population of the New World. Bartolomé de Las Casas (1474–1566) denounced, in numerous writings and letters, the cruel treatment of the indigenous peoples by the Spanish conquerors, and gave particular emphasis to Alvarado's cruelty. According to Las Casas, Alvarado had some four million people murdered. This figure may seem like a gross exaggeration today, but Alvarado's brutal behavior in the Highlands of Guatemala is confirmed by the trial records.

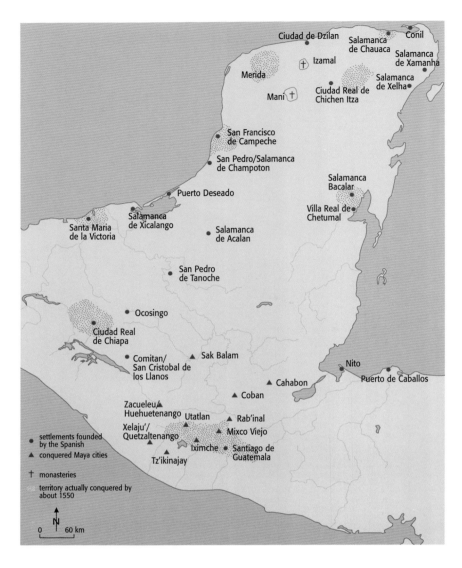

591 *Map showing the territory controlled by the Spaniards at the end of the 16th century*
In about 1548, after the last major revolt by the Maya against the new masters from Europe had been quelled, the Spaniards formally controlled the north of the

Yucatan peninsula. But by the end of the 16th century, only a few areas were officially recognized as being under their control. The map shows those regions that, at that time, were inhabited and administered by the Spaniards.

the land, the Spaniards and their allies had captured their city. The leaders of the defeated forces offered to be loyal subjects and pay tribute to the king of Spain. Alvarado's triumph over the ostensibly impregnable Tz'iknajay nipped in the bud any resistance on the part of neighboring villages and towns. Their leaders accepted Spanish authority, and it was possible to bring the area south of Lake Atitlan under control without a struggle.

After returning to the Guatemalan Highlands, Alvarado founded, on July 25, 1524, the first Spanish capital of Guatemala in Iximche, the former capital of the Kaqchikel Maya. This was not, however, destined to prosper (ill. 592). In his insatiable greed for gold, Alvarado demanded tribute in the form of gold and other valuables from the subjugated and allied Maya rulers. While Pedro de Alvarado was in Honduras, his brother Gonzalo took draconian steps against the indigenous inhabitants of Iximche that were not immediately willing to comply with Alvarado's demands, and killed many members of the ruling class. In 1526, the Kaqchikel – former allies of the Spaniards – rebelled against their oppressors, but were eventually forced to yield to their superior power. Notwithstanding their victory, the Spaniards left Iximche and, on November 22, 1527, established a new city at the foot of the Agua volcano, called Ciudad Vieja, which was buried beneath an avalanche of mud and rubble when the volcano erupted 14 years later.

Alvarado and his men are regarded by historians of Guatemala as ruthless adventurers in search of whatever wealth they could find. Twice, in 1527 and 1536, according to court records, Alvarado was obliged to justify his cruel behavior toward the indigenous peoples before a court in Spain. The monk Bartolemé de Las Casas (1474–1566) (ill. 589), famed for his intervention on behalf of the indigenous population, accused the conquistadors of the gravest crimes. According to Las Casas, Alvarado killed some four million indigenous people between 1524 and 1540. With a crucifix in one hand and a bible in the other, Las Casas and his fellow monks openly argued that the indigenous populations should be subdued and converted to the Christian faith by peaceful means.

It remains a historical fact that Pedro de Alvarado left far bloodier traces in his conquests, and set less store by negotiation than did Montejo the Younger in Yucatan. From our present-day point of view it can be seen that Alvarado was skilled in warfare and a good tactician, but a poor politician. Montejo the Younger, by contrast, can be seen to have been a soldier with political sensitivity and a skillful negotiator.

Alvarado and his men marched into Utatlan, but soon began to suspect an ambush and escaped to safety at the last minute. In the ensuing battle, Alvarado had two high-ranking members of the K'iche' nobility taken prisoner and burned. In order to overcome the last resistance of the Utatlan K'iche', Alvarado set fire to the city, and with his indigenous allies, who included Kaqchikel Maya, carried out attacks on other villages and towns in the area. By April 11, 1524, the region was basically under control and the K'iche' had been made subject to the Spanish crown, enabling Alvarado to devote himself to the conquest of the other parts of the country.

The Kaqchikel had offered the Spaniards an alliance, and had energetically contributed to the subjugation of the K'iche', described above, because their territory was already part of the area controlled by the Spaniards. Alvarado and his troops, agreeing to a proposal put forward by the Kaqchikel, set about "pacifying" another arch-enemy of the Kaqchikel, namely the Tz'utujil Maya, whose fortified capital of Tz'iknajay was situated on an island in Lake Atitlan and connected to the mainland by bridges. The inhabitants were taken by surprise by this assault, and before they could demolish these connections with

The conquest of Chiapas (1524–1527)

As in Guatemala, there were a large number of Maya peoples living in the province of Chiapas, including the Tzotzil, Tzeltal, and Lakandon; and the Chiapanek, who did not speak a Mayan language. When the Spaniards arrived at the beginning of the 16th century, the Maya peoples lived in autonomous regions, and intervened again and again in the struggle for supremacy in Chiapas. The territory formally belonged to the Spanish colonialists in Coatzacoalcos. After the *encomienda* had been introduced, the colonists were given the right to demand tribute from the indigenous inhabitants.

When, in 1522, the Chipaneks refused to pay tribute, Captain Luis Marín, on the orders of Hernán Cortés, launched a punitive expedition in 1524 against the "rebels," who were at that time the most influential ethnic group in Chiapas, even exacting tribute from their own Maya neighbors. With the aid of these Maya, who had allied themselves with the Spaniards and who saw an opportunity of taking action against their indigenous enemies, Marín eventually succeeded in quelling the "revolt" and ostensibly subjugating the inhabitants of Chiapas without the use of force. However, one of Marín's soldiers, acting without orders, tried to extort gold from the Chamula Maya. Failing to achieve this to the hoped-for extent, he killed their cacique. The Chamula thereupon refused to accept the authority of the Spaniards, thereby compelling Marín to take military action against them.

Despite his military resources, the captain did not manage to subjugate the area once and for all and establish a permanent Spanish presence in Chiapas. At the beginning of 1527, Captain Diego de Mazariegos was ordered to crush another revolt in Chiapas and to found a Spanish city there. With his troops and indigenous auxiliaries from central Mexico, he followed the same route that Marín had taken three years previously. At the Sumidero Canyon (ill. 593) to the north of Tochtla, the present-day Tuxtla Gutierrez, there was a military confrontation with the Tzotzil Maya, the so-called "Battle of Sumidero." The Tzotzil Maya fought ferociously against the resolute and well-equipped soldiers and their Mexican allies. In the course of the fighting, the Spaniards drove a group of 2,000 people, including women and children, to the edge of a steep cliff terrace above the River Grijalva. In their anguish, they threw themselves into the river, choosing death over Spanish enslavement. This mass suicide was the most extreme extent of indigenous resistance, while at the same time marking the end of the period of conquest in Chiapas.

The establishment of a permanent Spanish presence in Ciudad Real, the present-day San Cristobal de las Casas, marked the beginning of the colonial era in Chiapas. By strengthening their presence in the region, the Spaniards eventually succeeded, in 1695, in subjugating the Ch'olan Maya, bringing the whole of Chiapas under their control. Following the conquest of the Itzaj Maya in 1697, the tropical Lowlands and the Highlands were subject to Spanish administration – 195 years after the first contact between the Maya and the Spaniards (ill. 591).

KANEK' – THE LAST KING OF THE ITZAJ MAYA

Temis Vayhinger-Scheer

from Merida, Avendaño and his missionaries reached the shores of Lake Peten-Itzaj at midday on January 14, 1696. There, they waited to be ferried across to the place where, in 1623, during the previous attempt to carry out missionary work, a friar of the order, along with many companions, had been killed by the Itzaj. Avendaño reported:

"Over 80 canoes came, full of indigenous people in warpaint and battledress, with huge quivers of arrows. But they were all lying down in the canoes. They all shielded and accompanied their king, who came on land with an escort some 500 strong to receive us. They took us on board with the utmost eagerness, paying no attention to the playing of shawms with which we awaited him ... They cast loose immediately and went out with us onto the lake, which must have been about three *leguas* (more than 12 kilometers [seven-and-a-half miles]) wide at that point ... Suddenly, the king mentioned above placed his hand on my heart to see whether I was afraid, and asked me that same question. I was, on the contrary, very glad, because I could see that my desires were to be fulfilled and that my laborious journey was bearing fruit. I replied:

The Itzaj were among the last independent Maya in the southern Lowlands of the Yucatan peninsula. Two hundred years after the first meeting between Europeans and Maya, they were still managing to preserve their own way of life, their political organization, and their religion. Again and again, they had held off Spanish visitors and missionaries, even repelling them by force at times. The jungle, with its hot, humid, tropical climate and numerous swamps formed a natural barrier, which, especially during the rainy season, provided effective protection from potential invaders. According to sources from colonial times, the supreme representative of the Itzaj Maya was King Kanek', who lived on Noj Peten in the middle of Lake Peten-Itzaj, in what is now Guatemala (ill. 594). Military action against Kanek' began in 1695 with a large-scale road-building project initiated simultaneously from the north and the south. The driving force behind this project came from the Basque interim governor of the province of Yucatan, a man by the name of Martín de Ursúa y Arizmendi who had considerable political and economic influence.

This political context dictated the timing of a mission led by Basque-born Franciscan Father Andrés de Avendaño y Loyola who was born November 13, 1657 and baptized after 1705. Avendaño tried to reach Noj Peten before the soldiers and other priests. By way of credentials and as propaganda for his monastic order, the Franciscan sent the interim governor, Ursúa, an important eyewitness account of his meeting with Kanek' (ills. 595, 597). After marching for a month

594 Aerial photograph of Flores, Peten, Guatemala
This photograph shows the almost circular island of Flores, seen from the south-east. On the left the San Benito spit can be seen, top center the islet of Santa Barbara, and on the right the Tayasal peninsula. A traffic-bearing causeway some 500 meters in length links Flores with Santa Elena on the southern mainland. In central Peten, between the Usumacinta rivers and San Pedro in the west and Mopan and Belize in the east, there is a complex of lakes extending for about 100 kilometers. Lake Peten-Itzaj is the largest of these lakes, which were formed from hollows in the Yucatan karst. Their water level is subject to considerable fluctutation.

595 Map of the area around Lake Peten-Itzaj. From: Fray Andrés de Avendaño y Loyola, Relación de las dos entradas que hice a la conversión de los gentiles ytzáex, y cehaches; manuscript, after 1696
In 1695, the Franciscan monk Avendaño went to Lake Peten-Itzaj as a missionary. His account includes a sketch of Noj Peten showing the location of the lake between the Spanish province of Yucatan in the north and the Audiencia of Guatemala in the south. In addition to the route taken by the monk and his escort, the map shows the roads that were built from both directions during that year but which, according to Avendaño, failed to meet. The uncolonized area between them is described as *Prospero*. The map also gives the names of various indigenous groups living in this area.

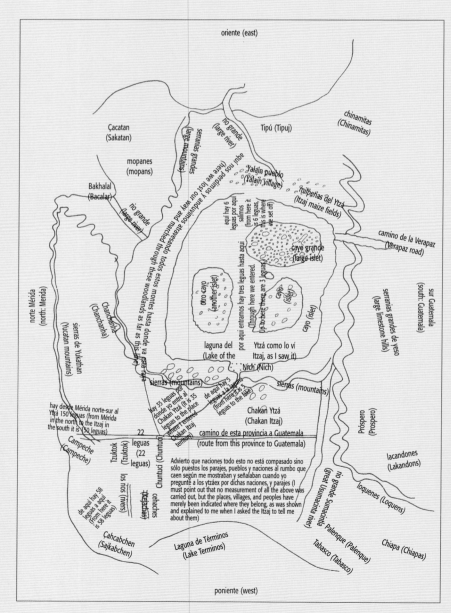

596 *Flores, view from Santa Elena*
The residence of the Itzaj ruler Kanek', on the present-day island of Flores, is located in the southern basin of Lake Peten Itzaj. On the east side of the main plaza, which occupies the highest point of the island, is the whitewashed church with its twin-tower façade, visible from afar. The Tayasal peninsula can be seen in the background. The provincial capital of Peten, at 36,000 km², (13,900 square miles), is the largest department in Guatemala, and is a favorite starting point for tours to Tikal and the other archeological Maya sites in the area.

'Why should my heart be uneasy? On the contrary, it is very glad. For I am the happy man who fulfils your prophecies, according to which you must become Christians ....'"

On the island, Kanek' performed the belated formal welcome of his guests. In an antechamber of his house, he had the maize drink *posole* given to them, to the lively interest of the inhabitants. Following this, Avendaño, speaking on behalf of his province and of the interim governor Ursúa, attempted to persuade the assembled Maya elite to embrace the Catholic faith and submit to the Spanish crown. The Maya asked for time to consider this request. But Avendaño was impatient. That same night, he attended an assembly of Maya priests and urged them to come to a decision. Kanek' answered on behalf of them all. He explained his hesitation in terms of his lack of familiarity with baptism. Eventually, the following morning, Kanek' gave the missionary permission to baptize the first of a total of 300 children.

Avendaño soon realized, however, that his enterprise was encountering far greater resistance from other quarters. Kanek' was not a sovereign monarch as the concept was understood in Europe. As the baptismal ceremony was being performed, the cacique Kowoj and other Maya warriors arrived on the island from nearby. Their opposition to the top Itzaj ruler and the priest broke out immediately. By his own account Avendaño was able, thanks to Kanek's support, to negotiate with the two Maya factions a waiting period of four months before the adults were baptized. In a kind of secret memorandum, Kanek' declared himself willing to

yield the area under his rule, on the condition that his political opponents, led by the cacique Kowoj, were removed by Ursúa.

It is hard to interpret these agreements because, at the end of December 1695, in Merida, an Itzaj delegation led by Aj Chan, Kanek's nephew, speaking on behalf of his uncle, declared their surrender and were baptized. These events raise questions. Were the Maya, faced with a military threat, adopting delaying tactics, and merely pretending to cooperate? Were Kanek' and Aj Chan looking for an ally in order to gain or retain power? Kanek was probably guided by both these considerations.

The agreement that was eventually reached was put in question the very same night by the cacique Kowoj. More and more Maya became openly critical of Kanek'. The Itzaj ruler's control over his subjects threatened to slip from his grasp. Outwardly, too, he appeared to be collaborating with the imperial power – he wore the Spanish uniform sent him by Ursúa, which must have looked absurd to the Maya! Kanek' warned the missionaries of a murder plot: his opponents wanted to prevent news of the agreement and knowledge of the missionaries' route from reaching the approaching detachment of road builders, or even getting through to Campeche or Merida. On the night of January 16, 1696, despite his wife's resistance, the Itzaj ruler took his guests to the eastern end of the lake. On their way back, they were deserted by their Maya guides and lost their way in the jungle. They failed to reach Tipuj, which was a journey of about 12 days. One of Avendaño's

companions died of exhaustion, and the others barely escaped starvation. When, shortly after Avendaño's escape, the Itzaj engaged a detachment of troops from the north in battle, and killed all the members of a Guatemalan expeditionary force, hope of a peaceful resolution vanished. Ursúa, who in the meantime had formed an alliance with the diocesan church, had a small galley built. After early morning mass, as day broke on March 13, 1697, the order to engage was given. Canoes filled the lake. The aggressors were met with a hail of arrows. On Noj Peten too the Maya fought for their independence. But they could not withstand the Spaniards, and eventually abandoned their island city and tried to swim to the mainland. The island was captured, and by the evening the soldiers had completed their destruction. In July 1697, Kowoj was shot for instigating a conspiracy. Kanek' was handed over to Ursúa by his nephew Aj Chan and taken to Santiago de Guatemala, in present-day Antigua, where he was placed under house arrest. His residence at Noj Peten was known as Flores from 1831, and is today part of the capital, of the same name (ill. 596). Most Itzaj perished or died of Spanish diseases, after being resettled in the cold Highlands. Today, there are 500 remaining Itzaj in two small locations on the north shore of Lake Peten. They cling to their language and culture, refusing to succumb to the overpowering Spanish culture.

597 *First MS page of Avendaño's "Relacíon," with its elaborate title page*
Along with the older genres of *historia* and *crónica*, the genre of *relación* came into being on the Iberian peninsula in the 15th century. This term, which is also a legal concept, comes from the Latin *relatio* and means report or narrative. The "Relación" is the only extant piece of writing by Avendaño. A contemporary copy may be found today as MS No. 1040 in the Ayer Collection of the Newberry Library in Chicago. The actual text is preceded, before Folio 1, by an elaborate title page with basic information concerning the venture.

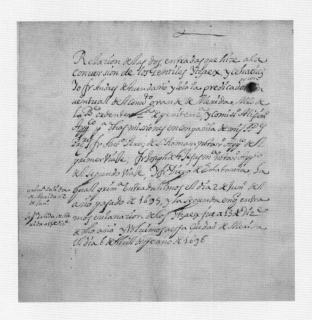

BETWEEN CONFORMITY AND REBELLION –
THE MAYA SOCIETY IN THE COLONIAL PERIOD (1546–1811)

Antje Gunsenheimer

In the conquerors' wake – the new political order

The Spanish conquest of the Maya area, and its subsequent administration as a colony, entailed for the Maya, as for all other peoples on the American continent, dramatic changes in their way of life. Following the end of the conquest (1546), the colonial power established itself by introducing Spanish administrative bodies and Christianizing the population. These political and religious changes were accompanied by new economic and social arrangements. Maya reaction to this upheaval ranged from resignation to insurrection, and was as diverse as the Maya area itself.

After the conquest had been concluded, it was initially the responsibility of the leaders of the expeditions to secure the areas concerned in both military and political terms. The transition to systematic colonization was accomplished by means of the institution of the *encomienda*. This allowed the landowner, the *encomendero*, to demand tribute and forced labor for themselves from the inhabitants of one or several villages, or of an entire region. The right of *encomienda* was granted for life as a reward for special achievement during the conquest. It soon developed, however, into a hereditary right. The *encomendero* undertook, for his part, to live in the area, secure it from military attack, and protect and Christianize the inhabitants.

Following disputes with the offspring of the first conquerors over land ownership and claims, the Spanish crown created a system of administration that was intended to help avoid large-scale land ownership overseas from becoming out of control. Between 1529 and 1559, a system of territorial administration by executive officials, based on the Spanish model, was developed. To prevent abuse, officials were appointed for fixed periods and were subject to regular checks. The system of administration was structured in hierarchic groups of organizations. The supreme authority was the Consejo de Indias ("Council of the Indies"), which was based in Spain. It was directly accountable to the king and responsible for the regulation of all matters. In the colonies, *audiencias* were created, which were courts of appeal constituting the supreme authority, headed by the viceroys of the various provinces. The viceroy deputized for the Spanish monarch, and had the corresponding rights and powers. The area of Maya settlement came under the authority of the province of New Spain and the Captaincy General of Guatemala (ill. 599). At regional level, this system of administration provided for the appointment of royal officials by the viceroy. They were made responsible for government and the administration

of justice in the indigenous communities. On the level of municipal administration, known as *cabildo*, the Maya enjoyed a high degree of administrative autonomy. Each village and town had a *cabildo* consisting of four public offices, namely governor, judge, councillor, and notary. Only the notary was paid a fixed salary. All offices, except for that of governor, could be staffed by more than one official (ill. 599). The officeholders had duties in various areas. To begin with, the demands of the Spanish authorities had to be met, for example the provision of runners for the system of posts and communications. Furthermore, they were responsible for the punctual delivery of tribute to the Spanish crown, consisting of fabrics, maize, beans, wax, turkeys, salt, pepper, and earthenware. They had to organize compulsory labor and were also responsible for settling legal disputes, keeping records of all local affairs in an archive, and for the maintenance of public institutions (village plaza, church, prison, guest house, and roads). This form of organization remained in force, with only minor changes, until about 1750.

599 *The hierarchy of offices in the Spanish overseas territories at the beginning of the 17th century*

King of Spain

Council of the Indies

officials of the Spanish crown — viceroy and/or captain-general and governor — church

regional authorities — audiencia — provincial governor — bishop

local administration — encomendero — corregidor or alcalde Mayor — priests

gobernador — local civil/religious offices

local indigenous authorities — Spanish cabildo — cabildo: alcaldes regidores — cofradia offices

clerk/notary — maestro cantor

→ authorized to issue instructions

- - - → authorized to issue instructions in particular matters

.... theoretical influence on bishop

598 *The monastery of San Francisco. Antigua, Guatemala; colonial era, early 17th century*
In the colonial era, Antigua was the intellectual and religious heart of Central America. It was well known as a city of churches and monasteries built in the plateresque baroque style that was typical for Spain at that time. As early as 1541, the newly founded city was destroyed by a volcanic eruption and an earthquake. It was rebuilt, but was struck once again by an earthquake in 1773.

599 *The hierarchy of offices in the Spanish overseas territories at the beginning of the 17th century*
Following the Spanish conquest, a system of administration for the new territories had to be developed. To begin with, the *Consejo de Indias* ("Council of the Indies") was established. The Council's instructions were issued to the viceroys or governors. At local level, the Spanish crown decided to transfer the model of Spanish municipal administration to the individual villages.

FRANCISCO DE MONTEJO'S CRUELTY TOWARD THE MAYA OF YUCATAN

Bartolemé de Las Casas, later Bishop of Chiapas, appealed to the Spanish crown for humane treatment of the Maya and called for an end to slavery. Although he often exaggerated his figures and accounts of events, the Spanish crown did concede certain rights to the indigenous peoples.

Translated from Bartolemé de Las Casas: "A brief account of the devastation of the West Indian lands."

In 1526, another cruel man was appointed as governor of the province of Yucatan, because he reported falsehoods to the King and made mendacious proposals. All tyrants there, as a rule, have acted in this way right down to the present day, in order to be appointed to office and receive orders enabling them to plunder with impunity ....

This barbarian, with the 300 men that he had with him, began by waging war in the most savage manner against the good, innocent people who lived peaceably in their dwellings and did not the slightest harm to anybody, and caused a large number of them to be murdered. Because this land contained no gold – for if he had found only a single piece of gold he would have sent them into the mines, where they would in any case have perished – he decided to transform these people, for whom Jesus Christ gave his life, body, and soul into gold. Accordingly, those that he did not kill, he made into slaves, down to the last man. And because wherever people got wind of slaves, there were plenty of ships available, he had the ships heavily laden with slaves and traded them for wine, oil, wine vinegar, bacon, items of clothing, horses – in a word, whatever he or his companions needed ....

In this empire, or this province of New Spain, Francisco Montejo was accustomed from time to time to catch rabbits and other such game with his dogs. One day he could not find anything to hunt, and his dogs seemed to him to be hungry. So he snatched a little boy from his mother, cut off piece after piece from the boy's arms and legs with his dagger and shared them out between the dogs. When they had devoured these pieces, he threw the little body onto the ground for them to eat up together. It can be seen from this how mercilessly the Spaniards have behaved in these lands, the very opposite of the purpose for which God sent them there, and how little respect they have for those human beings whom God also created in his image and for whom he shed his blood.

600 *Killing of indigenous peoples. From: Theodorus de Bry, "Ad Urbe Novo"* Theodorus de Bry, who himself never went to America, left a voluminous, lavishly illustrated work on the discovery and conquest of the entire American continent. In it, he accused the Spanish conquistadors of cruelty. Not having seen the New World for himself, he relied on letters, verbal reports, and writings about colonial rule, including those of Las Casas on the destruction of the West Indian lands.

Old and new elite

The new political system favored the old elite class of Maya society (ill. 601). The Spanish crown accorded native lords the rank of Castilian noblemen. Men from these elites were allowed to bear the title of Hidalgo and to be addressed as Don, while the women of the nobility were addressed as Doña. These titles entailed exemption from all taxation; Spanish intention was to obtain, as quickly as possible, the cooperation of the former masters of the land.

Something that made it easier to establish this system was the fact that various offices of the *cabildo* clearly corresponded to particular pre-colonial offices of Maya society. The title of governor, for example, is often also given as *batab* or *jalach winik* in contemporary documents. These were the names of leading political offices within the Maya society of Yucatan, carrying powers that clearly corresponded to the responsibilities of the Spanish governor. The office of councillor was seen as the equivalent of the pre-colonial *aj kuch kab*.

The fortunes of an indigenous noble family in the colonial era can be seen in the case of the Pech family. When the Spaniards arrived, the Pechs ruled over several settlements on the north-west coast of the Yucatan peninsula, in the province bearing their name, Ceh-Pech. During the conquest of Yucatan, they joined the Spanish side at an early stage and accepted conversion to Christianity. A strategy that was obviously successful. The *cabildo* documents of the Ceh-Pech region show that, in 1567, members of the Pech family held the office of governor in 21 out of 25 villages. In the 17th and 18th centuries, the Pechs are likewise known to have occupied the office of governor in the villages of Yaxkukul, Ixil, Motul, Chuburna, and Chicxulub. They were able to maintain their elevated status for many generations. Social and political prestige led, not least, to economic prosperity – in the village of Ixil, the Pech family owned by far the largest amount of land.

According to guidelines laid down by the Spaniards, officeholders in the *cabildo* were supposed to be re-elected annually. However, existing documents, such as those from the Yucatan village of Tekanto, give inadequate information as to who was entitled to vote. It seems to have been the village notables who, so to speak, elected themselves.

By cooperating with the Spanish colonial masters, Iskin Nijaib', a K'iche' Maya from Momostenango in Guatemala, was able to maintain his political and social position in both systems. Only a short time after the conquest, he had himself baptized and was given the name of Francisco Vico. He made great efforts to bring the people who had fled from the Spaniards back to Momostenango, and to expedite their Christianization. In Momostenango, he was appointed as the indigenous governor, with privileges such as the right to bear the title of Don and to carry a sword and wear Spanish clothing. The crown arranged for him to be accorded all pre-Hispanic rights within Maya society. He was assured of acknowledgment by the K'iche' population by being appointed their supreme leader (ill. 605).

The land of turkey and honey

The economic situation in the colonial era is easier to understand if a brief look is taken at the pre-Hispanic era. As can be gleaned from statements made by the inhabitants of Yucatan in about 1580, they produced maize, beans, and various vegetables, and they bred turkeys. Beekeeping and the production of honey were also an essential part of the economy, and large quantities of textiles were woven. For the most part, these products were for personal use and given as tribute to the local *batab*. The cotton needed for weaving was obtained by

barter in Xicalango on the Gulf of Campeche, in Bacalar, or in Nito on the Caribbean coast. In these places, there were central exchanges to which traders came from distant regions, even from the Aztec metropolis Tenochtitlan, to barter for products such as cacao, cotton, precious stones, and birds' feathers. In the Postclassic, slaves were a further, very important, trading commodity. Some of them came from central Mexico and were then sold to the Maya in Xicalango. Commodities introduced by the Spaniards, such as tools, beasts of burden (horses, mules, asses, and oxen), and other useful animals (chickens, goats, sheep, pigs, and cattle) were rapidly accepted by the Maya people. But this did not bring about a complete change in their patterns of production. Methods of agricultural cultivation in Yucatan have scarcely changed to the present day. Attempts to grow cereals for Spanish consumption failed because the climate, with its long dry season, proved unsuitable. Cattle breeding, on the other hand, was adopted with increasing success by indigenous fraternities (*cofradías*). They produced meat for the markets of the city dwellers of Merida and Valladolid. In the Guatemalan Highlands, a new branch of economy developed with the introduction of sheep. Both the Maya and the Spaniards succeeded in producing wool, and markets were regularly held for its sale.

601 *Family tree of the Xiu family. MS page dating from 1557; Cambridge Mass., Tozzer Library, Harvard University*
In 1557, with the intention of legitimizing their claim to the city of Uxmal and its surroundings before the new

Spanish masters, members of the princely Xiu family had a family tree sketched. It identified them as the legitimate successors of the legendary founder of the city, Hun Uitzil Chac Tutul Xiu, seen here reclining in front of his wife.

602 *"Mestizas yucatecas" – Yukatek women's costume.*
Engraving by Désiré Charnay, from: "Les anciennes villes
du nouveau monde," 1885
Women's costume in Yucatan consists, to the present
day, of a white petticoat (*pik*) and a chemise-like outer
garment (*iipil*), also white. Today, these are usually
made of a light cotton fabric. The length of the petticoat
varies between knee-length and calf-length, and the
outer garment is usually knee-length. The hem of both
garments is adorned with wide bands embroidered
with colorful floral patterns. In the case of more
elegant clothing, there is also a lace inset. The square
neckline is likewise adorned with braiding of this kind.
A wide silk shawl draped loosely over the shoulders
completes the costume.

603 *Sisal hacienda in Yucatan, 19th century*
Numerous abandoned sisal haciendas are to be found in
the north-west of the peninsula. It was not until the 19th,
and especially the 20th, century that sisal became the
"Yucatan gold" that was exported worldwide. But sisal
agave had been grown before this for the manufacture of
ropes and woven fabrics. The export of sisal brought
great wealth to Yucatan, but the profit went exclusively
to the plantation owners descended from old Spanish
families, not to the Maya, who were compelled, under a
form of serfdom, to provide life-long forced labor on the
huge plantations. Many of the luxurious haciendas were
abandoned after the Mexican revolution (1910–11), but
today they are being rediscovered and refurbished as
hotels and museums.

604 *Page from the Chilam Balam. Kaua, Yucatan,*
Mexico; colonial era, 19th century; preserved in Merida,
private collection
In the 19th century, several collections of Yucatan texts
came into the hands of scholars. Because of their
similarities, as regards themes and content, they were
given the generic designation of "Chilam Balam books,"
because the first manuscript of this kind to be found
bears the title "*el libro del Chilam Balam*" (The book
of Chilam Balam). The nine books that have been
discovered so far are identified by their provenance.
The drawing shown in the illustration is taken from
the Chilam Balam book of the village of Kaua (near
Valladolid). This manuscript, which probably came into
existence at the beginning of the 19th century, shows
particularly clearly the profound influence of Spanish
culture on the Maya, who, for example, took over the
European signs of the zodiac.

The sufferings of the conquered

Conquest always entails the seizure, by force, of land and of people, who are inevitably exposed to violence from their conquerors. In this respect, the Spanish invaders were no different from any other conquering armies. Any resistance was suppressed by force. Exorbitant demands in almost all areas of life made slaves of the conquered peoples (ill. 603).

A far greater misfortune for the entire population was caused by the diseases that were brought into the area by the Europeans; these included influenza, smallpox, measles, and scarlet fever. They were unknown on the American continent prior to contact with the Europeans, and during the first decades of colonization they caused epidemics on a large scale. It is estimated, for example, that, in the first 50 years following the conquest, Momostenango lost as much as 70 percent of its inhabitants as a result of imported diseases. In Yucatan as a whole, the population dropped by an estimated 2.3 million to less than half a million people. Whole villages were devastated by influenza or smallpox epidemics, and were abandoned by the few that survived. Further scourges follwed, resulting in the drastic decimation of the population, and taking effect right into the late colonial era. Disease, the occasional absence of the rainy season, and plagues of locusts constituted a disastrous combination, leading to widespread epidemics and fatal catastrophes.

New crafts and traditional division of labor

Fundamental changes to the Maya way of life were also brought about by new crafts introduced by the Spaniards: they became ironsmiths, goldsmiths, silversmiths, tailors, milliners, shoemakers, candlemakers, and soap boilers. Members of the indigenous population were allowed to learn and practise any of these crafts. This gave them the opportunity to acquire a respected position in Maya society by virtue of economic success, regardless of family background, and thus move up in the social hierarchy. In her will, the dressmaker Pasquala Matu, who died in the Yukatek village of Ixil on August 25, 1766, left a house with a plot of land and two wells, along with a total of 40 items of mens' and womens' clothing, to her heirs – her husband, four sons, and two daughters. In terms of the social and economic conditions under which the Maya lived in the 18th century, Pasquala Matu was a wealthy woman.

The craftsmen were not, however, permitted to join the Spanish guilds. From this it can be inferred that they produced goods predominantly for the indigenous market, as the example of Pasquala Matu also shows. The collection of clothes that she left in her will suggests that she probably made clothes exclusively to meet the demands of her fellow Yukatek Maya: trousers, belts, and shirts for the men; dresses, petticoats, and blouses for the women, such as are still worn today (ill. 602).

From the patterns of inheritance, it can be seen that the sphere of womens' work was predominantly in and around the domestic holding. They wove fabrics, cooked, looked after the children, bred animals, such as pigs and poultry, and tended the kitchen garden and the fruit trees in the vicinity of their house. The sphere of men's work comprised the production of timber, honey, and wax, and farming. Married couples were, therefore, separate producers but joint providers. The fabrics that the women produced, and the animals they reared, were also sold by them. Weaving in particular was of central importance, because textiles were the principal goods rendered as tribute to the Spanish crown. Any surplus production could then be sold on the home market.

Christianization: ancient religion in a new guise

Missionary activity began as early as 1519, with the expeditions of the conquistador Hernán Cortés, who during his sojourn on the island of Cozumel, had the first baptisms performed. Franciscans, Dominicans, and Augustinians – without exception mendicant orders – accompanied the expeditions of conquest or followed in their wake (ill. 606). In the years that followed, the orders rapidly established themselves in the newly conquered regions (ill. 608) by founding dioceses and monasteries (ills. 610, 611). The Franciscans in particular came in large numbers, and proved to be tenacious in their missionary efforts. This helped them to achieve rapid success within the first 30 years and to occupy a pre-eminent position in the process of Christianization.

At first, the missionaries tried to impart Christian teaching by way of particular gestures and ceremonies, such as making the sign of the cross, blessing with the hands, and kneeling in front of the cross. Later, when they had learned to speak the indigenous languages and were able to write them down using the Roman alphabet, they were able to translate teaching primers, catechisms, and the texts of sermons into the particular languages in question. An efficient way of steadily propagating and establishing Christianity was to build schools for the children of the nobility. People trained in this way were to act as role models for

606 *Allegory of the Spanish conquest and Christian mission. Copperplate engraving from: "Rethorica Christiana," Perugia 1579*
The ship with a crucifix as its mast is an allegory illustrating the close connection between the conquest and missionary work. Annexations were carried out in the sign of the cross. Indeed, the justification given for the expeditions of the conquistadors was not the hegemonic interests of the Hapsburg court. On the contrary, they were proclaimed as crusades to spread the Christian faith. The religious sanctioning of force and subjection was no different from the Maya's divine legitimation of wars.

605 *Diego Vico. Lienzo in the church of San Vincente Buenabaj, El Quiche, Guatemala; colonial era, 1st half of the 17th century*
Diego Vico was the most important indigenous cacique in Momostenango in the Guatemalan Highlands in the first half of the 17th century. His elevated social position was the result of his political activities and his economic prosperity, based on cattlebreeding. He donated, among other things, a silver chalice to the church of San Vicente Buenabaj, which can still be seen there today, along with his portrait.

the rest of the population and provide a new generation of lay preachers, helping to offset the chronic shortage of missionaries from the motherland (ill. 607).

In their own literature, the Chilam Balam books, the Maya described the change to the new religion as a change of clothes because, from their point of view, Christianization was associated with a compulsory dress code that required men to wear shoes, trousers, and shirts (ill. 604).

Missionary activity did not, however, bring about the complete loss of old religious ideas. Many indigenous people began to combine the newly learned tenets of the Christian faith with their own original religious traditions. Diego Vico (1595–1675), a K'iche' Maya and descendant of Iskin Nijaib' (ill. 605), encouraged the building of churches and monasteries in his native Momostenango. In his own home, however, he had a traditional altar set up, at which he performed the ancient ceremonies of the K'iche' Maya. Contemporary rumor in Momostenango had it that Diego Vico possessed a pre-Hispanic idol: a statuette of a double-headed black bird of prey. Those who envied him claimed that Diego owed his economic success purely to the protection of this *qab'awil*, "idol." It was not only in Central America that the Catholic clergy used the Inquisition to combat these "heretical" tendencies. They did not, however, succeed in completely suppressing the various local forms of religion.

607 *A Franciscan preaching to an indigenous audience. Copperplate engraving, from "Rethorica Christiana," Perugia 1579*
The Franciscan order took over the entire Yucatan peninsula for its missionary work, and would not tolerate any other order beside themselves. Further south, however, in Chiapas and Guatemala, Dominicans and Jesuits were also active, the latter especially in the northern Highlands of Guatemala. Even in the first five years, however, the claim to a monopoly, as regards the conversion of the Yukatek Maya, led to a shortage of monks and priests. In order to improve the situation, the Franciscans campaigned throughout Europe, in letters and other writings, for more friars from the order to be sent out. They also soon began to train indigenous lay preachers who, as *maestros cantores* (masters of the liturgy), assisted the Franciscans who were active in the villages.

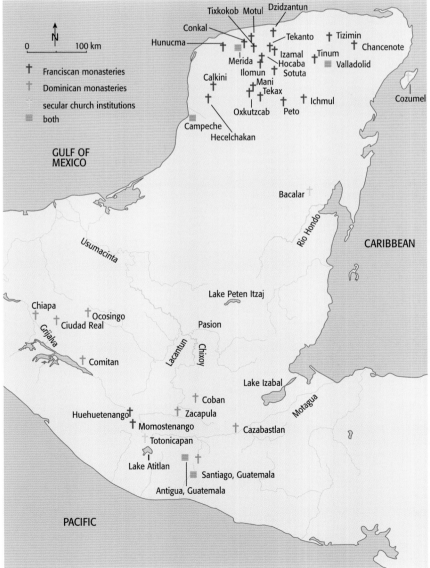

608 *Missions and centers of settlement in the Maya area in about 1600*
To begin with, Franciscans and Dominicans played a particularly prominent part in the spread of Christianity. The distribution of missionary and settlement centers shows the difficulty and precariousness of exploiting the conquered regions. In Yucatan, the Spaniards could regard their dominance as secure only in the north-west and on the coast. The inaccessibility of the still largely unknown territory in Chiapas and Guatemala led to the establishment of the first central missionary posts on the banks of rivers.

609 *"El Koche." Painting by Bernard Lemercier taken from a painting by Frédéric Waldeck; 1838; Mexico City, Fomento Cultural Banamex*
Sedan chairs were the favorite means of transport on the Yucatan peninsula during the colonial era. On impassable territory, where rocks and tree roots made it impossible to build straight roads, and where tropical downpours left deep holes full of mud, the Spaniards had themselves transported on sedan chairs carried on the shoulders of four Maya. The Maya word for sedan chair, *k'och*, was bowdlerized by them into *Koche*.

Rebellions

Adaptation was not the only reaction of the Maya to the conquest and occupation of the territory in which they lived. Quite the contrary: in no other region of Mesoamerica did as many insurrections occur as in the Maya regions.

The series of rebellions began in 1546, with an uprising in the east of the Yucatan peninsula. In this sparsely populated area, Maya groups from Cupol, Cochua, Sotuta, and Uaymil-Chetumal formed. They attacked and killed the few Spanish settlers. In retaliation, the ageing conqueror Francisco Montejo sent his son and his nephew off with troops from Campeche to march in an easterly direction. They eventually succeeded in quelling the insurrection and driving the Maya out of the occupied areas, which included the towns of Valladolid and Chetumal. The ringleaders were condemned to death by burning, but eventually pardoned following a plea by the Franciscan father Villalpando. In the Highlands of Chiapas, religious movements led, in the years 1708 to 1713, to unrest and finally to a bloody rising against Spanish rule. Its starting point was the emergence of religious cults involving saintly visions. For example, while working in the fields in the autumn of 1711, the Tzotzil Maya Dominica López

from Santa Marta had a vision of the Virgin Mary, who asked her for a solid house at the place where she had appeared. The Virgin Mary was allegedly seen repeatedly, with the result that more and more people became followers of her cult. Worship of the Virgin Mary became a self-sufficient phenomenon. The Tzotzil built a chapel and organized large-scale festivities to which pilgrims came from far and wide. Both the Spanish authorities and the church, which had lost control of these developments, suspected the existence of pagan rituals and banned the worship. Cults of this kind sprang up in the Tzotzil communities of Zinacantan, Santa Marta, and Chenalho. These movements were soon crushed by means of the persecution and suppression of their followers.

It was a different matter with the Tzeltal-speaking community of Cancuc. In May 1712, a young woman by the name of María de la Candelaria had a vision of the Virgin Mary in a small village outside Cancuc. The cult developed in a very similar manner to that in Santa Marta. It was condemned by the church, but this led to secession from the Catholic Church. The followers of the cult decided to have their ceremonies performed exclusively by indigenous curates, which was forbidden by the rules in force at the time. To counter the sanctions that were expected from the Spaniards, a number of settlements joined forces. Tension between the two camps – the allied Maya communities and the Spaniards – who began a buildup of arms, finally culminated when the Maya attacked the city of Ciudad Real de Chiapas. The struggle lasted until the middle of 1717, but eventually the government troops gained the upper hand and were able to disperse the cult and its host of followers. Whether the rebellion in Quisteil in Yucatan (1761 to 1762) was a genuine insurrection or merely a failed attempt to prolong a village festival, is still the subject of debate by scholars. When a Spanish trader refused the request of drunken men for more alcohol, he was fatally wounded in a scuffle. The rumor rapidly spread that the Maya of Quisteil were planning an insurrection. The conquerors immediately sent off a small detachment of soldiers, who came up against superior force from the Maya. Following this defeat, panic spread among the Spanish-speaking population. It was alleged that there were as many as 3,000 armed Maya troops, led by Jacinto Canek, who had himself proclaimed king. A far greater expeditionary force was sent by the Spaniards, and they eventually encountered a large number of Maya, who were, however, poorly equipped. The government troops were able to suppress the Maya rising with few casualties. Jacinto Canek and his followers were captured after a manhunt that lasted for days. He was put on trial and sentenced to death, along with eight of his followers. The speech that Jacinto Canek is said to have made before his assembled supporters became famous. He described the wretched situation of the Maya population, their exploitation and maltreatment, and the abuse of power by officials and clergy, who exacted tribute and forced labor in huge measure. Following these events, the village of Quisteil was raised to the ground and the soil made barren with salt. It was never resettled and to this day cannot be precisely located.

611 *Franciscan monastery. Izamal, Yucatan, Mexico; colonial era, 1553–'62*
"A pleasing sight, but also a scandal that St. Francis would certainly not have tolerated." Francisco Toral, the first Bishop of Yucatan, is reported to have said this when he saw the grand Franciscan monastery at Izamal. Even in the pre-Hispanic era, Izamal was a great religious center. It was thus a carefully considered decision, with a very specific purpose, to build an impressive work of architecture at this precise spot in order to demonstrate to the Maya people the greatness and splendor of the Christian faith. The architect of the monastery, Pater Juan de Mérida, followed, in all essential respects, the guidelines provided by the prelate Diego de Landa.

610 *The plaza in front of the monastery. Mani, Yucatan, Mexico; colonial era, building started in 1549*

Work on the massive monastery complex at Mani began in 1549. First, a large open chapel was built, in front of which the converts from the indigenous population assembled for outdoor mass. There were longhouse churches of this kind in many places; they were the first Christian buildings on the peninsula. The actual church was not added until later. On the plaza in front of the monastery, on July 12, 1562, Diego de Landa, the Bishop of Yucatan, had the Maya codices, which had been collected from many villages, burned. Prior to this, the cacique had been abused and tortured in order to extort confessions that they still worshipped the devil.

EXPLORATION

THE SEARCH FOR EVIDENCE – THE SCIENTIFIC DISCOVERY OF THE MAYA

Eva Eggebrecht

In the late summer of 1519, immediately before he was due to depart for the Mexican Highlands from the coast at Veracruz to conquer the Aztec empire, Hernán Cortés (1485–1547) despatched two couriers to Spain. Alonso Hernandez de Puertocarrero and Francisco de Montejo, one of the subsequent conquerors of Yucatan, were to convey a message to the Spanish court. Cortés wished to be assured of the king's good will and to be given approval for his plans for the conquest of Mexico. He needed to cover himself in this way because, at the time, he was in a state of rebellion against the Spanish crown, having gone against royal will and exceeded his powers by founding the city of Veracruz Llave.

The ship that was to convey news to the motherland had an extremely valuable cargo on board. In order to further his interests at court, Cortés sent the "fifth" that was due to the Spanish king, the first great treasure from the lands that, shortly afterwards, were to be named New Spain, with Cortés as their governor representing the Spanish crown (ill. 614). The treasure consisted of booty and bartered items that his expeditionary army, on its journey from Cuba around the Yucatan peninsula as far as the Mexican coast, had amassed in their "contact" with the indigenous population (ill. 613).

The most splendid showpieces in the treasure came from the Aztec ruler Montezuma in person. He had sent several detachments of fleet-footed bearers led by high ranking courtiers, to the coast, a journey of four days across the mountains. Their purpose was to offer lavish gifts as an inducement to Cortés and his expeditionary force in their bivouacs, to leave the country, or at least to keep him away from the metropolis at Tenochtitlan. Chroniclers of the period described the finest items received by Cortés in these words: "The first item was an extraordinarily fine piece of work, a golden disc, lavishly decorated, the size of a wagon wheel, which in the view of connoisseurs was worth 20,000 gold piastres. It represented the sun. Then came the moon, an even larger, heavy silver disc, decorated with numerous figures ... And finally the cacique handed over the helmet (a Spanish helmet that they had been given during a previous visit) filled to the brim with fine nuggets of gold that came straight from the goldmines. They were worth at least 3,000 piastres. But even ten times that amount would have meant less to us than the certainty that in this country there must be abundant gold and silver mines."

With his strategy of appeasement, Montezuma achieved the exact opposite of his goal. Instead of inducing the Spaniards to leave the coast at Veracruz with the gifts that they had been given, he spurred them on in their avarice and made them shift the search for gold, which had as yet been unsuccessful in Yucatan, to the Aztec empire. The conquest of Mexico, that is to say of the Aztec empire, was thus settled, because the Spanish court had been convinced by the splendor, artistry, and immeasurable value of the gifts.

Considering the dangers that crossing the Atlantic still entailed at the time, it was good luck that the ship and its costly cargo arrived safely in Spain.

612 *Stela A. Quirigua, Izabal, Guatemala, December 25, 775 A.D.; sandstone*
Quirigua was one of the first Maya cities to be explored in a systematic scientific fashion. The site was discovered by John Lloyd Stephens and Frederick Catherwood, and was visited a number of times in the late 19th century by Alfred Maudslay, who financed the first excavations at the center and photographed the stelae, which were several meters high. At the beginning of the 20th century, Edgar Lee Hewett and Sylvanus Morley uncovered the famous stone monoliths, which became known as "zoomorphs."

613 *Indigenous cacique present gifts to Cortés. Drawing from the "Historia de las Indias" by Diego Durán; 1588; Madrid, Biblioteca Nacional*
In his numerous encounters with the indigenous population of the Yucatan peninsula and the coast of the Gulf of Mexico, Hernando Cortés was, again and again, treated as a guest and presented with gifts, as can be seen in this 16th-century drawing. The indigenous nobles hoped thereby to induce the conquistador and his Spanish adventurers to leave the country, or at least to keep them away from the metropolis at Tenochtitlan. Many of these gifts were sent, as part of the "fifth" due to the crown, to Europe, where they later made up the nucleus of Mexican collections in museums.

In fact, Hernán Cortés' consignment caused a sensation throughout Europe. The historians of those early days recorded the event in their writings. The artistry of the gold and silver items, the precious stones, the hides and plumage of exotic animals, caused amazement in Seville, Valladolid, and Brussels, and were considered evidence of the unexpectedly high level of culture at the Aztec courts. They were seen by Albrecht Dürer, who wrote enthusiastically that he had never, in all his life, seen anything of comparable beauty. Ever since then, it has been a matter of frequent regret that he did not draw these objects.

There are surviving lists containing brief descriptions of the contents of this first great batch of ancient American works of art. Modern research has attempted to trace the route taken by these objects through the royal collections of works of art and rarities, with the disappointing result that none of the listed objects can now be identified with any certainty in present-day collections or museums. It is also hard to believe that the works of the Mesoamerican gold- and silversmiths could have survived the episodes of war and looting in Europe over the past 500 years. In many cases, textiles, feathers, and leather have probably rotted away through not being properly stored.

614 *Map of the Yucatan peninsula, the Gulf of Honduras, and the island of Cuba. End of the 16th/beginning of the 17th century; Seville, Archivo Real de las Indias*
The first maps of the Yucatan peninsula showed it as an island. It was not until the expeditions by Cortés and other Spanish adventurers that it was found to be joined to Mexico and the lands to the south, namely Honduras

and Nicaragua. This map shows that, to begin with, the Spanish cartographers knew only the position of the coastlines. The interior, in contrast, was to a large extent unexplored. The only signs of life in the "white patches" are the few newly founded cities and monastery complexes.

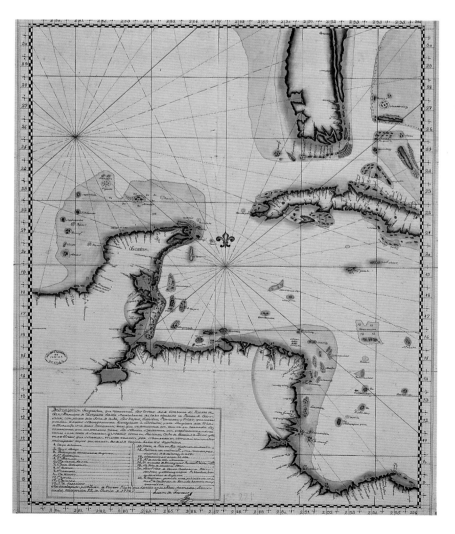

615 *Alexander von Humboldt. Oil painting by Georg Friedrich Weitsch, 1806; Berlin, Staatliche Museen Preussischer Kulturbesitz*
Alexander von Humboldt approached the American continent as a polymath. There was hardly any branch of scholarship in which he was not interested. He devoted himself to geography, geology, mining, zoology, biology,

the political situation of the Latin American countries, and finally their pre-Hispanic history. The journeys that he made in the years 1799–1804 never took him to the Maya area, but he rendered a great service to Maya research by publishing five pages of the Dresden Codex for the very first time.

Maya books in Europe

A certain Francisco López de Gómara (1511–c. 1566) was commissioned by the Cortés family around the middle of the 16th century to write "Historia de las Indias – Conquista de México." In it, he included an account of the Aztec objets d'art presented by his patron to the Spanish court. He dealt first with the items of gold and silver, the precious stones, and other things, but he also made the following remark: "Among all these objects there were also a few books with painted figures as used by the Mexicans for writing, folded together like fabric, made of agave leaves – an admirable thing. But since their meaning was not understood, no great store was set by them." Another source goes into more detail: "Mention should also be made of paintings, with a width of less than the size of a hand, folded in the form of a book that can be opened out. The letters

After a short visit to the Governor of British Honduras in present-day Belize, the two researchers pressed on to Copan. There, they described and drew architectural and sculptural remains that were visible beneath the dense plant growth. Catherwood used a camera lucida as a technical aid, in which a prism projected an object viewed by the eye on to a sheet of drawing paper laid horizontally. Thereby, he achieved a precision never before reached in the documentation of such monuments. Stephens described predominantly "those idols which give the distinctive character to the ruins of Copan," including a stela that Catherwood later hand colored as an etching (ill. 624):

"[The front of the statue] appears to represent the portrait of a king or hero, perhaps erected into a deity. It is judged to be a portrait, from certain marks of individuality in the features, also observable in most of the others, and its sex is ascertained by the beard .... It stands at the foot of a wall rising in steps to the height of thirty or fourty feet [nine or twelve meters]; originally much higher, but the rest fallen and in ruins. Its face is to the north, its height is eleven feet nine inches [360 centimeters], the breadth of its sides three feet [91 centimeters], and the pedestal is seven feet square [213 square centimeters]. Before it, at a distance of twelve feet [365 centimeters], is a colossal altar. It is of good workmanship and has been painted red – though scarcely any vestige of the paint remains and the surface is time-worn ... [It is] richly sculptured on all its sides. The front represents a death's head. The top is sculptured, and contains grooves, perhaps for the passage of the blood of victims, animal or human, offered in sacrifice."

Finally Stephens summarized his impressions:

"Of the moral effect of the monuments themselves, standing as they do in the depths of a tropical forest, silent and solemn, strange in design, excellent in sculpture, rich in ornament, different from the works of any other people, their uses and purposes, their whole history so entirely unknown, with hieroglyphics explaining all, but perfectly unintelligible, I shall not pretend to convey any idea. ...

In regard to the age of this desolate city I shall not at present offer any conjecture. Some idea might perhaps be formed from the accumulations of earth and the gigantic trees growing on the top of the ruined structures, but it would be uncertain and unsatisfactory. Nor shall I at this moment offer any conjecture in regard to the people who built it, or to the time when or the means by which it was depopulated, and became a desolation and a ruin; whether it fell by the sword, or famine, or pestilence. ... One thing I believe, that its history is graven on its monuments. ... The sight of this unexpected monument put at rest at once and forever, in our minds, all uncertainty in regard to the character of American antiquities, and gave us the assurance that the objects we were in search of were interesting, not only as the remains of an unknown people, but as works of art,

proving, like newly discovered historical records, that the people who once occupied the continent of America were not savages."

From Copan, Stephens traveled to Guatemala City, the formal location of the central government of the United Provinces of Central America, proclaimed in 1823 and comprising Guatemala, El Salvador, Nicaragua, Honduras, and Costa Rica. From 1826, the self-interests of the states, based on economics and the competition between their elite power groups, increasingly led to military conflicts between rivals, and to general social unrest. As a rule, the whole region found itself in a state of latent or open civil war, with disastrous effects on people of all social levels. Straggling groups of numerous disoriented soldiers and marauding bands caused general insecurity.

Stephens had not only to evaluate the political situation, but also to advance various contractual matters between Washington and the Central American States. He searched for the representatives of the central government in the various capital cities of the member states until finally concluding:

"I could not conceal from myself that the Federal Government was broken up; there was not the least prospect of its ever being restored, nor for a long time to come, of any other being organized in its stead. ... I ... made a formal return to the authorities of Washington, in effect, 'after diligent search, no government found.' I was once more my own master, at liberty to go where I pleased, at my own expense, and immediately we commenced making arrangements for our journey to Palenque."

Catherwood had been staying in Copan, and had then worked in Quirigua, which was, at that time, part of a Hacienda in private ownership and was completely unknown as a Maya site. This led Stephens to consider a truly adventurous plan.

"Besides their entire newness and immense interest as an unexplored field of antiquarian research, the monuments were but about a mile from the river, the ground was level to the bank, and the river from that place was navigable; the city might be transported bodily and set up in New-York [sic]."

From Guatemala City to Palenque was a distance of 1,620 kilometers (1,000 miles). Stephens would have to travel on mules, in the company of their more or less skillful drivers, on trails to the Atitlan lake bordered by volcanoes and over the Sierra Madre to the high plateau of Chiapas, and on to the north slope of the Tumbala mountains, where the land spreads out into the Tabasco plain. Rivers had to be crossed, together with the baggage, on precarious bridges of braided lianas or on tree trunks, whilst the animals were led over, swimming.

Stephens had arranged for a pass to be issued to him from the new power in Guatemala, Rafael Carrera. This became a protective shield and free ticket in matters of accommodation and subsistence for all participants in his small traveling company. But the country was not at peace, and in the Highlands Stephens sensed that the hour of revenge was near and that, amongst the indigenous peoples, the wish to bring a bloody sacrifice to the spirits of their ancestors and win back their inheritance prevailed.

The town of Santo Domingo de Palenque, which lay about 15 kilometers (nine miles) from the ruins, had experienced a definite economic boom because imports to Guatemala were previously reloaded there. But, the trade route had moved to Belize and a cholera epidemic had hit a large part of the population of the town. By the time that Stephens and Catherwood arrived, the wretchedness was overwhelming. Stephens realized that, in order to be able to work there, he must take up residence on site at the ruins and must secure the provision of food and supplies. As he and his small caravan cut a trail through the thick jungle, the first building of the palace of Palenque emerged before them.

624 *View of Copan, Stela D and altar. Hand colored lithograph by Frederick Catherwood, 1844*
Stephens understood how to express, in perfect style, often with a lightly ironic undertone, observations, feelings, and thoughts regarding "lost" Maya sites: "The people of Copan could not comprehend what we were about, and thought we were practicing some black art to discover hidden treasure ... and even the monkeys, these counterfeit presentments of ourselves, sometimes looked steadfastly at us. They seemed on the point of asking us why we disturbed the repose of the ruins."

625 *First sight of Kabah. Hand-colored pastel lithograph by Frederick Catherwood, 1844*
Their journeys through the north-west of the Yucatan peninsula also brought Stephens and Catherwood to Kabah in the present-day Mexican Federal State of Yucatan. Here, in one of the palaces, they found carved wooden door lintels, which they arranged to be sent to New York, where shortly afterwards they were destroyed in a fire.

626 *The Gate of Labna. Hand-colored pastel lithograph by Frederick Catherwood, 1844*
To complete architectural drawings as exactly as possible, Catherwood used a new instrument, the camera lucida. A prism mounted on a stand projects an image of the object viewed onto the paper on the easel so that the projection only has to be traced. This tool led to an even greater precision in the copying of the proportions of structures, which clearly shows in this example of the Gate of Labna in Mexican, Yucatan.

627 *The El Castillo of Chichen Itza. Hand-colored pastel lithograph by Frederick Catherwood, c. 1840*
In his original drawings for the lithographs, Catherwood not only hoped to achieve the correct representation to scale of architecture and sculptures, but also tried to capture the atmosphere of decay in a rampantly growing forest beneath a constantly changing sky. Both Stephens and Catherwood wanted, with their books, not only to excite the attention of science, but also to offer an entertaining read to the American and European middle classes.

628 *View of the Nunnery's Quadrangle and the Pyramid of the Magician in Uxmal. Hand-colored pastel lithograph by Frederick Catherwood, c. 1840, in: John L. Stephens, Incidents of Travel in Yucatan, 1843*
The view is from the Great Pyramid of Uxmal, in today's Mexican Federal State of Yucatan, to the Nunnery Quadrangle in the middle. Left of that stands the "Pyramid of the Magician," with its steep steps and oval plan, which no doubt struck Stephens and Catherwood as unusual.

Early research in Palenque

Of all the Classic Maya sites, Palenque has enjoyed the most enduring and greatest attention (ills. 629, 630). Since the middle of the 18th century, the inhabitants of the nearest large town, Tumbala, knew of the existence of "Casas de piedra" in the vicinity of Santo Domingo. The inhabitants described the fallen structures of their Maya ancestors as "stone houses" until well into the 19th century. At the beginning of the 1870s, the news of the ruins of Palenque reached José Estachería, the highest-ranking representative of the Spanish throne, in Guatemala City. Another decade elapsed before investigations were initiated on site, some of the first by the royal architect Antonio Bernasconi, whose reports

and drawings found their way to Spain only many years later. On March 15, 1786, Estachería received instructions to collect artifacts from Palenque and to undertake excavations on behalf of the Crown. In Europe as well, it was a time of growing devotion to scientific research of the past, the hour of archeology's birth.

Estachería became active amazingly quickly and dispatched artillery captain Antonio del Río and draftsman Ricardo Almendáriz to Palenque. With the support of a body of 100 men, recruited from the inhabitants of the district, del Rio went to work with axes, picks, and handspikes. The force of his attack has become legendary, although methods used at other sites – like at excavations in Egypt – were no more cautious. Results of del Río's work were already available in 1787.

"From the beginning, I held the opinion that excavations would be necessary (thereon I directed my attention above all), if one wants to form an idea of the first inhabitants and of the age of the buildings, if one wants to find medallions, inscriptions, or other monuments, which shine a light in the darkness; and so I went to work without waste of time ... Finally no window and no door was

629 *Palace and tower of Palenque. Lithograh from a drawing by Count Waldeck, 1886*
In Count Waldeck's strikingly Classic interpretation, the vegetation has become a tree that could also stand on the Appian Way. It covers the collapsed upper part of the Tower of Palenque and leaves the observer in doubt about the height of the structure. Also, the reliefs on the lintels of the entrances indicate antique themes. This manipulation corresponds with the unfounded theories that Waldeck disseminated about the origins of the American peoples.

630 *Palace and Tower of Palenque. Engraving from a drawing by Désiré Charnay, 1885*
Charnay took up the same motif as Waldeck in the drawing from which this engraving was produced. However, he reproduced the architecture, as well as the vegetation, far more objectively and realistically. The same can be said for the reliefs over the entrances, which Waldeck, in his interpretation, had purposely falsified. Charnay was sent to research and discover Maya sites by the French government and a rich benefactor.

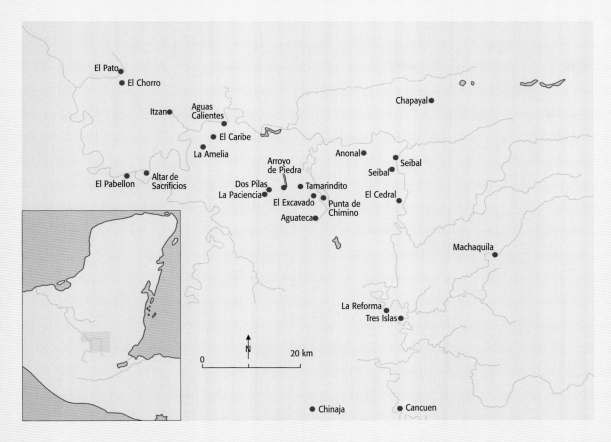

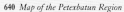

640 *Map of the Petexbatun Region*
The Petexbatun region in the south of the largest departments of Guatemala, the Province of Peten, which was originally completely covered with virgin forest, is especially rich in spectacular archeological zones. Although the district was poorly accessible for a long time, it has become densely populated in recent decades and, as a consequence, has been robbed of its natural vegetation. Today, only a few patches of rainforest still exist there. Meanwhile, settlers have penetrated even the protected zones around the archeological sites and have destroyed both forest and ruins.

rapidly. In contrast to the itinerant *chicle* collectors and the oil companies, the settlers searching for land came in much larger numbers and for the long term. Ever larger areas of undisturbed rainforest were used for agriculture. The formerly small agricultural settlements became towns.

The extensive exploitation of the Lowlands uncovered numerous, formerly entirely unknown, ruins. The agricultural use of overgrown ruins as a rule means their destruction. Establishment of maize fields, for example, requires the clearing of rain forest. In the present day, the trees are felled with chain saws and the whole area is burnt. The fire not only directly attacks the ruins, but also robs them of their protective plant cover. Regional authorities tried to put a stop to this development by the installation of nature reserves around the larger ruin locations. The fear of losing important archeological cultural monuments has recently become linked with efforts to protect the rainforests themselves. Nevertheless, development over the last years shows how limited the measures taken really are. Because the tropical soil is quickly leached out by agricultural use, the number of good and fertile fields is limited, with the result that land shortage is rife in the Lowlands once more. For settlers, the protected rainforests are particularly attractive, because the earth beneath them is untouched and promises high yields. It is not only the change in the natural environment of the ruined cities, through the careless incursions of people, that has had catastrophic consequences for the condition of these once glorious buildings. Since the international art trade discovered the Maya, there has been a worldwide demand for related artifacts. Only very few works of Maya art are made available for free sale in the art market by museums and private collectors. But valid national and international regulations are by-passed illegally time and time again in order to satisfy the rising public demand.

Maya art treasures have suddenly acquired a financial value to the present inhabitants of the Lowlands. The incentive for poor members of the population in the Maya Lowlands to increase their earnings by robbing an unfrequented ruin or burial is therefore large. A number of well-organized and well-equipped gangs are responsible for plundering ruins on a large scale.

The Petexbatun region is regarded as one of the most severely looted areas of Central America.

Today, there is hardly an intact ruin remaining; buildings are pulled apart and completely destroyed in the search for treasures and graves, and freestanding stone monuments are sawn into pieces and smuggled out of the country. There is often little more than a stump in the soils to bear witness to the existence of such a monument. In Aguateca, all of the better preserved stone monuments have been destroyed: they were cut up in such a way that the particularly fine pieces could be smuggled abroad (ill. 641). In Dos Pilas, in 1998, an outstandingly well-preserved hieroglyph stairway was pillaged, and a section of it was sawn off. When excavation at the site was complete, in the early 1990s, the stairway was reburied and only a few initiates knew its precise location. The looted fragment has not yet resurfaced.

641 *Stela 2. Aguateca, Peten, Guatemala, Structure L8-5, upper part; Late Classic, 736 A.D.; limestone; H. 290 cm, W. 93 cm, D. 33 cm*
The third ruler of the Dos Pilas dynasty is presented, on Stela 2 of Aguateca, as the victor over the ruler of Seibal. The monument was inaugurated in A.D. 736 and, at the rediscovery of Aguateca more than 40 years ago, was still outstandingly preserved. A cut from a saw, with which robbers attacked this stela in the mid '90s, can be seen to the left of the head of Ruler 3; the robbers were discovered and ran away.

II THE MAYA IN THE PRESENT

MAYA TODAY – FROM INDIOS DEPRIVED OF RIGHTS TO THE MAYA MOVEMENT

Nikolai Grube

Don Agapito wiped the sweat from his brow then once more thrust the digging stick into the thin topsoil of Yucatan and bored a hole in the earth in which he sowed maize kernels and beans. With a quick movement he filled the seed hole with earth, took a pace forward and used the digging stick again. It had been thus since the grayness of morning. Don Agapito must work quickly, for soon the first rains will come; then it would be too late for sowing on a new *milpa*.

Florentino Ajpacaja Tum swore. Once again the electricity to the small isolated mountain village of Santa Catarina Ixtahuacan in the Highlands of Guatemala was cut off. Just as he wanted to print off a couple of pages of his K'iche' encyclopedia on the new laser printer that he had bought with the money from the American foundation. No, his monumental work would not be a simple K'iche'-Spanish dictionary, of which there were already so many. Dictionaries, so thinks Don Florentino, were ever only vehicles for missionaries and conquerors; they were instruments to rob the Maya of their language and to hispanicize them. His encyclopedia shall not benefit foreigners, but the Maya themselves. It is exclusively written in K'iche', a monumental representation of the K'iche' culture through thousands of laboriously collected words.

Angelina Coyoc is gamekeeper in the Cockscomb Jaguar Reserve of Belize. She proudly explains to the party of travelers in the Creole English of her small country that 60 to 80 predatory cats live here in the only jaguar reservation in the world, the largest and most stable jaguar population in Central America. A good third of the country, she says, is protected as natural reserve, not least because her brothers and sisters in the south of the country, the Mopan and Q'eqchi' Maya of the richly forested Toledo District defended themselves so successfully against the international companies that wanted to convert the forest to furniture and paper on a large scale.

Three people in three countries: They are bound together by their identity as Maya. In the zone of tension between tradition and technology, assimilation and resistance, globalization and isolation, about eight million Maya still live today on the same soil that their ancestors prepared and cultivated for several thousand years. "Still" – this word has a trite aftertaste, because it assigns the Maya to the past, it implies a continuity in tradition and custom, a picture that barely reflects the real diversity. The Maya of the present are no longer just farmers who produce maize for their own consumption in isolated villages, or pose as exotic photo opportunities for the tourists' cameras. They are also politicians, factory workers, and university professors. The Maya identity has received a new meaning. This can best be recognized in Guatemala, where for ten years, a strong Maya movement led to an ethnic renaissance; but this consciousness of being Maya can also be seen in other countries.

Today, the land of the Maya is divided between five states: Mexico, Guatemala, Belize, Honduras, and El Salvador. In three of them, there is a noteworthy Maya population (ill. 643). In the small multi-ethnic state of Belize, the Maya form about 20 percent of the country's population. Numerically, the Maya in Mexico are far more significant. Although less than one percent of the total population of Mexico, in the southern Federal States of Chiapas, Tabasco, Campeche, Yucatan and Quintana Roo, they form a large part of the population, indeed the majority. The true land of the Maya is Guatemala. Of the roughly ten million Guatemalans, six million are Maya whose mother tongue is one of the 29 Mayan languages.

643 *The distribution of Mayan languages*
Around eight million people in the countries of Mexico, Belize, and Guatemala speak one Mayan language as their mother tongue. The 31 Mayan languages spoken today are as closely related to one another as, for example, the Romance languages. Guatemala is the country with the greatest number of speakers, which is where the K'iche' language group is to be found.

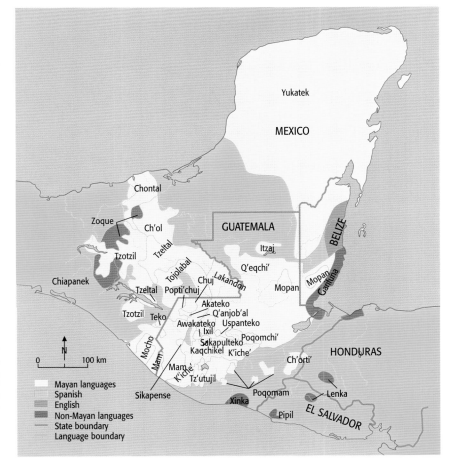

Previous double page
Yax Pasaj and Lolmay. Copan, Honduras, Temple 18; Photograph from 1992
Past and future: 500 years of colonialism, poverty, and open oppression have not been able to take identity or perspective away from the Maya people. Lolmay, who was baptized as Pedro García Matzar, has reassumed a Maya name. He is today a philologist, and one of the leading Maya intellectuals. He has learnt to read the hieroglyphic script: only he who knows history has a future.

642 *K'iche' Maya. Joyabaj, El Quiche, Guatemala*
Joyabaj, in the Highlands of Guatemala, is the center of K'iche' culture and language. The K'iche' are the largest language group in Guatemala and live in the central and western parts of the Highlands of Guatemala. They have preserved many elements of their old culture, including the 260-day calendar, which they call *chol q'iij* ("count of the days").

417

644 Coffee harvest in Escuintla, Guatemala.
Photograph from c. 1934
The Vagabond Law of President Rufino Barrios (1873–1885) – tightened up even more by his successors – forced the Maya of Guatemala to work for a decreed number of days on the plantations. Anyone who did not fulfill his duty was imprisoned. Children had to help too, to contribute to the feeding of the family. Even today, the economy of Guatemala is based on the export of a few main products, like coffee, sugar, and cardamom, the world prices of which are exposed to large swings.

The continuity of colonial relations

With the separation, in 1821, of the lands, governed by the former Viceroy of New Spain and the Captain General of Guatemala from the Spanish motherland, the countries where the Maya lived received formal autonomy and became sovereign states. Mexico was the first country to proclaim its independence, with many other Latin American countries following as soon as possible. But this did not lead to the recovery of freedom for the indigenous inhabitants. In Creole Mexico, Spanish oligarchy had long been formed and firmly established, and worldly wealth, such as that of the Catholic Church, held together to continue to enjoy all established privileges. In the new states, political subordination from outside fell away, internal subjection remained, and the minority ruled under the endless string of dictators.

The consequences of the plantation economy

A central problem for the village communities in the countries of Mexico and Guatemala was the question of land ownership, which was regulated by prescriptive law and not title deeds. In Guatemala and the adjoining Mexican Federal State of Chiapas, this led to the villages being defenseless and exposed to the acquisition of their land by the coffee barons during the coffee boom between 1870 and 1900. Above all, with strong German participation, the flourishing coffee cultivation caused a collapse of traditional agricultural economy throughout the Highlands. At the same time, the Lowlands of Guatemala and the adjacent countries of Central America fell under the growing influence of investors from the United States, through the establishment of banana plantations. Large fields are essential for producing both coffee and bananas. Church estates were secularized and indigenous community lands were systematically broken up and expropriated. The concentration of extensive estates in the hands of a small agrarian elite increased considerably. To satisfy the growing requirement for cheap laborers on the plantations in Guatemala, President Rufino Barrios (1873–1885) introduced the so-called Vagabonds Law: the indigenous people had to show evidence of a fixed number of working days on the plantations to avoid punishment – prison or forced labor building roads (ill. 644). This work service became established through blanket coverage military control under General Jorge Ubico (1931–1944). It led to large population displacements within the country, because the Maya settled in the vicinity of the plantations on which they worked (ill. 465). One consequence of these upheavals was the increasing significance of Spanish as a language of common understanding among the members of the various Maya groups within each plantation. Despite civil war and initial steps to reform, the neo-colonial system has not been overturned in Guatemala today. The country's economy still depends, to a large extent, on the export of the traditional products of coffee, bananas, and sugar, whose swinging world market prices induce dramatic economic and social tensions. The vast majority of the indigenous population is condemned to life on a pendulum between village self-sufficiency and work on the plantations.

The Caste War in Yucatan

Things were not much different for the Maya in the neighboring country of Mexico after the end of the colonial period. Here too, the old oligarchy was able to cement its power and support its economic success by, amongst other things, the incorporation of community lands. Throughout the Yucatan peninsula, large plantations were established on which sugar cane was produced. Another plant that thrived well on the meager karst soils was the sisal agave. With the dawn of industrialization in Europe and North America, the demand was growing for the fibers and ropes that could be extracted from their leaves. Both products (sugar and sisal) required large areas for cultivation, which meant that, from the middle of the 19th century, there was an increased demand for land.

The Spaniards controlled western Yucatan from 1542, but the colonial masters had never managed to obtain permanent domination over the east of the peninsula, which was difficult to access and covered with dense forests. Therefore, throughout the entire colonial era, groups of Yukatek Maya in this area had been able to retain extensive independence. But as the plantations continued to expand, these independent groups also fell within the sphere of influence of the plantation owners. In July 1847, near the town of Valladolid in the east of the present federal state of Yucatan, there was an uprising by the Maya – they resisted levies and taxes that were too high. The conflict really flared up when leaders of this revolt were executed. The Maya of the region organized themselves according to the model of the Yukatek militia and rose up against the white ruling class. Within a short time, armed only with muskets and machetes, they had conquered nearly the whole peninsula (ill. 646). In May 1848, the Maya soldiers stood before Merida, prepared to take the largest town in the peninsula by storm. But this triumph over colonial oppression did not materialize. In August, the Maya were defeated and within a short time they were driven back east. Even today, it is not entirely clear what prevented the seizure of Merida and thereby the almost certain victory of the Maya. The onset of the rainy season, and the need for the self-sufficient Maya to return to their fields to oversee maize planting, are often proposed as explanations for their sudden retreat. Another, and probably more plausible, explanation could have been disagreements between the Maya leaders, who may have found it impossible to agree on a long-term strategy.

645 *Payday on the Coffee Finca. Photograph from 1913*
Maya laborers have been used on the Coffee Fincas ever since coffee was first cultivated in Guatemala, predominantly with the participation of German and Swiss capital. Essentially, neither the working conditions nor the land ownership positions have changed. Today, the official minimum wage is about US $2 a day, but it is often less. 87% of the Guatemalans therefore live beneath the poverty line, and 73% of children under the age of 5 are malnourished.

An independent Maya state

Forced back into the impenetrable forests of the east, the surviving rebels were able to regroup. In 1850, in the vicinity of a cenote (at the entrance to which the so-called Holy Cross had been discovered), they founded the town of Noj Kaj Santa Cruz Xbalam Naj, which would soon become the capital city of an independent Maya state. In its center, following the pattern of a colonial church, a temple was built for the "Holy Cross," the honoring of which formed the religious focus for the rebels. The cross was credited with the ability to speak. The Maya perceived in it their Messiah, who had come to Earth just for them, to talk to them as the chosen people of God. To start with, a Maya with ventriloquist skills was hidden behind the "Speaking Cross." When he died, the Cross communicated only in writing. The communications would be found in the mornings at the base of the Cross, and were aimed directly at the rebels, inciting them to continue the fight. With its combination of Christian and indigenous religious elements, the Cult of the Cross was a typical product of contact with the colonial culture. Its messianic ideology, directed toward the re-establishment of a fictitious, healed, pre-Hispanic world, nevertheless proved to be so influential that resistance against the hated strangers (the colonists) remained the objective for many decades. The power of this Maya state was so great that they traded with the inhabitants of British Honduras, which was adjacent to the south of their district. The inhabitants of this small colony lived on trade in tropical timber, for which there was a great demand in Victorian England. The Maya permitted the British to fell mahogany and campeachy wood even in their distant virgin forests. In return, they received gunpowder, weapons, and foodstuffs, which enabled them to prevent the Mexican troops from marching in to pacify them.

Not until 1901 did the Mexican army in east Yucatan manage to advance and capture the rebels' capital. This was made possible because the soldiers had advanced into the border zone between the Maya country and the British colony, to cut off the supplies of weapons and other goods. The Maya, however, had deserted the capital long before the soldiers arrived, and had taken the "Holy Cross" to a hiding place in the forest. In most history books, the year 1901 is considered the end of the Caste War, but it was in fact only the year in which the Mexicans marched into an empty town. The battles continued, with violent confrontations occuring up to the 1940s. Even today, the Cruzo'ob Maya of Quintana Roo (as the descendants of the rebels are now known) refuse complete integration into the Mexican State. In the villages around Felipe Carrillo Puerto (the former rebel capital), armed companies still protect the Holiness of the Cross.

646 *Scene from the Caste War. Oil on canvas, c. 1850*
The painting shows the horrors of the Caste War. It probably represents an attack on a Yukatek village by the rebelling Maya, who tried to obtain weapons and other commodities in this way in the second half of the 19th century. Apart from the British colony of Belize, the rebels had no trading partners, so they had no choice but to loot from their neighbors.

The Caste War was the most successful and longest-lasting indigenous uprising on the whole American continent, but it was not, by any means, the only one. In Chiapas too, there were many years of armed rebellion, which from 1867 to 1870 involved the town of Chamula and the entire district surrounding the town of San Cristobal de las Casas. In other cases, however, the oppressed Maya were forced to fight against regimes from a hopelessly disadvantaged position. Many of these groups possessed no army, no infrastructure, and no financial resource, giving them little hope of measuring up to their opponents. Such repeated futile attempts at insurrection against superior forces make it easy to understand why the majority of the Maya chose physical isolation or cultural resistance rather than open conflict with the dominant regime. The most successful strategy proved to be compromise between the Maya and the missionaries and colonial officials – through which, little of the substance and value of their traditional beliefs was changed. This ability of the Maya to receive foreign cultural elements within their own life style, without destroying the integrity of their own culture, has contributed hugely to their survival.

Burnt earth – Guatemala in the civil war

The retreat of the Maya into the villages was a consequence of their political incapacitation. For many years, this isolated way of life meant protection from the hostile outside world. But it also prevented the establishment of politically effective pan-regional initiatives and representation of interests. This situation was changed in Guatemala in the second half of the 1970s, when the Catholic Church, especially in rural areas, became active in promoting the founding of indigenous cooperatives. At the same time,

revolutionary movements in Nicaragua and El Salvador had effects in Guatemala. In 1976, a huge earthquake hit wide regions of the Highlands. As a result of this, foreign aid organizations traveled to Guatemala to support the creation of self-help groups.

Indigenous communities came into direct contact with international organizations and, as a result of this, also encountered sources of income that

647 *Memorial for the murdered. Church of Nebaj, El Quiche, Guatemala; photograph from 1998*
More than 60 villages were leveled to the ground under Generals Romeo Lucas García and Efraín Ríos Montt in the Ixil triangle between the towns of Nebaj, Nenton, and Canton. Although the Ixil Maya tried to preserve tactical neutrality, they fell between the fronts of the guerilla movement and the military.

648 *"In front of the Sergeant's hut." San Lucas Toliman, Solola, Guatemala; photograph from 1913*
The increasing expansion of the export economy meant that other agrarian elites developed alongside the Creoles – the old families originally from Spain, consisting partly of members of the mestizo middle class, and partly of foreign immigrants. The term *ladino* was coined for the new, non-indigenous masters of the country. The term is still used today for the Europeanized upper class, and also for the population groups who are of native origin, but want to rid themselves of their Maya identity.

Text on crosses in image: TIBURCIO YOS CUMES, ANTONIO YOS CUMES, LAZARO SICAJAN TZAY, MELECIO C...

were independent of the State. A process of growth of awareness and emancipation began. In 1978, the union of agricultural laborers, CUC (Comité de Unidad Campesina), was formed, which within a short time was able to mobilize large parts of the Highlands. These trends, which at first were advanced only by a few officials, teachers, and priests in the villages, were seen, from the very beginning, as a threat by the power-holding elite in the country. The people in power retaliated with a repressive policy of resettlement, with the ultimate objective of eliminating indigenous life and culture. The military and the oligarchy saw, in the indigenous population, not only underdeveloped beggars, who stood in the way of the economic advance of the country, but also collaborators in revolutionary movements. The suppression of the native population in the early 1980s took on the dimensions of genocide. Union members, Catholic activists, and teachers were abducted by death squads and tortured and murdered. Maya demonstrations fell under storms of bullets, the entire male population of villages was shot and secretly buried in mass graves, women were raped, and children were forced into military service. Maya villages disappeared from the maps, and whole tracts of land (such as the Ixil region) were depopulated (ill. 647). Those who had survived and not fled were forcibly resettled into so-called model villages, whose chessboard patterns of streets were watched over by soldiers. The statistics convey an impression of the

649 *Widows at the cemetery of Xeatzan Bajo*
The human rights organization Amnesty International spoke, in 1981, of political murder as a government program in Guatemala. The mourners were predominantly Maya. The dead were hastily buried in secret in mass graves. It is only now that the graves and the dead are being identified. They are named and buried near to their relatives – the widowed wives and fatherless children.

extent of the blood bath and the human misery of these years, for which the Maya simply use the Spanish term *violencia*: 150,000 dead, at least one million refugees in their own country, and 400,000 refugees in neighboring countries, the USA and Europe (ill. 649).

It was only in 1983 and 1984, under pressure of world publicity, that these acts of horrific violence finally eased off. In 1986, the first free election was held in the area since 1954 – when the last democratically elected government of Jácobo Arbenz was toppled with the participation of the CIA. The main reason for this coup was the landowners' fear of the land reforms planned by the government. Right up to the present day, the new democratic government has not been able to change anything about the land ownership arrangements that date back to colonial times.

Between open oppression and creeping disdain

War, violence, social repression, and cultural alienation determined the life of the Maya in the colonial period, and things are not drastically different now. In Guatemala, the conflict is tangible, and divides the country into Maya and non-Maya. In the Mexican Federal State of Chiapas, a civil war that broke out in 1994 demonstrates that the Mexican Revolution of 1910/1911 (with its land reforms) never arrived here. In other regions, like on the Yucatan peninsula, the boundaries between Maya and non-Maya are less clearly drawn, but are nevertheless articulated in a subtler way. Ignorance of the Maya world and its history, as well as arrogance toward their culture, determines the behavior of the non-Maya, who set the tone in all state establishments (ill. 648). So that they did not have to deal with the Mayan languages, these were abruptly declared to be dialects, a pejorative term, which in Latin America means as much as "gibberish" or "stammering." The Mayan languages were repressed, supposedly, for the benefit of a unified national language and identity, through holding firmly to Spanish as the only official and written language. Although there are schools in Maya regions with bilingual education, in which instruction in the introductory years is also delivered in the respective Mayan language, the objective of most bilingual programs is to educate the young Maya to the use of Spanish at the expense of their mother tongue. The ruling ideology leaves no place for the indigenous people of the land to be Maya.

The national cultures rob them, not only of their linguistic identity, but also of their past (ill. 651). Not a single word about the time before the Spanish invasion is written in the schoolbooks of Mexico and Guatemala, and the view that the history of the region began with the conquest is still taught. Young Maya know about the French Revolution, but not who erected the buildings of Tikal. The erasure of Maya history went so far that the large ruined cities were explained as the work of other civilizations. Attempts to interpret the creations of the ancient Maya culture as those of one of the tribes of Israel, Hindu priests, or extraterrestrials are grist to the mill of those who want to drive a wedge between the present-day and pre-Columbian Maya. Others identify those living today as Indios or Indians, and give with their choice of words the understanding that there is no continuity between their identity and historical subjects. The cultural estrangement from their own roots goes so far that many people would like to lay aside all signs of indigenous identity. The strong influence of the North American popular culture, especially on the young, contributes to the separation of the Maya from their roots.

650 *Chuchqajaw in Chichicastenango, El Quiche, Guatemala*
In many places in Guatemala, religious brotherhoods, the so-called *cofradías,* still exercise a great influence on the community. They are not just trustees of holy statues and religious festivals, but also the bearers of political office. A grown man who wants to achieve social recognition must belong to a brotherhood and have fulfilled all of the official roles. Members of the Brotherhood of Santo Tomás in Chichicastenango collect donations on market days for their charitable purposes. They can be recognized by their costume, above all the head cloth, and call themselves *chuchqajaw,* "mother-father."

651 *A critical view of Maya kitsch, Palenque, Chiapas, Mexico*
A Maya head made from white concrete, gazing into the heavens, announces to the visitor to the modern town of Santo Domingo de Palenque that here the path to the ruins of the ancient Maya City branches off. Heroic monuments that glorify the pre-Columbian past are found all over Mexico. However, no monument is dedicated to the modern successors of King Pakal. The Maya of Chiapas are one of the poorest groups of people in Mexico.

As a matter of fact, the Maya culture is full of life. During the last decade, in Mexico, Guatemala, and Belize, Maya have founded their own organizations. They want to secure their past as much as their future. They demand the return of the cities of their ancestors, which were excavated by foreign archeologists and opened for tourists. The Maya publisher, Cholsamaj, prints scientific publications, schoolbooks in Mayan languages, and reproductions of the Maya codices. In Guatemala, the Maya have founded their own schools, in which the teaching is undertaken in the Mayan languages, K'iche', Tz'utujiil, or Q'anjob'al. Maya women and men have struggled to gain positions of authority. The sociologist, Amanda Pop, the elected parliamentary representative and leader of the organization for war widows, Rosalina Tuyuc, and also the Nobel Prize winner, Rigoberta Menchú Tum, appear confidently in their national costume: no longer shamefully burying their Maya identity, but acknowledging it openly (ill. 653). In Mexico, Maya authors join together to find new patterns of literary expression in their mother tongue. But people are also looking to the past. The quest for an identity, for origins, can only be answered by taking history into account. So archeology and historical research, and also epigraphy, have attained a new importance. What started as exotic science in the salons of the educated and in the libraries of Europe and North America is today of great meaning for the cultural renaissance of the Maya.

Catholic missionaries gave the Maya new names as a sign of their Christian baptism. Young Maya today have set their Christian names aside and use Maya names again, such as Nikte', Lolmay, and Ixkem as signs of their new old identity. But Don Florentino, the author of the encyclopedia, did not want to change his name. At 68 he was, he said, too old for it. However, he sat with the young Maya on the bus to visit the excavation of ruins of Copan. "The stelae of Copan have so much meaning for us," he said, "like the [Athenian] Acropolis for the Europeans." And whilst Lolmay was taking photographs near a relief with a representation of Yax Pasaj – the 16th king of the Copan dynasty – Don Florentino diligently noted the names of the kings of Copan in his *kematz'iib,'* the "writing-loom," as the word for "notebook" appears in K'iche' Maya. This shows that the newest achievements of our times are being incorporated into the Mayan languages.

652 *The Lakandon – the last "wild" Maya pose for the camera. Naha, Chiapas, Mexico; Photograph from 1998*
The roughly 300 Lakandon Maya, who today live in the villages of Naha and Lacanha in the Mexican Federal State of Chiapas, are erroneously regarded, on the basis of their traditional costume of white tunics and their long hair, as the last "wild" Maya. Many of them have actually been converted to Christianity. One group, in the 1960s, were converted by American Adventists to Protestantism, based on the literal truth of the Bible. They still pull on their long robes for tourists.

Cultural renaissance and the pan-Maya movement

In Guatemala, a strong Maya movement formed as a reaction to the civil war. In 1992, the Nobel Peace Prize was awarded to the K'iche' woman Rigoberta Menchú Tum, and a battle then raged in the newspapers and media about the authenticity of the Maya culture. Modern Maya priests are reproached on the basis that they freely avail themselves of convictions and spiritual practices borrowed from other religions. The Christian god has become a component of modern Maya religion, and Christian saints are called upon together with gods of pre-Columbian origin. Maya priests also use symbols from pre-Columbian times; reprints of hieroglyphic texts, above all the four surviving codices, are an important part of the rituals of some current *ajq'iij*, as the Calendar Priests in the Highlands are called. Critics of the Maya movement see in this, proof that the Maya religion practiced as it is today is no longer true but is rather a syncretistic belief that does not deserve the term "Maya." In contrast to this opinion, Maya intellectuals believe that it is precisely the flexibility and the ability of the Maya culture to integrate outside influences that are an indication of their vitality.

653 *Rosalina Tuyuc*
Maya women have assumed leading positions in the Guatemalan community despite strong resistance. Rosalina Tuyuc founded the widows organization CONAVIGUA (*Coordinadora Nacional de Viudas de Guatemala*) and is now, as then, its chairperson. She is also an elected member of Parliament and one of the few representatives of the Maya, who in Guatemala make up more than half of the population.

WE SEARCH FOR OUR IDENTITY

In 1992, 500 years after the official discovery of America, Rigoberta Menchú received the Nobel Peace Prize for her untiring efforts to gain equal rights for indigenous peoples. The fate of her family was shared by ten thousand other families and formed the basis of her autobiography.

Translated from: Rigoberta Menchú: "La nieta de los mayas," Madrid, El Pais-Aguilar, 1998

Many people think we Indígenas have only been spectators in these last 500 years and maintain that we are the defeated. In fact we have had to endure racism, discrimination, banishment, and oppression. We are a people, who can very precisely give a name to the consequences of colonization, of an unending measureless exploitation, of a degraded unbounded discrimination, and we will speak plainly about it. However, it is good to know that the indigenous peoples have built the great cities with their own hands. We have raised huge structures by the sweat of our brows. We have carefully planned all the steps and determined our own pace with the building. We have also contributed to the rich diversity of the peoples of America. And indeed to such an extent that no one could distinguish where the indigenous begins and where it stops. For the culture is in no way pure. It is dynamic and dialectic. It is moved and developed. One can not declare the one to be pure and the other to be impure because the purity does not permit itself to be defined. Think that our people were at no time uninvolved passive spectators. All achievements are due to us, because we have contributed to them, also to the most complex ethnic and cultural diversity ....

I believe that the conservation of fundamental thousand-year-old concepts of value is no more only an interest of the Indian peoples. I stumbled upon these ideas with the *ajq'iij* – the Maya priests. They do not concern themselves with the question whether our ancestors were better or worse, or the one was purer than the other, if the Ladinos were purer or less pure or should be Indígenas. They taught us that war destroyed the dignity of the Indígenas and unity. One could for example assert the following: when one belongs to a group, one is a true Indígena, otherwise not. The *ajq'iij* have not dissipated their energies with such subjects. The *ajq'iij* were very plain. They said: "The time is come, that the rain falls, that the rain lets the seed, our seed that lie dormant in the soil, sprout, and that our culture blooms, that the discord leaves us." They said, the time of the rain has come. The time of clearness. The brightness of our path began. The lucidity led us to identity and we began again to explore characters and to reconstruct our mental attitude. A circle was closed, one Age came to an end and a new one began.

APPENDIX

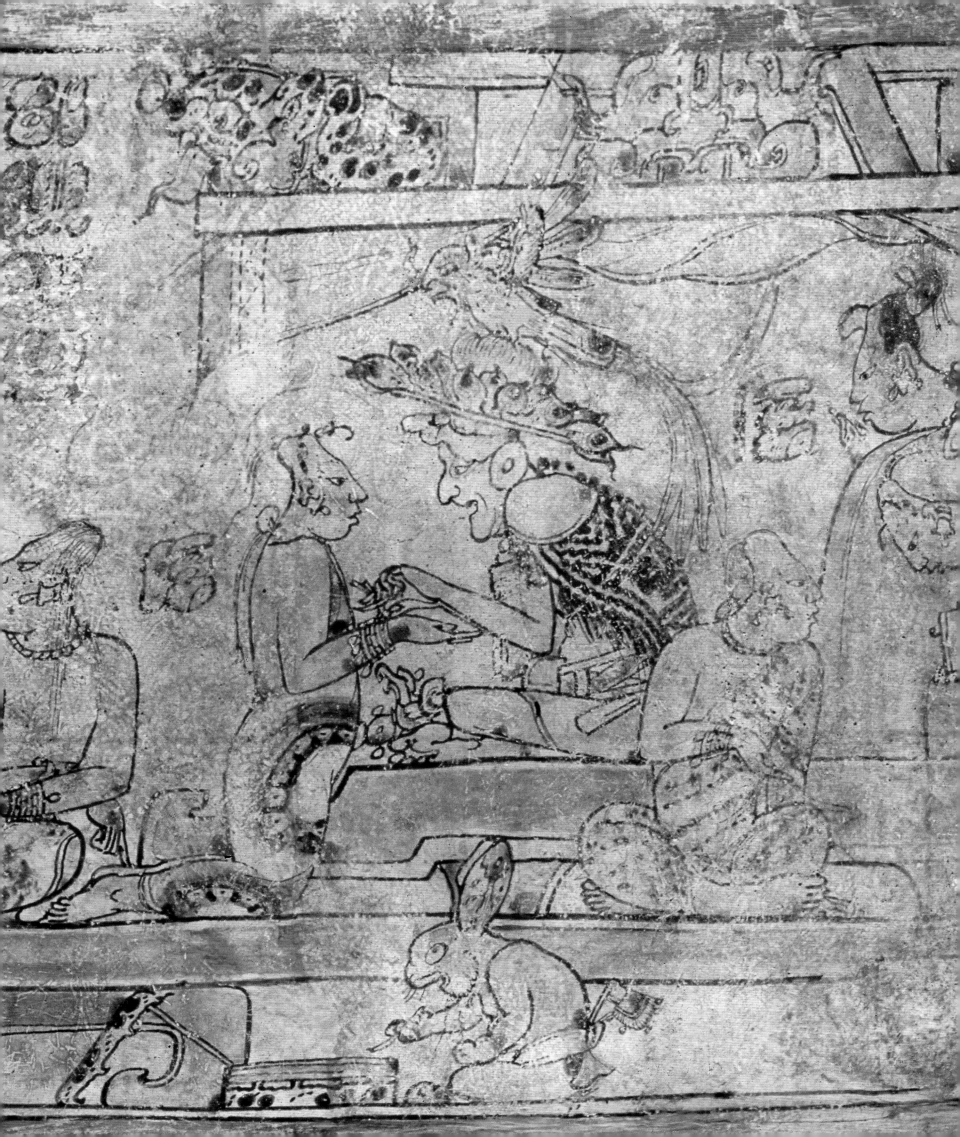

GLOSSARY

Daniel Graña-Behrens and Nikolai Grube

Head of the Maize God. Copan, Honduras, Structure 10L-22; Late Classic, 715 A.D.; tuff; H.32 cm; Copan, Centro Regional de Investigaciones Arqueológicas, Instituto Hondureño de Antropología e Historia

Achiote
A Spanish term for a tree of the *Bixa orellana* species, and also for the orange-yellow to reddish dye that is made from the seeds of this tree. Achiote is used in food preparation for its aroma.

Acropolis (Greek, "high city")
In Maya archeology, an acropolis describes any platform that serves as a base for several buildings. An acropolis could represent a place to honor the gods and ancestors (like the North Acropolis of Tikal), or equally, form a living complex (like the Central Acropolis of the same city).

Adobe (Spanish, "air-dried brick")
A type of clay brick that was used to build houses in pre-Columbian times. Because it was unfired, it weathered quickly.

Agave
A plant group with about 300 varieties. Present-day Maya still use the leaves to brew an alcoholic drink that was documented in Classic hieroglyphs. Agave leaves are sometimes depicted projecting from clay jugs on colorfully illustrated ceramic vessels; the content of these jugs is indicated by the inscription placed on them: *chi* (fermented agave drink).

Aguada (Spanish, "waterplace")
A funnel- or bowl-shaped → cenote filled with sand, in which rainwater collects.

Ajaw (Mayan, "Lord," "King")
A title for rulers, princes, kings, and general noblemen. In a narrower sense, *ajaw* describes the highest political office of the Maya in Classic times. The attribute *k'uhul* (divine) often follows the word *ajaw*, above all in → emblem glyphs. In the calendar, *ajaw* means both the last day in → Tzolk'in and the time unit for the → Short Count.

Akan (God A)
Akan is the god of alcoholic drinks, hallucinogenic substances, and presumably of the hallucinations themselves. In Paul Schellhas' list of gods, he is named as God A. His distinguishing marks are the signs for darkness, death, and magic on his head. Paintings on vases often show him at drinking orgies, where alcohol is administered both orally and rectally.

Altar
Before stelae, most round stone sacrifice tables lay on the ground or on three stone feet. It is thought that offerings and censers were placed on them. Square and rectangular altars seem to have first appeared in the Late Classic. Many are sculpted and inscribed with the year of their erection.

Apron molding
A special façade construction of a stepped pyramid base that was particularly popular in central Peten, Tikal, and Uaxactun. The front of the step was divided into an inclined zone at the top and an underlying recessed zone. Because the projecting section could be likened to an overhanging apron, this profile was named apron molding. The effects of light and shadow intensify the impact of the regular horizontal alternation.

Apse house
Typical Lowland farmhouses, built of wood or stone above an oval platform, had rounded, narrow sides – hence the term apse house. The roof was made of straw from the guano palm (*Sabal mexicana*).

Atole
A drink made from maize dough and water that is flavored with various additives, such as salt or honey. The term atole comes from Aztec, but Classic Maya ceramic vessels often have the term *ul* on them. The contents of these vessels are more closely defined as *sak ul* (white atole) or *sak ch'aj ul* (white, bitter or unsweetened atole).

Aztecs
The Aztecs are counted among the → Nahua

group of people in central Mexico, whose former capital Tenochtitlan is at the present center of Mexico City. In about 1300, the Aztecs expanded into the most politically powerful confederation in the region. They had an efficient administration at their disposal and forced the conquered peoples to pay tribute. In 1519, their well-known ruler Montezuma II received the conqueror Hernán Cortés who, with his forces, shortly afterwards incorporated the Aztec empire into the Spanish world empire.

Back loom
An appliance for weaving textiles. It is held in place by a strap, and is also known as a belt loom. One end of the strap is secured to a fixed object, while the other end is placed around the hips.

Bajo (Spanish, "Lowland")
A term for a loam-covered, often extensive depression in which water accumulates. In the south of the Yucatan peninsula, bajos form a marsh.

Bakab
A title with unknown meaning, which in the Late Classic was mostly reserved for the rulers. Some researchers equate it with the similar sounding term → Batab', which in the Postclassic in northern Yucatan identified an important office.

Bak'tun
A time interval of 144,000 days, comprised of 20 → K'atun of 7,200 days. In the → Long Count, it is normally the largest dating unit.

Balam (Mayan, "jaguar")
This is the largest predatory cat found in Mexico and Central America (*Felix onca*). In the Classic, the word Balam was frequently used as a component of rulers' names; for example, the prince of the city-state Tortuguero was called Balam Ajaw (Jaguar-Lord). The jaguar was certainly both feared and honored by the Maya. Therefore, portrayals of rulers enthroned on a jaguar pelt are found on numerous ceramic objects. But the jaguar is also a creature of the underworld (→ Xibalba); → Popol Wuj told of a mythological jaguar lair that was positioned somewhere in the cosmos, in which the Hero Twins were imprisoned as a test of their courage.

Balche'
A mildly alcoholic drink that is made by mixing water with the fermented bark of the Balche' tree (*Lonchocarpus longistylus*). Today, it is consumed only on ritual occasions, and honey is added for sweetness.

Ball game
A game with a rubber ball (→ Zapote), called *pitzil* by the Maya, which is played throughout Mesoamerica. The ball could not be touched with hand or foot, but, as is still the case in several parts of Mexico, was struck with the hips. In the Classic, the Maya laid out special I-shaped playing fields, with beveled boundary walls that allowed the ball to ricochet. Points were scored either when the ball flew through a ring fixed above the playing field or when it hit a marker stone on the ground. Nothing is known about team sizes in the Classic. Inscriptions often show the ruler of a city state as a ballplayer, such as *Aj Pitzil* ("He, the ballplayer"). Whether human sacrifice was offered in connection with the ball game, as is sometimes suggested, has not been proved beyond doubt.

Bark pestle
A corrugated stone slab, about the size of the palm of the hand, which was used in the production of paper. The tool was grooved at the edges to allow the operator to secure a good grip. The bark of the amate fig was worked with the pestle until a paper-like fibrous material resulted.

Batab'
Next to → Jalach Winik, this was the highest political office of the Postclassic in several Maya states in the Yucatan peninsula. The title is derived from the Yukatek Mayan word *bat* (stone axe) and means axe carrier. The Batab' office holder of the various federated states cited a common ancestor from time to time.

Head of a Pawajtuun. Copan. Honduras, Structure 10L-11; Late Classic, 769 A.D.; tuff; H. 80 cm

Blood sacrifice
This noble ritual was undertaken by politically important members of Maya society, by means of a perforator, and served to preserve dynastic interests and cosmic order. Blood was considered the most precious human possession and therefore the greatest possible sacrifice. As is illustrated from time to time, the blood was dropped onto paper strips, which would then be burned together with → copal.

Blowgun
A weapon made from a wood or bamboo, with which a projectile (clay pellet or dart) is delivered using expelled breath. The blowgun is known from a mythical event, displayed on ceramics of the Classic and told in → Popol Wuj of colonial times. According to Popol Wuj, the → Hero Twin Junajpu ("One-Blowgun") used this weapon to kill the bird of heaven, named → Itzam Ye in the Classic and →Wuqub' Kaqix in the Popol Wuj.

Breadnut
Also called ramon tree. A tall-growing tree (*Brosimum alicastrum*; Mayan, *ox*), the fruits of which possess a pleasant tasting pulp. Principally in hard times, the cores of these fruits were ground and added to maize paste.

Calabash
Large, pear-shaped fruit from the tree of the same name (*Crescentia cujete L.*). Because they are so hard, the rinds make suitable storage containers for liquid foods and drinking water. The fruits were hollowed out by the Maya for these purposes as early as the Classic, as evidenced by vase paintings.

Calendar Round
A mode of calendar specification that results from the combination and interdigitation of → Tzolk'in and → Haab calendars. Because of the structure of both calendars, a Calendar Round is first repeated after 18,980 days, or approximately 52 solar years. The day of world creation fell on 4 Ajaw (Tzolk'in) and 8 Kumk'u (Haab).

Capital (Latin, capitulum, "head")
The head of a column or pillar. They are differentiated, according to their decorative style, as leaf-, blossom-, or figure-capitals.

Caste War
A war between the Maya and the Yucatan government in the 19th century. In 1847, the Maya, whose political, social, and economic conditions had dramatically deteriorated after Mexican independence in 1821, rose up against the Yucatan-Mexican government troops. The armed uprising quickly escalated into a war between a fellowship split into two camps, hence the term Caste War. From 1847 to 1901, the Maya exercised military control over the eastern region of Yucatan and developed their own structures of state. The honoring of a reputed speaking holy cross (→ Cruzo'ob Maya) in Chan Santa Cruz, now Felipe Carrillo Puerto, was of central significance. After military defeat in 1901, the Maya moved the "speaking cross" to safety in Tixcacal Guardia.

Cedarwood
An extremely hard and termite-resistant wood which, in the pre-Columbian eras, was predominantly used for the manufacture of door lintels.

Ceiba
The ceiba tree (*Ceiba pentandra*), called *yaxche* (first tree) in the Mayan language and considered to be a symbolic "World Tree," represented the Earth's axis for the Maya and is still honored as a holy tree.

Cenote
A natural sinkhole filled with groundwater in the northern karst area of the Yucatan peninsula, which formed through the collapse of the overlying limestone strata. Cenotes, the name of which is borrowed from the Mayan word *tz'ono'ot*, form important drinking water reservoirs and influenced the choice of settlement sites in pre-Hispanic times (e.g. Chichen Itza, Dzibilchaltun, Mayapan).

Central America
While the terms "Mesoamerica" and "Middle America" can be defined in a cultural or geographic sense respectively, Central America is a politically determined term. It describes all the states on the isthmus between North America and South America. These are the states of Belize, Guatemala, Honduras, El Salvador, Nicaragua, Costa Rica, and Panama. These states are loosely tied to one another by various agreements and common institutions.

Chaak (God B)
The Postclassical Maya Rain God. In the earlier Classic, Chaak had various manifestations and numerous supplementary names like, for example, Yaxjal Chaak ("Greening of Chaak"), Muyal Chaak ("Cloud-Chaak"), → Jun Ye Nal Chaak (→ "Palenque Triad"), Ox Bolon Chaak ("Three-Many Nine-Chaak"), and Yax Bolon Chaak ("Green-One Nine Chaak"). Characteristics of this divinity are a long nose, usually bent downward, shell-shaped ear decorations, and a so-called shell diadem. Sometimes, snakes project from the corners of Chaak's mouth and he is often shown with an axe in his hand.

Chak Mo'ol (Mayan, "Red/Great Jaguar")
The name given to a particular type of stone sculpture, first introduced in 1875 by A. Le Plongeon. The sculptures are full relief human figures, which lie on the ground with their elbows propped up, their legs angled, and with their heads turned to one side. There is either a depression in the middle of the stomach or a bowl held there. It is possible that the heart was ripped out of Chaak Mo'ol figures condemned to death by ritual → human sacrifice.

Ch'ahom
A title from the Classic that was not strictly reserved for rulers, but was also carried by lesser nobility. The meaning of the title is still unknown.

Chenes
The Spanish plural of the Mayan word *ch'een,* "springs." Chenes is the eastern region of today's Mexican Federal State of Campeche, in which numerous places carry *ch'een* in their names, e.g. Bolonchen ("Nine Springs"). In architecture, this term is used to define the local pre-Hispanic style; characterized by façades overloaded with geometric motifs and building entrances in the shape of snake jaws, which symbolize access to the → underworld.

Chilam Balam (Mayan, "Jaguar-Translator," "Jaguar-Explainer")
This is the name of a Maya prophet who lived during the Spanish conquest. Numerous manuscripts (written down in the Yucatan language, but in the Roman alphabet) collected from north Yucatan in the 17th and 18th centuries were named after him. These manuscripts, collected together under the term "Chilam-Balam Books," were, for the most part, designated according to their place of origin. Best known are "Chilam Balam of Chumayel" and "Chilam Balam of Tizimin." The books contain myths about the origins of the world and historical reports, as well as prophetic and medical discussions. The history of the development of the Chilam-Balam texts is still unexplained. They contain both pre-Hispanic and Colonial cultural elements and it is proposed that oral records and old American picture writings were absorbed to the same extent as European observation and submissions.

Chochola ceramics
These are unpainted vessels made from black clay, usually engraved with lavish scenic depictions and hieroglyphic texts. In rare cases, the vessels may have been formed in molds. These ceramics, the only ones with figurative decoration from the Puuc region, are named after Chochola, the place in Yucatan where the first examples were found. As a matter of fact, however, inscriptions and artists signatures allow two centers of production to be determined, Xcalumkin and Oxkintok, from where, in the Late Classic, these artistically demanding clay wares were traded to distant parts of Yucatan.

Ch'ol
A Maya group in the Mexican Federal State of Chiapas, and also the name of their language, which belongs to the western branch of the Maya family of languages. The three languages – Ch'ol, → Ch'orti', and → Chontal – are closely related to one another and their common predecessor, proto-Ch'ol, was the language of the hieroglyphic script and of the nobility. Today, about 150,000 Ch'ol-Maya live in the vicinity of Tila, Tumbala, Palenque, and Yajalon. The shortage of land in their original settlement area led to many of them invading the virgin forest of Selva Lacondona to settle there permanently.

Chontal
A Maya group in the Mexican Federal State of Tabasco and the name of their language, which is closely related to the Ch'ol and Ch'orti' languages. Today, about 60,000 Chontal live not far from the Mexican Gulf coast, around Nacajuca.

Ch'orti'
A Maya group found in the east of the Guatemalan administration districts of

Altar with the portrait of the Jaguar god of the underworld. Copan, Honduras, Building 10L-24 (jaguar steps); Late Classic c. 750 A.D.; tuff; h. 170 cm

Chiquimula and Zacapa, and also the name of their language. About 60,000 Ch'orti' live in small villages, principally in the region around the towns of Jocotan, Camotan, and San Juan Ermita. Their language has retained to this day many elements of the written language of hieroglyphs and is perhaps, of all the Mayan languages, the most closely related to the courtly Mayan of Classical times. A few years ago, Ch'orti' could still be heard in the vicinity of the town of Copan in Honduras, but there are no longer any Ch'orti speakers to be found there today.

Chultun (Mayan, cisterns)
A bell-shaped underground storage chamber for water, or important basic foods like maize. These chambers were important, above all in areas with a low rainfall and in the dry season, to secure the supply of drinking water. Gutters were cut into the ground to channel rainwater into these reservoirs.

Cinnabar
A mineral (mercury sulfide) ranging from red through to black in color that is often found scattered in burials. It was probably used to seal the burial, but may also have symbolized blood as a life-giving substance.

Coa
This word, borrowed from Nahuatl, is used to describe a fire-hardened planting stick (→ digging stick).

Codex
A folding screen book prepared from the bark of the fig tree. Long strips are stuck together, covered with a lime base, and painted with multicolored → hieroglyphs and images. Only the Grolier Codex and three others from the Maya region, called after their repositories of Dresden, Madrid, and Paris, have survived.

They apparently originated in the Postclassic and at the time of the Spanish conquest; their content is prophetic as well as calendrical and astronomical.

Codex-style ceramics
In the Mirador basin of north Guatemala, the Maya produced ceramics in a wide variety of shapes, with fine black line drawings on a cream-colored base. The mythological scenes were apparently copied from codices, which is why they are known as "codex-style" ceramics.

Coffee
Contrary to popular opinion, coffee came originally from Ethiopia and not from Central America. Coffee plants were first naturalized in central America, principally by the German and Swiss, in the 19th century, when extensive production led to expropriation of Indian land. Since then, indigenous people have worked as underpaid helpers on the fincas. Even today, a large part of Guatemalan export earnings come from the coffee trade.

Cofradía (Spanish, "lay brotherhood")
These strongly hierarchical brotherhoods were attached to the Franciscan, Dominican, Augustinian, and Jesuit orders, but were led by the laity. Preeminently, they were pledged to fostering the cult of a saint after whom they also named themselves. Arriving from

Vessel with incised decoration. Provenance unknown; Late Classic, 600–900 A.D.; fired clay with scored decoration; H.15.5 cm, W.15.2 cm; New York, American Museum of Natural History (Kerr 2733)

Europe, these spiritual societies found a large following amongst the indigenous population in the Spanish colonial empire. This is explained by similar organizations in their pre-Hispanic structures. In time, further brotherhoods developed that were not authorized by the Church. Such societies have survived to the present day and determine religious life in many Maya communities in Guatemala and in the Highlands of Chiapas in Mexico.

Comal
A term derived from the Aztec for a clay plate used for baking tortillas (flat maize bread) that was placed directly over the fire. Today, these plates are usually made from tin-plate.

Copal
A term taken from the Aztec for incense, and which has been adopted in scientific language in favor of the Mayan term *pom*. Copal is valued for the highly aromatic smoke that arises when burned, and is still used today, but exclusively for ritual purposes. On Classic Maya monuments, copal can be seen lying as small balls on smoking vessels or in sacks waiting to be smoked.

Corbel vault
A roof construction that can also be referred to as false vault because, in a static sense, it is not load-bearing. With corbel vaults, the stone layers of the walls on both sides are brought progressively closer together until the vault closure is reached. The final stones are called vault cap stones. In the Classic, the Maya often painted these stones, which were centrally placed in the vault, and provided them with an inscription. Shoe stones, typical of the → Puuc style, make an especially elegant form of the corbel vault.

Copador ceramics
The Copador ceramics, manufactured at the eastern periphery of the Maya region and widely distributed in the Late Classic, are identified by their polychrome painting and so-called pseudo-hieroglyphs, which imitate the characters without being readable.

Correlation
The comparison of two or more different calendar systems like, for example, the Long Count of the Maya calendar and the Julian notation from Europe. If they are off-set, a correlation constant has to be calculated. This gives, with reference to each zero date, the exact number of days that separate the systems. In the case of the Long Count of the Maya and Julian notation, this value is 584,285 days, as derived by Goodman, Martinez, and Thompson (amended by Lounsbury), known as GMT 584,285 for short. This correlation constant permits the calculation of the Julian or Gregorian date for each and every date in the Maya time calculation, and vice versa.

Cozumalhuapa
A group of neighboring archeological sites in the Pacific coastal plain of Guatemala, and also the term for the cultural style originating there. Dates are still being discussed, but most scientists link it to the arrival of Nahua-speaking Pipil tribes early in the Postclassical period (900–1200 A.D.). Basalt sculptures and stelae with central Mexican-inspired imagery are especially characteristic of the Cozumalhuapa style.

Craquelé
A net of fine cracks intentionally made in the glaze of ceramics. Various thin layers of → engobe were spread on the outer surface of a vessel. The top layer contracted, and split apart during firing. This form of decoration is characteristic of the Middle Preclassic Mamom ceramics.

Cruzo'ob Maya
A term used to describe the rebeling Maya of

Urn with striped pattern. Punta Piedra, Quintana Roo, Mexico; Postclassic, 1000–1500 A.D.; H. 37 cm, W. 38 cm ; Cancun, Museo Arqueológico de Cancún

the → Caste War (1847–1901), who, in part of east Yucatan, paid homage to an alleged speaking holy cross. The center of the cult was Chan Santa Cruz Xbalam Nah, today's Felipe Carrillo Puerto. In 1847, the rebels organized themselves militarily under the sign of this cross to defend the interests of the Yukatek Maya. The name Cruzo'ob Maya came about as a result of this – the Spanish word *cruz* is combined with the Mayan plural form *o'ob*. This movement, coined from both Catholic and indigenous beliefs, tried to establish a religious as well as a sociopolitical order.

Day of World Creation
The pre-Columbian Maya believed that 4 Ajaw 8 Kumk'u (→ Calendar round, → Tzolk'in, → Haab) was the day on which the world was created. It corresponded with the date 13.0.0.0.0. in the → Long Count. Inscriptions report that, on this day, the jaguar, snake, and water thrones were erected at the heavenly site known as "first place of the three stones."

Digging stick
A wooden pole that tapers to a point or is fire-hardened at the end, which is exclusively used for work in the fields. It can be used to loosen earth, or can be pressed into the ground to create a furrow for sowing seeds into.

Distance Number
The term for a number or number sequence that expresses in days the interval between two dates. As in the → Long Count, the days are combined into periods to depict the distance number.

Double-headed serpent bar
A ritual staff in the form of a double-headed serpent, which, like the royal scepter, symbolizes the ruling power. The head of a divinity, for example one of the → Paddler Gods or the ruler's ancestors, protrudes from the jaws of each snake.

Dresden Codex
The finest and best-preserved of the four pre-Hispanic Maya folding screen books. This Late Postclassic codex, which has 78 pages and

a total length of 365 centimeters (144 inches), has been in Dresden since 1739, and is today exhibited in the Book Museum of the State Library of Saxony. Its 74 written sides contain complex astronomical tables used to foretell the positions of Venus and solar and lunar eclipses, as well as almanacs based on the 260-day ritual calendar. The tables served prognostic purposes, and determined good and unfavorable days for a range of affairs.

Dry season
One of the two main meteorological periods of the year. The dry season starts, with regional differences, between October and December and lasts until the end of May or the beginning of June, when the first heavy rains announce the start of the rainy season. March and April are the hottest months of the year. When north winds bring cold sea air and clouds over land, it can rain even during the dry season.

Dwarfs
Midgets apparently enjoyed high esteem in the Maya culture. They lived at the royal court, where they entertained the rulers, and were also their preferred servants. Dwarfs were believed to be the messengers of the underworld. Many stelae show them handing insignia, such as the → K'awiil scepter or flowers, to the king, probably on behalf of deceased ancestors with whom, according to the Maya understanding, they maintained in close contact.

Eccentric flint/eccentric obsidian
Bizarrely shaped → flint (silex) or obsidian objects that fulfilled no practical function, but nevertheless represented valuable sacrificial offerings. They are found in burials, under stelae and altars, and in sacrificial caches. They are often decorated with stylized anthropomorphic and zoomorphic entities.

Ecliptic
The circular path along which the sun appears to move through the sky when viewed from the Earth. Ancient Europeans believed that the sun passed 12 signs of the zodiac. In contrast, the Maya assumed, as can be extracted from the Paris → Codex, 13 zodiac signs, in which they included, amongst others, a turtle and an owl.

E Group
An architectural complex named after Group E of Uaxactun, where it was first identified. A western high pyramid with a square plan stands opposite three aligned buildings, as a rule on a communal platform, in the east. In between, there is usually a plaza containing monuments. Some of the E Groups were probably observatories, and served to fix sunrises. Viewed from the western construction, the two outer pyramids of the triad lie on the line of sight of the points at which the sun appears on the horizon at the June and December solstices. The middle construction was possibly used to fix sunrises on the equinoxes in March and September. Not all E Groups show these orientations, but they are undoubtedly important dynastic shrines, where the Maya went to venerate their deceased ancestors. Most were built at the transition from Late Preclassic to Early Classic. E Groups have been identified outside

Uaxactun at Naachtun, Güiro, Caracol, Yaxha, Tikal, and Calakmul.

Ejército Nacional Zapatista de la Liberación Nacional
(EZLN, Spanish, "National Zapatista Army of National Liberation")
This movement became militarily active in the Mexican Federal State of Chiapas at the start of 1994. It took the name of the legendary revolutionary Emiliano Zapata, who championed the cause of the peasants during the Mexican revolution at the beginning of the 20th century. The present-day Zapatistas fight, not just for land and freedom, but above all for cultural and political self-determination, as well as social justice for the Maya peoples in Chiapas. The conflict still continues, despite numerous efforts to restore peace.

Emblem Glyph
The term for a title composed of several → hieroglyphs. It identifies the bearer as K'uhul → Ajaw ("divine ruler") over a city-state or political federation, whose name is usually of geographic or mythological origin.

Encomienda (Spanish, "assignment," "protection")
The submission of the indigenous workforce to the conqueror through the Spanish throne for a restricted time and according to feudal law. In return, the occupant of an *encomienda*, the so-called *encomendero*, pledged to protect the assigned workers and to convert them to Christianity. The encomienda led to the ruthless exploitation of the original inhabitants and was changed, to the effect that the *encomendero* received taxes in place of work output.

Engobe
A multi-filtered slip of repeatedly sieved clay, with which ceramic vessels were covered before firing to make them waterproof, and to give them a smooth surface and even color.

Entrada (Spanish, "enter")
A term for the advance of Spanish soldiers or priests through unexplored and mostly jungle-covered regions of the Spanish colonial empire. The entrada aimed to conquer the region, convert the indigenous people living there, and consolidate colonial rule.

Epigraphy
The science concerned with → hieroglyphs in inscriptions. Epigraphy involves decoding the writing, the study of the historical development of writing and language, and the analysis of the historical testimony of texts. In contrast to the Egyptian study of inscriptions, Maya epigraphy covers all available material – codices, stone monuments, ceramics, and inscribed wall paintings.

Epi-Olmec
Following the end of the Olmec civilization, a culture developed on the Mexican Gulf coast, in the area from the Tehuantec isthmus to the Guatemalan Pacific coast. The Epi-Olmecs lived similarly to the Olmecs, but differed in some respects, as for example, in their use of hieroglyphic writing. The Epi-Olmecs made use of a highly developed

writing system, similar to that of the Maya. The most important textual evidence is the La Morraja stela from 156 A.D., which was discovered only in 1986, in the Mexican Federal State of Veracruz.

Equinox
March 21 and September 23 each year, when day and night are of equal lengths.

Esperanza phase
An epoch in the history of Kaminaljuyu in the Highlands of Guatemala. During the Esperanza phase (ca. 400–600 A.D.), the city experienced a cultural boom based on intensive contact with, perhaps even conquest by, Teotihuacan. During this time, various buildings were erected in Talud-Tablero style, which was characteristic of this distant Mesoamerican metropolis.

Ethnohistory
A science of history centered on specific population groups, but which, in contrast to traditional historiography, has recourse not only to written sources, but also to oral traditions and archeological objects.

Fine Orange
A term used to describe thin-walled ceramics with orange-yellow to reddish coloring and a smooth surface. Decoration is either completely absent or executed only by scoring. These ceramics are considered among the most important in the Maya region and were produced over a period of 950 years up to the Postclassic period.

Fire drill
A tool that was used to create fire. A spindle was placed vertically on a softwood board and twirled between the hands for as long as it took for the tinder to ignite. Fire drilling was an important ceremony for the → Aztecs in Mexico. After the completion of every calendar cycle of 52 years, fire was freshly kindled, which signaled the beginning of a new era. So far, however, the meaning of fire drilling to the Maya people, as displayed by various Maya deities on page 37 of the Madrid Codex, has not been interpreted conclusively.

Flint
A strongly siliceous sedimentary rock. Knapped flint was used to produce blades,

Lidded vessel with the representation of a macaw. Tikal, Peten, Guatemala; Early Classic, 300–600 A.D.; fired clay, painted; Guatemala City, Museo Nacional de Arqueología y Etnología

as well as spear and lance heads. The Maya also worked flint when making ritual artifacts for use in ceremonies. These so-called eccentric flints are an example of this type of work. They show human or supernatural creatures, sometimes given bizarre traits and features.

Fresco painting (Italian, fresco, "fresh")
The technique of painting a wall where colors are spread onto fresh, wet plaster. Because plaster dries quickly, only the part of the wall that the artist will be able to paint that day can

Vessel painting showing a war scene. Provenance unknown; Late Classic, 600–900 A.D.; fired clay, painted; H. 17 cm , W. 15.5 cm; private collection (Kerr 2352)

be plastered. This is the origin of the term day work. In comparison with → secco painting, which is applied to a dry base, frescos are more durable under good climatic conditions.

Glottochronology
A method of dating linguistics that compares related → languages in order to determine the date of their separation. The basic assumption of this method, which is currently viewed with great criticism, lies in the fact that the vocabulary of each and every language changes by 81 percent over 1,000 years.

Gold
There are no natural sources of gold in the Maya region, as was established by the fortune-seeking Spanish conquerors. The few gold artifacts that have been found there are imported goods from southern Central America or central Mexico. In the Postclassic, the Maya began to emboss and punch imported sheet gold. Their metalworking techniques went no further than this. Most gold objects in the Maya region were found in the cenote of Chichen Itza.

Grolier Codex
Only surviving in fragments, the Grolier Codex, named after the gallery where it was first exhibited, was found by art robbers three decades ago in a dry cave in the Mexican Federal State of Tabasco. At first, the eleven-sided manuscript was regarded as a fake

because its written characters are exclusively day signs and numbers. However, it was soon established that the artifact was pre-Columbian times and that, moreover, the manuscript, like the → Dresden Codex, contained a Venus calendar. Today, its authenticity is no longer in doubt.

Haab
The calendar of a solar year of 365 days, comprising 18 months, each of 20 days, and a supplementary month of five days. Each of the 19 months has its own name and hieroglyph. In inscriptions, the date information in the Haab calendar usually follows that in the → Tzolk'in calendar (→ Calendar Round).

Hacha (Spanish, "axe," "hatchet")
Two completely different items are covered by this term. The first is a conventional stone axe. It served in the Classic as a weapon of war as well as a ritual tool used, for example, for decapitation. The other hacha is a flat stone sculpture, which closely resembles the shape of an axe blade, and is thought by some researchers to be part of the equipment of a ballplayer.

Hallucinogens
Plant or animal materials that induce the disturbance of sensory perception. The Maya of the Classic probably consumed certain types of fungi, as well as fluids secreted from a species of toad. The fluid was mixed with tobacco and smoked as a cigar. The hallucinogens no doubt served the purpose of achieving a state of trance during rituals.

Hematite
Iron ore mineral comprising black crystals with a metallic luster.

Hero Twins
A heroic pair, whose deeds are fully described in → Popol Wuj, the holy book of the K'iche' Maya. The mythological twins successfully outwitted the gods of the underworld and established world order. After their work was done, they rose as the sun and moon in the firmament. In the Popol Wuj, they are referred to as Junajpu ("One blowgun") and Xb'alanke ("Jaguar"). On ceramic vessels of the Classic, they carry the names Hun Ajaw ("One master") and Yax Balam ("Green/first jaguar"). Black flecks on the naked torso and the blowgun are characteristic for Junajpu, and Xb'alanke is usually shown with the ears of a jaguar or a beard made from jaguar fur.

Hieroglyph
A character in a non-alphabetic → script, which in Mayan can be either a → logogram or a → syllable character. Should several hieroglyphs be gathered together to form a word or complete semantic unit, and optically form a continuum, this is termed as a hieroglyph block.

Hieroglyphic stairway
Hieroglyphic stairways, with glyphic signs either inscribed or painted on them, are always open steps leading from public plazas to platforms with temples or palaces, and usually report successful military campaigns. Occasionally, they also comprise the entire

dynastic history of a city, as on the famous Copan steps with their 2,200 hieroglyphs.

Holmul Dancer

A motif used on ceramic vessels from various pre-Columbian sites. It depicts one or more dancers, often in the style of the Maize God, carrying a very large back frame. Because such ceramic vessels were first excavated in Holmul, in eastern Peten in Guatemala, the constantly recurring figures became referred to as Holmul Dancers.

Hornstone → flint

Huaxtecs

A Maya group which split from other Maya peoples around 3,500 years ago, and moved to the north. In pre-Hispanic times they were renowned for their stone sculptures and conch work. Today around 70,000 Huaxtecs live on the Mexican Gulf coast in the states of Veracruz, San Luis Potosi, and Tamalipas.

Huipil or Wipil/Ipil

An Aztec term for the traditional outer-clothing of women indigenous to Mexico and Central America. It is a smock made from square, woven sections that are sewn together with a hole in the middle to slip it over the head. They are made using various techniques, but most often on the belt loom.

Human sacrifice

Human sacrifice, as practiced by the Maya from as early as the Classic up until the conquest era, is predominantly illustrated on ceramic vessels and only rarely displayed on stone monuments. The illustrations show mainly victims stretched out over an incense burner or stone, with a package stuck in their open chest, which probably was inserted after the removal of the heart. It should be understood that human sacrifice was a ritual act that served to uphold cosmic order and to worship the gods.

Hu'unal

The god of kingship. He is usually shown wearing a three-pointed headdress and, because of the similarity between that and the headgear worn by jesters from the Middle Ages, he is often termed Jester God. His actual name, Hu'unal, comes from the word *hu'un*, which means "head band." The image of this god was worn by kings on the diadem and occasionally also as a pectoral. In the pre-Hispanic era and beyond, kings often decorated themselves with flowers for special occasions, which is why the god of kingship was reputed to be the personification of a blossom.

Incense

Incense used by the Maya came from the resin of the copal tree (*Protium copal*; Mayan, *pom*), which would have been mixed with charcoal and burned in special incense burners. The aromatic smoke symbolized divine nourishment. Other sacrificial offerings, such as drops of blood on paper strips, were burned at the same time. Even today, incense sacrifice still represents an essential part of Maya ceremonies.

Incense burner

Ceramics that served to burn incense have been found throughout the Maya area, dating from the Late Preclassic onward. They vary from simple bowls and plates to vessels decorated with figures, like those occurring in Palenque and the Highlands of Guatemala. In the Postclassic, incense burners were produced in the Lowlands in the form of painted, multicolored divine figures. Even today, the Lakandon Maya practice the periodic renewal of their incense burners, which are decorated with pictures of their gods.

Initial Series

The introductory, (initial) calendar element of

Colonnade at the Temple of the Warriors. Chichen Itza, Yucatan, Mexico; Terminal Classic, 900–1000 A.D.

an inscription. It comprises an → introductory hieroglyph, the → Long Count, → the Calendar Round, and the → Supplementary Series.

Inner face of wall apertures

The vertical section of the wall openings for arches, windows, and portals.

Introductory hieroglyph

A block of → hieroglyphs that formally introduces an expanded Long Count date.

Itz'aat (Mayan, "wise man," "savant")

A title that indicates savants and artists, and also refers to an office. Maya rulers frequently held the Itz'aat title. It is not clear whether they would have been addressed as savant, wise man, or artist, or also held an appropriate office. In pictorial representations, a turban-like cloth, a point of which falls over the head, either to the front or to the back, identifies an Itz'aat. Often, a brush or writing stylus was shown protruding from the headdress.

Itzaj

A Maya group that lived at the northern edge of the Peten-Itza lake in the center of the Guatemalan administrative district of El Peten. The language of the same name belonged to the Yukatek branch of the Mayan languages and differed only slightly from the usual Mayan of the Yucatan peninsula. Today, roughly 300 Itzaj are settled in the village San Jose; and a small group emigrated to Belize in the last century and settled in Benque Viejo and San José Succotz. Only about 50 people can still speak the language, but efforts are being made to preserve it. The Itzaj play an important part in the pre-Columbian history of Yucatan. According to legend, they moved out of the southern Lowlands to the north, and founded Chichen Itza. After the fall of the city, some went to Mayapan and others back to the south, where they built a city on the island of Noj Peten in the Peten-Itaz lake. They managed to defend their independence against the Spanish conquerors until 1697.

Itzamnaaj (God D)

The Postclassic god of writers and artists. Inscriptions from the Classic onward refer to this god and name him Itzamnaaj, a word not yet translated definitively. Inscriptions report that he was present at the creation of the world, and thus a special role was assigned to him to make him stand out from the other gods. He is characterized by a hooked nose, the features of an old man, and a flowered headdress, which falls over his face.

Itzam Ye

A mythical bird of heaven. In the Classic, it was regarded as an aspect of the god → Itzamnaaj, and is often depicted enthroned at the top of the tree of the worlds (→ ceiba). It may be the same as the cosmic bird → Wuqub' Kaqix ("seven macaws"), which, according to the myth told in the → Popol Wuj, was killed by the Hero Twins.

Ix Chel (Goddess O)

The goddess of weaving and water. She is usually shown pouring water from a jug. Her characteristics are a wrinkled face and a hooked nose. In hieroglyphic texts, she is called Chak Chel ("red/colored/great rainbow, many rainbows"), but in the Chilam-Balam texts of colonial times she is called only Ix Chel ("rainbow woman").

Ixil

A Maya group in the mountainous north of the Guatemalan administration district El Quiche, and also the name of their language. Approximately 80,000 Ixil Maya live in the area between the three locations of Chajul, Nebaj, and Nenton, the so-called Ixil triangle. Here, during the Guatemalan civil war, which only ended in 1996, nearly all the Maya villages were leveled to the ground by the military.

Jade

A collective term for a mostly greenish lustrous ornamental stone made of jadeite or similar minerals. Because the stone was highly valued and reserved for the elite, and because the Maya in the Classic used jade exclusively from the Montagua River in south-eastern Guatemala, it was a coveted trade item. The Maya made varied ornamental pieces and ritual objects. Numerous death masks were also made of this material and would have symbolized the wealth and status of the deceased dignitary.

Jalach Winik (Mayan, "true man")

The title of the highest political office bearer in several provinces of Postclassic northern Yucatan. As ruler of a province, Jalach Winik simultaneously carried the → Ajaw title. If, at the same time, he held the title Batab', he was also administrator of the capital city of a state to whom all other Batab' titleholders were subordinated. In colonial times, the term was used for bishops, governors, and other high offices.

Jawante (Mayan, "wide dish")

Classic inscriptions define jawante as a completely flat dish that stands on three feet. In Classic illustrations on ceramic vessels, these dishes are shown containing → tamales.

Jester God

An interim name given to a supernatural being in human or animal form, because of its three-pointed head cover, which was reminiscent of the cap worn by European jesters in the Middle Ages. The headdress is also interpreted as a three-leaved plant symbol. The diadems of most Maya rulers carry a picture of the so-called Jester God, whose hieroglyphic name is Hu'unal.

Jun Ye Nal (Mayan, "one maize cob"; God E)

The Classic name for one form of the Maize God, who is associated with → Chaak (GI) and the ancestor of the → Palenque Triad. He is recognizable by his youthful face and his hairstyle, upon which the hieroglyph for maize, or maize cob, is sometimes placed. Depictions on ceramic vessels show the Maize God like a sprouting maize plant, rising or dancing from a crack in the turtleshell that symbolizes the Earth. Jun Ye Nal is sometimes depicted supported by the → Hero Twins. This scene is interpreted as the birth of maize and is seen as a renewal or rebirth, in connection with Maya belief.

Kalom

A title that conjointly denotes an office and, in the Early Classic, sometimes included the position of the most important → Ajaw title. A cardinal point is often placed in front of the

OVERVIEW OF HISTORICAL SITES

Christian Prager and Nikolai Grube

Abaj Takalik

Artificially raised earth platforms, public plazas, and courtyards surrounded by buildings form the center of this Preclassic site. There are more than 20 sculptures and inscribed stelae in Abaj Takalik, and they are regarded as the precursors of the stone monuments in Classic Maya Lowlands. They are dated between 37 B.C. and 126 A.D.

Acanceh

Beneath the modern township of the same name lies the archeological site of Acanceh, which had its heyday in the Late Preclassic and Early Classic. The core of the settlement is dominated by the main pyramid, on which monumental stucco masks have recently been exposed. To the south of this construction lies a second building, on which the stucco façade, ornamented with figures, reveals influence from Teotihuacan.

Aguateca

This site, on the high plateau of Lago Petexbatun, which falls away steeply on all sides, was discovered in 1957. The palace and ceremonial complex in the center of the city bear witness to the period in the late 8th century when Aguateca flourished. The region around Aguateca was, at this time, the scene of numerous warlike engagements, so the site needed to be protected with defensive measures. To add to the natural geological protection from the steep slope and the ravine that runs through the ceremonial center of Aguateca, the inhabitants built long palisade walls within and around the core of the settlement. Despite being well fortified, the city was conquered and burned at the end of the 8th century.

Ake

Ake, which lies about 35 kilometers (22 miles) east of Merida, was discovered by John Lloyd Stephens in 1842. Along with Acanceh and Izamal, Ake is one of the few sites in the northern Lowlands where the buildings originating in the Early Classic appear to still have been inhabited well into the Postclassic. Having said this, Ake was definitely at its peak in the Classic (300–950 A.D.).

Altar de Sacrificios

One of the earliest settlements in the central Lowlands, Altar de Sacrificios on Rio Usumacinta should be looked at in the light of its position on a major trading route. Finds, which came to light during the discovery of the site in the 19th century, indicate that it was founded in the Middle Preclassic. The complete excavation was not accomplished until the last third of the 20th century. Numerous stelae and other memorials, erected by its rulers between 455 and 849 A.D., indicate a cultural blossoming of the city during the late Classic.

Altun Ha

The earliest traces of a settlement in Altun Ha can be traced back to the Middle Preclassic, around 1,000 B.C. However, the monumental architecture still visible today originated in the Classic. With more than 300 identifiable buildings and a number of rich upper class burials in the city, it is likely that the rulers of Altun Ha profited from a trade network between the central Lowlands and the Caribbean coast. During this time of great wealth, 8,000 to 10,000 people would have lived in Altun Ha.

Balamku

With an area of just a square kilometer (less than a mile), Balamaku is a relatively small site, which comprises three architectural groups. The site was first discovered in 1990, and is held in particularly high regard due to the discovery of a spectacular stucco façade, which originates from between 300 and 500 A.D. The multicolored frieze of this façade, with a length of about 17 meters (56 feet) and a height of more than four meters (13 feet), counts as one of the finest stucco works of the Maya Lowlands.

Becan

The earliest traces of a settlement in Becan probably date back to the 7th century B.C. Between 200 and 600 A.D, the central area of the site was enclosed by a ditch and a defensive ring of palisade walls; seven bridges provided access to the center. In the Late Classic, between 600 and 730 A.D., the center was developed further, with the addition of extravagant palaces and temples. Becan, which was discovered in 1934, was inhabited until 1450 and is typical of the Rio Bec style of architecture.

Bonampak

The polychrome wall paintings of Bonampak (Mexico), discovered in 1946, are among the most important artworks of Mesoamerica. They are part of a group of pictorial and written testimonies that make it possible to reconstruct the course of wars, rituals, and other events in the life of the Maya nobility. The center of Bonampak comprises three large architectural building complexes dating from between 600 and 800 A.D. Inscriptions on the paintings, on the door lintel in Structure 1, and on the sculpted stela standing in the main plaza, report on the life of the rulers Yajaw Chan Muwaan and his son, who governed between 780 and 792 A.D. With the coming to power of Yajaw Chan Muwaan, the Bonampak dynasty received a boost, much needed after losing their independence to wars against Tonina hegemony in the previous decade.

Cahal Pech

The ruins of the significant medium-sized

Chichen Itza, Yucutan, Mexico. Tatiana Proskouriakoff's reconstruction drawing of the sacral center illustrating the imposing monumental architecture of this important site.

ceremonial center of Cahal Pech, which was discovered in the 1950s, are to be found above the modern town of San Ignacio in Belize. The site comprises 34 buildings, two ball courts, and many plain stelae. The site, which was settled in the late Preclassic, was abandoned in about 800 A.D.

Calakmul

Discovered in 1931, this is the largest of all Maya sites, and its significance is shown by the 117 stelae found here. Due to the poor state of preservation of the stelae – the inscriptions have weathered because of the poor quality of the local limestone – the history of the site remained unknown for many years. Although the building of both the main pyramids, Structure 1 and the 45-meter- (148-foot)-high Structure 2, was started in the Middle Preclassic, Calakmul is not identifiable as the seat of a prominent royal dynasty until about 500 A.D. Calakmul first became a pan-regional "superpower," capable of competing with Tikal, under Tuun K'ab Hix (c. 520–550 A.D.). Calakmul's influence reached its furthest extent under Yuknoom the Great. His son, Yuknoom Yich'aak K'ak' (686–695 A.D.) was, however, vanquished in 695 A.D. while battling Tikal. The sensational tomb chamber of this ruler was found in Structure 2 in 1997. The inscribed evidence of the site ends in the year 909 A.D., but coarsely executed miniature stelae indicate that the settlement existed beyond that time.

Cancuen

This site, discovered by Teobert Maler in 1908, lies about 40 kilometers (25 miles) south of Seibal on the Pasion river. Cancuen is the largest known ruin site along the course of this river. Its core comprises two or three large ceremonial complexes with pyramid temples and living areas for the elite. By referring to the stelae on site, the high point of the settlement can be estimated as between 790 and 800 A.D. There is also an indication of an earlier settlement of Cancuen around A.D. 741, city was made subject to the ruler Dos Pilas. Cancuen was able to liberate itself at the end of the 8th century.

Caracol

This, the largest archeological site in Belize, was first discovered in 1937 by woodcutters. Settled since the Late Preclassic, the beginnings of the local royal dynasty can be traced back to 331 A.D. Under the ruler Yajawte K'inich II (553–599) and his son K'an II (618–658), Caracol was able to free itself from the supremacy of Tikal and to become one of the most powerful cities of the eastern Lowlands. The center is dominated by the 46-meter-(150-foot)-high Caana pyramid, which was started in the Preclassic and successfully englarged in the Classic. The various acropolis complexes of the center are connected by long sakbe to the densely settled outskirts. Here, more than 3,000 house platforms have been discovered, but a total of 36,000 house platforms may have stood on the 88 square kilometers (55 square miles) of the settlement area. Inscriptions on 23 stelae and 23 altars describe the dynastic history of the city up to the year 859 A.D.

Cerros

The ruins of Cerros lie on a peninsula that projects into the Bay of Corozal in Belize. Thomas Gann discovered the site in about 1900, but it was first excavated in the 1970s and '80s. Between 50 B.C. and 100 A.D., Cerros was counted among the most important trade centers on the coast of the Yucatan peninsula. This theory is supported by the presence of more than 100 palace buildings and pyramids – some extravagantly decorated with stucco works – which form the settlement core of the site. The unique artwork and architecture from Cerros were way-markers for the iconography and architecture of the Lowland Maya of the Classic.

Chichen Itza

Next to Tulum on the east coast of Yucatan, Chichen Itza is the best-known ruined city in the north of the peninsula. Shortly after the invasion of the Spaniards, Montejo the Elder (1479–1548) occupied the ruins and established there the first Spanish capital city in Yucatan in 1532. After only a short time, the Spanish settlement had to be abandoned. The Maya ruins were never forgotten – they were first visited by European researchers in the middle of the 19th century and first understood archeologically at the beginning of the 20th century. Two styles of building dominate in Chichen Itza: the Puuc style (600–900 A.D.), named after the region of the same name, and the so-called Mexicanized style (900–1200 A.D.), which united influences from the Gulf coast, Oaxaca, and central Mexico. Famous buildings like the El Castillo, the Temple of the Warrior, and the Great Ball Court, are typical examples of the Mexican influence in Chichen Itza. With more than 50 epigraphic inscriptions, Chichen Itza is considered one of the most interesting places in north Yucatan. The most important, and most frequently mentioned, person in the settlement is K'ak'upakal, who ruled this metropolis in the mid-9th century.

Chinkultic

Despite the considerable number of inscribed stone monuments, which relate to the years between 591 and 897 A.D., the dynastic history of Chinkultic on the Chunujabab lagoon in Chiapas, has not been extensively researched. Worthy of note are the representations of prisoners on the stelae, which indicate that, at its high points, Chinkultic was a regional power that raised its reputation by the fact that it held foreign nobles captive in the city. Chinkultic was discovered at the beginning of the 20th century. The core of the settlement revealed more than 200 buildings, and the architecture, still visible today, originated in the Classic. Ceramic finds show that the settlement dates back to Late Preclassic times and lasted until the Postclassic.

Coba

With a settled area of about 43 square kilometers (27 square miles), Coba was the most important center in the north-east of Yucatan in the Late Classic. Individual building complexes are linked by 45 sakbe, with one leading to Yaxuna, 100 kilometers (62 miles) away. Massive temples and residential buildings testify to the power of the local elite, whose history is recorded on about 50 hieroglyphic inscriptions. Coba was already settled in 100 A.D., grew in size in the Late Classic, and was abandoned at the end of the Classic, although it was resettled in about 1200 A.D.

Comalcalco

Buildings constructed from clay bricks characterize this Late Classic archeological site in the alluvial plain of Tabasco. Because there was a shortage of stone in this region, the inhabitants were forced to resort to the material of the silty subsoil. Their hieroglyphic texts were also written on clay tiles. This settlement reached its greatest expansion in the Late Classic. Three great ceremonial complexes dominate – the large

Chichen Itza, Yucatan, Mexico, El Castillo (also called K'uk'ulcan pyramid). The monumental structure was excavated in the 1930s and reconstructed, when older precursor structures were found inside.

Dzibilnocac, Campeche, Mexico. This photograph was taken by Teobert Maler in1887 and shows the west face of the east flanking temple of the large temple palace of Dzibilnocac.

Dzibilnocac, Campeche, Mexico. A modern photograph of the same building in Dzibilnocac. The archeological definition reads Structure A 1.

Acropolis, the North Group, and the East Acropolis. Comalcalco maintained dynastic connections with the last rulers in Palenque.

Copan

Copan lies on the river of the same name in the far north-west of the Central American state of Honduras. It is the longest-known and best-researched Maya city. It was, above all, the precise illustrations of Frederick Catherwood, who visited Copan in 1839 with John Lloyd Stevens, that made this site famous. A sequence of comprehensive excavations and restoration works have been undertaken in the center of Copan since the start of the 20th century, during which the graves of early rulers, including that of the dynastic founder Yax K'uk' Mo' (c. 426–437 A.D.), have been uncovered. The settlement of the Copan valley can be traced back to the 13th century B.C. through ceramics found in local caves, and individual items found in the region of the alluvial plain of the Copan river. The dynastic history of Copan, reaching back to the time of the dynasty founder, can be read on its numerous stone monuments. In total, 17 rulers governed Copan during its 400-year existence. Most of the constructions visible today originated during the reign of the last three rulers (738–822 A.D.). The last monument, dated 822 A.D., was not completed. Copan attained fame predominantly because of the quality and fineness of its stelae, altars, and façade sculptures. During the rule of Waxaklajuun Ubaah K'awiil (695–738 A.D.), a sculptural style was developed that is unique in its graphic power and animation.

Dos Pilas

In 1954, inhabitants of the town of Sayaxche in the heart of the Petexbatun region discovered the ruins of Dos Pilas. In an area of just one square kilometer (less than a mile), 500 buildings were discovered, including large pyramid constructions and many smaller groups of living quarters. The history of the place can be almost completely reconstructed from the 35 or more inscribed monuments on site and in the region. The texts reveal that the ruling lineage in Dos Pilas was driven out of Tikal and settled further south to the Petexbatun. The earliest recorded historical date refers to the birth of Ruler 1 in the year 625 A.D. By about 731 A.D., the nearby center of Aguateca emerged as a "twin capital" of the Dos Pilas kingdom. The last reference to the people of Dos Pilas dates from about A.D. 807. As in other sites in the region, the rulers of Dos Pilas were constantly trying to strengthen their position of power and to extend their area of influence. Wars, political marriages, and personal contacts were tactical aids, which, especially in this region, were successful methods of gaining power.

Dzibanche

After Coba, Dzibanche is the largest ruin of the Mexican Federal State of Quintana Roo. Discovered in 1927 by Thomas Gann, it lies in the south of the country west of Bacalar. Excavations at the beginning of the 1990s showed that the site reached its zenith in the Early Classic, and was much more significant than previously assumed. The richly furnished burials of Dzibanche's elite indicate the importance of the local nobility, and hieroglyphic stairways decorated with representations of captives suggest that the site was a vassal state of Calakmul.

Dzibilchaltun

With an area of about 16 square kilometers (10 square miles) and a total of more than 800 buildings, Dzibilchaltun was one of the greatest centers in northern Yucatan. There is evidence of continuous settlement from 900 B.C. to colonial times. In about 250 B.C., the population began to increase rapidly, reaching its maximum in about A.D. 830. The majority of the surviving inscriptions, detailing the lives of local rulers and their dynastic connections, also originated at this time. Between 1000 and 1200, construction rates shrank in line with the population count. But, between 1200 and 1540, a new settlement emerged within the ruined center of Dzibilchaltun.

Dzibilnocac

Stephens and Catherwood discovered the remains of Dzibilnocac, which lie within the modern town of Iturbide in Campeche, in 1842. Although the site is in the Chenes region and its architecture is built in the Chenes style, there are buildings there that indicate Rio Bec influence. The largest is Structure A1, which would have served as both temple and palace. The site was settled in the middle of the Preclassic, but the architecture visible today originated in the late Classic. Dzibilnocac was abandoned in about 950 A.D.

Edzna

Although local people have known of Edzna for a long time, scientists did not become interested in researching it until the 1920s. Within the settled area of 3.7 kilometers (2.3 miles), the five-story main temple was the most conspicuous of the buildings. Because of its situation on an artificial platform, and its height of nearly 40 meters (131 feet), it offered an excellent long-distance view of the surroundings. About 40 inscribed stelae, panels, and a hieroglyphic stairway, contain information about the history of the site, which was already settled in about 400 B.C. and was not abandoned until 1500 A.D. Inscriptions on the earliest stela date to before 435 A.D., and the most recent of the monuments was erected in about 810 A.D. In the Late Classic, Edzalal may have come under the leadership of Calakmul, a Maya settlement then in its prime.

Ek Balam

Spectacular discoveries made in the last couple of years have awakened public interest in the ruins of Ek Balam. The core of the settlement extends over an area of about six square kilometers (four square miles), and is surrounded by two walls. Structure 1, in the site's center, is 150 meters (492 feet) long and is therefore the largest construction in the city. The excavations over the last two years have brought to light a well-preserved stucco façade and a flight of steps inscribed with hieroglyphs. Most of the buildings so far excavated date from the last part of the Classic. Other finds at Ek Balam from the Preclassic suggest that the site was already settled at this time.

El Baul

Located in the region of Santa Lucia

Cozumalguapa, El Baul belongs to a group of sites that share similar architectural features. The area was settled in the middle of the Preclassic (800–400 B.C.). Characteristic archeological finds of this region are heavy basalt stelae with a typical style of iconography, which shows influence from Mexico.

El Cayo
The ruins of the small El Cayo site lie on both banks of the Usumacinta, between Yaxchilan and Piedras Negras. El Cayo, which was founded in the Late Classic, profited between 600 and 800 A.D. from through trade on the river, and at that time was a strategic out-station of Piedras Negras. Teobert Maler found the ruins of El Cayo in 1897, and excavations followed in the 1950s and '90s. A sequence of inscriptions found on the site show that El Cayo was governed by viceroys of the Sajal rank, who took office under the aegis of the ruler of Piedras Negras.

El Meco
The ruins of El Meco lie to the north of Cancun. This old settlement, which was possibly that of Belma, in which Montjero the Elder established his quarters for several months in 1528, was discovered by August Le Plongeon in 1877. The main building in El Meco is the so-called Castillo, a five-stepped pyramid, which reached its present shape in the Late Classic. The settlement of El Meco was founded in about 250 A.D. and the site was abandoned c. 1100 A.D. Despite this, El Meco was still one of the most important trade centers of the region during the Late Postclassic.

El Mirador
Embedded deep in virgin forest in the north of Guatemala lie the immense remains of the earliest Maya metropolis, El Mirador, which reached its cultural high point between 150 B.C. and 150 A.D. During this time, the city limits covered an area of about 16 square kilometers (10 square miles). The center comprised a crowded collection of sacred and secular buildings. The absolute claim to power of the ruler of the time found expression in the

construction of the so-called El Tigre, an enormous building complex with a ground area of 5.6 hectares (138 acres) and a height that reached well above the canopy of the trees. El Mirador ruled and influenced political and economic events in Peten during the Late Preclassic.

El Peru
The ruins of the Maya city El Peru lie about 20 kilometers (12.5 miles) north-west of Laguna Perdida in the Peten. In the 1960s and '70s, this site fell victim to relentless art thieves, who sawed off and removed a large proportion of the stelae. After years of detective work, Ian Graham was able to track down several pieces and reassemble them in photographic form. El Peru's role in Maya civilization is so far only partly known, but it is certain that Tikal waged a war against this place and that the palanquins of the then rulers were taken to Tikal as spoils of war. It seems that El Peru was part of the Calakmul hegemony in the late Classic.

El Tabasqueno
Several buildings were found at Tabasqueno in 1895 by Teobert Maler. The Chenes style dominates the architecture of this site, as shown by Structure 1, which is among the most impressive constructions, and is dated to about 710 A.D.

El Zotz
The ruins of the small El Zotz site are found to the north of Lago Peten Itza. At the end of the 1960s, art robbers removed a carved wooden door lintel from a temple building, which, shortly afterwards, surfaced in the Denver Art Museum. The piece was returned to Guatemala in 1998. Carved and inscribed wooden door lintels are extremely rare and, so far, have been found only in Tikal, Dzibanche, and El Zotz.

Hochob
Teobart Maler discovered a group of eight buildings on a plateau near the town of Dzibalchen in Campeche in 1888. The architecture of the small site of Hochob is in

Chenes style, and because of its excellent preservation serves as an example for this building style. Although all of the remaining buildings probably originated in the Late Classic, settlement at this strategically important place can nevertheless be shown to date back to the Early Preclassic right up to the time of conquest.

Hormiguero
The ruins of Hormiguero in Campeche are counted among the most impressive and best-preserved constructions in the Rio Bec style. Structure 2, with its south façade constructed as gaping snake jaws, is one of the most important buildings at the site. The earliest traces of settlement here are thought to be Preclassic, from between 50 and 250 A.D. Structural forerunners built in the earlier Rio Bec style, which was used between 550 and 600 A.D., have been found beneath the buildings erected in the Late Classic. As in other Rio Bec cities, there are no hieroglyphic inscriptions at Hormiguero.

Itzan
Although hardly any excavations have been undertaken in Itzan, the site has become well-known because of its numerous inscriptions. Itzan lies 13 kilometers (eight miles) north-east of Altar de Sacrificios and was already settled in the Preclassic. Itzan managed to defend its independence well into the Late Classic, and in addition maintained dynastic connections with Dos Pilas. There were five generations of rulers at Itzan between 685 and 807 A.D. The latest inscription dates from the year 829 A.D.

Iximche
The ruins of the former capital city of the Caqchikel Maya lie to the west of the town of Chimaltenango in Guatemala. Groups of constructions made from dressed stone are arranged around four plazas. Originally, the walls were stucco and painted in the Mixteca Puebla style. The buildings, which clearly show Mexican influences, are described as epi-Toltec style. The place was first settled during the Late Postclassic. With the arrival of

the Spaniards, it was declared the capital city of Guatemala for a short time.

Ikkun
The influence of Ikkun, the regional power in the late Classic, which lies north of Poptun, lasted until after Naj Tunich. A sequence of inscriptions from the 8th century report on war campaigns against neighboring cities, an indication that Ikkun had a regional hegemony. However, such concentration of power was, as a rule, short-lived, because continuous intercity rivalry prevailed.

Ixlu
The small ruin site of Ixlu is to be found on the east bank of Lago Peten Itza, about 30 kilometers (11 miles) south of Tikal. Sylvanus Morely discovered the site in the 1930s; at that time, he documented two stelae and an altar, which were created between 859 and 879 A.D. The sites of Ixlu and Jimbal, on the periphery of Tikal, reached their cultural height at the end of the Classic, at a time when the gradual decline of Tikal had already begun. The latest monument of this region was erected in 889 A.D., only 20 years after the last ruler of Tikal had erected the last authenticated stela there.

Ixtutz
The relatively small site of Ixtutz, about ten kilometers (six miles) north of Machaquila, was very important during the Late Classic. Inscriptions there show that the site cultivated relationships with rulers from Dos Pilas and Aguateca, and had waged war against Machaquila, which lay only a short distance away.

Izapa
Izapa, on the Pacific coast of Chiapas, was already settled in about 800 B.C., although the structures visible today date from between 300 and 50 B.C. Typical of the construction method in Izapa are raised earth platforms, which are masked with undressed stone and carry a top layer of stucco or clay. Izapa is renowned because of its 89 stone stelae, the majority of which are not sculpted. Izapa is

Hochob, Campeche, Mexico. Snakehead Palace, south façade. This photo of the so-called Snakehead Palace from Hochob comes from the year 1887 and shows the entrance area of the central structure.

Hochob, Campeche, Mexico. About 100 years later, the state of preservation of the façade of the Snakehead Temple has not appreciably deteriorated.

among the most important centers with Late Preclassic sculptures, which are therefore often known as Izapa style. The Izapa style marks a transition between Olmec and Classic Maya iconography.

Jaina
In the Classic, the island of Jaina on the west coast of Campeche served, both regionally and pan-regionally, as a necropolis. Between 500 and 1000 A.D., about 20,000 graves were dug in the inhabited areas of the island. A ceremonial center with pyramids and domestic structures crosses Jaina from west to east. The domestic structures and three stelae, which are inscribed with images of prisoners, suggest that a local noble dynasty that also fulfilled an important regional role inhabited the site.

Kabah
In 1843, Stephens and Catherwood published the earliest information about the ruins of Kabah, which lie close to Uxmal. Large architectural complexes, such as the palace and the Temple of Pillars, which were erected in the Late Classic, form the center point of the site and display characteristic Puuc style. Another striking building, dating from between 830 and 1000 A.D., is the so-called Codz Poop, the south façade of which is decorated with about 400 stone masks of the Rain God. There are signs at Kabah too that the place was inhabited in Preclassic times.

Kaminaljuyu
The ruins of Kaminaljuyu, the largest archeological site of the Guatemalan Highlands, lie in soil under the present capital of Guatemala. The site was first settled by agricultural cultures at around 2,500 B.C. Kaminaljuyu's importance grew with the increasing obsidian trade between the Highlands and the Lowlands. The site played an important role in the Preclassic era as "Port of Trade" between Central Mexico and the Maya Region. Settlement can be traced back to 800 A.D.

Kohunlich
This site lies south of Quintana Roo, about 40 kilometers (25 miles) west of Chetumal. The Early Classic stucco masks of Structure 1 in Kohunlich are famous for being among the finest examples of their kind. The architecture was worked in Rio Bec style at the Terminal Classic, between 800 and 1050 A.D. Constructions from the first building phase at Kohunlich, however, originate from the Early Classic, between about 450 and 600 A.D.

Labna
Just as with many other sites in Yucatan, the relatively small Labna settlement was first made known to the general public in 1843 by Stephens and Catherwood. The most important buildings here are the palace, the portal arch, and El Mirador; they were all built in Puuc style. The Early Classic palace is, with a length of more than 120 meters (394 feet), the largest building on site. The other structures at Labna date from the Late Classic to Terminal Classic.

Lamanai
In the Late Preclassic and Early Classic,

Lamanai's location on the lagoon of the New River promoted it as an important trade center for the exchange of goods between the coast and the cities in the Peten. Most of the architecture still visible today (more than 718 buildings) originated during this time. The first phase of settlement began in the Early Preclassic. In contrast to other Maya cities, Lamanai was continuously settled from the Early Classic up until the arrival of the Spaniards.

Lubaantun
Unlike its neighboring sites (Pusilha, Nim Li Punit, and Uxbenka) Lubaantun was founded in the Late Classic and was inhabited only from 700 to 900 A.D. The site flourished during this time because of its position on the Rio Grande. Lubaantun was one of the most important trade centers in the south, profiting from trade between the south, east, and north of the peninsula. The ceremonial center is composed of 11 large buildings, which are grouped around five public plazas. Because most of the buildings on the top levels of the pyramids were made of stone that weathered easily, only the pyramid platforms are preserved to this day. Despite the pan-regional significance of Lubaantun, at the time of writing only three sculpted and inscribed ball game pitch markers have been discovered. There are no stelae at this site.

Machaquila
A geologist discovered the ruins of Machaquila by the river of the same name in 1957. As a tributary to the Rio de la Pasion, the Rio Machaquila served as a long-distance trade route in pre-Columbian times, and the site of Machaquila played no small part in this business. Trade also brought cultural acquisitions from central Mexico into the region, and Mexican influence can be identified here from the Terminal Classic onward. The 18 inscribed monuments at Machaquila report that, between 711 and 841 A.D., the site was a small independent

state, which founded its leadership in the region on marriage, politics, and war.

Mayapan
Mayapan was the most important ceremonial center in the north of Yucatan in the Late Postclassic. After Chichen Itza had lost significance in Yucatan in the 12th century, Mayapan established itself, between 1250 and 1450, as the most eminent trade center in the peninsula. Nevertheless, Chichen Itza retained its architectural influence, and Mayapan's El Castillo is clearly an imitation of its more famous precursor. To shield the settlement from attackers, the 3,600 buildings at the core of the city were surrounded by a wall eight kilometers (five miles) long.

Mixco Viejo
The capital of the Poqomam Maya, Mixco Viejo was built in the Guatemalan Highlands in the Late Postclassic (about 1250 A.D.) and was inhabited up until the arrival of the Spaniards. Pedro de Alvardo conquered the fortified city in 1525, and deported its inhabitants to another region. Pyramid structures, living accommodation, and ball game courts define the character of Mixco Viejo, which was rediscovered in 1896 by Karl Sapper.

Moral
Equally well-known by the names Balancan, Balancan-Morales, La Reforma, and Morales, this place is one of the most interesting ruins in the Mexican Federal State of Tabasco, by virtue of the inscriptions discovered here. The center of Moral comprises seven buildings, including both pyramids and living quarters. It can be deduced from the inscriptions that Moral was already an independent city-state by about 633 A.D., extending its sphere of power through warlike expansion. The 12 or so

inscribed monuments from Moral are now kept in the regional museum of Balancan.

Motul de San Jose
Teobert Maler discovered the ruins of Motul de San Jose in the year 1895. This small Late Classic center is located north of Lake Peten Itza. It is seen as the place of origin of many of the ceramic vessels stolen from the region because the emblem glyph of Motul de San Jose can be recognized on them. The inscriptions of Machaquila tell of a ruler of Motul de San Jose taken prisoner in 731 A.D.

Naachtun
The large and inaccessible Naachtun site, discovered in 1919 by Sylvanus Morley, has not yet been systematically investigated. The extensive E Group complex indicates a settlement in the Late Preclassic. Most of the 40 poorly preserved stelae date from the Early Classic.

Nadzcaan
At the start of the 1990s, Mexican archeologists found the remains of an enormous metropolis in Campeche. The stelae discovered so far suggest that the place had its own emblem glyph and was an important center during the Classic.

Nakbe
Roughly 13 kilometers (8 miles) south of El Mirador, lie the ruins of the Preclassic trade city of Nakbe. It was discovered during an aerial survey in 1930, and first investigated in 1962 by Ian Graham. The core settlement consists of two large building complexes from the Middle Preclassic, and is the first archeological site in the Peten in which buildings from this era have been identified. The small building platforms would have been built between 1000 and 600 B.C., and the massive buildings were erected between 600 and 200 B.C.

Labna, Yucatan, Mexico. This modern photograph shows the 120-meter long palace of Labna, which dates to the early Late Classic. A causeway or *sakbe* runs southward over the plaza.

Nakum

The ruins of Nakum, lying roughly 18 kilometers (11 miles) to the east of Tikal, were discovered in 1905 by Maurice de Périgny. The architectural remains of this relatively large ruin site originate from the Late Classic, and the stelae date from the mid-8th century. Temple A, with its round door arches, which were walled up at the Terminal Classic, is among the most interesting of the buildings in Nakum.

Naranjo

In the search for valuable grave goods, plunderers damaged many buildings at this site in the Peten by digging long tunnels and trenches through the structures. Many ceramic vessels with clear Naranjo provenance, which today can be found in the art trade, originated from this looted site. The stelae, found in good condition by Teobert Maler at the end of the 19th century, were sawn down in the 1960s and smuggled abroad. Inscriptions here tell us that, in the Late Classic, not only had Naranjo waged war on its neighbors, but it had also become the target of foreign attacks.

Nim Li Punit

In 1976, geologists discovered the ruins of Nim Li Punit 20 kilometers (12.5 miles) north-east of Lubaantun, in the Toledo district of Belize. On the central plaza of this Late Classic site, archeologists found 26 stelae, six of which have inscriptions. Lubaantun is seen as the economic and political center of this region, but it is assumed that Nim Li Punit was the dynastic cultural center of the ruling elite.

Nohmul

Thomas Gann discovered this site, which lies to the north of Orange Walk in Belize, in 1897. With a settled area of about 18 square kilometers (11 square miles) Nohmul is one of the most important Maya centers in the eastern Maya area. The large number of buildings at this site indicates a high population, which reached its maximum in the Late Preclassic. During this time, Nohmul maintained trade relationships with cities as far away as central Mexico.

Oxkintok

During the Classic, Oxkintok was a significant place in the Puuc region. The core of the site consists of three building complexes, which are each connected to one another by *sakbes*. One of the most interesting buildings is the so-called Satunsaat, because it shows a system of chambers that are linked by small doorways and narrow steps. Oxkintok has a large number of hieroglyphic texts, which record events between 474 and 859 A.D.

Palenque

The ruins of Palenque were discovered in the 18th century, but the excavations, which continue to this day, first began in the 1940s. Important finds, like the recently discovered throne in Temple 19 and the burial chamber in Temple 21, are continuously coming to light. With nearly 200 hieroglyphic texts, Palenque is among the most important sites for inscribed texts in the Maya area. The Temple of the Inscriptions, with its burial chamber, and the sarcophagus of the famous Maya ruler K'inich Janaab Pakal (625–683 A.D.), is one of the most spectacular archeological discoveries of the 20th century. Imposing architectural constructions, like the Temple of the Inscriptions, the Palace complex, the Great Plaza, and several smaller temples and living quarters (which are arranged around the plaza), form the settlement core of Palenque. The earliest traces of a settlement here date from the 3rd century A.D. Most of the architecture and façade decorations, however, were erected during the blossoming of Palenque between 600 and 800 A.D. This era saw the reign of the three most influential rulers of Palenque: K'inich Janaab Pakal and his sons, Kan Balam (684–702 A.D.) and K'an Joy Chitam (702–711 A.D.). This line of rulers was interrupted in about 711 A.D., with the capture of K'an Joy Chitam by Tonina, but continued again with K'inich Ahkal Mo' Naab III (721–736), from an adjacent line of the family, who commissioned Temple 19.

Piedras Negras

Teobert Maler discovered the remains of this center which, during the Late Classic, fought with other city-states for dominance and control of trade on the Usumacinta river. In the Classic, the site was called *yokib*. It was first settled in about 400 B.C. and was abandoned in about 800 A.D. The majority of the 60 or so sculpted stone monuments of Piedras Negras were made during the high point of the town, between 710 and 790 A.D. In the 1960s and '70s, a considerable number of monuments were stolen from the site, several of which subsequently resurfaced in the art trade.

Pomona

The ruins of the historical site of Pomona lie on the Usumacinta river, in close proximity to the modern town of Tenosique in Chiapas. Just like the other sites on the Usumacinta, this Late Classic site profited from the flourishing trade between the coast and the central Peten. In the ceremonial center of Pomona, a number of inscription fragments have been discovered. These have been carefully preserved and are on display today in a small museum at the site. In about 795 A.D., Pomona was conquered by Piedras Negras and, after that, fell under its influence.

Pusilha

The southernmost site in Belize where hieroglyphic texts have been found goes by the name Pusilha, and is only a short distance away from the Guatemalan border. Since it was discovered in 1926, 26 sculpted stone monuments (21 stelae, two fragments, and three altars), of which at least 13 are inscribed, have been found. All of these monuments were in the Stela Plaza.

Quirigua

The ruins of Quirigua in the Motagua valley were first made known to the general public in 1841 by Stephens and Catherwood. As a significant ceremonial and administrative center, this site dominated trade with the Caribbean coast and the Highland and Lowland regions in the Classic. The many splendid sculptured stelae, altars, and zoomorphs are among the most brilliant of all Maya stone carving. They document the history of Quirigua from 426 to 810 A.D. Most of the architectural monuments that are still visible today were produced under the aegis of K'ak' Tiliw, the most influential king of Quirigua. During his rule, he expanded his power over the region, managing in 738 A.D. to capture and kill Waxaklajuun Ubaah K'awiil (695–738 A.D.), the ruler of Copan. With the defeat of Copan, which was of great economic and political significance in the south of the Maya area, Quirigua acquired regional dominance from 740 to 810 A.D.

Rio Azul

Rio Azul, 80 kilometers (50 miles) north-east of Tikal, is one of the most significant Early Classic centers of the Peten. Along with Tikal and Uaxactun, the leading cities of the time, Rio Azul was able to climb to regional power in the north-east because of its position on a river important for trade. More than 5,000 buildings, as well as dams, canals, and defenses, were built on both sides of the river. Grave robbers looted numerous richly endowed burials in the 1970s and '80s. Archeologists managed to save their priceless wall paintings which belong to the finest examples of Early Classic art.

Rio Bec

The term Rio Bec covers 14 Late Classic ruin sites (Rio Bec A to N) that lie within an area roughly 20 kilometers (12.5 miles) south of Xpuhil in Campeche. Most of these building complexes, which often consist only of a single building, were found by Raymond Merwin in the 1920s. Some complexes have more buildings. The architectural style Rio Bec derives from the name given to these sites.

Sacul

Ian Graham mapped the ruins of Sacul, which lie west of the Rio Mopan area, for the first time in 1970, and also documented the six inscribed stone stelae. The monuments and a large proportion of the architecture have since been demolished or taken out of the country by art thieves. The stelae date from the period between 731 and 790 A.D., and mention other sites in the region such as Ucanal. Sacul is a good example of a growing trend in the Late Classic, where formerly small centers gained increasing wealth and power and were able to commission many more monuments.

Santa Rita Corozal

Due to its position close to the coast, Corozal controlled Classic trade routes both on the coast and on the rivers Rio Hondo and New River. These two rivers formed the main traffic axis for trade between the Maya city

Labna, Yucatan, Mexico. In 1886, Teobert Maler photographed the central structure and left wing of the palace installation of Labna before restoration.

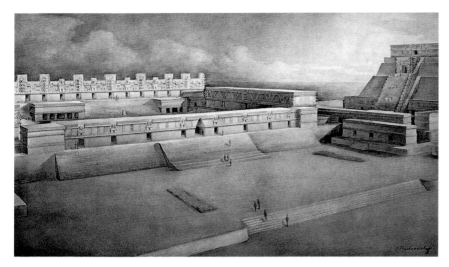

Uxmal, Yucatan, Mexico. This drawing by Tatiana Proskouriakoff reconstructs the center of Uxmal with the Nunnery Quadrangle on the left and the Pyramid of the Magician to its right.

Uxmal, Yucatan, Mexico. The present state of preservation of the Pyramid of the Magician. In the foreground are the remains of the ball court of Uxmal.

Lamanai and large settlements in the Peten. Once Mayapan had lost its significance in the Postclassic, Corozal ruled the trade, as can be seen from the goods from central and north Mexico that have been found there. Settled since 2000 B.C., Corozal was important predominantly in the Postclassic, when superb wall paintings (now lost) were created, and was continuously populated until the arrival of the Spaniards.

Santa Rosa Xtampak
The ruins of Santa Rosa Xtampak, on a plateau to the north-east of Hopelchen, were first documented by Stephens and Catherwood in 1843. Although the Chenes style dominates the architecture of the site, influences from Puuc and the Rio Bec region are also evident. The site shows a high building density and would have accommodated about 10,000 inhabitants in its heyday. The importance of Xtampak is underlined by the existence of about ten hieroglyphic texts containing information about its rulers and history.

Sayil
The settlement area of Sayil, nearly three square kilometers (two square miles) in extent, was inhabited by 9,000 people at the Terminal Classic. As at other sites in northern Yucatan, the water supply for such a large number of people was secured through artificial water collection basins – known as chultunes. The three-story palace in the north, and the stela group in the south of the site are some of the most noteworthy constructions in Sayil. The building of the palace started in A.D. 650 and was completed by about 900 A.D., when the top level was added. Most of the stelae date from the first third of the 9th century. This corresponds to the heyday of Sayil, between 800 and 1000 A.D.

Seibal
The center of Seibal, on the Pasion river, comprises three large architectural complexes in a area of about one-and-a-half square kilometers (one square mile). Seibal was settled towards the beginning of the Middle Preclassic, flowered in the Early Classic, and was abandoned in the middle of the 7th century. As revealed by the architecture and monumental art, Seibal and other parts of the Petexbatun were resettled by people from the Gulf Coast of Mexico in the Terminal Classic. Up until 930 A.D., a rejuvenated Seibal served as a trade center in the region, but was finally deserted in the middle of the 10th century. A third settlement followed, during which time Seibal became an important economic and political center for the Petexbatun region.

Tamarindito
Tamarindito, built close to the Lake Petexbatun, is one of the earliest settled places in the region. The Petexbatun area has innumerable small ruins, many of which consist of a small ceremonial center with few habitations. The dynastic history of Tamarindito is poorly known. In about 472 A.D., the birth of the first ruler was mentioned, and in about 762 A.D., the glyphic name of the city appeared for the last time. In 731 A.D., Dos Pilas assumed power over Tamarindito and the local ruling lineage lost its power.

Tancah
The remains of the site of Tancah lie to the north of Tulum. The earliest buildings were built in the Terminal Classic and the Early Postclassic (770–1200 A.D.); a series of other buildings was erected in the Postclassic (1200 to 1400 A.D.). In the structures from the Postclassic, archeologists found wall paintings bearing representations of various motifs. The style of these wall paintings is identical to the figures in the Madrid Maya Codex, which no doubt also originated in the Postclassic.

Tikal
With an area of more than 64 square kilometers (40 square miles), the settlement space at Tikal is one of the greatest contiguously settled areas of the Maya region. The mapped district alone covers 16 square kilometers (ten square miles) and comprises more than 3,000 individual structures, temples, and courtyard groups. Estimates suggest that, during the Classic, more than 50,000 people lived in Tikal. The metropolis was occupied during the period between 800 B.C. and 900 A.D., but the earliest architecture originates from the 4th century B.C. The nobility resided in the Central and North Acropolis, the administrative center of the city. This is also where some of the rulers found their last resting place. From the Preclassic to the 9th century, more than 39 rulers controlled the fate of the city, constantly fighting with other settlements – such as Uaxactun, Caracol, and Calakmul – over political and economic hegemony in the central Peten. In the Early Classic, the influence of the central Mexican metropolis Teotihuacan made itself felt, expressed in the architecture and imagery of Tikal. The Mexicans even founded a new dynasty in Tikal by enthroning a noble who may have come from Teotihuacan. During the Classic, the importance of Tikal grew, leading to conflicts with other expanding cities. The disputes peaked in the Late Classic with the capture of the ruler of Calakmul, Yuknoom Yich'aak K'ak' (686–695 A.D.) by the king of Tikal, Jasaw Chan K'awiil (682–734 A.D.).

Tonina
The acropolis of Tonina crowns a chain of hillocks above the Ocosino valley, near to the town of Ocosingo in Chiapas. As well as for its characteristic architecture of boulder blocks and stone chippings, Tonina has become especially well known because of its large number of inscribed stelae, altars, panels, and stucco friezes, which, for the most part, can still be seen on site or in the local museum. The inscriptions embrace the period between 495 and 909 A.D. The motif used on many of the monuments and stucco works is a representation of the captured men and women who fell into the hands of the Tonina rulers in regional and pan-regional campaigns in the 7th and 8th centuries. Archeologists have also discovered deposits of human bones, possibly the remains of sacrificed prisoners. Apparently, the rulers of Tonina constantly tried, by warlike means, to extend their area of influence and position of power in relation to the large centers in Chiapas, in Usumacinta, as well as in the Peten. The high point of their political power came with the capture of K'an Joy Chitam from Palenque (702–711 A.D.) in 711 A.D., and the capture of another noble from Calakmul, the other main center of power in Peten.

Tulum
In 1518, Grijalva sailed along the east coast of Yucatan and discovered, on the heights of Tulum and Tancah, a place called Tzama. Later authors assumed that this was Tulum itself. Because of its position right by the sea, the city of Tulum in the Postclassic was an important junction and landing place for the numerous traders who carried out long-distance trade from here. Even today, luxuriously formed buildings and numerous wall paintings testify to the former splendor and wealth of this place.

Uaxactun
About 23 kilometers (14 miles) north of Tikal, lie the remains of one of the earliest historical cities, which experienced its heyday predominantly in the Classic. Uaxactun was inhabited, with interruptions, from the Middle Preclassic to the Late Classic. The earliest recorded date was in the year 328 A.D., and the latest was in about 889 A.D. The Structure E-VII-B, which served as an observatory for astronomical calculations, is one of the best-known buildings in Uaxactun. It is a pyramidal structure with a flight of steps on each of its four sides, which are flanked by large stucco masks.

Ucanal
In 1914, Raymond Merwin discovered the small settlement of Ucanal, which lies about 35 kilometers (22 miles) south-west of the town of Melchor de Mencos on the western bank of the river Mopan. The latest identifiable date on the ten sculpted stone monuments is from the year 849 A.D. The hieroglyphs on these monuments show central Mexican influences, because the same foreign elements can be found on stelae in Ixlu and Seibal. The ruler of Ucanal was identified as *k'uhul k'an witznal ajaw*, which translates as "divine ruler of the yellow mountain place" – presumably the ancient name of Ucanal.

Utatlan
The K'iche' used the name "the place of the old reeds," or Q'umarcaaj, for their capital city. Utatlan, lying to the north-west of Chichicastenango, was erected on the peak of

a hillock surrounded by a ravine. It was these natural defenses that led to the founding of Utatlan in about 1400, and consolidated the ascendancy of the K'iche' Maya over their neighbors. Alvarado conquered Utatlan in 1524 and permitted the looting of the city.

Uxbenka
The monuments of Uxbenka, first located by Norman Hammond in 1975, are among the earliest Maya remains in present-day Belize. About ten years ago, archeologists discovered 22 stone stelae, nine with figure motifs and hieroglyphic texts, which led to the site being known as Stela Plaza. The stela texts tell of a powerful elite that developed in about 396 A.D., whose influence can be seen in inscriptions up to about 782 A.D. Relationships with other Maya sites in the region cannot be established because of the poor state of preservation of the monuments. It is possible that Uxbenka had its own emblem glyph.

Uxmal
The ruins of Uxmal rank alongside the best-known sites of the Puuc region. The architecture dates from the Terminal Classic, between 900 and 1000 A.D. Most of the buildings were built in Puuc style, but a few exceptions show Mexican motifs and three were erected in Chenes style. The most important of the buildings of Uxmal is the Pyramid of the Magician, a structure more than 34 meters (112 feet) high, composed of five building phases, which only reached its present height by the Terminal Classic. Uxmal also has a large number of inscribed monuments, including 17 stelae. They originated between 895 and 907 A.D., and because of their poor state of preservation hold only fragmentary information about the site's dynastic history.

Xcalumkin
About 13 kilometers (eight miles) east of the town of Hecelchakan (Campeche, Mexico), the archeological zone of Xcalumkin extends over an area of about two and a half square kilometers (one and a half square miles). The discovery of the Puuc style

ruins by Teobert Maler in March 1888 was followed by an investigation by the Carnegie Institution of Washington, lasting three weeks in 1935. Up until 1988, about 40 monuments with hieroglyphic texts from 728 to 744 A.D. had been excavated. All were found in the centrally located "Building of the Initial Series" and the "Hieroglyphs Group," a building complex to the south of the center. The texts of the monuments refer mostly to the consecration of particular structures within these building groups, and name their owners, who had the function of *sajal,* "govenor," of Xcalumkin. Opinion is still divided over the existence of an emblem glyph and the institution of *k'uhul ajaw,* "divine ruler," linked to it. Most of the sculpted monuments of Xcalumkin were taken to museums in Mexico City and Campeche to save them from destruction and robbery.

Xcaret
Xcaret (Quintana Roo, Mexico) became known to the Spanish conquistadors when they landed on the east coast of Yucatan in 1517 and went ashore there. Excavations in the 1950s and '60s have shown that Xcaret was already settled in the Late Preclassic. In the Postclassic, when the architecture that still exists today originated, Xcaret was a significant shipment point for trade with the religious centers of Cozumel. Numerous wall paintings from the Postclassic have survived in the buildings of Xcaret. These are stylistically similar to illustrations found in other sites on the east coast.

Xultun
Xultun, which was discovered in 1920 by a *chiclero,* was studied archeologically a short time later by the Carnegie Institution of Washington. Sylvanus Morley, the leader of this expedition, gave the site the name of Xultun. This means "the last stone," and relates to a stela erected in about 889 A.D. In the 1930s, this was thought to be the latest erected stone in the Maya area. By 1975, archeologists had found more than 20 stelae and altars, most of them displaying hieroglyphic texts and figurative repre-

sentations, but they are too weathered to reveal much about the dynastic history of the rulers of Xultun. It has been calculated that the stelae and altars originated over a period of about 300 years. Both the large architectural complexes (Group A and B) of this significant Maya site were connected by a causeway, roughly 200 meters (656 feet) long and just short of 20 meters (66 feet) wide. The original name of Xultun has yet to be deciphered.

Xunantunich
The center of Xunantunich lies on a hilltop high over the Belize River, and is composed of six large plazas with more than 25 palaces and temples. With a height of about 40 meters (131 feet), the Castillo is the highest building in Xunantunich. An elaborate stucco frieze runs around the top platform of the Castillo. Finds include ceramics dating from the Early Preclassic, and several buildings that originate from the Early Classic, but most of the buildings still surviving today, and the eight stelae, originated in the Late Classic. Xunantunich was abandoned in the 10th century, but in the Postclassic, people settled on the site again.

Yaxchilan
The ruins of Yaxchilan, which were found by Edwin Rockstroh in 1881, lie in the middle of a loop in the river at Usumacinta, and extend along the river inland on leveled hilltops. Because of its monumental architecture and unique sculpture, Yaxchilan is considered one of the most important archeological sites in Chiapas. The core area – the main plaza – comprises the large and the small acropolis. Within this built-up central zone, a total of 130 buildings have been found. Two rulers are largely responsible for building Yaxchilan: Itzamnaaj Balam (Shield Jaguar) II reigned between 681 and 742 A.D., his son Yaxuun Balam (Bird Jaguar) IV was king of Yaxchilan between 752 and 768 A.D. The latter gave the city its character that can still be admired today. Many of the more than 110 well-preserved hieroglyphic texts were completed during the reign of these two rulers and their successor. They contain evidence of the history of Yaxchilan between 359 and 808 A.D. and suggest

that the site played an important role in opposition to the city of Piedras Negras on the Usumacinta, which was conquered by Yaxchilan's last king K'inich Tatb'u Joloom.

Yaxha
The ruins of one of the greatest archeological sites in Guatemala, already called Yaxha in pre-Hispanic times, are found on the bank of the Yaxha lake. In the center of the settlement area, there are the remains of more than 500 buildings, including the only twin pyramid complex outside Tikal. The massive pyramid temple and the enormous living area for the nobility are conspicuous in the architecture of the site. Yaxha was settled towards the end of the Preclassic and first abandoned in the 10th century. More than 20 inscribed stelae provide information about the site's history.

Yaxuna
This relatively small discovery site lies 20 kilometers (12.5 miles) south of Chichen Itza. The pyramids of Yaxuna were some of the largest constructions in the northern Lowlands, erected by rulers in the Middle Preclassic and Classic. The longest known Maya causeway (*sakbe*) extends from Yaxuna to the great city of Coba, 100 kilometers (62 miles) to the east.

Zaculeu
The remains of the one-time capital of the Mam Maya (1250–1525 A.D.), the site Zaculeu is located near the town of Huehuetenango. The fortified city was conquered by Alvarado in 1525, and its inhabitants were driven away. Archeological remains suggest that Zaculeu was inhabited from the Early Classic, and that it served as a trade center for the long-distance trade with Mexico in the Postclassic. The architecture shows Mexican influences, and Mexican goods were unearthed during excavations.

Santa Rosa Xtampak, Campeche, Mexico. The west façade of the three-story temple palace of Santa Rosa Xtampak in a photo by Teobert Maler from 1891.

Santa Rosa Xtampak, Campeche, Mexico. The photo shows the current state of preservation of the west façade of the temple palace. Flights of steps inside lead to the upper stories.

SELECTED COLLECTIONS AND MUSEUMS

compiled by Elisabeth Wagner

Basel (Switzerland)
Museum der Kulturen

Dr Gustav Bernouilli, a doctor and naturalist from Basel, who in the course of an expedition through the Peten in 1877 also visited Tikal, laid the foundations for the finds from the Maya area that are displayed in this museum today. With the permission of the Guatemalan government, Bernouilli removed three wooden door lintels from Temples I and IV and shipped them to Basel; they arrived there in 1878, shortly after the death of the researcher. The middle piece of lintel 3, decorated in relief, originated from Temple I. Lintel 2, from Temple IV, is completely preserved except for one beam. All beam parts from lintel 3 from Temple IV, which was similarly dismantled, are present in the Basel museum: it is the most complete of the three lintels from Tikal. A painted dish with the portrait of the Maize God, which Bernoulli found in Tikal, also passed into the museum's possessions.

Berlin (Germany)
Ethnologisches Museum, Staatliches Museen zu Berlin, Preußischer Kulturbesitz

Maya relics form an essential component of the exhibition "American Archaeology" in the Ethnologisches Museum, Berlin. Since the foundation of the museum in 1873, this division has been constantly expanded. Adolf Bastian (1826–1905), the first director of ethnology at the museum, is to be thanked for the fact that, along with other acquisitions, the Jimeno collection from Yucatan was brought to Berlin in 1881. Numerous Jaina figurines belong to this collection. Other Maya objects

are ceramic figurines and vessels from Alta Verapaz, which were entrusted to the museum by Erwin P. Dieseldorff. Eduard Seler, who between 1890 and 1911 made many journeys to Middle America, also brought quite a few things to Berlin from the Maya area. Many of these objects originated in Chacula, which is also known by the name Quen Santo. Seler was also able to acquire the Alvarado collection for the Berlin museum, with items from the surroundings of the Guatemalan city of Antigua, as well as painted ceramics. Outstanding pieces in the collection include stelae in the Cozumalhuapa style from the ruin site of the same name in southern Guatemala. One of the most recent acquisitions of the Berlin Museum is an Early Classic vessel engraved with a burial scene.

Boston (MA, US)
Museum of Fine Arts

The Museum of Fine Arts in Boston holds one of the most outstanding collections of painted ceramic vessels of the various Maya cultures. The former private collection is available to the museum only as a long-term loan. One of the finest pieces is the "cosmic plate," decorated with the most complete representation of the Maya universe that is known.

Brussels (Belgium)
Musées Royaux d'Art et d'Histoire

The American division of the Musées Royaux d'Art et d'Histoire in Brussels accommodates an important collection of artifacts from Maya

times. A stela with a representation of a Maya ruler, and a fragment of a relief tablet with inscriptions from the region around Bonampak, as well as several fragments of sculpture from Copan, are among the treasures of the Brussels collection. The precise place of origin of numerous other items, such as the intricately painted and relief ceramic vessels and ceramic figurines, is, however, not known.

Cambridge (MA, US)
Peabody Museum of American Archeology and Ethnology

Much of the Mesoamerican stock of the Peabody museum in Cambridge is consolidated from several individual collections from the Maya area. Included here are numerous pieces that were assembled during early research trips commissioned by the museum. Furthermore, the collections of the archeological section of the Carnegie Institution of Washington, after its closure in 1958, were transferred to the stock of the Peabody museum. Edward H. Thompson, who led one of the early expeditions, brought to Cambridge artifacts made of jade, wood, and other materials, which he salvaged during the excavation of the Great Cenote of Chichen Itza. Sculptures from Piedras Negras, and relief tablets 1 and 2, were handed over to the museum by Teobert Maler. Above all, the collection contains the Copan sculptures, which were found not only during the early museum expeditions, but also from the excavations of the Carnegie Institution. These include a chair statue and several blocks of the Hieroglyph Stairway from Structure 10L-26, a

very impressive bust of the Maize God from Structure 10L-22, as well as numerous other façade sculptures. Archeological undertakings of the Peabody Museum and the Carnegie Institution since the 1920s have expanded the inventory of the museum with finds from the Maya sites of Altar de Sacrificios, Barton Ramie, Holmul, Labna, and Uaxactun. The excavations of the Carnegie Institution of Washington set the standards for quality of documentation and publication of finds.

Campeche (Mexico)
Museo de Las Estelas "Román Piña Chán"

An 18th century colonial fortification has served, since 1985, as a museum for the stone monuments that were found in the most important ruin site in the federal state of Campeche. The exhibits include stelae, door jambs, and door lintels from various discovery sites in Campeche like, for example, Xcalumkin, Edzna, Jaina, and Itzimte, as well as columns from Tunkuyi and Cansacbe. Further monuments from the ruins of the Chenes region also belong in the collection. The museum was dedicated to Román Piña Chán from Campeche, one of Mexico's most famous archeologists.

Chigago (IL, US)
Field Museum of Natural History

The Mesoamerican section of the Natural History Museum in Chicago houses, among others, an important collection of ceramic vessels, which were collected in the 1900s during various expeditions to Maya ruin sites in Yucatan and Belize. The pieces are of

Cleveland, The Cleveland Museum of Art; shell with a representation of a smoker; provenance unknown; Late Classic, 600–900 A.D.

Washington D.C., Dunbarton Oaks Research Library and Collection; jade pendant with the outline of a noble; provenance unknown; Early Classic, 250–400 A.D. (Kerr 2839)

Guatemala City, Museo Nacional de Arqueologia y Etnología; ocarina in the form of a noble with rattles; Nebaj, El Quiche, Guatemala; Terminal Classic, 800–900 A.D.

Zurich, Museum Rietberg; stela with a standing Maya noble; provenance unknown; Late Classic, 7th century A.D.

Denver, Denver Art Museum; ear ornament made from shell with depictions of captives; provenance unknown; Early Classic, 200–400 A.D. (Kerr 2817)

Merida, Museo Regional de Yucatán "Palacio Canton"; ceramic vessel in the form of a turtle; Mayapan, Yucatan, Mexico; Late Postclassic, c. 1250

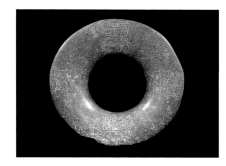

London, The British Museum: The Mexican Gallery; ear decoration of jade with inscription; provenance unknown; Late Preclassic, 50 B.C.–A.D. 50

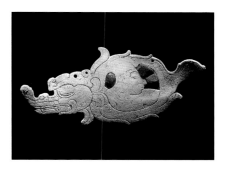

Copan Ruinas, Museo de Arqueología; shell pendant with jade and obsidian inlays; Copan, Honduras; Late Classic, 600–900 A.D.

special significance because their place of origin is known precisely. They were accurately documented (according to the technology available at the time). During the 20th century, the museum acquired a comprehensive collection of textiles from the Maya areas of Guatemala.

Cleveland (OH, US)
The Cleveland Museum of Art

The Cleveland Museum owns one of the largest and best quality collections of Maya art in whole of the United States. Stone monuments housed by the museum includes Stela 34 from El Peru, and a relief tablet from the area of El Cayo in the vicinity of Piedras Negras. The monuments show a representation of a noble lady, and display an unusually large number of sculptors' signatures. Smaller objects include painted ceramic vessels and ceramic figurines, as well as various works in jade. One of the finest Maya shell works so far discovered is the plaque with the finely engraved representation of a smoking Maya dignitary, which is shown here.

New York American Museum of Natural History; human bone carved with supernatural being; provenance unknown; Early Classic, 100–400 A.D.

Guatemala City (Guatemala)
Museo Ixchel del Traje Indígena

Named after the goddess of weaving, the Museo Ixchel was founded in 1973 as a private establishment. The only organization in Guatemala that devotes itself to the research and conservation of textiles of the present Maya in Guatemala is established here. The museum has an important collection of costumes and fabrics from about 120 Maya communities, predominantly from the Highlands of Guatemala. Since 1993, it has been in a new building on the campus of the Universidad Francisco Maroquín. Several exhibition rooms present costumes from the end of the 19th century to the present day.

Guatemala City (Guatemala)
Museo Nacional de Arqueología y Etnolgía

The permanent exhibitions in the six galleries of the National Museum of Guatemala give a comprehensive overview of the archeology and ethnography of all regions of pre-Hispanic Guatemala, from colonial times to the present. The rotunda in the center of the museum is a place for prominent display,

Princeton, The Art Museum, Princeton University; ceramic figurine of a captive; provenance unknown; Late Classic, 700–900 A.D

where numerous stelae, altars, relief panels, and other stone monuments from various sites in the Guatemalan part of the Classic Maya Lowlands are displayed. Reconstructions of several tomb structures from Tikal and Rio Azul can be seen here. Selected jade objects, predominantly from Tikal, are displayed in a specially secured room: the jade mask from Burial 160 and the wooden vessels with inlaid jade mosaic from Burials 116 and 196, are among the finest works of art from the Maya Classic.

Guatemal City (Guatemala)
Museo Popol Vuh

Along with a comprehensive collection of painted ceramic vessels from the Maya Lowlands, the Museo Popol Wuj in Guatemala also contains a series of stone sculptures from the Highlands, as well as from the Pacific coast area. The best known pieces in the museum include Altar 1 from Naranjo, with a portrait of the Death God as well as a long inscription and, above all, the large burial urns from the K'iche' Maya district. Apart from the objects from pre-Columbian times, the museum also has an important

New York National Museum of the American Indian; musical instrument in the form of a woman; Jaina, Campeche, Mexico; Late Classic, 600–900 A.D.

collection of art from the colonial era – the work of silversmiths, sculptors, and painters, as well as a folk-art collection of costumes – which were worn for dancing – and wooden masks from various Maya communities in Guatemala.

Cologne (Germany)
Rautenstrauch-Joest-Museum (Museum für Völkerkunde)

The Maya objects, which are conserved but not yet exhibited, at the Rautenstrauch-Joest-Museum in Cologne are part of the former Ludwig collection. The artworks acquired from the art trade by Peter and Irene Ludwig form one of the most significant and largest European collections of pre-Columbian art.

Leiden (Netherlands)
Rijksmuseum voor Volkenkunde

The Leiden museum for ethnology exhibits another significant stock of Maya artwork. The collection, matching any in Europe, has painted and molded ceramic vessels, ceramic figurines, stucco sculptures, and especially, the

Villahermosa, Museo Regional de Antropologia "Carlos Pellicer Camera"; base of an incense burner; Tapijulapa, Tabasco, Mexico; Late Classic

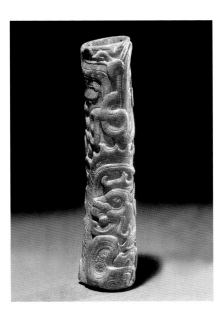

Leiden Plaque. This jade plaque, featuring engravings on both sides, was found in 1864 by a Dutch engineer during canal building work close to Puerto Barrios in Guatemala. On the front side of the plaque is a representation of a ruler, and the inscription on the other side reports on his enthronement. This event occurred in 320 A.D. Further important pieces are door lintel 2 from La Pasadita and a painted ceramic vessel in codex style bearing a representation of a ball game.

London (Great Britain)
The British Museum

The "Mexican Art" section of the British Museum in London owes the great variety of its collection principally to the expeditions of Alfred P. Maudslay, one of the great pioneers of Maya research. In the years 1881 to 1894, Maudslay set out for the Maya area eight times. He investigated and documented primarily the ruin sites of Copan, Quirigua, Yaxchilan, Chichen Itza, and Palenque. He photographed the monuments and prepared numerous molds, which he sent to England. The copies (more than 400) are today a part of the gigantic collection of casts in the British Museum, which documents just about all the cultures of the world. The heart of the Mesoamerican collection is, nevertheless, formed of original sculptures shipped to England by Maudslay: these include eight door lintels from Yaxchilan, as well as nine sculptures from Copan. Apart from the Maudslay collection, the museum contains numerous other objects that Thomas Gann brought back from his research trips, as well as several stelae from the Maya city of Pusilha, in present-day Belize.

Madrid (Spain)
Museo de América

The core pieces of the Maya collection in the Madrid Museo de América are the artifacts that Antonio del Río sent back to Spain from his expedition to Palenque in 1787. Prominent pieces of this, the oldest Maya collection, are various stone sculptures, perhaps the leg of a throne, the so-called "Stela of Madrid," and two relief panels with inscriptions from the palace of Palenque. By carrying out excavations, del Río also discovered a quantity of sculpted stucco fragments, as well as flint and obsidian objects that originate from various sacrifice depositories. A further treasure is preserved in the library of the museum: one of only four known Maya manuscripts, the Madrid Codex.

Merida (Mexico)
Museo Regional de Yucatàn "Palacio Cantón"

The regional museum of Merida has been located, since 1980, in the building known as "Palacio Cantón," which General Francisco Cantón Rosada had erected between 1909 and 1911 as a residence for himself. The objects displayed in the museum offer an overview of the archeology of pre-Hispanic Yucatan. Many stone monuments, from the best known ruin sites of the federal state of Yucatan, like Chichen Itza, Mayapan, Oxkintok, and Uxmal are exhibited. The wall paintings originate from Mulchic and Chacmultun, and numerous ceramics, jade, and other small artifacts were found in all parts of Yucatan and brought to the museum.

Mexico City (Mexico)
Museo Nacional de Antropología

The national museum in Mexico City was inaugurated in 1964. It houses 12 galleries on the ground floor, which in contrast to the ethnographic section on the upper floor, present archeological finds from all cultural regions and epochs of Mexico. Among them, a large area is dedicated to the Maya culture. The exhibited articles include stone monuments, ceramic vessels, small statues, artifacts of bone, shell, flint, and obsidian from all known large Maya cities of Mexico. A complete reconstruction of the burial chamber of the ruler Pakal of Palenque, from whose burial several gifts in the form of valuable jade jewelry are exhibited, is to be seen in the basement of the section. Another magnificent piece in the museum is a huge stucco relief from the façade of a temple, which was confiscated from art thieves in the 1960s – the exact provenance of this is not known.

New York (NY, US)
The Metropolitan Museum of Art

The ancient American division of this world famous museum in New York exhibits a comprehensive Maya collection: from painted and relief-ornamented ceramic vessels, through jade and shell jewelry to stone sculptures, all varieties of the Maya arts are represented. Stela 5 from Piedras Negras as well as a column ornamented in relief (of unknown origin), are the best known monuments of the exhibition. The Early Classic wooden sculpture of a sitting dignitary is one of the few wooden artifacts that have survived from pre-Columbian times.

Philadelphia (PA, US)
University Museum

The Maya artworks exhibited in the University Museum of Philadelphia come mainly from sites that the museum researched in several large projects in the 1930s and 1950s. Stela 14, which shows a ruler on a richly ornamented throne platform, came from the ruin site of Piedras Negras in Guatemala. Stelae 6 and 16, which show a ruler's portrait, a long inscription, and a sculpted altar were found in Caracol in present-day Belize. Other artifacts in the collection are a stone shield with a representation of the Fire God from Copan, figurines, and painted clay vessels.

Villahermosa (Mexico)
Museo Regional de Antropología "Carlos Pellicer Camera"

The Museo Regional de Antropología Carlos Pellicer houses archeological finds of the Mexican federal state of Tabasco, primarily artifacts of the Olmec and Maya cultures. Stone monuments, painted and molded ceramic vessels, and figurines, as well as small artifacts from various sites (Balancan Morales, Comalcalco, and Tortuguero) make up the main stock of the collection. Along with the Olmec finds, the museum also provides a good overview of pre-Hispanic cultural development in the present federal state of Tabasco.

Washington (D.C. US)
Dumbarton Oaks Research Library and Collection

The pre-Columbian section of Dumbarton Oaks is part of a large private collection, which is kept in the former residence of collectors Mr. Robert Woods Bliss and Mrs. Mildred Barnes Bliss. The collection contains objects from ancient cultures, including works of art from Columbia, Costa Rica, Guatemala, Mexico, Panama, and Peru. After Mr. Robert Woods Bliss' death, the collection was once more extended, through donations from his widow and other private collectors. Objects may also have been acquired from the art trade. The art of the Maya is represented in this extensive collection by a series of significant artifacts. These include stone monuments and two relief tablets from Palenque and El Cayo, door lintel 1 from Kuna Lacanja, the head of the Maize God from Temple 22 in Copan, painted and relief decorated ceramic vessels, an alabaster vessel, Jaina figurines, and jade jewelry.

Zurich (Switzerland)
Museum Rietberg

Mesoamerica is one of the focal points of the collection of the Rietberg museum, where the art of entire epochs and cultural areas of Mexico is especially well represented. The outstanding Maya artworks include Jaina figurines and a stela of unknown origin with a representation of a Maya ruler. A relief tablet, which on the basis of its style probably comes from the vicinity of Pomona (Tabasco, Mexico), shows a seated Maya dignitary.

Cambridge, Peabody Museum of American Archeology and Ethnology, Harvard University; face ornament; Chichen Itza, Yucatan, Mexico; Terminal Classic, 800–900 A.D.

Palenque, Museo "Alberto Ruz Lhuiller"; head of a noble in limestone with hieroglyph text; Palenque, Chiapas, Mexico; late Classic, 608 A.D.

Mexico City, Museo Nacional de Antropología; ceramic figurine with a representation of a god in a flower petal; provenance unknown; Late Classic, 600–900 A.D.

Guatemala City, Museo Popol Wuj; detail of a molded incense burner; provenance unknown; Early Classic, 250–600 A.D.

ADDRESSES

Australia

Canberra
Australian National Gallery
Parkes Place
Canberra, ACT, 2601
Melbourne
National Gallery of Victoria
285–321 Russell Street
Melbourne, VIC 3000

Austria

Vienna
Museum für Völkerkunde
Neue Hofburg
1014 Vienna

Belgium

Brussels
Museés Royaux d'Art et d'Histoire
Parc du Cinquantenaire 10
1000 Brussels

Belize

Belize City
Bliss Institute
Southern Foreshore
Belize City
Belmopan
Department of Archaeology
East Bloc
Belmopan

Canada

Montreal
The Montreal Museum of Fine Arts
Jean-Noël Desmarais Pavilion
1380 Sherbrooke Street West
Montreal, Quebec H3G 2T9

Toronto
Gardiner Museum of Ceramic Art
111 Queen's Park
Toronto, Ontario M5S 2C7
Royal Ontario Museum
100 Queen's Park
Toronto, Ontario M5S 2C6
Vancouver
*Museum of Anthropology at the
University of British Columbia*
6393 N.W. Marine Drive
Vancouver, British Columbia V6T 1Z2

Chile

Santiago
Museo Chileno de Arte Precolombino
Bandera 361
Santiago

Costa Rica

San Jose
Museo Nacional
Calle 17, Avenidas Central y Segunda
San Jose
Museo Nacional del Jade "Fidel Tristán Castro"
Instituto Nacional de Seguros (I.N.S),
Piso 11
Avenida 7, Calle 9 y 11
San Jose

Denmark

Copenhagen
Nationalmuseet
Ny Vestergade 10
1471 Copenhagen

El Salvador

San Salvador
*Museo Nacional de Antropología
Dr. David Joaquín Guzmán*

Avenida La Revolución/
Carretera a Santa Tecla
Col. San Benito
San Salvador
Chalchuapa
Museo Regional de Chalchuapa
Sitio Arqueológico Tazumal
Chalchuapa, Santa Ana
Ceren
Museo Joya de Ceren
Sitio Arqueológico Joya de Ceren
Ceren, La Libertad
San Andres
Museo de San Andrés
Sitio Arqueologico de San Andres
San Andres, La Libertad

Finland

Helsinki
Didrichsen Art Museum
Kuusilahdenkuja 1
00340 Helsinki

France

Bordeaux
Musée d'Ethnographie
Université Victor Segalen Bordeaux 2
3 Place de la Victoire
33076 Bordeaux
Paris
*Bibliothèque Nationale de France,
Département des Manuscrits, Richelieu-Louvois*
58 Rue de Richelieu et 2 Rue Louvois
75002 Paris
Musée de l'Homme
Musée National d'Histoire Naturelle
Palais de Chaillot, 17 Place du Trocadero
75116 Paris

Germany

Berlin
*Ethnologisches Museum, Staatliche
Museen zu Berlin, Preußischer Kulturbesitz*

Lansstraße 8
14195 Berlin
Dresden
Buchmuseum der Sächsischen Landesbibliothek,
Staats- und Universitätsbibliothek Dresden
Marienallee 12
01099 Dresden
Freiburg
Museum für Völkerkunde
Adelhauserstraße 33
79098 Freiburg
Hamburg
Hamburgisches Museum für Völkerkunde
Rothenbaumchaussee 64
20148 Hamburg
Cologne
Rautenstrauch Joest Museum für Völkerkunde
Ubierring 45
50678 Cologne
Mannheim
*Völkerkundliche Sammlungen der Stadt
Mannheim im Reiss-Museum*
Neubau D5
68159 Mannheim
Munich
Staatliches Museum für Völkerkunde
Maximilianstraße 42
80538 Munich
Stuttgart
Linden – Museum Stuttgart
Staatliches Museum für Völkerkunde
Hegelplatz 1
70174 Stuttgart

Great Britain

Liverpool
*National Museum and Galleries on Merseyside,
Liverpool Museum*
William Brown Street
Liverpool L3 8EN
London
British Museum, The Mexican Gallery
Great Russell Street
London WC1B 3DG

Copán Ruinas, Museo de Arqueología; eccentric flint with
a representation of the god K'awiil; Copan, Honduras;
Late Classic, 763 A.D.

Campeche, Museo Histórico Fuerte de San Miguel;
jade mask with obsidian and mother of pearl; Calakmul,
Campeche, Mexico; Late Classic, 600–900 A.D.

Mexico City, Museo Nacional de Antropología; ball game
court monument in limestone; Chinkultic, Chiapas, Mexico;
Early Classic, 591 A.D.

Mexico City, Museo Nacional de Antropología; ceramic
incense burner; Mayapan, Yucatan, Mexico; Late
Postclassic, c. 1350

Guatemala

Antigua
Museo Arqueológico
Hotel "Casa Santo Domingo"
3a Calle Oriente No. 28
Antigua Guatemala, Sacatepequez
Coban
Museo "Príncipe Maya"
Coban, Alta Verapaz
Escuintla
Museo Regional de Arqueología Olmeca y
Exposiciones Antropológicas,
Museo denominado Rubén Chávez Van Dorne
Escuintla, Escuintla
Guatemala City
Museo Ixchel del Traje Indígena
Universidad Francisco Marroquín
Campus Central
6a. Calle Final, Zona 10
Guatemala Ciudad 01010
Museo Nacional de Arqueología y Etnología
Parque La Aurora, Local 5, Zona 13
Guatemala Ciudad 01013
Museo Popol Vuh
Universidad Francisco Marroquín
Campus Central
6a Calle Final, Zona 10
Guatemala Ciudad 01010
Quetzaltenango
Casa de La Cultura
de la Antigua Guatemala
4a Avenida Norte y 4ta Calle Oriente
Quetzaltenango, Quetzaltenango
Museo Quezaltenango
7a Calle 11–09, Zona 1
Quetzaltenango, Quetzaltenango
Tikal
Museo Lítico
Parque Nacional Tikal
Tikal, El Peten
Museo "Sylvanus G. Morley"
Parque Nacional Tikal
Tikal, El Peten
Uaxactun
Museo "Juan Antonio Valdés" and
Stela park "Nikolai Grube"
Uaxactun, El Peten

Honduras

Copán Ruinas
Museo de Arqueología
Parque Central
Copan Ruinas, Copan
Museo de Escultura Maya
Parque Arqueologico
Copan Ruinas, Copan
La Entrada
Museo Arqueológico
La Entrada, Copan
San Pedro Sula
Museo de Antropología e Historia del Valle de Sula
3a. Avenida y 4a. Calle NO
San Pedro Sula, Cortes
Tegucigalpa
Museo Nacional Villaroy
Calle Morelos 3A
Barrio Buenos Aires
Tegucigalpa, Francisco Morazan

Hungary

Budapest
Néprajzi Múzeum
Kossuth Lajos ter 12
1055 Budapest

Israel

Jerusalem
Israel Museum
Ruppin Boulevard
Jerusalem 91710

Italy

Genoa
Museo Americanistico "F. Lunardi"
Villa De Mari-Gruber
Corso Solferino 25
16122 Genoa
Rome
Museo Nazionale Preistorico-Etnografico
"L. Pigorini"
Piazza Guglielmo Marconi 14
00144 Rome

Japan

Osaka
Minpaku – National Museum of Ethnology
10–1 Senri Expo Park, Suita
Osaka 565–8511

Mexico

Bacalar
Museo Regional de Bacalar
Fuerte de San Felipe
38 km northeast of Chetumal
Bacalar, Quinatana Roo
Campeche
Museo de Las Estelas "Román Piña Chán"
Museo de Escultura Maya
Baluarte de Virgen de la Soledad
Calle 8 s/n
Colonia Centro
Campeche, Campeche
Museo Histórico Fuerte de San Miguel
Avenida Escenica s/n
Campeche, Campeche
Museo Regional de Campeche
"Casa Teniente del Rey"
Calle 59 No. 40
Colonia Centro
Campeche, Campeche
Cancun
Centro Cultural Cancún
Avenida Kukulcan
Centro de Convenciones
Cancún, Quintana Roo
Chablekal
Museo del Pueblo Maya
Zona Arqueologica de Dzibilchaltun
Chablekal, Yucatan
Chichen Itza
Museo de Sitio de Chichén Itzá
Zona Arqueologica de Chichen Itza
Carretera Merida-Cancun-Tinum, km 120
Comalcalco
Museo de Sitio
Zona Arqueologica de Comalcalco
Comalcalco, Tabasco
Comitan de Dominguez
Museo Arqueológico del Valle de Comitán
2a. Avenida Oriente, esquina 1a. Calle Sur
Col. Centro
30000 Comitan de Dominguez, Chiapas
Casa de la Cultura de Comitán
Avenida Rosario Castellanos, esquina 1a
Calle Sur
Col. Centro
30000 Comitan de Dominguez, Chiapas
Cozumel
Museo de la Isla de Cozumel
Avenida Rafael Melgar, entre Calles 4 y 6
Norte
Cozumel, Quintana Roo
Emiliano Zapata
Museo Municipal
Emiliano Zapata, Tabasco
Hecelchakan
Museo Arqueológico del Camino Real
Domicilio Conocido
Hecelchakan, Campeche
Hopelchen
Museo Municipal
Hopelchen, Campeche
Izamal
Museo Comunitario de Itzamal Kavil
"Guacamaya de Fuego"
Calle 31 con 28,
Izamal, Yucatan
Jonuta
Museo Arqueológico Profesor Omar Huerta E.
Calle Juarez s/n
Jonuta, Tabasco
La Venta
Museo de Sitio
Calle Principal s/n, Ex-Pista Aérea
La Venta, Tabasco
Merida
Museo Regional de Yucatán "Palacio Cantón"
Calle 43 y Paseo Montejo
Merida, Yucatan
Mexico City
Museo Nacional de Antropología
Av. Paseo de la Reforma y Calzada Gandhi s/n
Col. Chapultepec Polanco
Delegacion Miguel Hidalgo
11560 Mexico D.F.
Oaxaca
Museo de Arte Prehispánico Rufino
Tamayo
Av. Morelos 503
Oaxaca, Oaxaca
Palenque
Museo "Alberto Ruz Lhuillier"
Palenque, Chiapas
Puebla
Museo Amparo
2° Calle Sur 708
Centro Historico
72000 Puebla, Puebla
San Cristobal de las Casas
Museo de los Altos de Chiapas
Avenida 20 de Noviembre s/n
Colonia Cerrillo
San Cristobal de las Casas, Chiapas
Tenosique
Museo de Sitio
Zona Arqueologica de Pomona
Tenosique, Tabasco
Tonina
Museo de Sitio
Zona Arqueologica de Tonina
Tonina, Chiapas
Tuxtla Gutierrez
Museo Regional de Antropología
Calzada de los Hombres Ilustres 885
29000 Tuxtla Gutierrez, Chiapas
Uxmal
Museo de Sitio de Uxmal
Zona Arqueologica de Uxmal
old road from Campeche to Santa Elena,
km 78
Valladolid
Museo San Roque
Calle 42/corner of Calle 38
Col. Centro
97780 Valladolid, Yucatan
Villahermosa
Museo Regional de Antropología
"Carlos Pellicer Camara"
Avenida Carlos Pellicer 511
Zona CICOM
Villahermosa, Tabasco
Parque Museo de la Venta
Avenida Adolfo Ruiz Cortines s/n
Villahermosa, Tabasco
Yaxcopoil
Antigua Hacienda y Museo
Federal Highway (Carretera Federal) 261,
km 33
Yaxcopoil, Yucatan
Zinacantan
Museo Tradicional "Ik'al Ojov"
Av. Insurgentes 4
29350 Zinacantan, Chiapas

Netherlands

Leiden
Rijksmuseum voor Volkenkunde
Steenstraat 1
2300 AE Leiden

Norway

Oslo
Universitetets Ethnographiske Museum
University of Oslo
Frederiks Gate 2
0164 Oslo

Spain

Barcelona
Museo Barbier-Mueller de Arte Precolombino
Montcada 14
08003 Barcelona
Madrid
Museo de América
Avenida Reyes Catolicos 6
Ciudad Universitaria
28040 Madrid

Sweden

Gothenburg
Etnografiska Museet I Goteborg
Avagen 24
3–402 Gothenburg
Stockholm
Nationalmuseum
Södra Blasieholmshamnen
10324 Stockholm

Folkens Museum Etnografiska
Djurgårdsbrunnsvägen 34
10252 Stockholm

Switzerland

Basel
Museum der Kulturen
Augustinergasse 2
4051 Basel
Geneva
Musée d'Ethnographie de la Ville de Genève
Boulevard Carl-Vogt 65
1205 Geneva
Musée Barbier-Mueller
Rue Jean-Calvin 10
1204 Geneva
Schaffhausen
Museum zu Allerheiligen, Ebnöther collections
Klosterplatz 1
8200 Schaffhausen
Zürich
Museum Rietberg
Gablerstrasse 15
8002 Zürich

United States

Boston
Museum of Fine Arts
465 Huntington Avenue
Boston, MA 02115–5523
Brooklyn
Brooklyn Museum of Art
200 Eastern Parkway
Brooklyn, NY 11238
Cambridge
Peabody Museum of American Archeology and Ethnology, Harvard University
11 Divinity Avenue
Cambridge, MA 02138
Chicago
The Art Institute of Chicago
111 South Michigan Avenue
Chicago, IL, 60603–6110
Field Museum of Natural History
1400 South Lake Shore Drive
Chicago, IL 60605–2496
Cleveland
The Cleveland Museum of Art
11150 East Boulevard
Cleveland, OH, 44106–1797
Dallas
Dallas Museum of Art
1717 N. Harwood Street
Dallas, TX 75201

Dayton
The Dayton Art Institute
456 Belmonte Park
Dayton, OH 45405
Denver
Denver Art Museum
100 West 14th Avenue Parkway
Denver, CO 80204–2788
Denver Museum of Natural History/ Denver Museum of Nature and Science
2001 Colorado Boulevard
Denver, CO 80205
Detroit
The Detroit Institute of Arts
5200 Woodward Avenue
Detroit, MI 48202
Durham
Duke University Museum of Art
Buchanan Boulevard at Trinity Avenue
Durham, NC 27708–0732
Fort Worth
Kimbell Art Museum
3333 Camp Bowie Boulevard
Fort Worth, TX, 76107–2792
Gainesville
Samuel P. Harn Museum of Art
University of Florida
SW 34th Street and Hull Road
Gainesville, FL 32611–2700
Houston
Houston Museum of Fine Arts
1001 Bissonnet
Houston, TX 77005
The Menil Collection
1515 Sul Ross
Houston, TX 77006
Kansas City
William Rockhill Nelson Gallery of Art – Atkins Museum of Fine Arts
4525 Oak St. 64111
Kansas City, MO 64111
Los Angeles
Los Angeles County Museum of Art
5905 Wilshire Boulevard
Los Angeles, CA 90036
Los Angeles County Museum of Natural History
900 Exposition Boulevard
Los Angeles, CA 90007
Milwaukee
Milwaukee Public Museum
800 West Wells Street
Milwaukee, WI 53233
Minneapolis
The Minneapolis Institute of Arts
2400 Third Avenue South
Minneapolis; MN 55404

New Haven
Yale University Art Gallery
1111 Chapel Street
New Haven, CT 06520
Peabody Museum, Yale University
170 Whitney Avenue
New Haven, CT 06520–8118
New Orleans
New Orleans Museum of Art
1 Collins C. Diboll Circle
New Orleans, LA 70179–0123
Middle American Research Institute
Dinwiddie Hall, 4th floor
Tulane University
New Orleans, LA 70118
New York
The Metropolitan Museum of Art
1000 Fifth Avenue at 82nd Street
New York, NY 10028–0198
National Museum of the American Indian – Heye Foundation/Smithsonian Institution
The George Gustav Heye Center
Alexander Hamilton U.S. Custom House
One Bowling Green
New York, NY 10004
American Museum of Natural History
Central Park West at 79th Street
New York City, NY 10024–5912
Ocala
The Appleton Museum of Art
4333 East Silver Spring Blvd
Ocala, FL 34478–3190
Orono
Hudson Museum
University of Maine
5746 Maine Center for the Arts,
Orono, ME 04469–5746
Philadelphia
University Museum
33rd and Spruce Streets
Philadelphia, PA 19104
Philadelphia Museum of Art
Benjamin Franklin Parkway and 26th Street
Philadelphia, PA 19130
Princeton
Princeton University Art Museum
Princeton University, McCormick Hall
Princeton, NJ 08544–1018
Princeton University Library
Princeton, NJ 08544
Raleigh
North Carolina Museum of Art
2110 Blue Ridge Road
Raleigh, NC 27607–6433
Redlands
San Bernardino County Museum

2024 Orange Tree Lane
Redlands, CA 92374
Richmond
Virginia Museum of Fine Arts
2800 Grove Avenue
Richmond, VA 23221–2466
Saint Louis
St. Louis Museum of Art
Forest Park
1 Fine Arts Drive
St. Louis, MO 63110
Salt Lake City
The Utah Museum of Fine Arts
University of Utah
1530 East South Campus Drive
Salt Lake City, UT 84112–0360
San Antonio
San Antonio Museum of Art
200 West Jones Avenue
San Antonio, TX 78215
San Diego
San Diego Museum of Art
Fine Arts Gallery of San Diego
Balboa Park
San Diego, CA 92112–2107
San Diego Museum of Man
1350 El Prado
Balboa Park
San Diego, CA 92101
San Francisco
De Young Museum
75 Tea Garden Drive
Golden Gate Park
San Francisco, CA 94118
Santa Ana
Bowers Museum of Cultural Art
2002 North Main Street
Santa Ana, CA 92706
Seattle
Seattle Art Museum
100 University Street
Seattle, WA 98101–2902
Tulsa
Gilcrease Museum
1400 Gilcrease Museum Road
Tulsa, OK 74127
Washington
Dumbarton Oaks Research Library and Collection
1703 32nd Street, N.W.
Washington, D.C. 20007

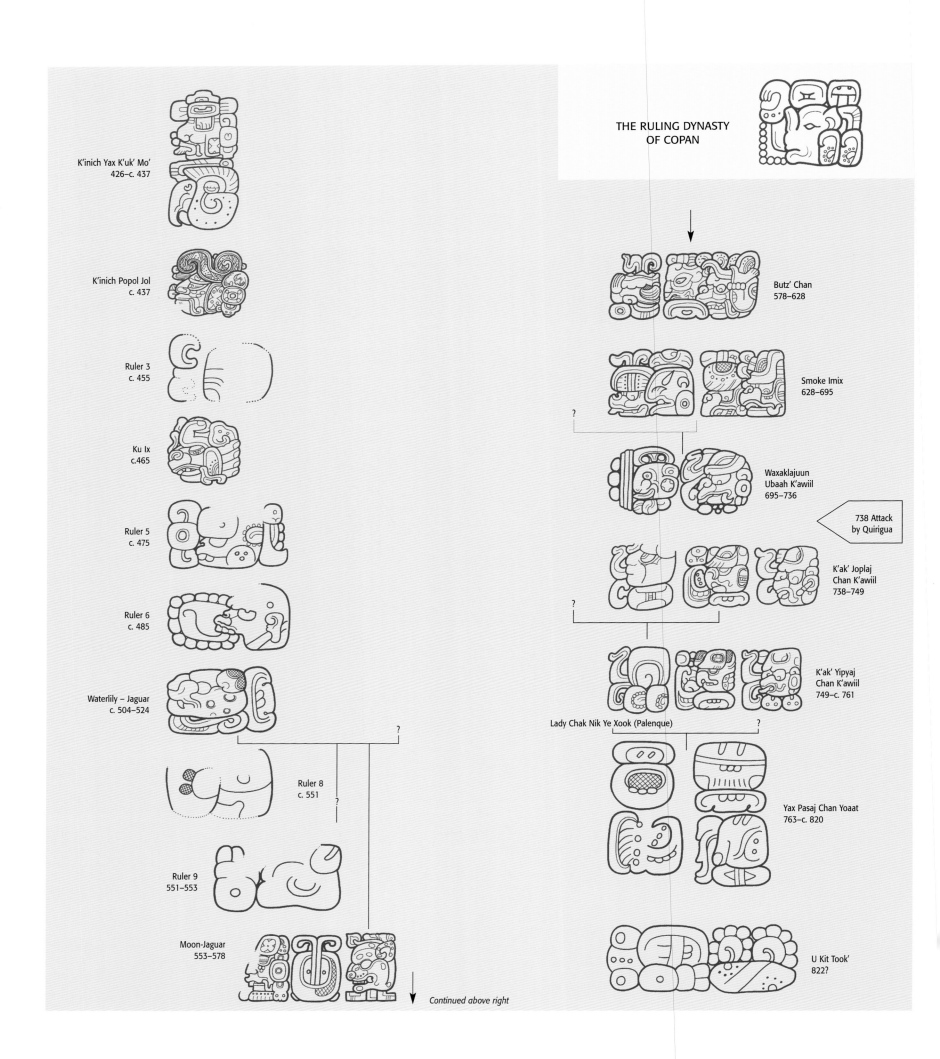

THE RULING DYNASTY
OF COPAN

K'inich Yax K'uk' Mo'
426–c. 437

K'inich Popol Jol
c. 437

Ruler 3
c. 455

Ku Ix
c.465

Ruler 5
c. 475

Ruler 6
c. 485

Waterlily – Jaguar
c. 504–524

Ruler 8
c. 551

Ruler 9
551–553

Moon-Jaguar
553–578

Continued above right

Butz' Chan
578–628

Smoke Imix
628–695

?

Waxaklajuun
Ubaah K'awiil
695–736

738 Attack
by Quirigua

K'ak' Joplaj
Chan K'awiil
738–749

?

K'ak' Yipyaj
Chan K'awiil
749–c. 761

Lady Chak Nik Ye Xook (Palenque)   ?

Yax Pasaj Chan Yoaat
763–c. 820

U Kit Took'
822?

456

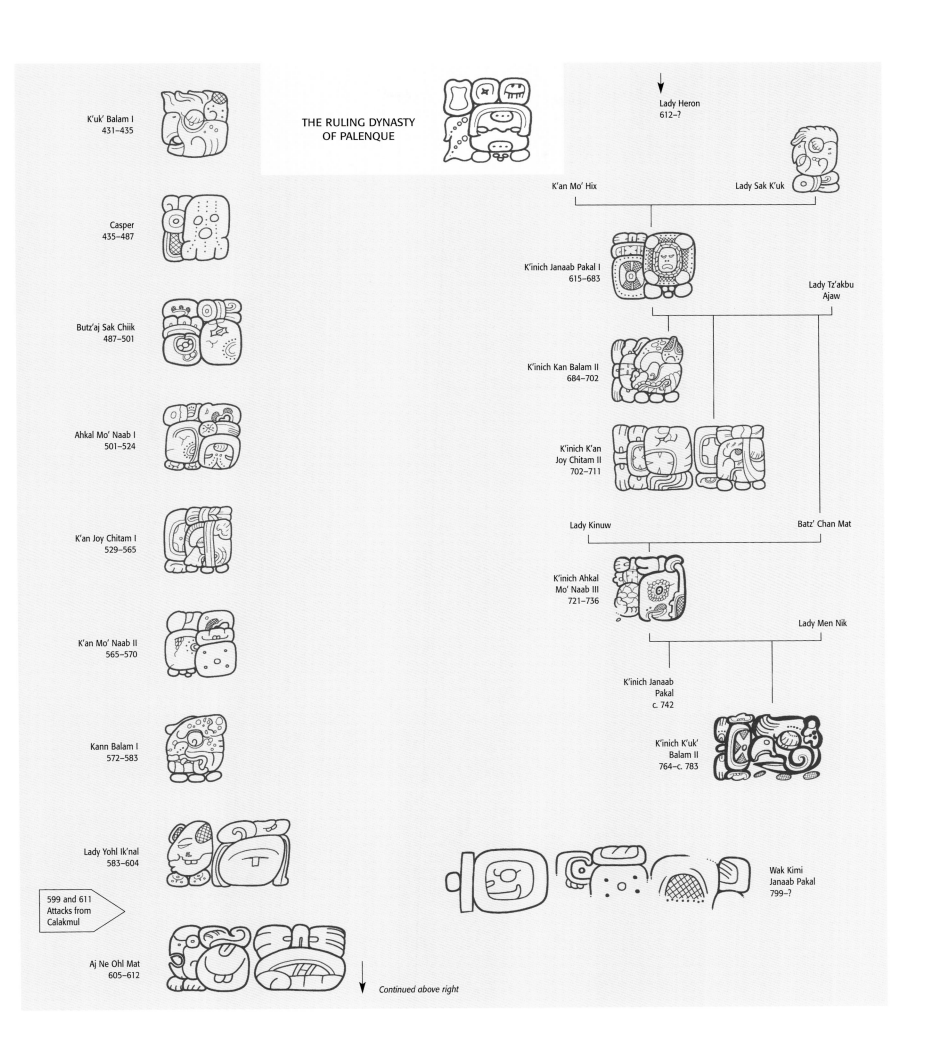

THE RULING DYNASTY
OF PALENQUE

K'uk' Balam I
431–435

Casper
435–487

Butz'aj Sak Chiik
487–501

Ahkal Mo' Naab I
501–524

K'an Joy Chitam I
529–565

K'an Mo' Naab II
565–570

Kann Balam I
572–583

Lady Yohl Ik'nal
583–604

599 and 611
Attacks from
Calakmul

Aj Ne Ohl Mat
605–612

Continued above right

Lady Heron
612–?

K'an Mo' Hix

Lady Sak K'uk

K'inich Janaab Pakal I
615–683

Lady Tz'akbu
Ajaw

K'inich Kan Balam II
684–702

K'inich K'an
Joy Chitam II
702–711

Lady Kinuw

Batz' Chan Mat

K'inich Ahkal
Mo' Naab III
721–736

Lady Men Nik

K'inich Janaab
Pakal
c. 742

K'inich K'uk'
Balam II
764–c. 783

Wak Kimi
Janaab Pakal
799–?

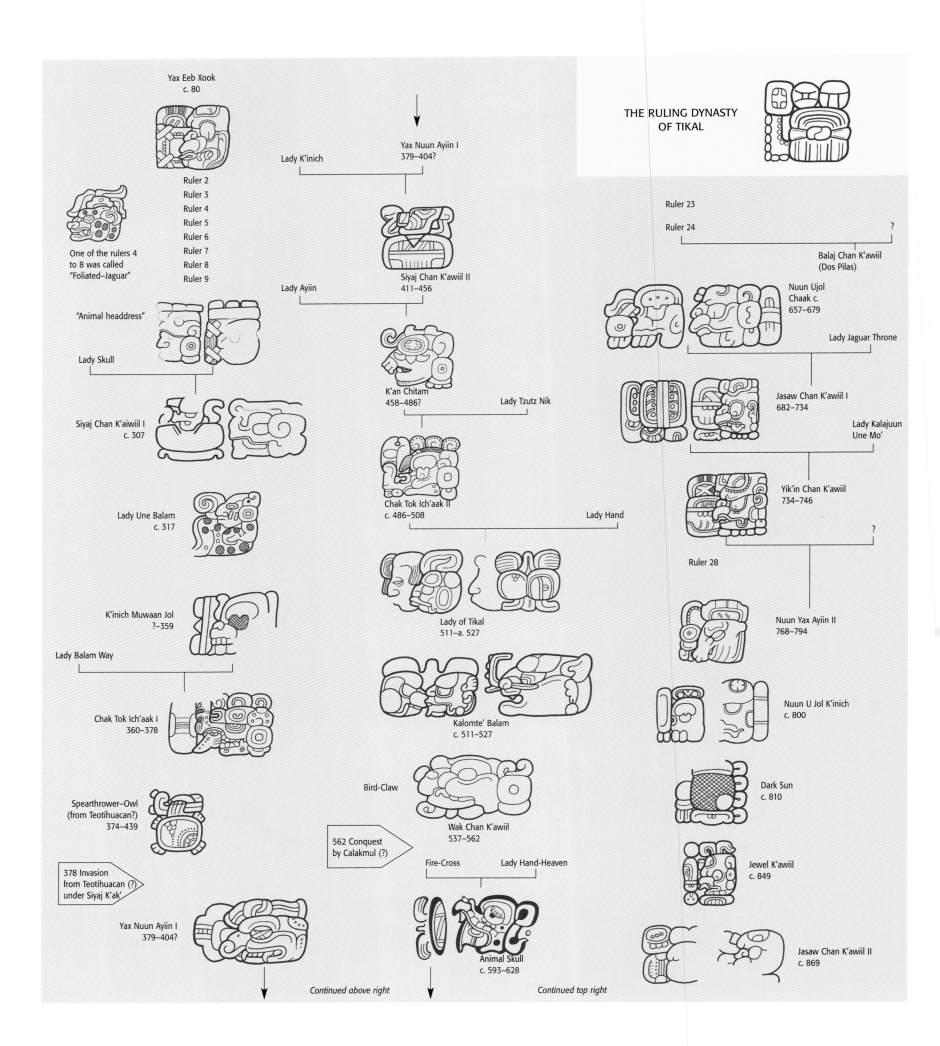

Yax Eeb Xook
c. 80

THE RULING DYNASTY
OF TIKAL

Lady K'inich

Yax Nuun Ayiin I
379–404?

Ruler 2
Ruler 3
Ruler 4
Ruler 5
Ruler 6
Ruler 7
Ruler 8
Ruler 9

One of the rulers 4
to 8 was called
"Foliated–Jaguar"

Ruler 23

Ruler 24   ?

Balaj Chan K'awiil
(Dos Pilas)

"Animal headdress"

Lady Ayiin

Siyaj Chan K'awiil II
411–456

Nuun Ujol
Chaak c.
657–679

Lady Skull

Lady Jaguar Throne

Siyaj Chan K'aiwiil I
c. 307

K'an Chitam
458–486?

Lady Tzutz Nik

Jasaw Chan K'awiil I
682–734

Lady Kalajuun
Une Mo'

Lady Une Balam
c. 317

Chak Tok Ich'aak II
c. 486–508

Lady Hand

Yik'in Chan K'awiil
734–746

?

K'inich Muwaan Jol
?–359

Lady of Tikal
511–a. 527

Ruler 28

Nuun Yax Ayiin II
768–794

Lady Balam Way

Chak Tok Ich'aak I
360–378

Kalomte' Balam
c. 511–527

Nuun U Jol K'inich
c. 800

Bird-Claw

Dark Sun
c. 810

Spearthrower–Owl
(from Teotihuacan?)
374–439

Wak Chan K'awiil
537–562

562 Conquest
by Calakmul (?)

Fire-Cross   Lady Hand-Heaven

Jewel K'awiil
c. 849

378 Invasion
from Teotihuacan (?)
under Siyaj K'ak'

Yax Nuun Ayiin I
379–404?

Animal Skull
c. 593–628

Jasaw Chan K'awiil II
c. 869

Continued above right   *Continued top right*

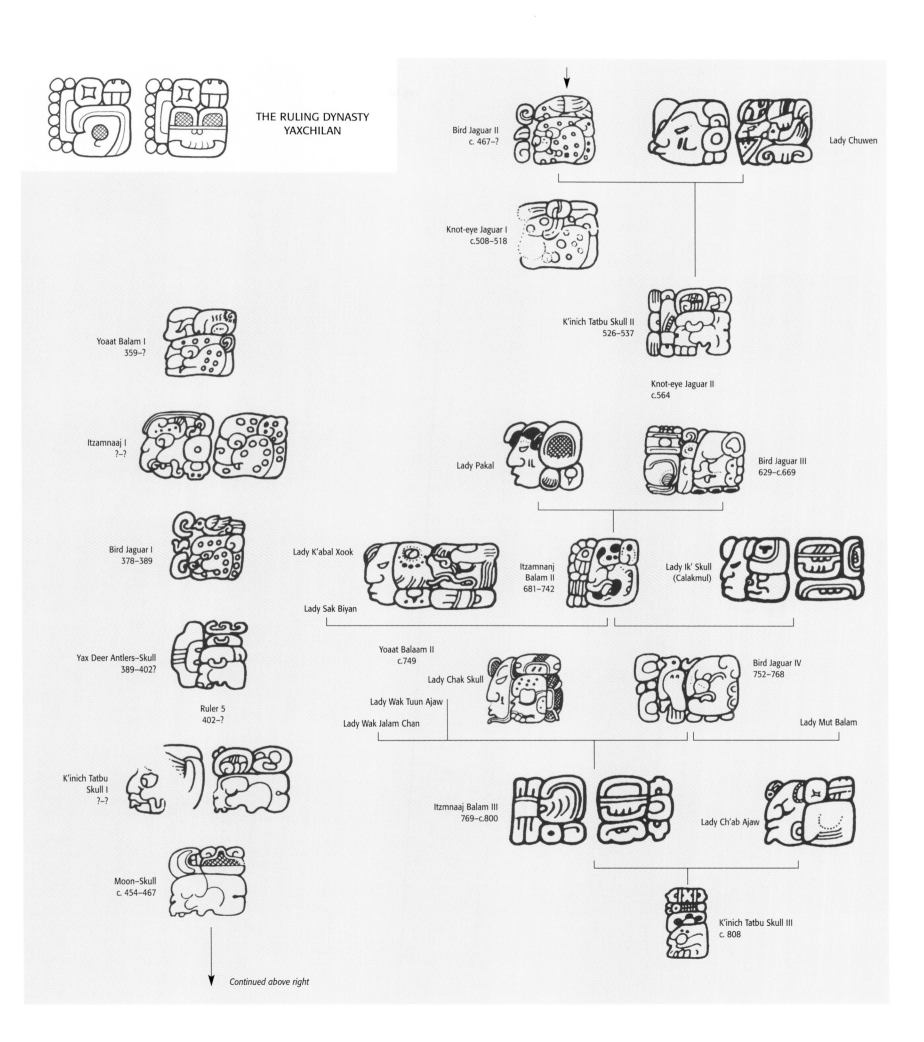

THE RULING DYNASTY
YAXCHILAN

Bird Jaguar II
c. 467–?

Lady Chuwen

Knot-eye Jaguar I
c.508–518

K'inich Tatbu Skull II
526–537

Knot-eye Jaguar II
c.564

Yoaat Balam I
359–?

Itzamnaaj I
?–?

Lady Pakal

Bird Jaguar III
629–c.669

Bird Jaguar I
378–389

Lady K'abal Xook

Itzamnanj
Balaam II
681–742

Lady Ik' Skull
(Calakmul)

Lady Sak Biyan

Yax Deer Antlers–Skull
389–402?

Yoaat Balaam II
c.749

Lady Chak Skull

Bird Jaguar IV
752–768

Lady Wak Tuun Ajaw

Ruler 5
402–?

Lady Wak Jalam Chan

Lady Mut Balam

K'inich Tatbu
Skull I
?–?

Itzmnaaj Balam III
769–c.800

Lady Ch'ab Ajaw

Moon–Skull
c. 454–467

K'inich Tatbu Skull III
c. 808

Continued above right

459

Northern Lowlands

During the last ice age, nomadic hunter-gatherers settled the American continent in several waves of immigration across the Bering Straits. Oldest finds in the Maya area from the time 9000–7000 B.C. include stone implements like flakes and spearpoints, together with the remains of animals that are extinct today, such as the mammoth. On the coasts, the settlers specialized in the collection of crustaceans and shellfish, and in about 5000 B.C., maize was planted for the first time. In about 2000 B.C., the first permanent settlements appeared, along with agriculture and the manufacture of ceramics.

Loltun Cave, c. 900 B.C.

Southern Lowlands

Head of figure from Cuello,
c. 1300 B.C.

Wedges from Cuello, 1800 B.C.

1000–600 Swasey ceramic in Cuello. Ear[ly] artistic epoch of the Maya culture in Beliz[e] stucco platforms, elaborate ceramics, use of cultivated crops

600–250 Heyday of Nakbe, one of the most important centers of the Middle Preclassic in central Peten, monumental architecture and sculpted stone monuments

Highlands

8000 Los Tapiales. Resting place for hunter-gatherers, earliest finds in Highlands of Guatemala, including flint spear points and flakes

Barra ceramic, oldest
Mesoamerican ceramic
c. 1600 B.C.

1500–1200 Ocos ceramic. Early Preclassic pottery on the Pacific coast gives clues to permanent settlement and villages with a population of fishermen and farmers

1000–500 Las Charcas phase of Kaminaljuyu. Population growth in Guatemala valley, production of figurines and sculpture

Monument 12 from
Chalchuapa, 1000–400 B.C.

Other civilizations/Mesoamerica

1200–900 San Lorenzo (Olmec city)

1200–800 Tlatilco culture in central Mexico

900–600 Classical epoch of La Venta (Olmec city)

Monument 3 from San Jose
Mogote, 900–400 B.C.

Europe/Africa/Asia

2040–1650 Egypt, Middle Kingdom

1700 Minoan Cretan writing as linear writing

1600 Phoenician alphabet

Minoan 17th century B.C.;
snake goddess; Fayence: Heraklion,
Arch. Museum

after 1555 Egyptian New Kingdom after expulsion of the Hyksos

Tutankhamun, gold mask from the inner
sarcophagus; c. 1347–1339 B.C.
Cairo, Egyptian Museum

Late Shang period, c. 1200–1000 B.C.
Ritual serving vessel; Peking,
National Museum

c. 960–925 King Solomon

814 Phoenicians from Tyre found Carthage

753 Founding of Rome

587 Destruction of Jerusalem by Nebucadn[ezzar]

551-479 Confucius founds an austere mora[l] philosophy

E C L A S S I C   L A T E   P R E C L A S S I C   (PROTOCLASSIC)

Northern Lowlands

Pot from Punta Piedra,
Quintana Roo, 400–100 B.C.

100 Relief in the entrance of the Loltun Cave: earliest dated Maya sculpture, representation of Maya rulers

Southern Lowlands

Figure from Uaxactun,
600–300 B.C.

ramic from Cuello, 900–400 B.C.

Gordon ceramic from Copan, 800–600 B.C.

Stucco mask from Chakanbakan,
Quintana Roo, 400–0 B.C.

1st century A.D. Founding of the Royal dynasty of Tikal

Jade mask from the Peten,
c. 200 A.D.

Fuchsite mask from Burial
85 in Tikal, 1st century A.D.

Highlands

Plate from Las Charcas, 1000–400 B.C.

500–200 Miraflores phase of Kaminaljuyu, most important settlement phase. The origin of much of the architecture visible today. Stone sculptures, richly furnished burials, flourishing trade

300–150 Izapa style. Large site with more than 80 temple platforms east of Tapachula, Chiapas. Artistic style on monuments of Tres Zapotes on the coast of Veracruz as far as the Pacific plains of Chiapas and Guatemala

Usulutan ceramic, 300 B.C.

36 A.D. Stela 1 from El Baul, Guatemala carries the earliest date in the Long Count in the Maya area, with time units each of 144,000 days, 9,600 days, 360 days, 20 days, and 1 day

200–400 Aurora phase of Kaminaljuyu

Monument from Izapa, 300 B.C.

EPI-OLMECS

Other civilizations/ Mesoamerica

from San Lorenzo, 1200–900 B.C.

500–900 Monte Alban in Oaxaca valley. Numerous massive stone buildings, unique abundance of sculptures with a scriptlike system of symbols. Religious and economic center of the Zapotecs

Stela from La Mojarra,
156 A.D.

36 B.C. Earliest date for Mesoamerica in Chapa de Corzo

30–220 Epi-Olmec culture

around 100 Sun Pyramid in Teotihuacan

c. 150 La Mojarra stela

View of Monte Alban

Incense burners from Cuicuilco, c. 100 B.C.

TEOTIHUACAN

Europe/Africa/Asia

Athens, Acropolis, Parthenon;
447–432 B.C.

448–368 Siddharta Gautama acquires status of Buddha

447–432 Building of Parthenon in Athens

336–323 Alexander the Great conquers Persia

c. 300 Laotse founds Daoism in China

221 Building of the Great Wall of China started

183 Hannibal's suicide

149–146 Destruction of Carthage by the Romans

0 Birth of Christ

64 Rome burns under Emperor Nero, persecution of the Christians

70 Destruction of Jerusalem by Titus

98–117 Emperor Trajan, the Roman Empire reaches its maximum extent

100–400 Gandhara Dynasty in India

170 Ptolemy's "Geographica"

chaemenid, Susa, Iran; c. 500 B.C.;
riffin from the Palace of Darius I the Great
22–486 B.C.); Paris, Musée du Louvre

Julius Caesar (100–44 B.C.), marble bust,
Naples, Museo Nazionale Archeologico

Khasneh or Treasury of the Pharaohs,
Petra, Jordan, probably 1st century B.C.

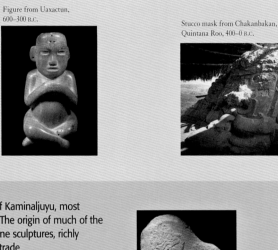

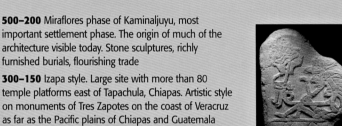

Northern Lowlands

Cántaro from Sayil, 250–550 A.D.

250–550 Pyramids with stucco façades in Acanceh: one of the earliest building and sculpture works in the northern Lowlands

Column temple of Ake, 250–550 A.D.

Stucco façade from Acanceh, 250–550 A.D.

Lintel II from Oxkintok, 475 A.D.

Teotihuacan vessel from Becan, 400–500 A.D.

Temple of the Seven Dolls in Dzibilchaltun, c. 700 A.D.

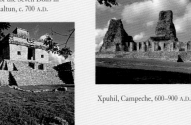

Xpuhil, Campeche, 600–900 A.D.

Southern Lowlands

292 First stela in Tikal

378 Conquest of Tikal by Siyaj K'ak' from Teotihuacan (?)

426 Enthronement of Yax K'uk' Mo' of Copan

Building E-VII-sub in Uaxactun

Siyaj K'ak' on stela 31 from Tikal, 445 A.D.

Tripod vessel from Copan, 250–500 A.D.

Fuchsite mask from Rio Azul, c.A.D. 500

Altar Q from Copan, 775 A.D.

562 Calakmul (?) conquers Tikal

599 Calakmul defeats Palenque

611 Calakmul defeats Palenque

631 Calakmul conquers Naranjo

695 Defeat of Calakmul by Tikal

736 Quirigua beheads the Copan king

Stucco portrait from Pal c. 690 A.D.

Highlands

250–900 Cozumalhuapa style. Unique occurrence in architecture and monumental art on the Pacific coast of Guatemala. Mexican and Maya influences, use of the 260-day ritual calendar, sculptural art with speech scrolls and a symbol system, often with the themes of death and the ball game.

400–600 Esperanza phase of Kaminaljuyu. Relationships with Teotihuacan in the architecture, the ceramics, and other artifacts, epoch of advance

Incense burner from Amatilan, 400–500 A.D.

Tripod vessel from Kaminaljuyu, 400–600 A.D.

C L A S S I C   V E

Other civilizations/ Mesoamerica

300–900 Classic Veracruz culture

0–600 Teotihuacan. One of the largest cities of Mesoamerica on the north side of the valley of Mexico, in its heyday covering more than 20 sq km. Famous regular road system, Sun and Moon Pyramids, murals. Widespread influence in central Mexico, into the Maya area

600–650 Collapse of Teotihuacan. Classic Veracruz culture on the Gulf Coast of Mexico with the center at El Rajin. Ceramic finds, monumental architecture (palaces, temples, stepped pyramids), and pictures of the ball game, war, and sacrifice

View of Teotihuacan, 250–550 A.D.

T E O T I H U A C A N

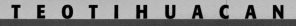

Europe/Africa/Asia

216 Building of the thermal bath of Caracalla

313 Constantine proclaims the "Edict of Milan" about freedom of religion

320–535 Gupta dynasties in north India

395 Final partition of the Roman Empire after the death of Theodosius the Great

439 Vandals conquer Carthage

476 Fall of the last of the western Roman emperors

537 Emperor Justinian rebuilds the Cathedral of Saint Sophia in Constantinople (Istanbul)

630 Mohammed occupies Mecca and the Kaaba

c. 706–751 Earliest evidence of printing

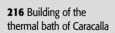

The Good Shepherd, Catacombs of Domitilla, Rome, 2nd–3rd century A.D.

Constantine Arch, Rome, 312–315 A.D.

Northern Wei Dynasty, 386–534 A.D., cave temple in Yungang, China

Christ giving benediction, St. Sophia, Istanbul, 6th century.

Borobudur, east side with main entrance, Java, Indonesia; 8th–9th century A.D.

SIC TERMINAL CLASSIC EARLY POSTCLASSIC

998 Latest date in Chichen Itza

905–915 Latest blossoming of Uxmal under King Chan Chaak

Governor's palace in Uxmal, 900–1000 A.D.   Warrior temple in Chichen Itza, 950–1050 A.D.

chola ceramic, 700–800 A.D.

Chenes building in Santa Rosa, Xtampak, c. 800 A.D.

Figurine from Jaina, 600–900 A.D.

Sotuta vessel, 1000–1200 A.D.

Northern Lowlands

c. 909 Tonina, latest stela with a date using the Long Count

e I in Tikal, A.D.

Codex style ceramic from Nakbe, 600–900 A.D.

Stela 10 from Seibal, 849 A.D.

Zoomorph from Quirigua, 795 A.D.

Monument 101 from Tonina, 909 A.D.

Southern Lowlands

From 800 A.D., new types of ceramics and style elements in art appear for the first time, which show foreign influences from central Mexico and the Gulf region. The ruling nobility of the cities disappeared, but the ordinary population stayed until about 1200 in the border areas. In the Highlands, earlier cities were abandoned and new ones founded, most as strongly defended settlements on elevated sites. The Pacific coast region developed its own style of sculpture (Santa Lucia Cozumalhuapa), because of foreign influences and the influx of Nahua-speaking population groups of the Pipil.

Stela from Cozumalhuapa, 800–900 A.D.

Incense burner from El Quiche, c. 900 A.D.

Highlands

CRUZ–CULTURE   TOLTECS

c. 900 Beginning of Tula's heyday

900–1100 Toltecs of Tula

1000–1521 Mixtecs, influential group in the Sierra of Oaxaca, who ruled a large territory in various small kingdoms. Widely distributed art style.

Mural, Cacaxtla, c. 800–900 A.D.

Other civilizations/ Mesoamerica

MIXTECS

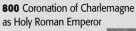

rabs defeated by s Martel at Tours itiers

800 Coronation of Charlemagne as Holy Roman Emperor

862 Norseman Rurik founds the Russian Empire

901 Vikings discover Greenland

962 Otto I becomes Emperor of the Holy Roman Empire of German nations

1066 Normans conquer England

1096–1099 First Crusade

c. 1100 Construction of Angkor Wat in Cambodia

1187 Saladin conquers Jerusalem

Patio del Yeso, Alcazar, Seville, 11th–12th century

The four Evangelists, book illustration from the *Treasury Gospels*. Beginning of 9th century; Aachen, cathedral treasure

Mexquita, Cordoba, 785–990 A.D.

Angkor Wat, View from the West, Cambodia, first half of 12th century

Europe/Africa/Asia

M I D D L E   P O S T C L A S S I C   LATE POST-CLASSI

Northern Lowlands

1283 Rise to power of Mayapan

Scepter from Chichen Itza, c. 1300

Mural in Tulum, 1400–1500

Incense burner from Mayapan, c. 1450

1517 Hernández de Córdoba
1528–1542 Conquest of Yuc

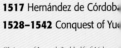
Cloisters of Izamal, 2nd half of 16th cen

Caracol of Mayapan, 1200–1450

Southern Lowlands

Incense burner from Dzibanche, 1300–1400

Temple in Topoxte, 1200

Mural from Santa Rita Corozal, c. 1400

Gold earflares from Santa Rita Corozal, c. 1400

1524 Cortéz crosses th Yucatan peninsula

Highlands

Gold chain from Iximche, 1200–1500

after 1400 K'iche' hegemony, the most powerful and influential Maya group of the Maya Highlands in the Postclassic

c. 1475 Founding of Iximche

Open snake jaws, Iximche ball game court, after 1475

Lead-glazed figure vessel, 1200–1500

T A R A S C A N S   /   A Z T E C S

Other civilizations/ Mesoamerica

1200 Axtecs settle in high valley of Mexico
1200–1521 Tarascans
1200–1521 Aztecs
1325 Founding of Tenochtitlan

Tlaloc, Mexica culture, 1325–1521

Ocelotl Cuauhxicalli, Mexica culture, 1502–1520

1519–1521 Conquest of Mexico by Cortéz
1542 New laws forbid Indi slavery

Sun stone, Mexica culture, Ocelotl Cuauhxicalli, 1325–1521

M I X T E C S

Europe/Africa/Asia

1275 Marco Polo visits China
1200–1546 Mali Empire in East Africa

Glass Window, Sainte Chappelle Paris, c. 1250

1302 Papal Bull 'Unam Sanctam': the Pope as supreme Lord of the World
1348 Black Death devastates Europe

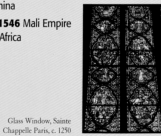
Petrarca Joos van Wassenhoove, gen. Justus of Gent; tempera on wood; Urbino, Palazza Ducale, 15th century

1453 Byzantium is conquered by the Turks
1492 Columbus lands on Guanahani

Jan van Eyck (1385–1441) side wing of the Gent altar, 1432, Gent, Sint Bavo.

Portrait of Christopher Columbus, Madrid, Museo de América

1504 Leonardo and Michaelangelo in Florence
1517 Luther's 95 theses
1555 Religious peace of A
1588 Destruction of the Sp Armada by English navy

Portrait of Phillip IV of Spain Velazquez (1599–1660),

1600	1700	1800	1900	2000

C O L O N I A L   T I M E S   MODERN NATIONAL STATES

1648–1650 Yellow fever epidemic

1847 to c.1936 Caste War in Yucatan

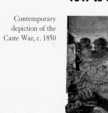

Contemporary depiction of the Caste War, c. 1850

Chilam Balam of Chumayel, c. 1750

View of Cancun

Northern Lowlands

1697 Conquest of Tayasal

18th century The English settle on the Caribbean coast (Belize)

1981 Belize becomes independent

...o Montejo
...Yucatan

Drawing from Catherwood, mid 19th century

Southern Lowlands

1712 Tzeltal Maya rebellion

1821 Independence for Guatemala

1868 Tzeltal Maya rebellion

1992 Nobel Peace Prize awarded to Rigoberta Menchú

1994 Zapatist uprising in Chiapas

1954–1996 Civil war in Guatemala

San Christóbal de las Casas, Chiapas, Dominican Church, 1547–1560, baroque restored

Antigua, Guatemala, Plaza Mayor, Cathedral 1565, restored after 1773

Rigoberta Menchua

Highlands

Hernán Cortéz, woodcut, 16th century

Map of the Americas with images of their conquerors, Theodorus de Bry, 1596

Alexander von Humboldt

1821 Mexico's independence

1845–1848 American-Mexican war

1846–1867 Emperor Maximilian

Emiliano Zapata (1879–1917)

1911–1920 Mexican revolution

20th century Research and excavation of Teotihuacan

Porfirio Diaz (1830–1915)

Other civilizations/ Mesoamerica

1600	1700	1800	1900	2000

1616 Death of Shakespeare

1618–1648 Thirty Years' War in Germany

1683 Turks beseige Vienna

1776 US becomes independent

1789 French Revolution

1815 Battle of Waterloo

1821 Mexico becomes independent of Spain

1848 First German parliament, in the Paulskirche in Frankfurt

1895 S. Freud and psychoanalysis

View of the Eiffel Tower and the World Exhibition ground, Paris 1889

1914–1918 First World War

1939–1945 Second World War

1991 dissolution of the Warsaw Pact and end of the Cold War

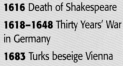

Johann Sebastian Bach (1685–1750), a sheet of music from the Matthew's Passion, Leipzig, University library

Jacques Louis David, The death of Marat, 1793, Brussels Musées Royaux des Beaux-Arts

Karl Marx (1818–1883) tinted portrait photograph, c. 1880

Europe/Africa/Asia

REMARKS ON THE WRITING AND PRONUNCIATION OF MAYAN

Nikolai Grube

In the family of Mayan languages, many sounds exist that, to an English-speaking reader, will seem unusual (as things that sound natural to us are strange to the Maya.) The first Spanish clerics began to learn the Mayan languages in the 16th century, and began to write grammars and dictionaries, with the intention of converting the Maya and incorporating them into the new colonial empire. They first had to create characters or character groups for the sounds that were unknown to them.

Because various orders preached in the Maya area and the individual languages were not alphabetically recorded together, several different methods of spelling developed. The rules that counted for one Mayan language could be quite irrelevant to another. An inclusive orthography for the alphabetic writing of all Mayan languages came about only in 1989. It was developed by the Maya themselves, to promote the communication and thereby the political and cultural cohesion of the various groups. At first, this official book of rules was followed only by the Maya of Guatemala. However, it has meanwhile also been accepted in Mexico and is being increasingly respected as the standard by researchers. The pronunciation of the letters is modeled extensively on Spanish, but has a list of peculiarities:

- In all Mayan languages, there are glottal as well as simple consonants; between their articulation and that of the following vowel, the glottis is closed for a fraction of a second. Glottal consonants are marked with an apostrophe('):

kab' "earth"	*k'ab'* "hand"
koj "puma"	*k'oj* "mask"
tzutz "lard"	*tz'utz'* "kiss"
pat "shape "	*p'at* "leave
something	something behind"

Vowels as well as consonants can be glottal. It sounds as though the breath is held for a short time immediately after pronunciation.

- In the Mayan languages of the Guatemalan Highlands, a guttural *q* is pronounced with the back of the tongue, near the soft palate; it sounds like a *k*.
- The letter combination *tz* indicates a silent sibilant in which the tongue tip presses against the back of the teeth.

- *x* represents phonetically the English *sh*.
- *ch* is pronounced as in Spanish, that is, like the English *tch* in kitchen.

- In many Mayan languages and also in the language of hieroglyphs, different meanings are linked to short or long vowels. Long vowels are shown by a repeated letter. Thus *chak* means red, whereas *Chaak* is the name of the Rain God.

- In hieroglyphic script, the background sound *j* would be distinguished from the glottal *h*. The latter would be softly pronounced and could in many cases even be dropped, but the former, as in Spanish, would sound similar to *ch* as in loch.

The spelling of Mayan words in this book is based on this orthography, except for a few place names like Dzibilchaltun (Tz'ibilchaltun) and Tikal (Tik'al), which have been established in this form for a long time. Standardization would be linguistically sensible, but would result in old and new maps no longer agreeing.

Most archeological sites, contrary to appearances, do not carry authentic old Maya names, but rather those that were given to them in the 19th or 20th centuries by the explorers or researchers. Many of the names are of Spanish origin like Caracol "snail," others are new Maya creations like Xunantunich "stone of the young woman." The original Maya names were forgotten before or during the Spanish invasion, and are only now being deciphered again. We have known for a while that Tikal was called *Mutul* in the Classic and Palenque was called *Lakamha'*. Even so, the familiar terms will continue to be used because a renaming of the archeological sites would lead to great confusion.

Examples for pronunciation of Mayan words for English speaking readers:

Xunantunich	shunantunitsh
Uxmal	ushmal
Kaminaljuyu	kaminalchuyu
Joyab'aj	choi ab-ach

AUTHORS

Dr. James Brady
Los Angeles, California State University, Department of Anthropology, Associate Professor; leader of excavation projects in caves in the Maya area, including Naj Tunich and the caves of Dos Pilas; research emphasis: cave archeology.

Dr. Pierre Robert Colas
Bonn, Rheinische Friedrich-Wilhelms-Universität, Institut für Altamerikanistik und Ethnologie, scholarship holder from the German Research Foundation (DFG); archeological and epigraphic field research on the Northern Vaca Plateau Geo-archeological Project in Belize as well as in cave archeology on Proyecto Arqueologico Piedras Negras in Guatemala, and ethnological field research on linguistic usage among the Maya of San Antonio, Cayo, Belize.

Dr. Nicholas Dunning
Cincinnati, Ohio, University of Cincinnati, Department of Geography, Associate Professor; research emphasis: archeology of settlements, agriculture, archeology of the Puuc region.

Markus Eberl, M.A.
Department of Anthropology, Tulane University, New Orleans, candidate for doctorate; research emphasis: archeology of the Lowlands, Maya script and eschatology.

Dr. Eva Eggebrecht
Hildesheim, Roemer- und Pelizaeus-Museum, co-worker; research emphasis: Egypt, World cultures, history of discovery.

Arq. Federico Fahsen Ortega
Guatemala City, Universidad del Valle, architect and town planner; 1980–1984 Ambassador in the United States, Vice Foreign Minister of Guatemala and Director of the Tourist Authority INGUAT. Since 1984, actively participating in Maya research with emphasis on hieroglyphic script and archeology of the Highlands.

Dr. Daniel Graña-Behrens
Bonn, Rheinische Friedrich-Wilhelms-Universität, Institut für Altamerikanistik und Ethnologie, scientific collaborator with a VW-Stiftung Tandem research project on scripts and ritual in Mesoamerica and China; research emphasis: Maya script, ritual and historiography in Mesoamerica.

Prof. Dr. Nikolai Grube
Bonn, Rheinische Friedrich-Wilhelms-Universität, Institut für Altamerikanistik und Ethnologie, university professor; research emphasis: archeology and history of Maya civilisation, Maya hieroglyphic script, Mesoamerican ethnology, resource use in the American tropics numerous book publications and essays on the script, history, and archeology of the Maya.

Marta Grube
Bonn, co-worker on various archeological projects in Belize.

Dr. Antje Gunsenheimer
Hanover, Volkswagen-Stiftung, examiner. Research emphasis: Yukatek Maya literature, Maya society in the early colonial times, Maya history in general.

Dr. Norman Hammond
Boston University, Professor of Archeology and Associate in Maya Archeology at the Peabody Museum, Harvard University; member of the British Academy and of the Society of Antiquaries of London; collaboration on various archeological projects in Belize, including Lubaantun, Nim Li Punit, Nohmul, Colha and Cuello. Since 1992, leader of the investigations in La Milpa in the north-west of Belize in cooperation with Gair Tourtellot.

Dr. Richard Hansen
Los Angeles, University of California, Regional Archeological Investigation of the North Peten, Guatemala, Project Director; leader of excavations at Nakbe, El Mirador, and numerous other sites in northern Peten; research emphasis: Preclassic.

Dr. Peter Harrison
Albuquerque, University of New Mexico, Anthropology Department, Adjunct Associate Professor; Research Associate with the Middle American Research Institute, Tulane University; participant and leader of excavation projects in Tikal, Quintana Roo (Mexico), and north Belize. Research emphasis: intensive agriculture of the Maya, architecture.

Prof. Dr. Annegrete Hohmann
Graz, Technische Universität, Institut fur Städtebau, Professor of Urban Planning; research emphasis: urban planning and layout among the Maya.

Simon Martin
Philadelphia, The University Museum, University of Pennsylvania, curator for Maya hieroglyphics, Epigrapher for the Calakmul archeological project, Campeche, Mexico; research emphasis: hieroglyphic script, religion, and history of the Classic Maya, numerous book publications and essays on the script, history, and archeology of the Maya.

Dr. Marilyn Masson
Albany, State University of New York, Department of Anthropology, Associate Professor; Director of excavations of Laguna On, Belize; research emphasis: archeology of the Postclassic period in the Lowlands, Zapotek inscriptions.

Dr. Mary Ellen Miller
New Haven, Yale University, Vincent Scully Professor of the History of Art; research emphasis: art history of Mesoamerica, iconography of the Bonampak murals.

Christian Prager, M.A.
Bonn, Rheinische Friedrich-Wilhelms-Universität, Institut für Altamerikanistik und Ethnologie, candidate for doctorate; research emphasis: hieroglyphic text, inscriptions of the southern Maya Lowland, Belize, ethnohistory of the colonial period in the Lowlands, religion of the Maya

Dr. Dorie Reents-Budet
Wilmington, The University of North Carolina, Director, Museum of World Cultures and Adjunct Associate Professor, Department of Anthropology; research emphasis: polychrome ceramics, iconography, and neutron activation of ceramics from the Classic period.

Frauke Sachse, M.A.
Bonn, Rheinische Friedrich-Wilhelms Universität, Institut für Altamerikanistik und Völkerkunde, candidate for doctorate; research emphasis: Mayan linguistics, ethnohistory, Xinca languages.

Temis Vayhinger-Scheer, M.A.
Heilbronn; research emphasis: ethnohistory of the scouthern Lowlands Itzaj Maya.

Dr. Karl Taube
Riverside, University of California, Department of Anthropology, Professor; research emphasis: Mesoamerican iconography, and religion.

Dr. Stefanie Teufel
Bonn, Rheinische Friedrich-Wilhelms-Universität, Institut für Altamerikanistik und Ethnologie, lecturer, collaborator with various archeological projects in Guatemala and Belize; research emphasis: iconography and hieroglyphic script of the Maya, especially of Piedras Negras.

Michael Vallo, M.A.
Bonn, Rheinische Friedrich-Wilhelms Universität, Institut für Altamerikanistik und Völkerkunde, candidate for doctorate; co-worker on Bonn University's archeological project of Xkipche, Yucatan; research emphasis: chronology of the Puuc region, ceramics.

Dr. Alexander W. Voß
Chetumal, Universidad de Quintana Roo, lecturer; research emphasis: hieroglyphic script, dynastic history of the Maya, archeology and history of civilization of Yucatan.

Elisabeth Wagner, M.A.
Bonn, Rheinische Friedrich-Wilhelms Universität, Institut für Altamerikanistik und Völkerkunde, candidate for doctorate; training as gemstone cutter and polisher; research interests: hieroglyphic scripts, dynastic history, religious iconography.

BIBLIOGRAPHY

General descriptions of Maya culture

Allebrand, Raimund (Ed.), Die Erben der Maya. Indianischer Aufbruch in Guatemala, Horlemann, Unkel 1997

Coe, Michael D., The Maya, Thames and Hudson, 5th Edition. London and New York 1998

Eggebrecht, Arne, Nikolai **Grube**, and Eva **Eggebrecht** (Ed.), Die Welt der Maya, Philipp von Zabern, Mainz 1992

Hammond, Norman, Ancient Maya Civilization, Rutgers University Press, New Brunswick 1982

Miller, Mary E., Maya Art and Architecture, Thames and Hudson, London and New York 1999

Riese, Berthold, Die Maya. Geschichte, Kultur, Religion, C. H. Beck, München 1995 (= Beck'sche Reihe Wissen, 2026)

Sabloff, Jeremy A., Die Maya. Archäologie einer Hochkultur, Spektrum der Wissenschaft, Heidelberg 1991 (= Spektrum Bibliothek, 29)

Schmidt, Peter, Mercedes **de la Garza** and Enrique **Nalda** (Ed.). Los Mayas, Ausst.-Kat. Conaculta, RCS-Libri, Milan and Mexico City 1998

Sharer, Robert J., The Ancient Maya, Stanford University Press, 5. Edition Stanford, CA 1994

Volcanoes and jungle – a richly varied habitat

Blake, Emmet R., Birds of Mexico, University of Chicago Press, Chicago 1953

Holdridge, Lawrence R., Mapa ecológico de América Central, Unidad de Recursos Naturales, Unión Panamericana, Washington D.C. 1969

Huntington, E., The Peninsula of Yucatan. In: Bulletin of the American Geographical Society, 44, 1912: 801–822

Murie, A., Mammals from Guatemala and British Honduras. In: University of Michigan, Museum of Zoology, Miscellaneous Publications, 26, 1935: 7–30

Pennington, Thomas D. and J. **Sarukhan**, Arboles tropicales de Mexico, Instituto Nacional de Investigaciones Forestales, Mexico 1968

Roys, Ralph L., The Ethno-Botany of the Maya, Department of Middle American Research, Tulane University, New Orleans 1931 (= Middle American Research Institute Publication, 2)

Sapper, Karl, Sobre la geografía física y la geología de la península Yucatán, Instituto de Geología, 3, Mexico 1896

Standley, Paul C., Flora of Yucatan, Field Museum of Natural History, Chicago 1930 (= Botanical Series, III, 3)

Stuart, L., Fauna of Middle America. In: Handbook of Middle American Indians, 1, 1964: 316–362

Wagner, P.L., Natural Vegetation of Middle America. In: Handbook of Middle American Indians, 1, 1964: 216–264

Ward, W.C., A.E. **Weidie** and W. **Black**, Geology and Hydrogeology of the Yucatan and Quaternary Geology of Northeastern Yucatan Peninsula, New Orleans Geological Society, New Orleans 1985

Cacao – the beverage of the gods

Coe, Michael D., The True History of Chocolate, Thames and Hudson, London 1996

Stuart, David, The Río Azul Cacao Pot. Epigraphic Observations on the Function of a Maya Ceramic Vessel. In: Antiquity, 62, 1988: 153–157

The origins of the Maya civilization – the beginnings of village life

Adams, Richard E.W. (Ed.), The Origins of Maya Civilization, University of New Mexico Press, Albuquerque 1977

Andrews V, E. Wyllys and Norman **Hammond**, Redefinition of the Swasey Phase at Cuello, Belize. In: American Antiquity, 55 (3), 1990: 570–584

Gerhardt, Juliette Cartwright, Preclassic Maya Architecture at Cuello, Belize, Oxford 1988 (= British Archaeological Research, International Series, 464)

Hammond, Norman, The Earliest Maya. In: Scientific American, 236 (3), 1977: 116–133

Hammond, Norman, Cuello. An Early Maya Community in Belize, Cambridge University Press, Cambridge, MA 1991

Hammond, Norman, Amanda **Clarke** and Sara **Donaghey**, The Long Goodbye. Middle Preclassic Maya Archaeology at Cuello. Belize. In: Latin American Antiquity, 6, (2), 1995: 120–128

Jones, John G., Pollen Evidence for Early Settlement and Agriculture in Northern Belize. In: Palynology, 18, 1994: 205–211

Kelly, Thomas C., Preceramic Projectile Point Typology in Belize. In: Ancient Mesoamerica, 4 (2), 1993: 205–227

Kosakowsky, Laura, Preclassic Maya Pottery at Cuello, Belize, University of Arizona Press, Tucson 1987 (= Anthropological Papers of the University of Arizona, 47)

Kosakowsky, Laura and Duncan C. **Pring**, The Ceramics of Cuello, Belize. A New Evaluation. In: Ancient Mesoamerica, 9(1), 1998: 55–66

Obsidian – the metal of the Maya

Clark, John E., Prismatic Blademaking, Craftmanship, and Production. An Analysis of Obsidian Refuse from Ojo de Agua, Chiapas, Mexico. In: Ancient Mesoamerica, 8 (1), 1997: 137–159

Hammond, Norman, Obsidian Trade Routes in the Mayan Area. In: Science, 178, 1972: 1092–1093

The first cities – the beginnings of urbanization and state formation in the Maya Lowlands

Ball, Joseph W. and E. Wyllys **Andrews V,** Preclassic Architecture at Becan, Campeche, Mexico, Tulane University, New Orleans 1978 (= Middle American Research Institute, Occasional Paper, 3)

Dahlin, Bruce H., A Colossus in Guatemala – The Preclassic Maya City of El Mirador. In: Archaeology, 37 (5), 1984: 18–25

Forsyth, Donald W., The Ceramics of El Mirador, Peten, Guatemala, Provo, Utah 1989 (= Papers of the New World Archaeological Foundation, 63)

Forsyth, Donald W., The Ceramic Sequence at Nakbe. In: Ancient Mesoamerica, 4 (1), 1993: 31–53

Freidel, David, Polychrome Façades of the Lowland Maya Preclassic. In: Painted Architecture and Polychrome Monumental Sculpture in Mesoamerica, edited by Elizabeth Boone, Dumbarton Oaks, Washington D.C., 1985: 5–30

Grube, Nikolai (Ed.), The Emergence of Lowland Maya Civilization. The Transition from the Preclassic to the Early Classic, Verlag von Fleming, Möckmühl 1996 (= Acta Mesoamericana, 8)

Hansen, Richard D., Excavations in the Tigre Complex, El Mirador, Peten, Guatemala, Provo, UH 1990 (= Papers of the New World Archaeological Foundation, 62)

Hansen, Richard D., An Early Maya Text from El Mirador, Guatemala, Center for Maya Research, Washington D.C. 1991 (= Research Reports on Ancient Maya Writing, 37)

Hansen, Richard D., Continuity and Disjunction. The Preclassic Antecedents of Classic Maya Architecture. In: Function and Meaning in Maya Architecture, edited by Stephen D. Houston, Dumbarton Oaks, Washington D.C. 1988: 49–122

Hansen, Richard D., Ronald L. **Bishop** and Federico **Fahsen**, Notes on Codex-Style Ceramics from Nakbe, Peten, Guatemala. In: Ancient Mesoamerica, 2(1), 1999: 225–243

Laporte, Juan Pedro and Juan Antonio **Valdés**, Tikal y Uaxactun en el Preclásico, Instituto de Investigaciones Antropológicas, Universidad Nacional Autónoma de Mexico, Mexico City 1993

Matheny, Ray T., Investigations at El Mirador, Peten, Guatemala. In: National Geographic Research, 2, 1986: 322–353

McAnany, Patricia, Living with the Ancestors. Kinship and Kingship in Ancient Maya Society, University of Texas Press, Austin 1995

Pendergast, David, Lamanai, Belize. Summary of Excavation Results, 1974–1980. In: Journal of Field Archaeology, 8 (1), 1981: 29–53

Ricketson, Oliver G. and Edith B **Ricketson**, Uaxactun, Guatemala, Group E, 1926–1931, Washington D.C. 1937 (= Carnegie Institution of Washington Publications, 477)

Jade – the green gold of the Maya

Digby, Adrian, Maya Jades, British Museum, London 1972

Lange, Frederick W., Precolumbian Jade. New Geological and Cultural Interpretations, University of Utah Press, Salt Lake City 1993

Proskouriakoff, Tatiana, Jades from the Cenote of Sacrifice, Chichen Itza, Yucatan, Harvard University, Cambridge, MA 1974 (= Papers of the Peabody Museum of Archaeology and Ethnology)

Maya agriculture

Adams Richard E.W., W.E. **Brown** and T. Patrick **Culbert**, Radar Mapping, Archaeology, and Ancient Maya Land Use. In: Science, 213, 1981

Fedick, Scott L. (Ed.), The Managed Mosaic. Ancient Maya Wetland

Harrison, Peter, D., The Rise of the Bajos and the Fall of the Maya. In: Social Process in Maya Prehistory, edited by Norman Hammond, London 1977: 469–508

Harrison, Peter, D., The Revolution in Ancient Maya Subsistence. In: Vision and Revision in Maya Studies, edited by Flora Clancy and Peter D. Harrison, University of New Mexico Press, Albuquerque 1990: 99–113

Harrison, Peter, D. and B.L. **Turner**, Pre-Hispanic Maya Agriculture, University of New Mexico Press, Albuquerque 1978

Harrison, Peter D. and Robert E. **Fry**, Pulltrouser Swamp. A Lowland Maya Community Cluster in Northern Belize. The Settlement Maps, The University of Utah Press, Salt Lake City 2000

Killion, Thomas W. (Ed.), Gardens of Prehistory. The Archaeology of Settlement Agriculture in Greater Mesoamerica, University of Alabama Press, Tuscaloosa 1992

Pohl, (Ed.), Ancient Maya Wetland Agriculture. Excavations on Albion Island, Northern Belize, Boulder 1990 (= Westview Special Studies in Archaeological Research)

Puleston, Dennis E., An Experimental Approach to the Function of Classic Maya Chultuns. In: American Anthropologist, 36, 1971: 322–335

Turner, B.L. and Peter D. **Harrison**, Pulltrouser Swamp. Ancient Maya Habitat, Agriculture and Settlement in Belize, University of Texas Press, Austin 1983

Tortillas and Tamales – the food of the maize people and their gods

Pilcher, Jeffrey M., Que vivan los tamales! Mexican Cuisine and National Identity, University of New Mexico Press, Albuquerque 1998

Taube, Karl A., The Maize Tamale in Classic Maya Diet, Epigraphy and Art. In: American Antiquity, 54, 1989: 31–51

From chiefdoms to statehood in the Highlands of Guatemala

Adams, Richard E.W., Routes of Communication in Mesoamerica. The Northern Guatemalan Highlands and the Peten. In: Mesoamerican Communication Routes and Cultural Contacts, edited by T.A Lee Jr. and C. Navarette, Brigham Young University, Provo, UH 1978 (= Papers of the New World Archaeological Foundation, 40)

Bove, Frederick, Formative Settlement Patterns on the Pacific Coast of Guatemala. A Spatial Analysis of Complex Societal Evolution, London 1989 (= British Archaeological Research, International Series, 493)

Bove, Frederick and Lynette **Heller** (Ed.), New Frontiers in the Archaeology of the Pacific Coast of Southern Mesoamerica, Arizona State University, Tempe 1989 (= Anthropological Research Papers, 39)

Braswell, Geoffrey E., La arqueología de San Martín Jilotepeque. In: Mesoamerica, 19 (35), 1998: 117–154

Demarest, Arthur A., The Archaeology of Santa Leticia and the Rise of Maya Civilization, Middle American Research Institute, Tulane University, New Orleans 1986 (= Middle American Research Institute Publication, 52)

Fahsen, Federico, La transcisión Pre-Clásico Tardío-Clásico Temprano. El desarrollo de los estados Mayas y la escritura. In: The emergence of Lowland Maya Civilization – the Transition from the Preclassic to the Early Classic, edited by Nikolai Grube, Verlag Anton Sauerwein, Mökmühl 1995 (= Acta Mesoamericana, 8)

Ichon, Alain und Rene **Viel**, La periode formative à La Lagunita et dans Le Quiche Meridional, Guatemala, Centre National de la Recherche Scientifique, Institut d'Etnologie, Paris 1984

Jones, Christopher, A Ruler in Triumph, Chocola, Monument I. In: Expedition, 28 (3), 1986: 3–12

Lowe, Gareth W., Thomas A. **Lee Jr.** and Eduardo **Martínez**, Izapa. An Introduction to the Ruins and Monuments, Brigham Young University, Provo, Utah 1982 (= Papers of the New World Archaeological Foundation, 31)

Parsons, Lee Allan, The Origins of Maya Art. Monumental Stone Sculpture of Kaminaljuyu, Guatemala and the Southern Pacific Coast, Dumbarton Oaks, Washington D.C. 1986 (= Studies in Pre-Columbian Art and Archaeology, 28)

Popenoe de Hatch, Marion, Kaminaljuyu/ San Jorge. Evidencia arqueológia de la actividad económica en el valle de Guatemala 300 AC a 300 DC, Universidad del Valle de Guatemala, Guatemala City 1997

Popenoe de Hatch, Marion, Los K'iche's – Kaqchiquiles en el altiplano central de Guatemala. Evidencia arqueológica del período clásico. In: Mesoamérica, 19 (35), 1998: 93-115

Sharer, Robert J. and David W. **Sedat**, Archaeological investigations in the Northern Maya Highlands, Guatemala. Interaction and the Development of Maya Civilization, The University Museum, University of Pennsylvania, Philadelphia 1987 (= University Museum Mono-graph, 59)

Shook, Edwin and Alfred V. **Kidder**, Mound E-III-3, Kaminaljuyu, Guatemala, Carnegie Institution of Washington, Washington D.C. 1952 (= Carnegie Institution of Washington Publication 596, Contributions to American Anthropology and History, 58)

Whitely, David S. and Marilyn P. **Beaudry** (Ed.), Investigaciones arqueológicas en la costa sur de Guatemala, Institute of Archaeology, University of California, Los Angeles 1989 (= Monograph 31)

The Insignia of power

Freidel, David A. and Linda **Schele**, Kingship and the Late Preclassic Maya Lowlands. The Instruments and Places of Ritual Power. In: American Anthropologist, 90 (3), 1986: 547–567

Schele, Linda and Mary E. **Miller**, The Blood of Kings, Kimbell Art Museum, Fort Worth 1986

Power in the West – the Maya and Teotihuacan

Berrin, Kathleen and Esther **Pasztory**, Teotihuacan. Art from the City of the Gods. Exhib.Cat. San Francisco Museum of Fine Arts, San Francisco, Thames and Hudson, London 1993

Foncerrada de Molina, Marta, Mural Painting in Cacaxtla and Teotihuacan Cosmopolitanism. In: Palenque Round Table Series, 3, 1978, Part 2, edited by Merle Green Robertson, Pre-Columbian Art Research Institute, San Francisco 1980: 183–198

Martin, Simon and Nikolai **Grube**, Chronicle of the Maya Kings and Queens. Deciphering the Dynasties of Ancient Maya, Thames and Hudson, London and New York 2000.

Pasztory, Esther, Teotihuacan. An Experiment in Living, University of Oklahoma Press, Norman 1997

Schele, Linda und David **Freidel**, Forest of Kings. The Untold Story of the Ancient Maya, William Morrow, New York 1990

Stone, Andrea, Disconnection, Foreign Insignia and Political Expansion. Teotihuacan and the Warrior Stelae of Piedras Negras. In: Mesoamerica after the Decline of Teotihuacan 700–900 A.D., edited by Richard A. Diehl and Janet C. Berlo, Dumbarton Oaks, Washington D.C., 1989: 153–172

Stuart, David, The Arrival of Strangers. Teotihuacan and Tollan in Classic Maya History. In: Mesoamerica's Classic Heritage, edited by David Carasco, Lindsay Jones and Scott Sessions, University Press of Colarado, Boulder 2000: 465–513

Sugiyama, Saburo, Rulership, Warfare, and Human Sacrifice at the Ciudadela. An Iconographic Study of Feathered Serpent Representations. In : Art, Ideology, and the City of Teotihuacan, edited by Janet C. Berlo, Dumbarton Oaks, Washington D.C., 1992: 205–230

Taube, Karl A., The Temple of Quetzalcoatl and the Cult of Sacred War at Teotihuacan. In: Res – Anthropology and Aesthetics, 21, 1992: 53–87

Taube, Karl A., The Writing System of Ancient Teotihuacan, Center for Ancient American Studies, Barnardsville und Washington D.C. 2000 (= Ancient America, 1)

Winning, Hasso von, An Iconographic Link between Teotihuacan and Palenque. In: Mexicon, 3 (2), 1981: 30–32

Hieroglyphs – the gateway to history

Berlin, Heinrich, El glifo „emblema" en las inscripciones mayas. In: Journal de la Société des Américanistes, 47, 1958: 111–119

Coe, Michael D., Breaking the Maya Code, Thames and Hudson, London 1992

Coe, Michael D. and Justin **Kerr**, The Art of the Maya Scribe, Thames and Hudson, London and New York 1998

Förstemann, Ernst, Die Maya-Handschrift der Königlich Öffentlichen Bibliothek zu Dresden, Richard Bertling, Dresden 1892

Grube, Nikolai, Die Entwicklung der Mayaschrift, Verlag von Flemming, Berlin 1991 (= Acta Mesoamericana, 3)

Houston, Stephen D., Maya Glyphs. Reading the Past, London 1989 (= British Museum Publications)

Houston, Stephen D., The Shifting Now. Aspect, Deixis, and Narrative in Classic Maya Texts. In: American Anthropologist, 99, 1997: 291–305

Houston, Stephen D., John **Robertson** and David **Stuart**, The Language of Classic Maya Inscriptions. In: Current Anthropology, 41 (3), 2000: 321–356

Justeson, John S. and Lyle **Campbell** (Ed.) Phoneticism in Maya Hieroglyphic Writing, Institute of Mesoamerican Studies, State University of New York at Albany, Albany 1984 (= Institute of Mesoamerican Studies Publication, 9)

Knorozov, Yurii V., Pis'menost Indeitsev Maiia, Akademie der Wissenschaften, Moskau und Leningrad 1964

Schele, Linda, Maya Glyphs. The Verbs, University of Texas Press, Austin 1982

Stuart, David, Ten Phonetic Syllables, Center for Maya Research, Washington 1987 (= Research Reports on Ancient Maya Writing, 14)

Thompson, John Eric S., A Catalogue of Maya Hieroglyphs, University of Oklahoma Press, Norman 1962

Bark paper books

Bricker, Victoria R. and Gabrielle **Vail** (Ed.), Papers on the Madrid Codex, Tulane University, New Orleans 1997 (= Middle American Research Institute Publication, 64)

Grube, Nikolai, Die Entzifferung der Maya-Handschriften. In: Die Bücher der Maya, Mixteken und Azteken, edited by Carmen Arellano Hoffmann and Peter Schmidt, Vervuert, Frankfurt 1997: 59–93

Thompson, John Eric S., A Commentary on the Dresden Codex, American Philosophical Society, Philadelphia 1972

Treiber, Hannelore, Studien zur Katunserie der Pariser Maya-Handschrift, Verlag von Flemming, Berlin 1987 (= Acta Mesoamericana, 2)

Astronomy and mathematics

Aveni, Anthony F., Skywatchers of Ancient Mexico, University of Texas, Austin 1980

Bricker, Harvey M. and Victoria R. **Bricker**, Zodiacal References in the Maya Codices. In: The Sky in Mayan Literature, edited by A. Aveni, Oxford University, New York and Oxford 1992: 148–183

Kelley, David, Deciphering the Maya Script

Kelley, David, Deciphering the Maya Script, University of Texas Press, Austin 1976

Lounsbury, Floyd, The base of the Venus Tables of the Dresden Codex and its Significance for the Calendar-Correlation problem. In: Calendars in Mesoamerica and Peru. Native Computations of Time, edited by Anthony Aveni and Gordon Brotherson, 44. International American Congress, Oxford 1883: 1–26 (= British Archaeological Research, International series, 174)

Lounsbury, Floyd, A Derivation of the Mayan-to-Julian Calendar Correlation from the Dresden Codex Venus Chronology. In: The Sky in Mayan Literature, edited by Anthony Aveni, Oxford University, New York and Oxford 1992: 184–206

Riese, Berthold Christoph L., Eine mexikanische Gottheit im Venuskapitel der Mayahandschrift Codex Dresdensis. In: Bulletin de la Société Suisse des Américanistes, 46, 1982: 37–39

Tedlock, Barbara, Time and the Highland Maya, University of New Mexico, Albuquerque 1982

Thompson, John Eric S., Maya Hieroglyphic Writing. An Introduction, University of Oaklahoma Press, 3. Edition Norman 1971 (= Civilization of the American Indian Series, 56) (First published in 1950 as Carnegie Institution of Washington Publication 589)

Solar eclipses – fearing the end of the world

Aveni, Anthony, Skywatchers of Ancient Mexico, University of Texas Press, Austin 1980

Bricker, Harvey M and Victoria R. **Bricker**, Classic Maya Prediction of Solar Eclipses. In: Current Anthropology, 24, 1983: 1–24

The dynastic history of the Maya

Berlin, Heinrich, El glifo „emblema" en las inscripciones mayas. In: Journal de la Société des Américanistes, 47, 1958: 111–119

Culbert, T. Patrick (Ed.) Classic Maya Political History, University of New Mexico Press, Albuquerque 1991

Fash, William L., Scribes, Warriors, and Kings. The City of Copan and the Ancient Maya, Thames and Hudson, London und New York 1991

Grube, Nikolai, Classic Maya Dance. Evidence from Hieroglyphs and Iconography. In: Ancient Mesoamerica, 3 (2), 1992: 201–218

Grube, Nikolai und Simon **Martin**, Política clásica maya dentro de una tradición mesoamericana. Un modelo epigráfico de organación política 'hegemónica'. In: Modelos de entidades politicas mayas, edited by Silvia Trejo, Mexico City 1998: 131–146

Houston, Stephen D., Hieroglyphs and History at Dos Pilas, University of Texas Press, Austin 1993

Houston, Stephen D. and David **Stuart**, Classic Maya Place Names, Dumbarton Oaks Research Library and Collection, Washington D.C. 1994. (= Studies in Pre-Columbian Art and Archaeology, 33)

Houston, Stephen D., Of Gods, Glyphs, and Kings. Divinity and Rulership among the Classic Maya. In: Antiquity, 70, 1996: 289–312

Houston, Stephen D., The Ancient Maya Self.

Personhood and Portraiture in the Classic Period. In: Res – Anthropology and Aesthetics, 33, 1998: 73–101
Houston, Stephen D. and Takeshi **Inomata** (Ed.), Royal Courts of the Ancient Maya, Westview Press, Boulder 2000
Martin, Simon, Calakmul y el enigma del glifo Cabeza de Serpiente. In: Arqueología Mexicana, 18, 1996: 42–45
Martin, Simon and Nikolai **Grube**, Maya Super States. In: Archaeology, 48, 1995: 41–46
Martin, Simon and Nikolai **Grube**, Chronicle of the Maya Kings and Queens, Thames and Hudson, London and New York 2000
Proskouriakoff, Tatiana, Historical Implications in a Pattern of Dates at Piedras Negras, Guatemala. In: American Antiquity, 25 (4), 1960: 455–475
Schele, Linda, An Epigraphic History of the Western Maya Region. In: Classic Maya Political History. Hieroglyphic and Archaeological Evidence, edited by T. Patrick Culbert, Cambridge University Press, Cambridge 1991: 72–101
Schele, Linda and David **Friedel**, A Forest of Kings. The Untold Story of the Ancient Maya, 2nd Edition. Morrow, New York 1992

Marriage diplomacy – women at the royal court

Proskouriakoff, Tatiana, Portraits of Women in Maya Art. In: Essays in Pre-Columbian Art and Archaeology, edited by Samuel K. Lothrop, Harvard University Press, Cambridge, MA 1961: 81–99

Under a deadly star – warfare among the Classic Maya

Brokmann, Carlos, Armamento y organización militar de los mayas. In: Arqueología Mexicana, 4 (19), 1996: 66–71
Chase, Arlen F. and Diane V. **Chase**, The Investigation of Classic Period Maya Warfare at Caracol. In: Mayab, 5, 1989: 5–18
Demarest, Arthur, Interregional Conflict and "Situational Ethics" in Classic Maya Warfare. In: Codex Wauchope. A Tribute Roll, edited by M. Giardino, B. Edmonson and V. Creamer, Department of Anthropology, Tulane University, New Orleans 1978:101–111 (= Human Mosaic, 12)
Friedel, David, Maya Warfare. An Example of Peer Polity Interaction. In: Peer Polity Interaction and Socio-Political Change, edited by Colin Renfrew and John F. Cherry, Cambridge University Press, Cambridge 1986: 93–108 (= New Directions in Archaeology)
Friedel, and Linda **Schele**, Forest of Kings. The Untold Story of the Ancient Maya, William Morrow, New York 1990
Martin, Simon and Nikolai **Grube**, Chronicle of the Maya Kings and Queens, Thames and Hudson, London and New York 2000
Proskouriakoff, Tatiana, Historical Data in the Inscriptions of Yaxchilan, Part I. In: Estudios de Cultura Maya, 3, 1963: 149–167
Puleston, Dennis E. and Donald W. **Callender Jr.**, Defensive Earthworks at Tikal. In Expedition, 9 (3) 1967: 40–48
Schele, Linda and Mary E. **Miller**, The Blood of Kings, Dynasty and Ritual in Maya Art, Kimbell Art Museum, Fort Worth

Stone, Andrea, Disconnection, Foreign Insignia, and Political Expansion. Teotihuacan and the Warrior Stelae of Piedras Negras. In: Mesoamerica after the Decline of Teotihuacan 700–900 A.D., edited by Richard A. Diehl and Janet C. Berlo, Dumbarton Oaks, Washington D.C., 1989: 153–172
Webster, David, The Study of Maya Warfare. What it tells us about the Maya Archaeology. In: Lowland Maya Civilization in the Eighth Century A.D., edited by Jeremy A. Sabloff and John S. Henderson, Dumbarton Oaks Research Library and Collection, Washington D.C., 1993: 415–444

A game of life and death – the Maya ball game

Friedel, David, Linda **Schele** and Joy **Parker**, Maya Cosmos. Three Thousand Years on the Shaman's Path, William Morrow, New York 1993
Leyenaar, Ted J. J. and Lee A. **Parsons**, Ullama, the Ballgame of the Maya and the Aztecs, Spruyt, Van Mantgem & De Does, Leiden 1988
Taladoire, Eric, Les terrains de Jeu de Balle, Mission Archéologique et Ethnologique Française au Mexico, Mexico D.F. 1981

Unity in space and time – the Maya architecture

Andrews, George F., Maya Cities. Placemaking and Urbanization, University of Oklahoma Press, Norman 1975
Andrews, George F., Pyramids and Palaces, Monsters and Masks. The Golden Age of Maya Architecture, 1: Architecture of the Puuc Region and the Northern Plains, Labyrinthos, Lancaster, CA 1995
Andrews, George F., Pyramids and Palaces, Monsters and Masks. The Golden Age of Maya Architecture, 2: Architecture of the Chenes Region, Labyrinthos, Lancaster, CA 1997
Andrews, George F., Pyramids and Palaces, Monsters and Masks. The Golden Age of Maya Architecture, 3: Architecture of the Río Bec Region and Miscellaneous Subjects, Labyrinthos, Lancaster, CA 1999
Gendrop, Paul, Los estilos Río Bec, Chenes y Puuc en la arquitectura maya, Universidad Nacional Autónoma de Mexico, Mexico D.F. 1983
Heydon, Doris and Paul **Gendrop**, Architektur der Hochkulturen Mittleamerikas, Belser Verlag, Stuttgart 1975
Hohmann, Hasso, Gewölbekonstruktionen in der Maya-Architektur. In: Mexicon, 1 (3), 1979: 33–36
Hohmann, Hasso and Annagrete **Vogrin**, Die Architektur von Copan (Honduras), Akademische Druck- und Verlagsanstalt, Graz 1982
Hohmann, Hasso, Die Architektur der Sepulturas-Region von Copan in Honduras, Academic Publishers, Graz 1995
Hohmann, Hasso, A Maya Palace in Mexico – Structure IV at Becan, Campeche, Academic Publishers, Graz 1998
Houston, Stephen D. (Ed.) Function and Meaning in Classic Maya Architecture. A Symposium at Dumbarton Oaks, 7th and 8th October 1994, Dumbarton Oaks Research Library and Collection, Washington D.C. 1998
Kubler, George, The Art and Architecture of Ancient America, Penguin Books, Baltimore, Maryland 1962

Pollock, Harry E. D., The Puuc. An Architectural Survey of the Hill Country of Yucatan and Northern Campeche, Mexico, Harvard University, Cambridge, MA 1980 (= Memoirs of the Peabody Museum of Archaeology and Ethnology, 19)
Potter, David F., Maya Architecture of the Central Yucatan Peninsula, Mexico, Tulane University, New Orleans 1977 (= Middle American Research Institute Publication, 44)
Proskouriakoff, Tatiana, An Album of Maya Architecture, Washington D.C. 1946 (= Carnegie Institution of Washington Publication, 558)

The history of a Maya settlement – research results from the excavations of Xkipche

Prem, Hanns J., Geschichte eines Mayapalastes. Ausgrabungen in Xkipche, Yucatán. In: Antike Welt, 30 (5), 1999: 545–554
Reindel, Markus, Xkipche, un asentamiento Maya en el norte de Yucatan, Mexico. In: KAVA. Beiträge zur Allgemeinen und Vergleichenden Archäologie, 17, 1997: 177–250

Maya architecture at Tikal

Coe, William R., Excavations in the Great Plaza, North Terrace and North Acropolis of Tikal, 6 Bde., University Museum, Philadelphia 1990 (= Tikal Report, 14)
Coe, William R. and Rudy V. **Larios**, Tikal. A Handbook of the Ancient Maya Ruins, Associación Tikal, Guatemala City, 1986
Harrison, Peter D., Tikal, Maya Rulers of Time, Thames and Hudson, London und New York 1999
Jones, Christopher, Excavations in the East Plaza of Tikal, 2 Bde., University of Pennsylvania, Museum of Archaeology and Anthropology, Philadelphia 1996 (= Tikal Report, 16)
Schele, Linda and Peter **Matthews**, The Code of Kings. The Language of Seven Sacred Maya Temples and Tombs, Scribner, New York

Processions, pilgrims and loadcarriers – the ceremonial roads

Benavides, Antonio, Los caminos prehispánicos de Cobá. In: XV. Mesa Redonda de la Sociedad Mexicana de Antropología, 2, 1977: 215–225
Chase, Arlen F. and Diane Z. **Chase** (Ed.), Studies in the Archaeology of Caracol, Belize, San Francisco 1994 (= Pre-Columbian Art Research Institute Monograph 7)
Villa Rojas, Alfredo, The Coba-Yaxuna Causeway, Washington D.C. 1934 (= Carnegie Institution of Washington Publication, 436)

Understanding the murals of Bonampak

Fuente, Beatriz de la (Ed.), La pintura mural prehispánica en Mexico, Vol. 2: Area Maya, Bonampak, 2 Bde., Universidad Nacional Autónoma de Mexico, Mexico City 1998
Mathews, Peter, Notes on the Dynastic Sequence of Bonampak, Part 1. In: Third

Palenque Round Table, 1978, edited by Merle Greene Robertson, University of Texas Press, Austin 1980: 60–73 (= Palenque Round Table Series 5)
Miller, Mary E., The Murals of Bonampak, Princeton University Press, Princeton 1986
Miller, Mary, E., The Boys in the Bonampak Band. In: Maya Iconography, edited by Elizabeth P. Benson and Gillet Griffin, Princeton University Press, Princeton 1988: 318–330
Ruppert, Karl J., John Eric S. **Thompson** and Tatiana **Proskouriakoff**, Bonampak, Chiapas, Mexico, Washington D.C. 1955 (= Carnegie Institution of Washington Publication, 602)

Grave robbers in the jungle

Messenger, Phyllis M. (Ed.), The Ethics of Collecting Cultural Property: Whose Culture? Whose Property? University of New Mexico Press, Albuquerque 1989
Meyer, Karl E., The Plundered Past, Atheneum, New York 1977

The art of Classic vase paintings

Adams, Richard E.W., The Ceramics of Altar de Sacrificios, Harvard University, Cambridge, Mass. 1971 (= Papers of the Peabody Museum of Archaeology and Ethnology, 63, 1)
Coe, Michael, The Maya Scribe and his World, Grolier Club, New York 1973
Coe, Michael, Supernatural Patrons of Maya Scribes and Artists. In: Social Process in Maya Prehistory. Studies in Honor of Sir Eric Thompson, edited by N. Hammond, Academic Press, London 1977:327–347
Coe, Michael, Lords of the Underworld. Masterpieces of Classic Maya Ceramics, The Art Museum, Princeton University, Princeton University Press, Princeton 1978
Coe, Michael and Justin **Kerr**, Art of the Maya Scribe, Thames and Hudson, London and New York
Grube, Nikolai, An Investigation of the Primary Standard Sequence on Classic Maya Ceramics. In: Sixth Palenque Round Table, 1986, edited by Virginia M. Fields, Pre-Columbian Art Research Institute, San Francisco 1990: 223–232 (= Palenque Round Table Series, 8)
Grube, The Primary Standard Sequence on Chocholá Style Ceramics. In: The Maya Vase Book, Vol. 4, edited by Justin Kerr, Kerr Associates, New York 320–330
Grube, Nikolai and Werner **Nahm**, A Census of Xibalba. A Complete Inventory of Way Characters on Maya Ceramics. In: The Maya Vase Book, Vol. 4, edited by Justin Kerr, Kerr Associates, New York: 686–713
Houston, Stephen and Karl A. **Taube**, Name Tagging in Classic Maya Script. In: Mexicon, 9 (2), 1987: 38–41
Houston, Stephen and David **Stuart**, The Way Glyph. Evidence for "Co-essences" among the Classic Maya. In: Research Reports on Ancient Maya Writing, 30, 1989: 1–16
Houston, Stephen, David **Stuart** and Karl **Taube**, Folk Classification of Ancient Maya Pottery. In: American Anthropologist, 91 (3), 1989: 720–726

470

Houston, Stephen, David **Stuart** and Karl **Taube**, Image and Text on the "Jauncy Vase". In: The Maya Vase Book, Vol. 3, edited by Justin Kerr, Kerr Associates, New York 1992: 498–512

Joyce, Rosemary, The Construction of the Mesoamerican Frontier and the Mayoid Image of Honduran Polychromes, Peabody Museum of American Archaeology and Ethnography, Harvard University, Cambridge, MA 1991

Kerr, Barbara and Justin **Kerr**, Some Observations on Maya Vase Painters. Paper presented at the Conference on Maya Funerary Ceramics, The Art Museum, Princeton University, Princeton 1981

Kerr, Barbara and Justin **Kerr**, Some Observations on Maya Vase Painters. In: Maya Iconography, edited by E.P. Benson and G.G. Griffin, Princeton University Press, Princeton 1988: 236–259

MacLeod, Barbara, Deciphering the Primary Standard Sequence. Department of Anthropology, University of Texas at Austin, Phil. Diss. 1990

Peterson, Susan, The Craft and Art of Clay, Prentice Hall, New Jersey 1992

Reents-Budet, Dorie, Elite Maya Pottery and Artisans as Social Indicators. In: Craft and Social Identity, edited by Cathy Costin and Rita Wright, Washington 1998 (= Archaeological Papers of the American Anthropological Association, 8)

Reents-Budet, Dorie, Ronald L. **Bishop** and Barbara **MacLeod**, Acercamiento integrada a la cerámica pintada clásica Maya. In: Simposio Investigaciones arqueológicas en Guatemala, 1992, edited by Juan Pedro La Porte, Héctor L. Escobedo and Sandra Villagrán de Brady, Museo Nacional de Arqueológica y Etnología, Ministerio de Cultura y Deportes, Instituto de Antropología e Historia and Asociación Tikal, Guatemala City 1993

Reents-Budet, Dorie, Ronald L. **Bishop** and Barbara **MacLeod**, Painting the Maya Universe. Royal Ceramics of the Classic Period, Duke University Press, Durham, New York and London 1994

Reina, Rubén E. and Robert M. **Hill**, The Traditional Pottery of Guatemala, University of Texas press, Austin 1978

Rhodes, Daniel, Clay and Glazes for the Potter, Chilton Book Company, Philadelphia 1973

Rice, Prudence, Pottery Production, Pottery Classification and the role of Physicochemical Analysis In: Archaeological Ceramics, edited by Jacqueline S. Olin and Alan D. Franklin, Smithsonian Institution Press, Washington D.C., 1982: 47–56

Stuart, David, The Rio Azul Cacao Pot. Epigraphic Observations on the Function of a Maya Ceramic Vessel. In: Antiquity, 62 (234), 1988: 153–157

Taschek, Jennifer and Joseph **Ball**, Lord Smoke Squirrel's Cacao Cup. The Archaeological Context and Sociological Significance of the Buenavista "Jauncy Vase". In: The Maya Vase Book, Vol. 3, edited by Justin Kerr, Kerr Associates, New York 1992: 490–497

The Classic Maya gods

Freidel, David, Linda **Schele**, and Joy **Parker**, Maya Cosmos. Three Thousand Years on the Shaman's Path, William Morrow, New York 1993

Grube, Nikolai and Werner **Nahm**, A Census of Xibalba. A Complete Inventory of Way Characters on Maya Ceramics. In: The Maya Vase Book, Vol. 4, edited by Justin Kerr, Kerr Associates, New York 1994:686–715

Hellmuth, Nicholas M., Monster und Menschen in der Maya-Kunst, Akademische Druck- und Verlagsanstalt, Graz 1987

Houston, Stephen, D. and David **Stuart**, The Way Glyph. Evidence for "Co-Essences" among the Classic Maya, Center for Maya Research, Washington D.C. 1989 (= Research Reports on Ancient Maya Writing, 30)

Miller, Mary, and Karl **Taube**, The Gods and Symbols of Ancient Mexico and the Maya, Thames and Hudson, London and New York 1993

Schele, Linda and Mary E. **Miller**, The Blood of Kings. Ritual and Dynasty in Maya Art, Kimbell Art Museum, Fort Worth 1986

Schellhas, Paul, Die Göttergestalten der Mayahandschriften. Ein mythologisches Kulturbild aus den alten Amerika, Verlag von Richard Bertling, Dresden 1897

Taube, Karl, A. The Maya Maize God. A Reappraisal. In: Fifth Palenque Round Table, 1983, edited by Virginia M. Fields, Pre Columbian Art Research Institute, San Francisco 1985: 171–181 (= Palenque Round Table Series, 7)

Taube, Karl A., The Major Gods of Ancient Yucatan. Schellhas Revisited, Dumbarton Oaks Research Library and Collection, Washington D.C. 1992 (= Studies in Pre-Columbian Art and Archaeology, 32)

Court dwarfs – the companions of rulers and envoys of the underworld

Houston, Stephen, D., A Name Glyph for Classic Maya Dwarfs. In: The Maya Vase Book, Vol. 3, edited by Justin Kerr, Kerr Associates, New York 1991: 526–531

Mayer, Karl Herbert, Zwergendarstellungen bei den präkolumbischen Maya. In: Das Altertum, 32 (4), 1986: 212–224

Miller, Virginia, E., The Dwarf Motif in Classic Maya Art. In: Fourth Palenque Round Table, 1980, edited by Elizabeth P. Benson, Pre-Columbian Art Research Institute, San Francisco 1986: 141–153

Maya creation myths and cosmography

Ashmore, Wendy, Site-Planning Principles and Concepts of Directionality among the Ancient Maya. In: Latin American Antiquity, 2 (3), 1991: 199–226

Ashmore, Wendy, Deciphering Architectural Plans. In: New nTheories on the Ancient Maya, edited by Elin C. Danien and Robert J. Sharer, The University Museum, University of Pennsylvania, Philadelphia 1992: 173–184 (= University Museum Monographs, 77; University Museum Symposium Series, 3)

Bassie-Sweet, Karen, At the Edge of the World. Caves and Late Classic Maya Worldview, University of Oklahoma Press, Norman 1996

Bricker, Victoria, Directional Glyphs in Maya Inscriptions and Codices. In: American Antiquity, 48 (2), 1983: 347–353

Coe, Michael D., A Model of Ancient Maya Community Structure in the Maya Lowlands. In: Southwestern Journal of Anthropology, 21, 1965: 87–119

Freidel, David, Linda **Schele** and Joy **Parker**, Maya Cosmos. Three Thousand Years on the Shaman's Path, William Morrow, New York 1993

Gossen, Gary H., Chamulas in the World of the Sun. Time and Space in a Maya Oral Tradition, Harvard University Press, Cambridge 1974

Schele, Linda, Religion und Weltsicht. In: Die Welt der Maya, edited by Arne Eggebrecht, Nikolai Grube and Eva Eggebrecht, Phillip von Zabern, Mainz 1992:197–214

Taube, Karl A., Aztec and Maya Myths, University of Texas Press, Austin 1994

Tedlock, Dennis, Popol Vuh. The Definitive Edition of the Mayan Book of the Dawn of Life and the Glories of Gods and Kings, Simon and Schuster, 2 Edition, New York 1996

Vogt, Evon Z., Zinacantan. A Maya Community in the Highlands of Chiapas, Belknap Press, Cambridge 1969

Vogt, Evon Z., The Zinacantecos of Mexico. A Modern Maya Way of Life, Holt, Rinehart and Winston, New York 1970 (= Case Studies in Cultural Anthropology)

Vogt Some Aspects of the Sacred Geography of Highland Chiapas. In: Mesoamerican sites and World Views, edited by Elizabeth P. Benson, Dumbarton Oaks Research Library and Collection, Washington D.C., 1981: 119–139

Intoxication and ecstasy

Furst, Peter D., Hallucinogens and Culture, Chandler and Sharp, San Francisco 1976

Smet, Peter de, Ritual Snuffs and Enemas in the Americas, Centrum voor Studie en Documentatie van Latijns Amerika, Amsterdam 1985 (= Latin American Studies, 33)

Stross, Brian and Justin **Kerr**, Notes on the Maya Vision Quest through Enema. In: The Maya Vase Book, Vol. 2, edited by Justin Kerr, Kerr Associates, New York 1990:349–361

Uncovering the dark secrets of the Maya – the archeology of Maya caves

Andrews V, E. Wyllys, Explorations in the Gruta de Chac. In: Middle American Research Institute Publication, 31: 1–21, Middle American Research Institute, Tulane University, New Orleans, 1965

Brady, James E., Settlement Configuration and Cosmology. The Role of Caves at Dos Pilas. In: American Anthropologist, 99 (3), 1997: 602–618

Brady, James, E. and George **Veni**, Man-Made and Pseudo-Karst Caves. The Implications of Sub-Surface Geologic Features Within Maya Centers. In: Geoarchaeology, 7, 1992: 149–167

Brady, James, E., Ann **Scott**, Allan **Cobb**, et al., Glimpses of the Dark Side of Petexbatun Regional Archaeological Project. The Petexbatun Regional Cave Survey. In Ancient Mesoamerica, 8 (2), 1997: 353–364

Brady, James, E., Gene A. **Ware**, Barbara **Luke** et al., Preclassic Cve Utilization near Cobanerita, San Benito, Peten. In Mexicon, 19 (5), 1997: 91–96

Brady, James, E. and Keith **Prufer**, Caves and Crystalmancy. Evidence for the Use of Crystals in Ancient Maya Religion. In: Journal of Anthropological Research, 55, 1999: 129–144

Broda, Johanna, Calendarios, cosmovisión y observación de la naturaleza. In: Temas Mesoamericanos, hrsg. von Sonia Lombardo und Enrique Nalda, Instituto Nacional de Antropología e Historia, Mexico 1996: 427–469

Carlson, Ruth and Francis **Eachus**, The Kekchi Spirit World. In: Cognitive Studies of Southern Mesoamerica, edited by Helen L. Neuenswander ND Dean E. Arnold, Summer Institute of Linguistics, Dallas 1977: 36–65

García-Zambrano, Angel J., Early Colonial Evidence of Pre-Columbian Rituals of Foundation. In: Seventh Palenque Round Table, 1989, edited by Virginia M. Fields, Pre-Columbian Art Research Institute, San Francisco 1994: 217–227

Gossen, Gary H., Chamulas in the World of the Sun. Time and Space in a Maya Oral Tradition, Harvard University Press, Cambridge 1974

Guiteras Holmes, Calixta, Sintesis de la visión del mundo de los altos de Chiapas. In: Los Mayas del Sur y sus relaciones con los Nahuas Meridionales. In: VIII. Mesa Redonda de la Sociedad Mexicana de Antropología, Mexico 1961: 303–308

Gurnee, Russell H., Seamay Cave (Caves of the Grand Staircase) Senahu, Alta Verapaz, Guatemala, C.A. In: National Speleological Society News, 23 (8), 1965: 114–117

Kubler, George, Pre-Columbian Pilgrimages in Mesoamerica. In: Fourth Palenque Round Table, 1980, edited by Elizabeth Benson, Pre-Columbian Art Research Institute, San Francisco 1985: 313–316

Manzanilla, L., L. **Barba**, R. **Chavez** et al., Caves and Geophysics. An Approximation to the Underworld of Teotihuacan, Mexico. In: Archaeometry, 36, 1994: 141–157

Martinez Marin, Carlos, Santuarios y peregrinaciones en el Mexico Prehispanico. In: Religión en Mesoamerica, edited by Jaime Litvak King and Neomi Castillo Tejeros, Mexico 1972:161–176 (= XII. Mesa Redonda de la Sociedad Mexicana de Antropología)

Mercer, Henry C., The Hill-Caves of Yucatan, The University of Oaklahoma press, Norman 1975 (Reprint of the Original Issue of 1896)

Schackt, Jon, The Tzuultak'a. Religious Lore and Cultural Processes among the Kekchi. In: Belizean Studies, 12 (5), 1984: 16–29

Schavelzon, Daniel, Temples, Caves or Monsters? Notes on Zoomorphic Façades in Pre-Hispanic Architecture. In Third Palenque Round Table, 1978, Part 2, edited by Merle Greene Robertson, University of Texas press, Austin 1980: 151–162

Seler, Eduard, Die alten Ansiedlungen von Chacula, im Distrikte Nenton des Departments Huehuetenango der Republik Guatemala, Dietrich Reimer Verlag, Berlin 1901

Stuart, David and Stephen **Houston**, Classic Maya Place Names, Dumbarton Oaks, Washington D.C. 1994 (=Studies in Pre-Columbian Art and Archaeology, 33)

Tedlock, Barbara, The Role of Dreams and Visionary Narratives in Mayan Cultural Survivals. In: Ethnos, 20, 1992: 453–476

Thompson, J. Eric S., The Role of Caves in Maya Culture. In: Mitteilungen aus dem Museum für Völkerkunde in Hamburg, 25, 1959: 122–129

Thompson, J. Eric S., Maya History and Religion, University of Oklahoma Press, Norman 1970

Vogt, Evon Z., Ancient Maya and Contemporary Tzotzil Cosmology. A Comment on some Methodological Problems. In: American Antiquity, 30, 1964: 192–195

Vogt, Evon Z., Tortillas for the Gods. A Symbolic Analysis of Zinacantan Ritual, Harvard University Press, Cambridge 1976

Wilson, Richard, Mountain Spirits and Maize. Catholic Conversion and Renovation of Tradition among the Q'eqchi' of Guatemala, University of London, Department of Anthropology, Phil. Diss. 1990

Jaina – the island necropolis

Piña Chán, Román, Jaina. La casa en el agua, Instituto Nacional de Antropología e Historia, Mexico City 1968

Schele, Linda und Jorge Pérez de Lara, Hidden Faces of the Maya, Alti Publishing, 1997

Death and conceptions of the soul

Eberl, Markus, Tod und Begräbnis in der Klassischen Mayakultur (Magisterarbeit), Seminar für Völkerkunde, Rheinische Friedrich-Wilhelms-Universität Bonn, Bonn 1999

Eberl, Markus, Ritos funerarios de los antiguos Mayas, Instituto Nacional de Antropología e Historia, Mexico City 2000 (= Euroamericans)

Gaida, Maria, „Er trat seinen Weg an". Zur Neuerwerbung eines frühklassischen Maya-Dreifußgefäßes. In: Museumsjournal. Berichte aus den Museen, Schlössern und Sammlungen in Berlin und Potsdam, 10 (1), 1996: 34–37

Ruz Lhuillier, Alberto, Costumbres funerarias de los antiguas mayas, Universidad Nacional Autónoma de México, Mexico City 1968

Long twilight or new dawn? Transformations of Maya civilization in the Puuc region

Andrews, George, Pyramids and Palaces, Monsters and Masks. The Golden Age of Maya Architecture. Vol. 1: Architecture of the Puuc Region and Northern Plains Areas, Labyrinthos, Lancaster, California 1995

Barrera Rubio, Alfredo and José Huchim Herrera, Architectural Restoration at Uxmal 1986–1987, University of Pittsburgh, Pittsburgh 1990 (= Latin American Archaeological reports 1)

Becquelin, Pierre, La Civilizacion Puuc vista desde la región de Xculoc. In: Hidden among the Hills. Maya Archaeology of the Northwest Yucatan peninsula, edited by Hans Prem, Verlag von Fleming, Mökmüll 1994: 59–70

Carrasco Vargas, Ramon, Formación socio-política en el Puuc. El Sacbé Uxmal-Nohpat-Kabah. In: Perspectivas Antropológicas en el Mundo Maya, edited by M. Josefa Inlesias Ponce de Leon and Francesco Ligorred Perramón, Sociedad Española de Estudios Mayas, Madrid 1993: 199–212 (= Publicaciónes de la Sociedad Española de Estudios Mayas, 2)

Charnay, Désiré, The Ancient Cities of the New World, Harper & Bothers, New York 1887

Dunning, Nicholas P., Lords of the Hills. Ancient Maya Settlement of the Puuc Region, Yucatan, Mexico, Prehistory Press, Madison 1992 (= Monographs in World Archaeology, 15)

Gill, Richardson, The Great Maya Droughts, University of Texas Press, Austin 1999

Graham, Ian, Corpus of Maya Hieroglyphic Inscriptions, Vol. 4, Part 2: Uxmal, Peabody Museum, Harvard University, Cambridge, Mass. 1992

Grube, Nikolai, Hieroglyphic Sources for the History of Northwest Yucatan. In: Hidden among the Hills. Maya Archaeology of the Northwest Yucatan Peninsula, edited by Hanns J. Prem, Verlag von Flemming, Möckmüll 1994: 316–358

Kowalsky, Jeff Karl, The House of the Governor. A Maya Palace at Uxmal, Yucatan, Mexico, University of Oklahoma Press, Norman 1987

Kowalsky, Jeff Karl, The Puuc as Seen from Uxmal. In: Hidden among the Hills. Maya Archaeology of the Northwest Yucatan Peninsula, edited by Hanns J. Prem, Verlag von Flemming, Möckmüll 1994: 93–120

Kowalsky, Jeff Karl, Alfredo Barrera Rubio, Heber Ojeda Más and José Huchim Herrera, Archaeological Excavations of a Round Temple at Uxmal. Summary Discussion and Implications for Northern Maya Culture History, edited by Martha Macri and Jan McHargue, The Pre-Columbian Art Research Institute, San Francisco 1993: 281–296 (= Palenque Round Table Series, 8)

Kowalsky, Jeff Karl and Nicholas Dunning, The Architecture of Uxmal. The Symbolics of State-making at a Puuc Maya Regional Capital. In: Mesoamerican Architecture as a Cultural Symbol, edited by Jeff Karl Kowalsky, Oxford University Press, Oxford 1999: 273–297

Maler, Teobert, Peninsula Yucatan. Aus dem Nachlass, edited by Hanns J. Prem, Gebr. Mann Verlag, Berlin 1997

Pollock, H.E.D., The Puuc. An Architectural Survey of the Hill Country of Yucatan and Northern Campeche, Mexico, Harvard University Press, Cambridge, Mass. 1980 (= Memoirs of the Peabody Museum of Archaeology and Ethnology, 19)

Rivera Dorado, Miguel, Los Mayas de Oxkintok, Ministerio de Educación y Cultura, Madrid 1996

Sabloff, Jeremy and Gair Tourtellot, The Ancient Maya City of Sayil. The Mapping of a Puuc Regional Center, Tulane University, New Orleans 1991 (= Middle American Research Institute Publication, 60)

Schele, Linda and Peter Mathews, The Code of Kings. The Language of Seven Sacred Maya Temples and Tombs, Simon and Schuster, New York 1998

Smyth, Michael, Christopher Dore and Nicholas Dunning, Interpreting Prehistoric Settlement Patterns. Lessons from the Maya Center of Sahil, Yucatan. In: Journal of Field Archaeology, 22, 1995: 321–347

Smyth, Michael, Josep Ligorred Perramón, David Ortegón Zapata and Pat Farrel, An early Classic Center in the Puuc Region. New data from Chac II, Yucatan, Mexico. In: Ancient Mesoamerica, 9, 1998:233–258

Tourtellot, Gair and Jeremy Sabloff, Community Structure at Sayil. A Case Study of Puuc Settlement. In: Hidden among the Hills. Maya Archaeology of the Northwest Yucatan Peninsula, edited by Hanns J. Prem, Verlag von Flemming, Möckmüll 1994: 71–92

...and then it was sculpted, the precious stone – the Maya stonemasons and sculptors

Stuart, David, A new Carved Panel from the Palenque Area, Center for Maya Research, Washington D.C. 1990 (= Research Reports on Ancient Maya Writing, 32)

The dynamics of maturing statehood in Postclassic Maya civilization

Andrews, Anthony P., Late Postclassic Lowland Maya Archaeology. In: Journal of World Prehistory, 7, 1993: 35–69

Bey, George J III, Craig A. Hanson and William M. Ringle, Classic to Post-Classic at Ek Bakam, Yucatan. Architectural and Ceramic Evidence for Defining the Transition. In: Latin American Antiquity, 8 (3), 1997: 237–254

Blanton, Richard E., Gary M. Feinman, Stephen A. Kowalewski and Peter N. Peregrine, A Dual Processual Theory for the Evolution of Mesoamerican Civilization. In: Current Anthropology, 37 (1), 1996: 1–14

Chase, Diane Z. and Arlen F. Chase, A Postclassic Perspective. Excavations at the Maya Site of Santa Rita Corozal, Belize, Precolumbian Art Research Institute, San Francisco 1988 (= Precolumbian Art Research Institute Monograph, 4)

Fox, John W., Late Postclassic State Formation, Cambridge University Press, Cambridge 1987

Freidel, David A. and Jeremy A. Sabloff, Cozumel. Late Maya Settlement Patterns, Academic Press, New York 1984

Jones, Grant D., The Conquest of the Last Maya Kingdom, Stanford University Press, Stanford 1998

Kepecs, Susan, Gary M. Feinman and Sylviane Boucher, Chichen Itza and its Hinterland, A World Systems Perspective. In: Ancient Mesoamerica, 5, 1994: 141–158

Landa, Friar Diego de, Landa's Relaciones de las Cosas de Yucatan, translated by Alfred Tozzer, Harvard University Press, Cambridge 1941 (= Papers of the Peabody museum of Archaeology and Ethnology, 18)

Masson, Marilyn A., In the Realm of Nachan Kann. Postclassic Maya Archaeology at Laguna de On, Belize, University of Colorado Press, Boulder 2000

Miller, Arhur D., On the Edge of the Sea. Mural Painting at Tancah-Tulum, Quintana Roo, Mexico, Dumbarton Oaks, Washington D.C. 1982

Prendergast David M., Stability through Change. Lamanai, Belize from the Ninth to the to the Seventeenth Century. Classic to Postclassic, edited by J. A. Sabloff and E. W. Andrews V, University of New Mexico Press, Albuquerque 1986: 223–250

Pollock, Harry E. D., Ralph L. Roys, Tatiana Proskouriakoff and A. L. Smith, Mayapan, Yucatán, Mexico, Carnegie Institute of Washington, Washington D.C. 1962 (= Carnegie Institute of Washington Publication, 619)

Rathje, William L., The Last Tango in Mayapan. A Tentative Trajectory of Production-Distribution Systems. In: Ancient Civilization and Trade, edited by J. A. Sabloff and C. C. Lamberg-Karlovsky, University of New Mexico Press, Albuquerque 1975: 409–448

Rice, Don S., The Peten Postclassic. A Settlement Perspective. In: Late Lowland Maya Civilisation. Classic to Postclassic, edited by J. A. Sabloff and E. W. Andrews V, University of New Mexico Press, Albuquerque 1986: 301–346

Rice, Prudence, M., Peten Postclassic Pottery Production and Exchange. A view from Macanche. In: Models and Methods in Regional Exchange, edited by R. E. Fry, Society of American Archaeology, Washington D.C., 1980: 67–82 (= Society for American Archaeology SSA Papers, 1)

Sabloff, Jeremy A. and William L. Rathje, The Rise of a Maya Merchant Class. In: Scientific American, 233, 1975: 72–82

Smith, Michael E. and Cynthia Heath-Smith, Waves of Influence in Postclassic Mesoamerica? A Critique of the Mixteca-Puebla Concept. In: Anthropology, 4, 1980:15–20

The art of weaving

Eggebrecht, Arne, Webkunst der Maya aus Guatemala, Philipp von Zabern, Mainz 1992

Mahler, J., Garments and Textiles of the Maya Lowlands. In: Handbook of Middle American Indians, 3, 1965: 581–593

Taylor, Dicey, Painted Ladies: Costumes for Women on Tepeu Ceramics. In: The Maya Vase Book, 3. Edited by Justin Kerr, Kerr Associates, New York 1992: 513–525

The martial dynasties – the Postclassic in the Maya Highlands

Anales de los Cakchiqueles, Memorial de Solalá o Anales de los Cakchiqueles, Traducción, introducción y notas de Adrián Recinos, Fondo de Cultura Económica, Mexico City 1980

reton, Alain, Rabinal Achi. Un drame dynastique maya du quinzième siècle, Société des Américanistes & Société d'Ethnologie, Paris 1994 (= Recherches Américanistes, 5)

Carmack, Robert M., The Quiché Mayas of Utatlan. The Evolution of a Highland Guatemalan Kingdom, University of Oklahoma Press, Norman 1981

Fox, John W., Quiche Conquest. Centralism and Regionalism in Highland Guatemalan State Development, University of New Mexico Press, Albuquerque 1977

Guillemin, Jorge F., The Ancient Cakchiquel Capital of Iximche. In: Expedition, 9 (2), 1967: 22–35

Hill, Robert M., Eastern Chajoma (Cakchiquel) Political Geography. Ethnohistorical and Archaeological Contributions to the Study of a Late Postclassic Highland Maya Polity. In: Ancient Mesoamerica, 7 (1), 1996: 63–87

Ichon, Alain, Organización de un centro Quiché protohistórico: Pueblo Viejo Chicaj, Instituto de Antropología e Histoia, Guatemala City 1975 (= Instituto de Antropología e Historia Publicacion Especial, 9)

Lehmann, Henri, Mixco Viejo. Guía de las ruinas de la plaza fuerte Pokoman, Tipografía Nacional, Guatemala City 1968

Wauchope, Robert, Zacualpa, El Quiche, Guatemala. An Ancient Provincial Center of the Highland Maya, Tulane University, New Orleans 1975 (= Middle American Research Institute Publication, 55)

The Spanish conquest of Yucatan and Guatemala in the 16th and 17th centuries

Bricker, Victoria R., The Indian Christ, the Indian King. The Historical Substrate of Maya Myth and Ritual, University of Texas Press, Austin 1981
Chamberlain, Robert S., The Conquest and Colonization of Yucatan, 1517–1550, Carnegie Institution of Washington, Washington D.C. 1948 (= Carnegie Institution of Washington Publication, 582)
De Vos, Jan, La paz de dios y del rey. La conquista de la Selva Lacandona (1525–1821), Fondo de Cultura Económica, Mexico City 1980
De Vos, Jan, Los enredos de remesal. Ensayo sobre la conquista de Chiapas, Consejo Nacional para la Cultura y las Artes, Mexico City 1992
Jones, Grant D., The Conquest of the Last Maya Kingdom, Stanford University Press, Stanford 1998
Las Casas, Bartolomé de, Kurzgefaßter Bericht von der Verwüstung der Westindischen Länder, Insel Verlag, Frankfurt am Main 1981
Morales Padrón, Francisco, Historia del descubrimiento y conquista de América, Editorial Gredos, Madrid 1990
Pietschmann, Horst, Die iberische Expansion im Atlantik und die kastilisch-spanisch Entdeckung und Eroberung Amerikas. In: Handbuch der Geschichte Lateinamerikas, Vol.1, edited by Horst Pietschmann, Verlag Klett-Cotta, Stuttgart 1994: 207–273
Straub, Eberhard (Ed.) Conquista. Amerika oder die Entdeckung des Menschenrechte, Communio, Cologne 1991
Termer, Franz, Quauhtemallan und Cuzcatlan. Der erste und zweite Bericht des Pedro de Alvarado über die Eroberung von Guatemala und El Salvador im Jahre 1524, Hansischer Gildenverlag, Hamburg 1948 (= Hamburger Romanistische Studien, Ibero-Amerikanische Reihe, 18)
Tozzer, Alfred M., Landa's Relación de las Cosas de Yucatán. A translation, Harvard University Press, Cambridge, Mass. 1941 (= Papers of the Peabody Museum of American Archaeology and Ethnology, 18)

Kanek' – the last king of the Itzaj Maya

Avendaño y Loyola, Andres, Relacíon de las dos entradas que hice a la conversíon de los gentiles Yzaex y Cehaches, edited by Temis Vayhinger-Scheer, Verlag von Flemming, Möckmüll 1996 (= Mexican Occasional Publication, 3)
Jones, Grant D., The Conquest of the Last Maya Kingdom, Stanford University Press, Stanford 1998

Between conformity and rebellion – the Maya society in the colonial period (1546–1811)

Bricker, Victoria R., The Indian Christ. The Indian King, University of Texas Press, Austin 1981
Carmack, Robert M., Rebels of Highland Guatemala. The Quiche-Mayas of Momostenango, University of Oklahoma Press, Norman und London 1995
Collins, Anne C., The Maestros Cantores in Yucatan. In: Anthropology and History in Yucatan, edited by Grant D.Jones, University of Texas Press, Austin 1977: 233–247
Farriss, Nancy M., Maya Society under Colonial Rule. The Collective Enterprise of Survival, Princeton University Press, Princeton 1984
Garza, Mercedes de la, et al.(Ed.), Relaciones histórico-geográficas de la gobernacón de Yucatán, 2 vols., Universidad Nacional Autónoma de México, México 1983
Oberem, Udo, Die Conquista und Indianer unter spanischer Herrschaft. In: Alt-Amerikanistik – Eine Einführung in die Hochkulturen Mittel- und Südamerikas, edited by Ulrich Kohler, Reimer Verlag, Berlin 1990: 493–518
Patch, Robert W., Maya and Spaniard in Yucatan, 1648–1812, Stanford University Press, Stanford 1993
Pietschmann, Horst, Lateinamerika. Die staatliche Organisation des kolonialen Iberoamerika. Teilveröffentlichung zum Handbuch der lateinamerikanischen Geschichte, Klett-Cotta, Stuttgart 1980
Restall, Matthew, Life and Death in a Maya Community. The Ixil Testaments of the 1760s, Labyrinthos, Lancaster, California 1995
Restall, Matthew, The Maya World. Yucatec Culture and Society 1550–1850, Stanford University Press, Stanford 1997

The search for evidence – the scientific discovery of the Maya

Humboldt, Alexander von, Vues de Cordillères et monuments des peuples indigènes de l'Amérique, Paris 1810
Palacio, Don Diego, Carta dirijida al rey de España, por el licenciado Dr. Don Diego Garcia de Palacio, Oydor de la real audiencia de Guatemala, Colección de Documentos Inéditos, Mexico City 1576
Stephens, John, L., Incidents of Travel in Central America, Chiapas, and Yucatan, 2 vols., Harper, New York 1841
Stephens, John, L., Incidents of Travel in Yucatan, 2vols., Harper, New York 1843

Maya cities – lost, excavated, and conserved

Inomata, Takeshi, The Last Day of a Fortified Classic Maya Center. Archaeological investigations at Aguateca, Guatemala. In: Ancient Mesoamerica, 8 (2), 1997: 337–351
Quintana, Oscar, Probleme der Konservierungt von Maya-Ruinen. In: Die Welt der Maya, edited by A. Eggebrecht, N. Grube and E. Eggebrecht, P. von Zabern, Mainz 1992: 139–141
Wurster, Wolfgang W., Erforschung und Erhaltung von Maya-Städten im zentralen Peten Guatemalas. Aktueller Stand des archäologischen Regionalprojektes „Triángulo Cultural Yaxhá-Nakum-Naranjo". In: Beiträge zur Allgemeinen und Vergleichenden Archäologie, 15, 1995: 203–227

Maya today – from Indios deprived of rights to the Indian awakening

Allebrand, Raimund, Renaissance der Maya. In: Die Erben der Maya. Indianischer Aufbruch in Guatemala, edited by von Raimund Allebrand, Horlemann, Unkel 1997: 69–135
Burgos, Elisabeth, Rigoberta Menchú. Leben in Guatemala, Lamuv, 11. edition, Göttingen 1991
Carmack, Robert M., Harvest of Violence. The Maya Indians and the Guatemalan Crisis, University of Oklahoma Press, Norman 1986
Cojtí Cuxil, Demetrio, Configuración del Pensamiento Politico del Pueblo Maya, 2 vols. Cholasamaj, Guatemala City 1993–1996
Fischer, Edward F. and R. McKenna **Brown** (Ed.), Maya Cultural Activism, University of Texas Press, Austin 1996
Grube, Nikolai, Im Zeichen des sprechenden Kreuzes. In: Damals, 31, 1999: 76–79
Janik, Dieter, Die langen Folgen der kurzen Conquista. Auswirkungen der spanischen Kolonisierung bis heute, Vervuert, Frankfurt am Main 1994
Le Bot, Yvonne, La guerre en terre maya. Communauté, violence et modernité au Guatemala, Karthala, Paris 1992
Oxlajuuj Keej Maya' Ajtz'iib, Maya Chii. Los idiomas Mayas de Guatemala, Cholsamaj, Guatemala City 1993
Stoll, David, Between two Armies in the Ixil Towns of Guatemala, Columbia University Press, New York 1991
Sullivan, Paul, Unfinished Conversations. Mayas and Foreigners between Two Wars, Knopf, New York 1989
Toledo Maya Cultural Council, Maya Atlas. The Struggle to Preserve Maya Land in Southern Belize, North Atlantic Books, Berkeley 1997
Warren, Kay B., Indigenous Movements and their Critics. Pan-Maya Activism in Guatemala, Princeton University Press, Princeton 1998
Wilson, Richard, Maya Resurgence in Guatemala. Q'eqchi' Experiences, University of Oklahoma Press, Norman 1995

INDEX

PICTURE ACKNOWLEDGMENTS

The publisher would like to thank the museums, collectors, archives, and photographers for their permission to reproduce their copyright and for their friendly support during the realization of this book. Up to the time of publication, the editor and publisher have made intensive efforts to locate all other owners of picture rights. Any persons or organizations who have not been approached, and who claim rights to illustrations used, should contact the publisher.

m = middle   a = above   b = below   l = left   r = right

2: Michel Zabé/AZA, Mexico City; 4/5/6/7: Justin Kerr, New York (NY); 8/9: Jorge Peréz de Lara, Mexico City; 10: Studio für Landkartentechnik, Norderstedt; 11: The British Museum, Museum of Mankind, London; 12: J. Pérez de Lara, Mexico City; 13 a: Michel Zabé/aza, Mexico City; 13 b: Archiv Eggebrecht, Hildesheim; 14/15: Michel Zabé/aza, Mexico City; 16: Stiftung Preußischer Kulturbesitz, Berlin; 17 a: Stephan Wagner, Munich; 17 b: Archiv Grube, Bonn; 18/19/20: H+Z Bildagentur GmbH, Hannover/B. & H. Röder; 21: John B. Garver Jr./Rolli Arts, Essen; 22 a: Herbert Wilhelmy/Peter Frese, Munich; 22 b: John B. Garver Jr./Rolli Arts, Essen; 23: Archiv Grube, Bonn; 24: John J. Bangma/Okapia, Frankfurt a. M.; 25 a/b: Henri Stierlin, Geneva; 26 l: Archiv Eggebrecht, Hildesheim; 26 r: Archiv Grube, Bonn; 27: Getty Images/Tony Stone Images, Munich/James Strachan; 28 a: Andreas M. Gross; 28 b: E. Thiem/Lotosfilm, Kaufbeuren; 29: Justin Kerr, New York (NY); 30 a/bl: Andreas M. Gross; 30 ml: Andreas M. Gross/jd Bildagentur, Munich; 31 al: Getty Images/Tony Stone Images, Munich/Art Wolfe; 31 am: Jack Swenson/Wildlife/Okapia, Frankfurt a. M.; 31 ar: M. P. L. Fogden/OSF/Okapia, Frankfurt a. M.; 31 b: Okapia, Frankfurt a. M./Lynn Stone; 32 a: Tandem Verlag GmbH, Königswinter/Günter Beer; 32 bl: Stockfood, Munich/Bernd Euler; 32 br: Archiv für Kunst und Geschichte, Berlin; 33 a: Nikolai Grube, Bonn/Peter Frese, Munich; 33 m: Andreas M. Gross; 33 b: National Geographic Society, Image Collection, Washington D.C./George Mobley; 34: E. Thiem/Lotosfilm, Kaufbeuren; 35: Thomas C. Kelly/Rolli Arts, Essen; 36 a: Harry D. Pohl/Rolli Arts, Essen; 36 b: Norman Hammond, Boston (MA); 37: Norman Hammond, Boston (MA); 38: Norman Hammond/Rolli Arts, Essen; 39/40 a: Norman Hammond, Boston (MA); 40 b: J. Lubinski, Medical College of Ohio; 41: Martha Cooper; 42: (1, 3–6): Norman Hammond, Boston (MA); (2): Stuart Rome; (7): Richard D. Hansen, Los Angeles (CA); (8): E. Thiem/Lotosfilm, Kaufbeuren; 43: E. Thiem/Lotosfilm, Kaufbeuren; 44 a: G. Büttner/Naturbild/Okapia, Frankfurt a. M.; 44 b: Charles H. Miksicek/Rolli Arts, Essen; 45 l: G. Büttner/Naturbild/Okapia, Frankfurt a. M.; 45 r: The Garden Picture Library, London; 46: E. W. Andrews, Boston (MA); 47 a: Juan P. Laporte/Rolli Arts, Essen; 47 b: Elisabeth Wagner, Bonn; 48 al: Michel Zabé/aza, Mexico City; 48 ar: John E. Clark/Rolli Arts, Essen; 48 b: Norman Hammond/Peter Frese, Munich; 49 a/bl: Michel Zabé/aza, Mexico City; 49 br: Justin Kerr, New York (NY); 50: National Geographic Society, Washington D.C./Stephen Northup; 51: Richard D. Hansen/Peter Frese, Munich; 52: Richard D. Hansen, Abel Morales, Lopez Wayn K./Rolli Arts, Essen; 53 al: F. R. Hillman; 53 ar: C. D. Bieber; 53 b/54 al: Richard D. Hansen, Los Angeles (CA); 54 ar: Andreas M. Gross, Munich; 54 bl: Richard D. Hansen, Los Angeles (CA); 54 br: F. R. Hillman; 55: Juan Luis Velasquez/Rolli Arts, Essen; 56 a: C. D. Bieber; 56 bl: Ortego/Richard D. Hansen/Rolli Arts, Essen; 56 br: F. R. Hillman; 57: Richard D. Hansen, Los Angeles (CA); 58 a: Richard D. Hansen/Rolli Arts, Essen; 58 b: National Geographic Society, Washington D.C.; 59: David Pendergast/Rolli Arts, Essen; 60: J. Pérez de Lara, Mexico City; 61 a: Terry Rutledge/Rolli Arts, Essen; 61 b: Linda Schele, David Freidel/Peter Frese, Munich; 62/63 a: Richard D. Hansen, Los Angeles (CA); 63 b: F. R. Hillman; 64 b./65: Richard D. Hansen, Los Angeles (CA); 66 a: Michel Zabé/aza, Mexico City; 66 b: Henri Stierlin, Geneva; 67 a: Henri Stierlin, Geneva; 67 bl: Michel Zabé/aza, Mexico City; 67 br: Justin Kerr, New York (NY); 68 a: Adrian Digby/Rolli Arts Essen; 68 m: © Tandem Verlag GmbH, Königswinter/Elisabeth Wagner/Rolli Arts, Essen; 68 bm/r: Justin Kerr, New York (NY); 68 bl: E. Thiem/Lotosfilm, Kaufbeuren; 68 ml: E. Thiem/Lotosfilm, Kaufbeuren, 69 a: University of Pennsylvania Museum, Philadelphia; 69 bm: Justin Kerr, New York (NY); 69 bl: Henri Stierlin, Geneva; 69 br: The Art Archive, London; 70: J. Pérez de Lara, Mexico City; 71: Andrew Harrison/Rolli Arts, Essen; 72 al: Getty Images/Tony Stone Images, Munich/David Hiser; 72 ar: Getty Images/Tony Stone Images, Munich/Jacques Jangoux; 72 br: Doro Schütze/Version, Cologne; 72 bl: Herby Sachs/Version, Cologne; 73: Akademische Druck- und Verlagsanstalt, Graz; 74 al: Peter D. Harrison, New Mexico; 74 ar: Marco Gross, Peten; 75 a: Peter D. Harrison, New Mexico; 75 b: Getty Images/Tony Stone Images, Munich/Paul Edmondson; 76 a: Peter D. Harrison, New Mexico; 76 b: Herbert Wilhelmy/Peter Frese, Munich; 77 l: Peter D. Harrison/Peter Frese, Munich; 77 r: B. L. Turner II.; 78/79 a: Robert Francis, South American Pictures; 79 b: Norman Hammond/Rolli Arts, Essen; 80/81 a: 2000 Macduff Everton, Santa Barbara (CA); 81 b: Justin Kerr, New York (NY); 82/83: Andreas M. Gross; 84/85: 2000 Macduff Everton, Santa Barbara (CA); 86: E. Thiem/Lotosfilm, Kaufbeuren; 87: Federico Fahsen/Rolli Arts, Essen; 88 a: Henri Stierlin, Geneva; 88 b: Getty Images/Tony Stone Images, Munich/Suzanne Murphy; 89: Archiv Eggebrecht, Hildesheim; 90 a: Elisabeth Wagner, Bonn; 90 b: © Tandem Verlag GmbH, Königswinter; 91 al: Robert J. Sharer; 91 ar: Archiv Eggebrecht, Hildesheim; 91 b: Federico Fahsen, Guatemala; 92 a: E. Thiem/Lotosfilm, Kaufbeuren; 92 b: Henri Stierlin, Geneva; 93: Henri Stierlin, Geneva; 94: Federico Fahsen/Peter Frese, Munich; 95: Collection Gaston Burmand, Geneva/Gérald Berjonneau, Paris; 96 a: Andreas M. Gross; 96 bl: E. Thiem/Lotosfilm, Kaufbeuren; 96 br: Justin Kerr, New York (NY); 97: Henri Stierlin, Geneva; 98: TCL/Getty Images/Bavaria Bildagentur, Düsseldorf; 99: Roger-Violett, Paris; 100 (1–4): Andreas M. Gross ;(5): TCL/Getty Images/Bavaria Bildagentur, Düsseldorf; 100 m: W. Haberland/Rolli Arts, Essen; 101: R. Kiedrowski, Ratingen; 102: Fine Arts Museum of San Francisco/Gift of Jack Tanzer, 1986.74, San Francisco (CA); 103 a: Fine Arts Museum of San Francisco/Bequest of Harald J. Wagner, 1985.104.9, San Francisco (CA); 103 b: Michel Zabé/aza, Mexico City; 104: © Tandem Verlag GmbH, Königswinter/Simon Martin/Peter Frese, Munich; 105: © Tandem Verlag GmbH, Königswinter/Simon Martin/Peter Frese, Munich; 106: Justin Kerr, New York (NY); 107 a: © Tandem Verlag GmbH, Königswinter/Nikolai Grube, Bonn/Peter Frese, Munich; 107 b: University of Pennsylvania/Rolli Arts, Essen; 108 l: Justin Kerr, New York (NY); 108 ar: © Tandem Verlag GmbH, Königswinter/Simon Martin/Peter Frese, Munich; 108 mr: © Tandem Verlag GmbH, Königswinter/Nikolai Grube, Bonn/Rolli Arts, Essen; 109 a: The Art Archive, London/Francesco Venturi; 109 b: Hans Zaglitsch, Muiden; 110: Justin Kerr, New York (NY); 111: Rafael Doniz, Mexico City; 112/113: J. Pérez de Lara, Mexico City; 114: The Art Archive, London/Francesco Venturi; 115: Bibliotheca del Palacio Real, Patrimonio Nacional, Madrid; 116: Stiftung Preußischer Kulturbesitz/Iberoamerikanisches Institut, Berlin; 117: Museum der Kulturen, Basel – Photo: Peter Horner 1997; 118 bl: Bayerische Staatsbibliothek, Munich – Photographic dept.; 118 am: President & Fellows of Harvard College, Peabody Museum, Harvard University, Cambridge (MA); 118 ar: Courtesy Peabody Museum, Harvard University, Cambridge (MA). Photograph by Carnegie Institution of Washington; 119 l: Hasso Hohmann, Graz; 119 r: President & Fellows of Harvard College, Peabody Museum, Harvard University, Cambridge (MA); 119 bm/120: Nikolai Grube, Bonn/Peter Frese, Munich; 121: Edizioni White Star, Vercelli; 122 a: Nikolai Grube, Bonn/Peter Frese, Munich; 122 b: H. Zaglitsch, Muiden; 123: Bayerische Staatsbibliothek, Munich – Photographic dept.; 124 a/br: © Tandem Verlag GmbH, Königswinter/Nikolai Grube, Bonn/Rolli Arts, Essen; 124 bl: © Tandem Verlag GmbH, Königswinter/Nikolai Grube, Bonn/Peter Frese, Munich; 125: Justin Kerr, New York (NY); 126 a: Michael D. Coe/Rolli Arts, Essen; 126 b: Justin Kerr, New York (NY); 127 a: Archiv Grube, Bonn; 127 b/128 a: Justin Kerr, New York (NY); 128 bl: Nikolai Grube, Bonn/Peter Frese, Munich; 128 br: Andreas M. Gross; 129 a: The Art Archive, London/American Museum, Madrid/Album, Joseph Martin; 129 b/130: Justin Kerr, New York (NY); 131: © Tandem Verlag GmbH, Königswinter/Alexander Voß/Rolli Arts, Essen; 132 a: J. Pérez de Lara, Mexico City; 132 bl: Henri Stierlin, Geneva/Rolli Arts, Essen; 132 br: Anthony Aveni/Peter Frese, Munich; 133 a: Andreas M. Gross/jd Bildagentur, Munich; 133 bl: Anthony Aveni/Rolli Arts, Essen; 133 br: © Tandem Verlag GmbH, Königswinter/Alexander Voß/Peter Frese, Munich; 134: © Tandem Verlag GmbH, Königswinter/Alexander Voß/Rolli Arts, Essen; 135: Justin Kerr, New York (NY); 136: Linda Schele/Peter Frese, Munich; 137: Akademische Druck- und Verlagsanstalt, Graz; 138: © Tandem Verlag GmbH, Königswinter/Alexander Voß/Rolli Arts, Essen; 139 a: Archiv Grube, Bonn; 139 b: © Tandem Verlag GmbH, Königswinter/Alexander Voß/Peter Frese, Munich; 140/141: Akademische Druck- und Verlagsanstalt, Graz; 142: © Tandem Verlag GmbH, Königswinter/Nikolai Grube/Rolli Arts, Essen; 143: Justin Kerr, New York (NY); 144 a: TCL/Getty Images/Bavaria Bildagentur, Düsseldorf; 144 b: University Museum of Philadelphia; 145 a/br: Akademische Druck- und Verlagsanstalt, Graz; 145 bl: © Tandem Verlag GmbH, Königswinter; 146/147: Justin Kerr, New York (NY); 148: The Art Archive, London/Archaeological Museum Copan Honduras/Dagli Orti, Paris; 150: Justin Kerr, New York (NY); 151: Nikolai Grube, Bonn/Peter Frese, Munich; 152 a: Alvaro Toepke Cáceres; 152 b: Justin Kerr, New York (NY); 153 l: Dallas Museum of Art, Gift of The Otis and Valma Davis Dozier Fund, Dallas (TX); 153 r: President & Fellows of Harvard College, Peabody Museum, Harvard University, Cambridge (MA); 154: The British Museum, London; 155 a: President & Fellows of Harvard College, Peabody Museum, Harvard University, Cambridge (MA)/Hillel Burger; 155 b: Justin Kerr, New York (NY); 156: The British Museum, London; 157 a: Andreas M. Gross, Munich; 157 b/158 a: Justin Kerr, New York (NY); 158 b/159: Linda Schele/Rolli Arts, Essen; 160: University of Pennsylvania Museum, Philadelphia (PA); 161: British Museum, London; 162: Simon Martin/Peter Frese, Munich; 163 a: University of Central Florida, Department of Sociology and Anthropology, Orlando (FL)/Arlen & Diane Chase; 163 b: Henri Stierlin, Geneva; 164 a: Enrico Ferrorelli/Focus, Hamburg; 164 b: Simon Martin/Peter Frese, Munich; 165: Stephen Houston/Peter Frese, Munich; 166: Peabody Museum, Harvard University, Cambridge (MA) /Hillel Burger; 167 l: Ian Graham, Courtesy of the Peabody Museum, Harvard University, Cambridge (MA); 167 r: University of Pennsylvania Museum, Philadelphia (PA); 168: Museum der Kulturen, Basel - Photo: Peter Horner, 1997; 169: Nikolai Grube, Bonn/Peter Frese, Munich; 170 l: Andreas M. Gross, Munich; 170 r: Courtesy of the Peabody Museum, Harvard University, Cambridge (MA)/Teobert Maler; 171: Ian Graham, Cambridge (MA); 172 a: Justin Kerr, New York (NY); 172 b: © Tandem Verlag GmbH, Königswinter/Nikolai Grube; 173: © Galerie Mermoz, Paris/Roger Asselberghs; 174: Justin Kerr, New York (NY); 175: Andreas M. Gross, Munich; 176 l: Justin Kerr, New York (NY); 176 r: Nikolai Grube, Bonn/Rolli Arts, Essen; 177: Justin Kerr, New York (NY); 178 a: Akademische Druck- und Verlagsanstalt, Graz; 178 b: © Tandem Verlag GmbH, Königswinter/Nikolai Grube, Bonn/Peter Frese, Munich; 179 a: Rafael Doniz, Mexico City; 179 b: Linda Schele & David Freidel/Rolli Arts, Essen; 180: Linda Schele/Rolli Arts, Essen; 181 a: Justin Kerr, New York (NY); 181 b: National Geographic Society, Washington D.C.; 182/183: Museum der Kulturen, Basel – Photo: Peter Horner 1997; 184: Justin Kerr, New York (NY); 185 a: City of Bristol Museum and Art Gallery, Bristol; 185 b: David Webster/Peter Frese, Munich; 186 a: The Art Archive, London/Archaeological Museum Copan Honduras/Dagli Orti, Paris; 186 b: Justin Kerr, New York (NY); 187 a: AKG, Berlin; 187 b: AKG, Berlin/Erich Lessing; 188 a/b: Ian Graham, Courtesy of the Peabody Museum, Harvard University, Cambridge (MA); 188 m: © Tandem Verlag GmbH, Königswinter/Nikolai Grube, Bonn/Peter Frese, Munich; 189 m: Tatiana Proskouriakoff; 189 b: Linda Schele/Peter Matthews/Peter Frese, Munich; 190 al: H. Zaglitsch, Muiden; 190 ar: Henri & Anne Stierlin, Geneva; 190 b: Konrad Wothe/Look, Munich; 191 a: Archiv Grube, Bonn; 191 b: Andreas M. Gross, Munich; 192/193: 2000 Macduff Everton, Santa Barbara (CA); 194: FPG/Getty Images/Bavaria Bildagentur, Düsseldorf; 195: William R. Coe II/Peter Frese, Munich; 196 a: Elisabeth Wagner, Bonn; 196 b: Annegret Hohmann-Vogrin, Graz; 197 a: Andreas M. Gross, Munich; 197 b: Frank Ducote/Nicholas Hellmuth/Peter Frese, Munich; 198 r: Archiv Grube, Bonn; 198 l: Andreas M. Gross, Munich; 199 a: Elisabeth Wagner, Bonn; 199 b: Hasso Hohmann, Graz/Peter Frese, Munich; 200: H. Zaglitsch, Muiden; 201 a: J. Pérez de Lara, Mexico City; 201 b: University of Pennsylvania Museum, Philadelphia (PA); 202 a: AKG, Berlin; 202 b: The Art Archive, London/Album/J. Enrique Molina; 203 al: Ignacio Marquina/Peter Frese, Munich; 203 ar: Herby Sachs/Version, Cologne; 203 b: Merle Greene Robertson/Peter Frese, Munich; 204 al: Picture Finders/Getty Images/Bavaria Bildagentur, Düsseldorf; 204 ar: Herby Sachs/Version, Cologne; 204 bl: Merle Greene Robertson/Rolli Arts, Essen; 204 br: Ignacio Marquina/Rolli Arts, Essen; 205: Konrad Wothke/Look; 206 a: Hasso Hohmann/Rolli Arts, Essen; 206 bl: Andreas M. Gross, Munich; 206 br: R. Kiedrowski, Ratingen; 207: Andreas M. Gross, Munich; 208 a: Hasso Hohmann, Graz/Peter Frese, Munich; 208 b: Henri & Anne Stierlin; 209 a: Archiv Eggebrecht, Hildesheim; 210 a: The Art Archive, London/Mirelle Vautier; 210 b: AKG, Berlin; 211: Archiv Eggebrecht, Hildesheim; 212: AKG, Berlin; 213 a: Edizioni White Star, Vercelli; 213 b: The Art Archive, London/Mireille Vautier; 214: FPG/Getty Images/Bavaria Bildagentur, Düsseldorf; 215 a: Images/Getty Images/Bavaria Bildagentur, Düsseldorf; 215 b: Ignacio Marquina/Peter Frese, Munich; 216 a: Michael Vallo, Bonn; 216 b: Michael Vallo/Carsten Deichmann/Hanns J. Prem, Bonn/Rolli Arts, Essen; 217: Michael Vallo/Carsten Deichmann/Hanns J. Prem, Bonn; 218: Getty Images/Tony Stone Images, Munich/Simeone Huber; 219: William R. Coe, Philadelphia (PA)/Peter Frese, Munich; 220 m: Peter D. Harrison, New Mexico/Peter Frese, Munich; 220 al: J. Pérez de Lara, Mexico City; 220 ar: Herbert Hartmann/Getty Images/Bavaria Bildagentur, Düsseldorf; 220 am: Nicholas Hellmuth, St. Louis (MO); 220 bm: Andreas M. Gross, Munich; 220 bl: Peter D. Harrison, New Mexico; 220 br: Archiv Grube, Bonn; 221: Roger-Viollet, Paris; 222: Nicholas Hellmuth, St. Louis (MO); 223 a: Peter D. Harrison, New Mexico/Peter Frese, Munich; 223 b: Peter D. Harrison, New Mexico; 224 al: Elisabeth Wagner, Bonn; 224 ar: J. Pérez de Lara, Mexico City; 224 b: Teobert Maler, Iberoamerikanisches Institut, Berlin; 225 a: Terry Rutledge from a drawing by Peter Spier/Peter Frese, Munich; 225 b: Archiv Grube, Bonn; 226: Andreas M. Gross, Munich; 227 a: Teobert Maler/

Iberoamerikanisches Institut, Berlin; **227 b:** Herbert Hartmann/Getty Images/Bavaria Bildagentur, Düsseldorf; **228 a:** J. Pérez de Lara, Mexico City; **228 b:** Roger-Viollet, Paris; **229:** Rolli Arts, Essen; **230 a:** H. Stanley Loten/Peter Frese, Munich; **230 b:** Peter D. Harrison, New Mexico/ Peter Frese, Munich; **231:** P. D. Harrison, New Mexico; **232 b:** Andreas M. Gross, Munich; **232 a:** Diane & Arlen Chase, Orlando (FL)/Peter Frese, Munich; **233 l:** © Tandem Verlag GmbH, Königswinter/Markus Eberl/Peter Frese, Munich; **233 b:** ISKA-Archiv, Berlin/Version, Cologne; **234:** National Geographic Society, Washington D.C./Enrico Ferrorelli; **235:** Andreas M. Gross, Munich; **236:** E.Thiem/Lotusfilm, Kaufbeuren; **237 a:** Christopher A. Klein/National Geographic Society, Washington D.C.; **237 m:** Andreas M. Gross, Munich; **237 ml/r:** National Geographic Society, Washington D.C.; **237 b:** Karl Ruppert/Peter Frese, Munich; **238 al:** Tatiana Falcón; **238 ar:** Henri Stierlin, Geneva; **239 a:** David Wooddell; **239 b:** National Geographic Society, Washington D.C.; **240/241:** H. Burger/Peabody Museum of Harvard University, Cambridge (MA); **241 b:** Henri Stierlin, Geneva; **242/243:** H. Burger/President & Fellows of Harvard College, Peabody Museum, Harvard University, Cambridge (MA); **243 a:** National Geographic Society, Washington D.C.; **244 a/m:** Andreas M. Gross, Munich; **244 b:** Stephan Wagner, Munich; **245:** Nikolai Grube, Bonn; **246:** Justin Kerr, New York (NY); **247/248:** Dorie Reents-Budet; **249 a:** Justin Kerr, New York (NY); **249 b:** Dorie Reents-Budet; **250 a:** E. Thiem/Lotosfilm, Kaufbeuren; **250 b:** Justin Kerr, New York (NY); **251:** Dorie Reents-Budet; **252 a:** Justin Kerr, New York (NY); **252 b:** Dorie Reents-Budet; **253 ar:** © Tandem Verlag GmbH, Königswinter/Elisabeth Wagner, Bonn; **253 al:** Justin Kerr, New York (NY); **253 ar:** Nikolai Grube, Bonn/Peter Frese, Munich; **253 b:** Justin Kerr, New York (NY); **254/255/256 a:** Dorie Reents-Budet; **256 bl:** Justin Kerr, New York (NY); **256 br:** Dorie Reents-Budet; **257:** Henri Stierlin, Geneva; **258/259:** Dorie Reents-Budet; **260/261:** Getty Images/Tony Stone Images, Munich/Robert Frerck; **262:** Justin Kerr, New York (NY); **263:** Günter Zimmermann/Rolli Arts, Essen; **264 a:** Justin Kerr, New York (NY); **264 b:** © Tandem Verlag GmbH, Königswinter/Elisabeth Wagner/Rolli Arts, Essen; **265:** Akademische Druck- und Verlagsanstalt, Graz; **266:** Andreas M. Gross, Munich; **267 al:** Elisabeth Wagner, Bonn; **267 ar:** H. Zaglitsch, Muiden; **267 b:** Linda Scheele; **268/269:** Justin Kerr, New York (NY); **270:** Elisabeth Wagner, Bonn; **271:** Hasso Hohmann, Graz; **272:** Rafael Doniz, Mexico City; **273:** Michel Zabé/aza, Mexico City; **274 a:** © Tandem Verlag GmbH, Königswinter/Elisabeth Wagner, Bonn; **274 b/275:** Justin Kerr, New York (NY); **276 a:** Elisabeth Wagner; **276 b/277:** Justin Kerr, New York (NY); **278 a:** E. Thiem/Lotusfilm, Kaufbeuren; **278 b:** Justin Kerr, New York (NY); **279 a:** J. Pérez de Lara, Mexico City; **279 b:** Justin Kerr, New York (NY); **280:** Herby Sachs/Version, Cologne; **281:** Andreas M. Gross, Munich; **282/283 b:** J. Peréz de Lara, Mexico City; **283 a:** © Tandem Verlag GmbH, Königswinter/Elisabeth Wagner/Peter Frese, Munich; **284:** Dorie Reents-Budet; **285 a:** Linda Schele/Rolli Arts, Essen; **285 b:** © Tandem Verlag GmbH, Königswinter/Elisabeth Wagner/ Rolli Arts, Essen; **285 m:** Peter D. Harrison, New Mexico; **286 a:** Dorie Reents-Budet; **286 b:** © Tandem Verlag GmbH, Königswinter/Elisabeth Wagner/Rolli Arts, Essen; **287 a:** Justin Kerr, New York (NY); **287 b:** Linda Schele/Peter Frese, Munich; **288:** © Tandem Verlag GmbH, Königswinter/Elisabeth Wagner/Rolli Arts, Essen; **289 l:** National Geographic Society, Washington D.C./George Mobley; **289 r:** Nikolai Grube, Bonn/Peter Frese, Munich; **290 a:** Peter D. Harrison, New Mexico/Rolli Arts, Essen; **290 b:** Henri Stierlin, Geneva; **291:** Nikolai Grube, Bonn; **292:** Bildarchiv Preußischer Kulturbesitz, Berlin; **293:** Elisabeth Wagner, Bonn; **294 l:** Nikolai Grube, Bonn/Rolli Arts, Essen; **294 r/b/295:** Justin Kerr, New York (NY); **296:** J. Pérez de Lara, Mexico City; **297:** Archiv Eggebrecht, Hildesheim; **298 a:** © Tandem Verlag GmbH, Königswinter/Nikolai Grube, Bonn/Peter Frese, Munich; **298 b:** Henry C. Mercer/Rolli Arts, Essen; **299 a:** Linda Schele/Peter Frese, Munich; **299 b/300 a:** J. Pérez de Lara, Mexico City; **300 b:** Andrea Joyce Stone/Peter Frese, Munich; **301 l:** George Veni; **301 r:** Enrico Ferorelli/Focus, Hamburg; **302 a:** J. Pérez de Lara, Mexico City; **302 b:** Teobert Maler/Rolli Arts, Essen; **303:** H. Zaglitsch, Muiden; **304:** E. Thiem/Lotosfilm, Kaufbeuren; **305:** Archiv Eggebrecht, Hildesheim; **306 al:** Chip & Jennifer Clark; **306 ar:** James E. Brady, Los Angeles; **306 b:** Justin Kerr, New York (NY); **307:** Thomas Höpker/Magnum/Agentur Focus, Hamburg; **308 a:** J. Pérez de Lara, Mexico City; **308 b:** Frank D. Pierce, Leonardo de la Luz Morino/Rolli Arts, Essen; **309 bl/bm:** J. Pérez de Lara, Mexico City; **309 br:** Henri Stierlin, Geneva; **310:** Claudia Obrocki/ Staatliche Museen zu Berlin, Berlin; **311:** Roger-Viollet, Paris; **312 a:** Nikolai Grube, Bonn/Rolli Arts, Essen; **312 b:** Justin Kerr, New York (NY); **313 al:** Elisabeth Wagner/Peter Frese, Munich; **313 am:** © Tandem Verlag GmbH, Königswinter/Markus Eberl/Peter Frese, Munich; **313 r:** President & Fellows of the Harvard College, Peabody Museum, Harvard University, Cambridge (MA); **314:** Merle Greene Robertson 1976; **315 l:** Herby Sachs/Version, Cologne; **315 r:** Frank Ducote, Nicholas Hellmuth/Rolli Arts, Essen; **316:** Karl Herbert Mayer, Graz; **317:** Justin Kerr, New York (NY); **318 a:** R. Doniz, Mexico; **318 b:** FPG/Getty Images/Bavaria Bildagentur, Düsseldorf; **319:** National Geographic Society, Washington D.C. /George Mobley; **320/321:** Getty Images/Tony Stone Images, Munich/Robert Frerck; **322:** AKG, Berlin/Werner Forman; **323:** Archiv Eggebrecht, Hildesheim; **324 a:** Nicholas Dunning, Cincinnati (OH); **324 b/325 a:** Nicholas Dunning, Cincinnati (OH)/Peter Frese, Munich; **325 b:** J. Pérez de Lara, Mexico City; **326/327 a/bl:** H. Zaglitsch, Muiden; **327 br:** George F. Andrews/Peter Frese, Munich; **328 a:** Nicholas Dunning, Cincinnati (OH)/Peter Frese, Munich; **328 b:** Picture Finders/Getty Images/Bavaria Bildagentur, Düsseldorf; **329 a:** Eduard Seler 1917/Peter Frese, Munich; **329 b:** H. Zaglitsch, Muiden; **330:** Picture Finders/Getty Images/Bavaria Bildagentur, Düsseldorf; **331:** BPK, Berlin; **332:** Henri Stierlin, Geneva; **333 m:** Ian Graham, Cambridge (MA)/Peter Frese, Munich; **333** (1): Henri Stierlin, Geneva; (2): H. Zaglitsch, Muiden; (3): J. Pérez de Lara, Mexico City; (4): J. Pérez de Lara, Mexico City; (5): Nicholas Dunning, Cincinnati (OH); (6): Photo Press/Rita; **334 a:** George F. Andrews/Rolli Arts, Essen; **334 b:** J. Pérez de Lara, Mexico City; **335 a:** The Art Archive, London/Album/J. Enrique Molina; **335 b:** Rolli Arts, Essen; **336:** Ian Graham, Cambridge (MA)/Peter Frese, Munich; **337 a:** Román Piña Chan/Rolli Arts, Essen; **337 b:** Justin Kerr, New York (NY); **338/339 a:** Andreas M. Gross; **339 b:** Ian Graham, Courtesy of the Peabody Museum, Harvard University, Cambridge (MA); **340:** J. Pérez de Lara, Mexico City; **341:** Marilyn Masson, Albany (NY)/Peter Frese, Munich; **342 a:** The University Museum, University of Pennsylvania, Philadelphia (PA); **342 b:** Dumbarton Oaks Research Library and Collections, Washington D.C./Painting by Felipe Dávalos; **343:** J. Pérez de Lara, Mexico City; **344 m:** Rolli Arts, Essen; **344 ar to bl:** (1): The Art Archive, London; (2): Henri Stierlin, Geneva; (3): Andreas M. Gross, Munich; (4): Henri Stierlin, Geneva; (5): TCL/Getty Images/Bavaria Bildagentur, Düsseldorf; (6): J. Pérez de Lara, Mexico City; (7): Archiv Grube, Bonn; **345 bl:** Archiv Grube, Bonn; **345 br:** Ulf Müller-Moewes, Königswinter; **346:** H. Zaglitsch, Muiden; **347 a:** Morris R. Jones/Rolli Arts, Essen; **347 b:** J. Pérez de Lara, Mexico City; **348:** Peabody Museum of Archaeology and Ethnology, Harvard University, Cambridge (MA); **349:** Marilyn Masson, Albany (NY); **350:** BPK, Berlin/Dietmar Katz; **351 a:** E. Thiem/Lotosfilm, Kaufbeuren; **351 b:** M. Masson, Albany (NY); **352 l:** Michel Zabé/aza, Mexico City; **352 r:** J. Pérez de Lara, Mexico City; **353:** E. Thiem/Lotosfilm, Kaufbeuren; **354 a:** Susanne Baizermann/Rolli Arts, Essen; **354 bl:** Doro Schütze/Version, Cologne; **354 br:** Michel Zabé/aza, Mexico City; **355 a:** Michael Ross/Peter Frese, Munich; **355 b:** H. Burger/The Peabody Museum of Harvard University, Cambridge (MA); **356:** E. Thiem/Lotosfilm, Kaufbeuren; **357:** Frauke Sachse, Ganderkesee/Rolli Arts, Essen; **358:** E. Thiem/Lotosfilm, Kaufbeuren; **359 a:** Peabody Museum of Archaeology and Ethnology, Harvard University, Cambridge (MA); **359 b:** Roger-Viollet, Paris; **360/361/362 a:** E. Thiem/Lotosfilm, Kaufbeuren; **364 a:** Rolli Arts, Essen; **364 b:** Bayerische Staatsbibliothek, Munich – Photographic dept.; **365:** R. Kiedrowski, Ratingen; **366 a:** Archiv Grube, Bonn; **366 b:** 2000 Macduff Everton, Santa Barbara (CA); **367:** © Tandem Verlag GmbH, Königswinter/Frauke Sachse, Ganderkese; **368 :** John Weeks/Rolli Arts, Essen; **368 b:** Archiv Grube, Bonn; **369:** The Newberry Library, Chicago (IL); **370/371:** Getty Images/Tony Stone Images, Munich; **372:** © Tandem Verlag GmbH, Königswinter/Christian Prager, Bonn/Rolli Arts, Essen; **373:** Courtesy, Special Collections Division, The University of Texas at Arlington Libraries, Arlington (TX); **374/375 l:** AKG, Berlin; **375 r:** Archivo Oronoz, Madrid; **376 l:** The Art Archive, London/Mireille Vautier; **376 r:** Hillel Burger/President & Fellows, Harvard University, Peabody Museum, Cambridge (MA); **377:** Andreas M. Gross, Munich; **378/379:** AKG, Berlin; **380 a:** © Tandem Verlag GmbH, Königswinter/Christian Prager/Rolli Arts, Essen; **380 b:** Andreas M. Gross, Munich; **381:** Archiv Eggebrecht, Hildesheim; **382 a:** Temis Vayhinger-Scheer, Bonn; **382 b:** Nach Fray Andrés de Avendaño y Loyola/Rolli Arts, Essen; **383 a:** Temis Vayinger-Scheer, Bonn; **383 b:** The Newberry Library, Chicago; **384:** E. Thiem/Lotosfilm, Kaufbeuren; **385:** © Tandem Verlag GmbH, Königswinter/Antje Gunsenheimer; **386:** BPK, Berlin; **387:** Tozzer Libray, Harvard College Library, Harvard University, Cambridge (MA); **388:** Bayerische Staatsbibliothek, Munich – Photographic dept.; **389 a:** Dr. H. J. Aubert, Bonn; **389 b:** BPK, Berlin; **390 l:** R. M. Carmack/State University of New York (NY) at Albany; **390 r/391 l:** Gilles Mermet/AKG, Berlin; **391 r:** Antje Gunsenheimer/Peter Frese, Munich; **392:** Fomento Cultural Banamex, Mexico City; **393:** J. Pérez de Lara, Mexico City; **394/395:** BPK, Berlin; **396:** Roger-Viollet, Paris; **397:** AKG, Berlin; **398 l:** SCALA Group S.p.A., Antella/Florence; **398 r:** AKG, Berlin; **399:** Akademische Druck- und Verlagsanstalt, Graz; **400:** BPK, Berlin; **401 a:** BPK, Berlin; **401 b:** The British Museum, London; **402 l:** Museo Comunitario de Itzamal Kawil/Izamal; **402 m:** Michael D. Coe; **402 r:** Bayerische Staatsbibliothek, Munich – Photographic dept.; **403:** AKG, Berlin; **404:** Archiv Eggebrecht, Hildesheim; **406/407 a:** AKG, Berlin; **407 b:** BPK, Berlin; **408:** Henri Stierlin, Geneva; **409 al:** Museo de América, Madrid/Javier Martínez de la Torre; **409 ar:** Biblioteca del Palacio Real, Patrimonio Nacional, Madrid; **410 a:** Bayerische Staatsbibliothek, Munich – Photographic dept.; **410 b:** Herby Sachs/Version, Cologne; **411 a:** Michael D. Coe./Thames and Hudson, London; **411 b:** Bibliothèque Nationale de France, Paris; **412:** Archiv Grube, Bonn; **413 a:** Peter Mathews, Calgary/Rolli Arts, Essen; **413 b:** Markus Eberl, Bonn; **414/415:** Thomas Hoepker/Focus, Hamburg; **416:** Ulli Stelzner/ISKA/Version, Cologne; **417:** © Tandem Verlag GmbH, Königswinter/Nikolai Grube, Bonn/Rolli Arts, Essen; **418/419:** ISKA-Archiv, Berlin/Version, Cologne; **420:** National Geographic Society, Washington D.C.; **421 a:** Thomas Hoepker/Focus, Hamburg; **421 b:** ISKA-Archiv, Berlin/Version, Cologne; **422:** Thomas Hoepker/Focus, Hamburg; **423 bl:** Andreas M. Gross, Munich; **423 br:** Ted Wood – Das Fotoarchiv, Essen; **424 a:** Cindy Carp – Das Fotoarchiv, Essen; **424 b:** Andreas M. Gross, Munich; **425:** dpa, Frankfurt a. M.; **426/427:** Justin Kerr, New York (NY); **428 a:** Henri Stierlin, Geneva; **428:** H + Z Bildagentur GmbH, Hannover; **429:** Andreas M. Gross, Munich; **430 l:** Justin Kerr, New York (NY); **430 r:** Michel Zabé/aza, Mexico City; **431 a:** Werner Forman/AKG, Berlin; **431 b:** Private Collection, Geneva; **432/433/434 a/b:** H. Zaglitsch, Muiden; **435:** Anne Stierlin, Geneva; **436 l:** The Art Archive, London/G. Dagli Orti, Paris/Museo de Arqueología, Copan; **436 r:** Andreas M. Gross, Munich; **437 l:** G. Dagli Orti, Paris/The Art Archive, London/Museo de Antropología, San Pedro Sula; **437 r:** Henri Stierlin, Geneva; **438/439:** Andreas M. Gross, Munich; **440/441:** Getty Images/Bavaria Bildagentur, Düsseldorf; **442:** Tatiana Proskouriakoff; **443:** Getty Images/Bavaria Bildagentur, Düsseldorf; **444 l:** BPK, Berlin; **444 r:** J. Pérez de Lara, Mexico City; **445 l:** BPK, Berlin; **445 r:** Archiv Grube, Bonn; **446:** H. Zaglitsch, Muiden; **447:** BPK, Berlin; **448 l:** T. Proskouriakoff; **448 r:** Jens Holst/Version, Cologne; **449 l:** BPK, Berlin; **449 r:** J. Pérez de Lara, Mexico City; **450:** (1, 2): Justin Kerr, New York (NY), (3): E. Thiem/ Lotusfilm, Kaufbeuren, (4): Museum Rietberg, Zurich/Wettstein & Kauf; **451:** (1, 3, 5, 8): Justin Kerr, New York (NY), (2): K. Furth, D. Heald/National Museum of the American Indian, New York (NY), (4): A.P. Andrews, (6): Justin Kerr, New York (NY), (7): Courtesy, National Museum of the American Indian, Smithsonian Institution/Karen Furth; **452:** (1): H. Burger/Peabody Museum of Harvard University, Cambridge (MA); (2, 3): Michel Zabé/aza, Mexico City, (4): Henri Stierlin, Geneva; **453:** (1, 2): Michel Zabé/aza, Mexico City, (3): Henri Stierlin, Geneva, (4): J. Pérez de Lara, Mexico City; **456–459:** Markus Eberl, Nikolai Grube, Bonn/Rolli Arts, Essen; **460/461:** **(Register 1)** (1): J. Pérez de Lara, Mexico City; (2): Michel Zabé/aza, Mexico City; **(Register 2)** (1): Norman Hammond, Boston (MA); (2): Martha Cooper; (3, 4, 7): E. Thiem/Lotosfilm, Kaufbeuren; (5): Department of Archaeology, Belmopan, Belize; (6): J. Pérez de Lara, Mexico City; (8): Justin Kerr, New York (NY); **(Register 3)** (1): John Clark, New World Archaeological Foundation; (2): Robert J. Sharer; (3): Michael D. Coe; (4): Michel Zabé/aza, Mexico City; (5): Museo Nacional de Antr., El Salvador; **(Register 4)** (1, 3): Rafael Doniz, Mexico City; (2): Getty Images/Tony Stone Images, Munich/Suzanne Murphy; (4): Fondo de Cultura, Mexico City; (5): George Stuart, Washington D.C., Center for Maya Research/Rolli Arts, Essen; **(Register 5)** (1): Erich Lessing/AKG, Berlin; (2, 3, 4): AKG/Lessing, Berlin; (5): John Hios/AKG, Berlin; (6): SCALA group S.p.A., Antella/ Florence; (7): Jean-Louis Nou/AKG, Berlin; **462/463:** **(Register 1)** (1, 5, 14): Michel Zabé/aza, Mexico City; (2): H. Zaglitsch, Muiden; (3, 6, 9, 11): J. Pérez de Lara, Mexico City; (4): Hasso Hohmann, Graz; (7): Henri & Anne Stierlin, Geneva; (8, 10): Justin Kerr, New York (NY); (12): The Art Archive, London/Mireille Vautier; (13): I. Groth, Mexico City; **(Register 2)** (1) Archiv Eggebrecht, Hildesheim; (2) Andreas M. Gross, Munich; (3): E. Thiem/Lotosfilm, Kaufbeuren; (4, 6) Henri & Anne Stierlin, Geneva; (5, 10): H. Zaglitsch, Muiden; (7): Peter D. Harrison, New Mexico; (8): Richard D. Hansen, Los Angeles (CA); (9): Ian Graham, Cambridge (MA); (11): R. Doniz, Mexico City; **(Register 3)** (1): J. Pérez de Lara, Mexico City; (2, 3): Stephan F. Borhegyi, Milwaukee Public Museum; (4): Michel Zabé/aza, Mexico City; (5): Andreas M. Gross, Munich; (6): E. Thiem/Lotosfilm, Kaufbeuren; **(Register 4)** (1): J. Pérez de Lara, Mexico City; (2): Andreas M. Gross, Munich; **(Register 5)** (1, 2, 4): SCALA group S.p.A., Antella/Florence; (3): AKG, Berlin; (5): Jean-Louis Nou/AKG, Berlin; (6). AKG, Berlin; (7, 8): Archivo Oronoz, Madrid; (9): Henning Bock/AKG, Berlin; **464/465:** **(Register 1)** (1): J. Pérez de Lara, Mexico City; (2): Symme Burstein, Peabody Museum, Harvard University, Cambridge (MA); (3): F. Davâlos/Dumbarton Oaks Research Library and Collection, Washington DC; (4): J. Pérez de Lara, Mexico City; (5): Patrick Frilet/Sipa-Image, Paris; (6): The University of Pennsylvania Museum, Philadelphia (PA); (7): National Geographic, Washington D.C.; (8): Getty Images/Tony Stone Images, Munich/Bob Krist; **(Register 2)** (1): Nikolai Grube, Bonn; (2): MichelZabé/aza, Mexico City; (3): Dietmar Katz/BPK, Berlin; (4): E. Thiem/Lotusfilm, Kaufbeuren; (5): BPK, Berlin; (6): Archiv Eggebrecht, Hildesheim; **(Register 3)** (1, 2): E. Thiem/Lotusfilm, Kaufbeuren; (3): Archiv Grube, Bonn; (4): Sipa Image/Patrick Frilet, Paris; (5): H + Z Bildagentur, Hannover; (6): dpa, Frankfurt a. M.; **(Register 4)** (1): Giovanni Dagli Orti, Paris; (2): Ana Casas Broda/ Museo del Templo Mayor, Mexico City; (3): Ana Casas Broda/Museo Nacional de Antropología, Mexico City; (4-6): AKG, Berlin; (7, 8): Ullstein Bilderdienst, Berlin; **(Register 5)** (1): Stephan Drechsel/AKG, Berlin; (2–5, 7): SCALA group S.p.A., Antella/Florence; (6, 8, 9): AKG, Berlin.

Endpaper:
Uaxactun, Guatemala, Group A and B, drawing by Tatiana
Proskouriakoff.
In the 1940s, the Russian-American art historian and architect Tatiana
Proskouriakoff produced graphical reconstructions of many Maya cities
and their architecture. Uaxactun is a significant Maya city north of Tikal
which reached its prime in the Early-Classic; however, both architectural
groups, connected by a raised causeway, were inhabited and developed
well into the End-Classic (9th century A.D.)
Photo: © 2006 Harvard University, Peabody Museum
Photo 58-34-20/45160 CIW 39-10-9

Frontispiece:
Mosaic mask. Calakmul, Campeche, Mexico, crypt from structure VII;
Late-Classic, 8th century A.D., jade, mussel shell; Campeche, Museo
Reducto de San Miguel
In December of 1984, a large tomb was discovered in a crypt under the
floor of structure VII in Calakmul which became famous above all for its
over-2000-year-old jade objects, among them this jade mask. Since no
hieroglyphic text was found in the tomb, the identity of the person inter-
red is not known, although it must have been an important man who died
between the age of 35 and 50.
Photo: © Michel Zabé/AZA, Mexico City

© 2006/2007 Tandem Verlag GmbH
h.f.ullmann is an imprint of Tandem Verlag GmbH

Art director: Peter Feierabend
Project management: Ute Edda Hammer; Kerstin Ludolph
Project assistance: Ann Christin Artel, Till Busse, Kerstin Dönicke,
Vera Diedrich
Coordination of the updated edition: Lucas Lüdemann
Scientific colaboration: Christian Prager, Bonn; Elisabeth Wagner, Bonn
Layout: Carmen Strzelecki, Cologne
Graphics: Peter Frese, Munich; Rolli Arts, Essen
Drawings: Mark van Stone (4 drawings for the syllabary table, p. 124)
Picture editing: Steffi Huber

Original title: *Maya. Gottkönige im Regenwald*
ISBN of the German edition: 978-3-8331-4447-9

© 2006/2007 for the English edition: Tandem Verlag GmbH
h.f.ullmann is an imprint of Tandem Verlag GmbH

Translation from German, editing and typesetting: Translate-A-Book,
Oxford,
Specialist editing: Michael Carrasco, Simon Martin, Mark van Stone
Project coordination: Alex Morkramer
Editing for the updated edition: Tim Welding

Printed in China

ISBN 978-3-8331-4339-7

10 9 8 7 6 5 4 3 2
X IX VIII VII VI V IV III II I

The publisher and editor would like to thank all the organizations and
experts who contributed to this book for their generous cooperation. Our
special thanks go to the Institut für Altamerikanistik und Völkerkunde
der Universität Bonn; the Department for Art and Art History, University
of Texas, Austin; the Department for Art and Archeology, Belmopan,
Belize; the Instituto Nacional de Antropología e Historia (INAH), Mexico;
the Instituto Hondure'o de Antropología e Historia (IHAH), Tegucigalpa;
the Instituto de Antropología e Historia de Guatemala; the Organización
Cultural Maya Mayaón and its coordinator, Bartolome Alonso Caamal,
Valladolid, Yucatan, and to the Oxlajuuj Keej Maya' Ajtz'iib' (OKMA),
La Antigua, Guatemala.

www.ullmann-publishing.com